THE ROUTLEDGE COMPANION TO TAX AVOIDANCE RESEARCH

An inherently interdisciplinary subject, tax avoidance has attracted growing interest of scholars in many fields. No longer limited to law and accounting, research increasingly has been conducted from other perspectives, such as anthropology, business ethics, corporate social responsibility, and economic psychology. This was recently stimulated by politicians, mass media, and the public focussing on tax avoidance after the global financial and economic crisis put a squeeze on private and public finances. New challenges were posed by changing definitions and controversies in the interpretation of tax avoidance concept, as well as a host of new rules and policies that need to be fully understood.

This collection provides a comprehensive guide to students and academics on the subjects of tax avoidance from an interdisciplinary perspective, exploring the areas of accounting, law, economics, psychology, and sociology. It covers global as well as regional issues, presents a discussion of the definition, legality, morality, and psychology of tax avoidance, and provides guidance on measurement of economic effect of tax avoidance activities. With a truly international selection of authors from the UK, North America, Africa, Asia, Australasia, Middle East, and continental Europe, with well-known experts and rising stars of the field, the contributors cover the entire terrain of this important topic.

The Routledge Companion to Tax Avoidance Research is a ground-breaking attempt to bring together scholarly research in tax avoidance, offering rigorous academic analysis of an important and hotly debated issue in a structured and balanced way.

Nigar Hashimzade is Professor of Economics at Durham University, Fellow of CESifo Research Network, and Research Fellow at the Institute for Fiscal Studies and at the Tax Administration Research Centre.

Yuliya Epifantseva is a US-based attorney with expertise in corporate tax law. After receiving her Ph.D. in economics from Cornell University and J.D. from NYU School of Law, she practiced law with Davis Polk & Wardwell LLP in New York. She is currently based in Boston.

'A collection of thoughtful, lively, and provocative essays on a topic of major policy importance.'
James R. Hines Jr., University of Michigan

ROUTLEDGE COMPANIONS IN BUSINESS, MANAGEMENT AND ACCOUNTING

For a full list of titles in this series, please visit www.routledge.com

Routledge Companions in Business, Management and Accounting are prestige reference works providing an overview of a whole subject area or sub-discipline. These books survey the state of the discipline including emerging and cutting edge areas. Providing a comprehensive, up to date, definitive work of reference, Routledge Companions can be cited as an authoritative source on the subject.

A key aspect of these Routledge Companions is their international scope and relevance. Edited by an array of highly regarded scholars, these volumes also benefit from teams of contributors which reflect an international range of perspectives.

Individually, Routledge Companions in Business, Management and Accounting provide an impactful one-stop-shop resource for each theme covered. Collectively, they represent a comprehensive learning and research resource for researchers, postgraduate students and practitioners.

PUBLISHED TITLES IN THIS SERIES INCLUDE:

THE ROUTLEDGE COMPANION TO CRITICAL ACCOUNTING
Edited by Robin Roslender

THE ROUTLEDGE COMPANION TO TRUST
Edited by Rosalind Searle, Ann-Marie Nienaber and Sim Sitkin

THE ROUTLEDGE COMPANION TO TAX AVOIDANCE RESEARCH
Edited by Nigar Hashimzade and Yuliya Epifantseva

THE ROUTLEDGE COMPANION TO INTELLECTUAL CAPITAL
Edited by James Guthrie, John Dumay, Federica Ricceri and Christian Neilsen

THE ROUTLEDGE COMPANION TO BEHAVIORAL ACCOUNTING RESEARCH
Edited by Theresa Libby and Linda Thorne

THE ROUTLEDGE COMPANION TO ACCOUNTING INFORMATION SYSTEMS
Edited by Martin Quinn and Erik Strauß

THE ROUTLEDGE COMPANION TO TAX AVOIDANCE RESEARCH

Edited by
Nigar Hashimzade and Yuliya Epifantseva

Routledge
Taylor & Francis Group

LONDON AND NEW YORK

First published 2018
by Routledge

2 Park Square, Milton Park, Abingdon, Oxfordshire OX14 4RN
52 Vanderbilt Avenue, New York, NY 10017

Routledge is an imprint of the Taylor & Francis Group, an informa business

First issued in paperback 2020

British Library Cataloguing-in-Publication Data
A catalogue record for this book is available from the British Library

Library of Congress Cataloging-in-Publication Data
Names: Hashimzade, Nigar, editor. | Epifantseva, Yuliya, editor.
Title: The Routledge companion to tax avoidance research / edited by Nigar
Hashimzade and Yuliya Epifantseva.
Description: New York : Routledge, 2018. | Includes index.
Identifiers: LCCN 2017016023 | ISBN 9781138941342 (hardback) |
ISBN 9781315673745 (ebook)
Subjects: LCSH: Tax evasion—Law and legislation. | Tax evasion—Prevention.
Classification: LCC K4486 .R69 2017 | DDC 343.05/23—dc23
LC record available at https://lccn.loc.gov/2017016023

ISBN: 978-1-138-94134-2 (hbk)
ISBN: 978-0-367-65616-4 (pbk)

Typeset in Bembo
by Apex CoVantage, LLC

CONTENTS

FIGURES

TABLES

CONTRIBUTORS

Giulio Allevato is a Lecturer of Tax Law at the SDA Bocconi School of Management. His research interests include international taxation, international finance, law and economic development, corporate taxation, individual income taxation, and comparative and EU taxation. He holds a PhD in International Law and Economics degree from Bocconi University, and an International Tax LL.M degree from the University of Michigan Law School. Before joining SDA Bocconi School of Management, he was Ernst Mach Scholar at the Institute for Austrian and International Tax Law of the Vienna University of Economics and Business Administration (WU).

Leyla Ateş is an Associate Professor of Tax Law at the Istanbul Kemerburgaz University and a member of IFA and the European Association of Tax Law Professors. Her research interests are in the areas of international tax law, income taxation and tax policy. Prior to her current position she has held academic posts at universities in Germany, Turkey, and Northern Cyprus. She co-chaired the G20 working group on "Governance" under the Turkish Presidency of the G20 in 2015.

Reuven S. Avi-Yonah is Professor of Law at University of California, Irvine, School of Law, specializing in corporate and international taxation. He has served as a consultant to the U.S. Department of the Treasury and the OECD on tax competition, and is a trustee of the American Tax Policy Institute, a member of the American Law Institute, a fellow of the American Bar Foundation and the American College of Tax Counsel, and also an international research fellow at Oxford University's Centre for Business Taxation.

William B. Barker is Polisher Family Faculty Scholar and Professor of Law, Penn State Dickinson Law. His research and teaching focusses on international and comparative taxation. His research reflects a strong normative approach to tax law that emphasizes the role of tax avoidance and important social values in the development of tax law in societies adopting free market, democratic systems in both the developed and emerging and transitional economies.

Karen Boll is an Associate Professor at the Department of Organization at Copenhagen Business School. Upon completing a degree in ethnology (cultural studies) she has worked as a civil servant at the Danish Ministry of Taxation, which stimulated her interest in the social and organisational aspects of taxation, and led to a research progamme on tax compliance, with the focus on Denmark and other Nordic countries.

Valerie Braithwaite is an interdisciplinary social scientist with a disciplinary background in psychology. Currently, she holds a professorial appointment in the Regulatory Institutions Network at the Australian National University, where she studies psychological processes in regulation and governance. She has published research articles and books on institutional practices and social relationships, including monographs *Defiance in Taxation and Governance: Resisting and Dismissing Authority in a Democracy* (Edward Elgar 2009), *Shame Management through Reintegration* (Cambridge University Press 2001), and edited collections *Trust and Governance* (Russell Sage 2003) and *Taxing Democracy: Understanding Tax Avoidance and Evasion* (Routledge 2003).

Allison Christians is the H. Heward Stikeman Chair in the Law of Taxation at the McGill University Faculty of Law. Her research and teaching focus on national and international tax law and policy issues, with emphasis on the relationship between taxation and economic development and on the role of government and non-government institutions and actors in the creation of tax policy norms.

Graeme Cooper is Professor of Taxation Law at the Law School of the University of Sydney. He studied in Australia and the US, and has taught at Law Schools in Australia, the US, Belgium and The Netherlands. He has worked for the OECD and as a consultant on projects for the UN, IMF, World Bank and the Australian Treasury, Audit Office and Taxation Office.

Steven A. Dean is a Professor at Brooklyn Law School and a member of the Executive Committee of the New York State Bar Association's Tax Section. His scholarship and teaching focus on tax law. His published work includes issues in taxpayer autonomy, the role of the law in the growth of social enterprise, and unconventional solutions to longstanding problems such as tax havens, regulatory complexity and tax shelters.

Yuliya Epifantseva is a US-based attorney with expertise in corporate tax law. After receiving Ph.D. in economics from Cornell University and J.D. from NYU School of Law, she practiced law with Davis Polk & Wardwell LLP in New York. She is currently based in Boston.

Alejandro Esteller-Moré is an Associate Professor at the Universitat de Barcelona (UB) in Spain, and the Director of the IEB research program on taxation. He holds a Master of Economics from Essex University (UK), and a PhD in Economics from UB. His research focuses on taxation.

Jane Frecknall-Hughes is Professor of Accounting and Taxation and Head of the Accounting Division at Nottingham University Business School. Jane's research focuses on taxation, especially from an interdisciplinary perspective. Prior to joining academia where she held posts at a number of UK universities she has worked as a chartered accountant and chartered tax consultant with KPMG. Jane's publication record on taxation includes books and articles in leading journals on taxation, among them a textbook, *The Theory, Principles and Management of Taxation: An Introduction* (Routledge, 2014).

Duccio Gamanossi degl'Innocenti is a post-doctoral research fellow at the Tax Administration Research Centre (University of Exeter and the Institute for Fiscal Studies). He holds a

PhD in Economics from the IMT School for Advanced Studies, Lucca, and a first class honours (magna cum laude) degree in Economics from the Università degli studi di Firenze. His research interests are in public economics, tax compliance, and game theory.

Carlo Garbarino is Professor of Taxation at Bocconi University Milan and an SDA Professor and the Director of the Tax Observatory at the SDA Bocconi School of Management, the Editor of *EC Tax Review*, Editor-in-Chief of *Fiscalità e Commercio Internazionale* (Kluwer), and the Director of the *Comparative and International Taxation* Series (Bocconi University Press). He is the author of *Manuale di tassazione Internazionale* (2008), *Judicial Interpretation of Tax Treaties* (Elgar 2016), three monographs, and over a hundred publications on comparative and international taxation.

Nigar Hashimzade is Professor of Economics at Durham University, Fellow of CESifo Research Network, and Research Fellow at the Institute for Fiscal Studies and at the Tax Administration Research Centre. She has published research papers in economic theory and econometric theory and co-edited two books on empirical research in economics. Her previous academic career was in theoretical physics.

John Hasseldine is Professor of Accounting and Taxation in the Peter T. Paul College of Business and Economics, University of New Hampshire, a Fellow of the Association of Chartered Certified Accountants, and the journal editor of *Advances in Taxation*. John has worked as an external expert at the International Monetary Fund. He has served on three government committees in the U.K. and was a contributor to the Mirrlees Review of the U.K. tax system conducted by the Institute of Fiscal Studies.

Tarun Jain is a professionally qualified lawyer actively engaged in main-stream tax litigation in India, currently engaged as Principal Attorney in BMR Legal. He is involved in and represents a wide range of clients in all varieties of tax fields before various forums in India including tax tribunals and constitutional courts. He regularly contributes to various law journals with his papers on finer nuances of tax laws.

Matthias Kasper is a social psychologist. His research analyses the institutional, social, and individual determinants of taxpayer behavior. He holds a PhD in International Business Taxation from Vienna University of Economics and Business and is currently Assistant Professor at the Department of Economic Psychology at the University of Vienna.

Erich Kirchler is Professor of Applied Psychology (economic psychology) at the University of Vienna. He has held invited professorial posts at universities in Europe, Australia, and the United States. His research focuses on money management in the household, expenditures and credit use, tax behaviour and well-being of working people, where he has published numerous research articles and books, including *The Economic Psychology of Tax Behaviour* (Cambridge University Press, UK, 2007).

Bodo Knoll is a lecturer at the Ruhr University Bochum in Germany. Prior to joining the Ruhr University, he worked as a research and teaching assistant at the University of Hohenheim in Stuttgart. His research covers a broad range of topics, including profit shifting of multinational firms, the impact of institutions on life satisfaction, public choice and the empirical assessment of occupation choices.

Christoph Kogler is an Assistant Professor at the Department of Social Psychology at Tilburg University. He studies economic decision-making applying different research methods as experiments, surveys, and methods to trace decision processes (fMRI, MouselabWEB etc.). His main research interests are the investigation of economic and psychological determinants of tax compliance with an emphasis on the influence of trust and fairness perceptions. He received a master's degree in psychology in 2002 and completed his postgraduate studies with his dissertation in 2006, both at the University of Salzburg, Austria and then worked as an assistant professor at the University of Vienna, Austria.

Gregory Morris is a Lecturer at the University of Exeter Business School and a Fellow of the Institute of Chartered Accountant. Prior to joining the University of Nottingham in 2008 to study for a PhD he had worked for many decades in business and in professional practice. Most recently he was head of the UK and EMEA tax practice of a large international law firm. His research interests are in the area of business, society and taxation.

Volker Nitsch is Professor of International Economics at Technische Universität Darmstadt. Prior to taking this position in 2009, he was Head of the International Economics Division at KOF Swiss Economic Institute at ETH Zürich, an Assistant Professor of Economics at the Freie Universität Berlin, and a Senior Economist at Bankgesellschaft Berlin.

Lynne Oats is Professor of Taxation and Accounting, University of Exeter Business School, Co-Director of the Tax Administration Research Centre. She worked at the Australian Taxation Office and has been a tax academic in Australia and the UK. Lynne is Managing Editor of *Journal of Tax Administration*, Assistant Editor (Accounting) of *British Tax Review*, and has published widely in the accounting and taxation fields. She co-authored and edited several books, including *Taxation Policy and Practice*, *Principles of International Taxation* and *Accounting Principles for Tax Purposes*, and *Taxation: A Fieldwork Research Handbook*.

Tadao Okamura is Professor of Tax Law at Graduate School of Law, Kyoto University, and a member of Japan's Government Tax Commission. He published numerous books and articles, including *Corporate Tax Law* (2007, Seibundo), *Corporate Taxation for the Future* (2007, Yuhikaku) (editor), and *The Developments in the Research on Tax Avoidance* (2015, Minerva) (editor). He is frequently invited to speak at conferences in Japan, Europe and the U.S.A.

Jerome Olsen is a Research Associate at the Faculty of Psychology, University of Vienna, Austria. His PhD project focuses on value added tax (VAT) compliance. Specifically, he investigates how VAT is socially represented by different actors in the field as well as factors influencing collaborative tax evasion of income tax and VAT by suppliers and consumers.

Henry Ordower is Professor of Law at Saint Louis University School of Law. His research and writing primarily focuses on U.S. and comparative taxation with emphasis on fairness in tax distribution and secondarily on the regulation of private investment companies. Professor Ordower maintains an active consulting practice advising in tax planning, hedge and private equity funds, and business structure, and providing expert testimony on taxation and business organizations in complex litigation matters. He has been elected to membership in the American College of Tax Counsel, the European Association of Tax Law Professors, and the International Academy of Comparative Law.

Dr. Amir Pichhadze is Lecturer at Deakin University's Law School. Amir obtained an S.J.D. and LL.M. (International Tax) from the University of Michigan Law School. He also obtained an LL.M. (Taxation) and LL.B. from the London School of Economics. Amir completed a judicial clerkship at the Tax Court of Canada. His legal research has been widely published in leading journals, and presented in numerous conferences around the world.

Amedeo Piolatto is a researcher at the Barcelona Economics Institute. His research area is public economics and political economy. He holds a PhD from Toulouse School of Economics, and prior to that he studied economics at Bocconi University (MSc) and the University of Turin (BSc). He has previously held positions at the University of Alicante, Autónoma de Barcelona, Collegio Carlo Alberto, and Tilburg University.

John Prebble, QC, BA, LLB (Hons) Auckland, BCL Oxon, JSD Cornell, Inner Temple, LEANZF, is a Professor of Law at the Victoria University of Wellington, New Zealand, Gastprofessor, Institut für Österreichisches und Internationales Steuerrecht, Wirtschaftsuniversität Wien, and Adjunct Professor of Law, Notre Dame University of Australia, Sydney. His main research interests include the application of analytical legal philosophy to income tax law, fundamental concepts of taxation law, international taxation, and tax avoidance.

Rebecca Prebble BA (hons), LLB (hons) (Victoria University of Wellington), LLM (Kent Scholar) (Columbia), is a senior analyst at the New Zealand Treasury, Wellington. Within that role she has worked in macroeconomic, regulatory, and criminal justice policy. Prior to that she worked for a New Zealand law firm.

Zoë Prebble BA (hons), LLB (hons) (Victoria University of Wellington), LLM (University of Michigan), is a PhD candidate at the Peter A. Allard School of Law at the University of British Columbia. Her doctoral research examines criminal statute law design, gendered violence and legal philosophy. Prior to that she worked for the New Zealand Law Commission.

Matthew D. Rablen is a Reader at the University of Sheffield and a former UK government economist advising on matters relating to tax compliance. He graduated with first class honours from the University of Nottingham and attained his PhD at the University of Warwick. He has published extensively on the economic theory of tax compliance.

Nadine Riedel is a Professor of Economics at the Ruhr University Bochum in Germany. Her current research interests comprise international corporate tax competition, taxation in developing countries and the empirical assessment of corporate tax effects on firm behaviour. Prior to joining the Ruhr University, she held teaching and research positions at the University of Oxford, the University of Munich and the University of Hohenheim (Stuttgart).

Takako Sakai is an Associate Professor of tax law at the Graduate School of Economics, Osaka Prefecture University. She acquired B.A. in 1995 from Yokohama City University, LL.M in 1999 and LL.D in 2007 from Kyoto University. She is the author of *Corporate Tax Attributes* (2011, Seibundo). Her recent research focus is general anti-avoidance rules.

Leonard Seabrooke is Professor of International Political Economy and Economic Sociology at the Copenhagen Business School. His most recent works include *Professional Networks in Transnational Governance* (co-edited with Lasse Folke Henriksen, Cambridge University Press,

2017), and *Global Tax Battles: The Fight to Govern Corporate and Elite Wealth*, co-authored with Duncan Wigan, and *Global Wealth Chains: Governing Assets in the World Economy*, co-edited with Duncan Wigan (both forthcoming in 2018 in Oxford University Press).

Farzaneh Shamsfakhr is a PhD candidate, research and teaching assistant at University of Duisburg-Essen, chair of Macroeconomics. She was a research student at the chair of Public Finance and Economic Policy in Ruhr University Bochum (RUB) in 2014–2015. Before joining RUB, Farzaneh has worked for Central Bank of Iran for several years.

Lawrence M. Solan is the Don Forchelli Professor of Law and Director of the Center for the Study of Law, Language and Cognition at Brooklyn Law School. Much of his writing is about the interpretation of statutes and contracts. He co-edited and co-authored several books, including *The Language of Judges, Speaking of Crime*; *The Language of Statutes: Laws and their Interpretation*; *The Oxford Handbook of Language and Law*; and *Speaking of Language and Law: Conversations on the Work of Peter Tiersma*.

Lukasz Stankiewicz is an Associate Professor of Law (maître de conférences) at the Jean Moulin Lyon III University (France), where he teaches tax law and public finance. He has given conference presentations and authored numerous articles in tax law and public finance both in French and in English. He also taught at Brooklyn Law School, at the Faculty of Law of the University of São Paulo, and at Paris I Panthéon Sorbonne University.

Jennifer Stark graduated from the University of Vienna, with a Master's degree in Psychology in 2012. Since then she has been working as a research and teaching associate and project collaborator at the Department of Applied Psychology: Work, Education, and Economy of the Faculty of Psychology at the University of Vienna. Currently, she is finalising her PhD in Psychology. Her research focus includes tax behaviour, intergenerational transfer of wealth, inheritance taxation, and social representations.

Miranda Stewart is Director of the Tax and Transfer Policy Institute at the Crawford School of Public Policy, Australian National University and a Professor at University of Melbourne Law School. Miranda has researched and published widely on tax law and policy. Recent publications address sham, abuse and economic substance in international tax and global tax reform. She co-edited two books, *Sham Transactions* and *Tax, Law and Development*.

Kristina Strohmaier is a research assistant at the Ruhr-University Bochum and the University of Hohenheim (Stuttgart). Her research focuses on applied microeconometrics in the fields of international tax competition, tax compliance and development economics.

Vokhid Urinov is Assistant Professor at University of New Brunswick, Faculty of Law (Canada) where he teaches tax and business law courses. Vokhid's research interests lie primarily in the areas of international tax. His most recent research works focus on the questions of tax compliance and administration in a globalized economy and the role of the emerging global automatic information exchange system in improving the taxpayer compliance.

Attiya Waris is an Advocate, Arbitrator, and Senior Lecturer of Tax Law and Policy at the Law School, University of Nairobi in Kenya where she has been teaching for over 10 years. She has published extensively on international and African regional tax law and policy as well as domestic tax in Kenya, Rwanda, South Africa and Bangladesh. Attiya has authored and co-authored several books on taxation, including *Tax and Development: Solving Kenya's Fiscal Crisis through Human Rights*.

Duncan Wigan is an Associate Professor in International Political Economy at the Department of Business and Politics, Copenhagen Business School. He is co-author, with Leonard Sea-brooke, of *Global Tax Battles: The Fight to Govern Corporate and Elite Wealth* and editor, also with Seabrooke, of *Global Wealth Chains: Governing Assets in the World Economy*.

Elea Wurth undertook her research on tax advisors as part of her PhD at the Regulatory Institutions Network, Australian National University, supported by the Australian Tax Office's Commissioner's scholarship 2008–10. Elea specialises in data science portfolio management and is now employed as a director of data science at the Australian Tax Office.

1

INTRODUCTION

Yuliya Epifantseva and Nigar Hashimzade[1]

Tax avoidance has traditionally been a subject of research in accounting and law. The past decade has witnessed growing interest in this subject in other disciplines, including anthropology, economics, psychology, and sociology. This was at least partly stimulated by politicians, mass media, and the public focussing on tax avoidance in many countries after the global financial and economic crisis put a squeeze on private and public finances. Changing definitions, controversies in the interpretation of concepts, new rules and policies have motivated researchers across disciplines to analyse tax compliance as decision-making in multilateral interaction among individuals, tax practitioners, governments, and broader society. In this book we have aimed to provide a comprehensive overview of the historical and contemporary matters in tax avoidance across several disciplines, including accounting, law, economics, psychology, and sociology.

The topics in tax avoidance research addressed in this *Companion* include global as well as regional issues, the aspects of legality, morality, and psychology of tax avoidance, and the challenges of measurement of economic effect of various tax avoidance activities. The volume is divided into five parts, each focussing on a specific set of topics. This division is, to a certain extent, arbitrary, as a number of important concepts and themes cut naturally across topics. Thus, the variable definition of tax avoidance and its distinction from tax evasion is discussed, along with related concepts, from the historical and foundational perspective in the first part, and from the social and ethical perspective in the final part. A variety of approaches to tackling tax avoidance is analysed as a conceptual framework in the second part, and as case studies in the third part. The role of tax intermediaries, or tax practitioners, is discussed in the final two parts, first as an interaction between individual tax practitioners and taxpayers in a social environment, and then from the viewpoint of ethical issues arising in the tax advice industry.

The first part of the *Companion* addresses the historical definitional aspects of various terms related to tax avoidance, and touches on their evolution in response to the increased public exposure and attention to issues of tax avoidance and evasion around the world. Because of the conflation of even the most basic definitions of tax avoidance and tax evasion both across English-speaking jurisdictions and within a variety of jurisdictions, by politicians, tax authorities

---

1 Views and opinions expressed herein are not intended to reflect views, positions or policy of any employer, organization or entity with which either of us is, or has ever been, affiliated.

and the media, it is crucially important to define and delineate the activities subject to the discussion before providing normative analysis. It is therefore not surprising that the themes of the chapters in this part echo the concluding part of the *Companion* that discusses societal aspects of tax avoidance.

In the opening chapter, Jane Frecknall-Hughes describes the fascinating history of taxation terminology, and in particular the intertwined semantic evolution of the key concepts of "tax avoidance" and "tax evasion" in the United States and UK. The chapter discusses the timing and reasons for the conceptual switch between these notions, perhaps shedding some light on the current fluidity and lack of coherence in their usage and connotations. It also discusses the evolving historical use of these concepts in law, tax administration, press, and other sources.

In the next chapter Henry Ordower explores the effect of legislative grants of economic incentives through the tax system on taxpayer behaviour and the resulting difficulty in drawing the line between legitimate and objectionable tax avoidance. He further argues that while the attempts to separate the two types of tax avoidance such as enacting general anti-avoidance rules (GAARs) and following general principles of economic substance may be partially successful, subsidies delivered through the tax system will inherently limit their effect. The resulting lack of clear delineation between legitimate tax planning and objectionable tax avoidance enables an even firmer embedding of 'the culture of tax avoidance' in the society, indirectly spilling over into lack of stigmatization for even the clearly illegal tax evasion activities.

As the word 'sham' is increasingly being used – and misused – in describing purported tax abuses, especially in the context of any tax haven activity of multinational corporations, it is very important to have a clear understanding of this term. The chapter by Miranda Stewart presents an exploration of the origin of the judicial doctrine of sham and its development in a variety of jurisdictions. It then explores the relationship between the doctrine of sham and tax avoidance and evasion, and also the GAARs.

The second part of the *Companion* contains a variety of perspectives on GAARs. It opens with Rebecca Prebble's and John Prebble's chapter that discusses the apparent conceptual conflict between GAARs and the broadly accepted values commonly referred to as the rule of law. GAARs violate the certainty principle embedded in the rule of law in that by their very nature their scope is not well defined. The chapter (i) examines the underlying values of the rule of law, (ii) argues that the very nature of the problem of impermissible tax avoidance warrants the departure from the rule of law, and (iii) argues that this departure does not weaken the rule of law but rather advances its importance.

The chapter by Graeme Cooper delivers a nuanced comparative analysis of one particular feature of many GAARs, namely, the requirement of a 'purpose', the term that GAARs use in different ways and to different results. The chapter discusses a number of challenges in designing GAARs that may prevent successful use of the 'purpose' feature to separate tax avoidance that aligns with legislative intent from impermissible tax avoidance.

The next two chapters present an in-depth analysis of the Canadian GAAR. Vokhid Urinov introduces the history and the development of the Canadian GAAR, and provides an in-depth discussion of its features. Reuven Avi-Yonah and Amir Pichhadze contrast the Canadian GAAR with the codified economic substance doctrine in the United States and identify the factors that should be used in analysing GAARs. The chapter goes on to discuss the application of these factors should the United States lawmakers consider implementing a GAAR.

The third part of the *Companion* presents regional approaches to addressing tax avoidance, both legislatively and judicially, as well as in cooperation between a tax authority and taxpayers. Along with an impressive evolutionary cross-comparison of the anti-avoidance approaches in the United States, the UK and France, the chapter by Steven A. Dean, Lawrence M. Solan, and

Lukasz Stankiewicz provides a number of general insights that echo the first two parts of the *Companion*. In particular, the chapter explores the similarities and divergence of the doctrines developed by courts when attempting to strike the balance between preserving the rule of law and giving the necessary tools to tax authorities to curb tax avoidance. This comparison is especially interesting in light of the different traditions of legislative-judicial interactions and doctrinal development in common law jurisdictions of the United States and the UK vis-à-vis the civil law system in France.

Tadao Okamura and Takako Sakai provide an in-depth analysis of addressing tax avoidance within the Japanese legal system, and the unique problems that stem from the importation, or partial importation, of German legal principles into Japanese law. In addition to discussing the issues unique to Japanese tax law, the chapter provides an illustration of challenges in addressing tax avoidance specific to a civil law jurisdiction.

The chapter by Giulio Allevato and Carlo Garbarino analyses the evolution of a civil law system in Italy in dealing with tax avoidance. Echoing the topics developed in the first and the second part of the *Companion*, this chapter explores how the Italian legal doctrines related to taxation evolved from the initial adherence to the certainty principle of the rule of law, which is especially salient in the civil law systems, to embracing a GAAR inspired by various developments in taxation within the European Union. The chapter also addresses briefly the new Italian tax compliance initiative designed to facilitate the implementation of the GAAR.

Leyla Ateş discusses the fascinating history of taxation in Turkey and describes how the evolution of tax law and administration in Turkey is informed by the challenges of a developing economy. The chapter argues that the mechanism of presumptive tax assessment in Turkey serves as evidence of the inadequate resources, lack of expertise, and lack of transparency in the Turkish taxation system.

Tarun Jain in his chapter sets forth an extensive survey and analysis of Indian tax law as it relates to tax avoidance, considering both the judicial and legislative approaches to these issues. The first part of the chapter describes the central role that Indian tax jurisprudence played in developing and implementing the anti-tax avoidance agenda, and analyses the varying and sometimes apparently inconsistent responses of the Indian courts. The second part of the chapter argues that the legislative reaction to tax avoidance has consisted of responses, usually through specific anti-avoidance provisions, to pro-taxpayer judicial decisions. The chapter also analyses the GAAR promulgated in response to the famous Vodafone decision, and describes the most recent anti-avoidance tax measures informed by the Base Erosion and Profit Shifting (BEPS) initiative.

Karen Boll's chapter on securing tax compliance by collaboration presents a novel approach used by tax authorities for large corporate taxpayers in several countries, usually referred to as 'cooperative compliance'. Karen Boll uses the institutional theory framework to analyse a case study of the cooperative compliance experience in Denmark. She argues that the Danish 'Tax Governance' system is a close copy of the cooperative compliance approaches employed elsewhere – notably, the Compliance Assurance Process in the United States, the Annual Compliance Agreement in Australia, and similar programmes in some European countries. Interestingly, the analysis shows that, while the cooperative compliance programmes are viewed as 'a cost-efficient way to secure tax compliance and to prevent future tax avoidance', measuring the outcomes of the programme remains a major challenge for the Danish tax authority.

This raises an important general issue of measurement. The success – or, indeed, the failure – of any policy intervention, including tax compliance policies, can only be assessed if the extent of the targeted activity can be accurately measured before and after intervention. Since taxpayers are seldom compelled, and have little incentive, to be fully transparent about their tax activities, empirical research in economics has demonstrated (though its conclusions have not been universally accepted) ingenuity in developing approaches to measuring tax avoidance and tax evasion. The next two chapters present the analysis of the important practical issue of quantifying the extent of the tax avoidance and evasion activities by firms and a review of some of these approaches.

The focus of the chapter by Bodo Knoll, Nadine Riedel, Farzaneh Shamsfakhr, and Kristina Strohmaier is on the issues of measuring tax avoidance and evasion in developing countries. The authors critically review the existing approaches in economic literature to the empirical estimation of the extent of tax avoidance and evasion, and present their own estimates based on the firm-level data for multinational corporations. The measured quantity is the corporate income shifting from 38 middle- and low-income countries (according to the World Bank classification). The authors find that an increase by one percentage point in the corporate tax rate in a host country is associated with a 1.7 per cent fall in the pre-tax profits reported by multinational firms, with yet stronger effect – a 2.1 per cent fall – for large corporations. The authors conjecture that the true effect might be even bigger, since the changes in the actual corporate tax rate faced by the multinationals are likely to be lower than the observed changes in the statutory tax rates. It is plausible that various forms of tax avoidance, such as the transfers to lower-taxed subsidiaries, debt shifting, and strategic location of intangible assets are responsible for this phenomenon.

The empirical estimation of the extent and consequences of trade misinvoicing as a form of tax avoidance and evasion activity is the subject of study by Volker Nitsch. Trade misinvoicing typically involves either using wrong classification of the goods or stating wrong quantities or values in the customs declaration. Ambiguities in tariff classification can be exploited to reduce import tariffs due, especially for newly introduced products. Developing countries are, therefore, more likely to be vulnerable to misclassification because of lack of resources, such as information, classification data, or local expertise. The chapter presents a discussion of the relative merits and drawbacks of various empirical methods employed by economists to estimate trade misinvoicing, and a comparison of estimates reported by different authors, primarily for the trade activities involving developing countries.

The analysis of the regional and global issues in tax avoidance is rounded up by two chapters written from the perspective of the international political economy. In these chapters the reader is introduced to a novel concept of Global Wealth Chains (GWCs), recently developed in the international political economy, along with the demonstration of how this framework qualitatively captures the nature of a variety of tax avoidance activities by multinationals.

The chapter by Leonard Seabrooke and Duncan Wigan outlines the GWC framework as a methodology for comprehensive analysis of the evolution of international capital which draws on and synthesises the approaches in institutional economics, economic geography, and international political economy to the study of finance and law, and economic sociology as it studies relations within networks that define market dynamics. They identify three factors that explain the variation in the governance of GWCs: (i) the complexity of information and knowledge transfer; (ii) the regulatory liability and the ease of intervention; and (iii) the capabilities of suppliers to solve or mitigate challenges posed by regulators. Based on these factors, the authors classify the GWCs into five different types: market, modular, relational, captive, and hierarchy, and link these types to the opportunities for tax avoidance activities in the world of international capital flows.

In the following chapter Leonard Seabrooke and Attiya Waris apply this framework to the analysis of GWCs in Africa, with special emphasis on the accountability and hierarchy of multinational businesses in the off-shore world. Improving the global value chains (GVCs), defined as the dispersal of production activities by multinational corporations, has been widely viewed as key to the development of African economies. There has been far less emphasis on upgrading financial institutions, or the role of aggressive tax planning and tax avoidance in how firms profit from their value chains. In the GVC research finance is generally tied to a defined development paradigm, such as microfinance, whereas the GWC framework takes a more general approach to the international flows of capital. The authors examine the attempts by different African states to create complex GWCs through the establishment of international financial centres, and discuss how these attempts can be characterized as a case of arrested development.

The analysis of an individual decision on tax avoidance and its perception in a society has been in the focus of research in cognitive and social sciences and across disciplines. The final two sections of the volume introduce the reader to the approach taken to this issue in psychology, economics, sociology, and law. In all these studies an individual decision is analysed in an interaction with the decisions of other individuals and with broader, societal attitudes and perceptions.

The chapter by Matthias Kasper, Jerome Olsen, Christoph Kogler, Jennifer Stark, and Erich Kirchler starts with a famous quote, attributed to John Maynard Keynes, one of the most influential economists in the modern time, about '[t]he avoidance of taxes' being 'the only intellectual pursuit that still carries any reward.' While the origin of this quote is still a subject of debate, the research presented in this chapter demonstrates that the effort put by an individual in such a pursuit is driven not only by a material reward but also, to a significant extent, by that individual's perception of fairness of the tax system and the social norms. The authors view tax avoidance as a social phenomenon arising from an interaction among individual decisions within a society. They introduce a concept of social representations as a theoretical framework, grounded in cognitive psychology, for the analysis of a dynamic interaction between individuals and their social environment. This framework is then used to discuss how the perception of fairness determines the social representations of tax avoidance (not necessarily illegal) and tax evasion (necessarily illegal). The empirical analysis is based on survey data collected by the authors. Among several interesting findings, the results suggest that, at least in the survey sample, tax avoiders are viewed more favourably in comparison to typical taxpayers and tax evaders. Along with other results, the study indicates that 'cheating on tax is not necessarily perceived as a crime, but rather as a game played by smart people' – seemingly in support of the aforementioned quote. The authors conclude that tax compliance policies should thus emphasize the negative social effect of tax avoidance and address the social acceptance of tax avoidance, in addition to restricting opportunities for avoidance and evasion.

Alejandro Esteller-Moré, Amedeo Piolatto, and Matthew D. Rablen present an overview of the theoretical and empirical literature in economics on taxation of high income-earners. While these individuals contribute a large portion of income tax revenue in a country, they are also highly mobile; they are also better informed and have better access to paid expertise that helps them exploit tax advantages across different countries. The authors synthesize the existing research and offer some avenues for further exploration in this area.

Elea Wurth and Valerie Braithwaite focus on the role of tax practitioners in tax avoidance. Their framework considers the relationship between a taxpayer and a tax practitioner as a micro-social process that is affected by social forces. The chapter offers an overview of several models of interaction between taxpayers and tax practitioners, along with an integrated framework for a broader study of tax avoidance industry. The authors use a survey of over 1,000 practitioners preparing and lodging returns for clients with the Australian Taxation Office to analyse how tax practitioners operate within the industry, with full knowledge of oversight by the tax authority. They outline the limitations of the traditional approach focussed on "battle" between tax practitioners and taxpayers for the attribution of responsibility for tax avoidance and evasion.

In a broader and more balanced social and economic relational model many other factors can be identified that influence the behaviour of a tax practitioner and that can be used to change this behaviour. Examples include public narratives, application of principles over rules, signalling of enforcement intent, and cooperation between professional practitioner networks and tax authorities.

An economic analysis of the design of an optimal tax enforcement system is presented by Duccio Gamannossi degl'Innocenti and Matthew D. Rablen. In contrast to the traditional economic theory, where a taxpayer can only reduce tax liability by illegal under-reporting of their income, in their framework individuals can, in addition to such evasion, participate, at a cost, in a tax avoidance scheme that permits them to further lower reported income. The role of the societal attitudes to tax non-compliance in either form is modelled as a social stigma cost. While the avoidance scheme is not explicitly illegal, it is deemed unacceptable to the tax authority, which will attempt to outlaw it after its use by taxpayers is discovered. An audited taxpayer is, therefore, penalised on the evaded tax, but not on the avoided tax, although the latter may be recovered once the scheme is outlawed. The authors characterise the optimal design of audits and penalty schemes when tax authority can only observe the declared income, with some interesting non-trivial implications. In particular, the model predicts that it is more difficult, that is, more expensive to the tax authority, to induce compliance of wealthier taxpayers. Also, when the penalty rate is higher for larger evasion, a lower reported income indicates that the taxpayer's preferred mix of avoidance and evasion is likely to have moved in favour of avoidance, because the competitiveness of the market for avoidance schemes increases, and the social stigma associated with tax non-compliance falls.

The final part of the *Companion* explores normative aspects of tax avoidance and the rhetoric surrounding it, offering a variety of perspectives and arguments. Zoë Prebble and John Prebble, in the chapter on tax avoidance and morality, and William B. Barker in the chapter on the ideology of tax avoidance, argue that tax avoidance and the legal framework that supports it are not morally justifiable. Thus, Zoë Prebble and John Prebble define tax avoidance as legal activity that goes against legislative intent and argue that tax avoidance is immoral. Their chapter identifies and dismantles the assumptions necessary to establish that tax avoidance is moral and concludes that because avoidance and evasion are factually similar, they are both immoral in a sense that is deeper than a mere breach of a duty to obey the law.

Complementing this perspective, William B. Barker also defines tax avoidance in terms of following the letter of the law while circumventing legislative intent. The chapter, a reprint of a 2009 journal article, considers tax avoidance that ultimately is detected and successfully challenged in court. The author takes issue with moral neutrality exhibited by the judiciary in the United States toward this type of tax avoidance, arguing that tax planning techniques which intentionally create and exploit ambiguities in tax statutes should not enjoy the degree of tolerance it currently does.

Continuing the discussion of ethical issues, Jane Frecknall-Hughes in the next chapter points out the added complexity of the moral and ethical considerations in the use of tax intermediaries, a broad group of service providers standing between a taxpayer and tax authority, as they serve or represent their clients. The chapter explores the variety of activities these professionals engage in and surveys the existing literature on tax intermediaries, including the literature on ethical aspects of their work.

A view counter to those expounded in the chapters by Zoë Prebble and John Prebble, by William B. Barker, and to some extent, by Henry Ordower, emerges in the last three chapters of the *Companion*. John Hasseldine and Gregory Morris discuss corporate tax avoidance and how it interacts with the notions of corporate social responsibility (CSR). The chapter carefully considers the definitional aspects of tax avoidance as it relates to corporate behaviour, the wider legal context of corporate behaviour, the principles of CSR, and goes on to describe and analyse corporate tax behaviour that has been regarded as "unacceptable". Their chapter concludes that, while some kinds of corporate behaviour obviously clash with the notions of CSR, in many cases moral and ethical assessments of corporate behaviour are not grounded in clearly articulated standards that take into account the legal and social nature of the corporate construct.

The chapter by Allison Christians, adapted for this book from her earlier work, also points out the conflation of tax avoidance and tax evasion, a phenomenon that has recently been on the rise. Echoing in some aspects the analysis of Henry Ordower in his chapter on tax avoidance culture, the chapter argues that moral assessment that relies on legislative intent to discern unacceptable tax behaviour is questionable when states and tax authorities create and maintain tax regimes, adopted through democratic legislative process, that facilitate and encourage tax avoidance. The author suggests that the legal system, and not notions of morality enforced by civic society, should bear responsibility for constraining taxpayer behaviour, and concludes by calling for transparency and accountability in governance.

In the final chapter of the *Companion* Lynne Oats and Gregory Morris use the tools of political science to take a close look at the origins and consequences of the recent shifts in discourse on tax avoidance, describing how various groups appropriated and adapted the concept to further their political goals. The resulting rhetoric that conflates different concepts, such as, for example, tax avoidance and tax evasion, or corporate compliance and individual compliance, affects not only policy makers, but also academic writings on taxation. This observation lends yet further support to our intention to bring under one cover in this volume the best examples of scholarly research in tax avoidance in several disciplines, offering rigorous academic analysis of an important and hotly debated issue in a structured and balanced way.

PART I

Tax avoidance

Definition and trends

2

HISTORICAL AND CASE LAW PERSPECTIVE ON TAX AVOIDANCE

Jane Frecknall-Hughes

Overview

Ways of not paying tax have a long history, and various activities/devices have been employed. However, the extent to which they constituted acceptable means of not paying tax has been debated even from early times. The mid to late nineteenth century and the early twentieth century appear to have been crucial periods in developing, in Great Britain, the distinction between *evasion* as illegal activity and *avoidance* as legal. This emerges from prior research undertaken on settlements, examination of minutes of government committees set up in the nineteenth century to examine tax issues and review of case law and periodicals.

The overall purpose of this chapter is to shed some light on the development of taxation terminology in relation to evasion and avoidance. This chapter considers especially the mid to late nineteenth and early twentieth centuries, as these appear to have been key periods in establishing a distinction whereby evasion came to denote a type of illegal activity and avoidance a legal activity. That distinction has been accepted for a long time, though it is not evident whence it is derived. As mentioned, the chapter considers Great Britain and thus has a common law focus. The chapter also considers possible reasons for the distinction arising and looks at contemporaneous source material such as government documents, case law reports and newspapers for further illumination. It is suggested that what drove the development of dualistic terminology, with specific legal meanings, was the need to separate out from *evasion* various activities, transactions, schemes and devices that might be different therefrom, but related. This development stemmed from normal usage of the word *avoidance* but subsequently displayed a semantic shift or shortcut into the meaning of the term as we understand it today. This has happened in other financial areas too, such as accounting (see Evans 2008), and it is still evidenced by recent developments in the tax area.

Taxation is a subject with an immense and very long history, possibly coincident with the beginning of advanced civilisation (see, for example, Burg 2004). Although there are many themes that emerge within tax history, they are all, arguably, different manifestations of one basic underlying theme, namely, the fundamental unpopularity of taxation. Rulers and governments always need tax revenues to provide public goods, to redistribute income and wealth, to promote economic stability and social and economic welfare, etc., but those taxed have often been very reluctant to pay. This has never been more succinctly expressed than in the remark attributed to Jean-Baptiste Colbert (1619–1683), the finance minister to King Louis XIV of France:

> The art of taxation consists in so plucking the goose as to obtain the largest amount of feathers with the least possible amount of hissing.[1]

The pervasiveness of taxation in daily life, combined with the complexity of taxes, rates, and the amount one has to pay, as well as issues of fairness, etc. – and the fact that taxation takes away personal property and income in a way which would be unacceptable if done by a body other than a recognised authority (such as a government) – means that taxes are often unpopular and people frequently resent their imposition. Some people pay taxes very willingly, appreciative of the uses to which taxes are put in the provision of public goods and conscious of a moral obligation towards the well-being of society. Unwilling taxpayers often engage in various kinds of activity, however, to keep as many of their feathers as possible, which leads us into consideration of tax planning, avoidance, and evasion. There is frequently a difference of opinion as to the meaning of terminology.

Definitions

A natural starting place is to look at the basic meanings of the words 'evade' and 'avoid'. The *Oxford English Dictionary (OED)* gives the following:

> 'Avoid' derives from the Old French 'esvuidier' or 'évuidier' and means 'empty' and 'make void/of no effect', but most usually 'keep clear of or away from, shun, refrain from' – meanings which it has borne since the 1300s.
> 'Evade' is an adoption of or adaptation from the French 'évader' and Latin 'evadere' and carries the meanings of 'escape by contrivance/artifice', 'contrive to avoid (doing something)'; from the 1700s 'get out of performing (a duty) or making a payment' and 'defeat the intention of (a law, stipulation, etc.), especially by specious compliance with its letter'.

The *OED* cites William Goldsmith's *Citizen of the World lxxx* from 1790 as showing the earliest use of the last meaning listed for 'evade'.

In terms of tax terminology development, this is interesting. If one refers to the *OED's* meaning of defeating the intention of a law by specious compliance with its letter, one might expect the activity we currently deem 'avoidance' to be deemed 'evasion', but contrarily, 'avoidance' seems to have been adopted as the descriptive term. The reason for this needs to be unravelled.

While there may be many definitions possible of tax evasion and tax avoidance, most people familiar with the terms would have no difficulty in accepting those put forward by Simon James (2012) in his *Dictionary of Taxation*:

> Tax evasion is the illegal manipulation of one's affairs with the intention of escaping tax. It is traditionally contrasted with legal *avoidance* of taxation.
>
> *(p. 98)*

---

1 One of the entries under "Taxation", in J. Vitullo Martin and J. R. Moskin (eds), *Executive's Book of Quotations* (Oxford and New York: Oxford University Press, 1994), 279.

> Tax avoidance describes the rearrangement of a person's affairs, within the law, in order
> to reduce tax liability.
>
> *(p. 23)*

Freedman (2004: 336) also defines the latter term similarly as meaning "all arrangements to reduce, eliminate or defer tax liability that are not illegal".

Sears in his 1922 book *Minimizing Taxes* suggests that the use of the terms 'evasion' and 'avoidance' with the meanings attributed to them today originated in the USA and was well established by the 1920s, with some sources[2] tracing this back to the comments of the American jurist Oliver Wendell Holmes in *Bullen v Wisconsin* (see discussion of that case later in this chapter).

The online version of the *OED*, with its entry for "tax evasion" (under "Tax, n[1]") supports the US origin of the modern use of "evasion", though no date or source appears to be given:

> **tax evasion** orig. *U.S.*, the reduction of tax payments by misstatement of income or other illegal means.

It is certainly arguable that the development is more complex and nuanced than is suggested and began much earlier than the 1920s.

Taxpayer activities to "get round" taxes

Perhaps a useful way to shed light on this phenomenon is to consider generally the ways and means of not paying tax that have been employed from a taxpayer perspective. These are many and varied, with a long history, and it is not proposed here to list them in any detail. The activities, transactions and devices that have caused problems over the years, however, fall into four broad categories, as outlined in the following sections.

Category 1: acceptable (or legitimate) tax avoidance

One might ensure that a tax does not apply by engaging in action or inaction that is uncontentious, such as not buying a good or service on which an excise has been imposed. In extreme circumstances, non-payment of taxes may be achieved by revolt or rebellion, though, depending on its nature, such action may constitute evasion. There are thousands of examples of tax revolts and rebellions against taxes perceived as unfair because of the way in which they were levied, the persons on whom they were levied, the rates that were applied, etc. Such resistance is one of the most dominant themes in worldwide tax history. David Burg, in his 2004 book entitled *A World History of Tax Rebellions*, covers a multitude of rebellions across many different time periods and countries. He comments (p. ix) that "[m]any major historic events, such as the *Magna Carta*, the American Revolution, and the French Revolution of 1789 originated largely as tax revolts" and that tax revolts often "subsume larger economic, political, social and even religious issues" as tax provides a focus for concerted opposition.

Less extreme, perhaps, is physical flight or escape. For example, in AD 212, many Egyptians fled their homeland in response to being left to bear the full burden of the Roman poll tax, after Caracalla, the Emperor, conferred Roman citizenship on virtually all those who lived in the

---

2 See, for example the article on "Tax avoidance and tax evasion" on Wikipedia.

provinces – except for the Egyptians (see Burg 2004: 36). Burg (2004: xii) also comments that in the light of barbarian attacks on the Roman Empire's northern borders, many poor people fled or deserted to the enemy to escape "intolerably burdensome taxes" and that the "heavy taxation to pay the costs of maintaining standing armies for protection against the barbarians was a major cause of the decline of the Roman Empire". This kind of flight is mirrored in modern times with companies, such as Starbucks, Amazon, Google and Facebook, re-locating their operations to jurisdictions where tax rates and rules are more favourable.

Exemption from payment may be seen as another form of escape. The aristocracy in France, for example, originally paid no direct taxes (but they actually levied taxes on those still tied to their estates by a feudal system which lingered on into the 1600s). While changes in the late seventeenth century meant that some direct taxes would apply to the nobility, they remained exempt from the taille (direct land tax, equating to a poll tax) which was paid by peasantry and non-aristocrats. Ironically, those who had money and could have paid taxes paid the least, if any at all.

In recent times, exemptions or reductions in taxes have more usually been made available to the less well-off in society (rather than to rich aristocrats) to alleviate the burden of tax or to encourage behaviour favoured by a government; for example, capital investment to support industrial development, for which various tax allowances might be given.

Legitimate tax planning is also a means of escaping or avoiding tax. For example, in the UK, inheritance tax may be charged on an individual's death where the value of assets in the estate, or given prior to death, exceeds certain exempt bands. In order to provide some relief, gifts taking place more than seven years before death are exempt, so it is possible to avoid paying some or all of the potential inheritance tax by making lifetime transfers of assets directly to the intended beneficiaries or indirectly into trusts. Hence, it is a normal part of inheritance tax planning to devolve estates so as to preclude a tax burden occurring on death, as this is legitimately avoidable. Such tax planning involves deliberately framing reality in a particular way to ensure that taxpayers are enabled to act pre-emptively in order to obtain future benefits which they would otherwise miss because of a lack of knowledge of the technicalities of tax law. People are also allowed to receive interest exempt of tax from certain specified forms of investments or to choose to do business by using one legal form in preference to another to minimise their tax burden.

The idea of 'legitimate avoidance' may seem rather odd if avoidance *per se* is "within the law" as the definition provided previously by James suggests (2012: 98). This contradiction was highlighted by Peter Wyman when Head of Tax at the accounting firm Coopers & Lybrand in 1997.

> Customs & Excise appears now to use the term 'legitimate avoidance' to distinguish between what they clearly believe to be 'illegitimate' avoidance and 'the legitimate desire to organise affairs in a tax efficient way'. These deliberate attempts to confer an aura of illegality to a legitimate activity is dangerous, and should not be allowed to continue unchallenged.
>
> *Wyman 1997: 3*

Thus there seems to be a deliberate attempt to shift appreciation of certain taxation issues such that avoidance should be regarded as ethically dubious. If avoidance is legally permitted, this approach casts doubt on the validity of the law permitting it by blurring terminology and shifting hitherto acceptable behaviour on to morally dubious ground by shifting the meaning of words. As a result, depending on what is encompassed in any particular means of avoidance,

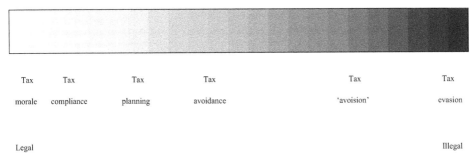

Tax	Tax	Tax	Tax		Tax	Tax
morale	compliance	planning	avoidance		'avoision'	evasion

Legal   Illegal

Figure 2.1 'Spectrum' approach.

Source: Adapted from Lymer and Oats 2012: 373.

it might be these days categorised by UK Revenue authorities as 'unacceptable', 'illegitimate', 'illegal' or 'abusive', which appears semantically rather odd if avoidance itself remains a legal concept and it is merely a (difficult) question of deciding where to draw a line between legality and illegality.

Tax activities and transactions have often been considered in terms of where they might lie on a spectrum ranging from uncontentious 'tax planning'[3] (such as deciding which form of business entity to use or using tax-exempt savings accounts) through to 'tax evasion', with colours from white to darkest black indicating their legality. Tax evasion is coloured black, indicating illegality, and taken to denote criminal offences such as the deliberate omission or understatement of income undertaken with the intention of not paying tax where such payments are required by law. A typical representation of this might be as shown above in Figure 2.1.

Tax morale refers to an individual's willingness to pay tax, even in circumstances where a failure to pay amounts due would not be detected. Tax compliance means complying with tax law.

Language used to describe activity as being on one side or the other of a "line" to denote avoidance or evasion is commonly found. For example, in the US case of *Bullen v Wisconsin*, Oliver Wendell Holmes stated,

> We do not speak of evasion, because, when the law draws a line, a case is on one side of it or the other, and if on the safe side is none the worse legally that a party has availed himself to the full of what the law permits. When an act is condemned as an evasion, what is meant is that it is on the wrong side of the line indicated by the policy, if not by the mere letter, of the law.
>
> *Bullen v Wisconsin 240 US 625 (1916), at 630–1*

In the 'spectrum or line' approach, it has always been less contentious where exactly a line should be drawn between tax planning and tax avoidance, as both are legal, than where it should be drawn between tax avoidance and tax evasion. The line beyond which avoidance becomes

---

3 It is not the purpose of this chapter to look at the distinction between 'tax planning' and 'tax avoidance' or the various terms, such as 'tax saving' or 'tax mitigation', which have been developed to characterise different types of acceptable avoidance, but to look at why illegal activity came to be called 'evasion' and legal activity 'avoidance'.

evasion (the grey area between the two is often referred to as 'tax avoision' – see Seldon 1979) is important in determining the legality of transactions. As Richard Broadbent, former chairman of HM Customs & Excise, said (2003: 127–8):

> There are cases we know of where transactions are completed solely for the benefit of a tax gain, which of course was not intended by Parliament. The question is, is it tax avoidance or does the activity go beyond avoidance and cross the boundary between avoidance and evasion? This can sometimes be difficult to decide. … It may be that as the legal principles of avoidance become defined in case law, a business which implements an avoidance scheme which has been held by the courts to be avoidance could be embarking on a course of conduct which amounts to evasion.

The 're-definition' referred to above in the quotation from Wyman may be interpreted as Customs & Excise trying to move the evasion-avoidance line farther into the grey area, or it may be interpreted as an attempt to taint hitherto acceptable activity with the illegality of evasion, as Wyman suggests. Not everyone agrees, however, that there is a dividing 'line' nor, if one exists, where it should be drawn. "One man's idea of acceptable tax planning is undoubtedly another man's idea of criminally subversive activity" (Gillett 1999: 1). Others think that there is no problem here at all and that "tax avoidance is a conceptual anomaly that exists in the mind of those whose sense of morality is violated by certain effective tax practices" (Orow 2004: 415). Avoidance occurs "where legislative intention and policy miscarried and failed to anticipate and reach the transaction under consideration" (*ibid.*).

Category 2: reverse "engineering"

One might do something which was subject to tax, then set about retrospectively seeking to "get out of" paying the amount due. It was, for example, not uncommon before the introduction of capital gains tax for individuals to try to claim that a sale of a good/asset had generated a capital, rather than a trading, profit, as a capital profit was then not taxable and a trading profit was.

Category 3: proactive physical means

Some sort of means of preventative means of "getting round" a tax might be employed. Such a means might be physical. For example, it was common to find windows bricked up so that the window tax levied in the years 1696–1851 did not apply (Dowell 1884: 168). Tax surveyors (the forerunners of tax inspectors) came periodically to count windows in houses, to assess the tax due. As the tax was levied on glazed windows, it did not apply if the glass was removed and the window bricked up. When the surveyor had left, the window could be re-glazed. Evidence of this can be seen today in many English stately homes, where the windows ultimately remained bricked up. It was not illegal to brick up a window, and a house owner might claim that this had been done for many reasons. A similar device was employed in the bricking up of hearths/chimneys as a way round the very unpopular hearth or chimney tax (1662–1688) (Marshall 1936), though legislation was introduced to render bricking up illegal.

Category 4: proactive use of the law

Another means would involve use of the law, in ways more or less equivocal. The extent to which transactions may be regarded as legitimate avoidance or illegitimate evasion (and so where the dividing line may be drawn) depends on the legal, social or political climate of the time. "Tax avoision" is a term coined (by Seldon 1979[4]) to describe activity, behaviour or transactions where it is unclear as to which side of a dividing line between legality and illegality they fall, especially if one considers that taxpayers should comply not only with the letter of the law but also with its spirit. However, in the early years of the last century, avoiding tax was viewed as a quite acceptable thing to do, as the following citations from two well known tax avoidance cases make clear:

> No man in this country is under the smallest obligation, moral or other, so to arrange his legal relations to his business or to his property so as to enable the Inland Revenue to put the largest possible shovel into his stores. The Inland Revenue is not slow … to take advantage which is open to it under the taxing statutes for the purpose of depleting the taxpayer's pocket. And the taxpayer is, in like manner, entitled to be astute to prevent, so far as he honestly can, the depletion of his means by the Revenue.
>
> *Lord Clyde, Ayrshire Pullman Services and D.M. Ritchie v CIR*
> *(1929) 14 TC 754 at 764–765*

> Every man is entitled if he can to order his affairs so that the tax attaching under the appropriate Acts is less than it otherwise would be. If he succeeds in ordering them so as to secure this result, then, however unappreciative the Commissioners of Inland Revenue or his fellow taxpayers may be of his ingenuity, he cannot be compelled to pay an increased tax.
>
> *Lord Tomlin, IRC v Duke of Westminster*
> *[1936] AC 1 at 19–20[5]*

When looking at this topic, many books inherently suggest that the issue of tax avoidance/ evasion began with the cases cited above. These cases take the idea of a "line" dividing acceptable behaviour from unacceptable behaviour into a new dimension, with the introduction (or re-introduction) of the idea of 'form over substance' and the use and development of schemes to exploit the law.

One of the characteristics attributed in the late twentieth and early twenty-first centuries to the more contentious forms of tax avoidance is the use of schemes which do not breach the letter of the law but do breach its underlying intention or spirit (e.g., the cases of *Ramsay (W.T.) Ltd v CIR* and *Furniss v Dawson* being typically cited examples of this). Perhaps the best definition of this sort of activity is Lord Templeman's in *Matrix-Securities v IRC*.

> Every tax avoidance scheme involves a trick and a pretence. It is the task of the Revenue to unravel the trick and the duty of the court to ignore the pretence.
>
> *[1994] STC 272, at 282*

However, this type of activity had been going on a long time, and was nothing new. Wheatcroft (1955: 209–10) cites an example of the use of land conveyances in the fifteenth and sixteenth

---

4 A. Seldon (ed.), *Tax Avoision: The Economic, Legal and Moral Inter-Relationships Between Avoidance and Evasion* (London: Institute of Economic Affairs, 1979).

5 Legal opinions were much the same in the USA at the time. See, for example, the comments of Judge Learned Hand, in the case of *Gregory v Helvering, Commissioner of Internal Revenue*, US Supreme Court (1935) (94-TNT-241-61).

centuries "to avoid incidents of manorial tenure", and the cases and sources reviewed later reveal other examples of this.

However, from a revenue authority perspective, such activities might be countered from a number of different standpoints, namely: (1) the "spectrum or line" approach, which has been discussed already; (2) the "smell" test; and (3) what revenue authorities might want. These last two standpoints are considered in more detail in the next section.

Revenue standpoints

The 'smell' test

This might be regarded as a version of 'substance over form', as evidenced in the well known case of *Ramsay (W.T.) Ltd v CIR*, which is often considered the first instance of the success of this argument, but there is another much earlier one which often escapes notice. Ferrier (1981: 303–4) reports on a 1783 scheme to "get round" the payment of a two pence Scot duty (a type of excise) payable in Glasgow on each pint of ale or beer brewed, brought in or sold in the city and suburbs, in *Magistrates and Town Council of the City of Glasgow v Messrs Murdoch, Warren & Co.* The brewers, based at Anderston, then far enough away to be considered as not in the city or suburbs, announced that they would cease to supply the city, and made a contract with a Mr Munro, who bought the beer and supplied it to customers from the Anderston premises. The case was taken to the House of Lords. Lord Mansfield was the foremost judge, and had no qualms about judging this a scheme which should not be allowed, and ignoring the "device of the intermediate contract with Munro" (Ferrier 1981: 306).

What revenue authorities might want

The approach now adopted by Her Majesty's Revenue & Customs (HMRC) seems to eschew the 'spectrum or line' and 'smell' test approaches, in favour of something that appears to go beyond these. For example, in an online version of the *International Tax Handbook* in 2007 it stated:

> [T]he expression 'tax planning' ... embraces a wide range of options from those which are merely 'mitigatory' to those which we would regard as 'avoidance' ... [F]ine distinctions between 'tax planning' and 'tax avoidance' are seen as being of less consequence than the overall effect on the yield to the Exchequer. This is particularly so where the apparent result is not in accordance with Parliament's intentions or which would not have been had Parliament addressed itself to the particular issue.

While it is undeniable that action to reduce a taxpayer's liability will result in a reduced tax take for the Government, regardless of how it may be categorised, does this then mean that words and definitions have been superseded by interpretation of actions in the light of the underlying intention of Parliament, even if, according to the above citation, Parliament has not expressed its intention? This may be to read too much into an isolated extract from an HMRC *Handbook*, but the underlying issue of what the law means or intends shows us that we have not really progressed very far in over 200 years, as the rest of this chapter goes on to demonstrate by reference to nineteenth and twentieth century and earlier source documents.

Nineteenth century terminology – government documents

In government documents, up to and including the early nineteenth century, references seem to be to 'tax evasion', rather than 'tax avoidance'. For example, the *General Alphabetical Index to the Printed Bills, Reports, Accounts and Papers* for the 1810–11 session of Parliament refers under Section P, under probates of wills, to "evasion of duty". It seems to be from the mid nineteenth century that the use of the word 'avoidance' starts to appear. Arguably the realisation that income tax was no longer a temporary tax, which the government aimed to abolish, contributed significantly to the emergence of a different perception, especially as increasing numbers of people were affected by it. Gladstone's government had intended to abolish the tax in 1860 – an intention signalled in the 1853 Budget – but it was retained, with Gladstone's last proposal for its abolition being recorded in 1874 (Sabine 1966: 90; Daunton 2001: 167). Gladstone himself was aware of the nature of the tax itself as "encouraging evasion and dishonesty" (Gunter and Maloney 1999: 336).

Income tax was often easy to avoid. Stopforth (1990) examines the use of the settlements legislation from 1799, when income tax was introduced, up to 1920. Owing to the way in which the legislation was drafted, it was possible to avoid the tax "by transferring assets to others within the family, granting annuities to them or creating trusts for their benefit" (Stopforth 1990: 1). The tax was also easily evaded (*ibid.*). As part of his research, Stopforth cites extensively from evidence given to the Select Committee on Income and Property Tax in June and July 1851 (the Hume Committee), which was concerned with eliminating evasion, but also discussed methods of avoidance. It is clear that Inland Revenue officials had begun to use the terms 'avoidance' and 'evasion' at this date to distinguish between legal and illegal activity. The problem is that officials do not use the terms with consistency of meaning, and it is clear that the terminology is in the process of development. Stopforth (1990: 2) cites the evidence of Charles Pressly, an Inland Revenue Commissioner:

> I made use of the word avoidance; a man having £160 a year may charge his estate with an annuity of £20 a year to his child; I do not call that an evasion of the duty at all; I think it is perfectly legitimate; I think he avoids the payment of the duty.
>
> *(This would be a Category 4 device, by reference to the list given earlier.)*

Similarly, Stopforth (1990: 2) also cites the evidence of Mr J. Hyde (a Surveyor of Taxes):

> I have only ways and manners in which parties get off; some in one way and some in another by contrivances, what we call avoidance.
>
> *(This would also be a Category 4 device.)*

However, when giving evidence as to a particular type of avoidance, Mr Hyde (Stopforth 1990: 2) comments:

> a farmer who is the owner and occupier of a farm at £140 per annum … would be assessed at £4/1/8d under Schedule A for the value and at £2/-/10d for the occupation, under Schedule D. His son, … was employed upon the farm; he ostensibly makes the son his tenant, by which means the father can claim the £140 for the value of the farm, and the son can claim under Schedule D as the occupier at £140. The exemption runs up to £300 a year … I believe that was done in Derbyshire to a great extent,

and in other parts of the country, after the first year. This is what I would describe perhaps as a legal avoidance; it is not a fraud; it is merely the management.

(Again, this would be a Category 4 device.)

It is, perhaps, regrettable that the term 'management' did not gain currency, as it could in theory have prevented the proliferation of numerous terms to describe various facets of tax avoidance. It would, in regard to business, have been a useful term, as tax is something which needs planning and active management. Stopforth (1990: 13, endnote 8) further comments, however, that in documents prior to the 1930s, officials often termed activity 'evasion' where we might sooner call it 'avoidance', though officials in the 1851 Select Committee did use avoidance in the sense we would use it today. Stopforth also comments (*ibid.*) that:

> [s]ubsequent documents [to the 1851 Select Committee minutes] show a blurring of the distinction and one wonders if whether this may have been deliberate policy on the part of officials in order to make avoidance appear to be less acceptable by tainting it with the illegality of evasion.

Nineteenth century terminology – cases

Another source of evidence for the use of terminology is the cases that were brought before the courts at the time. It is clear that the judges were subject to the same definition problems as the 1851 Select Committee witnesses. However, it is not easy to trace any logical development of definitions, though one can establish that some shift of meaning is occurring.

For example, Turner, LJ in 1860 in *Fisher v Brierly* stated:

> There is a marked distinction which perhaps has not been sufficiently attended to in some of the cases upon this subject, between evasion as it has been called and contravention, and it is against contravention, and not against what has been termed evasion, the power of this Court is directed. I agree with what was said by Lord Cranworth upon this subject in *Edwards v Hall* (6 De G. M. & G. 74).

(1860) 1 De Gex, Fisher & Jones 643, at 663

Lord Turner used 'evasion' here as we would now use 'avoidance' and 'contravention' to mean 'evasion'.

Lord Cranworth in *Edwards v Hall* in 1855 said that

> anyone has a right to evade a statute if his meaning is to place himself in such a situation as not to come within its purview.

(1855) 6 De Gex, Macnaghten& Gordon 74, at 84

Here, possibly, a Category 1 or 3 device is envisaged.

However, in *Yorkshire Wagon Co. v McClure*, in 1882, although not a tax case, Jessel, MR defined 'evade':

> that is, to do anything which is either expressly or impliedly prohibited by the Act of Parliament.

(1882) LR 21 ChD 309, at 316

Lord Jessel's definition of 'evade' is our 'modern' one, but Lord Turner and Lord Cranworth both seem to use the term 'evade' in a sense akin to the more usual definition of avoidance. They both seem to be thinking of an extension to the meaning of 'evade', viz., 'evade lawfully', which is made explicit in *Bullivant v AG* in 1901:

> This assumes that 'evade' means avoid by fraud, stratagem, trick, or underhand contrivance. But evade has two meanings: evade lawfully, and evade unlawfully. A man may evade a tax or duty by not doing the act which makes the impost applicable, and he may consult his solicitor how to avoid doing the act *[i.e., Category 1 or 3]*: such communications are privileged. The judgment of the Privy Council in *Simms v Registrar of Probates* pointed out that the word 'evade' was capable of two senses – one which suggests underhand dealing, and another which means nothing more than the intentional avoidance of something disagreeable. Their Lordships held that in the absence of evidence of some device or underhand contrivance the words 'with intent to evade the payment of duty' contained in an Australian statute imposed no penalty, not being applicable to innocent transactions.
>
> *[1901] AC 196, at 199*

Lord Lindley in the same case said,

> there are two ways of construing the word 'evade': one is, that a person may go to a solicitor and ask him how to keep out of an Act of Parliament – how to do something which does not bring him within the scope of it *[i.e., Category 1 or 3]*. That is evading in one sense, but there is nothing illegal in it. The other is, when he goes to his solicitor and says, 'Tell me how to escape from the consequences of the Act of Parliament, although I am brought within it.' That is an act of quite a different character *[i.e., Category 2]*.
>
> *[1901] AC 196, at 207*

In the case of *Simms v Registrar of Probates*, referred to in *Bullivant v AG* above, in 1900, it was stated:

> Upon the meaning of the term evasion as distinct from avoidance, the following cases were cited in the ruling judgments of the Court below:
>
> *Yorkshire Wagon Co. v McClure* (1); *Attorney-General v Beech* (2); *Harding v Headington* (3).
>
> *[1900] AC 323, at 325*

Later, Lord Hobhouse, speaking of an earlier judgment in the same case, said:

> He examines the meaning of the expression 'evade', and the conclusion he comes to is in the following terms: – 'I am thus driven to the conclusion that the word "evade" in s. 27 means to avoid by some direct means, by some device or stratagem *[i.e., Category 3]*. Without attempting, what is probably impracticable, to give an exhaustive definition of the phrase "with intent to evade the payment of duty hereunder," I am of opinion that the phrase would cover some arrangement, trust or other device, whether concealed, or apparent on the face of the non-testamentary disposition by which what is really a part of the estate of the deceased is made to appear to belong to somebody else in order to escape payment of duty.
>
> *[1900] AC 323, at 331*

Following up on *Yorkshire Wagon Co. v McClure*, in 1882, as referred to in *Simms v Registrar of Probates*, Lord Lindley, also one of the judges in *Bullivant*, said:

> There is always an ambiguity about the expression 'evading an Act of Parliament'. In one sense you cannot evade an Act of Parliament; that is to say, the Court is bound so to construe every Act of Parliament as to take care that that which is really prohibited may be held void. On the other hand, you may avoid doing that which is prohibited by the Act of Parliament and you may do something else equally advantageous to you which is not prohibited by the Act of Parliament *[i.e., Category 1]*. It appears to me that the transaction falls under the last of these two classes, it is a transaction as useful for the *Railway Company* as the other, but it is a real transaction, and is not struck at by the Act of Parliament at all.

This agrees, not surprisingly, with Lord Jessel's definition of 'evade', in the same case, which has been cited above, though Lord Jessel did not go on to define 'avoid', as Lord Lindley does here. There is thus a case for suggesting that the original meaning of avoidance is not 'avoidance of taxation' *per se*, but 'avoidance of doing something prohibited by law' – that is, the use of 'avoid' in its meanings of 'keep clear of or away from, shun, refrain from' – and doing something advantageous, which is not prohibited. However, it is but a short cut or a small shift in meaning to see this distinction become blurred because the very nature of the activities, transactions, schemes and devices employed was such that they had a dual role of refraining from prohibited activity at the same time as being designed to eliminate or reduce tax liability. That this occurred is clear by reference to *Harding v Headington* in 1873–4, though at first glance the terms appear used interchangeably without distinction of meaning. The case head note states:

> The respondent, being the occupier of a farm adjacent to a turnpike road, made a gap in the hedge a few feet on one side of a toll-gate at which tolls were authorized to be taken, and formed a semicircular road for a few yards over his farm, with a gap into the turnpike road a few feet on the other side of the gate. He then, with a horse and carriage, having passed more than 100 yards along the turnpike road, with the intention to avoid paying the toll, passed through one gap over the road on his own land, and back again by the other gap into the turnpike road, and then passed more than 100 yards along the turnpike road: –
>
> Held, that the respondent came within the exception in s. 41 [General Turnpike Act (3 Geo. 4, c. 126)], and was not liable to a penalty for evading the toll.
>
> *(1873–74) LR 9 QB 157, at 157*

Here though 'avoid' and 'evade' are used apparently to describe the same action, if the text is read carefully, it is clear that 'avoid' is used in the 'modern' sense and 'avoiding the toll' is not the same as the illegal action of 'evading the toll'. There are two instances in the report where 'evade' is used in the sense of 'legally evade', but the case report is not wholly the verbatim comments of the judges.

The whole issue of the meaning of these terms, though, could not, of course, be separated from the issue of the meaning of statutes themselves, and that of 'form over substance', as was made clear in the remaining case referred to in *Simms v Registrar of Probates*, namely *Attorney-General v Beech and Another*, in 1898, where Smith, LJ said:

> I cannot do better than quote the words of the Lord Chancellor (Lord Halsbury) in the House of Lords when dealing with a similar argument and addressed to the House upon a taxing Act in the case of *Tennant v Smith*. The Lord Chancellor said:

'... Cases, therefore, under the taxing Acts always resolve themselves into a question whether or not the words of the Act have reached the alleged subject of taxation. Lord Wensleydale said in In re Micklethwait:

It is a well-established rule that the subject is not to be taxed without clear words for that purpose; and also, that every Act of Parliament must be read according to the natural construction of its words.'

[1898] 2 QB 147, at 150

This was supported by Lord Cairns's comments in *Charles James Partington v Attorney-General* in 1869, where he based his opinion

upon form and also upon substance. I am not at all sure that, in a case of this kind – a fiscal case – form is not amply sufficient; because, as I understand the principle of all fiscal legislation it is this: If the person sought to be taxed comes within the letter of the law he must be taxed, however great the hardship may appear to the judicial mind to be. On the other hand, if the Crown, seeking to recover the tax, cannot bring the subject within the letter of the law, the subject is free, however apparently within the spirit of the law the case might otherwise appear to be. In other words, if there be admissible, in any statute, what is called an equitable construction, certainly such a construction is not admissible in a taxing statute, where you can simply adhere to the words of the statute.

(1869) LR 4 HL 100, at 122

The nineteenth century and before – terminology in newspapers and periodicals

Newspapers and periodicals are a good source of contemporary terminology, as they need to express opinions in language their readers will understand. It is evident, from even the briefest examination of newspapers and periodicals from the nineteenth century and before that a similar level of confusion appears. In an article entitled *An argument for the income-tax*, on 31 January 1857, *The Preston Guardian*, repeating material from *The Economist*, refers to it as a "tax liable to evasion and fraud", which is not altogether clear. Likewise, in an article entitled *Selling unstamped almanacks*, on 13 November 1831, *Police – The Examiner*, refers to evasion of stamp duty by the sellers, which is clearer as it seems to refer to documents being sold which should have been stamped, but were not. In 1829, *Bell's Life in London and Sporting Chronicle* reports on the excise on beer brewed by public brewers and how the rich can avoid this excise: they brew their own beer which the poor cannot, so the poor are taxed.[6] The remedy suggested was to impose an excise on malt, which all need to brew beer, hence all would be taxed. The idea of an excise being avoidable by not consuming an item on which an excise is imposed was, however, well understood. What constituted avoidance where a concept (such as income tax), not a physical object, was involved is less certain. The idea of tax avoidance, as we understand it today, was well understood, for example, in relation to the window tax. The eighteenth-century periodical,

---

6 Beer was not a drink of choice as it is today, but the poor drank it out of necessity. Water supplies, especially in cities, were often contaminated, and the brewing process involved boiling, so beer was safer to drink.

the *Observator*, carried an article on the window tax in its edition of 31 December 1709, which commented as follows:

> many People will stop up their present Windows, to avoid the tax … for we are not to doubt, but disaffected People, of whom there are too many, will take this Method to avoid the Tax.

If nothing else, the above article demonstrates that the concept of tax avoidance in its so-called 'modern' meaning is actually much older than the 1920s and does not originate in the USA.

Conclusion

It seems clear that 'avoidance' came into use in the mid nineteenth century as a term to differentiate legal activity from 'evasion', which was always clearly illegal. This development can be seen by reference to government documents and legal case reports of the period, and it would appear to have occurred earlier than some sources suggest. It is not specifically a US phenomenon. English cases do suggest that the semantic movement is from 'evasion' to 'legal evasion', thence to 'avoidance of prohibited activity', and finally to 'tax avoidance' as a result of what 'avoidance of prohibited activity' typically involved – and judges are careful in their use of the developing terms. Looking back to the definition of the two words as given by the *OED*, it does seem that 'evasion' might originally have carried the meaning that 'avoidance' now does, and that it is the legal need for distinction in terminology that has given the word 'avoidance' a meaning it did not originally possess. We should not be surprised at this, as it has happened in other areas, such as accounting, and remains a characteristic of the development of taxation terminology.

Acknowledgement

This chapter is drawn from several different sections of Frecknall-Hughes, J. (2014) *The Theory, Principles and Management of Taxation: An Introduction* (Oxford: Routledge), which are sometimes used *verbatim*.

Table of cases

Attorney-General v Beech and Another [1898] 2 QB 147.
Ayrshire Pullman Services and D.M. Ritchie v CIR 14 TC 754.
Bullen v Wisconsin 240 US 625 (1916).
Bullivant v AG [1901] AC 196.
Charles James Partington v Attorney-General (1869) LR 4 HL 100.
Edwards v Hall (1855) 6 De Gex, Macnaghten & Gordon 74.
Gregory v Helvering 293 US 465 (1935).
Fisher v Brierly (1860) 1 De Gex, Fisher & Jones 643.
Furniss v Dawson [1984] AC 474.
Magistrates and Town Council of the City of Glasgow v Messrs. Murdoch, Warren & Co. (1783) 2 Paton 615.
Harding v Headington (1873–74) LR 9 QB 157.
IRC v Duke of Westminster [1936] AC 1.
Matrix-Securities v IRC [1994] STC 272.
Ramsay (W.T.) Ltd. v CIR [1982] AC 300.
Simms v Registrar of Probates [1900] AC 323.
Yorkshire Wagon Co. v McClure (1882) LR 21 ChD 309.

References

"An argument for the income-tax". (1857). *Preston Guardian*, 31 January. British Newspapers 1600–1900 [Online]. Available at Gale Cengage Learning, by subscription [Accessed 15 August 2009]

Broadbent, R. (2003). "VAT compliance in the 21st century", *British Tax Review*, 2, 122–30.

Burg, D.F. (2004). *A World History of Tax Rebellions: An Encyclopedia of Tax Rebels, Revolts, and Riots From Antiquity to the Present*. New York and London: Routledge.

Daunton, M. (2001). *Trusting Leviathan: The Politics of Taxation in Britain, 1799–1914*. Cambridge: Cambridge University Press.

Dowell, S. (1884). *A History of Taxation and Taxes in England*, Vol. 3, 3rd ed. Reprint, New York: A.M. Kelly, 1965.

'Duty on Beer' (1829), *Bell's Life in London and Sporting Chronicle*, 1 December. British Newspapers 1600–1900. [Online]. Available from Gale Cengage Learning, by subscription. [Accessed 15 August 2009]

Evans, L. (2008). "Observations on the changing language of accounting" [Online]. Available at http://ssrn.com./abstract=1228525[Accessed 23 March 2008]

Ferrier, I. (1981). "The meaning of the statute: Mansfield on tax avoidance", *British Tax Review*, 5, 303–8.

Freedman, J. (2004). "Defining taxpayer responsibility: In support of a general anti-avoidance principle", *British Tax Review*, 4, 332–57.

"General alphabetical index to the printed bills, reports, accounts and papers: Session 1810–11", House of Commons Parliamentary Papers [Online]. Available at http://gateway.proquest.com/openurl?url_ver=Z39.88-2004&res_dat=xri:hccp&rft_dat=xri:hccp:fulltext:1810-002768:5 [Accessed 15 August 2009]

Gillett, P. (1999). "The consultative document on a general anti avoidance rule for direct taxes: A view from business", *British Tax Review*, 1, 1–5.

Gunter, C., and Maloney, J. (1999). "Did Gladstone make a difference? Rhetoric and reality in mid-Victorian finance", *Accounting, Business & Financial History*, 9(3), 325–47.

International Tax Handbook – ITH 103. (2007). "International tax planning: Avoidance in international context", HMRC [Online]. Available at www.hmrc.gov.uk/manuals/ithmanual/html/ITH0001/02_0007_ITH103.htm [Accessed 8 September 2007]

James, S. (2012). *Dictionary of Taxation*. Cheltenham: Edward Elgar.

Lymer, A., and Oats, L. (2012). *Taxation Policy and Practice*, 19th ed. Birmingham: Fiscal Publications.

Marshall, L.M. (1936). "The levying of the hearth tax, 1662–1668", *English Historical Review*, 51(204), 628–46.

'News' (1709), *Observator*, 31 December–4 January. British Newspapers 1600–1900. [Online]. Available from Gale Cengage Learning, by subscription. [Accessed 1 December 2013]

Orow, N. (2004). "Structured finance and the operation of general anti avoidance rules", *British Tax Review*, 4, 410–35.

Oxford English Dictionary (1993). Compact ed. BCA by arrangement with Oxford: Oxford University Press.

Oxford English Dictionary. "Tax, n¹". [Online]. Available at http://dictionary.oed.com/cgi/entry/50247781/50247781se44?single=1&query_type=word&queryword=tax+avoidance&first=1&max_to_show=10&hilite=50247781se44 [Accessed 16 August 2009]

Sabine, B.E.V. (1966). *A History of Income Tax*. London: George Allen & Unwin Ltd.

Sears, J.H. (1922). *Minimizing Taxes*. St Paul, MN: Vernon Law Book Co.

Seldon, A. (ed.) (1979). *Tax Avoision: The Economic, Legal and Moral Inter-Relationships Between Avoidance and Evasion*. London: Institute of Economic Affairs.

"Selling unstamped almanacks". (1831). *Police – The Examiner*, 13 November. British Newspapers 1600–1900 [Online]. Available at Gale Cengage Learning, by subscription [Accessed 15 August 2009]

Stopforth, D.P. (1990). "Settlements and the avoidance of tax on income – the period to 1920", *British Tax Review*, 7, 225–50.

"Tax avoidance and tax evasion", *Wikipedia* [Online]. Available at http://en.wikipedia.org/wiki/Tax_evasion [Accessed 9 June 2009]

Vitullo-Martin, J. and Moskin, J. R. (eds) (1994). *Executive's Book of Quotations*. Oxford and New York: Oxford University Press.

Wheatcroft, G.S.A. (1955). "The attitude of the legislature and the courts to tax avoidance", *Modern Law Review*, 18(3), 203–30.

Wyman, P. (1997). "Upholding the law", *Tax Journal* (10 November), 3–4.

3

PERSPECTIVES ON THE TAX AVOIDANCE CULTURE

Legislative, administrative, and judicial ambiguity

Henry Ordower

Introduction to the culture of tax avoidance

During the latter half of the twentieth century, a robust tax planning industry emerged in the United States and much of Europe.[1] Tax planners took to heart Judge Learned Hand's admonition that "[a]ny one may so arrange his affairs that his taxes shall be as low as possible; he is not bound to choose that pattern which will best pay the Treasury; there is not even a patriotic duty to increase one's taxes."[2] They developed tax minimization products and sold them to high income and high wealth taxpayers. Most of the products focused on reducing taxpayers' exposure to the steeply progressive income taxes, but some products also reached similarly progressive estate and gift taxes. Less frequently planning addressed excise- and consumption-based taxes. Despite Judge Hand's tax-avoidance-favorable rhetoric, he took a purposive approach to tax planning. In holding for the government in *Helvering v. Gregory*, Hand grafted a corporate-business-purpose requirement onto the tax-deferred reorganization statute:

> But the underlying presupposition is plain that the readjustment shall be undertaken for reasons germane to the conduct of the venture in hand, not as an ephemeral incident, egregious to its prosecution. To dodge the shareholders' taxes is not one of the transactions contemplated as corporate 'reorganizations.'[3]

Yet, Judge Hand's endorsement of intentional tax structuring to diminish one's taxes continues to hold sway as a cultural precept.

---

1 H. Ordower, "The Culture of Tax Avoidance", 55 *Saint Louis University Law Journal* 47, 55–9 (2010) ("Ordower, Culture" in the following).

2 *Helvering v. Gregory*, 69 F.2d 809, 810 (2d Cir. 1934), aff'd. as *Gregory v. Helvering, 293 U.S. 465 (1935)*. Judge Hand remained consistent about tax: "Over and over again courts have said that there is nothing sinister in so arranging one's affairs as to keep taxes as low as possible. Everybody does so, rich or poor; and all do right, for nobody owes any public duty to pay more than the law demands: taxes are enforced exactions, not voluntary contributions. To demand more in the name of morals is mere cant." *Commissioner v. Newman*, 159 F.2d 848, 851 (2d Cir. 1947) (dissent).

3 Gregory, id., 811. Assaf Likhovski, "The Duke and The Lady: Helvering v. Gregory and the History of Tax Avoidance Adjudication", 25 *Cardozo Law Review* 953 (2004).

A tax law dictionary equates the concept of tax avoidance with tax planning resulting in minimization of taxes – a legitimate practice[4] – as contrasted with tax evasion – illegitimate tax diminution.[5] Tax planning that violates no law is neither illegal nor, from Judge Hand's perspective, reprehensible. Participants in the tax planning industry have been impressively creative. They have designed tax-efficient transactional structures to assist their clients in minimizing taxes and have enabled their clients to defer or avoid tax. The last two Republican Party presidential candidates engaged in substantial tax planning. Mitt Romney used the carried interest technique[6] and Donald Trump sustained a very large net operating loss[7] that may have been available to offset his income for tax purposes for as many as eighteen years. The tax loss probably came from leveraged investments.[8] Unknown is whether the disclosure that Romney used the carried interest technique to diminish his taxes or the disclosure of Trump's very large net operating loss and his unwillingness to disclose his tax returns had any impact on the outcome in the presidential elections.[9] Trump's victory suggests that American voters applaud those who avoid taxes.

Acceptance of tax avoidance and even some tax evasion[10] in the United States is commonplace. Much of the tax evasion is trivial – an individual finds a ten-dollar bill lying on the sidewalk and keeps it without including the amount in the income reported on the annual tax return.[11] Probably most Americans would either be unaware of the requirement to report the ten dollars or would agree that the amount is too small to be of any significance. Failure to report nevertheless is unlawful. The cultural demarcation between avoidance and evasion tends to blur as the rhetoric surrounding tax avoidance and evasion conflates the concepts. Absence of a sharp line between avoidance and evasion contributes to, or perhaps causes, growth in the "tax gap."[12] If one lacks the sophistication or the wealth for complex tax planning, exclusion

---

4 Richard A. Westin, *WG&L Tax Dictionary* (Valhalla, 2002), 784.

5 Id., 786.

6 Described under heading "Some examples of simple tax planning", Example 2 below.

7 Section 172 of the Internal Revenue Code of 1986, as amended (the "Code"), 26 U.S.C.A. §172, (the excess of operating deductions over income for tax purposes is a net operating loss). Taxpayers at the time of Trump's loss could carry the loss back three and forward 15 years as a tax deduction. Current rules allow a two year carryback and a twenty year carryforward under IRC §172(b). This chapter will use IRC § followed by a number to refer to sections of the Code.

8 D. Barstow, S. Craig, R. Buettner and M. Twohey, "Donald Trump Tax Records Show He Could Have Avoided Taxes for Nearly Two Decades", The Times Found, *The New York Times* (1 October 2016), available at www. nytimes.com/2016/10/02/us/politics/donald-trump-taxes.html?_r=0. The information on Trump's tax reporting is scant, so the accuracy of the return remains in question. Whether the possible separation of the economic loss incurred by the lenders on the leveraged investments from the tax loss for Trump may have forced inclusion in Trump's income in a later year of an equal amount when the debt was discharged without payment is similarly uncertain, but Trump's creditors may have exchanged their debt for an equity interest in Trump's partnerships, thereby eliminating the cancellation of indebtedness income. D. Barstow, R. McIntire, P. Cohen, S. Craig and R. Buettner, "Donald Trump Used Legally Dubious Method to Avoid Paying Taxes", *The New York Times* (31 October 2016), available at www.nytimes.com/2016/11/01/us/politics/donald-trump-tax.html?emc=edit_na_2016 1031&nlid=54282593&ref=cta&_r=1.

9 Presidential candidates have no legal obligation to disclose their tax return, but disclosure has been customary since 1970. Tax Analysts, "Tax History Project: Presidential Tax Returns" (available at www.taxhistory.org/www/ website.nsf/web/presidentialtaxreturns).

10 See discussion under heading "Some examples of simple tax planning", Example 4: Sales and Use Tax.

11 I.R.C. §61 includes "all income from whatever source derived" so that the ten dollars is includable.

12 "Tax gap" refers to revenue lost as a result of taxpayers' failure to report accurately and completely, as opposed to "tax expenditures," which refers to features of the tax law that enable taxpayers to reduce their tax liability. See discussion of the tax gap below under heading "Tax gap and the tax avoidance culture" and tax expenditures, see also *infra* note 30 and accompanying text.

from planning opportunities well may serve to justify self-help to level the playing field just a bit with small-scale evasion. The individual who finds the ten-dollar bill and knows she should report the income does not report.

Troubling recent disclosures from the Panama Papers[13] that many politicians and other public figures invested offshore through opaque entities imply questionable behavior resulting in both legal and possibly unlawful tax structuring. Some politicians inevitably express their outrage in light of such disclosures. Resulting rhetoric may link loss of tax revenue to legitimate tax planning and indiscriminately mix tax avoidance with tax evasion by assigning negative connotations to legally acceptable tax avoidance. In a recent interview about the Panama Papers, the Australian assistant finance minister stated, "[I]f people are deliberately structuring their affairs to avoid paying tax in Australia that is clearly against the law."[14] While the statement was political, a rhetorical device to introduce criticism of the predecessor Labor government's failure to address tax planning adequately, the assistant finance minister used the term "tax avoidance" pejoratively and probably incorrectly. Even as the interviewer focused on the legitimacy of the practice, the finance minister emphasized the need for stronger anti-avoidance (not anti-evasion) legislation. On the other hand, when Hillary Clinton, the Democratic Party presidential candidate, suggested that perhaps Donald Trump was not paying taxes, Trump retorted, "That makes me smart."[15] Trump seemed to justify his nonpayment of taxes when Clinton remarked on failing US infrastructure because Trump does not pay taxes by saying, "It would be squandered, too, believe me."[16] Trump's rhetoric supports tax avoidance and possibly even tax evasion as he argues that the government wastes the tax revenue it gets. Implicit is the observation that smart taxpayers avoid – perhaps even evade – federal income taxes since only foolish taxpayers give the revenue to the government.[17]

Whether one views tax planning as a legitimate or improper activity, tax planning has become embedded into the economic culture.[18] In many places, tax avoidance has taken on a life of its own as the growing number of enactments of general anti-avoidance rules (GAARs) evidences.[19] Successful tax planning may make an investment profitable when the investment would have

---

13 The International Consortium of Investigative Journalists, "The Panama Papers: Politicians, Criminal and the Rogue Industry That Hides Their Cash", available at https://panamapapers.icij.org/ (describing the findings of leaked papers from a major Panamanian law firm representing business and investment interests worldwide).

14 Leigh Sales interview of Kelly O'Dwyer, "Assistant Treasurer Says Australia Cracking Down on Tax Avoidance and Evasion", 2016 WTD 66-21 (Release Date: APRIL 04, 2016) (Doc 2016–7195) (available at https://advance.lexis.com/document?crid=97eb19b4-0716-463c-bc3f-dac7ff9227b4&pddocfullpath=%2fshared%2fdocument%2flegalnews%2furn%3acontentItem%3a5JG5-BDP0-0063-32XD-00000-00&pdcontentcomponentid=6141&pdmfid=1000516&pdisurlapi=true)

15 R. Rubin, "Donald Trump on Not Paying Taxes: 'That Makes Me Smart'", *The Wall Street Journal* (26 September 2016), available at http://blogs.wsj.com/washwire/2016/09/26/donald-trump-on-not-paying-taxes-that-makes-me-smart/.

16 Id.

17 One might surmise that Trump would make large charitable gifts in order to redirect tax revenue to charitable donees so that the government will not squander the revenue, but there is little evidence of tax-planned charitable gifts from Trump. See H. Ordower, "Charitable Contributions of Services: Charitable Gift Planning for Non-Itemizers", 67 *Tax Lawyer* 517, 533 (2014) and section titled "Some examples of simple tax planning", Example 3: Charitable Deductions.

18 Ordower, Culture, see note 1 at 53.

19 C. Waerzeggers and C. Hillier, "Introducing a General Anti-Avoidance Rule (GAAR)", IMF Technical Note, IMF Legal Department (January 2016) (listing 12 countries but not including India, Ireland, and the United States, also having GAARs or their equivalent) available at www.imf.org/external/pubs/ft/tltn/2016/tltn1601.pdf. On general anti-avoidance rules (GAARs), see Part D of this book; Ordower, Culture, see note 1 at 94; R. Prebble and J. Prebble, "Does the Use of General Anti-Avoidance Rules to Combat Tax Avoidance Breach Principles of the Rule of Law? A Comparative Study", 55 *Saint Louis University Law Journal* 21 (2010).

been economically unsound without the tax benefits.[20] Capturing tax benefits becomes a primary investment objective rather than something incidental to another economic investment objective. Tax planners exploit three related types of tax structuring opportunities: (1) legislation offering tax incentives; (2) structural alternatives that generate differing tax outcomes without altering the non-tax economic consequences of the transaction; and (3) unintended statutory flaws and ambiguities, including legislatively sanctioned tax incentives exploited in ways not intended or not foreseen by the enabling legislation.[21] Both the existence of legislation delivering economic incentives through the tax system and opportunities to structure transactions producing substantially identical economic outcomes but differing tax outcomes create ambiguity concerning appropriate and inappropriate tax structuring. That ambiguity makes it difficult for tax administrators to combat what they perceive to be inappropriate tax planning and for courts to interpret ambiguous statutes as the legislatures may have intended them.

At all socioeconomic levels, and with respect to all taxes, attentiveness to opportunities to minimize taxes is common. Some techniques are legal, some questionable, others clearly illegal (whether or not enforced). Yet there is probably less uncertainty of applicable law for middle- and lower-income taxpayers than there is at the higher-income end. For example, the high audit rate for the earned income tax credit applicable to low-income, employed or self-employed taxpayers reflects substantial noncompliance by taxpayers and a relatively straightforward and unambiguous eligibility rule.[22] Similarly, failure to report income from services performed by middle- and lower-income taxpayers often is fraudulent – tax evasion rather than tax avoidance. A household worker or a laborer who receives payment in cash and does not report the income is evading, not avoiding, tax.[23] Barter exchange of services for services or services for property is unambiguously gross income to both parties to the exchange, although in many instances determining the correct amount to include in income may be difficult and securing voluntary reporting and compliance may be even more difficult.[24] In difficult valuation instances, generally toward the higher end of the income spectrum, the tax collector and the courts may choose not to confront the valuation issue, instead finding an exclusion from income[25] or fixing value at

20 During the 1970s and 1980s, promoters frequently sold tax sheltered investments to taxpayers in the U.S. that produced no independent economic return absent the associated tax benefits. Ordower, Culture, see note 1 at 55–8.

21 Categories (2) and (3) become the subject of the general and special anti-avoidance rules, see note 19 and accompanying text, and discussed below in text accompanying note 107.

22 In the tax years 2006–2008, only 1.6 percent of the returns claiming an earned income tax credit under IRC §32 were accepted as filed, 94.8 percent were subjected to an office or field audit. Internal Revenue Service, "Compliance Estimates for the Earned Income Tax Credit Claimed on 2006–2008 Returns" (2014), available at www.irs.gov/PUP/individuals/EITCComplianceStudyTY2006-2008.pdf.

23 In the case of some low income workers, failure to report their income from services is contrary to their best economic interests even if they never get caught underreporting income. Some forego the opportunity to claim the earned income tax credit under IRC §32 on their income from services. And underreporting and not reporting income from services may diminish or cause the individual not to qualify for social security benefits when the individual reaches the qualifying age. And, see, the discussion of the tax gap, in text accompanying and following note 137.

24 IRS, "Four Things to Know About Bartering", IRS Tax Tip 2012-33 (17 February 2012), available at www.irs.gov/uac/four-things-to-know-about-bartering-1). Consider a common babysitting exchange in many communities where parents log hours caring for other children in a pool of families and can draw hours having another parent care for his or her children. No money changes hands, just babysitting services. See also the discussion of the tax gap under heading "Tax gap and the tax avoidance culture" below.

25 *Benaglia v. Commissioner*, 36 B.T.A. 838 (1937) (holding meals and lodging provided for the convenience of the employer are excludable from gross income). Congress codified the result in the case in I.R.C. §119.

zero.[26] Likewise, conversion of income from services in the form of "carried interests" in partnerships from ordinary income to more favorably taxed capital gain is acceptable, nonfraudulent behavior.[27]

Some examples of simple tax planning

The following paragraphs present four simple and common examples of effective tax planning. Only the sales/use tax example benefiting a wide range of income groups represents impermissible planning that violates the law, although it generally remains unenforced. The others, benefiting relatively high-income taxpayers, are unquestionably legal. The "carried interest" example[28] has been the subject of legislative discussion on account of it being viewed by some commentators, including both US presidential candidates in 2016[29] and legislators as excessive and unjustified. Legislative elimination of the opportunity has been recommended but not enacted. There is nothing remarkable about the four opportunities. The legislature could make simple changes in the law to eliminate the opportunities, but it has not. The opportunities illustrate that elimination of tax avoidance requires action by the legislature but the legislature has no commitment to a consistent anti-avoidance plan. Legislative ambiguity tends to dominate as the public discussion in the legislature is critical of tax avoidance but the legislature continues to use the tax system to deliver subsidies, identifying them in budgeting as tax expenditures.[30]

Example 1: tax exempt bonds

Whenever the legislature delivers subsidies for an activity through the tax system, there is a risk that the subsidies will become misdirected. Capture of the tax-based subsidy in a manner relatively consistent with the legislative intent is unremarkable and difficult to criticize. And similarly, that observation remains valid even if the taxpayer who captures the subsidy is better off than he or she would have been if the legislature had chosen to deliver the subsidy directly. Economic inefficiency built into subsidies is not the fault of the taxpayer but represents an ambiguous and wasteful legislative choice. Tax exempt bonds for state and local governments exemplify such inefficient choices.[31]

The exemption from gross income of interest paid on bonds a state or local government issues enables the governmental debtor to pay a below-market rate of interest.[32] The difference between the interest the governmental unit would pay at a market rate and the amount it must

---

26 See note 50 and accompanying text. *Campbell v. Commissioner*, 59 TCM (CCH) 236 (1990), aff'd. in part, rvs'd. in part, 943 F2d 815 (8th Cir. 1991) (holding a profits interest to have indeterminate value and not includable in income). Rev. Proc. 93-27, 1993-2 C.B. 343 (treating the receipt of a profits interest for services as non-taxable when received, unless certain exceptions rendering valuation simple and straightforward apply). See the carried interest example below under heading "Some examples of simple tax planning", Example 2.

27 See *infra* note 40 and accompanying text which describes an opportunity arising from the failure to determine value.

28 Example 2, below, profits interest in a partnership.

29 See *infra* note 50.

30 US Department of the Treasury, "Resource Center: Tax Expenditures", available at www.treasury.gov/resource-center/tax-policy/Pages/Tax-Expenditures.aspx (defining the tax expenditure concept and estimating the amounts of tax expenditures each year).

31 I.R.C. §103 (exempting interest paid by a state or local government on its obligations from the gross income of its recipient/lender).

32 *South Carolina v. Baker*, 485 US 505 (1985), dispelled a common misconception that the Constitution prohibited the United States from taxing the interest state and local governments pay on their obligations.

pay at the tax exempt rate is intended as a subsidy to or revenue sharing with the state and local governments delivered through the federal income tax system. If the subsidy were efficient, the bondholder would receive the identical return on invested funds with comparable risk profiles[33] whether invested in the government obligation or a fully taxable obligation.

To illustrate: A taxpayer subject to a 40 percent marginal rate of tax[34] who invests $1,000 in taxable bonds paying 10 percent interest receives $100 of taxable interest income and has $60 remaining after tax. The tax exempt rate of interest for that taxpayer should be 6 percent if exempt bonds and taxable investments produced identical after-tax investment returns and the state or local bond issuer gets the 4 percent interest subsidy. Likewise, the rate for a 30 percent marginal-rate taxpayer should be 7 percent. State and local governments, however, may not set the interest rate on their obligations to the investors' differing tax characteristics or discriminate in rates paid among investors. These governments must choose an interest rate at which they can sell their bonds. Generally, there are insufficient buyers paying tax at the maximum marginal rate, so the governmental unit must set its rate higher to sell the bonds to below-maximum-marginal-rate taxpayers. If the rate is set for the 30 percent taxpayer (that is, 7 percent yielding $70), the 40 percent taxpayer receives a tax exempt bonus of $10 by buying the bond. The 40 percent investor gets a return approximately equal to an 11.67 percent taxable return. The state or local government receives a 3 percent subsidy, and the 40 percent taxpayer receives an additional 1.67 percent subsidy to her return on investment that the statute probably did not intend.[35]

It is possible that Congress concluded historically it had no power to tax the interest paid by state governmental units and that the statute simply codified that conclusion.[36] Congress could eliminate that inefficiency in delivery of the subsidy in a number of ways, including (a) providing a direct interest subsidy to state and local governments rather than the tax subsidy, or (b) substituting a tax credit for the exclusion.[37] But Congress does not do so[38] and the higher bracket taxpayer gets a tax subsidy greater than what the legislature intended – a form of tax avoidance inconsistent with but incidental to the intended subsidy.

Example 2: carried interests

One prominent example of successful tax planning that has received legislative attention, albeit without enactment of a legislative remedy, is the favorable taxation of private equity and hedge

---

33 In the case of publicly issued government and corporate bonds, Standard and Poor's, Moody's Investor Services and Fitch control the bulk of the bond rating business. Their ratings of the creditworthiness of the bond issuer enable the underwriters of the bonds to position the bonds for sale in the markets at a competitive interest rate so that a corporation with a AAA rating from Standard and Poor's should pay the same interest rate as a governmental unit with the same rating.

34 Tax rates are hypothetical to simplify the illustration, but in this instance the 40 percent rate is roughly the current 39.6 percent maximum rate imposed on the ordinary income of individuals under I.R.C. §1.

35 I.R.C. §103; and *see South Carolina v. Baker*, see note 32.

36 Compare I.R.C. §104(a)(2), excluding personal injury recoveries from gross income and originally codifying existing law. H. Ordower, "Schedularity in US Income Taxation and Its Effect on Tax Distribution", 108 *Northwestern University of Law Review* 905, 920 (2014).

37 Joint Committee on Taxation, "The Federal Revenue Effects of Tax-Exempt and Direct-Pay Tax Credit Bond Provisions", JXT-60-12 (2012), available at www.jct.gov/publications.html?func=startdown&id=4470.

38 Congress did rein in the ability of taxpayers to leverage their investments in tax exempt bonds by denying a deduction for interest paid to carry tax exempt investments under I.R.C. §265(a)(2), governmental units to leverage their exemption from tax under I.R.C. §115 with anti-arbitrage rules under I.R.C. §103(b)(2) (interest on arbitrage bonds not exempt) and to limit their ability to lend their borrowing power for private use with special rules applicable to private activity bonds under I.R.C. §§103(b)(3), 148 et seq.

fund managers on their "carried interests."[39] Private equity and hedge funds customarily operate as limited partnerships with the managers receiving 1 or 2 percent of the capital in the fund annually as a management fee and an additional amount of 10 to 20 percent of the increase in value of the fund as an interest in the profits of the partnership.[40] In most instances, the annual assets-based fee is ordinary income to the manager.[41] The performance allocation also would be characterized as a performance fee and generate ordinary income to the manager if it were paid in cash, but it is not. Instead the partnership determines the increase in the value of its assets periodically and allocates 10–20 percent of that amount to the manager's capital account. The amount allocated precedes the realization of gain by the partnership, and any final determination of the amount the manager will receive awaits the partnership's disposition of its assets even though the manager's interest in the partnership increases.[42]

As an interest in and a function of the profits of the partnership, that additional amount, referred to as a "carried interest" in the literature, often yields long term capital gain to the manager. Decisional law[43] and a procedural announcement from the Internal Revenue Service[44] treat profits interests received for services as having no value when received. The partnership's allocation to the manager of a distributive share of the partnership's taxable income and gain with respect to those profits interests under partnership rules preserves the character and source of income realized by the partnership as it is included in the partners' incomes.[45] In the case of a private equity fund particularly, that income will be capital gain when the fund ultimately sells its investment in the stock of a corporation in which it has invested. The manager's share of the gain therefore is also long term capital gain[46] rather than ordinary income from services. Distributions of cash with respect to those profits interests reduce the manager's adjusted basis in the

---

39 V. Fleischer, "Two and Twenty: Taxing Partnership Profits in Private Equity Funds", 83 *New York University Law Review* 1 (2008) (analyzing various arguments for taxing a profits interest but concluding that the private equity fund managers should have ordinary income from their profits interests in the private equity funds); H. Ordower, "Taxing Service Partners to Achieve Horizontal Equity", 46 *Tax Lawyer* 19 (1992) (arguing that the profits interests should be taxable as open transactions).

40 H. Ordower, "The Regulation of Private Equity, Hedge, and State Funds", 58 *American Journal of Comparative Law* 295, 304–5 (2010).

41 Private equity fund managers in some instances sought to convert the management fee into capital gain as well. For an explanation, see G. D. Polsky, "Private Equity Management Fee Conversions" (4 November 2008). FSU College of Law, Public Law Research Paper No. 337; FSU College of Law, Law, Business & Economics Paper No. 08-18, available at SSRN: http://ssrn.com/abstract=1295443 or http://dx.doi.org/10.2139/ssrn.1295443. In 2015, the IRS issued proposed regulations amending the I.R.C. §707 regulations to prevent conversions. IRS, Disguised Payments for Services, 2015-32 IRB (10 August 2015), available at www.irs.gov/irb/2015-32_IRB/ar09.html.

42 Customarily, the manager's interest in the partnership does not decrease if the partnership's assets lose value, but the manager often may not receive any further allocation under the profits interest until the partnership's value reaches the highest value with respect to which the manager received an allocation earlier. H. Ordower, "Demystifying Hedge Funds: A Design Primer", 7 *UC Davis Business Law Journal* 323, 359 (2007).

43 *Campbell v. Commissioner*, see note 26 (holding a profits interest to have indeterminate value and not includable in income).

44 Rev. Proc. 93–27, see note 26, 1993–2 C.B. 343 (treating the receipt of a profits interest for services as nontaxable when received, unless certain exceptions rendering valuation simple and straightforward apply, leaving the partner to receive a distributive share of the partnership's income).

45 IRC §702(b).

46 Long term capital gain becomes net capital gain to the extent it exceeds capital losses. I.R.C. §1222. For noncorporate taxpayers, net capital gain is taxed at significantly lower rates than ordinary income, currently a maximum rate of 20 percent rather than 39.6 percent for ordinary income. I.R.C. §1(h). Capital gain is also free from the social security tax and the Medicare tax but is now subject to the net investment income tax of 3.8 percent under I.R.C. §1411.

manager's interest in the partnership and yield gain from the sale or exchange of those interests if the distributions exceed the manager's basis.[47]

Proposals to alter the rules for private equity fund managers on carried interests suggest that some members of Congress view the favorable tax treatment as unjustified – a legislatively unsanctioned form of tax avoidance that benefits some very wealthy private equity fund managers. Yet the proposals to stop this seeming conversion of ordinary compensation income into long term capital gain have foundered.[48] There is apparently no legislative will to change tax rules favoring this small but wealthy taxpayer group of private fund managers. Very recently, some commentators have suggested that the president and the Department of the Treasury can change the tax outcome without the need for Congress to act,[49] and, as noted earlier, both presidential candidates expressed their intention to fix the carried interest problem.[50]

Example 3: charitable deductions for gifts of appreciated assets

Taxpayers in the United States who itemize their deductions[51] may deduct the amount of their charitable gifts[52] in determining their taxable income.[53] The charitable deduction diminishes the cost to the taxpayer of making the charitable gift by the amount of the gift multiplied by the taxpayer's maximum marginal rate of tax.[54] Accordingly, a taxpayer subject to the maximum rate of 39.6 percent bears only 60.4 cents of each charitable gift dollar because the federal treasury reimburses 39.6 cents through the deduction.[55] Taxpayers who do not itemize deductions secure no tax benefit from their contributions.[56]

In addition, the dollar amount of a charitable gift of property, other than money, is the fair market value of the property on the date of the gift.[57] If a donor who itemizes deductions gives appreciated property to charity, the donor not only gets a deduction equal to the fair market value of the donated property but also need not recognize and include in income the previously

---

47 I.R.C. §731.

48 See, "Ways and Means Committee Democrats, Carried Interest", available at http://democrats.waysandmeans. house.gov/issue/carried-interest.

49 D. J. Hemel, "The President's Power to Tax", 103 *Cornell Law Review* (forthcoming), available at http://papers. ssrn.com/sol3/papers.cfm?abstract_id=2773329 (arguing the President has the power to change the carried interest through regulatory action); G. Morgenson, "Ending Tax Break for Ultrawealthy May Not Take Act of Congress, Fair Game", *The New York Times* (6 May 2016), available at www.nytimes.com/2016/05/08/business/ ending-tax-break-for-ultrawealthy-may-not-take-act-of-congress.html?_r=0.

50 W. Elmore, "Clinton Would Ask Treasury to End Carried Interest Preference", 2016 TNT 116-3 (15 June 2016). Presidential candidate Trump expressed his intention to eliminate the carried interest opportunity. However, Trump also planned to reduce the rate of tax on all business income to 15 percent so that the rate of tax would be lower than currently imposed even on net capital gains.

51 I.R.C. §63(d) (allowing certain deductions, including the deduction for charitable gifts under I.R.C. §170, for noncorporate taxpayers to the extent the deductions aggregate more than the standard deduction amount).

52 I.R.C. §170 (charitable contribution deduction).

53 I.R.C. §63(a) (taxable income defined).

54 Or, if the deduction would cause the taxpayer's maximum rate to decline, all or part of the deduction will yield a deduction at the lower rate.

55 Ordower, "Charitable Contributions of Services", see note 18, at 519–21.

56 Charitable contribution deductions raise difficult policy issues since they enable donors to redirect government revenue through the deduction to charitable organizations, including religious institutions and churches, despite the separation of church and state under the First Amendment to the US Constitution.

57 Treas. Reg. §1.170A-1(c), 26 CFR §1.170A-1(c) (deduction for contribution of property is the fair market value of the property).

unrealized gain in the value of the donated property.[58] For example,[59] assume the 40 percent bracket taxpayer gives corporate stock to charity that has a value of $100 and an adjusted basis of $1. The taxpayer gets the deduction subsidy of $40, as in the preceding paragraph, plus an additional subsidy of the avoided $20 tax on the long-term capital gain that the taxpayer would have incurred upon the sale of the property.[60] Thus, the cost of the donation to the donor is only $40 for each $100 gift. If the donor also receives an intangible and nontaxable benefit from the charity – naming rights to a building, for example – the value to the donor of the charitable gift and deduction may even be greater.[61]

Consistent with the apparent legislative intent to encourage charitable giving, charitable donors contributing appreciated property receive a direct contribution subsidy through the charitable deduction and avoid the tax on appreciation in the value of property other than money they contribute. The value to a donor from the government subsidy of the charitable gift increases as the donor's marginal rate of tax increases so that the maximum charitable deduction benefit is available to the highest income taxpayers. Compare the Canadian model for charitable contributions that gives a substantially equal tax credit to all charitable donors without regard to their marginal tax rates. Canada pegs the credit to the maximum marginal rate of income tax.[62]

Congress has limited the deduction for appreciated property to the taxpayer's adjusted basis in two instances. In the case of property that would generate ordinary income when sold – inventory and depreciation recapture property, for example – the taxpayer's deduction, with exceptions, is limited to her adjusted basis in the donated property.[63] Similarly, in the case of property which would generate capital gain,[64] if the charitable recipient's use of donated tangible personal property is not related in service or use to its charitable purpose, the deduction also is limited to the taxpayer's adjusted basis in the donated property.[65] However, Congress has not sought to deny the benefit or require the donor to recognize gain on the donated property for even highly appreciated intangible property.

Example 4: sales and use tax – avoidance or evasion?

While the permissible tax planning opportunities described in the previous three examples are practical exclusively for some high- or moderately high-income taxpayers and are not available

---

58 I.R.C. §1001 (codifying the realization requirement and determining the amount of gain or loss realized on the sale or other disposition of property and including the gain or loss in income). For a discussion of the distributional effects of the realization requirement, see Ordower, "Schedularity", see note 36, at 910–12.
59 Amounts will be rounded for purposes of the illustration.
60 I.R.C. §1(h) (setting the maximum marginal rate for net capital gain, with limited exceptions, at 20 percent). In the case of a taxpayer selling a closely held corporation who has a religious obligation to tithe, the taxpayer must give the shares to the church first so that the taxpayer has made a gift of the property before sale yield a charitable contribution deduction equal to the value of the shares on the date of the gift. The church must agree independently to sell the shares to the buyer in order for the taxpayer to capture the full charitable deduction/exclusion benefit. If the taxpayer gives the proceeds of the sale to the church, the taxpayer rather than the church will be taxable on the gain and the taxpayer would not capture the benefit of the gain exclusion from a charitable gift.
61 W. Drennan, "Where Generosity and Pride Abide: Charitable Naming Rights", 80 *University of Cincinnati Law Review* 58, 66 (2012) (charitable naming rights have a zero value under current rulings).
62 Sec. 118.1(1) of the Income Tax Act (R.S.C. 1985, c. 1 (5th Supp.), available at http://laws-lois.justice.gc.ca/eng/acts/I-3.3/page-113.html#docCont. For an explanation, see Canada Revenue Agency's "Charities and giving" webpage, www.cra-arc.gc.ca/chrts-gvng/menu-eng.html.
63 I.R.C. §170(e)(1)(A), exceptions for certain inventory categories apply under I.R.C. §170(e)(3).
64 Includes I.R.C. §1231 gain.
65 I.R.C. §170(e)(1)(B).

to the bulk of taxpayers, moderate- and low-income taxpayers have been offered limited opportunities to avoid or evade some of their taxes. Without regard to their income or wealth, consumers who have computer and credit card access often favor purchasing goods over the internet from out of state vendors in order to avoid having to pay sales tax or the complementary use tax on their purchases.[66] Unless the state may impose the obligation to collect the state's use tax on the vendor shipping into the state, collection of the use tax is impractical because the state must rely on voluntary reporting and payment by the consumer.[67] If a vendor has no physical presence in the shopper's state of residence, the vendor need not collect the state sales or use tax at point of sale on shipments into the shopper's state, as US Supreme Court decisions prohibit states from imposing an obligation to collect use taxes on vendors that do not have a physical presence in the state.[68] The rapid growth of sales by internet retailers is attributable in part to the sales and use tax void that the physical presence test creates.

Some states have sought to collect the use tax through an attachment form to their state income tax return, but those efforts have met resistance and limited success with collection.[69] A growing number of states have enacted "Amazon laws" to close the void.[70] Those laws require many out of state vendors using in-state servicers or other types of affiliated businesses to solicit sales to collect the state's use tax on sales for shipment into the state.[71] The Supreme Court denied certiorari in a challenge to the "Amazon laws," thus allowing a state decision upholding the collection and reporting obligation to stand.[72] And, in the Supreme Court's most recent decision affirming the physical presence test, it stated in *dictum* that Congress has the power to modify the physical presence limitation.[73]

Unlike the previous three examples of tax avoidance, the consumer's failure to pay the use tax is more than tax avoidance. No legislation, administrative action or judicial decision sanctions the consumer's failure to report and pay the use tax. Judicial decisions only relieve vendors of the obligation to collect the tax at point of sale and pay it over to the state. Each state imposes a statutory obligation, often with an exemption amount, on all consumers to report and pay tax

66 Sales tax is an add-on tax a vendor is required to collect on in-state sales when it sells goods (and sometimes services) to a consumer. States that impose a sales tax also impose a complementary use tax at the same rate on consumers who purchase items outside the state but bring the items into the state for use in the state (includes items shipped into the state). Consumers who paid a sales tax in the state of purchase receive a credit for the tax paid at point of sale but not more than the amount of use tax payable in the state of use.

67 Except for items like automobiles which the buyer must register, so that the state may collect the tax at registration.

68 *Quill Corp. v. North Dakota*, 504 U.S. 298 (1992) (reaffirming the physical presence test requirement of the Commerce Clause and refusing to impose the obligation on an out of state vendor to collect the state's use tax on sales to residents of the state).

69 N. Manzi, *Use Tax Collection on Income Tax Returns in Other States*, Minnesota House of Representatives (2015), available at www.house.leg.state.mn.us/hrd/pubs/usetax.pdf.

70 The nickname "Amazon laws" is a reference to the online retailer Amazon.com.

71 New York and other states have enacted legislation imposing an obligation to collect use taxes on retail vendors that use a local affiliate to solicit sales in the state. N.Y. Tax Law §1101(b)(8)(i)(C)(I) (McKinney, 2013). The Supreme Court denied certiorari in a challenge to the New York law in *Overstock.com, Inc. v. New York State Dept. of Taxation & Fin.*, 134 S. Ct. 682 (2013). See generally E. K. Lunder and C. A. Pettit, "'Amazon Laws' and Taxation of Internet Sales: Constitutional Analysis", CRS Report (9 April 2015), available at www.fas.org/sgp/crs/misc/R42629.pdf (discussing click-through nexus for use tax).

72 *Overstock.com, Inc. v. N.Y. State Dep't of Taxation & Fin.*, 20 N.Y.3d 586, 987 N.E.2d 621, 965 N.Y.S.2d 61 (2013), *cert. denied*, 134 S. Ct. 682, 187 L. Ed. 2d 549 (2013) (upholding click-through nexus under NY CLS Tax §1101(b)(8)(vi)).

73 *Quill Corp. v. North Dakota*, see note 68, at 318. Note that 11 states joined in an amicus brief to the Supreme Court (release date 7 November 2016) urging the Court to grant certiorari in *Brohl v. The Direct Marketing Association* (16–458) to overrule *Quill*. 2016 STT 217-9 (9 November 2016).

on out of state purchases of goods that they use in the state.[74] Failure to report and pay is tax evasion, an illegal act, not lawful tax avoidance. Thus, the invitation to avoid taxes that the other opportunities offer is evasion in the case of consumers' failure to pay use tax.[75] This distinction between the use tax example and the private equity fund example is stark as it favors high-income individuals and protects their tax avoidance while lurking with possible penalties for the moderate- and low-income individuals.[76] While both opportunities originated in decisional law, the one affecting high-income and high-wealth taxpayers involves no illegality when the taxpayers exploit it. The one affecting all types of taxpayers involves tax evasion when the taxpayers at all income levels exploit it.

Yet ambiguity regarding consumers' obligation to pay the use tax persists. Many consumers may be unaware of their use tax obligation when out of state vendors do not collect the tax at point of sale.[77] Frequently, vendors openly have advertised that they did not collect the tax on their out of state sales.[78] And even the use tax statutes leave ambiguity regarding consumers' compliance obligations. The statutes may impose no criminal penalties on the consumer, and civil penalties are rarely imposed.[79] This ambiguity on compliance obligations in the absence of criminal penalties, along with the lack of effective enforcement at consumer level, contributes to wide-scale noncompliance.[80]

Tax benefit asymmetry: ambiguity in legislative purpose

The tax outcomes in the examples in the previous sections lack symmetry and rationality. In the tax exempt bond example, Congress chose to reduce the borrowing cost for state and local governments by making interest on their obligations free from federal income tax. In facilitating that interest rate subsidy, however, Congress selected an inefficient and wasteful tax structure. The subsidy transfers substantial value to high marginal tax bracket taxpayers who receive tax exempt interest in excess of any competitive market rate of interest. The inefficiency in delivery of the subsidy is manifest.

Yet Congress has not acted to make the subsidy more efficient or symmetrical across taxpayer groups. Congress could eliminate the asymmetry but does not. Perhaps Congress's inaction is attributable to the longevity of the exemption for state and local bond interest. No constituency in Congress is interested in revisiting the structure of the deeply rooted expectations the statute

---

74 For example, NY CLS Tax §1110 (imposing a compensating use tax equal to the sales tax).

75 Id., stating the obligation to pay use tax and offering a simplified computation of use tax based on income.

76 This is not to say that high-income individuals do not evade sales and use taxes. See, e.g., G. Bowley, "Lawsuit Accuses (Alec) Baldwin of Dodging Sales Tax", *The New York Times* C2 (28 October 2016). Use of the term "dodging" suggests tax avoidance, not evasion or acceptable evasion.

77 M. Cohn, "More States Expect Taxpayers to Report Their Use Tax", *Accounting Today* (13 April 2012), www.accountingtoday.com/blogs/debits-credits/States-Use-Tax-CCH-62331-1.html.

78 Recently vendors have retreated from such advertising and substituted complex description of the consumer's tax obligation with a link at the bottom of the webpage. See, e.g., www.tigerdirect.com/sectors/help/taxinfo.asp.

79 For example, NY CLS Tax §1817 (imposing criminal penalties but not on consumers for failure to report and pay). As to civil penalties, see, for example, the New York State approach in "Use Tax for Individuals (including Estates and Trusts)", *Tax Bulletin ST-913 (TB-ST-913)* (19 February 2016), available at www.tax.ny.gov/pubs_and_bulls/tg_bulletins/st/use_tax_for_individuals.htm.

80 Noncompliance on use tax is not indicative of noncompliance on other taxes, although wage earners are subject to withholding on income and social security taxes, interest and dividend income – the subject of third-party reporting – making the income tax and the social security tax more difficult to evade. See the discussion of the tax gap, below under heading "Tax gap and the tax avoidance culture".

offers, even though Congress has modified the statute on several occasions to limit the subsidy[81] and easily could tax the state and local bond interest and share revenue with the states to provide the subsidy the exemption currently intends.

Similarly, the charitable contribution deduction that favors high marginal bracket, itemizing taxpayers, especially those who own highly appreciated, intangible investment property, is long-standing and entrenched in the tax law. While Congress has acted to limit the deduction to tax basis in the case of certain types of property,[82] it has done nothing permanent to distribute the tax benefit symmetrically among taxpayer groups. The excess subsidy for charitable contribution could be eliminated by requiring taxpayers to include appreciation in income when they make a charitable gift of appreciated property or by limiting the deduction to the taxpayer's adjusted basis in the property – if a charitable deduction is worth preserving at all in the tax law.

In the private equity fund example, very high-income taxpayers convert income from services from the ordinary income classification generally applicable to income from services into long-term capital gain. This asymmetry in taxing some income from services as long-term capital gain and most income from services as ordinary income[83] encourages more sophisticated tax planning than the other examples. Structure is critical to defining the partnership interest as a profits interest in compliance with the administrative ruling.[84] While judicial and administrative decisions may have created the asymmetry, a legislative fix would be simple. Minimal amelioration of the asymmetry resulted from tax law changes under the Affordable Care Act[85] that removed the accompanying Medicare tax advantage from converting service income to investment income.[86] Investment income, including long-term capital gain received through a partnership, when the taxpayer's modified adjusted gross income exceeds $250,000, now is subject to a 3.8 percent Medicare tax.[87]

In the bond interest and charitable contribution examples, tax planning for the higher-bracket taxpayer seems unassailable. The taxpayer invested in the bond without any unusual investment structuring and received the unintended, but unavoidable, excess benefit. The investor is avoiding taxes on interest income by a straightforward selection of a tax exempt, rather than a taxable, bond. Both tax exempt and taxable bonds probably were available and open to all investors, and the investor was free to choose between them and among other available investments. The tax benefit simply was incidental to that investment choice for high marginal rate taxpayers. In the charitable contribution example, the high bracket taxpayer used generally available charitable contribution rules. Nothing questionable occurred. Additional tax planning might enable the taxpayer to gain additional advantages in the charitable context, but the basic charitable contribution fair market value deduction is uncomplicated. In both the bond interest and charitable contribution examples, one might disagree with the statutory design as it is wasteful of tax revenue, but the opportunity is generally available and discriminates only incidentally among taxpayers based upon their individual tax rate brackets. That type of discrimination in favor of high marginal bracket taxpayers is characteristic of any exclusion from income

---

81 Arbitrage rules and private activity bond rules. I.R.C. §103(b).

82 I.R.C. §170(e).

83 Under I.R.C. §1(h), net capital gain of individuals is taxed at a maximum rate roughly half the maximum rate for income from services – 20 percent rather than 39.6 percent.

84 Rev. Proc. 93–27, see note 44, 1993-2 C.B. 343.

85 Patient Protection and Affordable Care Act of 2010, 123 Stat. 119 (2010).

86 I.R.C. §1401(b) imposing a 2.9 percent hospital insurance tax on self-employment income; I.R.C. §3101(b) (similarly on wages) but not on investment income.

87 I.R.C. §1411 (tax on net investment income).

or deduction in yielding a greater amount of tax savings as the taxpayer's marginal income tax bracket increases. Similarly, the realization requirement that allows unrealized gain to remain untaxed until the taxpayer sells the appreciated property provides greater benefit from deferral to higher-bracket taxpayers.[88]

In the private equity, partnership profits interest example, judicial and administrative interpretation of tax law has yielded a valuable tax planning opportunity. Unlike the bond interest and charitable contribution examples, something does seem wrong in the conversion of ordinary service income into long-term capital gain. Both the Republican and Democratic 2016 U.S. presidential candidates agreed that there is something wrong with the conversion and said they planned to eliminate the opportunity when elected.[89] Yet Congress has not acted to eliminate the tax planning opportunity in partnership profits interests despite an array of possible solutions, including open transaction reporting for the receipt of partnership profits interests[90] and taxing part of the partnership's allocation and distribution to the manager as ordinary income.[91]

The three planning examples for high-bracket taxpayers highlight the lack of legislative resolve to eliminate tax planning opportunities that misdirect government revenue to private use by allowing some taxpayers to avoid all or a portion of their tax responsibility. In the examples, it is difficult to imagine a compelling policy reason for asymmetry in tax treatment of different taxpayers that results in inefficient delivery of intended tax subsidies. Even if there may have been a reason for offering an excess benefit originally or the opportunities to misdirect a benefit were not obvious to the legislature when it enacted the statute providing the benefit, permitting continuing asymmetry and inefficiency runs contrary to the presumptive legislative purpose to distribute tax burdens fairly and symmetrically. Instead only legislative intention to offer tax benefits to high income taxpayers is visible. In addition, when straightforward statutory adjustments might eliminate any misdirection of the benefit and unanticipated revenue loss, the continuing failure of the legislature to act encourages tax planners for the wealthy to seek other, perhaps less obvious and less permissible techniques to exploit flaws in the tax rules – understanding that the legislature will do little to prevent the exploitation and the courts, observing no legislative resolve to eliminate the flaws, are unlikely to interpret the tax laws to prevent tax avoidance.[92]

Perhaps reflecting the legislature's ambiguity most clearly has been its reluctance to fund the operations of the tax collector. Despite statistics that show that for each sum spent on the IRS, the additional tax collection is many times the amount spent,[93] Congress resists increasing the IRS's budget and frequently cuts the IRS's budget.[94] The legislative message remains murky. The legislature may want to correct many of the flaws in the tax law, but the legislature does not provide the government's administrative agency the resources necessary to collect even the flawed tax.

---

88 I.R.C. §1001 (measuring realized gain and loss and including it in gross income).
89 See note 50.
90 Ordower, "Taxing Service Partners", see note 40, at 36–7.
91 D. Weisbach, "The Carried Interest Problem", 124 *Harvard Law Review* 1773, 1774–5 (2011) (discussing a proposed 75/25 split of ordinary income and capital gain under a new section 710 of the Code).
92 For discussion of the courts' role, see Ordower, Culture note 1, at 86–7.
93 IRS, "National Taxpayer Advocate Delivers Annual Report to Congress; Focuses on Tax Reform", IRS Funding and Identity Theft, IR-2013-3 (9 January 2013), available at www.irs.gov/uac/newsroom/national-taxpayer-advocate-delivers-2012-annual-report-to-congress.
94 P. Bonner, "'Demanding Tax Season Likely Ahead', IRS Commissioner Tells AICPA", *Journal of Accountancy* (3 November 2015), available at www.journalofaccountancy.com/news/2015/nov/irs-commissioner-demanding-tax-season-ahead-2015.

And in the last example, an opportunity is available to all taxpayers, not just high-income taxpayers, and moderate- and low-income taxpayers seize the opportunity to escape paying a tax. Why should sales and use tax collection depend upon the physical presence of the vendor in the state in which the property purchased will be used? Judicial decisions under the Commerce Clause[95] ordaining such dependence may interpret the Constitution correctly, but those interpretations produce asymmetrical tax rules. Certain retail vendors may enjoy an advantage over others because they may offer a substantially tax-free price to the consumer by encouraging the consumer, albeit implicitly,[96] not to report. But the last example differs from the others because, in the avoidance of the state sales and use tax, consumers are evading, not just avoiding, the use tax they are obligated to pay. Consumers evade payment because the states lack any effective collection mechanism. At the same time, Congress has yet to act on the Supreme Court's invitation to eliminate the tax collection void.[97]

Like Congress, state legislatures have not provided the tools to prevent use tax evasion. The legislatures have not encouraged state revenue authorities to use their audit function aggressively to collect use tax from the consumer and have not enacted substantial civil and criminal penalties and funded enforcement to compel consumer reporting and payment of use tax. Increasing numbers of states have enacted "Amazon laws" to collect use taxes on out of state sales at point of sale. Despite widespread evasion by consumers of use taxes, no one has labeled individuals evading the use tax as scofflaws or morally corrupt, and there have been no use tax evasion prosecutions of consumers. The evasion behavior seems accepted and acceptable to the community at large. It is simply part of the culture of tax avoidance.

Tax avoidance: selecting among alternate structures

Tax planning that does not involve tax evasion is primarily the selection among possible structures for a transaction of the structure that yields more-favorable tax outcomes for one or more parties to the transaction than might have resulted without tax planning. Each of the four examples in the previous sections involves tax planning, although the last example relating to sales and use tax does involve tax evasion rather than avoidance. The bond investor chooses the tax exempt bond among investments because of the interest exclusion. The charitable donor may choose to make a charitable gift because the gift is deductible and may decide to give appreciated property, rather than selling the property and donating the proceeds, because the unrealized gain in the property will not be taxed to him. The private equity fund manager opts for an interest in profits rather than an immediate and taxable cash fee that he may invest in the partnership or elsewhere as he chooses. The consumer orders goods from out of state rather than going to a local vendor.

Sometimes the planning leads to more questionable manipulation and possibly evasion. The bond investor may borrow funds to invest in tax exempt bonds but not disclose the connection between the borrowing and the investment, thereby deducting the interest paid but excluding the interest income.[98] The charitable donor may overvalue the contribution, claiming a larger deduction than the law permits.[99] The private equity fund manager may monetize the profits

---

95 US Const. art. I, § 8, cl. 3.

96 Some advertise on their websites that they do not collect tax. And see note 78 supra and accompanying text.

97 See note 73.

98 I.R.C. §265(a)(2) (disallowing a deduction of interest incurred to carry tax exempt bonds).

99 I.R.C. §170(f)(8), (11) (substantiation requirements, generally, and appraisal requirements for property donations).

interest by borrowing against it without recourse so that he is not fully at risk in the partnership.[100] And the consumer, by not reporting the purchase in the state of residence and use, is evading the use tax. In each transaction, the non-tax economic outcome would be the same absent the tax planning. The bond investor would get a market rate return on investment. The charitable donor would give money to the charity (perhaps only the amount net of taxes payable on the gain). The private equity fund manager would receive 20 percent of the increase in the fund's value. The consumer would acquire the goods. The tax planning enhanced the economic value in each instance by transferring potential or actual tax revenues, hence tax expenditure, to private parties. Thus, tax planning augments the taxpayer's economic return from the investment by the amount of the tax the taxpayer avoids or by the reinvestment value of the deferred tax liability.[101]

Often the tax planned investment includes nonobvious or indirect structural variations that add value to the investment only by capturing a tax advantage that otherwise would not accompany the most logical and direct structure. Early in the development of the income tax, the US Supreme Court determined that the substance of a transaction, rather than its form, should control the transaction's tax characterization.[102] The holdings in early "substance over form" cases[103] suggest that tax planning should be of no avail. The substance of the transaction rather than its structure will control the tax outcome no matter how many possible structural permutations there may be that would reach the same economic outcome. And the "step transaction" corollary to the doctrine disregards unnecessary transactional steps that would alter the tax treatment but not the economic substance.[104]

Helvering v. Gregory[105] involved an example of an indirect structure designed to permit its sole shareholder to characterize what would be an ordinary income dividend as more favorably taxed capital gain. The unnecessary steps in the transaction were transparent, but together they fit within the tax characterization for which the taxpayer opted. The courts had some difficulty rejecting the taxpayer's characterization of her gain, and the novelty of the question allowed it to find its way to the Supreme Court. In *Gregory*, the Court applied the "substance over form" doctrine and held that a transaction structured as a tax deferred, divisive reorganization was a dividend in substance. The Court disregarded the reorganization form and taxed the shareholders on the receipt of a dividend according to the transaction's substance. Later Congress amended the

---

100 Rev. Proc. 93-27, see note 26, 1993-2 CB 343 (requires that the service partner not dispose of the interest within two years).

101 Many US tax shelters from the latter half of the twentieth century deferred but did not eliminate tax. The investing taxpayer reduced his or her tax liability in early years of the investment but absent rate changes would be liable for increased taxes when the tax benefits ended or for the amount of the deferred tax upon disposition of the investment. See discussion of deferral shelters in Ordower, Culture, s note 1, at 58 et seq.

102 *Weiss v. Stearn*, 265 U.S. 242 (1924); J. B. Donaldson, "When Substance-Over-Form Argument Is Available to the Taxpayer", 48 *Marquette Law Review* 41 (1964).

103 *Higgins v. Smith*, 308 US 473 (1940) (holding that a sale by a shareholder to his controlled corporation lacked economic substance to support a recognition of loss); later, *Knetsch v. United States*, 364 U.S. 361 (1960) (holding interest paid to carry a tax-deferred annuity product is not deductible where the otherwise tax deductible interest paid exceeds the nontaxable inside buildup in value, an economically unsound investment in the absence of the deduction for interest paid).

104 R. D. Hobbet, "The Step Transaction Doctrine and Its Effect on Corporate Transactions", 19 *Proceedings of the Annual Tulane Tax Institute* 102 (1970).

105 See note 2.

applicable statute to eliminate the opportunity to mischaracterize a transaction in that manner by including an active business requirement in corporate separations.[106]

As a precursor to the modern GAARs,[107] the "substance over form" doctrine has not worked well to limit opportunities for tax structuring designed to circumvent less favorable tax characterization of transactions. The doctrine's limitations do not bode well for the future success of GAARs. Tax avoidance structures manifest themselves in a wide variety of contexts. The preceding discussion of substance over form identifies one type of tax avoidance in transactions that take forms contrary to their economic substance. Use of fundamental structures like offshore corporations to avoid the incidence of worldwide taxation under US tax rules;[108] intentional flaws in tax rules like the structure of charitable contribution deductions[109] and tax exempt bonds;[110] special rules for specific activities, including real estate development,[111] low income housing,[112] oil and gas extraction,[113] purchase of durable goods;[114] and many other tax expenditures provide opportunities to plan transactions to exploit legislatively sanctioned tax benefits.

The United States has long used its tax system to deliver subsidies for investments the legislature deems beneficial. Accelerated depreciation,[115] for example, encourages taxpayers to invest in durable goods by permitting taxpayers to recover the cost of those goods for tax purposes by way of a deduction sooner than the goods economically waste as they produce income in the taxpayer's trade or business. The timing mismatch of economic waste and tax recovery gives the owner of the durable goods use of the depreciation tax savings for the additional time between tax recovery and economic waste – a temporary use of government funds without an interest charge. Encouraging purchase of durable goods is intended to stimulate the market for production and sale of durable goods as well as provide employment for those who produce the durable goods and, presumably, also for those using the durable goods. Tax planning consistent with the legislative subsidization of an activity through the tax system is unexceptional, so that a form over substance or step transaction analysis or a GAAR should not prevent the taxpayer from using an intended benefit in the way the legislature intended it to be used and even in ways incidental to the legislative intent like the tax exempt bond example previously given.

Against the backdrop of the broad array of subsidies delivered through the tax system, why would tax planners not seek to get a piece of those subsidies and stretch the rules as much as is possible to do so? The existence of the subsidies indeed stimulates the tax planning industry. The tax function that used to play a supporting role in the business world developed into a profit center as minimization of taxes became an independent goal for managers. As competition

---

106 The current statute prevents the spin-off of a corporation holding only liquid assets. I.R.C. §355(b) (requiring both the distributing and the distributed corporation to be engaged actively in the conduct of a business).

107 See note 19, general anti-avoidance rules.

108 The United States taxes its domestic corporations, citizens and residents on their worldwide income. Treas. Reg. §1.1-1(b). If, however, the US owner operates a business through a foreign corporation, the foreign corporation's income is not taxable in the United States until the corporation distributes its income to its US shareholder. Special anti-avoidance rules apply, including the controlled foreign corporation provisions, I.R.C. §951 et seq., to impose tax on the US owners of the foreign corporation under certain circumstances.

109 I.R.C. §170, discussed above in Example 3.

110 I.R.C. §103, discussed above in Example 1.

111 I.R.C. §168 (depreciable lives shorter than economic lives); I.R.C. §465 (exemption from at risk rules for borrowed funds).

112 I.R.C. §42 (low-income housing credits).

113 I.R.C. §263(c) (exception to capitalization for intangible drilling costs).

114 I.R.C. §179 (election to expense purchase and placement in service of tangible personal property).

115 I.R.C. §§168, 179.

within the tax planning industry grew and continues to grow, enormous amounts of creative effort have been and continue to be devoted to constructing transactions to capture tax benefits, whether intended for the specific transaction or not, probably with a loss of potential creative resources in actual production.[116] Distinguishing the intended use of a tax subsidy from the misuse of that subsidy, however, often proves elusive, as its use is buried in complex transactional structures. Even when tax avoidance can be identified in a transactional structure, concluding that the chosen structure is inconsistent with the delivery of the subsidy through the tax system may not be easy.

The delivery of subsidies through the tax system creates ambiguity as to legislative purpose. Some tax subsidies, used as intended, render transactions profitable that otherwise might not be because without the subsidy the activity is risky and uncertain so that necessary investors may be unavailable without the subsidy. Even the relatively new statutory economic substance requirement[117] must yield in situations in which the subsidy is intended to guarantee profitability and willing investors for the activity. Courts may be reluctant to disallow tax benefits where there is ambiguity as to the legislative intention except in instances in which the abuse of the tax benefits is most blatant and outrageous.

The preceding paragraphs do not argue that efforts to use general tax principles like economic substance and GAARs are futile. Rather the discussion is intended to highlight the limitations of those tools in staunching tax avoidance in all its forms. There are instances in which the tax planners overreach in structuring tax avoidance transactions and general tax avoidance principles and rules are effective. Taxing agencies certainly have enjoyed some limited successes in deploying general anti-avoidance tools. The courts continue to apply economic substance principles and GAARs in recent years to prevent tax avoidance through artificially constructed loss generating transactions involving financial products. For example, in June 2016, the Irish Supreme Court released its opinion disallowing a taxpayer's net tax loss from foreign currency straddles and gilts that the taxpayer used to offset much of the taxpayer's gain from real property sales. The taxpayer's economic loss from the structured transactions was less than 5 percent of that artificially generated loss.[118] Similarly artificial loss generating transactions using currency options and other complex financial products were disallowed in the "son-of-boss" initiative.[119] Taxpayers in some of those cases incurred substantial penalties.[120]

---

116 K.-D. Drüen, "Unternehmerfreiheit und Steuerumgehung [Entrepreneurial Freedom and Tax Avoidance]", 2008 *Steuer und Wirtschaft [STUW]* 154, 158 ("Steuerumgehung volkswirtschaftlich betrachtet den Wettbewerb und führt zur ineffizienten Allokation von Ressourcen, weil beträchtliches Personal in Unternehmen, Steuerberatung und Staat fern von wirtschaftlicher Nutzenmaximierung gebunden wird.") ["From an economic perspective, tax avoidance disrupts competition and leads to inefficient allocation of resources as considerable personnel in business, tax planning industries, and the state remain far from economic production maximization activity" (author's translation).] Footnote quoted from Ordower, Culture, see note 1, 48.

117 I.R.C. §7701(o) (economic substance requirement as a condition to claiming tax benefits).

118 *McNamee v. The Revenue Commissioners* [2016] IESC 33, available at www.supremecourt.ie/Judgments.nsf/1 b0757edc371032e802572ea0061450e/bf972756bfa84ce880257fdb0053ec31?OpenDocument (dismissing the appeal challenging the application of the Irish GAAR, s. 811 of the Revenue Act of 1997).

119 I.R.S. Announcement 2004-46, 2004-21 I.R.B. 964 (offering a settlement initiative for taxpayers who engaged in certain sophisticated, capital loss generating structures that allowed them to deduct their expenses as long-term capital losses).

120 *United States v. Woods*, 571 U.S., 134 S. Ct. 557, 187 L. Ed. 2d 472 (2013) (upholding penalties for overstating basis in sham partnerships).

Tax gap and the tax avoidance culture

When Judge Hand made clear that "there is not even a patriotic duty to increase one's taxes,"[121] he provided a rhetorical boost for the tax avoidance culture. But Hand surely would have agreed that there is a patriotic duty to pay the taxes one owes. Commitment to that duty seems to be on the wane. There is constant anti-tax noise, and many seem to view state and federal tax administrative agencies as enemies. Federal legislators lay blame for the tax laws they enacted on the tax administrative agency by referring to them as the "IRS Code."[122] The Commissioner of Internal Revenue has been demonized and threatened with impeachment.[123] Politicians pledge that they will not increase taxes.[124] In some states, voters through initiative ballots have amended state constitutions to limit the state's ability to increase revenue to meet state expenses,[125] motivating state and local tax agencies to increase collection efforts and local governmental units to rely on tax substitutes such as revenue-based policing.[126]

With declining recognition of an obligation to pay taxes, a discredited and disdained tax collector, and an intricate, complex and often inconsistent body of tax law and interpretation, taxpayers at all income levels lose sight of the national and local importance of the taxing function. Instead they glean from the enormous amounts of professional resources devoted to tax compliance[127] and avoidance[128] that to avoid paying taxes is the principal goal of those who can afford the professional assistance. Taxpayers see legislatures that are unwilling to fund tax enforcement; they experience the enforcement efforts that do emerge targeting disproportionally the economically weak, low-income income taxpayers;[129] they learn that some at the very top of the political ladder, major parties' presidential candidates, engage in aggressive and controversial tax reduction planning; and they hear a continual barrage of anti-tax rhetoric.[130] Conflation of tax evasion and tax avoidance leaves a conceptual muddle. It seems little wonder that the culture of tax avoidance becomes ever more firmly embedded in the United States.

Moderate- and lower-income taxpayers, without tax law training and without the services of tax professionals, are unable (or unwilling) to distinguish legal tax avoidance from illegal tax

---

121 *Helvering v. Gregory*, see note 2.
122 M. Y. H. Lee, "Who Wrote the 'IRS Code'? Hint: It Wasn't the Internal Revenue Service", *Washington Post* (13 April 2015), available at www.washingtonpost.com/news/fact-checker/wp/2015/04/13/who-wrote-the-irs-code-hint-it-wasnt-the-internal-revenue-service/.
123 M. DeBonis, "Impeachment Vote Averted by Promise of IRS Commissioner's Testimony", *Washington Post* (15 September 2016), available at www.washingtonpost.com/news/powerpost/wp/2016/09/15/impeachment-vote-averted-by-promise-of-irs-commissioners-testimony/.
124 Some commentators believe that George H. W. Bush's violation of his pledge "Read my lips, no new taxes" cost him the presidency in 1992. See Top 10 Unfortunate Political One-Liners, *Time*, available at http://content.time.com/time/specials/packages/article/0,28804,1859513_1859526_1859516,00.html.
125 The 1980 Hancock Amendment in Missouri, Mo. Const. art. X, §§ 16–23, for example.
126 H. Ordower, K. Warren and O. Sandoval, "Out of Ferguson: Misdemeanors, Municipal Courts, Tax Distribution and Constitutional Limitations", 61 Howard L.J. (forthcoming), Saint Louis University School of Legal Studies Research Paper No. 2016–14, available at SSRN: https://ssrn.com/abstract=2854372.
127 GAO, "Tax Policy Summary of Estimates of the Costs of the Federal Tax System" (2005), available at www.gao.gov/new.items/d05878.pdf.
128 Drüen, "Unternehmerfreiheit", see note 116.
129 See discussion of the high audit rate for the earned income credit under I.R.C. §32, see note 22 and accompanying text.
130 Compare Trump's remarks, see notes 15 and 16 and accompanying text. Many moderate- and low-income taxpayers even support repeal of the estate tax they never will have to pay, a repeal that may be contrary to their own economic interests, just because of anti-tax rhetoric.

evasion. With the limited exceptions of the earned income credit,[131] various small family credits[132] and, if they are fortunate enough to have sufficient income to carry a home mortgage, the generally available mortgage interest deduction,[133] these are not the taxpayers who may capture significant legal tax subsidies. They may be taxpayers who conclude that if it is all right for wealthier individuals to avoid taxes, it only is fair that they of moderate means also should seize every opportunity to avoid tax. The increasingly blurred distinction between legal and illegal tax minimization may escape taxpayers' understanding or they may choose to evaluate the tax evasion opportunities on the basis of risk of detection and punishment – self-help tax minimization if the risk of detection and punishment seems remote. Given the opportunity not to pay a tax, taxpayers do not pay even if not paying violates the law.

Failure to pay use tax on out of state purchases seems to be in that confused category.[134] Failure to report exchanges of services for services and goods also may fall into a realm of taxpayer uncertainty if not simple inattention to rarely enforced tax principles. Use of cash payments to avoid complex and time-consuming reporting obligations often facilitates completion of necessary tasks like home repairs when the worker prefers undetectable cash payments.

Nonpayment of taxes otherwise owed supplements lawful tax planning as an element of the culture of tax avoidance. Whether with simple, straightforward and obvious techniques, or creative, sophisticated structures that enable high-income and high-wealth taxpayers to diminish what otherwise might be their tax liability, failure to report strains collection of tax revenue. In addition to categorized tax expenditures,[135] some available to a wide range of taxpayers like the mortgage interest deduction and the earned income tax credit, some the focus of attention for creative tax planners (such as intangible drilling costs and complex financial products), there also is a substantial amount of potential tax revenue that escapes taxation because taxpayers fail to report income and overstate deductions. The IRS estimates that the amount of the revenue lost to nonreporting and the overstating of deductions for 2008–2010 runs to $458 billion annually.[136] This is the "tax gap." The tax gap measures noncompliance with the tax laws, as opposed to active but sometimes questionable reporting with tax planning, and it consists of all federal taxes: personal income, corporate income, estate and gift, excise and employment taxes. Repercussions from underreporting are few and no societal opprobrium attaches to such behavior. Instead, rank-and-file noncompliance tends to be socially accepted and acceptable behavior as taxpayers chat casually and openly about small-scale noncompliance with friends and acquaintances.

There are numerous nonstatutory opportunities not to pay taxes. Many of those nonpayments permanently escape taxation. Taxpayers regularly engage in economic activities and transactions but do not report despite the obligation to do so. The IRS estimates the voluntary compliance rate to be only 83.1 percent.[137] Absent withholding or third-party reporting, exclusions from and understatements of inclusions in tax bases are commonplace. The estimates of failure to pay self-employment tax are nearly five times as great as the employment tax because there is third-party

131 I.R.C. §32 and discussion at note 22.
132 Childcare credits under I.R.C. §21; child credit under I.R.C. §24.
133 I.R.C. §163(h)(2).
134 See Cohn, "More States", note 77.
135 See note 30 for Treasury estimates of tax expenditures.
136 IRS, "The Tax Gap: Tax Gap Estimates for Tax Years 2008–2010", available at www.irs.gov/uac/the-tax-gap. See generally M. G. Allingham and A. Sandmo, "Income Tax Evasion: A Theoretical Analysis", 1 *Journal of Public Economics* 323 (1972); S. Yitzhaki, "A Note on Income Tax Evasion: A Theoretical Analyis", 3 *Journal of Public Economics* 189 (1974); S. E. Agbi, "The Size of the Tax Evasion Problems on Self-Employment Income: An Examination of Effects of Tax Policies on Compliance", 2 *International Journal of Business and Management Review* 73 (2014).
137 Id.

withholding of the employment tax.[138] Similarly, overstatements of deductible amounts and tax basis are also common and reduce the amount of tax paid. For example, it is not unusual for a taxpayer who purchases an item at a charitable auction to claim a charitable contribution for the amount paid or a taxpayer receiving a benefit in conjunction with a charitable contribution to deduct the full amount of the payment to charity undiminished by the value of the benefit. Where the transactions involve payments for services, failure to report involves nonpayment of income tax as well as applicable employment taxes.[139] With respect to income taxes, much of that tax gap results from the underground economy where transactions consist of payments in cash or the bartering of goods or services. Often individuals exchange household services or pay for a household service in cash, and neither party reports the transaction. While the charitable claim and the payment for services may involve small amounts, they reflect anti-taxation and anti-compliance attitudes.

Without the banking system assisting the flow of payments, the transactions are difficult to identify and trace. Indirect methods of tracing payments by observing the spending behavior of individuals occasionally detect the failure to report income and pay taxes but are a vastly inadequate substitute for honest and complete taxpayer reporting and third-party information reporting. The culture in many countries, including the United States, does not stigmatize the failure to report completely and honestly. Rather the economic culture emphasizes avoidance of taxes as an acceptable choice whenever possible and imposes no moral obligation of tax compliance on the citizenry. Congress's reluctance to fund the IRS makes the resources necessary to detect tax evasion scarce and fortifies the perception that avoidance and even evasion of tax is acceptable behavior.

Conclusion – satisfying revenue needs

Tax avoidance and tax evasion shift the distribution of tax burdens from those with greater income and wealth to those least able to avoid or evade tax payment. Generally, individuals whose source of income primarily is wages that are subject to third-party tax withholding[140] and investment income subject to third-party information reporting[141] are least able to avoid payment of tax. Tax avoidance and tax evasion do not diminish governmental need for tax revenue. With limited exceptions like the use tax on out of state purchases, avoidance and evasion of tax historically has concentrated on the income tax.

The tax avoidance culture has exerted downward pressure on the progressive tax rates. Over the last several decades, maximum marginal rates of income tax have declined in the United States and Europe. In Europe, governments rely heavily on regressive value-added taxes collected throughout the production and distribution process and wage taxes collected from employers to replace revenue shortfalls.

While the United States has introduced new and increased fees for various governmental services that previously were cost free and has increased deficit spending to provide needed resources, it has not followed Europe's model of the value-added tax to produce federal revenue. Collection of income tax in the United States is critical to meeting revenue needs. Whether

---

138 IRS, "Tax Gap Estimates for Tax Years 2008–2010", Table 2, available at www.irs.gov/PUP/newsroom/tax%20 gap%20estimates%20for%202008%20through%202010.pdf.

139 For low wage taxpayers, failure to report income from services may be detrimental since the taxpayers may not claim the earned income tax credits to which they are entitled under I.R.C. §32. See note 23.

140 I.R.C. §3402.

141 I.R.C. §6041–§6049.

economic growth with the accompanying revenue produced from taxing the income generated along with deficit spending will suffice to satisfy revenue needs in the United States in light of anti-tax pressures remains uncertain. Limited efforts to collect additional income tax from high-net-worth and high-income individuals do exist. The recent enactment of the Foreign Account Tax Compliance Act (FATCA)[142] does seek to identify high-net-worth US taxpayers[143] who are secreting assets offshore in jurisdictions with strong bank secrecy laws and compel those taxpayers to disclose their offshore assets and report their income from those assets. FATCA relies on information reporting by foreign financial institutions and imposes sanctions on the institutions that do not agree to disclose US beneficial ownership and report those owners' income from the foreign accounts. Since the United States taxes its citizens and residents on their worldwide income, coercing financial institutions abroad to identify and disclose beneficial ownership by US persons of foreign financial accounts was anticipated to generate revenue to offset additional tax expenditures. At the time of passage, FATCA was estimated to generate $8.7 billion over 10 years.[144] The IRS offered an offshore voluntary compliance initiative under that legislation.[145] The initiative trades freedom from criminal prosecution for tax evasion and some penalties for voluntary reporting and payment of unpaid tax to the United States. It encouraged many US taxpayers to disclose their offshore investments on which they were not paying applicable federal income taxes.[146]

Yet, other than major offshore investors subject to FATCA, detection of failure to report many small transactions is low risk and such non-compliance has become an accepted part of the culture of tax avoidance.[147] Absent ethical compulsion which seems largely absent, there is no compelling obligation to report and pay honestly when one will not get caught. While seemingly an enforcement problem, non-reporting and intentional, but low risk of detection, false reporting is more a cultural determination that, on some level, taxes are unfair and malevolent. Accordingly, if one can get away with not paying, non-payment is all right. In that cultural context, the tax administrator is an adversary, not an agent working for the benefit of all. That perception of the IRS in the United States has resulted in the demonization of the agency both by Congress[148] and segments of the public at large. Congress rejecting its own tax agency tends to legitimize anti-tax and anti-reporting behavior. In that legislative context, the culture of tax avoidance in the United States is unlikely to change and tax avoidance and evasion likely to flourish.

142 Generally referred to as FATCA, added as a revenue offset provision, Title V, 124 Stat. 97, of the Hiring Incentives to Restore Employment Act of 2010, Pub. L. 111-47, 124 Stat. 71 (18 March 2010).
143 Foreign accounts less than an inflation-adjusted $50,000 are not subject to the FATCA reporting rules.
144 Joint Committee on Taxation, "Estimated Revenue Effects of the Revenue Provisions Contained in Senate Amendment 3310, The "Hiring Incentives to Restore Employment Act," Under Consideration By the Senate, JCX-5-10 (23 February 2010), available at www.jct.gov/publications.html?func=startdown&id=3649.
145 See generally IRS, "Offshore Voluntary Disclosure Program Frequently Asked Questions and Answers" (2014), available at www.irs.gov/individuals/international-taxpayers/offshore-voluntary-disclosure-program-frequently-asked-questions-and-answers-2012-revised.
146 IRS, "Offshore Voluntary Compliance Efforts Top $10 Billion; More Than 100,000 Taxpayers Come Back into Compliance", IR-2016-137, Oct. 21, 2016 (available at https://www.irs.gov/uac/newsroom/offshore-voluntary-compliance-efforts-top-10-billion-more-than-100000-taxpayers-come-back-into-compliance).
147 Although it is in fact not avoidance but evasion.
148 S. Dinan, "House Republicans Slash IRS Budget, Move Toward Commissioner's Impeachment", *The Washington Post* (24 May 2016), available at www.washingtontimes.com/news/2016/may/24/house-kicks-path-impeaching-irs-commissioner/. Members of Congress frequently disavow their responsibility for the tax laws in referring to the Code as the "IRS Code." M.Y. H. Lee, "Who Wrote the 'IRS Code'? Hint: It Wasn't the Internal Revenue Service", see note 127.

At local level, the tax avoidance culture and governmental inability to increase taxes has strained municipal budgets and led municipalities to enlist their police and municipal courts into revenue production. Police are encouraged to increase traffic stops for moving violations and non-compliant vehicles and to increase random stops to determine whether drivers are validly licensed. In all instances the focus is not on public safety but generation of revenue through the municipal courts' imposition of fines and court fees. The distribution of the fines and fees has tended to be regressive and possibly discriminatory because the traffic stop targets seem to consist disproportionally of people of color.[149] This revenue production development is exceptionally troubling. As the "tax" that they are, fines and court fees are not uniformly and predictably distributed. Instead distribution is arbitrary and undermines the citizenry's respect for the police and faith in the United States as governed by the rule of law.

To modify the tax avoidance culture is difficult but FATCA is an important step. Broad publicity that the IRS is targeting high worth individuals with FATCA may help to alter the perception among moderate and low income taxpayers that the wealthy can escape taxes, but the poor cannot. Expanded information reporting requirements on investment products and better funding for the IRS to provide more audit resources for the examination of high income taxpayers are critical to further diminish impressions that tax collection is centered on lower income taxpayers because high income taxpayers have the resources to resist taxes successfully. Along those lines adopting the European model for low and moderate income taxpayers that would make annual tax return preparation unnecessary for many taxpayers would eliminate most audits in the lower income ranges and moderate the tax collector as enemy characterization.[150] More uniform distribution of tax subsidies by favoring tax credits over tax deductions also would help and even better would be the diminished use of the tax system to deliver investment subsidies – a very unlikely change in policy. Nothing can be accomplished without the willingness of legislators to embrace the need to change the culture even if those changes impact their campaign donors adversely. Modification in thinking and rhetoric necessary to bring about those alterations in attitude seem remote possibilities. A more radical economic crisis that cannot be ameliorated with deficit spending may be required to bring about the required fundamental shift in legislative attitudes to enact sufficient pro-tax compliance and collection modifications to overcome embedded cultural opposition to taxation, including providing for an extensive pro-compliance advertising campaign. One might envision successful educational advertising similar to anti-drug, anti-smoking, and pro-seat belt use campaigns that helped to modify public behaviors.

---

149 Ordower, Warren, Sandoval, "Out of Ferguson", see note 126.
150 See, M.J. Graetz, *100 Million Unnecessary Returns: A Simple Fair and Competitive Tax Plan for the United States* (New Haven, CT: Yale University Press, 2008).

4

SHAM TRANSACTIONS AND TAX AVOIDANCE

Miranda Stewart

The word "sham" is used in a popular way to refer to fake, disguised or artificial transactions that aim to avoid tax. An example is tax haven transactions, such as those by wealthy individuals and multinational companies, identified in the Panama Papers.[1] The popular concept of "sham" here refers to a deliberate fraud.

A more specific judicial doctrine of "sham" transactions is applied by courts in many countries to address transactions that avoid tax. Judges use phrases such as "trompe l'oeil"[2] or "a cloud of words"[3] to describe sham transactions. This judicial doctrine is the subject of this chapter.

The judicial doctrine of "sham" has a long history. It is recognized and applied by courts across the common law world, as demonstrated in a recent collection which discussed the existence and application of the doctrine in the UK, Australia, Canada, NZ, India, South Africa and the US, across a wide range of areas of law, including taxation law, employment law, migration law, partnership and trust law, sale of goods, contract law and family law.[4] Similar judicial concepts have developed in civil law countries to counter tax abuse including *fraus legis* ("fraud on the law") or *abus de droit* ("abuse of law"). These judicial doctrines all address, to a greater or lesser degree, an intention of the taxpayer to deceive or defraud the Revenue, or an abuse of the tax law, without rising to the level of tax evasion or criminal fraud. Thus, they exist in between the concepts of tax avoidance and tax evasion.

The judicial doctrine of "sham" and similar doctrines do not automatically carry criminal or civil penalties and they are also narrower than the statutory General Anti-Avoidance Rules (GAARs) that are increasingly applied in tax laws across the world. Thus, while a judicial

---

1 See, e.g., "Isle of Sham: Tales From a Canadian Tax Haven", available at www.taxfairness.ca/en/news/isle-shamtales-canadian-tax-haven.

2 *Antle v. R* 2010 DTC 7304 (Canada; French report).

3 *Cam & Sons Pty Ltd v. Sargent* (1940) 14 ALJ 162 (High Court of Australia), 163 per Dixon J.

4 E. Simpson and M. Stewart (eds), *Sham Transactions* (Oxford: Oxford University Press, 2013). See also R. Rohtagi, *Basic International Taxation, Volume II: Practice*, Ch.6 "Anti-avoidance Measures", which surveys the wide practice and approach of many countries including India; N. Musviba, "Anti-Avoidance Provisions on Sham Transactions", *South African Tax Guide*, available at www.sataxguide.co.za/anti-avoidance-provisions-on-sham-transactions/; *CSARS v. NWK* 2011 (2) SA 67 (South African Supreme Court); E. Marais, "An Update on Tax Avoidance Principles in South Africa – January 2015", *African Tax Journal* (15 January 2015), available at www.africataxjournal.com.

doctrine of sham is widespread, it tends to be a narrow doctrine as developed and applied by courts. The doctrine of "sham" may be particularly narrow in those countries which have a GAAR in the tax legislation. For example, Australia and NZ have long had a statutory GAAR. The doctrine of sham exists in both countries but it has been described by an Australian judge as existing on the "periphery" of tax law.[5] In some countries, however, especially where there is no GAAR, the doctrine of sham has a wider meaning. For example, as explained below, US courts established early in the 20th century a "sham transaction" doctrine. It is one of several important judicial doctrines aimed at overriding the form of transactions and reflecting their economic substance for tax purposes. In the UK, the narrow doctrine of sham was developed by the courts but has been applied by the courts in recent decades, together with broader purposive approaches to interpreting tax legislation, so as to defeat tax avoidance schemes. The UK has now enacted a legislative GAAR.

What is a sham?

The particular formulation of the sham doctrine differs across countries and over time. However, there is a common element of deceit. A court may apply the doctrine if it finds that a purported legal transaction is used as a "cover-up".[6] A sham transaction is "a transaction constructed to create a false impression in the eyes of the tax authority".[7] The legal form is established in written documentation and other evidence as a cloak or a pretence to hide the real transaction (and its tax consequences) so as to deceive the Revenue.

For example, an arrangement may purport to be a business partnership at law, but it is in reality an employee-employer relationship.[8] A "letter-box company" in a tax haven that is established for tax avoidance purposes may be a sham.[9] A transaction may have the legal form of a loan that carries tax-deductible interest expense. However, a court may apply the doctrine of sham to recharacterise it as equity on which a non-deductible dividend is paid. The court may do this, if it concludes on the basis of all the facts and evidence, that this is the true legal intention of the parties to the transaction and is the more normal or commercial form of the transaction.[10]

Therefore, a finding of "sham" involves a court determining that a taxpayer or parties established documents or acts intended to establish the appearance of one legal form so as to attract a specific tax consequence, but which the taxpayer and other parties do not intend to carry out, so that in reality they have different or no legal consequences. The doctrine concerns the legal intention of the parties and it therefore applies to a transaction, prior to the application of any taxation law. A court will generally require evidence of an intention of the parties to deceive the Revenue in establishing this "false" legal form, in order to apply the doctrine. If a sham is found, the court will treat the "sham transaction" as void and will identify the true legal transaction of

---

5 Sharrment Pty Ltd & Ors v. Official Trustee in Bankruptcy (1988) 82 ALR 530, 536 per Lockhart J (Aus).
6 Rohtagi, *supra* n. 4.
7 *CIR v. Challenge Corporation Ltd* (1987) 2 WLR 24 (NZ), Lord Templeman, Privy Council.
8 In Australia: *Cam & Sons Pty Ltd v. Sargent* (1940) 14 ALJ 162 (High Court of Australia); in the US, e.g. *ASA Investerings Partnership v Commissioner* 201 F.3d 505 (DC Cir. 2000).
9 See, e.g. J. Kessler, "What Is (and What Is Not) a Sham" *Offshore International Tax Review* (2000) 9.2.2; *Bywater Investments Ltd v. Commr of Taxation* [2016] HCA 45 (High Court of Australia).
10 See, e.g. Frank van Brunschot, "Fraus legis and the Multinational Enterprises" (IBFD Bulletin, August/September 1988); Jacques Malherb, Simulation, Fraus Legis and Business Purpose Under Belgian Tax Law (IBFD Bulletin for International Taxation, August/September 1987); Rohtagi, *supra* n 4.

the taxpayer and other parties based on the evidence before it. The court then applies the tax law to the true legal transaction.

A widely cited interpretation in common law jurisdictions of a "sham", described as a "popular and pejorative word", was made half a century ago in *Snook*, an English case concerning sales of goods law. Lord Justice Diplock said of "sham":

> [I]f it has any meaning in law, it means acts done or documents executed by the parties to the 'sham' which are intended by them to give to third parties or to the court the appearance of creating between the parties legal rights and obligations different from the actual legal rights and obligations (if any) which the parties intend to create. But one thing, I think, is clear in legal principle, morality and the authorities ... that for acts or documents to be a 'sham,' with whatever legal consequences follow from this, all the parties thereto must have a common intention that the acts or documents are not to create the legal rights and obligations which they give the appearance of creating.[11]

These remarks are cited in many tax cases across the common-law world, except in the US which earlier developed its own judicial concept of sham.

The origins of sham, fraus legis *and* abus de droit

The doctrine of sham has earlier origins. The term "sham" in English law originates as "a late seventeenth-century slang expression which passed into legal usage in the 1690s".[12] It first appeared in English law reports in 1691.[13] The concept of "sham" is applied in the cases alongside a variety of related expressions, including "colourable", "fraud or practice apparent", and "simulation". The common law notion of "sham" can be traced to even older civil law and Roman law concepts, especially *fraus legis* and *abus de droit* or *fraude a la Loi*.

The concept of *fraus legis* dates back to the Roman Jurist Paul:

> Contra legem facit, qui id facit quod lex prohibit, in fraudem vero, qui salvis verbis legissententiam eius circumvenit *translated as:*
> He acts contrary to a statute, who does what the statute prohibits; he acts in fraud [of a statute], who sticks to the words of the statute but circumvents its sense.[14]

The historical relationship between sham and *fraus legis* (fraud of a statute, or fraud on the law) is explained by Macnair, who concludes that English law used to have such a doctrine but abandoned it during the 19th century, when the narrower doctrine of sham gained ascendance.[15]

---

11 *Snook v. London and West Riding Investments Ltd* [1967] 2 QB 786, 802, per Diplock LJ (UK).
12 M. Macnair, Sham: Early Uses and Related and Unrelated Doctrines, in Simpson and Stewart (2013), *supra* n. 4, p. 29.
13 *Nightingale v. Bridges* (1691) 1 Show KB 135; 89 ER 496 (UK).
14 Macnair, *supra* n. 12, p. 40. A. Watson (ed.), *The Digest of Justinian* (Philadelphia, PA: University of Pennsylvania Press, 1998), translates (Macnair suggests "mistranslates") as: "It is a contravention of the law if someone does what the law forbids, but fraudulently, in that he sticks to the words of the law but evades its sense".
15 Macnair, *supra* n. 12, p. 40.

However, courts in civil law countries still apply a general concept of *fraus legis* (or *fraude a la Loi*) or *abus de droit* inherited from Roman law.[16] There is also a doctrine of "simulation" in civil law,[17] which is similar to the concept of a "cloak" or fake transaction – in this case, the judge may pull aside the cloak to identify the true transaction. These doctrines are all applied by courts to recharacterise transactions that are entered into for purposes of tax avoidance, where the court finds an artificial or simulated legal form.[18] Rohtagi explains as follows:

> Re-characterisation is often used in tax law to bridge the differences between private law and tax law. The methods used vary from country to country. The most common are sham or simulation and written or unwritten general anti-avoidance rules in civil law countries. Similar principles are also followed in common law countries but practice varies. For example in Canada re-characterisation is permitted only if the label does not properly reflect its actual legal effect. Australia, Canada and New Zealand often reject economic substance unless stated in the tax statute. The UK Courts only re-characterise the legal facts of the transactions. The concept used often depends on the interpretation of the law. For example, what is legal and what is commercial depends on what parliament intended; however, because of the complexity of the law, most concepts tend to be legal in substance. The United States is an exception where economic substance usually prevails under its judicial doctrines.[19]

These doctrines have been extended to the level of the European Union, as a concept of abuse of law has been applied by the Court of Justice of the European Union in Value Added Tax (VAT) law.[20]

The application of "sham" to tax avoidance

This section surveys the application of the doctrine of "sham" to tax avoidance in several common law countries including the UK, US, Australia, Canada and NZ.

In the UK, the judicial doctrine of sham originally had a narrow compass and was rarely used in the tax context. However, in the last few decades, a broader concept of sham that refers to the substance of the transaction, combined with an approach of purposive interpretation of tax laws was developed by the courts to address tax avoidance transactions. These approaches (variously explained depending on the approach and timing as *fiscal nullity*, or more recently the *Ramsay* doctrine) were developed in a series of cases, the meaning of which has been much debated. There has been ongoing debate about the effectiveness, or

---

16 See, e.g. J. Prebble, "Abus de Droit and the General Anti-Avoidance Rule of Income Tax Law: A Comparison of the Laws of Seven Jurisdictions and the European Community" (2008).

17 Macnair, *supra* n. 12, p. 43, for a discussion see M. D. Blecher, "Simulated Transactions in the Later Civil Law", 91 *South African Law Journal* 358 (1974).

18 F. Zimmer, "Form and Substance in Tax Law", IFA Cahiers, Vol. 87A, General Report (2002).

19 Rohtagi, *supra* n 4.

20 R. de la Feria and S. Vogenauer (eds), *Prohibition of Abuse of Law: A new General Principle of EU Law* (Hart Publishing, 2011: Oxford).

not, of judicial approaches.[21] This debate finally led to the enactment of a GAAR in the UK five years ago.[22]

In the US, the concept of "sham" has a long history as a doctrine applied across a wide range of areas of law including marriage, leases and bankruptcy, as well as tax law.[23] The concept has similar features of pretence, disguise and intention to deceive as in other common law jurisdictions. However, the US differs from other common law jurisdictions in the adoption of a broader concept of sham in tax law.

Blank and Staudt explain, "US courts use a variety of judicially-created doctrines, such as the sham doctrine, the step transaction doctrine, the economic substance doctrine" to address tax avoidance transactions.[24] A court applying a "sham transaction" doctrine would disallow a tax arrangement on the basis that the substance of the transaction had no purpose other than tax avoidance.[25] The leading case, *Gregory v. Helvering*, is well-known in many jurisdictions around the world. In this case, the US Supreme Court overturned a tax avoidance transaction on the basis that it was a sham.[26] Justice Learned Hand said:

> All these steps were real, and their only defect was that they were not what the statute means by a "reorganization", because the transactions were not part of the conduct of the business of either or both companies; so viewed they were a sham, though all the proceedings had their usual effect.[27]

The US judicial anti-abuse doctrines including the broad concept of sham have been important in protecting its federal income tax over the last century. In addition, recently, US courts have resuscitated a narrower concept of "sham", enabling them to strike down abusive transactions without necessarily establishing the economic substance of the transaction as required by the broader doctrine. A "sham partnership" doctrine has been applied by US federal courts to overturn corporate tax shelters by finding an "illusory" intent of the taxpayers to create a genuine partnership. The Revenue has won several hard-fought and lengthy court cases in which the court applied the sham doctrine to defeat tax schemes of large corporations, which proliferated during the 1990s and which "were typically structured as a financing transaction in which a US corporation leased its own assets back from a partnership, generating a stream of deductible

---

21 See, e.g. J. Tiley, "Judicial Anti-Avoidance Doctrines", *British Tax Review* 196 (1988), 63–103; 108–45; J. Vella, "Sham Tax Avoidance and 'A Realistic View of the Facts' in the UK", in Simpson and Stewart (2013), *supra* n. 4, 259; J. Vella, "Sham Transactions", 4 *LMCLQ* 488 (2008); M. Gammie, "Tracing the Boundaries of Sham and Ramsay", in Simpson and Stewart (2013), above n. 4, 211.

22 See Tax avoidance: General Anti-Abuse Rule guidance HM Revenue and Customs (2014), available www.gov. uk/government/publications/tax-avoidance-general-anti-abuse-rules, viewed 28 June 2017.

23 J. D. Blank and N. Staudt, "Sham Transactions in the United States", in Simpson and Stewart (2013), *supra* n. 4, p. 68; referring to, e.g. Timothy Hall, "Denial of Social Security Retirement Benefits to Member of Family Business on Ground That Retirement Was Sham Designed to Qualify for Benefits", 102 *ALR* 25 (1991); S.-Y. Oei, "Context Matters: The Recharacterization of Leases in Bankruptcy and Tax Law", 82 *American Banker Law Journal* 635 (2008).

24 Blank and Staudt, *supra* n. 23, p. 69.

25 E.g. ASA Investerings *Pship v. Commr of Internal Revenue* 201 F.3d 505, 516 (DC Cir 2000); *Goodstein v. Commr*, 267 F.2d 127, 131–2 (1st Cir 1959).

26 *Gregory v. Helvering* 55 S Ct 2766 (1935) (US).

27 *Helvering v. Gregory* 69 F. 2d 809 (1943) (US Supreme Court). This anti-avoidance doctrine is widely discussed in US commentary; see e.g. L. Lederman, "W(h)ither Economic Substance", 95 *Iowa Law Review* 389 (2010); J. L. Cummings Jr., "The Sham Transaction Doctrine", 145 *Tax Notes* 1239 (15 December 2014).

business expenses while shifting taxable income to a tax-indifferent party such as a foreign bank."[28]

While the judicial doctrines in the US are quite robust and are supported by numerous specific or targeted anti-abuse rules, the US Congress recently codified its economic substance doctrine, imposing strict penalties on taxpayers for violating this and similar doctrines.[29]

In contrast to the broad judicial doctrine in the US, most other common law countries apply the narrower doctrine inherited from the UK. In Australia, the judicial doctrine of "sham" has been applied from time to time to overturn tax avoidance schemes over the last century.[30] The doctrine was affirmed in 2008 by the High Court in the *Raftland* case.[31] In *Raftland*, complicated legal arrangements relating to a trust and loss trading were held to be a sham, so the High Court applied the tax law to the arrangements they identified as reflecting the true legal intention of the taxpayer, which was then liable to substantially greater tax. The High Court also upheld the highest rate of tax penalty for "recklessness", which with interest more than doubled the assessment of tax.

The term "sham" is applied in Australia to taxpayers who enter into an ostensible transaction as a disguise to conceal their true transaction.[32] It is the "legal effect" and not the "economic" effect that is crucial and the "true nature" of the transaction "is to be determined by reference to all of the evidence".[33] The majority judgment in *Raftland* (Gleeson CJ, Gummow and Crennan JJ) emphasized that the purpose of "securing a fiscal benefit" of the taxpayer was "of significance in the identification of the legal rights created".[34] The court concluded that the documents prepared by the taxpayer and other parties were not to be taken at face value but it was cautious about finding deliberate deception.[35] Other judges have taken a stronger line. In a separate judgment in the same case, Kirby J referred to the "well understood" doctrine of sham:[36]

> it is perfectly proper for Australian courts, and other decision-makers, to invoke the concept of sham in legal analysis, as acknowledged in *Equuscorp*. It may be helpful in revenue cases so long as the need for intentional deception is kept in mind.[37]

A "sham" is thus a transaction "intended to be mistaken for something else … a spurious imitation, a counterfeit, a disguise or a false front. It is not genuine or true, but something made in imitation of something else or made to appear to be something which it is not."[38]

---

28 K. Burke and G. MP McCouch, "Sham Partnerships and Equivocal Transactions" *The Tax Lawyer* (Spring 2016: American Bar Association) discuss these marketed and very substantial corporate tax shelters, including two major tax avoidance schemes entered into by Dow Chemicals: *Chemtech Royalty Assoc., L.P. v. United States*, 2013-1 U.S.T.C. 83,496 111 A.F.T.R.2d 953, 955 (M.D. La. 2013); *Chemtech Royalty Assoc., L.P. v. United States*, 766 F.3d 453, 455–59 (5th Cir. 2014).

29 Internal Revenue Code Section 7701(o) (US).

30 For a discussion of the doctrine in Australia, see G.T. Pagone, "Sham Trusts", 41 *Australian Tax Review* 119 (2012); M. Kirby, "Of Sham and Other Lessons for Australian Revenue Law", 32 *Melbourne University Law Review* 27 (2008); A. Slater, "Sham and Substance", 28 *Australian Tax Review* 197 (1999); J. Glover, "Sham, Raftland and the Return of Economic Equivalence", 43 *Taxation in Australia* 21 (2008).

31 *Raftland Pty Ltd as trustee of the Raftland Trust v. Commissioner of Taxation* (2008) 238 CLR 516 (Aus).

32 (2006) 62 ATR 49, 66, para [77] per Kiefel J (Aus).

33 (2006) 62 ATR 49, 66, para [79], [89].

34 (2008) 238 CLR 516, 531, para [34] (Aus).

35 Ibid.

36 (2008) 238 CLR 516, 545, para [86].

37 (2008) 238 CLR 516, 558, paras [130], [134]–[136].

38 *Sharrment Pty Ltd and Ors v. Official Trustee in Bankruptcy* (1988) 82 ALR 530, 536 (Full Federal Court); *Scott v. FCT (No. 2)* (1966) 40 ALJR 265, 279.

In spite of its application with some success in tax avoidance cases, the sham doctrine is quite weak and in many countries, experience shows the Revenue agency often does not succeed. For example, in the early case of *Purcell*,[39] the weakness of "sham" in addressing tax minimisation is shown. Mr Purcell declared a trust of his farm and chattels one third each to his wife and daughter, and one third to himself, while ensuring that he would retain full control over the assets and conduct of the business. The trust was upheld as effective at law and for tax purposes, enabling him to minimize taxation. The majority rejected the Revenue's argument:

> [T]he Commissioner insisted that the declaration, if in form it created a trust, was in fact a mere sham, a device whereby property belonging to the settlor is made to appear to belong in equity to someone else in order to escape taxation ... The question is one of fact. The Chief Justice found that the declaration was not a sham, and that the respondent did in fact intend by the document to benefit his wife and daughter, although he ... was to some extent influenced by the fact that the disposition would reduce the burden of taxation.[40]

The Australian judges have emphasised that factors which are often seen as markers of tax avoidance do not necessarily indicate a "sham", including: circularity of transactions; use of nonrecourse debt; and complexity or artificiality of transactions and legal entities.[41] In contrast, Australia's statutory GAAR operates objectively on the legal transactions of the parties, although factors such as "form and substance" must be taken into account in ascertaining a sole or dominant purpose of obtaining the tax benefit.[42]

Recent authority suggests that a more robust judicial approach to finding of the facts of a transaction can be successful in countering tax avoidance. In a case decided in 2016, *Bywater Investments*, the High Court of Australia held that a company that was established by the taxpayer with a corporate residence in a tax haven was not, as a matter of fact, resident there for tax purposes.[43] A complicated set of companies, directors and an associated paper trail had been established, but these were found by the trial judge to involve directors and board meetings that were "fake" and "mere window dressing" consisting of "rubber stamping"; and the management structure of one entity was an "illusion". As a result, the true central management and control of the company, and hence its tax residence, was in Sydney. These judicial findings were upheld on appeal, without need for recourse to the doctrine of sham as technically defined.

In Canada, the doctrine of sham has been recognized in taxation law at least since the 1970s.[44] The doctrine has been seemingly expanded and narrowed in different cases over the years. Overall, the more narrow approach to the doctrine of sham has prevailed, although some recent cases appear to expand its application. Canadian courts of different provinces may apply a civil law (French) legal approach, or a common law (Anglo) approach to the doctrine of sham

39 *Purcell v. DFCT* (1920) 28 CLR 77; *DFCT v. Purcell* (1921) 29 CLR 464 (Aus). But see recently *Kennon v. Spry* (2008) 251 ALR 257; [2008] HCA 56.
40 *DFCT v. Purcell* (1921) 29 CLR 464, 472 (Aus).
41 *Sharrment Pty Ltd & Ors v. Official Trustee in Bankruptcy* (1988) 82 ALR 530, 536 (Aus).
42 Section 177D of Income Tax Assessment Act 1936 (Cth).
43 *Bywater Investments Ltd v. Commr of Taxation* [2016] HCA 45 (Aus).
44 *Minister of National Revenue v. Cameron* [1974] Supreme Court of Canada Reports 1062; see G. Loutzenhiser, "Sham in the Canadian Courts", in Simpson and Stewart (2013), *supra* n. 4, p. 243.

in applying the income tax law. Recent cases of *Faraggi*[45] and *Antle*[46] arose in Quebec and the Courts in these cases appear more willing to find a deception by the taxpayer and hence apply the doctrine to void the transaction. In French-language reports of the cases, the expression "trompe-l'oeil" – to deceive or trick the eye – is sometimes used. In the 2010 case of *Antle*, the taxpayer gifted shares to a discretionary trust set up in the tax haven of Barbados, which would then sell the shares to the taxpayer's wife who would sell them to an unrelated purchaser (there were also other complexities including reliance on the Canada-Barbados tax treaty). The goal of the whole transaction was to avoid capital gains tax on the share sale. The Canadian federal Court upheld the Revenue argument that the gain was taxable because the trust was not validly created in the tax haven. Some judicial comments indicated that the judges considered the trust was a "pretence" and concluded that the taxpayer had an intention to deceive, so this was a sham (which is not as steep a threshold as required at criminal law for fraud or deceit).[47]

In NZ, the sham concept was first applied by the courts in the context of commercial transactions but it has also been argued quite often in tax matters by the Revenue authority.[48] The courts have held that a sham exists where the transaction or document is a mask, cloak, or façade concealing the true position between the parties.[49] The NZ Supreme Court in *Ben Nevis* in 2008 affirmed that in the NZ context "a sham is a pretence":

> A document will be a sham when it does not evidence the true common intention of the parties. They either intend to create different rights and obligations from those evidenced by the document or they do not intend to create any rights or obligations. ... [a sham is] designed to lead the taxation authorities to view the documentation as representing what the parties have agreed when it does not record their true agreement.[50]

The NZ Supreme Court confirmed that "an allegation of 'sham', being akin to an allegation of fraud, should not be lightly made".[51]

The relationship between sham, substance, evasion and GAAR

The judicial doctrine of sham is applied at an earlier stage of analysis than a statutory GAAR. This is because "sham" concerns the legal, rather than economic substance and requires a finding of the legal intention of the taxpayer and other parties based on all the evidence. Although the concept of "sham" requires a finding of an intention to deceive, this does not rise to the level of criminal fraud which would be subject to criminal or administrative tax penalties or prosecution. In common law, the *mens rea* or criminal intent to defraud is not established. This is

---

45 *Faraggi v. R* 2008 FCA 398; 2009 DTC 5023 (Can).

46 *Antle v. R* 2010 FCA 280; 2010 DTC 7304 (Can).

47 Loutzenhiser, *supra* n. 44, p. 256.

48 S. Griffiths and J. Palmer, "Sham, Tax Avoidance and a GAAR: A New Zealand Perspective", in Simpson and Stewart (2013), *supra* n. 4, p. 228. See, e.g. *Bateman Television Ltd v. Coleridge Finance Co Ltd* [1969] NZLR 794, affirmed on appeal to the Privy Council at [1971] NZLR 929; *Paintin and Nottingham Ltd v. Miller Gale and Winter* [1971] NZLR 164; *Re Securitibank Ltd (No 2)* [1978] 2 NZLR 136; *Marac Finance Ltd v. Virtue* [1981] 1 NZLR 586; D. McLauchlan, "Agreements to Buy One's Own Goods – Implied Preceding Sale or Sham?" 1 *NZ Business Law Quarterly* 21 (1995).

49 *Paintin and Nottingham Ltd v. Miller Gale and Winter* (n. 48) 168; *Bateman Television Ltd v. Coleridge Finance Co Ltd* (n. 48) 803.

50 *Ben Nevis Forestry Ventures Ltd v. Commissioner of Inland Revenue* [2008] NSZS 115, para [33].

51 *Ben Nevis Forestry Ventures Ltd v. Commissioner of Inland Revenue* [2008] NSZS 115, para [39].

also relevant to the burden of proof. In a criminal matter, at least in common law jurisdictions, the burden to prove fraud would lie on the prosecutor or Revenue agency, whereas the issue of whether a tax assessment is correct may require proof by the taxpayer or the Revenue, depending on the jurisdiction.

The courts in Australia, NZ and Canada have had to analyse the relationship between "sham" and a GAAR, so as to decide how to apply the judicial doctrine or statutory rule to tax avoidance transactions.

Australia's federal income tax has always had a statutory GAAR and the question of the relationship between the doctrine of sham, and the GAAR arose a century ago. The case of *Jaques*[52] concerned a scheme to convert an existing company into two new companies, in such a way as to generate a tax deduction for the shareholders as well as saving other taxes on the transaction. The Commissioner argued that (1) the transaction was a sham, (2) it was an evasion of the tax law and (3) it was a breach of the GAAR. The taxpayer's defence stated that the GAAR was merely a statutory enactment of the sham doctrine, which the taxpayer argued it did not breach. The High Court concluded that the GAAR was intended to apply to transactions to avoid tax, even if these were legally effective and not a sham. One judge concluded, referring to earlier English case law:

> Numerous judicial decisions have dealt with the subject of sham transactions and transactions said to be "evasions" of the law. There is always great difficulty in determining in any particular case whether a transaction is a lawful or unlawful "evasion" of a statute. ... Parliament, in passing sec 53, recognized the difficulties ... It laid down its own test of avoidance for its own purposes. Therefore, what I have to do is not to consider the question of "evasion" by the light of the standard authorities on that subject. Nor do I see on the facts before me how I can treat what has been done as an unreality. Sec 53 regards the "contract, agreement, or arrangement" as possibly a very real one, but attaches consequences to the purpose or effect.[53]

The appeal court concluded that the GAAR would apply *even if* the transactions were legally effective and not a sham.

NZ has had a statutory GAAR in its tax law since 1891. The Revenue has argued and Courts have applied both the doctrine of sham and the GAAR in numerous cases.[54] The NZ Supreme Court has held that the GAAR and the doctrine of sham co-exist. However, Griffiths and Palmer identify significant confusion in NZ cases about the doctrine of sham, the concept of economic substance and the application of the GAAR. They suggest that the doctrine of sham is no longer ideal for addressing tax avoidance, serving "only to muddy the waters of an already difficult area"[55] and that the statutory GAAR alone should be applied to address this problem.

A similar argument has been made about the approach of the Revenue and courts in Canada. Recent cases appearing to strengthen the sham doctrine but there are questions about whether this is the better approach, or whether in the tax context, it would be better just to apply the GAAR. Loutzenhiser suggests that the additional requirement of deceit which must be

---

52 *Jaques v FCT* (1923–24) 34 CLR 328 (High Court of Australia), considering application of s 53 of the Income Tax Act 1915 (Cth), which was the first statutory GAAR.
53 (1923–24) 34 CLR 328, 338.
54 Currently in section BG1 of Income Tax Act 2007 (NZ).
55 Griffiths and Palmer, *supra* n. 48, p. 242.

established for "sham" may be a disadvantage and the doctrine will have "quite limited practical utility", as the Canadian tax authorities can use a range of other tools including specific anti-avoidance rules, an "ineffective transaction" judicial doctrine, and the GAAR.[56]

In the UK, although it is where the doctrine of "sham" originated, Revenue agencies may not want to rely on a narrow doctrine of "sham" because it is difficult to establish the taxpayer's legal intention. The broader judicial doctrine of purposive interpretation of the tax law (*Ramsay* approach), and ultimately the new GAAR enacted in the UK may be more useful.[57]

The relevance of sham to tax avoidance in future

The doctrine of sham has a narrow application in most countries. However, the doctrine still performs an important function in upholding the tax law. The doctrine can rescue the judge "from being led by the nose" by taxpayers.[58] The doctrine of sham protects the taxation law by ensuring that the rules for finding the intention of the parties to a transaction, and the interpretation of written documents, are properly applied. Thus, the doctrine of sham helps protect the rules of legal construction from deceit, bad faith or fraudulent intent. The doctrine of sham can also prevent the evasion of a legislative regime, such as the tax law, by taxpayers who construct disguised or fake transactions. As a result, the doctrine of sham may be used by the courts as a necessary companion to the purposive interpretation of the tax law with reference to its policy.

The most difficult aspect of the doctrine of sham is how to understand its relationship with fraud. Sham sits in law uneasily between evasion and avoidance, fraud and commercial dealing. The cases demonstrate, from the earliest history, that some finding of intentional deceit is important. This is why a sham transaction is void, so that a court can ignore it and apply the tax law to the "true" legal transaction of the taxpayer. However, courts are ambivalent as to the extent of dishonesty or fraud that is required for sham.

There is increasing public attention to international tax avoidance and evasion activities by high wealth individuals and multinational enterprises, especially legal transactions and entities in tax havens. The judicial doctrine of "sham" discussed here may be too narrow and cumbersome to address the current plague of tax haven activity, fake or controlled directors of trusts and companies in havens.[59] In order to ensure that Revenue agencies can address these fraudulent activities, systematic reforms are needed. These include law reforms to ensure transparency and disclosure of beneficial ownership of companies, trusts, bank accounts and bearer shares, and increased co-operation, data exchange and assistance in tax administration between revenue agencies in different countries.

Courts are finding other ways to identify the true facts of a transaction, for example whether a company board of directors is "fake", as in the recent Australian case of *Bywater Investments*. A robust approach to the facts can help to identify the true transaction, without necessarily requiring all the elements of "sham" to be established. There will remain a place for the judicial doctrine of sham in countering major tax avoidance activity, together with civil law doctrines of

---

56 Loutzenhiser, *supra* n. 44, p. 257–8.

57 Gammie, *supra* n. 21.

58 (2008) 238 CLR 516, para [151] per Kirby J.

59 B. Brinkmann, F. Obermaier and B. Obermayer, "The Secret World of Sham Directors, Panama Papers", available at http://panamapapers.sueddeutsche.de/articles/5718f882a1bb8d3c3495bcc7/. Often, sham directors are ordinary people who have themselves been deceived by tax evaders and those conducting other criminal activity.

fraus legis and *abus de droit*. Recent cases in many countries indicate that courts may be strengthening their approach, while the US courts have demonstrated "resourcefulness and versatility" in addressing new forms of tax abuse by large corporations, by rejuvenating the older legal doctrine of "sham".[60]

Today, the judicial doctrine of sham should be only one part of the armoury of the Revenue authorities and the courts in the fight against tax abuse. It increasingly is buttressed with statutory GAARs and specific anti-abuse rules that apply if a taxpayer is found to have a purpose of avoiding taxation, or rules that focus on economic substance or commercial reality of transactions. The new GAARs emphasise the objective facts; do not require a finding of subjective intention to deceive the Revenue; and enable a focus on the economic or commercial substance of a transaction as opposed to its legal form.

60 Burke and McCouch *supra* n. 28.

PART II

General anti-avoidance rules

5

GENERAL ANTI-AVOIDANCE RULES AND THE RULE OF LAW

Rebecca Prebble and John Prebble

Introduction

The rule of law and tax avoidance

"The rule of law" is a compendious term for a number of related values that people generally think good laws should adhere to. Dicey's familiar formulation held that the rule of law requires "the absolute supremacy or predominance of regular law as opposed to the influence of arbitrary power."[1] It is theoretically possible to interpret this condition as requiring merely that there should be laws, as opposed to a series of isolated commands. Nevertheless, theorists writing since Dicey have supplemented Dicey's basic formulation with a number of additional requirements that the basic formulation logically must entail if it is to be of value. In the present context, the most important of these is that the law should be capable of guiding people. In order to guide people, laws must be relatively clear and their application relatively certain; otherwise no one will know what is permitted and what is forbidden. The criterion of relative certainty has proven very difficult to satisfy when it comes to formulating rules that combat tax avoidance.

Tax avoidance is a problem for every country. Avoidance is not evasion. Evasion means lying about one's income. For example, a cash business may under-state its takings or fail to file any return of tax at all. Avoidance is not mitigation. "Mitigation" is not a term of art, but in this chapter, and generally in the present context, it means reducing one's tax in ways that a governing statute clearly encourages or permits; for example, taking a deduction for a gift to charity.[2]

Avoidance is between the two. Avoidance means, approximately, contriving transactions, typically but not necessarily artificial in nature, to reduce tax that would otherwise be payable according to what appears to be the policy of the taxing provision in question. This is a description rather than a definition. Terminology in the area is controversial. Some people deny that we can draw a meaningful distinction between avoidance and mitigation. Some people deny that the word mitigation has any right to exist as a meaningful term in this context.[3]

---

1 A.V. Dicey, *Introduction to the Study of the Law of the Constitution*, 10th ed. (London: Macmillan, 1960), 202.
2 J. Freedman, "Defining Taxpayer Responsibility: In Support of a General Anti-Avoidance Principle", *BTR* 332, 350 [2004].
3 See, e.g., *Miller v. CIR* [2001] 3 NZLR 316, 326 Lord Hoffman (PC).

As a general rule, the law does not require people to arrange their affairs so that they incur the greatest possible tax liability. When faced with two possible ways in which to organise their money, taxpayers are entitled to choose the option that requires them to pay the lesser amount of tax. There comes a point, however, where governments begin to think that taxpayers are going too far in their attempts to decrease their tax liability: at this point, taxpayers cease to engage in legitimate tax mitigation and embark on unacceptable tax avoidance.

Tax avoidance is perhaps best understood through examples, rather than by analysis. Examples of tax avoidance transactions from different jurisdictions abound. They tend to have a number of identifiable features, for example, artificiality,[4] lack of business or economic reality,[5] lack of true business risk,[6] and the exploitation of statutory loopholes.[7] Avoidance often involves taxpayers exploiting rules that were designed to reduce unfairness in the tax system[8] or using existing legal structures in enterprising ways that the legislature, had it thought about the matter, would not have approved.[9]

To help to recognise avoidance, take, for example, *Inland Revenue Commissioners v. Bowater Property Developments Ltd*,[10] a United Kingdom case that the House of Lords decided in 1988. That case involved development land tax, a kind of capital gains tax that applied to land sales if the development value component of the sale was valued at more than £50,000. In a transaction potentially caught by the tax, Bowater proposed to sell land for more than £250,000, to a company called Milton Pipes Limited.

Instead of selling the land as one parcel, Bowater segmented the land into five undivided shares. It sold one share to each of five sibling companies in the Bowater group for £36,000 per share. Land in undivided shares looks just like land: there was no subdivisional survey. There were no separate titles. The five Bowater companies owned the land in one title, just as a married couple owns their home in one title. The Bowater companies were a sort of modern marriage with five spouses. These five sales had no effect on the beneficial ownership of the land (using "beneficial" in its substantive sense rather than with the meaning that obtains in trust law). Both before and after the sales, the ultimate owners of the land were the shareholders in the Bowater group.

The five Bowater companies then sold their undivided shares to Milton Pipes for £50,000 each. That is, each company bought for £36,000 and sold for £50,000, making a profit of £14,000, well under the threshold of £50,000.

---

4 *FCT v. Gulland* (1985) 160 CLR 55, 109 Dawson J; *FCT v. Spotless Services Ltd* (1996) 186 CLR 404, 425 McHugh J.

5 *Mangin v. CIR* [1971] NZLR 591, 596–8 Lord Donovan (PC), quoting Turner J in the court below.

6 *Challenge Corporation Ltd v. CIR* [1986] 2 NZLR 513, 561 Lord Templeman (PC).

7 See generally N. Orow, *General Anti-Avoidance Rules: A Comparative International Analysis* (Bristol: Jordan Publishing Limited, 2000), 18.

8 E.g., *Challenge Corporation Ltd v. CIR* [1986] 2 NZLR 513 (PC) involved a corporate group taking advantage of rules that allowed it to consolidate the affairs of its members and to pay tax only on the resulting net profit. The group tried to minimise tax by buying an outside company that had suffered a loss and subtracting that loss from the profits of the original group.

9 E.g., *Mangin v. CIR* [1971] NZLR 591 (PC) involved an arrangement whereby the taxpayer each year leased the profitable part of his farm, which was a different section each year, to a family trust. The trust would then pay out the income from the section of the land to its beneficiaries, who were the taxpayer's wife and children. The artificial element in this arrangement was that the part of the farm leased to the trust changed year by year, with the trust always receiving almost all of the farm's income for that year. The result of the arrangement was that each beneficiary received a fraction of the farm's income. The income was therefore taxed at a lower rate than it would have been had it been entirely derived by the taxpayer.

10 [1989] AC 398 (HL).

Legally, there were five separate sales from Bowater and five more sales to Milton Pipes. Economically, there was just one sale from Bowater to Milton Pipes. Ignoring this economic reality, however, the House of Lords treated the transactions as genuine. Bowater accordingly escaped development land tax.

General anti-avoidance rules

Typically, governments combat avoidance by adding specific and often very detailed rules to tax legislation, being rules that frustrate one kind of avoidance transaction or another. For instance, jurisdictions might allow taxpayer companies to carry losses forward and to set them off against the profits of future years. As an anti-avoidance measure, such jurisdictions tend to require certain minimum continuity of ownership between the loss year and the profit year.[11] Tax statutes are replete with such closely targeted rules. However, specific anti-avoidance rules cannot combat the more creative forms of tax avoidance that employ transactions that governments cannot predict. Consequently, many tax systems feature general anti-avoidance rules in addition to specific ones.

There is considerable variation in the form that general anti-avoidance rules take in different countries. Nevertheless, the various forms have roughly the same effect, at least in theory. General anti-avoidance rules allow tax authorities to disregard schemes that would otherwise reduce tax liability. The transactions to which they apply are void for tax purposes. A transaction being void, the tax lies where it falls, although modern general anti-avoidance rules often allow tax authorities to reconstruct a transaction to reflect the economic reality of the circumstances and to tax the taxpayer on the basis of the reconstructed transaction.[12]

An example of a typical general anti-avoidance rule is section 99 of NZ's Income Tax Act 1976 (NZ's current rule is not so readily quotable because it is disaggregated into several elements,[13] but it has roughly the same meaning and effect). Section 99 relevantly read:

> Every arrangement made or entered into, whether before or after the commencement of this Act, shall be absolutely void as against the Commissioner for income tax purposes if and to the extent that, directly or indirectly, –
>
> (a) Its purpose or effect is tax avoidance; or
> (b) Where it has 2 or more purposes or effects, one of its purposes or effects (not being a merely incidental purpose or effect) is tax avoidance, whether or not any other or others of its purposes or effects relate to, or are referable to, ordinary business or family dealings, –
>
> whether or not any person affected by that arrangement is a party thereto.

Countries that have anti-avoidance rules broadly similar in form to New Zealand's include Canada,[14] South Africa,[15] Hong Kong,[16] and France.[17] The rule in Australia was formerly similar,[18]

---

11 New Zealand, for example, requires companies to have a minimum continuity of ownership of 49 per cent between loss year and profit year, Income Tax Act 2007, s IA 5(2).
12 See, for example, Income Tax Act (New Zealand) 2007, s GB 1.
13 Income Tax Act 2007, s BG 1, incorporating s GB 1 and certain definitions in s YA 1.
14 Income Tax Act 1988 (Can.), s 245.
15 Income Tax Act (SA), s 103.
16 Inland Revenue Ordinance (HK), s 61.
17 Livre de Procédure Fiscale, article L 64.
18 Income Tax Assessment Act 1936 (Aust) section 260.

but since 1981 has been framed in much more detail.[19] The United Kingdom enacted a general anti-*abuse* rule in 2013.[20] At first impression "abuse" suggests that, to be caught by the rule, taxpayers' arrangements must be somewhat more egregious than those caught by a typical anti-*avoidance* rule. However, the definition of "abusive" arrangements appears to embrace the same kinds of transactions and structures that typically fall to anti-avoidance rules. In general, arrangements are "abusive" if entering into them or carrying them out "cannot reasonably be regarded as a reasonable course of action in relation to the relevant tax provisions, having regard to all the circumstances."[21]

Until 2013 the United Kingdom operated a judicially developed anti-avoidance rule that could sometimes have roughly the same effect as a statutory general anti-avoidance rule. This United Kingdom common law anti-avoidance doctrine was first propounded by the House of Lords in *WT Ramsay Ltd v. IRC*.[22] At the risk of gross over-simplification, one can say that the common law anti-avoidance doctrine essentially allowed the court to look at a series of transactions and to determine whether the transactions had any economic purpose other than the avoidance of tax.

Until 2010, the United States resisted pressure to enact a statutory general anti-avoidance rule.[23] Instead of a statutory anti-avoidance rule, the United States had a judicially developed anti-avoidance rule, which was first established by the Supreme Court in *Gregory v. Helvering*.[24] The rule is often referred to as the economic substance doctrine. It operated in a similar manner to the United Kingdom judge-made rule. In 2010 the United States codified its economic substance doctrine. It did so by means of a somewhat improbable vehicle: the Health Care and Education Reconciliation Act of 2010,[25] which was primarily concerned with sweeping changes to the United States healthcare system. The United States' new statutory general anti-avoidance rule had not yet been tested when this chapter went to press, but it is expected to operate in much the same way as statutory rules in other countries.

Some civil law countries rely on the "abuse of rights" concept, which forbids the use of rights for improper purposes.[26] Others have statutory general anti-avoidance rules with broadly the same effect as those found in common law countries.[27] The different forms that general anti-avoidance rules take do not affect associated rule of law issues; problems and justifications that concern general anti-avoidance rules are equally relevant to all of them.

19 Income Tax Assessment Act 1936 (Aust.), Part IV A, ss 177A-177G. See further below, text accompanying footnote 65.
20 Finance Act 2013 ss 206–215 (UK).
21 Finance Act 2013 s 207(2) (UK).
22 [1982] AC 300.
23 Proposals to introduce a statutory general anti-avoidance rule to the United States have come before the United States House of Representatives on a number of occasions. See, e.g., Rep. Lloyd Doggett's "Abusive Tax Shelter Shutdown and Taxpayer Accountability Act of 2003", H.R. 1555, 108th Cong., 1st Sess. (2 April 2003).
24 (1935) 293 US 465.
25 The Health Care and Education Reconciliation Act of 2010 added new Code § 7701(o), 1 1Pub. L. No. 111-152, § 1409, 124 Stat. 1029 (30 March 2010).
26 N. Orow, *General Anti-Avoidance Rules: A Comparative International Analysis* (Bristol: Jordan Publishing Ltd, 2000), 373.
27 J. Prebble and Z. Prebble, "Comparing the General Anti-Avoidance Rule of Income Tax Law With the Civil Law Doctrine of Abuse of Law", 62(4) *Bulletin for International Taxation* 151 (2008).

How do general anti-avoidance rules breach the principles of the rule of law?

The exact content of the concept of the rule of law is the focus of a continuing debate between legal theorists.[28] Nevertheless, as far as certainty is concerned there is near unanimity: most, or probably all, legal philosophers consider that a law must be relatively certain in order to conform to the principles of the rule of law.[29] It is this requirement of certainty that general anti-avoidance rules offend.

The uncertainty surrounding tax avoidance stems from the fine line that separates unacceptable tax avoidance from acceptable tax mitigation. Lord Templeman in *Challenge Corporation Ltd v. CIR*[30] considered the two concepts with reference to section 99 of the Income Tax Act 1976, as the New Zealand general anti-avoidance rule was then numbered. His Lordship took an example from United Kingdom practice, namely a covenant to assign income. At the time, if in due form and for a duration of at least six years, a covenant to assign could shift liability for tax from the assignor to the assignee. He said:[31]

> Income tax is mitigated by a taxpayer who reduces his income or incurs expenditure in circumstances which reduce his assessable income or entitle him to reduction in his tax liability. Section 99 does not apply to tax mitigation because the taxpayer's tax advantage is not derived from an "arrangement" but from the reduction of income which he accepts or the expenditure which he incurs.
>
> Thus when a taxpayer executes a covenant and makes a payment under the covenant he reduces his income. If the covenant exceeds six years and satisfies certain other conditions the reduction in income reduces the assessable income of the taxpayer. The tax advantage results from the payment under the covenant.
>
> …
>
> Section 99 does not apply to tax mitigation where the taxpayer obtains a tax advantage by reducing his income or by incurring expenditure in circumstances in which the taxing statute affords a reduction in tax liability.
>
> Section 99 does apply to tax avoidance. Income tax is avoided and a tax advantage is derived from an arrangement when the taxpayer reduces his liability to tax without involving him in the loss or expenditure which entitles him to that reduction. The taxpayer engaged in tax avoidance does not reduce his income or suffer a loss or incur expenditure but nevertheless obtains a reduction in his liability to tax as if he had.

Although it is generally accepted that general anti-avoidance rules apply to tax avoidance and not to tax mitigation, drawing the line between the two is often problematic. A literal application of general anti-avoidance rules would catch many legitimate transactions.[32] General anti-avoidance rules therefore mean something more than their bare words.

---

28 See further, J. Waldron, "Is the Rule of Law an Essentially Contested Concept (in Florida)?", 21 *Law and Philosophy* 137 (2002).

29 There is abundant support for this proposition, in particular see F. A. Hayek, *The Constitution of Liberty* (London: Routledge, 1960), 144; John Rawls, *A Theory of Justice* (Cambridge, MA, The Belknap Press of Harvard University Press, 1971), 235.

30 *Challenge Corporation Ltd v. CIR* [1986] 2 NZLR 513, 562.

31 Ibid., 562.

32 See, e.g., J. Richardson in *Challenge Corporation Ltd v. CIR* [1986] 2 NZLR 513, 546 (CA) alludes to the somewhat paradoxical consequence situation of a literal interpretation of a general anti-avoidance rule being quite obviously not what Parliament intended.

Why are general anti-avoidance rules especially bad?

The preceding sections of this chapter have demonstrated that general anti-avoidance rules are vague. However, all legislation is vague to some extent. There will be boderline cases even for the most specific of rules. Why, then, do some people single general anti-avoidance rules out as particularly egregious breaches of the rule of law?[33] Drafters of most laws cannot foresee all relevant fact situations. As Hart pointed out, all laws admit of "core" situations, where the law will definitely apply, and "penumbra", where it is less certain whether the law will apply.[34] To criticise general anti-avoidance rules because it is not clear whether they apply in some situations appears to subject them to a higher standard than we demand of law in general.

The difference is that general anti-avoidance rules have far larger penumbras than most laws. Arguably, general anti-avoidance rules are nothing but penumbra. The reason why legislators decide that they need general anti-avoidance rules is that situations where the rules may be needed cannot be defined in advance. The fact that general anti-avoidance rules exist at all is evidence that policy-makers and legislators themselves cannot predict what structures taxpayers will eventually contrive in order to avoid tax. The following sections of this chapter examine the deeper values that the requirement of certainty seeks to preserve, and consider whether general anti-avoidance rules truly offend those values. If they do so, are there situations in which the rule of law must give way to countervailing considerations? And is tax avoidance one of those situations? An important factor is public tolerance of general anti-avoidance rules. It appears that the rule of law is seen as more important in some areas of law than in others. This chapter examines why this is so.

The underlying values of the rule of law

Guidance

The rule of law requires that the law must be certain so that it can provide guidance.[35] Generally, laws that are as vague as general anti-avoidance rules attract considerable criticism because they fail to provide people with sufficient information about what is and is not permitted to allow them to plan their lives. For example, on 29 August 1935 the Senate of the Free City of Danzig decreed an amendment to the Danzig Penal Code that criminalised acts "deserving of penalty according to the fundamental conceptions of a penal law and sound popular feeling."[36] In an uncomfortable common law echo, the House of Lords in the English case of *Shaw v. Director of Public Prosecutions* decided that it had jurisdiction to create new offences in order to punish acts that were contrary to public morals, but that had not previously been held to be illegal.[37] The Danzig legislation, which was enacted in order to align the city's criminal law with that of Nazi Germany, is sometimes known as the "Danzig Decree". Article 386 of the Criminal Code of

33 For example, the conference *The Rule of Law and Anti-Avoidance Rules: Tax Administration in a Constitutional Democracy* was convened in Sydney in 1995 to explore the apparent tension between anti-avoidance rules and the rule of law. Papers from the conference are collected in G. Cooper (ed.), *Tax Avoidance and the Rule of Law* (Amsterdam: IBFD Publications BV, 1997).
34 H. L. A. Hart, "Positivism and the Separation of Law and Morals", in H. L. A. Hart (ed.), *Essays in Jurisprudence and Philosophy* (Oxford: Clarendon Press, 1983), 49, 63.
35 See, e.g., J. Raz, The Rule of Law and Its Virtue, in J. Raz (ed.), *The Authority of Law: Essays on Law and Morality* (Oxford: Oxford University Press, 1979), 210, 213.
36 Decree of the Senate of the Free City of Danzig (29 August 1935), Article 2.
37 *Shaw v. Director of Public Prosecutions* [1962] AC 220 (HL).

the Qing Dynasty, which ruled China from 1644 to 1912, furnishes an interesting comparison to the Danzig Decree. The Qing code contained a long list of specific offences, but taking a form very similar to the decree of the Senate of Danzig, Article 386 provided that "[Doing] that which ought not to be done" was an offence. It is hard to think of a norm that claims to be a rule of law that could authorise more arbitrary action on the part of the authorities. Even the Nazi rule incorporated the (admittedly spurious) criterion of "sound popular feeling".

Both the Danzig Decree and *Shaw v. Director of Public Prosecutions* have been heavily criticised. For example, the Permanent Court of International Justice delivered an opinion condemning the amendment to the Danzig Penal Code.[38] People criticise *Shaw* for similar reasons.[39] Should we be concerned that the reasons that make the Danzig Decree, the decision in *Shaw*, and Article 386 of the Qing Code objectionable appear to apply equally to general anti-avoidance rules?

It is difficult to know what effect general anti-avoidance rules have on people's actions. It has been suggested that they act *in terrorem*, in that people are discouraged from constructing tax avoidance schemes because of the risk of being caught by the general anti-avoidance rule.[40] While this consequence may be what governments hope for when they resort to general anti-avoidance rules, such an effect is not what scholars mean when they argue that the law should be capable of guiding people. However, to demonstrate that general anti-avoidance rules offend the rule of law it is not sufficient simply to show that they do not guide people's actions. To see what may be objectionable about general anti-avoidance rules it is necessary to examine the underlying values of the rule of law, and to reveal why it is important that people should be able to rely on its principles to guide them.

Liberty

The relationship between liberty on one hand and laws that can be relied upon on the other is a key part in many theorists' conceptions of the rule of law. For Rawls, people must know exactly what legal rights they can claim because, "If the bases of these claims are unsure, so are the boundaries of men's liberties."[41] An essential part of being free, then, is knowing exactly how free one is. This argument has particular resonance when we look at general anti-avoidance rules. The argument is that general anti-avoidance rules' truly objectionable aspect is that no one really knows how far they extend. People are prevented from taking action that might be allowed, the argument continues, because they do not want to take the risk of their action being disallowed.

Hayek also stresses the connection between the rule of law and liberty, but his conception of liberty is slightly different from that of Rawls. Where Rawls would describe knowledge of the degree of liberty that the law allows as an essential component of liberty itself,[42] Hayek simply sees liberty as the absence of coercion. If people know what the law is in advance, they can choose to put themselves in the position of being subject to it. Subjection to the law is therefore a wilful act.[43] This argument is particularly relevant to general anti-avoidance rules. Since no one

38 Permanent Court of International Justice Advisory Opinion of 4 December 1935.
39 E.g., C. C. Turpin, "Criminal Law – Conspiracy to Corrupt Public Morals", 144 *Cambridge Law Journal* 144–146 (1961).
40 See, e.g., M. O'Grady, "Acceptable Limits of Tax Planning: A Revenue Perspective", KPMG Tax Conference, Ireland (November 2003), 6.
41 J. Rawls, *A Theory of Justice* (Cambridge, MA: The Belknap Press of Harvard University Press, 1971), 235.
42 Ibid.
43 F. A. Hayek, *The Constitution of Liberty* (London: Routledge, 1960), 144–5.

knows exactly when general anti-avoidance rules will apply, people who are caught by them have not made a conscious decision to be subject to them, and are therefore coerced.

The arguments in the preceding paragraphs appear to support the proposition that general anti-avoidance rules offend the rule of law as Rawls and Hayek explain that doctrine. But when tax professionals make this argument they are likely to put it in more specific terms, viz, that the existence of a general anti-avoidance rule has a chilling effect on legitimate tax planning, and that fear of general anti-avoidance rules prevents investors and businesses from utilising effective business structures that appear to be economically sensible. There may be some truth in this claim, but it is not borne out by reported cases.

Human dignity

For Raz, the criterion that the law should be capable of guiding action is closely linked to human dignity. The law must assume that people are capable of rational thought, and that they therefore want to plan their lives with the knowledge of what the law is.[44] Raz sees this factor as even more important than the rule of law's connection with freedom.[45] Laws that do not conform to the rule of law are an affront to human dignity because the law "encourages autonomous action only to frustrate its purpose."[46] Raz might well charge general anti-avoidance rules with such an offence. The detailed formality of tax law encourages people to find ways to circumvent it, but general anti-avoidance rules may frustrate their efforts.

Effective law and fuller

It is unlikely that Lon Fuller would disagree with Rawls's argument that the rule of law protects liberty or Raz's proposition that it protects dignity. Fuller, however, focuses his argument on the theory that certain formal criteria of the rule of law must all be sufficiently satisfied in order for law properly so called to exist.[47] Laws must be public, prospective, understandable, non-contradictory, possible to conform to, relatively stable, there must be congruence between how the rules are written down and how they are enforced, and laws must be rules as opposed to ad hoc decisions.[48]

In order to demonstrate how continuous breaches of the rule of law reduce the effectiveness of legal systems, Fuller gives us the example of King Rex. King Rex is a ruler who tries but fails to make law on eight separate occasions. Each time that Rex attempts to make law, he manages to breach one of these eight criteria. For example, on one occasion Rex publishes a legal code that is so convoluted that no one can understand it and on another occasion he announces that all cases will be decided retrospectively.

Naturally, Rex's subjects are dismayed at their king's disregard for the rule of law, and are annoyed at the way the consequences of that disregard affect them.[49] For present purposes, however, the interesting point is the consequence for Rex. Rex is unable to rule effectively because his rules are incapable of being followed. There is really no point in Rex having laws at all,

44 J. Raz, "The Rule of Law and Its Virtue", in J. Raz (ed.), *The Authority of Law: Essays on Law and Morality* (Oxford: Oxford University Press, 1979), 210, 221.
45 Ibid.
46 Ibid., 222.
47 L. Fuller, *The Morality of Law*, 2nd ed. (New Haven, CT: Yale University Press, 1964), 168.
48 Ibid.
49 Ibid., 167.

because his laws do not guide the behaviour of his subjects.[50] However much his subjects might want to obey Rex's laws, they cannot. Fuller's examples show that laws that do not conform to the rule of law can therefore be just as frustrating to law-makers as they are to law-followers.

Are general anti-avoidance rules effective?

General anti-avoidance rules tend to be counterexamples to Fuller's general theory of effective law. They are frustrating to the citizen, but they are useful to governments. When general anti-avoidance rules work they are undeniably effective, because they allow governments to collect tax that they would otherwise lose. Nevertheless, the experience of some countries with general anti-avoidance rules reveals that they can sometimes be ineffective for reasons very similar to those that plagued King Rex.

For example, when Sir Garfield Barwick was Chief Justice of Australia the Commissioner was seldom successful in litigation where he deployed the general anti-avoidance rule.[51] Barwick CJ felt very strongly that "[i]t is for Parliament to specify, … with unambiguous clarity, the circumstances which will attract an obligation on the part of the citizen to pay tax."[52] The Chief Justice had little time for the vagueness of the general anti-avoidance rule, and tended to find for the taxpayer even in cases of the most blatant tax avoidance.[53]

Barwick CJ's pro-taxpayer stance reached its apogee in the case of *Cridland v. FCT*,[54] which involved a scheme designed to take advantage of a rule that allowed primary producers to average their incomes over a number of years and to pay tax on that average. The rule was intended to make the tax system fairer for people like farmers, whose income often varies considerably from one year to the next. (Where there is a progressive scale, people with variable incomes can find themselves propelled unfairly into very high bands of tax, bands that do not reflect their average income calculated over several years.) The scheme relied on rules that made anyone with even a small amount of farming income a primary producer, and that allowed for averaging of all primary producer income, not farming income alone. Subscribing to the scheme, Cridland, a university student, bought a share in a unit trust. The trust was a primary producer. Cridland's interest as a beneficiary of the trust was only one dollar a year. The years in which he was a beneficiary straddled his time as a student and also time as a salaried graduate, when his income was much higher. Cridland claimed to be a primary producer and therefore to average his income, spreading much of it back into his impecunious years as a student. Despite the general anti-avoidance rule, the Barwick court upheld the claim, with Mason J delivering the leading judgment. *Cridland* was almost certainly a case where Australia's general anti-avoidance rule should have applied, but court found that the taxpayer had not avoided tax.

In response to this judicial attitude, which rendered Australia's general anti-avoidance rule almost useless, the Australian Parliament in 1981 enacted a new type of general anti-avoidance

---

50 Ibid., 168.
51 At the time, Australia's general anti-avoidance rule was contained in s 260 of the Income Tax Assessment Act (Cth) 1936.
52 *FCT v. Westraders Pty Ltd* (1980) 54 ALJR 406, 461 Barwick CJ.
53 See further, G. Lehman, "The Income Tax Judgements of Sir Garfield Barwick: A Study in the Failure of the New Legalism", 9 *Monash ULR* 115, 135 (1983). Lehman argues Sir Garfield Barwick did not deprive Australia's general anti-avoidance rule of all effect, because to do so would invite speedy law reform. Barwick CJ allowed the former section 260 to continue to operate where an "antecedent transaction" was involved, see *Mullens v. FCT* (1976) 135 CLR 290, 302.
54 *Cridland v. FCT* (1977) 140 CLR 330.

rule that attempts to attain more precision of detail. Generally known as "Part IVA", it is certainly more prolix.[55] As if responding to Barwick CJ's injunction to specify "with unambiguous clarity, the circumstances which will attract an obligation on the part of the citizen to pay tax,"[56] the Australian Parliament has several times supplemented or amended its general anti-avoidance rule, with the result that Part IVA now employs 8500 words, which cover 20 pages of the statute book. Part IVA decreasingly qualifies to be called a "general" anti-avoidance rule. There are, for instance, special rules about exploitation of deductions,[57] losses,[58] profit-stripping,[59] and franking credits.[60] In hindsight, Parliament's action was possibly not necessary: following Sir Garfield Barwick's retirement, the High Court was able to re-inject some force into section 260, Australia's then general anti-avoidance rule.[61] However, having turned its back on a truly general rule, opting instead to dig itself into the hole of a reductionist, detailed regime, Australia seems condemned to go on digging. The history of how section 260 fared during Sir Garfield Barwick's term as Chief Justice is an interesting example of how the rule of law defects of general anti-avoidance rules can make them ineffective.[62]

It is interesting to note that when general anti-avoidance rules are ineffective, this ineffectiveness is not due primarily to taxpayers being inadequately guided. Rather, when general anti-avoidance rules are ineffective it is because the judiciary do not know what to make of them. To return to general anti-avoidance rules' sinister counterpart, the amendment to the Danzig Penal Code, it seems that the Nazis had a similar experience to that of the Australians with Sir Garfield Barwick. The same rule applied in Germany, as well as in Danzig, but it ultimately led to very few prosecutions in either jurisdiction, because its terms were too vague for even the compliant judges of the Nazi era to make much sense of them.[63]

There appears to be a parallel with Article 386 of the Qing Dynasty Criminal Code. A penalty that was rather limited for the times mitigated the wide embrace of the language of the rule. The punishment for breach of Article 386 was caning with the *banzi*.[64] For this reason, it was generally understood that the catch-all Article 386 was intended to apply only to relatively minor misdemeanours.[65] Knowledge of the operation of the criminal law under the Qing is limited, but it may not be drawing too long a bow to suggest that Article 386 is another demonstration of Fuller's thesis. Uncertainty as to its coverage may have stunted the operation of what, on its face, was a rule that offered unlimited scope for oppression.

---

55 Income Tax Assessment Act 1936 (Aust), Part IVA, ss 177A–177G.

56 *FCT v. Westraders Pty Ltd* (1980) 54 ALJR 406, 461 Barwick CJ.

57 Income Tax Assessment Act 1936 (Aust), Part IVA, s 177C(2)(b).

58 Income Tax Assessment Act 1936 (Aust), Part IVA, s 177C(2)(c) and (ca).

59 Income Tax Assessment Act 1936 (Aust), Part IVA, s 177E.

60 Income Tax Assessment Act 1936 (Aust), Part IVA, s 177EA. "Franking credits" are an artifact of the New Zealand and Australian systems of company taxation, whereby tax paid by companies can be "imputed" to shareholders by means of credits distributed along with dividends.

61 See *FCT v. Gulland* (1984) 160 CLR 55.

62 The United Kingdom's experience with a judicially developed anti-avoidance doctrine might be used to illustrate the same point. The doctrine, as developed from its original formulation by Lord Wilberforce in *WT Ramsay Ltd v. IRC* [1982] AC 300, 323–6, is so vague that no one seems to be certain whether it even exists. Its application can therefore appear somewhat haphazard, see further, The Right Honorable Lord Walker of Gestinghope "Ramsay 25 Years On", 120 *LQR* 412 (2004).

63 M. Broszat, *The Hitler State* (London: Longman, 1981), 339.

64 See, e.g., J. Bourgon, "Abolishing 'Cruel Punishments': A Reappraisal of the Chinese Roots and Long-Term Efficiency of the Xinzheng Legal Reforms", 37 *Modern Asian Studies* 851–62 (2003).

65 Several scholars of Chinese law have confirmed this point to the authors.

General anti-avoidance rules in the tax area furnish a marked contrast to rules like the Danzig Decree and the Qing Article 386: situations where statutory general anti-avoidance rules are ineffective are relative rarities. The majority of jurisdictions that have general anti-avoidance rules find them to be a reasonably effective though not foolproof tool for frustrating tax avoidance.[66]

It is difficult to know what conclusion to draw from the fact that general anti-avoidance rules tend to be relatively effective. Fuller's argument that laws are more effective when people know what they require certainly seems uncontroversial and likely to be true in most situations. While Fuller does not demand that legal systems must satisfy each of his criteria perfectly in order to conform to the rule of law;[67] it is unlikely that Fuller would approve of the protracted and unapologetic breaches that accompany general anti-avoidance rules.

This point is even clearer if we use Fuller's framework to assess individual laws, as opposed to entire legal systems. A state with some laws that offend Fuller's criteria may still be able to be governed effectively, but, according to Fuller's thesis, an individual rule that continuously breaches many of his criteria ought not to be effective. It is an interesting feature of general anti-avoidance rules that their criteria for effectiveness are almost the exact opposite of the effectiveness criteria of other laws.

Are general anti-avoidance rules justified despite breaching the rule of law?

Problems of income taxation

The intuitive alternative to a general anti-avoidance rule is a system of very many specific rules that detail exactly what is and is not subject to income tax. Of course, all tax systems already have such specific rules in at least some areas of economic activity, whether or not they also have general anti-avoidance rules. Unfortunately, however, the more specific and detailed a system's rules become, the more ways people will find to circumvent those rules.[68] Tax law is unusual in two key respects. First, there are very few other areas of law that people so aggressively try to avoid.[69] Second, the nature of tax law means that tax legislation contains a large number of potential loopholes.[70] The result is that in the absence of a general anti-avoidance rule, there is apt to be a great deal of tax avoidance that the government is powerless to stop.

It is tempting to suggest that if legislators cannot frame a tax avoidance rule that conforms to the rule of law they should not have an anti-avoidance rule at all. Governments should just put up with the adverse consequences. This suggestion overlooks the fact that tax avoidance is not a problem for governments alone; it is a problem for society generally. Avoidance undermines two key purposes of a tax system. First, the principle of horizontal equity states that people in

---

66 Examples of cases where a general anti-avoidance rule has misfired include *Cridland v. FCT* (1977) 140 CLR 330, discussed earlier in this chapter and *Peterson v. CIR* [2005] UKPC 5 (PC), to be discussed below.

67 L. Fuller, *The Morality of Law*, 2nd ed. (New Haven, CT: Yale University Press, 1964), 170.

68 J. Freedman, "Defining Taxpayer Responsibility: In Support of a General Anti-Avoidance Principle", *BTR* 332, 346 [2004].

69 But see, for some examples of such areas of law, V. Fleischer, "Regulatory Arbitrage", *Legal Studies Research Paper Series*, Working Paper No. 10–11 (March 2010).

70 For an explanation of why tax law is more susceptible to loopholes than other areas of law, see R. Parsons, "Income Taxation – An Institution in Decay", 3 *Australian Tax Forum* 233 (1986), as developed in J. Prebble, "Income Taxation: A Structure Built on Sand", 24 *Sydney Law Review* 303 (2002).

the same economic position should be taxed at the same rate.[71] Tax avoidance makes horizontal equity difficult to achieve, because successful tax avoidance results in some people being taxed less than others who are in the same economic position. In other words, people who avoid tax are not paying their fair share as measured by their wealth. Second, tax avoidance makes it more difficult for tax systems to be economically neutral. Economic neutrality demands that tax systems should distort the normal workings of the market as little as possible; that is, that people should not make decisions for purely (or even partially) tax reasons. The existence of opportunities for tax avoidance frustrates this goal. To illustrate, consider the case of *Peterson v. CIR*,[72] which the Privy Council decided in 2005. *Peterson* was a case in which films were funded principally by non-recourse loans. Pursuant to a scheme, Mr. Peterson and others invested in films and deducted their investment from their other income. The deductions took the form of allowances for depreciation, which permitted investors in films to amortize the cost over two years when caluculating assessable income.

The promoters of the film told the investors that the cost of the film was (say) $2,000, while in fact it was only (say) $1,000. To fund their investment in the films, Mr. Peterson and his co-investors borrowed. The borrowing was in the form of non-recourse loans; that is, loans that were repayable only if the films were successful. Interest was not charged. Loans on such favourable terms naturally attract questions, and indeed it was found as a fact that the money was never borrowed at all.[73] The fact that the extra money from investors was not available did not bother the film's promoters, because they had overstated the cost of the film anyway.

The reason for the overstatement of the cost of the films was the tax saving that it led to. Instead of being able to write off $1,000 over two years, investors were able to write off $2,000, even though they had never actually spent the second $1,000 (and, except on paper, had not even borrowed it). Whether or not the films were successful, the investors would gain a tax advantage. This tax advantage meant that a scheme that would not ordinarily be attractive to investors became worthwhile.

This situation is a clear example of the tax system creating market distortions: the transactions in *Peterson* were not attractive for their intrinsic merits; they were attractive because of tax advantages. Jurisdictions that have general anti-avoidance rules are able to counteract the effect of this distortion to some extent: to the extent that investors see the tax advantages of a particular scheme as unlikely to stand up to close scrutiny and therefore refrain from investing in it, the market will not be distorted.

The aims of the tax system are related to the more general point about the purpose of tax systems. Governments do not tax people only to amass wealth. Rather, tax is necessary to keep states functioning. Governments must provide public services such as defence and education. Furthermore, most societies use tax to redistribute wealth to some extent. Tax avoidance reduces the effectiveness of welfare systems,[74] a matter that is particularly important in the light of the public perception (which is probably accurate) that most tax avoidance is perpetrated by the rich or by people who are relatively well off. Though few people have reasoned the issue through to a sufficient depth to put it this way, the wide spread of general anti-avoidance rules, either statutory or judge-made, indicates that countries may consider that the negative results from

---

71 See, e.g., R. E. Krever, "Structure and Policy of Australian Income Taxation", in R. E. Krever (ed.), *Australian Taxation: Principles and Practice* (Melbourne: Longman Cheshire Pty Ltd, 1987), 1, 11.

72 *Peterson v. CIR* [2005] UKPC 5 (PC). The Privy Council in fact found that New Zealand's general anti-avoidance rule did not apply to this scheme.

73 *Case U32* (2000) 19 NZTC 9,302 [80].

74 R. A. McLeod, "Tax Avoidance Revisited", 6 *NZJTLP* 103 (2000).

not having a general anti-avoidance rule outweigh the breaches of the rule of law that general anti-avoidance rules entail.

This balancing exercise reveals much about the nature of the rule of law and its values. Adherence to the rule of law can often interfere with a society's other goals. Some philosophers insist that the rule of law must be preserved without compromise.[75] Other writers, such as Raz, stress than the rule of law is only one yardstick against which a legal system may be measured.[76] Just as a society's conformity to the rule of law does not ensure that the society is good, a breach of the rule of law does not make that society bad.[77] Rawls expands on this point, saying that a breach of the rule of law may be "the lesser of two evils."[78] Tax avoidance is a very real evil for society: a breach of the rule of law seems to be a necessary remedy.

In democracies that follow a Western model, there is seldom anything sinister about legislators breaching the rule of law. As Fuller observes, laws tend to be most effective when they conform to the rule of law;[79] so governments have a vested interest in making sure their laws conform to its values. In situations where laws offend the rule of law, it will often be the case that the alternative is even less desirable.

The importance of certainty

Certainty is clearly an important rule of law value. Usually certainly is important for both the law-follower and the law-maker. Most laws are more effective when people can be certain what they are meant to do or not do. That is, in most cases the rule of law helps to promote effective law. General anti-avoidance rules are therefore an aberration: it is their very vagueness that makes them effective.[80] This characteristic, together with the fundamental problems of tax law, plus what many see as the dubious moral standing of tax avoiders, prompts some commentators to argue that certainty is simply an inappropriate value for general anti-avoidance rules to strive for.[81]

Challenge Corporation Ltd v. Commissioner of Inland Revenue[82] is an example of the negative effect that certainty can have on the utility of an anti-avoidance rule. Challenge Corporation, the taxpayer company, acquired a subsidiary that had suffered heavy losses. Challenge Corporation then purported to set the subsidiary's losses off against its own profits.

At the time, the provisions that allowed intra-group loss consolidation did not require any continuity of shareholding between loss year and profit year. Challenge Corporation had therefore complied with the letter of the law. Without a general anti-avoidance rule, companies in the situation of Challenge Corporation would be able to take deductions despite having suffered no economic loss.

---

75 See, e.g., F. A. Hayek, *The Constitution of Liberty* (London: Routledge, 1960).

76 J. Raz, "The Rule of Law and Its Virtue", in J. Raz (ed.), *The Authority of Law: Essays on Law and Morality* (Oxford: Oxford University Press, 1979), 210, 211.

77 Even Fuller, who is strongly committed to the rule of law, accepts that isolated breaches do not automatically condemn a legal system. See L. Fuller, *The Morality of Law*, 2nd ed. (New Haven, CT: Yale University Press, 1964), 170.

78 J. Rawls, *A Theory of Justice* (Cambridge, MA: The Belknap Press of Harvard University Press, 1971), 242.

79 L. Fuller, *The Morality of Law*, 2nd ed. (New Haven, CT: Yale University Press, 1964), 168.

80 As mentioned above under the heading "The rule of law and tax avoidance", there are some cases that are definitely tax avoidance (although these cases are mainly ones that have been judicially decided to be tax avoidance); so general anti-avoidance rules' sphere of application is not entirely unknown. Nevertheless, it is true to say that general anti-avoidance rules depend on their vagueness for their effectiveness.

81 E.g., J. Freedman, "Defining Taxpayer Responsibility: In Support of a General Anti-Avoidance Principle", *BTR* 332, 346 [2004].

82 *2 NZLR* 513 (1986).

Where the principles of the rule of law negatively influence a law's effectiveness, it is necessary to weigh the consequences of not having the law in question against the possibility that some people will be surprised by the manner in which the law operates. Certainty and related rule of law values are therefore extremely important where criminal sanctions are imposed, but are less important where the issue is tax avoidance.[83]

The morality of tax avoidance

In the face of such an obvious breach of the rule of law, the fact that so many countries have general anti-avoidance rules seems difficult to account for. The idiosyncrasies of tax law no doubt make general anti-avoidance rules necessary, but it is unlikely that the public tolerance of general anti-avoidance rules is caused by knowledge of these idiosyncrasies. Tax law is extraordinarily complicated, but it is unrealistic to suppose that most people see it as different in kind from other branches of the law. How, then, can we account for the lack of public condemnation of general anti-avoidance rules? The explanation may be a perception of tax avoidance as being questionable from a moral perspective.

A number of cases have held that people have the right to arrange their money in such a way as to pay as little tax as possible, even holding that there nothing immoral about tax avoidance.[84] Relying on such decisions, lawyers tend to assume that tax avoidance is morally unimpeachable as a matter of law. Chapter 23 of this book examines the contentious moral status of tax avoidance in some detail and argues that it is a logical error to say that on the assumption that tax avoidance is not immoral as a matter of law, avoidance is not immoral in any sense. Whether a certain act is moral cannot be a question of law. This question can be determined only as a matter of ethics: tax avoidance, like tax evasion, is immoral in a substantive sense, whether avoidance is contrary to the law or not.

As a matter of morality independent of law, people know that they have a duty to pay tax; so seeking to pay less tax than they otherwise might can appear to be shirking that duty.[85] General anti-avoidance rules do not set out to catch individual taxpayers trying earnestly to comply with complex tax laws. People who are ultimately caught by general anti-avoidance rules almost always know that they have engaged in something that they would at least concede to be "tax planning" – usually aggressive tax planning – even if they do not expect to be called to account. Taxpayers who engage in tax avoidance schemes are consciously putting other taxpayers at a relative disadvantage and may be criticised on moral grounds.[86] Perhaps it may be said that in the area of tax avoidance the benefits to society of relative certainty and conformity with the rule of law are outweighed by the detriments that arise from tax avoidance.

---

83 While taxpayers are usually extremely annoyed if their tax avoidance schemes are disallowed because of the operation of general anti-avoidance rules, general anti-avoidance rules do not impose *criminal* penalties, although some penalties are involved. It is arguable that it is more important for laws that impose criminal penalties to conform to the rule of law, see, J. Rawls, *A Theory of Justice* (Cambridge, MA: The Belknap Press of Harvard University Press, 1971), 241.

84 Probably the most famous statement on the morality of tax avoidance comes from Lord Tomlin in *CIR v. Duke of Westminster* [1936] AC 1, 19–20 (HL), where his Lordship stated that "every man is entitled if he can to order his affairs so that the tax attaching under the appropriate Act is less than it otherwise would be."

85 Nevertheless, the exact amount of tax the each individual should pay is open to debate. It is questionable whether taxpayers who have paid the amount of tax specified by black-letter law can really be shirking a duty. See further, J. Freedman, "Defining Taxpayer Responsibility: In Support of a General Anti-Avoidance Principle", *BTR* 332, 337 [2004].

86 See further, The Right Honourable Lord Templeman "Tax and the Taxpayer", 117 *LQR* 575, 575 (2001).

The argument that the detriments of the rule of law in a particular area outweigh its benefits is nevertheless unsatisfactory. At least, it would not satisfy Hayek, although it might satisfy Rawls or Raz. Hayek would argue that the merits of the rule of law should not be evaluated on a case-by-case basis, leaving us free to disregard its principles where those principles are inconvenient. Rather, one of the reasons why societies value the rule of law is that it applies despite its resulting in a net societal detriment from time to time. Societies commit to adherence to the rule of law for the very reason that there will be instances where it is tempting to tolerate breaches.

This argument echoes David Cole's criticism of Richard Posner's *Not a Suicide Pact: The Constitution in a Time of National Emergency*.[87] In his book, Posner argues that the protections offered by the United States Constitution should be interpreted flexibly in order to allow the government to address the threat of terrorism. Posner argues, for example, that the United States Administration's wiretapping of international telephone calls should be considered a "reasonable" search in the context of the threat of terrorism. Cole, however, points out that allowing the provisions of the Constitution to be interpreted more strictly or less strictly according to administrative convenience misses the point of having a constitution in the first place.[88] A constitution like that of the United States, and the rule of law, should be adhered to notwithstanding that doing so is not beneficial to society in every case. Any kind of cost-benefit analysis is simply inappropriate where the Constitution is concerned. The same considerations apply in respect of the rule of law.

It would follow from the principles advanced by Hayek and by Cole that the disbenefit to society at large that can accompany adherence to the rule of law when it is a matter of tax avoidance does not seem to explain the apparent acceptance of general anti-avoidance rules even among well-informed sectors of the public. Nor would that disbenefit justify the breach of the principle of the rule of law entailed in the uncertainty of general anti-avoidance rules. What, then, may be the explanation and the justification?

In respect of the public acceptance of general anti-avoidance rules, tax avoiders appear to be, and are seen as, fundamentally different from criminals. Generally speaking, when criminals break the law, they simply break it; they do not try to find ways to circumvent the law in order to avoid technical breaches. In contrast, there is an entire industry devoted to manipulating fiscal laws with a view to obtaining tax advantages without incurring a corresponding economic loss. In the light of this difference, the fact that the informed public appears to accept general anti-avoidance rules[89] despite their shortcomings as far as the rule of law is concerned is not surprising.

In respect of the justification for the breach of the rule of law, unlike criminal behaviour, tax avoidance takes advantage of the very nature of law itself. In particular, it takes advantage of law's adherence to formality. The formality of law in general and of tax law in particular is an essential pre-requisite for contriving artificial transactions that enable the authors of the transactions or their clients to avoid tax. These are transactions that shift income from higher taxed people to lower taxed people, that enable revenue to capital conversions, that achieve the deferral of receipts or the acceleration of expenditure, that, through international arbitrage, permit the recharacterization of receipts or expenditure, and so on.

---

87 (Oxford: Oxford University Press, 2006).

88 D. Cole, "How to Skip the Constitution", Review of Richard Posner, *Not a Suicide Pact: The Constitution in a Time of National Emergency*, 53 *New York Review of Books* 18 (16 November 2006).

89 People who move in the same circles as tax advisors may dispute this statement. But who has heard of a mainstream political party campaigning for support to repeal a general anti-avoidance rule?

The quality of relying on the formality of the law while circumventing the law's policy distinguishes tax avoidance from criminal behaviour, being the area where rule of law questions tend to be most prominent. While it is true that there are difficult cases at the edges of criminal law (assisted suicide of very sick people and certain practices in cultures other than our own being prime examples) most criminal activity is clearly wrong by the lights of most people, whether or not there is law to forbid it. In contrast, tax avoidance exploits the formality of the law and, in doing so, exploits the values of the rule of law itself. It attacks those values while pretending to honour them. Enacting a general anti-avoidance rule to frustrate that exploitation presents as a justifiable counter-measure.

Conclusion

General anti-avoidance rules demonstrate that the rule of law is not an unqualified good. As with all principles, the rule of law can be outweighed by competing considerations. General anti-avoidance rules give an example of what those competing considerations might be. Furthermore, while general anti-avoidance rules themselves are justified, they are useful in showing exactly why we value the rule of law. Most societies with developed legal systems tend not to breach the rule of law very often. As a rare example of a breach, general anti-avoidance rules are a useful reminder of why values such as certainty are important.

Acknowledgements

This chapter draws on R. Prebble and J. Prebble, "Does the Use of General Anti-Avoidance Rules to Combat Tax Avoidance Breach Principles of the Rule of Law? A Comparative Study", 55 St Louis University Law Journal, Symposium Issue, Sanford E. Sarasohn Memorial Conference on Critical Theory in Taxation 21–45 (2011). The authors thank Z. Radhi and H. van Oeveren for their invaluable editorial assistance.

List of authorities

Books

M. Broszat, *The Hitler State* (London: Longman, 1981), 339.
G. Cooper (ed.), *Tax Avoidance and the Rule of Law* (Amsterdam: IBFD Publications BV, 1997).
A. V. Dicey, *Introduction to the Study of the Law of the Constitution*, 10th ed. (London: Macmillan, 1960).
L. Fuller, *The Morality of Law*, (2nd ed. (New Haven (CT): Yale University Press, 1964).
H. L. A. Hart, "Positivism and the Separation of Law and Morals" in H.L.A. Hart, *Essays in Jurisprudence and Philosophy* (Oxford: Clarendon Press, 1983), 49.
F. A. Hayek, *The Constitution of Liberty* (London: Routledge, 1960)
N. Orow, *General Anti-Avoidance Rules: A Comparative International Analysis* (Bristol: Jordan Publishing Limited, 2000), 18.
R. Posner, *Not a Suicide Pact: The Constitution in a Time of National Emergency* (Oxford University Press, 2006).
J. Rawls, *A Theory of Justice* (The Belknap Press of Harvard University Press, 1971).
J. Raz, "The Rule of Law and Its Virtue" in J. Raz, *The Authority of Law: Essays on Law and Morality* (Oxford: Oxford University Press, 1979), 210.

Journal articles

J. Bourgon, "Abolishing 'Cruel Punishments': A Reappraisal of the Chinese Roots and Long-term Efficiency of the Xinzheng Legal Reforms" (2003) 37 Modern Asian Studies, 851–862.

D. Cole, "How to Skip the Constitution" review of Richard Posner *Not a Suicide Pact: The Constitution in a Time of National Emergency*, New York Review of Books, 53:18, 16 November 2006.

J. Freedman, "Defining Taxpayer Responsibility: In Support of a General Anti-Avoidance Principle" [2004] BTR 332.

R. E. Krever, "Structure and Policy of Australian Income Taxation" in Richard E Krever (ed.), *Australian Taxation: Principles and Practice* (Melbourne: Longman Cheshire Pty Ltd, 1987).

G. Lehman, "The income tax judgements of Sir Garfield Barwick: A study in the failure of the new legalism" (1983) 9 Monash ULR 115.

R. A. McLeod, "Tax Avoidance Revisited" (2000) 6 NZJTLP 103.

M. O'Grady, "Acceptable Limits of Tax Planning: A Revenue Perspective" KPMG Tax Conference, Ireland, November 2003.

R. Parsons, "Income Taxation – An Institution in Decay" (1986) 3 Australian Tax Forum 233.

J. Prebble and Z. Prebble, "Comparing the General Anti-Avoidance Rule of Income Tax Law with the Civil Law Doctrine of Abuse of Law", Bulletin for International Taxation, 151 (2008).

The Right Honourable Lord Templeman, "Tax and the Taxpayer" 2001 117 LQR 575.

C. C. Turpin, "Criminal Law – Conspiracy to Corrupt Public Morals" [1961] Cambridge Law Journal 144, 144–146.

J. Waldron, "Is the Rule of Law an Essentially Contested Concept (in Florida)?" (2002) 21 Law and Philosophy 137. J. Prebble, "Income Taxation: a Structure Built on Sand" (2002) 24 Sydney Law Review 303.

Cases referred to

Case U32 (2000) 19 NZTC 9,302 (TRA).

Challenge Corporation Ltd v. CIR [1986] 2 NZLR 513 (PC).

CIR v. Duke of Westminster [1936] AC 1, 19–20 (HL).

Cridland v. FCT (1977) 140 CLR 330 (HCA).

FCT v. Gulland (1985) 160 CLR 55 (HCA).

FCT v. Spotless Services Ltd (1996) 186 CLR 404 (HCA).

FCT v. Westraders Pty Ltd (1980) 54 ALJR 406 (HCA).

Inland Revenue Commissioners v. Bowater Property Developments Ltd [1989] AC 398 (HL).

Mangin v. CIR [1971] NZLR 591 (PC).

Miller v. CIR [2001] 3 NZLR 316 (PC).

Mullens v. FCT (1976) 135 CLR 290 (HCA).

Peterson v. CIR [2005] UKPC 5 (PC).

Shaw v. Director of Public Prosecutions [1962] AC 220 (HL).

W T Ramsay Ltd v. IRC (1935) 293 US 465 (HL).

6

THE ROLE AND MEANING OF 'PURPOSE' IN STATUTORY GAARS

Graeme Cooper

Background

Governments confronted with tax practices they regard as abusive can challenge that behaviour using a variety of weapons. Some countries will be content to rely upon judicial doctrines and the pragmatism of the judiciary (Arnold 2008). Others will point to doctrines (perhaps substantive and perhaps principles of statutory interpretation) such as *abus de droit* or *fraus legis* as appropriate mechanisms to direct the judiciary in characterising transactions and interpreting tax statutes. Some will confer extensive discretionary powers on the revenue authorities. And some countries will repeatedly enact targeted special-purpose rules directed at the latest form of abusive structure or transaction. Many papers compare how combinations of these tools are constructed in practice (Orow 2000; Mo 2003; Tooma 2008; Orow 2011; Brown 2012).

The experience of many countries is that these weapons have not proved sufficiently robust in the face of increasingly sophisticated taxpayer behavior and the limitations of administrative and judicial processes. Consequently, statutory general anti-avoidance rules ('GAARs') are becoming an increasingly common legislative tool to empower both administrators and judges in countering tax avoidance especially in the developing world (Mo 2003; Rosenblatt 2014; Waerzeggers and Hillier 2016). Examples can be seen in the tax legislation of Australia,[1] Canada,[2] China,[3] Ireland,[4] Hong Kong,[5] Malaysia,[6] New Zealand,[7] Singapore,[8] South Africa[9] the United Kingdom,[10] and other countries, and inserting a GAAR into domestic law has been under

---

1 Income Tax Assessment Act 1936, Pt IVA (Australia).
2 Income Tax Act, RSC 1985 c1 (5th Supp.), s. 245 (Canada).
3 Corporate Income Tax Law of the People's Republic of China, 2008, art 47 (PRC).
4 Taxes Consolidation Act 1997, Pt 33 (Ireland).
5 Inland Revenue Ordinance, ch 112, s. 61A (Hong Kong).
6 Income Tax Act 1967, s. 140 (Malaysia).
7 Income Tax Act 2007, part G (New Zealand).
8 Income Tax Act ch 134, s. 33 (Singapore).
9 Income Tax Act 1962, s. 80A (South Africa).
10 Finance Act 2013, c. 29 (UK), s. 206 (UK).

consideration in India for some time (Expert Committee 2012).[11] Officials from the IMF have recently published guidance for countries on how they might conceptualise the elements of a GAAR (Waerzeggers and Hillier 2016), and explicit GAARs are even becoming fashionable in international instruments such as the OECD's Model Income Tax Convention (OECD/G20 2015: 55), the EU Parent-Subsidiary Directive[12] and the European Council Directive of 12 July 2016, 'Laying down rules against tax avoidance practices that directly affect the functioning of the internal market' (Council Directive (EU) 2016/1164). Some countries have not enacted a GAAR in the form that will be described in this chapter such as South Korea[13] and the United States (McMahon 2008),[14] but have instead codified an alternative proposal – an 'economic substance' or 'substance over form' rule in their statutes (though some doubt the effectiveness of the US approach (Libin 2010)), and some continental European countries following the example of Germany[15] have enacted a codified anti-abuse rule which attacks choosing a legal form or invoking a legal right that produces a tax advantage (Schön 2008). These approaches are treated as different from the rules analysed here because they do not explicitly invoke and turn upon a notion like purpose or intent or motive.

At least in the common law world, the designs of modern statutory GAARs tend to follow common patterns, an outcome which is to be expected where the decision to enact the GAAR has been informed by the practice observed in other countries. The focus of this chapter is on the notion of 'purpose' commonly used in a GAAR. Purpose is typically a critical component of the rule, and in many ways it is the most problematic.[16] The 'purpose' component is the deeply mysterious black box at the centre of most GAAR rules and many GAAR disputes.[17] While some GAARs have chosen to emphasise 'effect' rather than (or perhaps in addition to)

---

11 A GAAR was included as part of the proposals for a Direct Taxes Code since at least 2010. See for example *Direct Taxes Code 2013* ch XIII, General Anti-avoidance Rule, available at http://incometaxindia.gov.in/Documents/direct-taxes-code-2013-31032014.pdf. The proposed Direct Taxes Code, which would have replaced the current Income Tax Act, 1961 (India), appears to have been abandoned by the Indian Government in the 2015 Budget. The proposed GAAR was deferred but, given the protracted gestation, there must be some doubt whether the GAAR will ever be enacted.

12 Council Directive (EU) 2015/121 (27 January 2015) amending Directive 2011/96/EU on the Common System of Taxation Applicable in the Case of Parent Companies and Subsidiaries of Different Member States (requiring Member States not to grant benefits under the Parent Subsidiary Directive where an arrangement has been put into place for a main purpose of obtaining a tax advantage and the arrangement is not genuine having regard to the facts and circumstances).

13 Basic Act for National Taxes, art 14 (South Korea).

14 Internal Revenue Code 1986, s. 7701(o) (USA).

15 Fiscal Code of Germany, art 42 (Germany).

16 Other parts of a GAAR will commonly include the annihilation provision to undo the effects of the abusive arrangement, some collection of safe harbours made immune from challenge by the GAAR, a reconstruction power allowing the revenue authority to impose tax on some substitute transaction, structure or person, a power (or perhaps obligation) to make compensating adjustments, some mechanism to establish the primacy of the GAAR over other provisions in the tax legislation including its interaction with any dedicated specific anti-avoidance provisions and some mechanism providing taxpayers with review rights, typically by challenge to a court. The rule may also be accompanied by special penalty provisions, particular rules about the burden of proof and special administrative procedures to be followed in order to invoke the GAAR.

17 This topic is plagued by synonyms. Commentators will often insist on using terms such as 'objective', 'intention', 'motive', 'goal', 'reason' or some other term. Criminal law, for example, often distinguishes between 'motive' (what a person was hoping to achieve by their action) and 'intention' (the actions which were done were deliberate). In tax, commentators will often see subtle distinctions in the selection of one term in preference to another. These distinctions can seem strained, often confusing and not always able to be sustained. This chapter will refer just to the term 'purpose' and will try to map the contours of that term as it is the word most commonly found in a GAAR.

purpose,[18] and some countries have contemplated anti-avoidance rules with a 'purpose-free' design (Cooper 2001),[19] the element of purpose remains common and significant in the design of modern GAARs. It is worth noting that making 'purpose' the fulcrum of a modern statutory GAAR is a direct legislative repudiation of the position taken by the UK House of Lords in the famous *Duke of Westminster* case that 'if [a taxpayer] succeeds in ordering them so as to secure this result, then, however unappreciative the Commissioners of Inland Revenue or his fellow tax-payers may be of his ingenuity, he cannot be compelled to pay an increased tax.'[20]

In many ways, a GAAR is an admission of legislative and administrative defeat. In ordinary situations, many tax laws, even those directed at avoidance, can be crafted with a reasonable degree precision – controlled foreign company rules, thin capitalisation regimes or dividend stripping rules are examples. But by enacting a GAAR, the legislator concedes they are unable to foresee future structures or transactions with sufficient clarity to be able to proscribe them, or declares themselves unwilling to invest further legislative time to react to them once discovered. Instead, they enact a GAAR to try to render ineffective something they neither foresee nor delineate. They do this by resorting to other integers such as purpose. But purpose is a deeply flawed and vexed criterion to use. It is a most curious way to set up a tax system to insist that tax benefits are only available to those who happen upon them accidentally or in ignorance.

The objective of this paper is to unravel some of the nuances about the way that 'purpose' is employed in the various designs and the problems to which it is susceptible. While 'purpose' may be unruly and unpredictable, though perhaps falling short of challenging the very notion of law (Prebble and Prebble 2010; Cooper 1997), governments may well feel that some rule, even a defective one, is worth the difficulties because the social benefits from increased tax compliance are greater than the private costs from increased legislative uncertainty (McMahon 2003) and this is currently the best design on offer.

Some examples

In order to set the stage for the discussion that follows, this section examines some of the contours of the way in which the notion of 'purpose' appears in statutory form in the GAARs of various countries. While the following extracts are not exhaustive, they are representative of the

18 See for example, Income Tax Act, ch 134, s. 33 (Singapore) (referring to arrangements with 'the purpose or effect' of altering the incidence of tax); Income Tax Assessment Act, 1936 s. 260 (Australia) (referring to contracts with the 'purpose or effect …' of avoiding tax); Income Tax Act 2007 s.YA 1 (New Zealand) (defining a 'tax avoidance arrangements' as 'an arrangement … that directly or indirectly has tax avoidance as its purpose or effect'). Similarly, Australia's GAAR for the value-added tax (the GST) applies where, 'an entity … entered into [a] scheme … with the sole or dominant purpose of … getting a GST benefit from the scheme or the principal effect of the scheme … is that the avoider gets the GST benefit …' A New Tax System (Goods and Services Tax) Act 1999 (Australia) s. 165–5.

19 One can think of fixed-ratio thin capitalisation rules or transfer pricing rules as specific purpose-free anti-abuse rules. The US toyed with a broader purpose-free rule at the beginning of this century. The US rule would have been driven by analysing the size of tax benefits in the commercial returns from an outlay. See Cooper 2001. Australia has a limited purpose-free rule in Income Tax Assessment Act, 1936 s. 82KL (Australia). Similar to the ill-fated US proposal, it purports to reverse the tax benefits from an outlay if the taxpayer recoups the entire outlay in tax deductions and commercial return. By way of example, assume the taxpayer outlaid $100 for some acquisition. If the outlay is immediately deductible and the relevant tax rate is 40%, the taxpayer will be denied a deduction if it enjoys both a tax saving of $40 and some 'additional benefit' worth at least $61 (in addition to the observable acquisition being paid for).

20 *Duke of Westminster v. Commissioners of Inland Revenue* [1936] AC 1, per Lord Tomlin.

common law world. The discussion presents them in roughly chronological order to reveal some of the refinements made to the basic design of a GAAR that have occurred during its (presumably conscious) transplant from one national legal environment to another.

Australia

In 1981, Australia replaced its long-standing GAAR with a new model. The lore in Australia is that the former Australian GAAR, dating from 1915, had become ineffective due largely to restrictive interpretations placed upon it by various judgments of Australia's High Court (Lehmann 1983; Cooper 2006).[21]

The substituted GAAR differed in many respects from its predecessor but retained a reliance upon purpose. Indeed, the new GAAR was further amended in 2013 in an attempt to emphasise even more clearly the pivotal role that 'purpose' was to play in the interpretation of the GAAR. Section 177D now provides –

Scheme for purpose of obtaining a tax benefit

(1) This Part applies to a scheme if it would be concluded (having regard to the matters in subsection (2)) that the person, or one of the persons, who entered into or carried out the scheme or any part of the scheme *did so for the purpose* of:

  (a) enabling a taxpayer (a relevant taxpayer) to obtain a tax benefit in connection with the scheme; or
  (b) enabling the relevant taxpayer and another taxpayer (or other taxpayers) each to obtain a tax benefit in connection with the scheme;

whether or not that person who entered into or carried out the scheme or any part of the scheme is the relevant taxpayer or is the other taxpayer or one of the other taxpayers.[22]

At first glance, the Australian provision seems to focus on the intention of a person, possibly the taxpayer though perhaps some other person, who has the requisite purpose. However, the qualification in the chapeau directs that the conclusion about 'purpose' is to be drawn, 'having regard to the matters in subsection (2).' Subsection (2) contains a list of eight factors or circumstances which are to be examined in forming the view about purpose:

(a) the manner in which the scheme was entered into or carried out;
(b) the form and substance of the scheme;
(c) the time at which the scheme was entered into and the length of the period during which the scheme was carried out;
(d) the result in relation to the operation of this Act that, but for this Part, would be achieved by the scheme;

---

21 The former GAAR purported to render void, 'every contract, agreement, or arrangement made or entered into, orally or in writing, whether before or after the commencement of this Act, shall so far as it has or purports to have the purpose or effect of in any way, directly or indirectly (a) altering the incidence of any income tax; (b) relieving any person from liability to pay any income tax or make any return; (c) defeating, evading, or avoiding any duty or liability imposed on any person by this Act; or (d) preventing the operation of this Act in any respect …' Income Tax Assessment Act, 1936 s. 260 (Australia).
22 Income Tax Assessment Act, 1936 s. 177D(1) (Australia).

(e) any change in the financial position of the relevant taxpayer that has resulted, will result, or may reasonably be expected to result, from the scheme;

(f) any change in the financial position of any person who has, or has had, any connection (whether of a business, family or other nature) with the relevant taxpayer, being a change that has resulted, will result or may reasonably be expected to result, from the scheme;

(g) any other consequence for the relevant taxpayer, or for any person referred to in paragraph (f), of the scheme having been entered into or carried out;

(h) the nature of any connection (whether of a business, family or other nature) between the relevant taxpayer and any person referred to in paragraph (f).[23]

The Hong Kong GAAR follows a similar design, with a list of apparently objective circumstances to which regard must be had in seeking the purpose of the person who entered the scheme.

This structure in the legislation creates an obvious tension which will be examined more fully in the next section of this chapter – how to reconcile an essentially subjective conception (the purpose of a particular person) with the objective facts and circumstances listed in subsection (2) (for example, the time at which the scheme was entered into).

Canada

Section 245 of the Income Tax Act, 1985 (Canada) was enacted in 1988. It allows the revenue authorities to vary the tax consequences of an 'avoidance transaction' and to substitute other consequences 'determined as is reasonable in the circumstances in order to deny a tax benefit that … would result, directly or indirectly, from that transaction …'[24] The notion of 'purpose' is found in the definition of 'avoidance transaction:'

(3)(a) An avoidance transaction means any transaction that, but for this section, would result, directly or indirectly, in a tax benefit, unless the transaction may reasonably be considered to have been undertaken or arranged *primarily for bona fide purposes other than to obtain the tax benefit* …[25]

The Canadian provision approaches 'purpose' from the other direction. Rather than impugn a transaction that was undertaken for an improper purpose, it blesses a transaction that was undertaken primarily for a bona fide purpose.

There are echoes of this design in the Irish provision. It defines a 'tax avoidance transaction' as arising where 'the transaction was not undertaken or arranged primarily for purposes other than to give rise to a tax advantage.'[26] However, the Irish provision also has echoes of the Australian legislation in that it looks as well to other more objective factors such as 'the results of the transaction, its use as a means of achieving those results, and any other means by which the results or any part of the results could have been achieved …'[27]

---

23 Income Tax Assessment Act, 1936 s. 177D(2) (Australia).
24 Income Tax Act, RSC 1985 c1 (5th Supp.), s. 245(2) (Canada).
25 Income Tax Act, RSC 1985 c1 (5th Supp.), s. 245(3) (Canada).
26 Taxes Consolidation Act, 1997 s. 811 (Ireland).
27 Taxes Consolidation Act, 1997 s. 811 (Ireland).

The Canadian provision also contains an important qualification to the primacy often given to subjective conscious purpose. Subsection (4) constrains the operation of the annihilation provision so that it can be enlivened –

> ... only if it may reasonably be considered that the transaction would, if this Act were read without reference to this section, result directly or indirectly in a misuse of the provisions of any one or more of this Act ... or would result directly or indirectly in an abuse having regard to those provisions, other than this section, read as a whole.[28]

Again, this aspect appears in the Irish legislation.[29] The two step structure seen in the Canadian and Irish formulations pose quite nicely another issue that will be examined more fully in the next section of this chapter – are there cases in which the taxpayer ought to be immune from the GAAR even though it is engaging in activities for the principal purpose of securing a tax advantage?

South Africa

South Africa replaced its existing GAAR in 2006 with a rule which permits the Commissioner to, 'determine the tax consequences under this Act of any impermissible avoidance arrangement ...' The definition of an impermissible avoidance arrangement employs generic purpose-based tests although expressed differently depending upon whether the transaction occurs in a business context or not:

> [an arrangement where the] sole or main **purpose was to obtain a tax benefit** and ... it was entered into or carried out by means or in a manner which would not normally be employed for bona fide business purposes ... or it lacks commercial substance ...[30]

The South African legislation is thus structured around two tests. In order to be an 'impermissible avoidance arrangement' it must be the case that the sole or main purpose of the 'arrangement' (perhaps in distinction to the purpose of some person) was to obtain a tax benefit, but purpose alone is insufficient. It is also required that there be an external, more objective indicator – the manner in which the transaction was carried out, and its commercial substance, must also be examined. This is not quite the eight-factor list seen in the Australian legislation but it has a similar feel, involving listed observable facts and circumstances as the indicator of purpose.

Second, the South African legislation also employs the Canadian notion of the misuse or abuse of the provisions of the legislation. In South Africa, the transaction will be an 'impermissible avoidance arrangement' if its sole or main purpose was to obtain a tax benefit and 'it would result directly or indirectly in the misuse or abuse of the provisions of this Act ...'[31] Purpose

---

28 Income Tax Act, RSC 1985 c1 (5th Supp.), s. 245(4) (Canada).

29 Taxes Consolidation Act, 1997, s. 811(3)(b) (Ireland) ('the transaction was undertaken or arranged for the purpose of obtaining the benefit of any relief, allowance or other abatement provided by any provision of the Acts and that transaction would not result directly or indirectly in a misuse of the provision or an abuse of the provision having regard to the purposes for which it was provided ...').

30 Income Tax Act 1962, s. 80A (South Africa).

31 Income Tax Act 1962, s. 80A (South Africa). Structurally, the notion of misuse or abuse must be satisfied in conjunction with purpose in order to trigger the GAAR, rather than as in the Canadian legislation where misuse serves as a defence in the presence of purpose.

alone is insufficient; an arrangement becomes impermissible through the combination of both purpose and defeating legislative intent.

Finally, the South African legislation supplements these generic tests with an alternative non-purpose-based list: the section can be enlivened in a business context if the transaction, 'lacks commercial substance, in whole or in part, taking into account the provisions of section 80C.'[32] Three special circumstances are listed in section 80C:

the inclusion or presence of –

(i) round trip financing as described in section 80D; or
(ii) an accommodating or tax indifferent party as described in section 80E; or
(iii) elements that have the effect of offsetting or cancelling each other.[33]

Each of these concepts is further elaborated. This combination of a generic purpose-based notion as the trigger for avoidance and a list of structures or transactions presumed to involve avoidance was a new departure in the South African legislation. It has influenced the design suggested for the Indian GAAR which also combines purpose-based tests and a more specific list.

United Kingdom

The UK enacted its GAAR in 2013 after a long process of soul-searching (Bowler 2009; Edgar 2008: 836).[34] The UK rule permits HMRC to make 'just and reasonable' adjustments 'to counteract the tax advantages' arising from 'tax arrangements that are abusive' in respect of 'any … tax to which the general anti-abuse rule applies.'[35]

The concept of a 'tax arrangement' is defined in terms of purpose –

> Arrangements are "tax arrangements" if, having regard to all the circumstances, it would be reasonable to conclude that the obtaining of a tax advantage was the main purpose, or one of the main purposes, of the arrangements.[36]

The notion of 'purpose' thus forms a gateway to the GAAR, but it is important to note that (like South Africa) the 'purpose' notion is applied to 'the arrangements' rather than any of the actors involved in devising, implementing or benefiting from the arrangement. The obvious contrast is with a GAAR which looks to uncover the purpose of persons involved in the scheme. The idea that a transaction can have a purpose is not new in the jurisprudence of the common law world. In 1958, Denning LJ went to some effort in *Newton's case* to explain the difference, and how it emerged from the text of the section he was examining –

> … the section is not concerned with the motives of individuals. It is not concerned with their desire to avoid tax, but only with the means which they employ to do it. It affects every 'contract, agreement or arrangement' … which has the purpose or effect of avoiding tax. In applying the section you must, by the very words of it, look at the arrangement itself and see which is its effect – which it does – irrespective of

---

32 Income Tax Act 1962, s. 80A (South Africa).
33 Income Tax Act 1962, s. 80C (South Africa).
34 Finance Act 2013, c. 29, ss. 206–215 (UK).
35 Finance Act 2013, c. 29, s. 209 (UK).
36 Finance Act 2013, c. 29, s. 207(1) (UK).

the motives of the persons who made it … In order to bring the arrangement within the section you must be able to predicate – by looking at the overt acts by which it was implemented – that it was implemented in that particular way so as to avoid tax.[37]

Prebble describes this as a test directed to 'the mechanics of implementation … rather than the motives of the individuals concerned' (2015: 1017). This dichotomy is picked up by the OECD/G20 in the *Final Report* on BEPS Action 6 (OECD/G20 2015: 55). The *Report* recommends that access to treaty benefits be constrained by a 'principal purpose test'. Treaty benefits would not be available,

> if it is reasonable to conclude, having regard to all relevant facts and circumstances, that obtaining that benefit was one of the principal purposes of any arrangement or transaction that resulted directly or indirectly in that benefit …

This distinction between the purpose of the actors involved in generating an abusive tax structure and a purpose attributed to the structure itself is explored more fully later in this chapter.

The second element in the UK legislation requires that the tax arrangement also be 'abusive.' A tax arrangement becomes 'abusive' if –

> the entering into or carrying out of [the tax arrangement] cannot reasonably be regarded as a reasonable course of action in relation to the relevant tax provisions, having regard to all the circumstances including –

> (a) whether the substantive results of the arrangements are consistent with any principles on which those provisions are based (whether express or implied) and the policy objectives of those provisions,
> (b) whether the means of achieving those results involves one or more contrived or abnormal steps, and
> (c) whether the arrangements are intended to exploit any shortcomings in those provisions.[38]

This element has echoes of the misuse or abuse notion in the Canadian and Irish legislation. The outcomes secured by the tax arrangement must be compared to the principles and policies (and any shortcomings) in 'the relevant tax provisions.'

Exploring more fully the contours of 'purpose'

The previous discussion has already hinted at some of the ideas, and the permutations and combinations of ideas, with which this chapter is concerned. While all of the provisions extracted

---

37 *Newton v. Federal Commissioner of Taxation* [1958] UKPCHCA 1, para 15. He then proposed several transactions where, in his view, one could not infer an improper purpose from examining the transaction (the transfer of shares cum dividend, arranging for a private company to become a non-private company for tax purposes and a declaration of trust made by a father in favour of his wife and daughter) and transactions where one could infer the transaction had an improper purpose (transactions where amounts spent were returned to the payers in other forms).
38 Finance Act 2013, c. 29, s. 207(2) (UK).

previously employ the term 'purpose,' it is clear that they are not using the term in the same way. Moreover, one sees in these rules combinations of three elements often used in combination or in juxtaposition – ideas about someone's state of mind, the existence and level of artifice involved and some notion of legislative intent, but how these ideas are assembled differs significantly between countries. And, to make matters more confusing, in some cases it seems the ideas merge so that what appear to be discrete ideas in fact reflect a single idea expressed several times but in different ways.

Purpose as a conscious mental state

As noted in the extracts above, 'purpose' can feature in the design of a GAAR in several ways. It can make a difference to the analysis whether a Court is trying to identify an (unacceptable) purpose of securing a tax advantage, or is instead attempting to discern an (acceptable) bona fide purpose, and it may matter whether 'purpose' plays the role of a precondition to challenge by a GAAR, or it is available as a defence against challenge by the GAAR.

The most common design of a GAAR seeks to identify whether some actor possesses a tainted purpose, and so an obvious analogy for lawyers is to see purpose as a concept akin to *mens rea* in criminal law: the conscious intent or plan of one or more of the persons involved to accomplish an outcome that was desired rather than unintended or unexpected. Other terms such as 'intention' or 'motive' can be used but all these terms refer to a conscious mental state – to ideas inside the relevant actor's mind which motivate his or her actions. The French rule speaks of actions that have been inspired by no other motive than that of avoiding or mitigating a tax burden.[39] The Aaronson Report (Aaronson 2011: para 5.13) in the UK, which led to its GAAR, stated the concept as –

> In many overseas GAARs … the approach has been to target arrangements which have the sole or main purpose of achieving a tax advantage. There are many variants in the language, but the underlying concept is the same: if one of the objects of the arrangement is to achieve a tax advantage, then for that very reason the tax advantage should be denied.

Used in this way, evidence of someone's 'purpose' might be found in the incautious letter or email, the instructions to advisers, or the unguarded answer given in the witness box. The best evidence would come from the actor's own writings and utterances, but it might come from others – from their evidence of correspondence or conversations with the actor, for example. These pieces of evidence would be the external indicia of what is essentially an internal matter.

A conscious purpose?

Used in this way, 'purpose' is essentially a subjective matter: it involves the conscious mind of some person. But even if no direct evidence existed of a state of mind, or did exist but the actor disowned it or attempted to explain it away, this would not be fatal. Judges routinely find the evidence of a state of mind without direct evidence in the form of documents or confessions. They infer the presence (or absence) of a state of mind from the evidence of the events that

39 Tax Procedure Code, art L. 64 (France).

occurred, often expressed in the idea that a person intends (or purposes) the natural consequences of their acts.[40]

The distinction is sometimes made in this area between 'objective' and 'subjective' mental states. This distinction can cause some confusion. It may be that the references to 'objective purpose' are simply identifying an evidentiary matter; that the identification of the actor's purpose or intention is to be proved objectively, and in particular without regard to direct and likely self-serving evidence from the taxpayer about their own reasons. Instead, 'purpose' has to be proven by other means. In this sense, the quest for 'objective purpose' is still to establish a subjective state of mind, but from objective evidence and logical inference.

But the term 'objective purpose' could be meant to have substantive implications. It may be intended to imply a rather different idea, namely that purpose is to be discerned by examining some fictitious person other than the actual taxpayer or some of the real actors. An 'objective purpose' might be perhaps an unconscious intent. Used in this sense, an objective 'purpose' is the purpose of some notional person perhaps akin to the fictitious 'reasonable person' from tort law. Seeking the 'objective purpose' would thus be akin to asking, what would a reasonable person, who implemented the acts actually undertaken by the taxpayer and confederates, have been seeking to accomplish? This objective purpose would have to be inferred by the judge from events and circumstances because it is not the conscious subjective state of mind of a real person. Used in this way, the fate of the actual taxpayer turns on what a judge decides would have been the purpose of this putative person. The Courts in Australia have interpreted their GAAR to operate in this way. For example, one judge has said of the Australian rule –

> The conclusion to be reached is not a finding on the evidence that one of the persons contemplated by the section had the requisite purpose [the dominant purpose of securing a tax benefit] but that such a purpose is to be attributed to one of those persons by analysis of objective criteria without regard to the actual purpose or motive, ultimate or otherwise, of the relevant scheme participants.[41]

Whose purpose?

GAAR designs also differ about just whose mind, or how many minds, are to be interrogated. The text so far has used the term 'actor' because a GAAR will sometimes deliberately cast a wide net in the defining range of persons whose purpose will be examined. For example, the Australian and Hong Kong GAARs contemplates the tax benefit being conferred on 'a person (in this section referred to as the relevant person)' but the purpose to be examined is that of 'the person, or one of the persons, who entered into or carried out the transaction' to establish whether their purpose was, 'enabling the relevant person, either alone or in conjunction with other persons, to obtain a tax benefit.'[42]

---

40 See for example *Crofter Hand Woven Harris Tweed Co v. Veitch* [1942] AC 435 ('in some branches of the law, "intention" may be understood to cover results which may reasonably flow from what is deliberately done, on the principle that a man is to be treated as intending the reasonable consequence of his acts'). This idea crops up in contexts other than criminal law: *Crofter Hand Woven Harris Tweed* involved an action against a union for interference with trade; *Deery v. Deery* [1954] HCA 4 is an application in the field of family law.

41 *Orica Limited v. Commissioner of Taxation* [2015] FCA 1399, para 19.

42 Inland Revenue Ordinance, s. 61A (Hong Kong).

This formulation deliberately tries to attract the GAAR where one person has the requisite purpose but the tax benefit is enjoyed by another. This might be needed, for example, where there is some form of income shifting between spouses or with other family members. In this situation, while the tax saving is enjoyed by the spouse with the reduced income (and tax), it may be hard to discern whether the relevant plans and purposes emanated from the assignor or recipient. More importantly, the presence of such a rule allows a GAAR to attach to mass-marketed investment schemes where the promoter has constructed a product with the return to investors driven by the tax benefits, but those investors have little real appreciation about how the return is achieved. Where the GAAR looks only to the purpose of the taxpayer who enjoyed the tax benefit and not beyond that to the motives of promoters or associates, the effectiveness of the GAAR must be somewhat problematic. On the other hand, there must be very real question whether it is appropriate to impugn an unwitting taxpayer unaware of the purposes of others.

The purpose of inanimate legal constructs

Despite the drafting in countries like South Africa, Canada and New Zealand and their attempts to discern the purpose of 'arrangements', the word 'purpose' as a linguistic usage must involve examining the state of mind of some 'person' – whether the taxpayer or some other person. When the drafting says the 'purpose' to be uncovered is that attached to an inanimate legal construct (an 'arrangement'), some other meaning must be intended but it is not obvious what it is. Humans can have subjective intentions, motives and desires; legal structures do not. This formulation – the purpose of an 'arrangement' or transaction – was used in Australia until 1981 and is proposed for the principal purpose test to be used in bilateral income tax treaties. It is also used in the UK and Canadian rules which refer to 'the main purpose, or one of the main purposes, of the arrangements.' It is still used in the New Zealand rule which applies to, 'an arrangement … that … has tax avoidance as its purpose or effect.'[43]

When the word 'purpose' is consciously and deliberately connected to an inanimate legal construct, there are several conceivable ways that the phrase might be read. First, the purpose of the 'arrangement' might simply be a direction to examine the purposes of those humans who designed and implemented it. But it seems more likely that this is meant to direct the ultimate inquiry away from conclusions about the minds of human beings, whether the taxpayer or others. Since arrangements cannot have purposes, this formulation might instead be referring to other notions like artifice and contrivance: an arrangement has a 'purpose' of securing a tax advantage if it displays a design contrived to achieve that result. While written in the language of 'purpose,' the meaning would have been better conveyed if it had referred to the idea of artifice. This is certainly an idea that drafters might have intended to capture by this inelegant usage. The notion that an arrangement has a purpose is linguistic nonsense, but arrangements can definitely be artificial or contrived.

Knowledge v. ignorance and accident

It is central to this idea of the subjective and conscious 'purpose' of 'persons' that the relevant actor (be they the actual taxpayer, an objectified actor or a confederate of the taxpayer) desired a particular outcome – any tax saving was deliberate and intended. This suggests that the actor

---

43 Income Tax Act 2007, s. YA 1 (definition of 'tax avoidance arrangement') (New Zealand).

involved, acting unaided, might need to have some knowledge and appreciation of tax law and of how the attractive tax outcome would come about.

Or to put it the other way, if part of the notion of purpose involves accomplishing an outcome that was desired, then it would seem to be a plausible defence to triggering a GAAR if the actor could demonstrate that the tax benefit achieved was unintended and unexpected, something which a lay person may have more scope to argue convincingly. Indeed, the very notion of an evil purpose as a precondition to triggering the GAAR implies the reverse – that tax benefits will remain available to those who happen upon them accidentally or in ignorance.

However, it is not entirely inconsistent with the notion of 'purpose' that the actor sought the outcome, albeit without appreciating just how or why it was being accomplished and it is likely that a court could be persuaded to this view – intending the outcome without understanding the means is sufficient.

But to be consistent, this argument would presumably not be available if the design of the GAAR requires a Court to discern a bona fide purpose because the design uses purpose as a defence against attack. In the face of such a rule, taxpayers presumably would bear an onus of showing a conscious decision to act in a particular way.

Multiple and conflicting purposes

Another important aspect of any discussion of purpose is how to deal with taxpayers who profess multiple purposes. Taxpayers who invest in marketed tax shelters will typically claim that their investment was motivated by the high commercial returns on offer, even though one portion of the return arises from the tax effects. Taxpayers who restructure their business vehicles to shift income into the hands of partners and children will often claim that their actions were motivated by a desire to give the partner a degree of financial independence, protect their assets and the business' assets from potential creditors should the business fail, or the action is a form of estate planning undertaken while alive, even though it has the effect of splitting the household's income more evenly among the members (Loutzenhiser 2013). Taxpayers who restructure a foreign corporation to relocate its headquarters to another foreign location may claim that they are doing so to avoid changes to foreign tax laws or foreign regulatory changes, even though the restructuring is done in a way which produces tax advantages for the shareholders in their jurisdiction.

No doubt tax considerations can be more or less influential in the minds of taxpayers and GAARs often try to quantify in linguistic terms just how important the purpose of securing the tax benefit needs to be among all the considerations that might have influenced the actor's behaviour. These linguistic formulae try to express a spectrum: it might be required that securing the tax advantage is 'the purpose' or the 'sole purpose' for which the taxpayer acted, it might be required that tax considerations were the 'dominant' or 'primary' purpose even though other objectives existed, tax considerations might be 'one of the [group of] principal purposes' that motivated the taxpayer's actions or the taxpayer might be able to escape the GAAR if tax considerations were 'merely incidental.' In practical terms, these phrases are probably trying to capture one of four ideas – that tax considerations were the sole motivating factor, that tax was the most influential of all the competing considerations, that tax was one of the group of considerations which were most influential in the actor's thinking, that tax considerations were present but were not significant.

A final consideration is how to handle competing purposes where the test is a subjective conscious purpose and multiple actors are involved. (Where purpose is to be found by examining the arrangement, this consideration ought not arise.) It was noted previously that some

GAARs search for the offending purpose in the minds of other actors, as well as the taxpayer. This formulation is often seen as a way of handling taxpayer ignorance – that the taxpayer will be imputed with the intent of those of advise, devise or implement the transaction, even where the taxpayer had no conscious understanding or appreciation of the effects of the transactions it was undertaking, or the effects of what was being done for its benefits by others. But widening the field of potential minds to explore raises the possibility of conflicting considerations – the taxpayer who invests in a marketed tax shelter may well be motivated exclusively by the higher commercial return being promised, oblivious to the fact that tax plays any part in how it arises. But it is conceivable that the promoter of the shelter (especially one that is more than usually unscrupulous), who appreciates the tax effects are significant, may nevertheless be driven primarily by the desire to secure its fee income for its own benefit, and be rather less interested in whether the tax advantages follows as promised.

'Purpose' and the element of artifice

The extracts above showed that a notion of artifice often appears as a second element in the design of GAARs. The use of artifice appears to be an attempt by the legislator to ground the GAAR in something observable about the features of the transaction or structure, and definitely more concrete than a mere state of mind.

Sometimes this idea of artifice is expressed in general terms – the transaction lacks commercial substance, it involves steps that are contrived or abnormal, the substance of the arrangement differs from its form, or it is not genuine – it has a *caractère fictive* in the words of the French GAAR. Sometimes the element of artifice is more carefully delineated – the South African rule, for example, itemises 'round trip financing,' transactions with tax indifferent parties and transactions with have offsetting effects.[44] The rule proposed for India would expand this list of dubious transactions (Expert Committee 2012: 26–7).[45] The Australian and Hong Kong laws list various factors to which 'regard' must be had. This suggests the items in the list are not prescriptive as in the South African rule, but they are meant to catalogue circumstances that are suggestive of artifice.[46]

Observing artifice

Notions such as 'commercial substance' and 'contrived or abnormal' are not without their own difficulty. There are many examples one could imagine: is a sale-and-leaseback arrangement to be viewed as artificial because it has the substance of secured borrowing but is not structured in that form? Is a repurchase agreement (REPO) a contrived borrowing? What about a long term lease classified as a finance lease for financial accounting but which meets the tests of an operating lease for tax purposes? These are all relatively common commercial dealings and yet one could say of all of them that they display disparity between the legal forms and the commercial substance of the transactions.

So does the test of artifice ultimately become a question about the current state of commercial legal practice – the transaction that was rare 5 years ago and is now common is now

---

44 Income Tax Act 1962, s. 80C (South Africa).

45 The Indian proposal adds transactions conducted through persons which disguise the value, location, source, ownership or control of funds and transactions involving a party without any substantial commercial purpose.

46 Income Tax Assessment Act, 1936, s. 177D (Australia); Income Tax Ordinance, s. 61A (Hong Kong).

no longer contrived? The UK rule appears to contemplate this kind of pragmatic approach in its references to arrangements that, 'cannot reasonably be regarded as a reasonable course of action …'[47] However, the document prepared by the UK Government implied the test of artifice in the UK rule was instead directed to the state of commercial legal practice at the time the legislation was prepared – the transaction is contrived if it was not common practice at that time (Secretary of the Exchequer 2012: para 2.2):

> The GAAR aims to target artificial and abusive tax avoidance schemes which, because they are often complex and/or novel, could not have been contemplated directly when formulating the tax legislation …

Combining these ideas

Having within the GAAR both a purpose element and an artifice element creates an obvious problem in framing how these ideas interact. Does an actor only have a requisite purpose when the tax benefits are difficult to accomplish? What happens if there is an extreme level of complexity to a structure but the taxpayer attributes this to commercial or regulatory considerations?

In theory, there are several ways that the artifice aspect and the purpose dimension could fit together. One possibility is that they are structured as prerequisites of equal importance – the GAAR is triggered only where both the transaction is undertaken for the purpose of avoiding tax and the transaction or structure displays evidence of contrivance or artifice. Where purpose and artifice are both present the GAAR would be triggered, but if one were missing the GAAR would not be enlivened: a transaction which lacks artifice would provide protection against the application of the GAAR so that artifice becomes an escape route for an actor whose mental state is tainted. And a transaction which appears artificial will nevertheless escape the GAAR where an actor can convince a Court that their purpose is untainted.

Alternatively, they might function as substitutes – the GAAR is triggered if either the transaction is undertaken for the purpose of avoiding tax or the transaction or structure displays evidence of contrivance or artifice.

But purpose and artifice are connected ideas in a linguistic sense – labelling something as contrived or artificial conveys also the connotation that it was done with an improper purpose. So another possibility is that these two ideas are somehow functionally interdependent and symbiotic – that artifice is the proof of purpose, or perhaps that purpose without artifice is innocuous. For example, the Greek GAAR allows the revenue authorities to ignore 'any artificial arrangement … under way with the main purpose of avoiding taxation,' but defines an arrangement as 'artificial' if 'it lacks commercial substance.'[48] Circumstances may arise where it is necessary to decide which is paramount. For example, if the test is ultimately a matter of purpose, and purpose is *prima facie* established by examining the degree of artifice evident in the transaction, it might nevertheless be possible to establish purpose in other ways – the 'smoking gun' letter or the admission under cross-examination. On the other hand, if artifice were more important, while the inquiry might still appear to examine the relevant actor's purpose, actual purpose would become irrelevant if it can be established only by contrivance. Such a reading in effect renders purpose otiose, but it is a reading which would make a GAAR less unpredictable

---

47 Finance Act, 2013, s. 207(2) (UK).
48 Tax Procedure Code, art 37 (Greece).

in operation and was recommended for the UK for this reason. The Report's author rejected the use of purpose as the trigger for a GAAR and proposed to rely on artifice instead –

> The starting point should be to see whether the arrangement is abnormal, in the sense of having abnormal features specifically designed to achieve a tax advantageous result. If an arrangement has such an abnormal feature or features then it becomes in effect 'short listed' for consideration as a potential target for the GAAR. Conversely, if there is no such feature then it is immediately dismissed from consideration.
>
> *Aaronson 2011: para 5.15.*[49]

This debate is more than academic because there are likely to be many situations where there is evidence of purpose but the transaction shows no contrivance. One stark example is a taxpayer who, at the end of the tax year, decides to write off a debt as bad. It is hard to think of a transaction which is more obviously undertaken for the purpose of generating a tax benefit. Indeed, writing off a bad debt achieves nothing but the tax benefit.[50] Because the mere fact of writing off a bad debt, uncommunicated to the debtor, has no commercial consequences between the parties, it must therefore be true, almost by definition, that it was done for the purpose of securing the tax benefit. If the GAAR were activated by purpose alone, then the transaction must be susceptible.

There are many other examples of the same problem evident throughout tax law, although they present the matter less starkly. Consider, for example, the decision by a private company to make a tax-favoured voluntary contribution to a pension fund for an employee, who also happens to be the sole director and principal shareholder. While making the contribution does have observable commercial consequences for the company, it does seem likely that the purpose of the company making the contribution would likely include the desire for the tax concession. Or consider a taxpayer who is employed, has some savings which generate income and a partner not currently in the paid workforce. The taxpayer gives some capital to the spouse who then invests the money, benefits from a tax-free threshold and the household enjoys a lower marginal tax rate. Again, this transaction does have commercial consequences, but it seems plausible that a Court could conclude this transaction was done for the purpose (at least in part) of avoiding tax. Or consider a company which decides to set up an in-house dining facility where sales staff entertain clients (the cost of which is a deductible business expense) rather than pay for meals at local restaurants (the cost of which is not deductible). There are commercial ramifications to the decision, but again a Court might conclude that the facility was set up for the purpose of avoiding tax.

At some point the designers will have to decide how to combine the ideas of purpose and artifice. Just how are these two ideas to be integrated? Are they functionally independent? Is one an indicator of the other? Is one the proof of the other? If so, is it just one proof, or the only proof? These are the questions that the legislative history should address.

---

49 Interestingly, the Report then re-instated a purpose test as a safe harbour – a transaction which was regarded as contrived, would nevertheless be excluded from the GAAR if it could be demonstrated that the 'arrangement [was] entered into entirely for non-tax reasons ...' (Aaronson 2011, para 5.31).

50 In order for the debtor to be formally relieved of the liability to pay it will typically be necessary that there be some consideration or the transaction be effected by Deed, although in some cases an estoppel might arise which might impede effective recovery by the creditor.

Assembling the pieces: tainted purpose and legislative intent

The legislative extracts quoted above showed the design in several countries contains a third element to the GAAR: that the outcome achieved by the taxpayer represents the exploitation of a shortcoming in the legislation, the misuse or abuse of a provision or the contradiction of some presumed policy objective or legislative intent behind a provision.

Again, it is not always obvious how the idea of a taxpayer's purpose and the purpose of the legislature are meant to fit. The 2016 EC Directive 'Laying down rules against tax avoidance practices ...' targets 'arrangements which, having been put into place for the main purpose or one of the main purposes of obtaining a tax advantage that defeats the object or purpose of the applicable tax law, are not genuine having regard to all relevant facts and circumstances' (Council Directive (EU) 2016/1164, art 7). This text could be expressing one idea or two or even three, all of which have to be met *seriatim*.

If this third element is a precondition to triggering the GAAR, or provides a defence against the operation of the GAAR, then again purpose alone is insufficient: an actor can have a deliberate, conscious and tainted purpose but the tax advantage is not to be impugned by a GAAR because enjoying that advantage does not represent exploitation, misuse, abuse or contradiction. Indeed, the taxpayer's acts may well be the furtherance of some legislative policy, and the intended reward comes in the form of the tax advantage which the taxpayer actively seeks.

Finding legislative intent

Formulations which refer to exploitation, misuse, abuse or the contradiction of policy or intent assume that these things can be ascertained by a Court, and that the text of the legislation does not currently capture it, even with the leeway that creative judicial interpretation may allow. Freedman, for one, has doubted that judges have the skills and competence for this task (Freedman 2007). Further, the idea that the meaning appearing from the text of the legislation is not the complete and authoritative statement of the legislative intent is clearly a controversial proposition in many legal cultures (Aaronson 2011: para 5.21).[51]

These formulations may also prove problematic because they contain an inherent paradox. The task of statutory interpretation already requires a judge to find Parliament's intent, and to do so from the words of the statute. Judges may be permitted to refer to external sources to confirm or modify their views about how the provisions are to be read and applied. The judge presumably concludes that they have come to a sensible reading of the primary section involved in the dispute, which gives effect to Parliament's intent. If it is a reading that allows the tax concession and the tax benefit is *prima facie* available, the revenue authority must resort to the GAAR. The judge must revisit the principal section and is now being asked to conclude that the original interpretation was wrong. Yet when applying the GAAR, it seems the judge is being asked to apply exactly the same criterion the judge applied the first time – to examine and interpret the section in order to uncover the underlying purpose or legislative intent. It is hard to believe that the judge will come to a different view about Parliament's intent when applying the GAAR from the view reached when first interpreting the section.[52]

---

51 Aaronson refers to 'the established principle of statutory interpretation in the UK, which requires the legislative "intention" to be established solely from the wording of the legislation ...' (2011, para 5.21).

52 This conundrum can be seen in the Canadian decision, *Copthorne Holdings Ltd v. Canada*, 2011 SCC 63.

Further, it is not immediately obvious what the judge is being asked to discern by these phrases. There is clearly a difference between asking a judge to ascertain what Parliament intended to say but failed, and asking the Court to second-guess what Parliament would have said if it had thought about the matter. Given that a GAAR is almost by definition directed at transactions and structures the legislator concedes they were unable to foresee (if they could predict the future they could write a precise rule instead), a GAAR is almost always going to be invoked in cases where Parliament has not thought about the matter, and there is no existing legislative intent to be found. The Court may often find itself in the position of having to second-guess what Parliament would have concluded had the matter been raised. This is rather different to the usual tasks of statutory interpretation.

Nor is it always obvious that there will be a legislative intent to be found. For example, in a tax system where the individual tax rate is higher than the corporate rate, is there a legislative intent to allow or to deny individuals the opportunity to form personal holding companies to derive investment income that would otherwise be earned directly by the individuals?[53] Similarly, in a tax system where the tax unit is the individual (rather than the family), is there a legislative intent to allow or to deny partners the opportunity to transfer assets between them so that the investment income is derived by the individual with the lower marginal rate? And these problems are not restricted to such structural items as tax rates or the tax unit. Does a legislative restriction denying a deduction for the cost of meals while entertaining clients at restaurants reveal any legislative intent about deducting the cost of catering services purchased for a client function held in-house?

Perhaps for that reason, the Australian GAAR sets the bar rather higher allowing an exception only where the taxpayer is, 'making … an agreement, choice, declaration, agreement, election, selection or choice, the giving of a notice or the exercise of an option [and that choice etc is] *expressly provided for by this Act* …'[54] (emphasis added).

Explicit tax incentives

Nevertheless, such a provision seems a sensible component of a GAAR and it is surprising that it is not more widely adopted to deal consciously with the issue of incentives. In the absence of such a requirement, it would seem that taxpayers who respond to the allure of tax incentives ought to be denied them – they have acted for the purpose of securing the promised tax benefit. It would be nonsensical to induce taxpayers to change their behavior by offering the inducement of tax reduction and then for a GAAR to deny it for that very reason and so some exception to that conundrum has to be found. Insisting on such an element in the design of the GAAR presents a more convincing way of answering one of the examples given in the previous section – the taxpayer who contributes to an employee pension fund is presumably giving effect to a legislative intent to encourage saving for retirement (and within the highly regulated environment of employee pension funds).

Of course there will be cases where the taxpayer's behavior ought not to be protected by the argument that its purpose is to secure a tax saving it was meant to enjoy – the legislative intent is usually qualified by conditions on the kind of retirement savings vehicle which can accept

---

53 The US considered it needs a dedicated specific regime for this purpose. The personal holding company rules impose a further tax on the undistributed profits of closely-held companies which derive predominantly passive income. Internal Revenue Code 1986, ss. 541 ff (USA).
54 Income Tax Assessment Act, 1936, s. 177C(2) (Australia).

tax-favoured contributions, the characteristics of the contributor, the size of the contributions, and so on. Schemes which are put in place to undermine these kinds of restrictions are presumably still within the scope of a GAAR.

Conclusions

History suggests GAARs are likely to be an increasingly common feature of the tax legislative landscape, both in domestic legislation and even international instruments, and some notion of purpose is likely to remain a dominant element of the design of a GAAR. The discussion above has tried to demonstrate some of the problems of this unruly concept. But in the absence of a more robust, perhaps purpose-free, design the best that can be hoped is that some of these conundrums can be addressed through careful structuring of a GAAR and its components.

References

Aaronson, G. (2011). 'A study to consider whether a general anti-avoidance rule should be introduced into the UK tax system'. Available at http://webarchive.nationalarchives.gov.uk/20130129110402/http://www.hm-treasury.gov.uk/d/gaar_study_supp_report_250612.pdf

Arnold, B. (2008). 'A comparison of statutory general anti-avoidance rules and judicial general anti-avoidance doctrines as a means of controlling tax avoidance', in J. Avery Jones, P. Harris and D Oliver (eds), *Comparative Perspectives on Revenue Law: Essays in Honour of John Tiley*. Cambridge: Cambridge University Press.

Bowler, T. (2009). *Countering Tax Avoidance in the UK: Which Way Forward?* London: Institute for Fiscal Studies.

Brown, K. (ed.) (2012). *A Comparative Look at Regulation of Corporate Tax Avoidance*. New York: Springer.

Cooper, G. (1997). 'Conflicts, challenges and choices – the rule of law and anti-avoidance rules', in G. Cooper (ed.), *Tax Avoidance and the Rule of Law*. Amsterdam: IBFD.

Cooper, G. (2001). 'International experience with general anti-avoidance rules', *Southern Methodist University Law Review*, 54, 83.

Cooper, G. (2006). 'The emerging high court jurisprudence on part IVA', *Tax Specialist*, 9, 235.

Cooper, G. (2009). 'Design and structure of general anti tax avoidance regimes', *Bulletin for International Taxation*, 63, 26.

Cooper, G. (2011). 'Predicting the past – the problem of the counterfactual in part IVA', *Australian Tax Review*, 40, 185.

Cooper, G. (2013). 'Taxing by analogy', *Australian Tax Review*, 42, 255.

Council Directive (EU) 2016/1164 (2016). 'Laying down rules against tax avoidance practices that directly affect the functioning of the internal market', 12 July.

Edgar, T. (2008). 'Building a better GAAR', *Virginia Tax Review*, 27, 833.

European Commission 2016, COM(2016) 2016/0011 (2016). 'Proposal for a council directive laying down rules against rax avoidance practices that directly affect the functioning of the internal market', 28 January.

Expert Committee (2012). 'Final Report on General Anti Avoidance Rules (GAAR) in Income-Tax Act, 1961'. Available at http://finmin.nic.in/reports/report_gaar_itact1961.pdf [Accessed 15 February 2016]

Freedman, J. (2007). 'Interpreting tax statutes: Tax avoidance and the intention of parliament', *Law Quarterly Review*, 123, 53.

Gammie, M. (2008). 'The judicial approach to avoidance: Some reflections on *BMBF* and *SPI*', in J. A. Jones, P. Harris and D. Oliver (eds), *Comparative Perspectives on Revenue Law: Essays in Honour of John Tiley*. Cambridge: Cambridge University Press.

Gammie, M. (2013). 'When is avoiding tax not abusive? Comparative approaches to a GAAR in Australia and the United Kingdom', *Australian Tax Review*, 42, 279.

Lehmann, G. (1983). 'The income tax judgments of Sir Garfield Barwick: A study in the failure of the new legalism', *Monash University Law Review*, 9, 115.

Libin, J. (2010). 'Congress should address tax avoidance head-on: The internal revenue code needs a GAAR', *Virginia Tax Review*, 30, 339.

Loutzenhiser, G. (2013). 'Tax avoidance, private companies and the family', *Cambridge Law Journal*, 72, 35.

McMahon, M. (2003). 'Beyond a GAAR: Retrofitting the code to rein in 21st century tax shelters', *Tax Notes*, 98, 1721.

McMahon, M. (2008). 'Comparing the application of judicial interpretive doctrines to revenue statutes on opposite sides of the pond', in J. A. Jones, P. Harris and D. Oliver (eds), *Comparative Perspectives on Revenue Law: Essays in Honour of John Tiley*. Cambridge: Cambridge University Press.

Mo, P. (2003). *Tax Avoidance and Anti-Avoidance Measures in Major Developing Economies*. Westport, CT: Praeger.

OECD/G20 (2015). *Preventing the Granting of Treaty Benefits in Inappropriate Circumstances – Action 6, 2015 Final Report*. Paris: OECD.

Orow, N. (2000). *General Anti-Avoidance Rules: A Comparative International Analysis*. Bristol: Jordan.

Orow, N. (2011). *Comparative Approaches to Cross Jurisdictional Tax Avoidance*. New York: Kluwer.

Prebble, J. (2015). 'Predication: The test of tax avoidance in New Zealand from *Newton* to *Ben Nevis*', *Victoria University of Wellington Law Review*, 46, 1011.

Prebble, R., and Prebble, J. (2010). 'Does the use of general anti-avoidance rules to combat tax avoidance breach principles of the rule of law? A comparative study', *Saint Louis University Law Journal*, 55, 21.

Rosenblatt, P. (2014). *General Anti-Avoidance Rules for Major Developing Countries*. Amsterdam: Wolters Kluwer.

Samtani, P., and Kutyan, J. (2014). 'GAAR revisited: From instinctive reaction to intellectual rigour', *Canadian Tax Journal*, 62, 401.

Schön, W. (2008). 'Abuse of rights and European tax law', in J. A. Jones, P. Harris and D. Oliver (eds), *Comparative Perspectives on Revenue Law: Essays in Honour of John Tiley*. Cambridge: Cambridge University Press.

Secretary of the Exchequer (2012). 'A general anti-abuse rule: Consultative document'. Available at http://webarchive.nationalarchives.gov.uk/20131002164056/http:/customs.hmrc.gov.uk/channelsPortalWebApp/channelsPortalWebApp.portal?_nfpb=true&_pageLabel=pageLibrary_ConsultationDocuments&propertyType=document&columns=1&id=HMCE_PROD1_032113 [Accessed 15 February 2016]

Tooma, R. (2008). *Legislating Against Tax Avoidance*. Amsterdam: IBFD.

Waerzeggers, C., and Hillier, C. (2016). 'Introducing a General Anti-avoidance rule (GAAR) – ensuring that a GAAR achieves its purpose', Tax Law IMF Technical Note 2016/1. Available at www.imf.org/external/pubs/ft/tltn/2016/tltn1601.pdf [Accessed 14 February 2016]

7

GENERAL ANTI-AVOIDANCE RULE IN CANADA

History, scheme, source, and enforcement

Vokhid Urinov

Introduction

When the Income Tax Act (ITA) was first introduced in Canada in 1917, the law was merely around 10 pages long and comprised 24 sections.[1] Since then the ITA has grown to just over 3,300 pages and 269 sections, written in a style incomprehensible to the average person.[2] Today the law is considered to be one of the largest and most complex laws in the country. It undergoes amendments and additions almost every year and with every federal budget announcement.[3] This constant increase in size and complexity of the tax law is largely due to the fact that the legislator often reacts with more detail and technical rules whenever taxpayers discover ways to circumvent the law. However, once an amendment is announced, taxpayers and their advisers come up with new strategies to beat the new rules.

In reality, it is impossible for the legislator, when enacting a particular tax law provision, to fully anticipate all possible ways taxpayers may attempt to avoid that provision. Accepting this reality, in 1987 the Canadian Parliament decided to take a different approach. It introduced a set of general provisions to the ITA that are commonly known as the General Anti-Avoidance Rule, or GAAR. The main purpose of the GAAR is to negate tax benefits derived from any arrangement that complies with a literal interpretation of the ITA but violates its intent and spirit. It is a statutory means to fight against abusive tax avoidance transactions.

This paper provides a brief review of the Canadian GAAR, its history, legislative scheme, and the enforcement mechanism.

---

1 Canadian Taxpayers Federation, News Release, available at www.taxpayer.com/news-releases/you-re-already-out-of-time-to-read-the-income-tax-act-before-filing-deadline--ctf.

2 See Income Tax Act (ITA), 1985 (2016) (Can.), available at http://laws-lois.justice.gc.ca/PDF/I-3.3.pdf.

3 The Canadian federal budget is the federal government's financial plan and forecast of its revenues and spending in the fiscal year. It is presented in the House of Commons by the Minister of Finance at the beginning of every year. The budget is then voted on by the House of Commons. It must be noted that the government's fiscal year runs from 1 April to 31 March.

Tax avoidance and general anti-avoidance rule in Canada

Duke of Westminster principle

Generally, taxpayers have the right to order their affairs in such a way as to reduce the tax otherwise payable. This principle originates from the often-quoted dictum in a landmark British case of 1936, and is commonly known as the "Duke of Westminster principle".[4] In this case, Lord Tomlin of the British House of Lords held that

> every man is entitled … to order his affairs so that the tax attaching under the appropriate Acts is less than it otherwise would be. If he succeeds in ordering them so as to secure this result, then, however unappreciative the Commissioners of Inland Revenue or his fellow taxpayers may be of his ingenuity, he cannot be compelled to pay an increased tax.[5]

Canadian courts regard the Duke of Westminster principle favourably, and the Supreme Court of Canada (SCC) cites the principle in many of its tax cases.[6] Thus, under the Canadian income tax system taxpayers are considered to have a legitimate right to engage in tax planning. However, in the recent decades there has been a proliferation of cases where taxpayers have aggressively pursued this right beyond the limits the Canadian Parliament had intended when it enacted the tax laws.[7] It has since been recognized that allowing taxpayers to pursue unconstrained tax planning may undermine the tax system.[8] Therefore, to reconcile these two conflicting premises, the Canadian income tax system now distinguishes between legitimate and illegitimate forms of tax avoidance. Distinguishing between these two forms is at the core of the Canadian GAAR, and leads us to the discussion of the concept of tax avoidance in Canadian tax law.

Concept of tax avoidance

The definition of tax avoidance under the Canadian tax system has been fairly broad. The Report of the Royal Commission on Taxation of 1966 (the "Carter Report"), one of the most comprehensive and influential tax reform studies in Canadian history, describes tax avoidance as "every attempt by legal means to prevent or reduce tax liability, which would otherwise be

---

4 *Inland Revenue Commissioners v. Duke of Westminster* (1936) (HL, UK). In this case, the taxpayer had a number of servants. Under the British tax law, wages for household servants were not tax deductible. However, the law allowed a deduction of annual payments made in pursuant of a legal obligation. The taxpayer, therefore, entered into deeds of covenant with its servants according to which he undertook to pay each of them annual sums for a period of 7 years. The payments were supposed to be made irrespective of whether services are performed by the servants. Overall purpose of the arrangement was to convert the non-deductible wages into deductible annuity obligations. The House of Lords ruled the case in favour of the taxpayer.

5 Ibid., 19.

6 See *Pioneer Laundry & Dry Cleaning Ltd. v. The Minister of National Revenue*, SCR 1 (1938); *Canada China Clay Ltd. v. Hepburn*, [1945] SCR 87 (Can.); *Stubart Investments Ltd. v. The Queen*, [1984] 1 S.C.R. 536 (Can.); *Hickman Motors Ltd. v. Canada*, [1997] 2 SCR 336 (Can.); *Canada Trustco Mortgage Co. v. Canada*, 2005 SCC 54 (Can.); *Imperial Oil Ltd. v. Canada; Inco Ltd. v. Canada*, [2006] 2 SCR 447 (Can.); *Lipson v. Canada*, [2009] 1 SCR 3 (Can.); *Copthorne Holdings Ltd. v. Canada*, [2011] 3 SCR 721 (Can.).

7 *Minutes of Proceedings and Evidence of the Standing Committee on Finance and Economic Affairs on June 29, 1987*, Vol. 76 (Ottawa: House of Commons, 1987), 76:6. The Department of Finance representative, Mr. Jim Wilson's testimony at the House of Commons' Standing Committee on Finance and Economic Affairs.

8 M. H. Wilson, *White Paper: Tax Reform 1987* (Ottawa: Ottawa Ministry of Finance, 1987), 1.

incurred, by taking advantage of some provision or lack of provision in the law."[9] This defini-tion encompasses almost every transaction by taxpayers that involves a reduction of taxes which might otherwise become payable under the tax law. The Carter Report also listed 3 common methods of tax avoidance: (1) willfully avoiding earning income, e.g., when taxpayers prefer leisure over labor, or when taxpayers prefer savings over investment; (2) taking advantage of some preferential tax schemes, elections, or incentives expressly allowed in the tax statute; (3) exploiting various technical provisions and devices of the tax statute in order to fall outside of the tax statute.[10]

The Carter Report reads, "if a man gives up the right to income and to any control over the income or the source of income, even with the avowed purpose of reducing his tax liabil-ity, he should not be taxed on that income. However, if he contrives matters in such a way that he continues to enjoy the benefits of income, or if he continues to control the source or disposition of income, he should not be allowed to reduce his liability below what a taxpayer in similar circumstances receiving the income would normally expect to pay under the tax system. The taxing statute should contain sufficient provisions to prevent this latter type of avoidance."[11]

The Carter Report condemned the latter type of tax avoidance for the following reasons:

- the loss of revenue to the government,
- the "fruitless expenditure" of intellectual efforts by some of the country's ablest lawyers, accountants and administrators in the economically unproductive tax avoidance battle,
- the "sense of injustice and inequality" felt by those who are unable (e.g., salary or wage earners) or unwilling to benefit from it,
- the "deterioration of tax morality" when widespread tax avoidance may foster tax evasion by taxpayers who cannot benefit from tax avoidance, and
- the unfair shifting of the avoided tax burden to other taxpayers.[12]

The definition of and attitude toward tax avoidance under the Canadian tax law has not changed much since then. The Canadian tax law and scholarship still defines tax avoidance broadly but they do not condemn all of its forms.[13] Today's definition of tax avoidance includes strategies both expressly allowed by the tax law, which can be called "legitimate tax avoidance", and those achieved through exploiting some deficiencies or inconsistencies in the law, which are often referred to as "abusive tax avoidance".

Legitimate tax avoidance

In Canada taxpayers can take advantage of tax benefits by putting their money into certain forms of savings plans: tax-free savings account (TFSA),[14] registered retirement savings plan

---

9 *Report of the Royal Commission on Taxation*, Vol. 3 (Canada: Ottawa Royal Commision 1966), 538, available at http://publications.gc.ca/collections/collection_2014/bcp-pco/Z1-1962-1-3-3-eng.pdf
10 Ibid., 539–40.
11 Ibid., 542.
12 Ibid., 541–2.
13 P. W. Hogg, J. E. Magee and J. Li, *Principles of Canadian Income Tax Law*, 8th ed. (Toronto: Carswell, 2013), 635–6.
14 ITA § 146.2 (2016) (Can.). According to the TFSA rules, a certain amount of money contributed to the account accumulates tax-free in the account and will not be taxed when withdrawn).

(RRSP),[15] and registered education savings plan (RESP).[16] Likewise, certain individuals, corporations and partnerships can also benefit from so-called "rollover" rules, which allow them to defer the recognition of income or gains on qualified corporate reorganizations or transfers of property when they elect for such deferrals.[17] The law also allows certain corporations to benefit from a preferential tax regime under the "small business deduction" rules.[18]

ITA prescribes these tax relief schemes for social, economic, or other policy reasons. Government believes that without the inducement offered by the statute, such investments may not be undertaken by taxpayers. Technically, these are legitimate tax avoidance schemes as the law manifestly offers them; and the taxpayers are free to elect for them and, if they do, may avoid paying a substantial amount of taxes.

Abusive tax avoidance

Then there are abusive avoidance schemes, which occur as a result of taxpayers employing sophisticated schemes that often involve series of transactions and the combined application of various technical provisions of ITA to these transactions to produce a tax advantage that the legislator has neither prescribed for nor intended it to occur. These transactions not only attempt to obtain a tax benefit, but do so in a manner that is inconsistent with the intent of the legislator. These are the types of tax avoidance schemes that the Canadian GAAR targets.

History of GAAR

The introduction of GAAR into the Canadian tax law is often linked to the SCC's 1984 decision in *Stubart Investments Ltd. v. Revenue.* The facts of the case were relatively simple:[19] A parent company had two subsidiaries: Stubart Investments Ltd (Stubart) and Grover Cast Stone Co. Ltd (Grover). Stubart operated a profitable business of manufacturing food flavorings, while Grover operated an unprofitable business with substantial losses manufacturing construction products. Grover's losses had accumulated and been carried over to future years without much hope for their utilization.

Considering the prospect of losses going to waste, the parent company devised and executed the following tax plan: in 1966 Stubart sold the assets of its profitable business to Grover. Having acquired the assets, Grover appointed Stubart as its agent to operate the acquired business. Stubart thus continued to operate the business as usual but now as Grover's agent and paid its

---

15 ITA § 146(5) (2016) (Can.). The RRSP is a private retirement savings plan that can be established by individuals for their own retirement. A certain amount of money can be contributed annually to the account. The contribution is tax-deductible, and the account accumulates tax-free but any withdrawal from the account is subject to tax.

16 ITA § 146.1 (2016) (Can.). The RESP is designed to enable taxpayers to save for post-secondary education of their beneficiaries. Under the RESP rule, an amount of money contributed to the RESP accumulates tax-free in the account and the accumulated income is taxed only when withdrawn from the account.

17 ITA § 85 (2016) (Can.) (tax-deferred transfer of property to a corporation), ITA § 97(2) (2016) (Can.) (tax-deferred transfer of property to a partnership), ITA § 85.1, § 86(1) (2016) (Can.) (tax-deferred exchanges).

18 ITA § 125 (2016) (Can.). The basic federal corporate tax rate in Canada is 38%, which will be reduced to 28% after the application of 10% provincial abatement. Under the small business deduction rules, certain Canadian-controlled private corporations (CCPCs) are entitled to claim a small business deduction of 17.5% on active business income earned in Canada. This brings the net federal corporate tax rate for active business income of these corporations to 10.5%.

19 See *Stubart Investments Ltd. v. The Queen,* 1 S.C.R. 536 (1984) § 3–6.

profits over to Grover. Grover declared the income for tax purposes at the end of the 1966, 1967 and 1968 fiscal years, respectively, but it offset its accumulated losses from its construction business against the income from the food flavoring business it purchased from Stubart. Once Grover's accumulated tax losses had been fully utilized, the business assets were supposed to be sold back to Stubart.

The revenue authorities reassessed Stubart, and allocated the income from the food flavoring business back to Stubart, thereby rejecting the claim that the profits belonged to Grover. Stubart challenged the reassessment and initiated an appeal. After all the lower level courts upheld the tax authority's position, the case ultimately reached the SCC.

The case-specific question before the court was whether a corporate taxpayer with the purpose of reducing its taxes can establish an arrangement whereby future profits are routed through a sister subsidiary in order to avail itself of the latter corporation's loss carry-forward. The tax authorities argued that the *bona fide* business purpose doctrine[20] must be used to resolve the issue as the facts of the case and the taxpayer openly admitted that the undertaken transaction had no purpose other than the utilization of losses in the sister corporation, i.e. the taxpayer had undertaken the transactions only to avoid the tax. Therefore, more general questions before the court were whether the tax authority is entitled to ignore the sale transaction between Stubart and Grover on that ground alone, and whether the *bona fide* business purpose doctrine is a part of Canadian tax law to curtail tax avoidance transactions. The court rejected the application of the business purpose test and upheld the taxpayer's position on a number of grounds.

First, the court noted that using the business purpose test to decide the case at hand was a complete rejection of the Duke of Westminster principle,[21] which was too entrenched in Canadian tax law, and it would be improper for the judiciary to undermine this principle without a proper legislation.[22]

The court also refused to challenge the transaction between Stubart and Grover on the sole reason that it was entered into by them without an independent or *bona fide* business purpose. The court recognized that the tax statute today is a mix of fiscal and economic policy. The economic policy element of the Act sometimes takes the form of an inducement to the taxpayer to undertake or redirect a specific activity. Without the inducement offered by the statute, the activity may not be undertaken by the taxpayer for whom the induced action would otherwise have no *bona fide* business purpose. Requiring the taxpayers' decisions always to have *bona fide* reasons may therefore run counter to the apparent legislative intent of the Parliament.[23]

The SCC suggested that rather than searching for a *bona fide* business purpose in a transaction, it would be more appropriate to look at the object and spirit of the relevant provisions of the tax law to determine whether the taxpayer's transaction would frustrate this object and spirit. This would involve analyzing the Parliament's express intention behind the relevant tax provisions. This approach later became known as "purposive approach" to statutory interpretation.[24]

---

20 The business purpose doctrine was originally developed by the US judiciary in *Gregory v. Helvering* and forms a part of tax law principles in the US. The main idea behind the doctrine is that no transaction is valid in the income tax computation process that has not been entered into by the taxpayer for a *bona fide* business purpose. By definition, an independent business purpose does not include tax reduction for its own sake. See *Gregory v. Helvering*, 293 US 465 (1935); *Knetsch v. United States*, 364 US 361 (1960).

21 See above for a brief discussion on the Duke of Westminster principle.

22 *Stubart Investments Ltd. v. The Queen*, 1 SCR 536 (1984), para. 71–72.

23 Ibid., para. 55.

24 *Canada Trustco Mortgage Co. v. Canada*, 2005 SCC 54 (Can.), para. 40–62.

In the case of *Stubart*, the court found that neither the loss carry-forward provisions nor any other provision of ITA had been shown to reveal a parliamentary intent to bar the taxpayer from entering into such a binding transaction and make the payments to Grover. Once the tax loss concept is included in the statute, the revenue collector is exposed to the chance, if not the inevitability, of the reduction of future tax collections to the extent that a credit is granted for past losses.[25] The court could not discern that the utilization of the carried over loss within a non-arm's length corporate group was inconsistent with the object and spirit of the provision of the ITA.

Concerned with these implications, the Department of Finance began to seriously examine ways to address the problem of tax avoidance post *Stubart*.[26] Traditionally, whenever the Canada Revenue Agency (CRA) discovers a major aggressive tax avoidance scheme, it requests the Department of Finance to propose a corresponding legislative change to outlaw the scheme. The Carter Report called this the "sniper" approach, in the sense that the approach contemplates the enactment of specific provisions, which identify with precision the type of transaction to be dealt with and prescribe with precision the tax consequences of such a transaction.[27] Sometimes the Department of Finance waited to see if the courts would remedy the issue rather than proposing a specific legislative change. However, in *Stubart* this did not quite happen. So, there was a need for another legislative reaction. Now, the question was how the legislative reaction ought to be devised.

The Department of Finance could follow its tradition of proposing a specific anti-avoidance rule, but the Department was already very frustrated with the implications of this approach. First, specific anti-avoidance rules do not effectively deal with transactions completed before the amendments introduced. In most cases any completed, and partially completed, transactions get "grandfathered" in under the specific anti-avoidance rules.[28] Krishna calls this situation "closing the barn door after the horses have bolted".[29] Second, although such detailed rules are sometimes required, they make ITA tremendously complex. Finally, the Department was also concerned with the fact that specific anti-avoidance rules, in some cases, constitute a roadmap for sophisticated taxpayers. In other words, any particularization of the tax law breeds avoidance. Specific anti-avoidance rules show taxpayers what the government has thought about, and the limits of the rule with fair precision, and thereby enable tax advisers to plot their way around the edge.[30]

Hence, one viable option before the Department of Finance was to propose a general rule to be enacted in ITA intended to curtail what ITA, the specific anti-avoidance rules, and the judiciary failed to curtail. Thus, in 1987 the Department of Finance released the White Paper

---

25 *Stubart Investments Ltd. v. The Queen*, 1 SCR 536 (1984), para. 67.

26 M. H. Wilson, *The Budget Speech Delivered in the House of Commons: Securing Economic Renewal* (Ottawa, 1987), 10, available at www.budget.gc.ca/pdfarch/1987-sd-eng.pdf.

27 Canada, *Report of the Royal Commission on Taxation*, Vol. 3 (Ottawa: Ottawa Royal Commision, 1966), 552, available at http://publications.gc.ca/collections/collection_2014/bcp-pco/Z1-1962-1-3-3-eng.pdf.

28 *Minutes of Proceedings and Evidence of the Standing Committee on Finance and Economic Affairs on June 29, 1987*, Vol. 76 (Ottawa: House of Commons, 1987), 76:6. The Department of Finance representative, Mr. Jim Wilson's testimony at the House of Commons' Standing Committee on Finance and Economic Affairs.

29 V. Krishna gives a thorough description of these challenges in his seminal work on tax avoidance. See V. Krishna, *Tax Avoidance: The General Anti-Avoidance Rule* (Toronto: Carswell, 1990), 28–30.

30 The Department of Finance representative, Mr. J. Wilson's testimony at the House of Commons' Standing Committee on Finance and Economic Affaires. See *Minutes of Proceedings and Evidence of the Standing Committee on Finance and Economic Affaires on June 29, 1987*, Vol. 76 (Ottawa: House of Commons, 1987), 76:6–7.

on Tax Reform.[31] The White Paper contained a proposed general rule on anti-avoidance.[32] Even though the House of Commons Standing Committee on Finance and Economic Affairs disagreed with the initial formulation of the rule, it acknowledged that such a rule was necessary.[33]

---

31 M. H. Wilson, *The White Paper: Tax Reform 1987* (Ottawa: Minister of Supply and Services, 1987).

32 The initial draft of the proposed legislation was tabled with the Parliament on June 18, 1987. The legislation reads as follows:

"1. Subsection 245(1) of the Income Tax Act is repealed and the following substituted therefor:

General Anti-Avoidance Provision. 245(1). Notwithstanding any other provision of this Act, where a transaction is an avoidance transaction, the income, taxable income, tax payable or other amount payable of or refundable to any person under this Act shall be determined as is reasonable in the circumstances ignoring the transaction.

Avoidance transaction. 245(2). An avoidance transaction includes:

(a) any transaction that results in a significant reduction, avoidance, deferral or refund of tax or other amounts payable under this Act, unless the transaction may reasonably be considered to have been carried out primarily for *bona fide* business purposes; or

(b) any transaction that is part of a series of transactions or events, which series results in a significant reduction, avoidance, deferral or refund of tax or other amount payable under this Act, unless the transaction may reasonably be considered to have been carried out primarily for *bona fide* business purposes.

Interpretation. 245(3). For the purpose of this section,

(a) "transaction" includes an arrangement, scheme, or event; and

(b) for greater certainty, the reduction, avoidance, deferral or refund of tax or other amount payable under this Act shall not be considered to be a *bona fide* business purpose.

Adjustments. 245(4). Where subsection (1) applies, in determining the income, taxable income, tax payable or other amount payable of or refundable to any person under this Act as is reasonable in the circumstances, without restricting the generality of the foregoing,

(a) any deduction in computing income, taxable income, or tax payable or any part thereof may be disallowed in whole or in part;

(b) any such deduction, and any income, loss or other amount or part thereof may be allocated to any other person; and

(c) the nature of any payment or other amount may be recharacterized.

Adjustments by the Minister or on request. 245(5). For the purpose of this section,

(a) the Minister, in order to eliminate double taxation, may make any adjustment to income, taxable income, tax payable, or other amount payable or refundable under this Act of any person other than a person referred to in subsection (4), and the Minister shall notify the person of the adjustment within a reasonable time;

(b) Any person other than a person referred to in subsection (4) shall be entitled, within 90 days of the day of mailing of any notice of assessment to any person for the year in which the avoidance transaction occurred, to request the Minister to make an adjustment pursuant to paragraph (a), and where the Minister refused to make an adjustment the person shall be notified of such refusal within a reasonable time; and

(c) The provisions of paragraph 56(1)(l) and 60(o) and Division I and J, as they relate to an assessment or a reassessment and to assessing and reassessing tax, are applicable, with such modifications as the circumstances required, to a refusal to make an adjustment under paragraph (b).

Purpose. 245(6). The purpose of this section is to consider artificial tax avoidance."

33 Some major changes that the Finance Committee recommended to the House of Commons as a result of their review of the proposed legislation on GAAR were: (a) the word "significant" be dropped from the definition of avoidance transactions so that any artificial or undue deferral of tax could be considered an avoidance transaction; (b) denied to incorporate the business purpose test into ITA, thus eliminating the need for the business purpose test in a transaction or a series of transactions because the test is not suitable for the structure of ITA that often serves as an instrument of socio-economic policies. *House of Commons Finance Committee Report on the Proposed General Anti-Avoidance Rule*, House of Commons Standing Committee on Finance and Economic Affairs (16 November 1987).

The revised draft legislation was introduced as part of Bill C-139, and it received Royal Assent on 13 September 1988. Thus, 4 years after the SCC's decision in *Stubart*, GAAR was introduced into the Canadian income tax law.

Having reviewed *Stubart*, one may wonder whether there was any need for GAAR in Canada in the first place, given the court's recommendation for the purposive interpretation of taxing statute in deciding tax avoidance cases in the future, and given that the current GAAR simply crystalized this common law principle into a law without much modification. However, a closer analysis of the decision may reveal some controversies within the decision that the legislature wanted to address:

"(a) The court expressly affirmed the Duke of Westminster principle as a good law in Canada.[34] Even though the court affirmed the principle in relation to the business purpose doctrine, the result was still a big victory for taxpayers and their advisers;

(b) The court also endorsed the purposive approach in construing the tax statute in relation to tax avoidance schemes. The court hoped that such interpretation would be "appropriate to reduce the action and reaction endlessly produced by complex, specific tax measures aimed at sophisticated business practices, and the inevitable, professionally-guided, and equally specialized taxpayer reaction" and would therefore reduce aggressive tax avoidance schemes in the future.[35] This part of the decision gave some comfort to CRA.

(c) The court rejected the business purpose doctrine as a standalone test in determining abusive tax avoidance schemes. The result of this rejection would expose all taxpayers, even those who enter into a transaction with *bona fide* purposes, to a more broadly stated object and spirit test."

These elements of the decision may bring a person into confusion, especially when (a) and (b) read together. It was quite debatable to see the two fairly conflicting interpretation principles being affirmed within the same decision. The Duke of Westminster principle generally suggests that a person is subject to tax only if the taxpayer is within the clear meaning of the words of the tax statute; the object and spirit of the provision or its purpose are irrelevant. On the other hand, as will be discussed later in this chapter, the purposive approach to statutory interpretation suggests that the literal, ordinary, or plain meaning of the tax provision alone is not determinative and that the interpretative task must also consider its context and purpose.

After all, result of the case was its further contribution to the existing uncertainty in the Canadian tax law. This time, the uncertainty played well for the benefit of some taxpayers. A quick review of the jurisprudence occurred between 1984 and 1988 (i.e. the time between the release of the *Stubart* decision and the introduction of GAAR) confirms judges' reluctance

---

34 *Stubart Investments Ltd. v. The Queen*, [1984] 1 S.C.R. 536, § 61 (Can.), para. 71–72. Justice Estey states: "The question then is whether the Minister is entitled to ignore it on that ground alone. If he is, then a massive inroad is made into Lord Tomlin's dictum that "Every man is entitled if he can to order his affairs so that the tax attaching under the appropriate Acts is less than it would otherwise be". Indeed, it seems to me that the business purpose test is a complete rejection of Lord Tomlin's principle … I think Lord Tomlin's principle is far too deeply entrenched in our tax law for the courts to reject it in the absence of clear statutory authority. No such authority has been put to us in this case.

35 Ibid., para. 66: "These interpretative guidelines, modest though they may be, and which fall well short of the *bona fide* business purpose test advanced by the respondent, are in my view appropriate to reduce the action and reaction endlessly produced by complex, specific tax measures aimed at sophisticated business practices, and the inevitable, professionally-guided and equally specialized taxpayer reaction. Otherwise, where the substance of the Act, when the clause in question is contextually construed, is clear and unambiguous and there is no prohibition in the Act which embraces the taxpayer, the taxpayer shall be free to avail himself of the beneficial provision in question." See also para. 60.

to apply or properly apply the "purposive interpretation".[36] Instead, the courts continued to implicitly or explicitly rely on the Duke of Westminster principle. It is against this background that the government decided to intervene with a legislative reaction, i.e. the introduction of GAAR that would limit taxpayers' and the court's reliance on the principle and that would statutorily crystalize the purposive approach to interpretation.

Statutory scheme and interpretation of the Canadian GAAR

Main rule

The Canadian GAAR is complex and involves a multi-stage determination process. The main provisions are contained in Part XVI (Tax Avoidance) of ITA: subsections 245(2), 245(3), and 245(4) of ITA.

Subsection 245(2) stipulates the general tax consequence when a transaction is found to be subject to GAAR; subsection 245(3) sets the main conditions that a transaction must meet for GAAR to apply; subsection 245(4) is a provision that relieves certain transactions that otherwise would be subject to GAAR from the scope of the rule. These rules will be described in detail below.

The general rule of anti-avoidance is contained in subsection 245(2) of ITA. It reads as follows:

> Where a transaction is an avoidance transaction, the tax consequences to a person shall be determined as is reasonable in the circumstances in order to deny a tax benefit that, but for this section, would result, directly or indirectly, from that transaction or from a series of transactions that includes that transaction.

This provision, in effect, denies the taxpayer any tax benefit resulting from a transaction or from a series of transactions that includes the avoidance transaction. In other words, avoidance transactions are ignored for tax purposes and the taxpayer's position is determined without reference to that transaction. The language of the provision may suggest that subsection 245(2) is actually a charging provision on its own right; however, some commentators argue that the provision is not a charging provision but merely an interpretative tool. This is because GAAR applies only where it is clear that a tax otherwise payable under specific provisions of ITA has been reduced, avoided, or deferred in circumstances amounting to a misuse or an abuse.[37]

Conditions

As stipulated in subsection 245(2) above, GAAR applies where a transaction is classified as an "avoidance transaction". The ITA lists the main conditions for a transaction to be considered as avoidance transaction under Subsection 245(3). It stipulates as follows:

"An avoidance transaction means any transaction

    (a) that, but for this section, would result, directly or indirectly, in a tax benefit, unless the transaction may reasonably be considered to have been undertaken or arranged primarily for *bona fide* purposes other than to obtain the tax benefit; or

---

36 *Farrell v. Minister of National Revenue*, [1985] 2 C.T.C. 2222; *Shore v. Minister of National Revenue*, [1986] 1 C.T.C. 2360; *R. v. Parsons*, [1984] 2 F.C. 909.

37 T. E. McDonnell, *Conference Report on Legislative Anti-Avoidance: The Interaction of the New General Rule and Representative Specific Rules* (Toronto: Canadian Tax Foundation, 1988), 29.

(b) that is part of a series of transactions, which series, but for this section, would result, directly or indirectly, in a tax benefit, unless the transaction may reasonably be considered to have been undertaken or arranged primarily for *bona fide* purposes other than to obtain the tax benefit."

This provision sets two important conditions for a transaction to be considered an avoidance transaction:

Tax benefit

The first step in determining the avoidance transaction is to establish whether there is a tax benefit that results directly or indirectly from a transaction or a series of transactions.[38] This is often referred to as the "tax benefit" test. ITA defines a "tax benefit" as "a reduction, avoidance or deferral of tax or other amount payable under this Act or an increase in a refund of tax or other amounts under this Act, and includes a reduction, avoidance or deferral of tax or other amount that would be payable under this Act but for a tax treaty or an increase in a refund of tax or other amount under this Act or as a result of a tax treaty".[39] A tax benefit can be achieved through deferring the recognition of income, accelerating the recognition of deductions, re-characterizing income from highly taxed categories (e.g. employment or investment income) into non-taxable (e.g. windfall or gift) or lightly taxed (e.g. capital gains, active business income) categories, and shifting income or losses between taxpayers (e.g. income splitting).

Whether a tax benefit exists is a question of fact made initially by CRA, and on review by the courts. In most cases, establishing the existence of a tax benefit is relatively straightforward, but in other cases, the courts have used a comparative approach.[40] If the comparative approach was used, the courts found a tax benefit by comparing the taxpayer's situation with an alternative arrangement.[41] The alternative approach must be the one that might reasonably have been carried out but for the existence of the tax benefit. For example, characterization of an amount as a capital gain, rather than as business income or investment income would result in differential tax treatment under the Canadian tax system as only one half of a capital gain is taxable.[42] The burden is generally on the taxpayer to rebut the existence of the tax benefit. And the quantum of the benefit is not relevant for the determination of tax benefit.

Non-tax purpose

The second condition in determining whether a transaction is an avoidance transaction is that the transaction has not been undertaken or arranged primarily for *bona fide* purposes but only

---

38 The concept of a series of transactions is found in ITA § 248(10) (2016) (Can.) and generally means any related transactions or events completed in contemplation of the series.

39 ITA § 245(1) (2016) (Can.).

40 *Canada Trustco Mortgage Co. v. Canada*, 2005 SCC 54, § 18–20 (Can.); *Copthorne Holdings Ltd. v. Canada*, [2011] 3 SCR 721, § 34–38 (Can.).

41 Ibid.

42 ITA § 38 (2016) (Can.).

to obtain the tax benefit.[43] In other words, subsection 245(3) indicates that a transaction is not considered an avoidance transaction if it can reasonably be considered to have been undertaken or arranged primarily for *bona fide* non-tax purposes. Here the term "primarily" ensures that a transaction will not be considered to be an avoidance transaction simply because it results in a tax benefit. Therefore, if the transaction has tax and non-tax purposes, the primary purpose must be established.[44] The *bona fide* non-tax purposes may be business, investment, family, or personal purposes. If the analysis reveals that the transaction that results in a tax benefit has been motivated purely or primarily by tax reasons, the transaction is considered to be an "avoidance transaction", and is moved to the next level of analysis, which is discussed in the following section. The overall purpose of this determination was to remove from the grasp of the GAAR transactions or series of transactions that have been undertaken or arranged primarily for non-tax purposes.[45]

Relieving provision

Labeling a transaction as an avoidance transaction under subsection 245(3) is not by itself sufficient to apply GAAR. This is especially true given the fairly low threshold for establishing the existence of a tax benefit and the absence of a *bona fide* purpose. Subsection 245(4) of ITA provides that avoidance transactions, as determined under subsection 245(3) of ITA, are subject to GAAR only if they meet one more condition. This final condition functions as an exception to the application of GAAR. The provision reads:

"Subsection (2) applies to a transaction only if it may reasonably be considered that the transaction

(a) would, if this Act were read without reference to this section, result directly or indirectly in a misuse of the provisions of any one or more of

(i) this Act,
(ii) the Income Tax Regulations,
(iii) the Income Tax Application Rules,
(iv) a tax treaty, or
(v) any other enactment that is relevant in computing tax or any other amount payable by or refundable to a person under this Act or in determining any amount that is relevant for the purposes of that computation; or

(b) would result directly or indirectly in an abuse having regard to those provisions, other than this section, read as a whole."

This provision suggests GAAR applies to an avoidance transaction only if it would result directly or indirectly in a misuse of the provisions of the Act, the Regulations or a tax treaty; or would result in an abuse of the provisions read as a whole. Otherwise, it exempts the transaction from the ambit of GAAR.

---

43 ITA § 245(3) (2016) (Can.). In statutory interpretation, this requirement is often referred to as "business purpose test". The first judicial reference to the "business purpose test" is seen in the Exchequer Court's decision in *Smythe v. MNR*, [1967] C.T.C. 498 (Can.). In this case, the court held that a transaction was not *bona fide* as it did not have a legitimate business purpose.
44 *OSFC Holdings Ltd. v. Canada*, 2001 DTC 5471 (FCA, Can.).
45 *Canada Trustco Mortgage Co. v. Canada*, 2005 SCC 54, § 21 (Can.); Evans, 2005 DTC 1762 (TCC, Can.).

In practice, subsection 245(4) sets a very high and difficult test to apply GAAR. The provision involves a two-stage determination process:[46]

(a) identifying and interpreting the relevant provision or provisions of ITA relied upon by the taxpayer to obtain the tax benefit and determining object, spirit, and purpose of the provision. This step requires the court to look beyond the text of the provision and determine parliament's express purpose when adopting the provision. The idea is to determine the rationale that underlie the applicable provision;[47] and

(b) analyzing the taxpayer's transaction or series of transactions to determine whether the impugned transaction would frustrate the underlying purposes that have been identified under the first stage. The terms "abuse" and "misuse" are integral part of the determination in this process.

Thus, the application of subsection 245(4) relies heavily on statutory interpretation. In the absence of subsection 245(4), the *bona fide* purpose test under subsection 245(3) would expose many purely or primarily tax motivated transactions to GAAR. As noted by the court in *Stubart*, this may be contrary to the object of ITA, which as a matter of tax policy, envisages or condones some activities which may be primarily or purely tax-motivated. Thus, this final determination process allows certain tax-motivated transactions from the ambit of GAAR if they do not "abuse" and "misuse" the specific tax provision.

Overall, the Canadian GAAR functions under a cascade mechanism. First, one must determine whether there is a tax benefit resulting from a transaction. If not, the transaction automatically falls out of the scope of GAAR. If there is a tax benefit, the next question to be asked is whether this tax benefit results from a transaction that is motivated by tax or *bona fide* non-tax reasons. Subsection 245(3) relieves transactions arranged purely or primarily for *bona fide* non-tax purposes from GAAR. The transactions that are arranged purely or primarily for tax reasons are labeled as "avoidance transactions" and are brought to the next level of analysis under subsection 245(4). Subsection 245(4) then requires analyzing these transactions to see if they may reasonably be considered to have resulted, directly or indirectly, in a misuse of specific taxing provision or an abuse having regard to those provisions read as a whole.

In other words, the GAAR targets only a transaction that (a) results in a tax benefit, and (b) has been motivated primarily by tax reasons, and, finally, (c) has resulted, directly or indirectly, in a misuse of specific provisions of ITA.

When transaction is challenged under GAAR, the burden of proof under subsection 245(3) rests with the taxpayer, while the burden under subsection 245(4) rests with the tax authority.[48] This requires the taxpayer to be able to refute the tax authorities' factual assumption on the existence of a tax benefit. Since the taxpayer has knowledge of the factual background of the transaction, it is also the taxpayer who has to show the existence of a *bona fide* non-tax purpose in the transaction. On the other hand, tax authorities must identify the object, spirit or purpose of the provisions that it claims to have been frustrated or defeated by the transaction.

---

46 *OSFC Holdings Ltd. v. Canada*, 2001 DTC 5471, § 44 (FCA, Can.). Ibid., at § 38.
47 *Copthorne Holdings Ltd v. R*, vol. 2 C.T.C. 29, § 70 (2012) (SC, Can.).
48 *Canada Trustco Mortgage Co. v. Canada*, 2005 SCC 54, para. 63–64 (Can.).

Sources of the Canadian GAAR

The SCC decided the case of *Stubart* in favor of the taxpayer, but the decision also laid the groundwork for the construction of the Canadian GAAR.[49] The GAAR reflects all the key common law doctrines that were extensively discussed in *Stubart*. These include the *"bona fide* business purpose doctrine", "step transactions doctrine," and finally the SCC's own "legislative purpose and intent doctrine". This section briefly examines the integration of these doctrines into the Canadian GAAR.

Bona fide business purpose doctrine

As discussed previously, the first test for the application of GAAR is that the transaction must be an avoidance transaction. One of the crucial elements of the avoidance transaction is that it has been undertaken or arranged not primarily for *bona fide* purposes but to obtain a tax benefit.[50] This provision in essence aims at sorting out artificial tax avoidance transactions from those transactions that are motivated primarily by legitimate commercial or personal reasons.

The doctrine was first introduced in the United States in *Gregory v. Helvering*.[51] In its pure form, the *bona fide* business purpose doctrine assumes that the tax law has been drafted to deal with business or commercial transactions, and a transaction must be ignored for tax purposes if the only reason for undertaking it is to save taxes. As discussed previously, the Canadian court rejected to apply the business purpose doctrine in *Stubart* on two grounds: (a) potential conflicts that may result from the application of the doctrine and the government economic policies to be achieved through some provisions of the tax statute (i.e. discussed elsewhere in this article); (b) the applicability of the doctrine only to transactions occurring in a business context. In relation to the latter reasoning, the court notes "the business purpose doctrine is an appropriate tool for testing the tax effectiveness of a transaction, where the language, nature and purposes of the provision of the tax law under construction indicate a function, pattern and design characteristic solely of business transactions".[52]

Following the court's rejection of the business purpose doctrine in *Stubart*, the Canadian GAAR adopted a principle that reflect some elements of the doctrine. Subsection 245(3) contains the term *"bona fide* purposes". The main reason for this modification is that the ITA defines the word "business" strictly to mean activities of commercial nature.[53] Hence, a reference to the business purpose in the ITA would refer to a business context and therefore transactions carried out in a non-business context may fail to meet the business purpose test, even if they are carried out primarily for non-tax purposes, e.g. social or economic purposes. On the other hand, the term *"bona fide* purpose" explicitly encompasses all purposes other than tax.[54]

---

49 *Stubart Investments Ltd. v. The Queen*, [1984] 1 S.C.R. 536, para 65 (Can.).

50 ITA § 245(3) (2016) (Can.).

51 *Gregory v. Helvering*, 293 U.S. 465 (1935).

52 Ibid., 65.

53 See definition of business under ITA § 248(1) (2016) (Can.). "Business" includes a profession, calling, trade, manufacture or undertaking of any kind whatever and, except for the purposes of para. 18(2)(c), section 54.2, subsection 95(1) and para. 110.6(14)(f), an adventure or concern in the nature of trade but does not include an office or employment.

54 B. J. Arnold and J. R. Wilson, "The General Anti-Avoidance Rules – Part 2", 36:5 *Canadian Tax Journal* 1123, 1155 (1988).

Step transactions doctrine

Generally, an avoidance transaction is a single transaction carried out primarily to obtain a tax benefit; however, in practice such transaction may involve multiple independent steps. Courts developed the step transactions doctrine to analyze the existence of tax avoidance in such multi-transactional schemes. The leading two cases that developed and comprehensively applied the doctrine were *W T Ramsay Ltd v. IRC* and *Furniss v. Dawson*, both UK cases.[55]

The facts of the landmark UK case, *Ramsay Ltd v. IRC* [1981] are interesting and very useful to explain the basic concept of step transactions. The taxpayer was a farming company, which realized a large taxable capital gain (£187,977) on the sale of its land. In order to avoid paying taxes on the capital gain, the taxpayer purchased a ready-made tax avoidance scheme, which involved a number of steps. According to the scheme, Ramsay purchased the shares of a newly formed investment company. At the same time, the taxpayer extended to the new company two shareholder loans of equal amount (£218,750 each) at an interest rate of 11%. Under the terms of the loan agreements, the interest on one loan could be increased as long as there was a corresponding decrease in the interest rate charged on the other loan. As soon as the loans were extended, the parties reduced the interest rate on one loan to zero and increased the interest rate on the other loan to 22%. Following a decision that the company should be wound up, the zero interest loan became repayable to the taxpayer at par, while the loan with 22% interest became repayable at a price of £394,673. As a result of these transactions, the value of the shares of the company was drastically reduced and resulted in an artificial capital loss to Ramsay. By applying the step transactions doctrine and analyzing the transactions as a whole, the House of Lords concluded there was neither a gain nor a loss to the taxpayer as a result of this multi-step scheme. The ultimate purpose of this circular, self-canceling scheme was nothing more than to create an artificial capital loss to offset Ramsay's capital gain realized on the sale of the land.

Thus, the idea behind the step transactions doctrine as applied in *Ramsay* was relatively simple. First, in examining the tax consequences of a series of transactions, it is suggested that each component part of the series of transactions is looked at as part of a collective whole in order to determine if the overall purpose of the transactions is to achieve a tax avoidance.[56] If tax avoidance is ascertained, the particular steps are disregarded for tax purposes as transitory events to achieve the overall purpose.

Conversely, each transaction is analyzed in isolation as if it were independent of the others. If at least one transaction in the series is an avoidance transaction, then the tax benefit that results from the series may be denied under GAAR. Thus, the fact that some of the transactions in the series of transactions have *bona fide* purposes does not preclude the tax-motivated transaction that form part of the series from being held as an avoidance transaction.

The Canadian GAAR reflects both forms of the step transactions doctrine. Subsection 245(3)(b) indicates that where a taxpayer, in carrying out a series of transactions, inserts a transaction that is not carried out primarily for *bona fide* non-tax purposes and the series results in a tax benefit, the transaction may be considered an avoidance transaction.[57] Thus, where a series of transactions result in a tax benefit, that tax benefit would be denied unless the primary purpose of each transaction in the series is to achieve some *bona fide* purpose. This consequence requires

55 *W T Ramsay Ltd v. IRC*, 2 W.L.R. 449 (1981) (HL, UK); *Furniss v. Dawson*, 1 All E.R. 530 (1984) (HL, UK).
56 *W T Ramsay Ltd v. IRC*, 2 W.L.R. 449, 180 (1981) (HL, UK).
57 CRA, Information Circular IC88–2: General Anti-Avoidance Rule – Section 245 (1988), § 4, available at www.cra-arc.gc.ca/E/pub/tp/ic88-2/ic88-2-e.html.

each transaction in the series of transactions to be tested for its purpose. The purpose test under subsection 245(3)(b) applies at the transaction level, not the series level.[58]

Earlier Canadian cases that applied the step transactions doctrine subsequent to the adoption of GAAR are *Lutheran Life Insurance Society v. Canada, RMM Canadian Enterprises Inc. et al. v. Canada, Singleton v. Canada, OSFC Holdings Ltd, Copthorne Holdings Ltd. v. R.*[59]

Legislative object and spirit doctrine

In reviewing the judicial doctrines applicable to tax avoidance in *Stubart*, the Supreme Court of Canada condemned the strict interpretation of tax statutes. The court quoted Dreidger: "Today there is only one principle or approach, namely, the words of an Act are to be read in their entire context and in their grammatical and ordinary sense harmoniously with the scheme of the Act, the object of the Act, and the intention of Parliament".[60] The court viewed the approach as an effective tool to fight against tax avoidance and to decrease legislative complexity. It noted:

> Such an approach would promote rather than interfere with the administration of the Income Tax Act, in both its aspects without interference with the granting and withdrawal, according to the economic climate, of tax incentives. The desired objective is a simple rule which will provide uniformity of application of the Act across the community, and at the same time, reduce the attraction of elaborate and intricate tax avoidance plans, and reduce the rewards to those best able to afford the services of the tax technicians.[61]

The doctrine was referred to as the "modern rule", and it was used to analyze the facts of the case. Therefore, *Stubart* also marks a change in the interpretation of the Canadian tax statutes from the traditional strict interpretation towards a more purposive one.

The Canadian Parliament decided that the modern rule or the "object and spirit" doctrine was embodied in GAAR under subsection 245(4) of ITA.[62]

Enforcement of the Canadian GAAR

One of the biggest challenges to apply the GAAR and counter abusive tax avoidance is to identify abusive avoidance transactions. CRA traditionally identified such transactions through its field audits and taxpayer applications for advance tax ruling. However, monitoring abusive tax avoidance through these very limited administrative strategies is insufficient to control the increasingly number of tax avoidance transaction. Under these circumstances, a significant number of abusive tax avoidance arrangements could escape unchecked as long as they do not fall into CRA's narrow "administrative radar".

---

58 P. Bleiwas and J. Hutson, *Taxation of Private Corporations and Their Shareholders*, 4th ed. (Toronto: Canadian Tax Foundation, 2010), 16:104.

59 *Lutheran Life Insurance Society v. Canada*, 91 DTC 5553 (1991) (FCTD, Can.); *RMM Canadian Enterprises Inc. et al. v. Canada*, 97 DTC 302 (1997) (TCC, Can.); *Singleton v. Canada*, 2001 DTC 5533 (SCC, Can.); *OSFC Holdings Ltd. v. Canada*, 2001 DTC 5471 (FCA, Can.); *Copthorne Holdings Ltd. v. R.*, SCC 63 (2011) (SCC, Can.).

60 *Stubart Investments Ltd. v. The Queen*, [1984] 1 S.C.R. 536, § 61 (Can.).

61 Ibid., §56.

62 Information Circular IC88–2: General Anti-Avoidance Rule – Section 245 (1988), § 5, available at www.cra-arc. gc.ca/E/pub/tp/ic88-2/ic88-2-e.html.

Reportable transactions

In order to identify potentially abusive tax avoidance transactions in an efficient and timely manner so that they can be properly reviewed, monitored and, if appropriate, challenged, the 2010 Federal Budget introduced for public consultation a new information reporting regime.[63] The new information reporting regime took effect in June 2013 and applies to certain avoidance transactions entered into after 2010. This reporting regime is contained in section 237.3 of the ITA and imposes a requirement for "reportable transactions" to be disclosed to the CRA on an annual basis.

Under this regime, reportable transactions are transactions that meet two requirements: first, the transaction must meet the conditions of avoidance transactions within the meaning of subsection 245(3); second, at any time the transaction must meet two of any of the following three hallmarks in respect of that avoidance transaction: (1) the tax advisor is remunerated with a "fee" based, at least in part, on the dollar value of the tax benefit resulting from the transaction or is contingent upon the obtaining of a tax benefit that results, or would result but for the GAAR, from the avoidance transaction,[64] (2) the tax advisor requires that the transaction remain confidential.[65] This is generally evidenced by the existence of an agreement that prohibits the participant from disclosing the details or structure of the transaction to any person; (3) the taxpayer or the advisor obtains "contractual protection".[66] The contractual protection means any form of protection against failure of the trans-

---

63 J. M. Flaherty, *Canada's Federal Budget Tabled in the House of Commons on 4 March 2010: Leading the Way on Jobs and Growth* (Ottawa, 2010), 382–4, available at www.budget.gc.ca/2010/pdf/budget-planbudgetaire-eng.pdf.

64 ITA § 237.3(1) (2016) (Can.). The provision reads:
"'fee', in respect of a transaction or series of transactions, means any consideration that is, or could be, received or receivable, directly or indirectly in any manner whatever, by an advisor or a promoter, or any person who does not deal at arm's length with an advisor or promoter, for –

(a) providing advice or an opinion with respect to the transaction or series;
(b) creating, developing, planning, organizing or implementing the transaction or series;
(c) promoting or selling an arrangement, plan or scheme that includes, or relates to, the transaction or series;
(d) preparing documents supporting the transaction or series, including tax returns or any information returns to be filed under the Act; or
(e) providing contractual protection."

65 ITA § 237.3(1) (2016) (Can.). The provision reads:
"'confidential protection', in respect of a transaction or series of transactions, means anything that prohibits the disclosure to any person or to the Minister of the details or structure of the transaction or series under which a tax benefit results, or would result but for section 245, but for greater certainty, the disclaiming or restricting of an advisor's liability shall not be considered confidential protection if it does not prohibit the disclosure of the details or structure of the transaction or series."

66 ITA § 237.3(1) (2016) (Can.). The provision reads:
"'contractual protection', in respect of a transaction or series of transactions, means

(a) any form of insurance (other than standard professional liability insurance) or other protection, including, without limiting the generality of the foregoing, an indemnity, compensation or a guarantee that, either immediately or in the future and either absolutely or contingently,
   (i) protects a person against a failure of the transaction or series to achieve any tax benefit from the transaction or series, or
   (ii) pays for or reimburses any expense, fee, tax, interest, penalty or similar amount that may be incurred by a person in the course of a dispute in respect of a tax benefit from the transaction or series; and

(b) any form of undertaking provided by a promoter, or by any person who does not deal at arm's length with a promoter, that provides, either immediately or in the future and either absolutely or contingently, assistance, directly or indirectly in any manner whatever, to a person in the course of a dispute in respect of a tax benefit from the transaction or series."

action or that pays for any expense, including tax, interest, penalties, or similar amounts, that may be incurred during a dispute about the tax benefit in respect of the transaction.

Even though these conditions are not themselves evidence of aggressive tax avoidance, their presence often indicates that the underlying transactions carry a higher risk of abuse of ITA.

The information reporting obligation is imposed on (a) the person for whom a tax benefit could result from an avoidance transaction or series, (b) any person who enters into an avoidance transaction for the benefit of another person (i.e. nominee or agent) and (c) any advisor or promoter who is entitled to a "fee" in circumstances described in the definition of "reportable transactions", and (d) any person not dealing at arm's length with an advisor or promoter with respect to the transaction and who is entitled to the fee described in (c) above.[67] Since the reporting obligation is imposed on multiple parties to the same transaction, a full and accurate disclosure of the reportable transaction by one of these parties is generally deemed to be the filing by every other party required to report the same transaction.[68]

The disclosure of a reportable transaction would not be considered in any way as an admission that GAAR applies to the transaction. The reporting requirement is simply intended to assist CRA in monitoring tax avoidance transactions in the light of GAAR. Non-compliance with the reporting obligations may entail strict penalties. Failure to report allows CRA to deny the tax benefit, ignoring the misuse and abuse test under subsection 245(4).[69] In other words, CRA would not have to argue that there is a misuse or an abuse of ITA to deny the tax benefit. If full and accurate disclosure is not made, ITA also imposes a penalty equal to the total of all fees that have been received by anyone in respect of the transaction.[70] Generally, persons who fail to fully satisfy their reporting obligations are jointly and severally liable for the penalty subject to a due diligence defense. A person is not liable to a penalty if the person has exercised the degree of care, diligence and skill to prevent the failure to file that a reasonably prudent person would have exercised in comparable circumstances (subsection 237.3(11)). Whether a person has exercised the degree of care, diligence and skill will be determined based on the facts and circumstances of each case.

Review for GAAR

Apart from the information obtained under subsection 237.3, the CRA also identified abusive tax avoidance transactions through referrals from the field auditors. In fact, until the new reporting mechanism was introduced, the majority of GAAR referrals originated from auditors' conducting regular audits[71] or from the CRA's Income Tax Rulings Directorate.[72] When CRA considers that a taxpayer is engaged in abusive tax avoidance, it first determines whether any (i.e. a technical or a specific anti-avoidance) provision contained in ITA can be applied to the transaction; if so, it reassesses the taxpayer based on that provision. If this is not possible, CRA determines whether GAAR can be resorted to.

67 ITA § 237.3(2) (2016) (Can.).
68 ITA § 237.3(4) (2016) (Can.).
69 ITA § 237.3(6) (2016) (Can.).
70 ITA § 273.3(8) (2016) (Can.).
71 Boyle, P., Gulliver, S., Lalonde, J., Lévesque, A.-M., and Lynch, P., "The GAAR Committee: Myth and Reality in Report of Proceedings of the Tax Conference" (2002), Conference Report at 2.
72 CRA, "Information Circular on Advance Income Tax Rulings and Technical Interpretations" (IC70-6R7) (22 April 2016), available at www.cra-arc.gc.ca/E/pub/tp/ic70-6r7/ic70-6r7-15e.pdf. The Income Tax Rulings Directorate is a department withn the CRA whose mandate is to provide CRA's technical interpretation of the Income Tax Act, the Income Tax Regulations and related statutes including Income Tax Conventions and provide advance income tax rulings on definite transactions or transactions that a taxpayer is contemplating.

If CRA considers it appropriate to reassess the taxpayer using GAAR, the case will be referred to CRA Headquarters for approval before issuing a reassessment. The tax offices are generally transparent to the taxpayers in their GAAR referral decisions and inform them of their intention to submit the case to the Headquarters and verify if the information to be forwarded for a GAAR review is accurate. Any additional submissions received from the taxpayer or the taxpayer's representative are required to be forwarded to the Headquarters in their entirety.[73] Once the case has been received by the CRA Headquarters, it will be referred to the GAAR Committee, unless the issue is substantially similar to one of the previously reviewed by the Committee.

The GAAR Committee is an ad hoc body, comprised of senior members from CRA, the representatives of the Department of Finance, and the Ministry of Justice, who all act in an advisory capacity.[74] The Committee meets periodically, normally biweekly. The meetings allow the Committee members to discuss the referred cases and provide ultimate recommendations on the application of GAAR. The taxpayers are not allowed to participate in the committee meetings. This is because of the committee's concerns that it does not intend to become a quasi-judicial and formal forum.[75]

If the committee is satisfied that there is enough information and a consensus is reached, the decision is to recommend whether GAAR should or should not be applied. If the recommendation is that GAAR should be applied, then there is a second step: deciding what the redetermined tax consequences should be.[76] CRA is not legally bound by the recommendations of the Committee but it is highly unlikely that it will proceed with a GAAR reassessment where the Committee does not recommend the GAAR application. As a result of the review process, the taxpayer receives a written response from CRA. This response will be to the submissions filed by the taxpayer.

Since 1988 through September 2013, the GAAR Committee has recommended that GAAR be applied in a total of 897 out of 1,163 cases (77% of all cases referred). Of them, 54 files made their way to the court where the Crown won in 28 cases and the taxpayer in 26 cases.[77] Historically, the four issues to which the GAAR Committee has most commonly recommended GAAR are surplus stripping, income splitting (including kiddie tax), loss creation via stock dividends, and issues involving cross-border taxation.[78]

Conclusions

Until the enactment of the Canadian GAAR, the line between legitimate and illegitimate tax avoidance was drawn largely by courts through statutory interpretation but often to the detriment of the tax authorities. The Duke of Westminster principle played a major role in this paradigm. The introduction of GAAR in 1988 has changed the paradigm. GAAR has set the

73 Boyle, P., Gulliver, S., Lalonde, J., Lévesque, A.-M., and Lynch, P., "The GAAR Committee: Myth and Reality in Report of Proceedings of the Tax Conference" (2002), Conference Report at 3.

74 W. Adams, "The General Anti-Avoidance Rule (GAAR) Committee in in Report of Proceedings of the Forty-Seventh Tax Conference" (1995), 1995 Conference Report, 1.

75 Ibid., 2.

76 Ibid., 6.

77 Auditor General of Canada, *2014 Spring Report on Aggressive Tax Planning* (Ottawa, Office of Auditor General of Canada, 2014), 8, available at www.oag-bvg.gc.ca/internet/English/parl_oag_201405_03_e_39334.html.

78 P. Hickey, "Canadian Tax Foundation's Annual Conference: CRA's GAAR Update" (2013), Canadian Tax Highlights.

statutory limit within which the Duke of Westminster would operate. It essentially shifted the boundaries of the taxpayers' right to engage in tax planning from the literal wording of the tax statute to what is believed to be its object and spirit.

Hence, one unique feature of the Canadian tax system may be that even though transactions are motivated purely or primarily by tax reasons, they may still escape from the application of GAAR as long as they can be swallowed by the provision's object and spirit. However, the determination of the legislative object and spirit has been an extremely difficult task and the law left this task largely to the courts. Thus, the Canadian courts have to deal with this complex task every time when they review the GAAR case.

Overall, even though GAAR has changed the way the Canadian courts traditionally viewed and approached tax avoidance transactions, it has not changed the fundamental principle that it is still the courts that determine the boundaries of acceptable and unacceptable tax avoidance. The rule has just clarified, somewhat modified and statutorily crystallized some fundamental interpretation principles that the Canadian courts were either uncertain or reluctant to apply to the avoidance transactions in the past. It provided them a statutory guidance in deciding on tax avoidance transactions in the future.

References

Adams, W. (1995). "The General Anti-Avoidance Rule (GAAR) Committee in in report of proceedings of the forty-seventh tax conference", 1995 Conference Report.

Arnold, B. J., and Wilson, J. R. (1988). "The general anti-avoidance rules – part 2", *Canadian Tax Journal*, 36(5), 1123.

Auditor General of Canada (2014). *2014 Spring Report on Aggressive Tax Planning*. Ottawa: Ottawa Office of Auditor General of Canada.

Bleiwas, P., and Hutson, J. (2010). *Taxation of Private Corporations and Their Shareholders*, 4th ed. Toronto: Canadian Tax Foundation.

Boyle, P., Gulliver, S., Lalonde, J., Lévesque, A.-M., and Lynch, P. (2002). "The GAAR Committee: Myth and reality in report of proceedings of the tax conference", 2002 Conference Report.

Canada (1996). *Report of the Royal Commission on Taxation*, Vol. 3. Ottawa: Ottawa Royal Commision.

Canada Trustco Mortgage Co. v. Canada, 2005 SCC 54, (Can.).

Copthorne Holdings Ltd v. R, vol. 2 C.T.C. 29 (2012) (SC, Can.).

CRA, "Information Circular on Advance Income Tax Rulings and Technical Interpretations" (IC70-6R7) from April 22, 2016

Flaherty, J. M. (2010). *Canada's Federal Budget Tabled in the House of Commons on March 4, 2010: Leading the Way on Jobs and Growth*. Ottawa: House of Commons.

Furniss v. Dawson, 1 All E.R. 530 (1984) (HL, UK).

Gregory v. Helvering, 293 U.S. 465 (1935).

Hickey, P. (2013). "Canadian tax foundation's annual conference: CRA's GAAR update", Canadian Tax Highlight.

Hogg, P. W., Magee, J. E., and Li, J. (2013). *Principles of Canadian Income Tax Law*, 8th ed. Toronto: Carswell.

House of Commons Finance Committee Report on the Proposed General Anti-Avoidance Rule. (1987). House of Commons Standing Committee on Finance and Economic Affairs.

Income Tax Act, 1985 (2016) (Can.).

Inland Revenue Commissioners v. Duke of Westminster (1936) (HL, UK).

Knetsch v. United States, 364 US 361 (1960).

Krishna, V. (1990). *Tax Avoidance: The General Anti-Avoidance Rule*. Toronto: Carswell.

Lipson v. Canada, [2009] 1 SCR 3, § 21 (Can.).

Lutheran Life Insurance Society v. Canada, 91 DTC 5553 (1991) (FCTD, Can.).

McDonnell, T. E. (1988). *Coference Report on Legislative Anti-Avoidance: The Interaction of the New General Rule and Representative Specific Rules*. Toronto: Canadian Tax Foundation.

Minutes of Proceedings and Evidence of the Standing Commitee on Finance and Economic Affaires on June 29, 1987, Vol. 76. (1987). Ottawa: House of Commons.

OSFC Holdings Ltd. v. Canada, 2001 DTC 5471 (FCA, Can.).

RMM Canadian Enterprises Inc. et al. v. Canada, 97 DTC 302 (1997) (TCC, Can.).

Singleton v. Canada, 2001 DTC 5533 (SC, Can.).

Stubart Investments Ltd. v. The Queen, [1984] 1 S.C.R. 536 (Can.).

W T Ramsay Ltd v. IRC, 2 W.L.R. 449 (1981) (HL, UK).

Wilson, M. H. (1987a). *The Budget Speech Delivered in the House of Commons: Securing Economic Renewal.* Ottawa: House of Commons.

Wilson, M. H. (1987b). *The White Paper: Tax Reform 1987*. Ottawa: Minister of Supply and Services.

8

FORMULATING A GENERAL ANTI-ABUSE RULE (GAAR) IN TAX LEGISLATION

Insights and recommendations

Reuven S. Avi-Yonah and Amir Pichhadze

The tools used to combat tax avoidance schemes

Courts around the world have repeatedly stated that taxpayers are "free to use their ingenuity to reduce their tax bills by any lawful means, however contrived those means might be and however far the tax consequences might diverge from the real economic position."[1] Yet, problems arise when, through tax avoidance schemes, tax law is misused to achieve a tax advantage that was not intended by the legislature. As the UK's HMRC explains, a tax avoidance scheme "often involves contrived, artificial transactions that serve little or no purpose other than to produce this advantage. It involves operating within the letter – but not the spirit – of the law."[2]

Tax avoidance schemes contribute, albeit in part, to the difference between, on the one hand, the amounts of tax that should be collectable by tax authorities and, on the other hand, the amount that actually gets collected. This difference, which represents a loss of otherwise taxable revenue, is referred to as a tax gap.[3] In the UK, for example, HMRC estimated that, for 2008–09, the tax gap was £42 billion, 17% of which is estimated to be the result of tax avoidance schemes.[4]

---

1 HM Revenue and Customs (2015), *GAAR Guidance*, para B2.1, 4, available at www.gov.uk/government/uploads/system/uploads/attachment_data/file/399270/2__HMRC_GAAR_Guidance_Parts_A-C_with_effect_from_30_January_2015_AD_V6.pdf. In the UK, for example, see: *Duke of Westminster v CIR* [1936] AC 1 at 19–21: "Every man is entitled if he can to order his affairs so as that the tax attaching under the appropriate Acts is less than it otherwise would be. If he succeeds in ordering them so as to secure this result, then, however unappreciative the Commissioners of Inland Revenue or his fellow taxpayers may be of his ingenuity, he cannot be compelled to pay an increased tax." See also *Fisher's Executors v. CIR* [1926] AC395; *Ayrshire Pullman v. CIR* (1929) 14 TC 754, 763–4. In the US, see *Gregory v Helvering*, 293 U.S. 465, 14 AFTR 1191 (1935), 469: "The legal right of a taxpayer to decrease the amount of what otherwise would be his taxes, or altogether avoid them, by means which the law permits, cannot be doubted."
2 HMRC, "Tackling Tax Evasion and Avoidance" (March 2015), 6, available at www.gov.uk/government/publications/tackling-tax-evasion-and-avoidance.
3 Ibid., 5.
4 Ibid., 7.

Not surprisingly, governments around the world attempt to combat aggressive tax avoidance schemes. In the UK, for example, the government has recently stated that it "has cracked down on those determined to break or bend the rules with radical initiatives. It has changed the economics of tax avoidance by introducing ground breaking measures that reduce the incentives for entering into avoidance schemes and worked to ensure that HMRC have the tools and powers they need to address evasion and avoidance. Many more evaders have been found by HMRC or have come forward to put their tax affairs in order. And many avoiders have sought to pay up or decided not to engage in further schemes."[5]

For some, "the appropriate response is for Parliament to introduce specific rules to block such attempts."[6] Such rules are commonly referred to as Specific Anti-Avoidance Rules ("SAARs"). While SAARs are commonly used around the world, they are problematic because they tend to produce overly complicated and technical tax rules,[7] which can become burdensome on taxpayers.[8] They may also be counterproductive because "the more detailed the rules, the more opportunity there may be for those wishing to do so to find and exploit loopholes."[9] Moreover, they merely provide a reactive response to known schemes,[10] leaving tax authorities to play a "never-ending cat and mouse game" that involves "drafting a specific rule anytime a new avoidance arrangement is uncovered."[11]

Rules targeting specific known schemes are not the only tools available in the battle against tax avoidance. Legal systems also use measures that apply generally. Such measures may be developed by the courts in the form of judicial doctrines.[12] One such doctrine, which is discussed in Part 2 of this chapter, is the "economic substance" doctrine.

As Xiong and Evans recently pointed out, "although such judicial doctrines can be used to deal with various aspects of complicated tax abuse, judges tended sometimes to limit and sometimes to enlarge the scope of jurisprudential interpretation, leading to substantial uncertainty and risk."[13] One way to limit the discretionary power of judges and overcome the uncertainty

---

5 Ibid., 5.

6 Q. C. Aaronson, "GAAR Study: A Study to Consider Whether a General Anti-Avoidance Rule Should Be Introduced Into the UK Tax System" (2011), para 3.1, available at: www.tax.org.uk/Resources/CIOT/Docu ments/2012/01/111111_GAAR_final_report.pdf.

7 Institute for Fiscal Studies, "Countering Tax Avoidance in the UK: Which Way Forward?" TLRC Discussion Paper No. 7 (2009), para 2.9, available at: www.ifs.org.uk/comms/dp7.pdf (herein-after the "TLRC Discussion Paper"). See also: R. S. Avi-Yonah and O. Halabi, "U.S. Treaty Anti-Avoidance Rules: An Overview and Assessment", University of Michigan Law & Econ, Empirical Legal Studies Center Paper No. 12–001; University of Michigan Public Law Working Paper No. 261 (13 January 2012), 29, available at SSRN: http://ssrn.com/abstract=1984700 or http://dx.doi.org/10.2139/ssrn.1984700.

8 TLRC Discussion Paper, Ibid., 7, paras 2.1, 2.9.

9 Ibid., para 2.1.

10 A reactive response reflects on a legislature's inability to pre-emptively identify and address every imaginable type of avoidance scheme that may and will be devised. As was recognized by the court in *FCT v. Hancock* ((1961) 8 A.I.T.R. 328), "the resource of ingenious minds to avoid revenue laws has always proved inexhaustible and for that reason it is neither possible nor safe to say in advance what must be found" (p. 333).

11 C. Silvani, "GAARs in Developing Countries: IFA Research Paper" (2013), 5, available at www.ifa.nl/Docu ment/Research%20Papers/IFA%20Research%20Paper%20on%20GAARs%20in%20Developing%20Coun tries%20(IFA%20Research%20Paper).pdf.

12 Weeghel identifies some of the typical doctrines as follows: "sham, legally ineffective transactions, substance over form, abuse of law, fraus legis, or simply as the general anti-avoidance rule" (S. van Weeghel, "General Report", *Tax Treaties and Tax Avoidance: Application of Anti-Avoidance Provisions*, Vol. 95a (IFA Cahiers, 2010), 22).

13 W. Xiong and C. Evans, "Towards an Improved Design of the Chinese General Anti-Avoidance Rule. A Comparative Analysis", 68:12 *Bulletin for International Taxation*, 688 (December 2014).

apparent in their judgments is by formalizing the doctrines, as the US has done by codifying the "economic substance" doctrine in 2010.

Part 2 also points out that focusing on the taxpayer's intentions is another limitation of the doctrine. Part 3 then proceeds to explain that this limitation could be overcome by adopting a statutory General Anti-Abuse Rule ("GAAR"). GAARs also impose generally applicable limits on what constitutes acceptable (legitimate) tax arrangements. But they do so based on whether the arrangements are consistent with the legislature's intentions, as they were conveyed in the tax provision which the taxpayer is relying on for achieving the tax advantage in question. Note that "by confining legitimate tax avoidance to schemes that are not inconsistent with the policy underlying the statutory provision invoked by the taxpayer, GAAR effectively limits the scope of the principle in *Commissioners of Inland Revenue v. Duke of Westminster* ... that '[e]very man is entitled if he can to order his affairs so that the tax attaching under the appropriate Acts is less than it would otherwise be.'"[14] Where an arrangement violates the rule, its tax consequences may be invalidated. Moreover, the deterrent effect of the rule could be strengthened by also imposing a penalty.[15]

The purpose of this chapter is to identify notable factors which are relevant to the formulation of a GAAR. These factors are distilled from the Canadian experience with a GAAR. Part 4 of the Chapter identifies two such factors. First is the need to have legislatures clearly identify their intended purpose(s) and policies. Second is the need to have legislatures formulate the GAAR in a way that will overcome the risk of having the constitutional validity of the rule challenged.

Based on these factors, Part 5 concludes with recommendations for the formulation of a statutory GAAR. For the purpose of example, these recommendations are applied to the US, where the option of adopting a statutory GAAR could, and arguably should, be considered. Yet, it should be emphasized that these recommendations could also be relevant to other countries, regardless of whether they do or do not already use a GAAR.

Limitations in the use of an economic substance doctrine to combat tax avoidance: lessons from the United States

The origins of anti-tax avoidance doctrine: Gregory v. Helvering (1935)

The evolution of anti-tax avoidance doctrine in the US begins with the seminal case of *Gregory v. Helvering*, decided by the US Supreme Court in 1935. Evelyn Gregory was the owner of all the shares of a company called United Mortgage Company ("United"). United Mortgage in turn owned 1,000 shares of stock of a company called Monitor Securities Corporation ("Monitor"). Mrs. Gregory wanted to sell the Monitor shares and to obtain the cash in her own hands, but having United sell the shares and distribute the cash or having United distribute the shares for her to sell would both have resulted in a dividend taxed at high rates with no offset for her basis. Instead, on 18 September 1928 Mrs. Gregory created Averill Corp and three days later United transferred the 1000 shares in Monitor to Averill. On 24 September Mrs. Gregory dissolved Averill and distributed the 1000 shares in Monitor to herself (a taxable

---

14 *Canada v. Imperial Oil Ltd.*, 2004 FCA 36 (CanLII), para 32.

15 In the UK, for example, the government, in its Budget 2015, "announced that it would strengthen the deterrent effect of the General Anti Abuse Rule (the GAAR) by introducing a penalty ... The new penalty will be based on the amount of tax people sought to avoid in a GAAR case" (see n.2, p. 18).

liquidation resulting in a capital gain), and on the same day sold the shares for $133,333.33. She claimed there was a cost basis of $57,325.45, and she should be taxed on a net capital gain on $76,007.88.

On her 1928 federal income tax return, Gregory treated the transfer of Monitor shares to Averill as a tax-free corporate reorganization, under Revenue Act of 1928 section 112. The Commissioner of Internal Revenue argued that in economic substance there was no business reorganization, and that the sole purpose of the transaction was to enable Mrs. Gregory to pay tax on the value of the Monitor shares at the favorable capital gains rate with an offset for her basis, rather than at the higher rate that would have applied to the entire amount had United distributed Monitor shares worth $133,333.33 to her as a dividend.

In the ensuing litigation, the Board of Tax Appeals (a predecessor to today's United States Tax Court) ruled in favor of the taxpayer. See *Gregory v. Commissioner*, 27 B.T.A. 223 (1932). On appeal, the United States Court of Appeals for the Second Circuit reversed. In his opinion, Learned Hand J used the following frequently quoted words:

> [A] transaction … does not lose its immunity, because it is actuated by a desire to avoid, or, if one choose, to evade, taxation. Anyone may so arrange his affairs that his taxes shall be as low as possible; he is not bound to choose that pattern which will best pay the Treasury; there is not even a patriotic duty to increase one's taxes.
>
> […]Nevertheless, it does not follow that Congress meant to cover such a transaction, not even though the facts answer the dictionary definitions of each term used in the statutory definition. … [T]he meaning of a sentence may be more than that of the separate words, … and no degree of particularity can ever obviate recourse to the setting in which all appear, and which all collectively create.
>
> […]The purpose of the section is plain enough: men engaged in enterprises … might wish to consolidate … their holdings. … But the underlying presupposition is plain that the readjustment shall be undertaken for reasons germane to the conduct of the venture in hand. … To dodge the shareholders' taxes is not one of the transactions contemplated as corporate "reorganizations.

The Supreme Court affirmed. It held that although the letter of the law might arguably have been complied with, the intention of the Act was not to allow reorganizations merely for the purpose of tax avoidance. In the course of its judgment, the Court said the following:

> It is earnestly contended on behalf of the taxpayer that since every element required by [the statute] is to be found in what was done, a statutory reorganization was effected; and that the motive of the taxpayer thereby to escape payment of a tax will not alter the result or make unlawful what the statute allows. It is quite true that if a reorganization in reality was effected within the meaning of [the statute], the ulterior purpose mentioned will be disregarded. The legal right of a taxpayer to decrease the amount of what otherwise would be his [or her] taxes, or altogether avoid them, by means which the law permits, cannot be doubted. […] But the question for determination is whether what was done, apart from the tax motive, was the thing which the statute intended. The reasoning of the court below [i.e., the reasoning of the Court of Appeals] in justification of a negative answer leaves little to be said.
>
> When [the statute] speaks of a transfer of assets by one corporation to another, it means a transfer made 'in pursuance of a plan of reorganization' […] of corporate

business; and not a transfer of assets by one corporation to another in pursuance of a plan having no relation to the business of either, as plainly is the case here. Putting aside, then, the question of motive in respect of taxation altogether, and fixing the character of the proceeding by what actually occurred, what do we find? Simply an operation having no business or corporate purpose-a mere device which put on the form of a corporate reorganization as a disguise for concealing its real character, and the sole object and accomplishment of which was the consummation of a preconceived plan, not to reorganize a business or any part of a business, but to transfer a parcel of corporate shares to the petitioner. No doubt, a new and valid corporation was created. But that corporation was nothing more than a contrivance to the end last described. It was brought into existence for no other purpose; it performed, as it was intended from the beginning it should perform, no other function. When that limited function had been exercised, it immediately was put to death.

In these circumstances, the facts speak for themselves and are susceptible of but one interpretation. The whole undertaking, though conducted according to the terms of [the statute], was in fact an elaborate and devious form of conveyance masquerading as a corporate reorganization, and nothing else. [… T]he transaction upon its face lies outside the plain intent of the statute. To hold otherwise would be to exalt artifice above reality and to deprive the statutory provision in question of all serious purpose.

As Assaf Likhovski has shown, *Gregory* needs to be understood against its historical background.[16] The election of Franklin Delano Roosevelt in 1932 was followed by sharp increases in the tax rates on the rich, especially in 1935–36, and by hearings that exposed massive tax avoidance by rich individuals like former Secretary of the Treasury Andrew Mellon. Thus, it is not surprising that Judge Hand ruled in favor of the government or that the Supreme Court affirmed.

The Gregory decision set the background for all that followed. It should be noted, however, that there was a subtle shift in emphasis between Judge Hand's opinion and the Supreme Court one. While Hand emphasized that what Mrs. Gregory had done was not what Congress intended, The Supreme Court, while repeating Hand's formulation, also emphasized the taxpayer's lack of business purpose, and it was the latter formulation that eventually led to the development and ultimate codification of the "economic substance" doctrine in 2010.

The development of the judicial economic substance doctrine, 1935–1978

In the years following Gregory, the Supreme Court decided a series of economic substance cases. In most of them, it followed *Gregory* in ruling that a transaction lacked economic substance if the taxpayer could not establish a non-tax business purpose [cites]. A good example is *Knetsch* (1960), in which the taxpayer borrowed at 3.5% to invest in an annuity paying 2.5%, because he could deduct the interest on the loan at a tax rate of over 90%, converting a before tax loss to an after-tax profit.

---

16 A. Likhovski, The Duke and The Lady: Helvering v. Gregory and the History of Tax Avoidance Adjudication, 25 *Cardozo Law Review* (Spring 2004), available at SSRN: http://ssrn.com/abstract=430080 or http://dx.doi.org/10.2139/ssrn.430080.

The "modern" economic substance doctrine is based on the Supreme Court's opinion in *Frank Lyon* (1978), in which the Court stated that:[17]

> [W]here, as here, there is a genuine multiple-party transaction *with economic substance* which is compelled or encouraged by *business* or *regulatory realities*, is imbued with *tax-independent considerations*, and is not shaped solely by tax-avoidance features that have meaningless labels attached, the Government should honor the allocation of rights and duties effectuated by the parties.

As many critics have pointed out, the Court got its economics wrong.[18] But more importantly, there is no reference at all to Congressional intent, which was the basis of the decision in *Gregory*. The entire emphasis shifts to the taxpayer's purpose.

This led to the development of the economic substance doctrine in the Courts of Appeal, which defined it as having two prongs: Whether the taxpayer intended the transaction to be profitable before tax (the subjective prong), and whether there was in fact a reasonable chance of making a profit (the objective prong). In some Circuits, the doctrine was applied in the conjunctive form (the taxpayer had to satisfy both prongs), while in others it was applied in disjunctive form (satisfying either prong was sufficient).[19] Notably, neither prong depended on Congressional purpose.

The first tax shelter wave, 1970–1986

Between 1970 and 1986, a series of "tax shelters" were developed by promoters and marketed to tens of thousands of taxpayers that had income that was not subject to withholding tax, such as physicians, dentists and lawyers. The typical "first wave" shelter involved a leveraged investment in property such as real estate, livestock, or films that was subject to favorable depreciation rules. Under the Supreme Court's decisions in *Crane* (1952) and *Tufts* (1983), the taxpayer could include borrowed amounts in its basis even if the loan was non-recourse, and even if the amount borrowed ultimately exceeded the value of the property. Taxpayers received both interest and depreciation deductions in the early years of the investment, which they could use to shelter their other income, while any gain came much later in the form of lower taxed capital gains.

The IRS tried to combat the shelters using economic substance, but with a few exceptions (e.g. *Estate of Franklin*) it was not very successful. In addition, there were too many shelter cases, which overwhelmed the Tax Court. Eventually, Congress took a successive series of steps that gradually eliminated the benefits of this type of shelter: the recapture provisions (IRC 1245), the at-risk rule (IRC 465), and especially the passive activities loss rule (IRC 469) of 1986, which led to massive contraction of the tax shelter industry.[20] In addition, the rate reduction from 50%

---

17 *Frank Lyon v. United States*, 1978. 435 US 561, pp. 58104.
18 B. Wolfman, Supreme Court in the Lyon's Den: A Failure of Judicial Process, 66 *Cornell Law Review* 1074 (1981).
19 Y. Keinan, The Economic Substance Doctrine – Past, Present and Future, 47 *Tax Management Memo* 259–279 (26 June 2006).
20 The shelters were built on the ability to borrow, acquire property with the borrowed funds, obtain interest and depreciation deductions, and later sell the property with a lower capital gains rate. The provisions mentioned eliminated the capital gains treatment, excluded losses due to borrowing when the taxpayer was not at risk, and segregated passive losses from active income.

to 28% and the elimination of the ordinary income/capital gains differential in the Tax Reform Act of 1986 helped reduce the motivation for tax avoidance.

The second tax shelter wave, 1993–2006

By 1991, however, the ordinary income and capital gains rate began to diverge, and the Clinton tax hike (1993) and Congress cutting the capital gains rate (1997) created the background for the second tax shelter wave.

Unlike the first wave, which was mass marketed to individual taxpayers, the second tax shelter wave was aimed at corporate and a few high net worth individual taxpayers. Moreover, while the tax shelters in the 1970s and 1980s were devised by small promoters, most of the tax shelters of the 1990s cycle were devised or at least promoted by the major accounting firms, all of which participated in helping their clients to engage in tax shelters.[21]

The IRS initially responded to this tax shelter activity by requiring registration of the tax shelters under IRC 6111, listing some tax shelters under IRC 6112, and requiring disclosure of certain transactions under IRC 6011. Each of these provisions sought to increase transparency as to the identification of transactions that the IRS might seek to challenge. For example, under IRC 6111, some transactions that met certain tax-advantaged criteria had to be "registered" through the use of disclosure forms filed with the IRS. IRC 6112, the "list maintenance" provision, required advisors on specified types of transactions to maintain lists of the transactions and those who engaged in them, available for possible inspection by the IRS.

At the same time, the IRS began to litigate against specific tax shelters in the courts, using the economic substance doctrine. However, before 2003 the IRS's litigation record was mixed: It won the *ACM, Winn-Dixie, ASA* and *Saba* cases but lost *Northern Indiana Public Service Co., Boca, Compaq, IES* and *UPS*.[22] As a result, the staff of the Joint Committee on Taxation in its February 2003 report on tax shelters engaged in by Enron Corporation before its bankruptcy was of the opinion that many of the Enron tax shelters would have been upheld by a court if the issue was litigated.[23]

In November 2003, the Permanent Subcommittee on Investigations of the US Senate held widely publicized hearings on individual tax shelters.[24] All of the Big Four announced that they were discontinuing their tax shelter activities. Some individuals associated with the tax shelter

---

21 See generally the discussion of the second wave of shelters in a symposium issue of the *Tax Law Review* (2001).

22 *Northern Indiana Public Service Co. v. Commissioner*, 115 F.3d 506 (7th Cir. 1997); *ACM Partnership v. Commissioner*, 157 F.3d 231 (3rd Cir. 1998); *ASA Investerings Partnership v. Commissioner*, 201 F.3d 505 (D.C. Cir. 2000); *Saba Partnership v. Commissioner*, 273 F.3d 1135 (D.C. Cir. 2001); *Boca Investerings v. Commissioner*, 167 F. Supp. 2d 298 (D.D.C. 2001); *Winn-Dixie Stores, Inc. v. Commissioner*, 254 F.3d 1313 (11th Cir. 2001); *IES Industries, Inc. v. United States*, 253 F.3d 350 (8th Cir. 2001); *Compaq Computer Corp. v. Commissioner*, 277 F.3d 778 (5th Cir. 2001); *United Parcel Service v. Commissioner*, 254 F.3d 1014 (11th Cir. 2001). See also *Gitlitz v. Comm'r*, 531 U.S. 206 (2001), in which the Supreme Court endorsed a literal approach to the Code similar to the technical arguments underlying tax shelters.

23 "Report of Investigation of Enron Corporation and Related Entities Regarding Federal Tax and Compensation Issues, and Policy Recommendations" (Joint Committee on Taxation, February 2003); see also "Tax Law Review Symposium Issue on Corporate Tax Shelters", 55 *Tax Law Review* 125 (2002), in which many distinguished tax professors expressed doubts that the IRS could prevent the tax shelter activity or successfully challenge many of the tax positions taken under existing law and regulations.

24 US Tax Shelter Industry, "The Role of Accountants, Lawyers, and Financial Professionals, US Senate Permanent Subcommittee on Investigations Minority Staff" (November 2003).

activities of the late 1990s faced criminal charges related to a variety of tax shelter activities. The IRS also promulgated new ethics rules that prevented law firms from giving opinions on tax shelters unless they independently verified the business purpose of each transaction, thereby making the lawyers into an independent supervisor of the shelters.[25]

From 2003 onward, the IRS began winning a series of tax shelter cases with increasing momentum, using economic substance.[26] This eventually led former Assistant Secretary of the Treasury for Tax Policy Pamela Olson to declare in 2006 that "the tax shelter war is over and the IRS has won." One should note, in fact, that most tax shelters were settled under a series of IRS initiatives without penalties, so that the taxpayers did not lose (they just paid the tax they would have paid absent the shelter, plus interest at a lower rate than what they could earn in the interim). And in the case of some shelters, the taxpayers also got to keep some of the tax benefits.

Codification and its critics, 2006–2010

In 2010, Congress codified the economic substance doctrine as Internal Revenue Code section 7701(o). The main change in the codified version was that it mandated following the conjunctive version of the doctrine in all the Circuits, and imposed stiff penalties for transactions lacking economic substance.

However, many critics remain skeptical of codification, which has not yet been tested in the courts.[27] The main concern is that the codified version, even more than the judicial version, provides a road map to successful avoidance. What is needed is (a) a credible taxpayer bolstered by contemporaneous documentation to satisfy the subjective prong, and (b) a reasonable chance of making a profit built into the transaction. A good example of a transaction that managed to pass muster under this test is the Caterpillar restructuring, which was never challenged by the IRS although it was clearly tax motivated [cite PSI report].

As many critics (e.g. Leandra Lederman) have pointed out, the basic problem with economic substance is the focus on the taxpayer's motivation, which goes all the way back to the Supreme Court's opinion in *Gregory*.[28] If the focus were instead on Congressional motivation, it is hard

25 The IRS first changed the regulations to limit the defenses available to taxpayers facing the accuracy-related penalty for certain returns filed after 31 December 2002. Treas. Reg. 1.6664-4(d) (2002). Second, the IRS changed the standards governing written opinions under Circular 230, the ethical standards governing practice before the IRS, effective 20 December 2004. Circular 230, 31 CFR 10.35(e)(2) (2004). In 2007, the IRS finalized regulations relating to the disclosure and registration of "reportable transactions" (which include listed transactions like COBRA, transactions entered into under conditions of confidentiality, transactions involving refundable or contingent fees, certain transactions involving significant losses, and other transactions of interest). 72 Fed. Reg. 43,157 (3 August 2007). In addition, Congress amended the tax return preparer penalty rules under IRC 6694 to raise the standard all return preparers must meet to "more likely than not," and a similar standard has been adopted under Circular 230. IRC 6694 (2007); Circ. 230, sec. 10.34 (2007).
26 *Boca Investerings v. Commissioner*, 314 F.3d 625 (D.C. Cir. 2003); *Long Term Capital Holdings v. United States*, 330 F. Supp. 2d 122 (D. Conn. 2004), aff'd, 150 Fed. App. 40 (2d Cir. 2005); *Dow Chemical Co. v. United States*, 435 F.3d 594 (6th Cir. 2006) (reversing district court judgment); *Black & Decker Corp. v. United States*, 436 F.3d 431 (4th Cir. 2006); *Coltec Industries, Inc. v. United States*, 454 F.3d 1340 (Fed. Cir. 2006) (reversing district court finding); *TIFD III-E Inc. (Castle Harbor) v. United States*, 459 F.3d 220 (2d Cir. 2006); cf. also *Times Mirror v. Comm'r*, 125 T.C. 110 (2005); *Merrill Lynch & Co. v. Comm'r*, 386 F.3d 464 (2d Cir. 2004).
27 See B. Wolfman, "Why Economic Substance Is Better Left Uncodified", 104 *Tax Notes* 445 (2004).
28 L. Lederman, "W(h)ither Economic Substance?" 95 *Iowa Law Review* 389 (2010); Indiana Legal Studies Research Paper No. 128, available at SSRN: http://ssrn.com/abstract=1345388.

to see how transactions like the tax shelter upheld by the Courts of Appeal in *Compaq* and *IES* could survive an IRS challenge.[29]

A third tax shelter wave, 2010–?

While it is too early to say with confidence, there may be a third tax shelter wave going on at present. A good indicator is the rise of so-called inversion transactions that exploit loopholes in IRC section 7874 to enable US corporations to become subsidiaries of foreign corporations and thereafter distribute their earnings out of the US as deductible interest or royalties. These transactions are clearly tax motivated but dressed up to appear as if they had a business purpose, thereby satisfying economic substance. We expect Congress will have to act again soon if the corporate tax base is to be preserved.[30]

Overcoming the limitations using a statutory GAAR

By now, numerous countries have already adopted statutory GAARs.[31] As suggested by Aaronson's GAAR Study Group, a GAAR can be justified on the basis that "levying of tax is the principal means by which the state pays for the services and facilities which it provides for its citizens,"[32] and thus it is "reasonable to *impose some limit* on the ability of taxpayers to escape their share of the tax burden by looking for loopholes or weaknesses in the tax rules, and then constructing elaborate schemes designed to exploit them. To be consistent with the rule of law *this limit* should be imposed by legislation."[33]

As Weeghel explained, "[a]lthough the precise features of GAARs differ, the common elements required for their application seem to be (a) a transaction or set of transactions that is solely or predominantly aimed at tax avoidance, and (b) if given effect the object and purpose of the applicable tax law would be violated."[34] Focusing on the second element, note that for a tax arrangement to be acceptable (legitimate) it must be consistent with the legislative intent which underlies the tax provision being relied on for the tax advantage in question. An 'abuse' of that legislative intent would constitute tax avoidance, notwithstanding that the arrangement is otherwise in compliance with a literal interpretation of the tax provision.[35]

---

29 The specific loophole underlying this shelter has been closed, but not the type of analysis that led the courts to approve of a shelter with no opportunity for profit before taxes.

30 While it is true that US tax law has recently been tilted toward defending the competitiveness of US based MNEs, including provisions like check the box and the CFC to CFC payment rule that openly try to help multinationals shift income from high to low tax jurisdictions abroad, this attitude should not preclude the US from adopting a GAAR. The provisions relied upon by most US multinationals are part of the tax law and represent the intent of Congress, and therefore relying on them is appropriate and would not be affected by the GAAR. What Caterpillar did was however abusive and not in accordance with Congressional intent, which is why it is currently under criminal investigation for tax fraud. The codification of the economic substance doctrine was adopted on a bipartisan basis and there is no reason why a GAAR that is narrowly drafted to apply only to transactions that are truly abusive and inconsistent with Congressional intent cannot receive similar bipartisan support.

31 *GAAR Rising: Mapping Tax Enforcement's Evolution* (Ernst & Young, 2013), 3, available at www.ey.com/Publication/vwLUAssets/GAA_rising/$FILE/GAAR_rising_1%20Feb_2013.pdf [accessed June 2015].

32 Graham Aaronson's GAAR Study, see n.6, para 3.3. See also *R (Huitson) v. HMRC* [2011] EWCA Civ 893, para 94.

33 Graham Aaronson's GAAR Study, see n.6, para 3.4.

34 Weeghel, see n.12, at p.22. See also *GAAR Rising*, *supra* at n.31, pp. 10–11.

35 *Canada Trustco Mortgage Co. v. Canada* (2005) 2 SCR 601, 2005 SCC 54 (CanLII), paras 13, 16, 49.

The UK's GAAR, for example, states that a "tax arrangement"[36] must not be "abusive". Tax arrangements are "abusive" if:[37]

> they are arrangements the entering into or carrying out of which *cannot reasonably be regarded as a reasonable course of action* in relation to the relevant tax provisions, having regard to all the circumstances including –
>
>> (a) whether the substantive results of the arrangements are *consistent with any principles on which those provisions are based (whether express or implied) and the policy objectives of those provisions,*
>>
>> (b) whether the means of achieving those results involves one or more contrived or abnormal steps, and
>>
>> (c) whether the arrangements are intended to exploit any shortcomings in those provisions.

Where, but for the application of the GAAR, the abusive tax arrangement would result in a "tax advantage",[38] that advantage is "to be counteracted by the making of adjustments,"[39] subject to the Act's specified conditions and limitations (e.g. the adjustment would have to be "just and reasonable.").[40]

Similarly in Canada, a transaction (or a series of transactions) is an "avoidance transaction" where, but for the GAAR in s.245 of the Income Tax Act ("ITA"), it "would result, directly or indirectly, in a tax benefit."[41] If the Minister of National Revenue ("Minister") alleges that a transaction is an "avoidance transaction",[42] the burden is on the taxpayer to prove otherwise on the basis that the transaction can "reasonably be considered to have been undertaken or arranged primarily for *bona fide* purposes other than to obtain the tax benefit."[43] If the taxpayer fails to prove that the transaction is not an "avoidance transaction" then the Minister has the burden of proving, on a balance of probabilities, that the avoidance transaction would result in an "abuse and misuse"[44] (either directly or indirectly) of a provision in any of the instruments specified in s.245(4), which includes the ITA.[45] As explained by the SCC,[46]

> [t]his analysis will lead to a finding of abusive tax avoidance when a taxpayer relies on specific provisions of the *Income Tax Act* in order to achieve an outcome that those

---

36 "Arrangements are 'tax arrangements' if, having regard to all the circumstances, it would be reasonable to conclude that the obtaining of a tax advantage was the main purpose, or one of the main purposes, of the arrangements" (S.207(1), Finance Act 2013). The arrangement could be in the form of "any agreement, understanding, scheme, transaction or series of transactions (whether or not legally enforceable)" (S.214, Finance Act 2013).
37 S.207(2), Finance Act 2013.
38 "A 'tax advantage' includes: (a) relief or increased relief from tax, (b) repayment or increased repayment of tax, (c) avoidance or reduction of a charge to tax or an assessment to tax, (d) avoidance of a possible assessment to tax, (e) deferral of a payment of tax or advancement of a repayment of tax, and (f) avoidance of an obligation to deduct or account for tax" (S.208, Finance Act 2013).
39 S.209(1), Finance Act 2013; HMRC GAAR Guidance, see n.1, para B3.2.
40 S.209(2), Finance Act 2013.
41 S.245(3)(a), Income Tax Act.
42 The elements of an avoidance transaction are set out in s.245(3) of the Income Tax Act.
43 S.245(3)(a), Income Tax Act.
44 As the SCC clarified, "determinations of 'misuse' and 'abuse' under s. 245(4) are not separate inquiries. Section 245(4) requires a single, unified approach to the textual, contextual and purposive interpretation of the specific provisions of the *Income Tax Act* that are relied upon by the taxpayer in order to determine whether there was abusive tax avoidance" (*Canada Trustco*, see n.35, para 43).
45 *Lipson v. Canada*, [2009] 1 SCR 3, 2009 SCC 1 (CanLII), para 21.
46 *Canada Trustco*, see *supra* n.35, para 45.

provisions seek to prevent. As well, abusive tax avoidance will occur when a transaction defeats the underlying rationale of the provisions that are relied upon. An abuse may also result from an arrangement that circumvents the application of certain provisions, such as specific anti-avoidance rules, in a manner that frustrates or defeats the object, spirit or purpose of those provisions. By contrast, abuse is not established where it is reasonable to conclude that an avoidance transaction under s. 245(3) was within the object, spirit or purpose of the provisions that confer the tax benefit.

If the Minister fails in this task, the taxpayer would not be denied the tax benefit even though the transaction was an "avoidance transaction".[47] But if the Minister proves that the avoidance transaction *abused* the relevant provision, then the taxpayer can be denied the tax benefits from the transaction.[48] The Minister's determination of the denied tax benefits must be "*reasonable in the circumstances*".[49]

Factors to consider in the formulation of a statutory GAAR: lessons from Canada

The need to clearly identify the legislature's intended policies and objectives

As the SCC explained in *Canada Trustco*, determining whether an avoidance transaction abused the statutory provision (being relied on for a tax advantage) involves a two-part inquiry: "The first step is to determine the *object, spirit or purpose of the provisions* of the *Income Tax Act* that are relied on for the tax benefit, having regard to the scheme of the Act, the relevant provisions and permissible extrinsic aids. The second step is to examine the factual context of a case in order to determine whether the avoidance transaction defeated or frustrated the object, spirit or purpose of the provisions in issue."[50]

Subsequently, in *Copthorne Holding Ltd. v. Canada*, the SCC further clarified this task of interpretation in the GAAR analysis:[51]

> The object, spirit or purpose can be identified by applying the same interpretive approach employed by this Court in all questions of statutory interpretation – a "unified textual, contextual and purposive approach" (*Trustco*, at para. 47; *Lipson v. Canada*, 2009 SCC 1 (CanLII), [2009] 1 S.C.R. 3, at para. 26). While the approach is the same as in all statutory interpretation, the analysis seeks to determine a different aspect of the statute than in other cases. *In a traditional statutory interpretation approach* the court applies the textual, contextual and purposive analysis *to determine what the words of the statute mean. In a GAAR analysis* the textual, contextual and purposive analysis is employed *to determine the object, spirit or purpose of a provision.* Here meaning of the words of the statute may be clear enough. *The search is for the rationale that underlies the words that may not be captured by the bare meaning of the words themselves.* However, determining the rationale of the relevant provisions of the Act should not be conflated with a value

---

47 *Lipson,* see *supra* n.45, para 25; *Canada Trustco,* see *supra* n.35, para 36.
48 S.245(2), Income Tax Act.
49 S.245(2), (5), Income Tax Act.
50 *Canada Trustco,* see *supra* n.35, para 55.
51 [2011] 3 SCR 721, 2011 SCC 63 (CanLII), para 70.

judgment of what is right or wrong nor with theories about what tax law ought to be or ought to do.

While the GAAR requires the courts to go "behind the words of the legislation to determine the object, spirit or purpose of the provision or provisions relied upon by the taxpayer,"[52] that "object, spirit or purpose" must be clearly conveyed by the legislation. The courts will not invent a legislative purpose which was not clearly conveyed in the tax provision that the taxpayer relied on for claiming a tax advantage. As the SCC explained:[53]

40   There is but one principle of interpretation: to determine the intent of the legislator having regard to the text, its context, and other indicators of legislative purpose. The policy analysis proposed as a second step by the Federal Court of Appeal in *OSFC* is properly incorporated into a unified, textual, contextual, and purposive approach to interpreting the specific provisions that give rise to the tax benefit.

41   The courts cannot search for an overriding policy of the Act that is not based on a unified, textual, contextual and purposive interpretation of the specific provisions in issue. First, such a search is incompatible with the roles of reviewing judges. The *Income Tax Act* is a compendium of highly detailed and often complex provisions. To send the courts on the search for some overarching policy and then to use such a policy to override the wording of the provisions of the *Income Tax Act* would inappropriately place the formulation of taxation policy in the hands of the judiciary, requiring judges to perform a task to which they are unaccustomed and for which they are not equipped. Did Parliament intend judges to formulate taxation policies that are not grounded in the provisions of the Act and to apply them to override the specific provisions of the Act? Notwithstanding the interpretative challenges that the GAAR presents, we cannot find a basis for concluding that such a marked departure from judicial and interpretative norms was Parliament's intent.

42   Second, to search for an overriding policy of the *Income Tax Act* that is not anchored in a textual, contextual and purposive interpretation of the specific provisions that are relied upon for the tax benefit would run counter to the overall policy of Parliament that tax law be certain, predictable and fair, so that taxpayers can intelligently order their affairs. Although Parliament's general purpose in enacting the GAAR was to preserve legitimate tax minimization schemes while prohibiting abusive tax avoidance, Parliament must also be taken to seek consistency, predictability and fairness in tax law. These three latter purposes would be frustrated if the Minister and/or the courts overrode the provisions of the *Income Tax Act* without any basis in a textual, contextual and purposive interpretation of those provisions.

Accordingly, in determining whether the avoidance transaction in question had to have real economic substance in the *Canada Trustco* case, the SCC construed the *object, spirit or purpose* of a provision which was relied on by the taxpayer, and restrained itself from inventing and imputing some underlying legislative rational that was not actually conveyed by Parliament within that provision. The court explained its analysis as follows:

57   Courts have to be careful not to conclude too hastily that simply because a non-tax purpose is not evident, the avoidance transaction is the result of abusive tax avoidance. Although the

---

52 *Pièces automobiles Lecavalier Inc. v. The Queen*, 2013 TCC 310 (CanLII), para 21.
53 *Canada Trustco*, see *supra* n.35, paras 40–42.

Explanatory Notes make reference to the expression "economic substance", s.245(4) does not consider a transaction to result in abusive tax avoidance merely because an economic or commercial purpose is not evident. As previously stated, the GAAR was not intended to outlaw all tax benefits; Parliament intended for many to endure. The central inquiry is focussed on whether the transaction was consistent with the purpose of the provisions of the Income Tax Act that are relied upon by the taxpayer, when those provisions are properly interpreted in light of their context. Abusive tax avoidance will be established if the transactions frustrate or defeat those purposes.

58　Whether the transactions were motivated by any economic, commercial, family or other non-tax purpose may form part of the factual context that the courts may consider in the analysis of abusive tax avoidance allegations under s. 245(4). However, any finding in this respect would form only one part of the underlying facts of a case, and would be insufficient by itself to establish abusive tax avoidance. The central issue is the proper interpretation of the relevant provisions in light of their context and purpose. When properly interpreted, the statutory provisions at issue in a given case may dictate that a particular tax benefit may apply only to transactions with a certain economic, commercial, family or other non-tax purpose. The absence of such considerations may then become a relevant factor towards the inference that the transactions abused the provisions at issue, but there is no golden rule in this respect.

59　　Similarly, courts have on occasion discussed transactions in terms of their "lack of substance" or requiring "recharacterization". However, such terms have no meaning in isolation from the proper interpretation of specific provisions of the Income Tax Act. The analysis under s. 245(4) requires a close examination of the facts in order to determine whether allowing a tax benefit would be within the object, spirit or purpose of the provisions relied upon by the taxpayer, when those provisions are interpreted textually, contextually and purposively. Only after first, properly construing the provisions to determine their scope and second, examining all of the relevant facts, can a proper conclusion regarding abusive tax avoidance under s. 245(4) be reached.

60　A transaction may be considered to be "artificial" or to "lack substance" with respect to specific provisions of the Income Tax Act, if allowing a tax benefit would not be consistent with the object, spirit or purpose of those provisions. We should reject any analysis under s. 245(4) that depends entirely on "substance" viewed in isolation from the proper interpretation of specific provisions of the Income Tax Act or the relevant factual context of a case. However, abusive tax avoidance may be found where the relationships and transactions as expressed in the relevant documentation lack a proper basis relative to the object, spirit or purpose of the provisions that are purported to confer the tax benefit, or where they are wholly dissimilar to the relationships or transactions that are contemplated by the provisions.

61　A proper approach to the wording of the provisions of the Income Tax Act together with the relevant factual context of a given case achieve balance between the need to address abusive tax avoidance while preserving certainty, predictability and fairness in tax law so that taxpayers may manage their affairs accordingly. Parliament intends taxpayers to take full advantage of the provisions of the Act that confer tax benefits. Parliament did not intend the GAAR to undermine this basic tenet of tax law.

62　The GAAR may be applied to deny a tax benefit only after it is determined that it was not reasonable to consider the tax benefit to be within the object, spirit or purpose of the provisions relied upon by the taxpayer. The negative language in which s. 245(4) is cast indicates that the starting point for the analysis is the assumption that a tax benefit that would be conferred by the plain words of the Act is not abusive. This means that a finding of abuse is only warranted where the opposite conclusion – that the avoidance transaction was consistent with the object, spirit or purpose of the provisions of the Act that are relied on by the taxpayer – cannot be reasonably entertained. In other words, the abusive nature of the transaction must be clear. The GAAR will not apply to deny a tax benefit where it may reasonably be considered that the transactions were carried out in a manner consistent with the object, spirit or purpose of the provisions of the Act, as interpreted textually, contextually and purposively.

Challenges to the constitutional validity of a GAAR

When drafting a GAAR, consideration should also be given to ensure compliance with domestic constitutional requirements. GAARs are particularly at risk of being challenged on the basis of constitutional validity because, by their nature, they are conveyed using vaguely phrased standards so that they can be flexibly applies generally. Vagueness, however, may come into conflict with constitutionally protected rights and freedoms. There are examples of both successful and unsuccessful constitutional challenges of GAARs.

In Poland, for example, the Polish Constitutional Court found that article 24b §1 of the Tax Ordinance Act ("TOA"), which set out a GAAR, was unconstitutional.[54] It was found to be "in breach of article 2 (the principle of the rule of law) in conjunction with article 217 (the principle of legislative base for tax liability) of the Polish Constitution, and therefore declared it to be null and void. In consequence of this judgment, GAAR was repealed from the TOA."[55]

In Canada, term 'abuse' in s.245(4) of the ITA was challenged as being unconstitutionally vague, but this was rejected by the FCA in *Kaulius v. Canada*.[56] The court held as follows:[57]

> As stated in *Ontario v. Canadian Pacific Ltd.*, 1995 CanLII 112 (SCC), [1995] 2 S.C.R. 1031, the question is whether a law provides the basis for legal debate and coherent judicial interpretation. If judicial interpretation is possible, an impugned law is not vague … In the case of section 245, the Tax Court and this Court have, on several occasions, had occasion to interpret the section and apply it. Indeed, on the facts in *OSFC* which are, for practical purposes, the same facts applicable to this case, the Court was able to interpret subsection 245(4) and apply it. Subsection 245(4), having been interpreted and applied on numerous occasions by the Courts, is capable of supporting legal debate and coherent judicial interpretation. It is therefore not unconstitutionally vague.

Applying the factors to the formulation of a GAAR in the US

Based on the Canadian experience with the GAAR, this chapter identified factors which ought to be considered and addressed when formulating a statutory GAAR. These factors may be

54 Ref. K 4/03 (11 May 2004).
55 B. Kuźniacki, "Sustainable Development in Poland and Anti-Avoidance Provisions: The Rational for Introducing CFC Rules Into the Polish Tax Law System", in *Social and Environmental Dimension of Sustainable Development: Alternative Models in Central and Eastern Europe* (Friedrich Ebert Stiftung e. V., 2012), 151, available at: http://fesprag.ecn.cz/img_upload/72ff215dde4b7f046a6aa04d2af13196/myphd_2012_opt_1.pdf.
56 2003 FCA 371 (CanLII), para 31.
57 Ibid., at paras 31–32. See also: *Canada v. Gregory*, 2000 CanLII 16315 (FCA).

relevant for countries in which a statutory GAAR already exists as well as for countries, such as the US, where the option of adopting a GAAR could (and arguably should) be considered. Next, for the purpose of example, these factors will be applied and considered in the context of the US, where a statutory GAAR could supplement[58] existing tools (for combating tax avoidance) by enabling the IRS to deny tax benefits arising from arrangements that are inconsistent with Congressional intention, rather than having to base their challenge on the taxpayer's intentions.

As Dr. Aviv Pichhadze and Dr. Amir Pichhadze have observed, the SCC's approach to statutory interpretation is consistent with a similar trend taken by the top courts in other countries, such as in the U.K. and the US.[59] In *Gitlitz v. Commissioner of Internal Revenue*, for example, it was suggested that without judicial intervention the transaction would produce a 'double windfall' for shareholders; "they would be exempted from paying taxes on the full amount of the discharge of indebtedness, and they would be able to increase basis and deduct their previously suspended losses."[60] Yet the Supreme Court of the United States held that "because the Code's plain text permits the taxpayer here to receive these benefits, we need not address this policy concern."[61] Postlewaite has suggested that the reason for this trend in statutory interpretation is the courts' "fear of usurping the role of the legislative branch."[62]

Shortly after *Gitlintz*, the Courts of Appeal in the US reaffirmed this approach of judicial restraint. In *Coggin Automotive Corp. v. C.I.R.*, for example, the US Court of Appeals for the Eleventh Circuit noted that "perhaps the tax court is straining to extend its interpretation of the legislative histories of Section 1373 and Section 1363(d) in order to close what it perceives to be a loophole in the case of holding companies that own no inventory yet elect S corporation status."[63] Yet, as the court went on to explained,[64]

> [i]n *Gitlitz v. Com'r*, 531 U.S. 206, 121 S.Ct. 701, 148 L.Ed.2d 613 (2001), in a case dealing with a potential double windfall to S corporation shareholders due to a discharge of indebtedness, the Supreme Court held that "[b]ecause the Code's plain text permits the taxpayers here to receive these benefits, we need not address this policy concern." *Id.* at 710. "[T]he result is required by statute." *Id.* at n. 10. If "this is an inequity in the United States Tax Code … only Congress or the Secretary (as the holder of delegated authority from Congress) has the authority to ameliorate" it. *Hillman v.*

---

58 On the question of whether a GAAR would apply to an arrangement that has already been subject to a SAAR, E&Y observes that "there seems to be little or no consistency among countries on this question." (GAAR Rising, see n.27, p. 16) In Canada, the FCA explained that "[t]he purpose of GAAR is to prevent abusive tax avoidance to which more specific anti-avoidance rules do not apply: Vern Krishna, *The Fundamentals of Canadian Income Tax*, 7th ed. (Toronto: Carswell, 2002), 862. Thus, if a taxpayer does not satisfy the statutory requirements of a provision on which the taxpayer relies, the Minister need not resort to GAAR. Similarly, GAAR is not needed if a more specific anti-avoidance rule applies … In other words, GAAR is the anti-avoidance provision of last resort." (*Canada v. Imperial Oil Ltd.*, 2004 FCA 36 (CanLII), paras 30–31). This was repeatedly reaffirmed by the SCC (e.g. Lipson, see n.45, para 119).
59 A. Pichhadze and A. Pichhadze, "Economic Substance Doctrine: Time for a Legislative Response", 48:1 *Tax Notes International* (1 October 2007). The trend towards textualism is also noted in N. B. Cunningham and J. R. Repetti, "Textualism and Tax Shelters", 24:1 *Virginia Tax Review* (Summer 2004).
60 *Gitlitz v. C.I.R.*, 531 U.S. 206, 220, 121 S. Ct. 701, 709–10, 148 L. Ed. 2d 613 (2001).
61 Ibid.
62 P. F. Postlewaite, "The Status of the Judicial Sham Doctrine in the United States", 15:1 *Revenue Law Journal* 147 (2005).
63 *Coggin Auto. Corp. v. C.I.R.*, 292 F.3d 1326, 1332 (11th Cir. 2002).
64 Ibid.

Internal Revenue Service, 250 F.3d 228, 234 (4th Cir.2001); *see also Brown Group, Inc. v. Com'r*, 77 F.3d 217, 222 (8th Cir.1996) (where the Eighth Circuit reversed the tax court's use of the aggregate method of partnership taxation to close what it perceived to be a loophole in the Internal Revenue Code in that "such a tax loophole is not ours to close but must rather be closed or cured by Congress.).

Following the *Gitlitz* case, Lipton commented that "the Supreme Court's decision in *Gitlitz* shows tax advisors that they do not need to shy away from taking a position that is clearly mandated by the Code, even if the result is unduly beneficial to the taxpayer. Put simply, Congress makes the law, and the Supreme Court said that when Congress has spoken clearly, taxpayers can rely on what Congress has said."[65] More recently, however, Lipton revisited this issue, raising concern that, notwithstanding *Gitlitz*, lower courts have been aggressively applying the economic substance doctrine in order to disallow tax benefits which appear to be "too good to be true", even where the transaction had a real business purpose.[66] In effect, as Lipton explains, "the judicial doctrines have been expanded into what appears to be a new provision in the Code – Section 'I Don't Like it'."[67] Lipton rightly cautions that this is a very worrisome development which undermines certainty in tax planning; certainty "which usually can be found by applying the rules in the Code and the Regulations."[68] Lipton goes on to conclude as follows:[69]

> The courts appear to be intent on reaching what they view is the 'right' result, even if the literal provisions of the Code do not help them. The economic substance doctrine is the crutch they have used to assist them in their analysis.
>
> What makes this approach even more interesting is that the one court that matters the most – the Supreme Court – has previously taken a more stringent approach in applying the literal words of the Code. The most recent example of this was *Gitlitz*, 531 U.S. 206, 87 AFTR2d 2001–417 (2001), in which the interaction of the rules for computing the basis of stock in an S corporation, when combined with the exclusion of COD income for an S corporation, resulted in a large tax benefit – a basis increase with no income! The IRS argued that this result was contrary to Congress's intent (which it clearly was), but the Court had no problem dismissing that argument. According to the Court: 'Because the Code's plain text permits the taxpayers here to receive these benefits, we need not address this policy concern.'
>
> The approach taken by the Supreme Court in *Gitlitz* does not appear to be matched by the language applied today in the lower courts, which seem focused on whether or not a result is 'fair' (in the court's opinion) and consistent with the way that Congress intended the law to operate (or, more often, would have intended if Congress actually had thought about the issue). The problem with the lower courts' approach, however, is that any certainty that is generated by a Code-based system is effectively eliminated by the courts' substitution of their own views of how the law should operate in place

65 R. M. Lipton, "Supreme Court Hands Taxpayers a Victory in Gitlitz, But Will Congress Take It Away?" 94 *Journal of Taxation* 133, 138 (March 2001).
66 R. M. Lipton, "Tax Shelters and the Decline of the Rule of Law", 120 *Journal of Taxation* 82, 82, 96 (2014).
67 Ibid.
68 Ibid., 83.
69 Ibid., 96.

of what the statute literally says. Cases with identical facts can lead to wildy different results – witness the STARS decisions.[70]

Notwithstanding the criticisms that some have expressed towards the SCC's approach in the *Canada Trustco* case,[71] these developments in the US support the SCC's restrained approach to statutory interpretation in order to preserve a "balance between the need to address abusive tax avoidance while preserving certainty, predictability and fairness in tax law so that taxpayers may manage their affairs accordingly."[72]

Yet, even in the US, Lipson's alarm should not be over-exaggerated. One can take some comfort, for example, by the recent decision of the US Court of Appeals for the Third Circuit in *Ball ex rel. Ball v. C.I.R.* In this case, "the Tax Court noted that any conclusion other than a holding that 'unrecognized gain from a Qsub election does not constitute an item of income or tax-exempt income under §1366(a)(1)(A),' would lead to 'absurd results' and 'open the door to a myriad of abusive transactions'."[73] Yet, as the Court of Appeal held:[74]

> The Supreme Court in *Gitlitz*, however, refused to address this policy argument when the text of the Code was clear. *Gitlitz*, 531 U.S. at 220, 121 S.Ct. 701 ("Because the Code's plain text permits the taxpayers here to receive these benefits, we need not address this policy concern."). Although statutory text cannot be read in a way that creates an absurdity, the payment of some taxes and not others is not an absurdity, but rather a policy choice rightly left to Congress. *Id*. Indeed, Congress, subsequent to *Gitlitz*, made changes to the statute at issue in that case to prevent further uses of the tax code loophole.

It can therefore be expected that, should the US Congress decide to also adopt a statutory GAAR, the US courts would (and arguably should) exercise judicial restraint in their statutory interpretation, similar to the SCC's approach in *Canada Trustco*. It would thus be necessary for Congress to clearly convey its intentions, otherwise courts would not (and arguably should not) invent and give effect to an intention which was not conveyed.

The risk is that the legislature's intentions may not be clearly conveyed. In Canada, for example, Arnold observed that "very few statutory provisions explicitly refer to economic substance; therefore, economic substance is unlikely to be an important factor in the application of the GAAR if the Supreme Court's approach is adhered to strictly by the lower courts."[75] Consequently, as Freedman explained, "a GAAR will not operate properly unless the underlying law is based on a clearly stated principle, because without such a principle or

---

70 These decisions refer to cases in which the economic substance doctrine was used to challenge the tax benefits from substantial business transactions. In these cases the taxpayer applied what is referred to as a STARS structure, as exemplified by the transaction in *Bank of New York Mellon Corporation*, 140 TC 15 (2013) (BNY). For more info, see: R. M. Lipton, "Tax Shelters and the Decline of the Rule of Law", 120 *Journal of Taxation* 82, 82, 93–6 (2014).

71 B. J. Arnold, "The Long, Slow, Steady Demise of the General Anti-Avoidance Rule", 52:2 *Canadian Tax Journal* (2004); B. J. Arnold, "Reflections on the Relationship Between Statutory Interpretation and Tax Avoidance", 49:1 *CTJ* (2001), 1-39; J. Li, "'Economic Substance': Drawing the Line Between Legitimate Tax Minimization and Abusive Tax Avoidance", 54:1 *CTJ* (2006), 23–56.

72 *Canada Trustco*, see *supra* n.35, para 61.

73 *Ball ex rel. Ball v. C.I.R.*, 742 F.3d 552, 562 (3d Cir. 2014).

74 Ibid.

75 B. J. Arnold, "The Canadian Experience With a General Anti-Avoidance Rule", available at www.sbs.ox.ac.uk/centres/tax/Documents/events/Arnold.pdf.

objective it is impossible to decide whether there has been abuse of the legislation."[76] In this sense, Freedman is correct in suggesting that GAARs could actually improve the underlying tax legislation.[77]

As for the second factor, the US Congress would need to draft the GAAR in a manner that is consistent with constitutionally protected rights and freedoms, in order to avoid having the rule challenged on constitutional grounds. A GAAR could, for example, be challenged for being unconstitutionally vague on due process grounds. "The concept of unconstitutional vagueness means no prohibition can stand or penalty attach where an individual could not reasonably understand his contemplated conduct is proscribed … Any statute, including a rule or regulation of an administrative agency, which forbids an act in terms so vague persons of common intelligence must necessarily guess at its meaning and differ as to its application, violates the first essential of due process of law … This principle requires the statute provide explicit standards to prevent arbitrary and discriminatory enforcement."[78]

In the context of tax legislation, the Court of Appeal for the Sixth District similarly explained that: "An enactment may be declared unconstitutionally vague under the due process clauses of the United States Constitution and the California Constitution … 'if it fails to provide people of ordinary intelligence a reasonable opportunity to understand what conduct it prohibits [or] if it authorizes or even encourages arbitrary and discriminatory enforcement.' A tax law in particular 'must prescribe a standard sufficiently definite to be understandable to the average person who desires to comply with it.'"[79]

"The degree of vagueness that the Constitution tolerates – as well as the relative importance of fair notice and fair enforcement – depends in part on the nature of the enactment … Specifically, vagueness in statutes with criminal penalties is tolerated less than vagueness in those with civil penalties because of the severity of the potential consequences of the imprecision."[80] "Where economic or commercial interests are involved, a lesser standard is utilized for determining vagueness."[81]

Yet, while a GAAR could be challenged on constitutional grounds in the US, doing so would expectedly be an uphill battle. "Laws are entitled to a 'strong presumption of constitutionality,' and any party challenging the constitutionality of a law 'bears the burden of proving that the law is unconstitutional beyond a reasonable doubt.'"[82] Moreover, it should be noted that "the void-for-vagueness doctrine 'does not require statutes to be drafted with scientific precision.' Rather, 'it permits a statute's certainty to be ascertained by application of commonly accepted tools of judicial construction, with courts indulging every reasonable interpretation in favor of finding the statute constitutional.' The bar is not a high one, and a 'civil statute that is not concerned with the First Amendment is only unconstitutionally vague if it is 'so vague and indefinite as really to be no rule [or standard] at all' or if it is 'substantially incomprehensible.'"[83]

76 J. Freedman, "Designing a General Anti-Abuse Rule: Striking a Balance", 20:3 *Asia-Pacific Tax Bulletin* 168 (May/June 2014).

77 Ibid., 168.

78 *Stastny v. Bd. of Trustees of Cent. Washington Univ.*, 32 Wash. App. 239, 252–53, 647 P. 2d 496, 505–06 (1982).

79 *Patel v. City of Gilroy*, 97 Cal. App. 4th 483, at 486.

80 *Shew v. Malloy*, 994 F. Supp. 2d 234, 253–54 (D. Conn. 2014) aff'd in part, rev'd in part sub nom. *New York State Rifle & Pistol Ass'n, Inc. v. Cuomo*, 804 F.3d 242 (2d Cir. 2015).

81 N. Singer and S. Singer, *Sutherland Statutory Construction*, 7th ed., St. Paul, Minn.: Thomson/West (2007), § 21:16.

82 *Buckley v. Wilkins*, 2005-Ohio-2166, ¶ 18, 105 Ohio St. 3d 350, 353, 826 N.E.2d 811, 815.

83 *Buckley v. Wilkins*, 2005-Ohio-2166, ¶ 19, 105 Ohio St. 3d 350, 353–54, 826 N.E.2d 811, 815–16.

In tax legislation, some degree of vagueness is to be expected and would be tolerated. As the Supreme Court of California explained:[84]

> Many, probably most, statutes are ambiguous in some respects and instances invariably arise under which the application of statutory language may be unclear. So long as a statute does not threaten to infringe on the exercise of First Amendment or other constitutional rights, however, such ambiguities, even if numerous, do not justify the invalidation of a statute on its face. In order to succeed on a facial vagueness challenge to a legislative measure that does not threaten constitutionally protected conduct – like the initiative measure at issue here – a party must do more than identify some instances in which the application of the statute may be uncertain or ambiguous; he must demonstrate that 'the law is impermissibly vague *in all of its applications.*'

When applying the 'void for vagueness' doctrine, the US Supreme Court cautioned that "the fact that Congress might, without difficulty, have chosen '(c)learer and more precise language' equally capable of achieving the end which it sought does not mean that the statute which it in fact drafted is unconstitutionally vague."[85]

---

84 *Evangelatos v. Superior Court*, 44 Cal. 3d 1188, 1201, 753 P. 2d 585, 592–93 (1988).
85 *United States v. Powell*, 423 U.S. 87, 94, 96 S. Ct. 316, 321, 46 L. Ed. 2d 228 (1975).

PART III

Regional and global perspectives in tax avoidance

9

TEXT, INTENT AND TAXATION IN THE UNITED STATES, THE UNITED KINGDOM AND FRANCE

Steven A. Dean, Lawrence M. Solan, and Lukasz Stankiewicz

Introduction

This chapter considers judicial safeguards against tax avoidance in three jurisdictions. Avoidance presents a grave challenge to the income tax that each employs. Taxpayers can – and do – treat even the most carefully designed set of rules as an invitation to minimize their tax burden. To combat that behavior, tax authorities can invoke anti-avoidance judicial doctrines and statutes designed to ensure that taxpayers remain faithful to both the letter and spirit of tax laws.

Such interventions risk upsetting a delicate balance. In a jurisdiction that paid too little attention to the text of tax statutes, allowing the government to impose whatever tax obligations suited its whim, taxpayers would face crippling uncertainty. The result would burden taxpayer autonomy, inhibiting business transactions and investment. An entirely literal approach would leave authorities powerless in the face of obvious mischief. Each jurisdiction struggles to navigate a path between excessive and inadequate textual fidelity.[1]

Surprisingly, a jurisdiction's ease with purposivism makes a middle ground suited to the unique demands of the tax law elusive. Judicial restraint offers an explanation for the contrast between the relative strength and weakness of tax purposivism in the United States and across the Atlantic in the United Kingdom and France, respectively. This Chapter is not the first to note the relatively permissive attitude of jurisdictions such as the United Kingdom and France toward tax avoidance. Remarkably, prior work has not attempted to reconcile that textualist impulse either with (i) those jurisdictions' broader rejection of textualism or (ii) the inversion of that relationship – with courts giving more deference to legislative intent in tax matters – in the United States.

This Chapter begins by describing the roles of textualism, intentionalism and purposivism in the United States, the United Kingdom and France. Next, it considers the potency of judicial anti tax-avoidance doctrines in each jurisdiction. The final portion of the chapter then reconciles the relative weakness of anti tax-avoidance measures in the United Kingdom and France

---

1 See generally S. A. Dean and L. M. Solan, "Tax Shelters and the Code: Navigating Between Text and Intent", 26 *Virginia Tax Review* 879, 880 (2007) (concluding "that the problem of tax shelters would exist, more or less in the same form, regardless of how judges approach statutory interpretation").

with the primacy of legislative intent outside the tax arena. Simply put, preserving taxpayer autonomy by hobbling the potent purposivism UK and French courts ordinarily deploy to safeguard legislative intent produces a different balance than the one that emerges as US courts work on a relatively clean – i.e. textualist – slate.

Textualism, intentionalism and purposivism

The three legal systems we discuss here have more in common than in conflict when it comes to ordinary principles of statutory interpretation. All three give deference to the legislature by enforcing the plain language of a statute, unless doing so leads to absurdity. All three take into account the intent of the legislature that enacted a law. All three employ a systemic approach to interpretation – construing statutes to create coherence both among related legislative provisions and among situations in which the same statute applies. And all three attempt to locate the mischief that a law was meant to address and construe the law in accordance with that purpose.

Yet there are differences, and these differences produce very different styles of judicial decisions. The United States and the United Kingdom share the common law tradition. The result is that many decisions rely heavily on prior judicial decisions, including the application of various canons of construction in the earlier cases. Less so in France, with its civil law tradition in which judicial decisions are important, but do not constitute "making law" in the same sense as in common law jurisdictions.

The United Kingdom and France both have parliamentary systems of government, whereas the United States has a government structured around a much more pronounced division between the legislative and executive branches. France and the UK are more comfortable with purposive analysis than is the US, where fierce legislative debates and at times a president unwilling to sign a bill into law bring less of a sense of a single purpose and more of a sense of expedient compromise. In contrast, the US focuses a great deal on linguistic nuance, with many cases analyzed on the basis of small differences in meaning among statutory terms, and small markers of pronunciation, such as where commas are placed. Each of the legal systems discussed here concern itself with legislative language, so the point is more a matter of degree than of kind.

Each system has its own peculiarities when it comes to permitting evidence of legislative intent. In the US, there is general debate about whether a statute's legislative history should be brought before a court at all, but there is no actual doctrine separating various moments in that history. In France, transcripts of legislative debates are not used in court. However, reports accompanying proposed legislation are routinely relied upon, without controversy. The UK is far more nuanced than either France or the United States in this regard. Certain commission reports are accepted as evidence to assist in disambiguating statutory language or to provide clues to legislative purpose. Parliamentary debates, however, were banned from being used in court proceedings until the 1990s, still play a limited role, and remain controversial.

In the next three sections are brief summaries of the three approaches to interpretation, focusing on similarities and differences that become relevant when we return to the world of taxation.

Textualism in the United States

For the past quarter century, American judges and legal scholars have engaged in a war over words in the interpretation of statutes. The catalyst in these debates was Justice Antonin Scalia, appointed to the Supreme Court by President Reagan in 1986. In both his judicial opinions[2] and his extra-judicial writings,[3] Scalia argued forcefully that respect for the democratic process demands that judges pay maximum attention to statutory language and eschew, to the extent possible, such extra-textual material as legislative history in construing laws. Dubbed "the new textualism" by legal scholar William Eskridge,[4] this approach to statutory interpretation elevates nuanced argument about statutory language over other sources of information about what the legislature intended. Judicial opinions, in turn, focus on such things as dictionary definitions of various words contained in laws,[5] subtle differences in wording between one provision and another,[6] and database searches of the use of words and phrases by ordinary people or by judges.[7]

Not all commentators and judges agree with this approach. Supreme Court Justice Stephen Breyer argues for a more purposive approach to statutory interpretation, and would enlarge the types of evidence available to judges to include legislative history.[8] Breyer believes that such a stance is more faithful to the intent of the legislature than is the textualist approach, which is more susceptible to rulings based on linguistic happenstance. US Court of Appeal Judge Robert Katzmann argues for a similar approach, based more on the realities of the legislative process, in which delegation to legislative committees and the role of sponsors in enacting legislation are central.[9] Academic commentators have been similarly critical of textualist methodology.[10]

To illustrate, consider the Supreme Court's decision in *Circuit City Stores, Inc., v. Adams*, decided in 2001.[11] Plaintiff Adams, who worked for Circuit City, a national chain of electronics stores, sued for employment discrimination. At the time he began working there, he signed the obligatory agreement in which he consented to arbitrating all disputes between him and his employer. Based on that agreement, Circuit City moved to have the case dismissed in favor of arbitration, relying on the Federal Arbitration Act, which requires the enforcement of agreements to arbitrate disputes arising under a contract "evidencing a transaction involving

---

2 See, e.g. *West Univ. Hosps. v. Casey*, 499 U.S. 83 (1991); *Chisom v. Roemer*, 501 U.S. 380, 418 (1991) (Scalia, J., dissenting); MCI Telecommunications *Corp. v. AT&T Co.*, 512 U.S. 218 (1994); *King v. Burwell*, 135 S. Ct. 2480, 2496 (2015) (Scalia, J., dissenting).

3 A. Scalia, *A Matter of Interpretation: Federal Courts and the Law* (Princeton: Princeton University Press, 1998); A. Scalia and B. Garner, *Reading Law: The Interpretation of Legal Texts* (St. Paul: Thomson/West, 2012).

4 W. N. Eskridge, Jr., "The New Textualism", 37 *UCLA Law Review* 621 (1990).

5 See, e.g. *Muscarello v. United States*, 524 U.S. 125 (1998) (majority and dissenting justices arguing over which dictionary best defines the word "carry" where dispute is over whether "carrying a firearm" in a criminal statute implies carrying it on one's person). For discussion of the Supreme Court's reliance on dictionaries, see J. J. Brudney and L. Baum, "Oasis or Mirage: The Supreme Court's Thirst for Dictionaries in the Rehnquist and Roberts Eras", 55 *William & Mary Law Review* 483 (2013), and references cited therein.

6 *Circuit City Stores, Inc. v. Adams*, 532 U.S. 105 (2001) (holding that "evidencing" interstate commerce in one provision of the Federal Arbitration Act was intended to have broader meaning than "engaged in" interstate commerce in another provision of the same act).

7 *See Muscarello*, 524 U.S. at 129 (reporting search of New York Times database to determine that people often use the expression "carry a gun" to refer to hauling the weapon in a vehicle, and not only to carrying it on one's person.

8 S. Breyer, *Active Liberty: Interpreting Our Democratic Constitution* (New York: Vintage Books, 2005).

9 R. A. Katzmann, *Judging Statutes* (Oxford: Oxford University Press, 2014).

10 W. N. Eskridge, Jr., "The New Textualism and Normative Canons" (reviewing A. Scalia and B. Garner, *Reading Law: The Interpretation of Legal Text*), 113 *Columbia Law Review* 531 (2013); J. R. Siegel, "The Inexorable Radicalization of Textualism", 158 *University of Pennsylvania Law Review* 117 (2009); A. R. Gluck and L. S. Bressman, "Statutory Interpretation From the Inside – An Empirical Study of Congressional Delegation, Drafting, and the Canons: Part I", 65 *Stanford Law Review* 901 (2013); Lawrence M. Solan, The Language of Statutes: Laws and Their Interpretation (especially ch. 4) (Chicago: University of Chicago Press, 2010).

11 532 U.S. 105 (2001).

commerce."[12] An exception exempts from enforcement "contracts of employment of seamen, railroad employees, or any other class of workers engaged in foreign or interstate commerce."[13] The issue in this case was whether the exception applies to Adams' agreement to arbitrate.

The exception is ambiguous: it can be understood as shorthand for just those workers who would have been deemed to engage in interstate commerce at the time the law was written, i.e. principally transportation workers; or it could be understood to include whichever workers are deemed to be engaged in interstate commerce at the time that the exception is being called upon. By 2001, that category had grown considerably as the result of changes in the economy and almost a century of commerce clause jurisprudence by the Supreme Court.

In a five-to-four decision, the Supreme Court held in favor of the employer, construing the arbitration requirement broadly and the exception narrowly. Its arguments were largely linguistic. The Court found that "evidencing a transaction" is a broader statement than the exception's "engaged in foreign or interstate commerce," suggesting that Congress intended the exception to the arbitration requirement to apply only to a subset of cases between employers and employees. Second, the Court relied on the canon *ejusdem generis*, which calls for "any other class of workers engaged in interstate commerce" in the exception to be construed as referring to transportation workers, since the statute specifically lists others in that category: seamen and railroad employees. The majority also pointed out that the Federal Arbitration Act was enacted to combat judicial hostility to arbitration in the early twentieth century, and that the Supreme Court had developed a jurisprudence of strong support for arbitration in recent decades.

The dissent focused on wholly different issues. The dissent was far more interested in the purpose of the exception, which was to keep the courthouse doors open to decide employment disputes, which are generally considered local affairs. Thus, the dissent was more concerned with both the social and legislative history surrounding the enactment of the exception than it was concerned about inferences drawn from subtle differences in the wording of the two provisions or in the more recent history of pro-arbitration court decisions.

The contrast between the two sides in this case well illustrates the tension between text and purpose in the practice of US courts in construing statutes. No judge claims a willingness to thwart the purpose of a statute, but many judges are willing to find the purpose only by searching very narrowly.

Notwithstanding these intramural battles, which at times become quite passionate, a growing body of literature suggests, correctly in our opinions, that there is a growing consensus around some of the major tenets of statutory interpretation in the United States. A study by Professor Abbe Gluck[14] shows that despite the vociferous bickering on the US Supreme Court, many states have settled on a "modified textualism" by which courts give statutory language priority, but are willing to resolve residual uncertainties in meaning with a variety of extra-textual inquiries. Moreover, although the disputes over the use of legislative history to resolve disputes over meaning remain heated, there is no serious disagreement among US judges and legal scholars over the use of the canons of construction, the precedential effect of earlier decisions, coherence with other provisions in the code, and the use of social history as background. All of these are fair game in an effort to divine the intent of the enacting legislature.[15]

---

12 9 U.S.C. § 2.
13 9 U.S.C. § 1.
14 A. R. Gluck, "The States as Laboratories of Statutory Interpretation: Methodological Consensus and the New Modified Textualism", 119 *The Yale Law Journal* 1750 (2010).
15 For discussion of the similarities among the various competing approaches, see J. T. Molot, "The Rise and Fall of Textualism", 106 *Columbia Law Review* 1, 30–46 (2006); Solan, see n.10 (especially ch. 3).

By the same token, most of the US judges and scholars who would regard themselves more as intentionalists or as purposivists are no more wedded to ignoring the plain language of the law than are the committed textualists. All sides are willing, on occasion, to correct clear legislative errors in drafting, but this concession more or less sets the limit when it comes to substituting judicial language for that of the legislature.[16] Thus, most of the actual disagreement comes within the ambit of how to resolve ambiguity in statutory language, where both sides have colorable positions with respect to the legislative language itself. As we shall see, other legal systems are more comfortable focusing directly on effectuating a statute's purpose than on linguistic nuances.

Purposivism in the United Kingdom

The United Kingdom struggles between textualism and purposivism. Its methods are, generally, eclectic and context driven. As one writer notes, courts typically first determine the purpose of the statute, and then construe the language of the statute, within its permissible range of legitimate interpretations, consistent with that purpose.[17] Yet, whether the court emphasizes the language or the purpose in its decision is by no means uniform.[18] Moreover, unlike US legal doctrine, judges in the UK have license to add or subtract language to the ordinary meaning of statutory language when doing so appears to be necessary to effectuate Parliament's purpose in enacting the law when no reading of the language as written seems to do so.[19]

Purposive interpretation is nothing new in British law. US and UK law students continue to be introduced to purposive interpretation through the rule in *Heydon's Case*,[20] a sixteenth century case in which the court held that in interpreting statutes it was necessary to consider the mischief that motivated the enactment of the statute and to rule in a manner that advances that purpose. Yet, over time, British law has had its periods of the text overriding purpose even when the latter is abundantly clear.[21] Thus, the trend toward purposivism taking hold in the mid-twentieth century in the UK has simultaneously deep roots and the feel of modernity.

The United States, in contrast, limits such authority to correcting clear errors in drafting, or in rejecting absurdity. The difference between the two systems is more a matter of degree than of kind, however.

In the United Kingdom, the largest issue in statutory interpretation is the legitimacy of consulting extra-textual material, in particular legislative history contained in *Hansard*, the official record of parliamentary debates. Courts are willing to consider explanatory notes published aside new legislation, although not part of that legislation.[22] In addition, reports of various commissions and law reform committees are admissible in UK courts to clarify the purpose of a statute and to resolve ambiguity.[23] Far more controversial is reference to Hansard. This was

---

16 See, e.g. *X-Citement Video v. United States*, 513 U.S. 64 (1994); J. Siegel, "What Statutory Drafting Errors Teach Us About Statutory Interpretation", 69 *The George Washington Law Review* 309 (2001).

17 W. Twining and D. Miers, *How to Do Things With Rules: A Primer of Interpretation*, 5th ed. (Cambridge: Cambridge University Press, 2010), 249.

18 *Id*. at 250.

19 *Id*. at 252.

20 76 Eng. Rptr. 637, 638 (1584).

21 See I. McLeod, "Literal and Purposive Techniques of Legislative Interpretation: Some European Community and English Common Law Perspectives", 29 *Brooklyn Journal of International Law* 109, 113–14 (2004).

22 See *Westminster City Council v. National Asylum Support Service*, [2002] 4 All ER 634 at [5].

23 See Twining & Myers, see n.17 at 260; J. J. Brudney, "Below the Surface: Comparing Legislative History Usage by the House of Lords and the Supreme Court", 85 *Washington University Law Review* 1, 7 (2007).

forbidden prior to 1993 when the House of Lords decided *Pepper v. Hart if*,[24] a case studied on both sides of the Atlantic. The details of the case and subsequent debates over its scope exceed the scope of this brief discussion. The limitations placed on the use of Hansard are relevant here, however, as illustrations of the UK's ambivalence toward finding extrinsic evidence of legislative intent. First, the admission of statements from Hansard was intended to be limited to statements by ministers or other sponsors of the bills that eventually became law. Second, the statements had to make clear that they related to a particular purpose that the law was intended to address. Finally, the statements could be used only for the limited purposes of resolving linguistic uncertainty to avoid absurd results.[25]

The UK doctrine in this matter is in different ways both more permissive and less permissive than practice in the US. The UK distinguishes between various commission reports on the one hand, and parliamentary debates on the other. In the US, those who oppose the use of legislative history as a general matter make no distinction between the reports of congressional committees and statements from the floor of the houses of Congress, transcribed in the Congressional Record.

Teleology in France

Let us compare the heavy reliance on textual nuance in the United States with the more purposive perspective of French courts. European courts in general, including French courts, are far more comfortable relying on the general purpose of a statute than are their US counterparts. Many codes are very old, and even those that are not old are often derived from codes enacted in the nineteenth century. The result is that judges are routinely confronted with situations that the drafters of the code did not anticipate. Yet, the codes were deemed to be complete statements of the law, requiring judges, whether reasoning by analogy from one code provision to another, or relying on the overall structure of the code, or inferring how the values reflected in relevant code provisions can best be advanced today, to make decisions that result in updating old laws. This is not considered judicial activism. Rather, the system was designed with this activity in mind.[26]

Because of the primacy of the code, judges regard themselves as playing a deferential role to the legislature, much as do US judges based on its own system of separation of powers. This deference, however, does not display itself by preferring nuanced textual analysis to the examination of legislative history. The search for a single meaning that will make such historical investigation irrelevant is less a part of the legal culture.[27] On the contrary, legislative history (travaux préparatoires), is more or less uncontroversially fair game in the interpretation of French statutes. This is especially the case for newer statutes, when the plain language does not yield a single, clear interpretation.

This is not to say that French judges ignore the language of a statute whereas US judges pay attention to it. European judges follow the text literally when the text is clear, absent absurdity

---

24 [1993] 1 All E.R. 42 (H.L. 1992).

25 *Id.* at 69 (summarizing the three limitations).

26 For an excellent description of how French judges and legal scholars reconcile the need for judges to make decisions in individual cases with a perspective that denies their being the ultimate source of law in the common law sense, see M. de S. – O. – l'E. Lasser, *Judicial Deliberations: A Comparative Analysis of Transparency and Legitimacy* (Oxford: Oxford University Press, 2009), 172–3.

27 See K. Zweigert and H.-J. Puttfargen, "Civilian Statutory Interpretation", 44 *Tulane Law Review* 704, 713 (1970).

or intervening historical development.[28] This is especially true when it comes to newer statutes, where there can be no legitimate argument that either the language or the society have changed extensively since the law's enactment. In fact, as Peter Strauss observes, the differences in rhetoric about the degree of deference to the legislature between the civil law and common law approaches to statutory interpretation may be far more profound than differences in substance.[29]

As for style, the biggest difference is the incessant reference to case law in US statutory decisions, a practice not followed in France. In the US, the "canons of construction" are almost all judge-made, and courts refer to various cases in which they were articulated to justify using them. In France, interpretive methods are not part of the Civil Code, although some European countries do include methodology in the code itself.[30] The practice, however, is not to recite and distinguish methods contained in judicial decisions in construing statutes, but rather to rely upon important legal treatises that articulate the interpretive principles. US law students learn that it is acceptable to cite as being tantamount to law certain universally recognized secondary sources, such as the American Law Institute's *Restatements* of the law. In civil law systems, the practice is similar, although it happens without apology to the common law tradition. Reference to cases and treatises varies from one legal system to another. Regardless, creating a coherent body of law that makes sense of the code as a whole is an important civil law value, and judges are well-versed in the important cases with which they will need to reconcile subsequent decisions. Thus, French courts pay very close attention to cases as the law develops, but tend not to make reference to them as sources of law.[31]

Just as US courts are especially comfortable devoting most of their statutory decisions to discussing prior cases, French courts are comfortable speaking of a law's purpose, especially an older law whose application to a new situation is in dispute.[32] Called the *teleological approach* to statutory interpretation, this purposive perspective is deeply embedded in the civil law tradition. As noted previously, French courts are no more likely than US courts to override the plain language of a statute to broaden its scope to better effectuate its purpose. Nonetheless, French courts are less likely to engage in minute analysis of language for the purpose of construing a law narrowly in a manner that will undermine its purpose. The orientation toward being responsible for applying codes written in general language to new and complex situations more or less mandates investigation into the purpose behind the law. The legislature could not have had a specific intent with respect to novel situations, and the language does not answer the question on its own.

Responses to tax avoidance

The puzzle at the heart of this chapter is not simply why courts otherwise willing to embrace purposivism become hesitant in the tax context. It is not hard to imagine, after all, that – given the pernicious impact of uncertainty – tax might simply be uniquely incompatible with

---

28 See C. M. Germain, "Approaches to Statutory Interpretation and Legislative History in France", 13 *Duke Journal of Comparative & International Law* 195, 201 (2003).

29 P. Strauss, "The Common Law and Statutes", 70 *University of Colorado Law Review* 225, 234–6 (1999).

30 Spanish Civil Code, Article 3, World Intellectual Property Organization (2009), English translation, available at www.wipo.int/wipolex/en/text.jsp?file_id=221319.

31 See l'E. Lasser, see n.26 at 173; M. Troper, C. Grzegorczyk and J.-L. "Gardies, Statutory Interpretation in France", in D. N. MacCormick and R. S. Summers (eds), *Interpreting Statutes: A Comparative Study* (Brookfield, VT: Dartmouth, 1991), 171, 188–9.

32 See C.M. Germain, see n.28 at 202.

purposivism. The more compelling mystery is how the converse can simultaneously also be true, so that courts in the United States enjoy more freedom to effectuate the purpose of tax statutes than they might in another context.

US, UK and French courts will not hesitate to strip tax benefits from a transaction that amounts to little more than a "simulation" or "hollow device," but US courts go further, demanding a "business objective," even when a transaction satisfies every statutory require-ment.[33] That judicial power – and the solicitude toward legislators that it implies – resonates more closely with French teleology than with US textualism. Although the differences among the interpretive styles described previously may in some respects be no more than skin deep, with respect to tax the differences are substantive and precisely the opposite of those the preced-ing discussion might suggest.

Common law anti-avoidance measures

Courts in the United States have crafted an array of interrelated anti-avoidance doctrines.[34] Those doctrines variously insist that transactions have economic substance and serve a business purpose while weighing them as potential shams or mere steps in a broader transaction. The pre-cise impact of these doctrines on taxpayer behavior defies easy description, but in the aggregate they serve as an important deterrent against taxpayer abuses. As described later in this chapter, the experience across the Atlantic has been quite different.

In *Gregory v. Helvering*, the US Supreme Court firmly rejected the notion that merely satisfy-ing the technical requirements of relevant statutes would be sufficient to qualify for legislative tax benefits.[35] The taxpayer in that case had scrupulously observed the formal requirements of the statute but was doomed by her inability to demonstrate that those steps served a meaningful business objective. Invoking the "plain intent of the statute," the Court concluded that allowing her to claim those benefits "would be to exalt artifice above reality and to deprive the statutory provision in question of all serious purpose."[36] As with the other anti tax-avoidance doctrines employed by US courts, the focus on legislative intent in *Gregory v. Helvering* echoes UK and French (non-tax) purposive inclinations.

The proliferation of common law anti-avoidance measures in the United States indicates both strength and weakness. One could easily imagine courts gladly exchanging their cluttered doctrinal toolbox for a single dependable anti-avoidance device. At first glance, each device might seem relatively straightforward, but a closer inspection reveals significant complexity.

Like *Gregory v. Helvering*'s business purpose doctrine, the economic substance doctrine requires that taxpayers not merely follow the letter of the tax law, but also be able to demon-strate that a given transaction has consequences and motivations for the parties involved that extend beyond taxation. Long before the codification of the doctrine in 2010, courts scrutinized

---

33 In each jurisdiction, some transactions are ignored. In the United States, the business purpose served by a transac-tion tends to receive greater attention as proof that a transaction merits respect. See, e.g. *Waterman Steamship Corp. v. Commissioner*, 430 F.2d 1185, 1196 (5th Cir. 1970) (concluding that "a subsidiary's dividend declaration immedi-ately before the complete disposition of the parent's interest in the stock of the subsidiary seems a hollow device lacking any business objective other than the extraction of earnings and profits without dividend consequences").

34 J. Bankman, "The Economic Substance Doctrine", 74 *Southern California Law Review*, 5, 12 (2000) (noting that "the economic substance doctrine is closely related to common law doctrines of sham transaction, substance over form, business purpose, economic profit, and step transaction").

35 293 U.S. 465 (1935).

36 *Id.* at 470.

transactions that satisfied each of the law's requirements for subjective and objective evidence of economic substance.

The economic substance doctrine calls for transactions to be as they appear, but also demands more. The objective leg of the doctrine looks for proof that a transaction has "some nontax effect."[37] Despite its apparent simplicity, the objective aspect of the economic substance doctrine raises a host of questions.[38] Coupled with that objective test comes an examination of "the taxpayer's expectations and motives."[39] The subjective test collides with the same types of fundamental uncertainties as its objective counterpart.[40]

Beyond the subtle differences that inevitably mark doctrines embraced by many courts and still more judges, different circuits adopted conflicting visions of the doctrine. Before codification homogenized it, one might even have said that more than one economic substance doctrine existed. The most striking inconsistency may have been that some jurisdictions demanded that a taxpayer show both objective and subjective evidence of economic substance[41] while others accepted just one, so that "the court must find that the taxpayer was motivated by no business purposes other than obtaining tax benefits in entering the transaction, and that the transaction has no economic substance because no reasonable possibility of a profit exists" to deny taxpayers their sought-after result.[42]

Each of the US judicial anti-avoidance doctrines shares traits with others. The complex relationships among the doctrines make it difficult to differentiate them.[43] Although the economic substance and business purpose doctrines stand alone, courts occasionally refer to the subjective economic substance prong as the business purpose test of the economic substance doctrine. Such inconsistencies and overlapping edges tend to be grudgingly accepted as the price of a robust anti-avoidance arsenal.

At the start of the twentieth century, both US and UK courts tended to resolve ambiguities in favor of taxpayers.[44] Since then the experience of US and UK courts with respect to what one member of the House of Lords derided as "spooky jurisprudence" has been strikingly different.[45] As the US income tax began to mature and its common law anti tax-avoidance

37 See Bankman, n.34.

38 See *id*. at 12–26.

39 See *id*. at 27. The subjective inquiry, sometimes referred to as the business purpose prong of the economic substance doctrine, focuses on "whether the taxpayer was induced to commit capital for reasons only relating to tax considerations or whether a non-tax motive, or legitimate profit motive, was involved": *Shriver v. Commissioner*, 899 F.2d 724, 726 (8th Cir. 1990).

40 See *id*. at 27 (noting that the question of "[h]ow significant must the nontax purpose be?" went long "unanswered by the courts, for the same reason that the cognate question in the objective leg of the economic substance test is left unanswered: The transactions thus far challenged by the government have served no plausible nontax purpose").

41 See, e.g. *United Parcel Serv. v. CIR*, 254 F3d 1014, 1018 (11th Cir. 2001) ("Even if the transaction has economic effects, it must be disregarded if it has no business purpose and its motive is tax avoidance").

42 *Rice's Toyota World v. Commissioner*, 752 F.2d 89, 91 (4th Cir. 1985).

43 See M. McMahon, "Comparing the Application of Judicial Interpretive Doctrines to Revenue Statutes on Opposite Ends of the Pond", in John Avery Jones, Peter Harris, J. David B. Oliver (eds), *Comparative Perspectives on Revenue Law: Essays in Honour of John Tiley* (Cambridge: Cambridge University Press, 2008), 40, 61 ("The economic substance doctrine is usually said to have originated in the Supreme Court's 1978 decision in *Frank Lyon Co. v. United States*, but as the doctrine has evolved … it in some way builds on the *Knetsch* legal sham and *Goldstein* purposive activity variants of the business purpose doctrine").

44 See A. Likhovski, "The Duke and the Lady: Helvering v. Gregory and the History of Tax Avoidance Adjudication", 25 *Cardozo Law Review* 953 (2004) (relying on tax treatises published in 1876 and (just before *Helvering v. Gregory*) in 1934 to pinpoint the timing of the divergence caused by the US embrace of anti-avoidance doctrines).

45 See *Norglen Ltd. v. Reeds Rains Prudential Ltd.* [1999] 2 AC 1 (HL) 14.

doctrines began to emerge in cases such as *Gregory v. Helvering*,[46] UK law followed a different path with *I.R.C. v. Duke of Westminster*.[47] Since before the Second World War, US tax law has maintained that a transaction's economic substance matters above all. UK courts have – at the risk of understatement – given transactional form greater weight.

One mildly hyperbolic formulation of the doctrine that has long set the tone for UK law urged that in the tax context "the court must look to the form of the transaction and not its substance."[48] The US Supreme Court concedes that "[a]ny one may so arrange his affairs that his taxes shall be as low as possible; he is not bound to choose that pattern which will best pay the Treasury; there is not even a patriotic duty to increase one's taxes,"[49] but US courts place great weight on substance. In the United Kingdom, courts adopt a permissive stance on tax avoidance to such an extent that what would be considered a marginal transaction in the United Kingdom "would not have been attempted in the United States."[50]

Beginning in the 1980s, it appeared that UK courts might be reversing course. *W.T. Ramsay Ltd. v. C.I.R.*,[51] particularly as interpreted by *Furniss v. Dawson*,[52] came to be seen as possible rejection of the longstanding *Westminster* doctrine by requiring courts to look beyond a transaction's form.[53] With the benefit of hindsight, the impact of *Ramsay* appears to be more modest. Several decades on, it has become evident that "*Ramsay* did not" – as some had perhaps hoped – "develop into a business-purpose doctrine along the lines of the US doctrine" which would have required that "taxpayers have a reason other than the avoidance of taxes for undertaking a transaction or a series of transactions if their actions are to be tax effective."[54]

From a US perspective, the modern *Ramsay* doctrine[55] most closely resembles neither the business purpose nor the economic substance doctrines but the US step transaction doctrine.[56] Rather than looking beyond taxpayers' actions to their motivations, the *Ramsay* "composite transaction" and the US step transaction doctrines merely redraw the boundaries of a transaction to prevent a taxpayer from securing unwarranted tax benefits. Like a quotation isolated from its context, a taxpayer might present a fragment of a transaction in a way that is entirely inconsistent with the broader sweep of the taxpayer's activities. These doctrines work to restore the missing context. In that sense, the *Ramsay* doctrine represented a relatively modest departure from

---

46 See text accompanying nn.35–36.
47 [1936] A.C. 1.
48 J. Tiley and G. Loutzenhiser, *Introduction to UK Tax Law; Income Tax; Capital Gains Tax; Inheritance Tax*, 111 (Oxford: Hart Publishing, 2012) (the authors note that this formulation is "misleading" and point out that despite courts' emphasis on form over substance that "documents cannot be used to deny proven facts").
49 *Gregory v. Helvering*, 293 U.S. at 811.
50 J. Tiley and E. Jensen, "The Control of Avoidance: The United States Experience", *British Tax Review* 161 (1998).
51 [1982] A.C. 300.
52 [1984] A.C. 474.
53 *See* J. Freedman, "Interpreting Tax Statutes: Tax Avoidance and the Intention of Parliament", 123 *Law Quarterly Review* 52, 53 (2007) ("For a time it seemed that this new approach was firming up into a judicial doctrine or at least a principle attempting to counter tax avoidance").
54 See J. Freedman, n.53 at 57; Tiley and Loutzenhiser, n.48 at 117 (noting that the House of Lords "quickly and decisively rejected the view that *Furniss v. Dawson* should be taken as the beginning of a general anti-tax avoidance jurisprudence").
55 See J. Freedman, n.53 at 57 (the "*Ramsay* 'approach' ... required the court to ascertain the legal nature of the transaction ... by looking at a series or combination of transactions intended to operate as such rather than in isolation from each other (known as a 'composite transaction')").
56 M. McMahon, "Comparing the Application of Judicial Interpretative Doctrines to Revenue Statutes on Opposite Sides of the Pond", in John Avery Jones, Peter Harris, J. David B. Oliver (eds), *Comparative Perspectives on Revenue Law: Essays in Honor of John Tiley* (Cambridge: Cambridge University Press, 2008), 40, 45.

Westminster. After all, (re)integrating one element of a transaction with its counterparts does less violence to a taxpayer's autonomy than negating some of the taxpayer's actions entirely.

Ramsay's current status remains the subject of contention.[57] *Ramsay*'s impact had already been limited by a relatively contemporaneous decision[58] and a more recent pair of cases has heightened the uncertainty.[59] Even in its strongest incarnation, the *Ramsay* doctrine would find itself the weakest weapon in the US common law anti-avoidance arsenal if it somehow found its way across the Atlantic.[60]

Legislative anti-avoidance efforts

When the terrain shifts from common law anti-abuse doctrines to statutory anti-avoidance measures, so too does the relationship among the three jurisdictions under consideration. Until quite recently, neither the United States nor the United Kingdom relied on general anti-abuse legislation to combat tax avoidance. By contrast, French authorities have long relied primarily on statutory anti-avoidance authority. Not only have French courts generally declined to adopt anti-abuse doctrines – which on its own might not be surprising for a civil law jurisdiction – but also they have, at times, actively curbed legislative anti-abuse efforts.

Less than a decade after *Duke of Westminster* and *Gregory* set the tone for UK and US tax law respectively, France codified its principal anti-avoidance provision.[61] The abuse of fiscal law statute plays the same part in France that the economic substance and its companion doctrines do in the United States.[62] Courts in the United States and the United Kingdom arrived at starkly different results, but they both shouldered the primary burden of balancing taxpayer autonomy against the need to curb tax avoidance. In France, the legislature has long taken a more prominent role, even if the intervention of the courts appears decisive at critical moments.

The 1941 codification of the abuse of law[63] concept bolstered a longstanding judicial practice of disregarding "simulations" (transactions that a US court might label a "hollow device").[64] Rather than the statute being a substantive shift in the law governing abusive tax planning, the statute's history suggests it was aimed at procedural shortcomings, which it sought to address by instituting a severe penalty[65] and implementing a new assessment procedure. From a comparative

---

57 See J. Freedman, n.53 at 63 ("the House of Lords applied the [*Ramsay*] principle in the *Scottish Provident* case on the very same day that it denied it" in BMBF).

58 See *Craven v. White*, [1989] A.C. 398. See Judith Freedman at 61 (noting that *Craven* suggested that there was no *Ramsay* principle and that *Ramsay* "was in truth a rule of statutory construction").

59 *Barclays Mercantile Business Finance Ltd v. Mawson* [2004] UKHL 51; [2005] 1 A.C. 684; [2005] S.T.C. 1 ("BMBF"); *IRC v. Scottish Provident Institution* [2004] UKHL 52; [2004] 1 W.L.R. 3172; [2005] S.T.C. 15.

60 Although *Scottish Provident Institution* demonstrates that the *Ramsay* doctrine retains some measure of potency, BMBF downplays its power. BMBF at 33 citing Lord Steyn in Mcgukian at 915 ("the *Ramsay* case simply rescued tax law from 'some island of literal interpretation' and brought it within generally-applicable principles.").

61 V. Thuronyi, *Comparative Tax Law* (The Hague: Kluwer Law Int'l, 2003), 188.

62 See Thuronyi, n.61 at 160–95 (describing "general anti-avoidance rules" in various jurisdictions and focusing on the economic substance and other doctrines in the United States, *Westminster* and *Ramsay* in the United Kingdom and the 1941 codification of the abuse of fiscal law provision in France).

63 Act of 13 January 1941 codified under article 156 *quinquies* of the ancient General Code of Direct Taxes (*Code général des impôts directs*), subsequently amended.

64 "Simulations" were disregarded on the tax plane well before the Act of 1941. There are cases which go back well into the XIX century in the field of registration duties: e.g. Cass. civ., 20 August 1867, Legrand c. enreg.

65 Initially, 200% of the amount of the assessment. The penalty was scaled down by the Act of 8 July 1987 to 80%, where it stands today. However, in 2008 a milder 40% penalty was introduced in case it is not proved that the taxpayer was the principal initiator of the scheme or that she was its principal beneficiary.

perspective, the procedural dimension is the most striking legacy of the 1941 text.[66] When disregarding transactions under the abuse of tax law provision, tax authorities must follow a special procedure which offers both the administration and the taxpayer an opportunity to refer the case to a special committee for its recommendation.[67] The recommendation of the committee is not binding but, if favorable to the administration, will shift the burden of proof to the taxpayer in case of litigation before courts.[68]

The wording of the 1941 text was ambiguous, limiting its practical impact.[69] Perhaps most importantly, academics and courts held generally that the abuse of law rule was limited to "*simulations*" and did not embrace the concept of "*fraude à loi.*"[70] *Fraude à loi* is a general theory in civil law countries,[71] pervading all branches of law, which, as applied in France, deprives of legal effect transactions that meet the letter of the law but violate its spirit.[72] The refusal to embrace *fraude à la loi* in the tax context set the tax law apart. The resulting textualist approach to construing tax statutes echoed *Duke of Westminster*'s reluctance to hold taxpayers responsible for following rules legislators perhaps should have, but did not, write.[73]

---

66 Codified today under article L. 64 of the Code of Tax Procedures (*Livre des procedures fiscales*).

67 Named, as of 2009, Committee of the Abuse of Tax Law (*Comité de l'abus de droit fiscal*). It is composed of three senior judges, issued each from the *Conseil d'Etat, Cour des comptes* and *Cour de cassation*, and of an attorney, a notary, a certified accountant and a professor of university.

68 While the Committee was created to favor tax authorities, it turned out to be a boon to taxpayers. Between 2011 and 2015, between 20 to 40% of the recommendations were favorable to the taxpayer. While not legally bound to follow those recommendations, in many instances the administration chose to abandon the assessment, preventing the litigation before courts. Making matters worse, unless authorized by some specific anti-avoidance rule, the administration cannot disregard or recharacterize taxpayer's transaction outside of the abuse of tax law procedure. The opportunity to have the case heard before the Committee is recognized as a substantial guarantee of taxpayer's rights that tax authorities must honor.

69 It stipulated the administration could recharacterize transactions which "dissimulated the real nature of a contract or convention".

70 Simulation is a civil law concept which consists in "creating an apparent juridical act which does not correspond to the reality of things" (*Dictionary of the Civil Code* [Paris: LexisNexis, 2014], 525). The apparent act can be fictitious such as in case of a gift in which the donor subsequently retains control of sums apparently disposed of. Another common example is that of a gift disguised as a sale. In principle, tax considerations are irrelevant in characterizing simulations since, as a legal sham, the transaction can be disregarded as a matter of civil law, even if simulated transactions are frequently entered into for tax reasons. In contrast, "*fraude à la loi*" applies to transactions that are regular under civil or commercial law. For instance, as a general rule, a company will not be fictitious if corporation law's forms are respected (i.e. proper accounts are kept, the board meets, etc.) but it can be disregarded under *fraude à la loi*, if it had been artificially introduced in a flow of income with the sole objective to avoid taxation, as the case may be in the treaty shopping devices in international taxation.

71 *Fraude de ley* in Spain, *fraus legis* in the Netherlands, *Gesetzumgehung* in Germany. The German term evokes literally the circumvention of law.

72 The modern expression of "*fraude à la loi*" originates in private international law. Every French law student knows the case of Princesse de Bauffremont (*Cour de cassation*, Req., 18 mars 1878), who in order to circumvent the – then applicable – prohibition of divorce in French law, took the nationality of the German Duchy of Saxe-Altenburg. Fraudulent, her new nationality as well as her divorce celebrated abroad was disregarded in France. In administrative law, "*fraude à la loi*" was firmly recognized as a general principle of law in a case where the court disregarded a fraudulent marriage celebrated with the sole objective to obtain a residence permit (Conseil d'Etat, 9 October 1992, n° 137342, Abihilali: Rec. 1992, p. 363).

73 *E.g.*, Maurice Cozian, one of the leading tax academics of his generation, in an article published as late as in 1980 ("La gestion fiscale de l'entreprise", *Revue de la jurisprudence fiscale*, 5/1980, pp. 202–206), underlines that the administration cannot second-guess taxpayer's intentions and that authors that allow for the application of the theory of *fraude à la loi* in tax law are isolated.

A significant shift occurred in 1981, initiated not by legislators but by the Conseil d'Etat.[74] While the statutory text remained unchanged, the court added a second prong to its construction of the principal French anti-abuse statute, recognizing the theory of *fraude à loi* in the tax context.[75] After that expansion, the statute targeted not only simulations in which a transaction fails to meet muster even in terms of its form, but also transactions that meet the letter of the law but violate its spirit. However, such a violation would only be found when a transaction was entered into for the sole motive of avoiding taxation.

After 1981 it remained unclear whether *fraude à la loi* applied to taxes not specifically covered by the 1941 statute. The Conseil d'Etat resolved that uncertainty with its 2006 *Janfin* decision.[76] *Janfin* held that the general anti-avoidance statute codified *fraude à la loi* as it applies to tax, rather than introducing *fraude à la loi* to the tax law. As a result, the statute merely offered a framework for implementing – along with penalties for violating – *fraude à la loi* principles within the legislation's clearly defined scope.

If the general anti-avoidance statute is one day abolished, *Janfin* suggests that the concept of *fraude à la loi* would, like a balloon, recover its full shape in tax law. The French Parliament reacted in 2008, redrafting the 1941 text to embrace *Janfin's* expansive vision of the potential of *fraude à la loi* in the tax context.[77] In practical terms, that redrafting accomplished two ends. First, the revised statutory definition of abuse copies the 2006 *Janfin* judgment word for word. Second, the abuse of tax law procedure and penalties has been generalized to all taxes.

The 1941 and 1981–2008 expansions dovetailed with judicial efforts to combat tax avoidance. Nevertheless, both prior to and even after Janfin's embrace of *fraude à la loi*, French courts have demanded significantly less of taxpayers than a US court would.[78] Only transactions motivated solely by tax benefits fall short. Legislative efforts to moderate that requirement, even so far as to ban transactions with a principal purpose of tax avoidance, have foundered. The *Conseil Constitutionnel* recently struck down a legislative principal purpose test as conferring excessive discretionary power to the administration which, given the severe penalties attached to the abuse of law procedure, violated the constitutional objective of "intelligibility" of law and the principle of legality of criminal offenses and sanctions.[79]

---

74 *Conseil d'Etat* is the French Supreme Administrative Court. France has no single supreme court but two, which reflects the organization of the French judiciary, split between the "judicial" and the administrative court systems. The former, topped by the *Cour de cassation*, hears disputes in private and criminal law cases, whereas the latter, headed by the *Conseil d'Etat*, reviews the legality of administrative acts (individual decisions and regulatory acts). As a matter of public law, most tax disputes (income taxes, VAT, etc.) are heard by administrative courts. However, both supreme courts lack the capacity to review the constitutionality of statutes, which belongs to a specialized court: the *Conseil consitutionnel*.

75 Conseil d'Etat, 10 June 1981, n°19079, referred to the "case of the vineyard of Bordelais".

76 Conseil d'Etat, 27 September 2006, n°260050, min. c/Sté Janfin.

77 Act n° 2008–1443 of 30 December 2008, art. 35. The new wording of the abuse of law rule can be translated as follows:
    In order to restitute their true character, the Administration can disregard (…), acts [i.e. transactions of taxpayer] constituting abuse of law, either when these acts are fictitious or when, searching to benefit from a textual application of texts or decisions against the objectives pursued by their authors, they [these acts] could not have been inspired by no other motive that than to avoid or attenuate (…) [taxes] that the taxpayer, given her situation or her real activities, would have been charged with if these acts were not (…) realized.

78 It establishes a higher bar than that set by *Duke of Westminster* but a significantly lower one than *Gregory v. Helvering*. The debate in the context of *Gregory's* business purpose test is whether the necessary business objective must be the primary motivation for the transaction. By contrast, French legislators have been unsuccessful in blocking transactions in which tax avoidance is the primary motivation (to date, only transactions with a sole purpose of tax avoidance are treated as violating a tax law's spirit).

79 Conseil constitutionnel, 29 December 2013, *Loi de finances pour 2014*, n°2013–685 DC.

The question remains whether it is the principal purpose test that, in and of itself, is unconstitutional or it was considered so because it had been embedded in a special procedure triggering the application of penalties of a quasi-criminal nature. Most commentators agree the latter proposition reflects the law, especially given the most recent case in which the constitutionality of a specific anti-abuse rule using the principal purpose test was upheld:[80] the administration can enforce this rule, protecting the intragroup dividend exemption regime, pursuant to the standard assessment procedure, without penalties for abuse of law.

The French general anti-abuse rule operates clearly as a last resort "safety valve"[81] that recharacterizes transactions only a purely textualist approach to tax statutes would accommodate. French courts, despite having finally accepted the "transplant" of *fraude à la loi* in tax law, display great reluctance to go further by shifting from a sole purpose to principal purpose test.[82] This traditional French stance is, however, under strain from European Union law and the OECD's BEPS Project conclusions which advocate for the principal purpose approach.[83]

The French picture of a judiciary respectful of legal certainty must be reconciled with the relative ease with which specific anti-abuse rules pass through the French Parliament.[84] Because France relies on a parliamentary system, there is little opportunity for discord between legislators and the executive. Given that relationship, important loopholes identified by the tax administration are eagerly closed by Parliament.

The real hurdle to change is not Parliament but the constitutional review of the statute by the *Conseil Constitutionnel*. Legislative loophole-closing can only work prospectively, which encourages aggressive statutory drafting intended to anticipate taxpayer response. The detailed anti-abuse rules that result, accounting for much of the complexity of tax law, are in turn strictly construed. The result – taxpayers winning on apparent technicalities – is familiar to any common law lawyer, reinforcing the notion that statutory interpretation is textual in the tax field.

To some extent, the complexities of the relationship between the courts and the legislature are mirrored in both the United States and the United Kingdom. Within the past decade, both the United States and the United Kingdom codified a general anti-avoidance rule (GAAR). In each case, though, the anti-abuse statute outlawed transactions that the French statute would not. The codified US economic substance doctrine resolved some, but not all, of the uncertainties associated with the doctrine and added a stiff penalty.[85] The United Kingdom's GAAR built on a blank slate, taking advantage of the resulting flexibility by introducing its "completely unique" double reasonableness test for abuse.[86]

---

80 Conseil constitutionnel, 29 December 2015, *Loi de finances rectificative pour 2015*, n°2015–726 DC.

81 The number of cases referred annually to the Committee of Abuse of Tax Law is a good indicator of the frequency of the use of the general anti abuse rule by the French Tax Administration. Accordingly, only 25 cases were referred to it in 2015 (38 in 2014, 54 in 2013 and 52 in 2012).

82 *E.g.*, one of the most senior judges of Conseil d'Etat, specialized in tax law, wrote that, in the eyes of the judge, there was an "abyss" between the "exclusive" and "principal" purpose tests (O. Fouquet, "Fraude à la loi: l'explicitation du critère subjectif", 30–35 *Droit Fiscal* (2009), act. 428).

83 See Action 6 of the BEPS Project or the Directive (EU) 2015/121 of 27 January 2015 amending Directive 2011/96/EU on the common system of taxation applicable in the case of parent companies and subsidiaries of different Member States.

84 Since 2011, one could list new limits on deduction of intragroup debt, on deferral of capital gains on tax-free contributions of shares, on the use of a short-term capital loss on disposal of shares of a corporation previously stripped of its earnings through a tax-free intragroup dividend distribution.

85 See I.R.C. § 7701(o) (requiring both subjective and objective evidence of economic substance and imposing a strict liability penalty for transactions lacking economic substance).

86 J. Freedman, "Designing a General Anti-Abuse Rule: Striking a Balance", *Asia-Pacific Tax Bulletin* 20, 167, 170 (2014) (noting that the unique formulation targets abuse by "ensur[ing] that the judgement is not one of pure

Taken together, the judicial and legislative actions of these three jurisdictions present a series of contradictions. French courts, ordinarily deferential to legislatures, not only decline to embrace teleological methods to resolve tax disputes against taxpayers, but also at times affirmatively strike down anti-abuse legislation. Although often viewed as a stronghold of textualism, the United States boasts a variety of the purposive anti-abuse doctrines that UK courts deride. The next section suggests that these striking juxtapositions of textualism and purposivism offer a compelling answer to the many questions they raise.

The sparrow and the cannon

In one sense, the different approaches of US, UK and French judges in the context of tax avoidance efforts offer few surprises. That the impressive array of anti tax-avoidance doctrines available to US courts has no counterpart in France seems entirely consistent with the modest role courts play in the French legal system. Likewise, UK courts have long had a fraught relationship with the legislative history that fuels the US anti-avoidance doctrines.

Looking beyond such obvious differences among these legal systems reveals a more intriguing pattern. French judges embrace the concept of teleology, which elevates the intent of legislators. For hundreds of years, British courts have employed the "mischief rule" derived from *Heydon's Case* to ensure that legislative intent does not wilt like a hothouse flower when a statute ventures beyond the confines of Parliament.

Given the textualist threads woven deeply into the fabric of US common law, it hardly seems a foregone conclusion that US courts would display the greatest zeal in the defense of legislative intent by combating tax avoidance schemes. Differences in governmental architecture could explain the apparent contradiction. A parliamentary system may obviate the need for judicial intervention by offering a streamlined process for crafting legislative remedies to tax avoidance strategies as they emerge.[87] That would, of course, also be true outside of the tax context, raising the larger question of why legislators would need judges to speak for them in other substantive areas under the banner of *Heydon's Case* or teleology.

In essence, the strength of UK and French purposive weapons made them unappealing. As the German saying goes, using teleology or the mischief rule to combat tax avoidance would be like shooting a sparrow with a cannon. At the time of *Gregory v. Helvering*, US courts enjoyed a considerable degree of freedom to strike a sustainable balance between fidelity to statutory text and legislative purpose. Serendipitously, the income tax arrived[88] during "a time of transition in the realm of statutory interpretation" in the United States marked by "the recognition that the language of a statute cannot resolve all disputes over its applicability to unforeseen cases. ..."[89] Neither UK nor French courts enjoyed that luxury as the income tax rose to prominence long

---

statutory interpretation" but "looks at a range of additional factors ... including the principles and objectives of the underlying legislative provisions and any shortcomings in them"). Freedman notes that although it employs the standard acronym the UK G.A.A.R. narrowly targets *abuse* rather than mere avoidance. *Id.*, 167.

87 A more active – and assertive – legislature has also been cited as an explanation for the reverse (greater judicial willingness to intervene). See McMahon, n.43 at 42 (relying in part on the work of John Tiley in attributing the "substantial" differences in "judicial interpretive approaches in the UK and the US" in part to "the greater frequency with which the US Congress reacts to tax avoidance schemes").

88 Although each income tax has a unique history, the US, UK and French income taxes all rose to prominence at roughly the same time and for the same reason. In each jurisdiction, the Great War – and its considerable fiscal demands – made the income tax a critical revenue raising tool.

89 L. M. Solan, "Law Language and Lenity", 40 *William & Mary Law Review* 57, 100–1 (1998).

after their relatively potent purposive practices took shape. Confronted with the stark reality of a mischief rule or teleology applied to taxation, UK and French judges simply may have balked.

The income tax has enjoyed a century of prominence as a fiscal tool despite its susceptibility to abuse. Compared to alternatives such as property taxes and consumption taxes, the income tax is complex and therefore vulnerable to strategic behavior on the part of taxpayers. Some amount of tax planning tends to be accepted as a valid expression of taxpayer autonomy.[90] Curbing the aggressive behavior of even a relatively small number of taxpayers heightens compliance burdens on all taxpayers. Balancing the risks and costs of too much or too little taxpayer autonomy may be the greatest challenge presented by the income tax.

Enjoying the advantage of working on a relatively blank canvas, US courts crafted an array of anti-abuse doctrines tailored to suit the demands of the income tax. In theory, UK courts could have done likewise, choosing substance (*Gregory v. Helvering*) rather than form (*Duke of Westminster*). That they did not is clear. Why they did not might initially seem puzzling.

Given their long history of emphasizing legislative purpose at the expense of fidelity to statutory language, they easily could have embraced substance-over-form principles. In fact, that long tradition gave UK courts cause to worry that such a carefully calibrated response might be elusive, creating a threat to taxpayer autonomy. A relatively modern UK decision articulated precisely that skepticism that moving too far from the statutory text would irretrievably disrupt the integrity of the income tax. Developing a US-style arsenal of anti-avoidance doctrines would open the Pandora's box of "spooky jurisprudence" by imbuing tax statutes with "a penumbral spirit which strikes down devices or stratagems designed to avoid its terms or exploit its loopholes."[91]

French courts have displayed a similar concern for taxpayers. As described previously, concerned that only when taxpayers have tax avoidance as their sole objective would transactions be identified as abusive, legislators substituted a requirement that the tax motive merely be a principal purpose for engaging in the transaction.[92] The *Conseil Constitutionnel* deemed even such a legislatively crafted penumbra to be too spooky for its taste, instead preserving the requirement that tax avoidance be the sole purpose of a transaction in order for it to be deemed abusive.[93] For a jurisdiction steeped in a teleological approach, such concern for the impact of a principal purpose test on taxpayer autonomy seems anomalous.

Conclusion

The available evidence suggests that otherwise purposive jurisdictions may reject tax purposivism because of – rather than despite – their relative comfort with purposivism. If correct, so that brute strength effectively precludes the precision required to achieve the necessary balance, that observation raises the further question of whether this outcome was inevitable (or desirable). On the one hand, the resultant textualist outpost in an otherwise purposive landscape might reflect a rational concern fueled by the uniquely fragile complexity of the income tax.[94] An income tax

---

90 See text accompanying nn.44–47.
91 See *Norglen Ltd. v. Reeds Rains Prudential Ltd.* [1999] 2 AC 1 (HL) 14.
92 Article 100 du projet de loi de finances pour 2014.
93 See text accompanying n.79.
94 Future scholarship could allay or confirm such concerns, perhaps by determining whether similar lacunae exist in other complex substantive areas (so that, for example, UK and French courts seem equally hesitant to employ purposive tools in contexts such as securities regulation or bankruptcy).

simply might not be compatible with teleology, thus posing an unexpected obstacle to ongoing reform efforts (such as BEPS).

On the other hand, that outcome could represent a triumph of fear over logic. French courts could embrace a modified teleology calculated to address concerns about taxpayer autonomy. US anti-abuse doctrines have not proven incompatible with the freedom of taxpayers to invest and otherwise to conduct their affairs. Understanding whether taxpayer autonomy would wither at the touch of teleology could help to tip the balance in current debates such as that over the principal purpose test recently rejected by the *Conseil Constitutionnel*. More broadly, solving the mystery of what seems a Möbius strip of purposivism and textualism offers a unique opportunity to understand the relationship between them.

10

TAX AVOIDANCE IN JAPAN

Tadao Okamura and Takako Sakai

Introduction

Japan, a country that is situated at the east edge of Asia, experienced a long period of Asian feudalism. In those days, taxation was a means by which feudal loads deprived people of the fruits of their efforts, primarily agricultural products such as rice. People hated taxes and always thought less taxation was a good policy.

Soon after World War II, Japan was democratized with the establishment of the Constitution in 1946. Articles 30 and 84 of the Constitution provide the foundation for statute-based taxation. Accordingly, the government cannot levy any taxes without a statutory provision that prescribes the taxing conditions.[1] If a taxpayer's conduct or attributes do not satisfy the relevant statutory taxing conditions, a tax cannot be levied. Statutory taxing conditions must provide the following five features: who is the potential taxpayer (and who is exempted), what is the object of the tax (and what is not), to whom the object is attributed, how the tax base is calculated, and the tax rate. The statutory text that prescribes taxing conditions should be interpreted literally and unassertively, without expanding or shrinking the meanings of its words or concepts.[2]

The constitutional principle of statute-based taxation rests on two premises.[3] First, the design of the national tax system, including its tax bases and the intensity of its burden, should be discussed and decided through the people's representatives in the Diet. This premise reflects the idea of democracy in the Constitution. In designing the tax system, its effect on redistribution of wealth is important. Second, the tax burden should be foreseeable with reasonable accuracy. This premise stems from the idea of protecting taxpayers' economic activities from a nation's taxing power. Without being able to foresee the tax burden, taxpayers could not carry on business transactions. If people always have to worry about an unexpected tax burden, economic development would be severely deterred. These two premises sometimes conflict with each other. For example, the tax agency can attain more accurate foreseeability through administrative rulings

---

1 H. Kaneko, The Principle of Statute-Based Taxation in Japan: Trends of Scholars' Opinion and Case Law, 32:1 *International Tax Review* 17 (2004).
2 H. Kaneko, *Sozei-ho* [Tax Law], 22th ed. (2017, Koubundou), 116; T. Okamura, T. Watanabe, and Y. Takahashi, *Basic Zei-ho* [Basic Tax Law], 7th ed. (2013, Yuhikaku), 37.
3 Kaneko, n.1, p. 26.

for specific cases or agreements with taxpayers, but such procedures lack the process of a democratic discussion. However, it is hard for the Diet to examine and enact every detailed rule, thus administrative notices prescribe important rules. Although notice-based taxation conflicts with the democratic premise of the principle of statute-based taxation, it improves the foreseeability of a tax burden.

As will be discussed in the next section, there is no single, clear definition of tax avoidance in Japan. However, there is one common feature among the definitions; that is, tax avoidance does not satisfy any taxing conditions. If it does, it is not avoidance but evasion of tax that is entirely illegal. Thus, under the principle of statute-based taxation, the relevant taxing conditions and their legal interpretation draw the line between tax avoidance and evasion.[4] For example, because a statute provides that those who "own" depreciable assets should be allowed the depreciation deduction, the interpretation of the word "own" determines whether those who acquire the assets without any economic risk of ownership can deduct its depreciation. If we interpret the word "own" broadly, the scope of tax avoidance broadens and tax evasion shrinks, and vice versa. When a taxpayer's conduct is classified as tax avoidance, and not tax evasion, it is generally respected and not subject to tax, because it does not satisfy the conditions to tax. In this sense, tax avoidance does not differ from tax saving. However, there are some exceptions where taxation without meeting the taxing conditions is permitted to prevent tax avoidance, as discussed later.

In our opinion, in comparison with other developed countries, the interpretation of taxing provisions in Japan is strict and formalistic, which provides more opportunities to avoid tax. This may well stem from the long history of anti-tax sentiment among the Japanese.

The definitions

Japan imported the concept of tax avoidance from pre-World War II Germany, as it did with many other legal concepts in civil and public laws. The German concept of tax avoidance (Steuervermeidung) is based on the statutory provision, the Reichsabgabenordnung (RAO) of 1919 Article 5. It is the origin of the current general anti-avoidance rule (GAAR), now the Abgabenordnung (AO, General Tax Code) of 2008 Article 42 Clause 1.[5] The original provision, which differs a little from the current version, stated that "[t]he tax burden cannot be avoided or reduced by abusing the possibility of a legal formulation in civil law. Tax shall be assessed on the abusive formulation as if it was done economically in an ordinary formulation."

This provision suggests that an abusive civil legal formulation reduces a tax burden. This is because the taxing conditions of German tax law are constructed on the premise of the formulation of civil legal relationships. Germany enacted a national civil code (Bürgerliches Gesetzbuch, BGB) in 1900, and has never been a common law country. With the BGB, it was convenient for German legislators to enact a tax law by incorporating civil legal relationships into the taxing conditions, instead of developing the conditions from scratch. For example, if a taxpayer obtains legal title to an asset in civil law, tax law treats her as its owner for tax purposes. However, the legislators cannot think of all the possible means to obtain and keep the title or the possible economic status of taxpayers with the title. Indeed, titleholders in sale-leaseback transactions or leveraged acquisitions with nonrecourse loans were surely unknown to German legislators in

---

4 K. Kiyonaga, *Sozeikaihi no Kenkyu [Studie der Stererumgehung]* (1995, Minervashobou), 111, 389.

5 See, e.g. W. Schon, "Statutory Avoidance and Disclosure Rules in Germany", in J. Freedman (ed.), *Beyond Boundaries – Developing Approaches to Tax Avoidance and Tax Risk Management* (2008), 47–55, available at SSRN: http://ssrn.com/abstract=1590814.

those days. Because taxing conditions are supposed to be formulated on normal and ordinary civil legal formulations, unusual, unknown formulations that do not satisfy taxing conditions might well be thought abusive. Note that what is abused here is not tax law, but civil law.

The aforementioned features and relationships of tax law, taxing conditions, and civil law are common to Japan. Japan also has a national civil code that was enacted in 1899, one year before Germany's was enacted, and many basic concepts in tax law are borrowed from the civil code, such as the definitions of "spouse," "child," and "sale." Based on these features, the most accepted definition of tax avoidance in Japan, which we call "the major definition," consists of the following three necessary requirements:[6]

(i)   It employs an unusual legal formulation in civil law that does not satisfy the relevant taxing condition;

     Some scholars add "without reasonable business purpose" to this requirement, which restricts the scope of tax avoidance.[7]

(ii) It achieves almost the same economic consequences as the ordinary formulation does; and
(iii) It eliminates or reduces the tax burden from the amount assessed upon the ordinary formulation that satisfies taxing conditions.

This definition indicates the strong influence of German law, where the concept of tax avoidance is based on an abusive formulation in civil law.[8] However, there is an important difference between the two countries with respect to the concepts. Although the German definition is based on the statutory language of the GAAR (AO Art. 42), the Japanese definition is not, because Japan has no such GAAR; i.e. the Japanese definition is not statutory.[9] Thus, we speculate that Japanese tax scholars who learned about the German GAAR and the German avoidance concept artificially borrowed the concept. This kind of partial import from Germany often occurred in the development of Japanese law.

We think that this borrowing has led the Japanese theory of tax avoidance to considerable confusion that will be explained in this chapter. But for now, let us mention the functions these concepts perform. While the German concept functions to single out those legal formulations that are subject to the GAAR, the Japanese concept cannot because Japan has no GAAR. The Japanese concept could be of theoretical nonpractical use only, but it has been often argued and cited in court cases with the term "tax avoidance." For example, taxpayers often argue that the transaction at issue should be respected for the litigated tax assessment because it has a legitimate business purpose and is not tax avoidance. This kind of argument displays a serious error, because tax assessments should implement taxing conditions literally under the principle of statute-based taxation, but there are no such terms as "business purpose" or "tax avoidance" in the tax laws.

There is another influential definition that we call "the alternative definition." It tries to find its foundation in the statute. Although Japan has no GAAR, there are several so-called anti-avoidance provisions with limited scope. Their scope covers closely held family corporations, corporate reorganizations, consolidated tax returns, and a foreign corporation's income

---

6 K. Kiyonaga, *Zei-ho* [Tax Law], rev. ed. (2013, Minervashobou), 42.
7 Kaneko, n.2, p. 127.
8 Kiyonaga, n.4, p. 369.
9 See as legislative background, Y. Masui, "The Responsibility of Judges in Interpreting Tax Legislation: Japan's Experience", 52:2 *Osgoode Hall Law Journal* 506–7 (2015).

attributable to the permanent establishment.[10] These provisions include the same expression: "if the tax authority recognizes a conduct or calculation that results in an improper reduction of the tax burden, the authority can levy the tax notwithstanding the conduct or calculation." The only condition these anti-avoidance provisions have to apply is the "improper reduction of the tax burden." Based on this statutory phrase, a leading academic theory defines tax avoidance as the "improper" reduction or elimination of tax. Although this definition is very broad, this theory does not condemn tax avoidance at all. Instead, it admits that tax avoidance is legal, and that taxpayers have legitimate entitlements to reduce their tax burdens even by means of tax avoidance, unless these statutory anti-avoidance provisions prohibit the conduct.[11]

Now, let us explain how confusion occurs about the major definition. It confuses the meaning of tax avoidance with the ability to apply these anti-avoidance provisions. The major definition's logic is probably that because these provisions are anti-avoidance provisions, their applicable scope should be limited to "tax avoidance" in the meaning of the major definition (not the statutory words "improper reduction of tax"). However, under the principle of statute-based taxation, this interpretation is unacceptable because the anti-avoidance provisions do not state all of the requirements of the major definition.

The alternative definition eliminates this defect in the major definition, but it inevitably entails the vagueness of the statutory word "improper". In some court cases, taxpayers challenged the constitutionality of one of the anti-avoidance provisions because their words are too vague to be a taxing condition and then those are violating the principle of statute-based taxation. However, courts totally have rejected these challenges.[12]

The approaches

When a transaction is found to be a "tax avoidance" scheme, how does the tax authority deal with it? There are two ways.

In Germany or Japan, a taxpayer's actual but abusive legal formulation is disregarded and substituted by a normal formulation as determined by the authority. The treatment of tax avoidance is "deemed taxation" since it is not based on real facts but on assumed ones.[13] And because this anti-avoidance assessment is made without satisfaction of taxing conditions, which is highly exceptional to the normal application of law, there must be an anti-avoidance provision authorizing such an assessment.

In contrast, the tax authorities in the United States and probably in the United Kingdom pursue actual facts and economic realities against tax avoidance transactions beyond the veil of their forms. This pursuit is called "substance over form", which is a part of the common law in taxation.[14] Until recently the United States and the United Kingdom did not have statutory GAARs. We think this is because such an assessment is the ordinary application of law with no need for any special rules.

The difference between the two treatments comes from the structure of tax law. On the one hand, Germany and Japan have a national civil code that is the basis of taxing conditions. In other words, taxing conditions consist of two layers, the bottom layer is the civil legal relationship, and the upper layer is the taxing factors that are picked up from the bottom. The legislature

---

10 Arts 132, 132–2, 132–3, 147–2 of the Corporate Tax Law.

11 Kiyonaga, n.6, p. 44.

12 Supreme Court, Judgement, 21 April 1978, 24 Sho-getsu (8) 1694 [1978].

13 Kiyonaga, n.4, pp. 111–13.

14 Bittker and Lokken, *Federal Taxation of Income, Estates and Gifts*, ¶4.3.

makes taxing conditions that usually rely on civil legal formulations, not actual facts and their economic effects. This formality provides ample room for taxpayers to employ such civil legal formulations that avoid satisfying taxing conditions. For example, the line between a sale and a lease is drawn by civil law in repossession transactions and sale-and-leaseback transactions unless tax law provides special measures.

On the other hand, in those countries without a national civil code, taxing conditions cannot be based on a civil code, and have to be created from scratch. They try to rely on actual facts and the economic substance of transactions, although there are some exceptions; they are sometimes connected to the legal formulation in civil law. For example, to be recognized by the US Internal Revenue Code, a so-called "A- reorganization" (named after the section of the Code) must be a merger or consolidation under the applicable state law.[15]

So viewed, the difference between the two groups of countries and between taxation on a deemed legal formulation and taxation on actual economic substance is just on the surface. Both pursue economic reality, but those with a national civil code that provides the basis of taxing conditions need the authority to disregard the civil legal formulation.

Yahoo Inc. v. District Director of Azabu[16] marks the recent developments in the Japanese anti-avoidance provisions. The case is about loss carryovers in a corporate merger. For an acquiring corporation to make use of the losses carried over from the target corporation, the Corporate Tax Law requires that the merger should not only be a qualified tax-free reorganization, but also satisfy the business continuity requirements, including the continuity of certain directors of the target after the merger, which was at issue in the case. Just three months before the merger, the acquiring corporation, Yahoo, installed Mr. I who was a very able president of Yahoo into the target, CS, as one of the CS's directors. Also, on the occasion of the merger, all of the CS's original directors left the office. Even so, these conducts satisfied the requirement of the continuity of certain directors in the wording of the statutory provision.

According to the explanation by the Ministry of Finance, the purpose of the continuity of business requirement is to secure the acquirer's continuity of the target's business that has caused the losses. Therefore, the idea of the continuity of certain directors can be explained by the relationship between the directors' responsibility and the carryover losses. However, the continuity of certain director requirement specifies neither the term of the director's service before and after the merger nor any number of the target corporation's directors to continue to serve. The requirement may appear absurd in the first place, because it gives an incentive to keep those directors who have caused the losses and should be replaced. Yahoo's installation of Mr. I with dismissing the former CS directors surely made sense from a business perspective.

The tax authority denied the loss carryovers by virtue of the anti-avoidance provision for corporate reorganizations, and accessed the deficiency. Yahoo sued the assessment. The point at issue was whether Yahoo's aforementioned conduct was the phrase of the provision: "conduct or calculation that results in an improper reduction of corporate tax burden."

Both the district court and Tokyo High Court held for the tax authority.[17] The Tokyo High Court stated that the "improper reduction of tax" could be caused not only by (i) the conduct that was economically unreasonable and unusual but also by (ii) the conduct that was contrary to the purport and purpose of the corporate reorganization tax system or its individual provisions even though the conduct had a business purpose. The court observed that the case belonged to

15 I.R.C. sec. 368(a)(1)(A).
16 Supreme Court, Judgement, 29 February 2016, 70 Minshu (2), 242 [2016].
17 Tokyo District Court, Judgement, 18 March 2014, 2236 H.J. 25 [2014], Tokyo High Court, Judgement, 5 November 2014, 60 Sho-getsu (9) 1967 [2014].

second category, and stated that since the principal purpose of Mr. I's installation was the usage of the carryover losses and the installation was just superficial, Yahoo's actions as a whole were contrary to the purpose of the legislation and could be disregarded by virtue of the statutory anti-avoidance provision.

The Tokyo High Court's extension of the scope of the anti-avoidance provision was criticized. First, the court's reasoning cannot comply with the major definition of tax avoidance mentioned previously. According to the theory of this definition, the reason why tax avoidance should be nullified is because the legislators were unable to expect tax-avoiding conduct in enacting the taxing conditions. In other words, taxing conditions are enacted on the basis of ordinary, usual, and reasonable legal formulations. If we permit avoiding tax by a conduct that is so unusual or unreasonable that the legislators could not put it onto any taxing conditions, fairness of taxation becomes impaired. For the purpose of the fairness in this sense, more precisely, equality between the taxpayers with usual conduct and those with unusual tax avoidance should be nullified. Thus, the anti-avoidance provisions and the phrase "improper reduction of tax" should be interpreted in this way. This means the provision can apply to type (i) cases, but not type (ii) cases that do not demonstrate unusual taxpayer conduct. Indeed, no court cases before have approved the application of any anti-avoidance provisions to type (ii) cases.[18]

Second, applying the provision to type (ii) cases casts a serious question. How can we calculate the "reduction" in the provision? What is the criterion? The major definition would calculate the amounts using deemed normal and usual conduct, but type (ii) conduct may be normal. Note that the alternative definition does not have such an answer. It might say that the criterion can be calculated according to the purport and purpose of the tax system, which is vague.

The Supreme Court approved the lower courts, but changed the reasoning, probably in response to the criticism. The Court said that the phrase "the conduct or calculation that result improper reduction of corporate tax burden" should be interpreted as conduct or calculation that abused statutory rules of reorganization by making the rules devises of tax avoidance. It then stated that such abuse should be recognized by judging (a) whether the conduct or calculation was intended to reduce tax burden through the reorganization, and (b) whether the application of the reorganization rules deviated from the purport and purpose of such rules, taking into account (i) whether the conduct or calculation was abnormal and unusual, and (ii) whether the conduct or calculation had business purpose or other reasonable cause. In short, the Court required both (a) tax avoidance intent, and (b) deviation from the purport and purpose of such rules, and both (i) abnormality and (ii) business purpose of the conduct were elements to be considered in judging (a) and (b). Compared with the Tokyo High Court, the Supreme Court attached greater importance to the taxpayer's intention than the provision's purport and purpose. The Court stated the installation of Mr. I was under such intention and the application of the continuity of director rule deviated from the purport and purpose of the rule.

Yahoo has another point to be mentioned. Was the assessment approved by the court "deemed taxation"? If so, what was the amount? Here, no deemed taxation occurred because the tax authority only denied the loss carryover. This assessment was inevitable, since what should be deemed is a normal, usual and reasonable conduct, to which the legislators have connected the taxing condition. The major definition also criticizes this non-deemed assessment.[19]

18 Kaneko, n.2, p. 498–499.
19 T. Okamura, "Soshiki-saihensei to Kouikeisan-hinin (2) [Corporate Reorganization and Anti-Avoidance (2)]", 179 *Zeiken* 67 (2014).

The extensions

Although Germany adapts "deemed taxation" to deal with tax avoidances, the substance-oriented application of tax law is not unknown. There used to be a statutory provision, the Reichsabgabenordnung (RAO) of 1919 Article 4, and its successor, the Steueranpassungsgesetz of 1934 Article 1 Clause 3, which are relevant to this discussion.[20] The original provision's content was: In judging the facts for the application of taxing conditions, the worldview of the social state, the purpose and the economic meaning of the tax law, and change of circumstance should be considered. Although this provision was abolished on the last day of 1976, its principle on the judgment of facts is said to remain unchanged. The principle corresponds to the doctrine of substance over form in the United States. It pursues the economic reality of actual facts in the application of tax law, although what "the worldview of the social state" means is very ambiguous.

The relationship between this principle or the abolished provision and the GAAR was discussed a great deal in Germany. Although there are a variety of theories, one important feature deserves attention from the perspective of Japan that has no GAAR but has anti-avoidance provisions with limited scope; that is, if there was such a principle, it would work outside the scope of the anti-avoidance provisions, and the tax authority can in effect disregard and reconstruct tax avoidance transactions without an anti-avoidance provision. This effect should be taken into consideration in Japan.

In Germany the principle constitutes one of three parts of the famous German doctrine, "wirtschaftliche Betrachtungsweise" (economic observation method). Another provision that also forms part of the doctrine was the Steueranpassungsgesetz of 1934 Article 1 Clause 1. This provision is about the interpretation of tax law, stating the same principle as the provision for the judgment of facts. Here, we can find an effect similar to the one mentioned above.[21] If there was such a principle of legal interpretation, the tax authority can in effect deal with tax avoidance without an anti-avoidance provision, which should be carefully considered in Japan.

The last provision that forms part of the doctrine "wirtschaftliche Betrachtungsweise" is AO Article 42 GAAR. Thus, this doctrine consists of (i) factual judgments, (ii) legal interpretations, and (iii) deemed taxation. These three components share features. By employing one of them, the tax authority can levy a tax burden on the conduct or attributes that do not satisfy any taxing conditions without taking the three components of the doctrine into consideration. In short, the doctrine works for taxation without satisfaction of taxing conditions. Therefore, the doctrine seems to come into conflict with the principle of rule of law. However, the doctrine is authorized by statutes (or a statutory principle as for a judgment of facts) in Germany.

In contrast, Japan has never enacted any statute to authorize such a doctrine. Also, the Japanese Constitution, not statutes provides the principle of statute-based taxation that requires taxation according to taxing conditions, although courts have approved exceptions when a couple of anti-avoidance provisions apply. As such, does "no taxation without taxing conditions" hold in Japan?

Anti-avoidance factual finding

The answer is no, and here is why. Japan's Civil Code Article 94 (Fictitious Manifestation of Intention) Clause 1 provides "Any fictitious manifestation of intention made in collusion with another party(ies) shall be void." Although Clause 2 provides "The nullity of the manifestation

---

20 Kiyonaga, n.4, p. 364.
21 Ibid., 138, 210.

of intention pursuant to the provision of the preceding paragraph may not be asserted against a third party without knowledge," the tax authority is not a "third party" in this clause. Thus, if the tax authority can nullify a transaction that is suspected of tax avoidance by means of this civil law provision, it can deal with tax avoidance outside the scope of anti-avoidance provisions of tax law. In applying Article 94, the tax authority usually argues that because the parties enter the tax-avoiding scheme not for a business purpose but for eliminating or reducing a tax burden, there is no or not enough *bona fide* intention to engage in the legal conduct (the tax sheltering transaction) required by Article 94. This makes the alleged legal conduct void. Because the legal conduct in civil law no longer exists, tax law cannot find any fact that satisfies the tax-reducing conditions. The sheltering transaction is thus re-characterized according to its true legal nature in civil law and the taxpayer's attempt fails. Note that the application or interpretation of civil law, not tax law, defeats the attempt to avoid tax. In other words, without any anti-avoidance provision the tax authority can nullify tax avoidance. This measure is called "the denial by factual finding in civil law", because the tax authority denies tax avoidance by finding the fact that the legal conduct does not exist.[22] The result is if there is no business purpose, the transaction can be denied, which resembles to the business purpose test in the United States and other countries.

A vulnerability of this approach lies at its core, the factual finding of "fictitious manifestation of intention" of Article 94. Does a tax reduction purpose or a lack of business purpose make the intention of legal conduct fictitious? Does it taint the legal validity of transactions in civil law? Some scholars firmly deny this possibility. Suppose a taxpayer donates money to a charity only for the purpose of acquiring a charitable deduction. Does this purpose make the donation void? Of course not. In civil law theory, the purpose of reducing a tax burden is just a "motive" of this legal conduct (the donation), not its "intention". Even if the taxpayer's mind is focused exclusively on tax reduction and lacks sincere charitable intent, she still has the genuine intention to donate money, because without the donation, she cannot acquire the tax reduction. She surely has a real, nonfictitious intention of the end result, i.e., the transfer of money to the charity. Article 94 cannot make such a donation void. It is a tax policy issue whether to make such a donation eligible for a charitable deduction. The same goes for the acquisition of assets for the purpose of deducting accelerated depreciation or expensing, and other transactions undertaken only to achieve preferred tax treatment. Whether to afford tax preference to such transactions is an issue of taxation, not civil law. In short, the opposing view argues that a lack of business purpose does not affect the intention required by civil law. Whether to require a business purpose, and to what extent, is a tax law issue, not a civil law issue. And there are no taxing conditions in Japan stating anything about business purposes or tax avoidance purposes.

The distinction between the two laws exposes the issue. What the denial by factual finding does at the civil law level should be done instead at the tax law level, and to do so, an anti-avoidance provision is necessary. Applying Article 94 mixes up the two and misplaces the application of tax avoidance principles. Remember taxing conditions consist of two layers; the bottom layer consists of the civil legal relationship and the upper layer consists of the taxing factor. By manipulating the factual finding in the bottom layer for taxation, taxpayer's civil legal conduct gets drawn into the taxing area in the upper layer. This is clearly shown by the fact that although the denial alleges the taxpayer's legal conduct to be null and void, the tax authority can never make, and has never made, its legal effect void between the private parties in the legal conduct.

---

22 M. Nakazato, "Kazeinogare-shohin nitaisuru Sozeiho no Taiou [Response of Tax Laws for Tax Shelter]", 1169, 1171 *Jurist* 116, 86 (2000).

This approach was disputed in a well-known film lease case, *A Partner of Empyrean v. Nishinomiya District Director*.[23] According the scheme devised by Merrill Lynch Capital Markets, the taxpayer formed a partnership, Empyrean, with other investors, and purchased two movie films, one of them entitled "Casualties of War". The films were produced by Columbia Pictures for a substantial amount of money that was raised by a nonrecourse loan by Dutch Bank. The taxpayers leased the films to an American distributing agency, IFD, with a distribution contract that gave IFD a comprehensive right to the films, including giving and changing the titles, editing the content, and making foreign editions. Empyrean received consideration for the lease and distribution contract in the amount of the interest for the nonrecourse loan plus some portion of the profit from the distribution. IFD transferred the comprehensive right to Columbia Pictures, the original producer, which operated the films. The taxpayers' purpose for the transaction was to acquire the depreciation deduction for the films. The durable period was only 2 years. The nonrecourse loan and the consideration eliminated all of the risk in this film investment from the taxpayers.

The tax authority denied the depreciation, arguing that since the taxpayers did not have a real intention to acquire the films, they did not own the depreciable assets of the films. The district court and Osaka high court approved the tax assessment. The high court said that "tax-avoiding transactions should be scrutinized and be subject to taxation based on the parties' real intention in making the civil legal formulation in their agreements." This reasoning clearly shows an anti-avoidance factual finding. However, the Supreme Court used different reasoning to reach the same result, saying that "Even if Empyrean acquired the title of the films, most of their rights were transferred to IFD on the same day, and in substance, Empyrean lost the rights to use the films and earn profits from them, or to dispose of them. Adding the fact that Empyrean did not share any risk in the borrowed money, and the taxpayers did not seem to have any interest to earn profits from the distribution, the films were not assets to create earnings, and therefore they were not assets in use in the business. Thus, they did not come under the "depreciable asset" provided in the statutory provision providing depreciation deduction." In this holding the Supreme Court seems to avoid the denial by a factual finding. Rather, this reasoning resembles the anti-avoidance interpretation explained in the next section.

Anti-avoidance interpretation

This two-layer analysis reveals further possibilities for this anti-avoidance approach. Many legal terms exist in both tax and civil laws. They include "ownership," "to acquire," "sale," "exchange," "lease," and so on. This shows that tax law has borrowed those words and their concepts or meanings from civil law, not vice versa. Those borrowed terms are meant to convey the same concepts as in civil law, because in drafting the tax law the legislators of tax law have used the words knowing their concepts in civil law. It is natural to assume that if the legislators embody a different concept in a word common to civil law, it would have specifically defined the concept in tax law. Japanese cases and generally accepted theories that state borrowed concepts do not change their meanings in coming into tax law.

However, legal terms, including those borrowed by tax law, need interpretation. For example, in repossession transactions, what a "sale" is and how it differs from "lease" need to be clarified by an interpretation. In the two-layer system, this interpretation is supposed to be made in civil law, not tax law. However, a civil law interpretation differs considerably from a tax law

23 Supreme Court, Judgement, 24 January 2006, 60 Minsyu (1) 252 [2006].

interpretation that should be literal and unassertive. Civil law permits and often requires a teleological interpretation. Thus, if the tax authority makes a teleological interpretation with a taxation purpose, the principle of rigid interpretation in tax law cannot be maintained. If courts approved the interpretation, the tax authority can defeat the attempt of avoidance without an anti-avoidance provision.

However, "pure" civil law interpretation, without any consideration of other law fields is almost impossible. The Japanese two-layer system might not be compatible with the literal interpretation principle in tax law, and further, the principle of statute-based taxation provided by the Constitution.

The aforementioned two approaches are interchangeable. For example, there is a famous case called the "sale or exchange case."[24] In simple terms, taxpayer A transfers Blackacre to taxpayer B, and sometime thereafter, B transfers Whiteacre to A. Whether there are two sales or one exchange significantly alters the tax consequences under the Income Tax Act. The taxpayers alleged there were two sales while the tax authority assessed that just one exchange existed. The authority could have brought forth two arguments. First, the authority could have argued that the taxpayers lacked the intention to carry out two sales, but their true intention was for an exchange to occur. This is the "denial by factual finding in civil law" approach. Second, the authority could have argued that the "sale," one of the typical contract categories provided in the Civil Code, did not cover the transaction at issue but instead it fell under an "exchange," another typical contract category. Both approaches attempt to grasp the real nature of the transactions, not to reconstruct civil legal conduct. Note that if an anti-avoidance provision applied to this transaction, the bona fide sale in civil law is disregarded for tax purposes, and an exchange is deemed to have occurred and becomes the basis of taxation. Thus, the end result of an anti-avoidance provision would be the same as the results of the two approaches.

One Supreme Court case, *Risona Bank Corp. v. District Director of Higashi*,[25] exhibits the characteristics of an anti-avoidance interpretation. A New Zealand corporation, A, established a wholly owned subsidiary, B, in the Cook Islands, a tax haven, in order to invest A's funds raised from investors. However, if B received the funds directly from A, its return would be subject to Cook Islands' taxation. A could avoid this taxation by using a conduit. That is, if A lent the funds to a Cook Islands' corporation, C, not controlled by A (A was a 28% shareholder), and then C lent them to B, the tax would not apply. However, this scheme would incur a different tax. When B paid interest to C, the payments would be subject to withholding tax by the Cook Islands. So, a consulting firm thought up an arrangement, which inserted a Japanese major bank, Risona, between B and C to facilitate a back-to-back loan. That is, Risona borrowed the money from C, and at the same time Risona lent the same amount to B. B's interest payments to Risona were, of course, subject to the withholding tax. However, Risona grossed up this withholding tax, and paid this amount of interest to C while deducting a slight commission for itself. For example, B pays an interest of 100 to Risona, but the Cook Islands' government withholds 20, so Risona receives only 80. Nevertheless, Risona is supposed to pay 99 (100 minus 1 as its commission) to C. Risona accepted the offer of this arrangement and participated into it.

Why is Risona willing to pay more than it receives? Because the Japanese government pays the difference. That is, this amount comes from the Japanese foreign tax credit.[26] Since Risona pays the foreign tax to the Cook Islands (although it is withheld by B, the legal tax obligator is

---

24 Tokyo High Court, Judgement, 21 June 1999, 52 Kosai Minshu 26 [1999].
25 Supreme Court, Judgement, 19 December 2005, 59 Minsyu (10) 2964 [2005].
26 Art. 69(1) of the Corporate Tax Law.

Risona), that amount is credited from the Risona's amount of tax due to Japan. The tax credit is limited to a certain amount, but Risona had enough margin within the limit.

It could be alleged that Risona's use of the credit abused the foreign tax credit system and improperly reduced its tax burden, but no anti-avoidance provision covered this arrangement. However, the tax authority denied the credit and claimed both of the extended approaches in court. First, in terms of the anti-avoidance factual finding, it argued that the back-to-back loan was void because the parties did not have a real intention of making loans, but only the intention to avoid the tax. The tax authority further argued that even if the back-to-back loan was not void, what was really carried out in the arrangement was to "sell" the foreign tax credit margin of Risona, so tax consequences should follow this substantive arrangement. Second, using the anti-avoidance interpretation approach, the tax authority argued that Risona 's "payment" of the Cook Islands' tax did not meet the statutory definition of a "payment" under the foreign tax credit, because the arrangement had no business purpose. The Supreme Court took the second approach, but the reasoning was tougher. The Court said that "When we observe the whole arrangement, Risona paid the Cook Islands' tax that ought to be paid by the foreign parties, shifted the burden to our government by means of the foreign tax credit at issue, and earned the commission. By this arrangement, Risona avoided its tax burden by our foreign tax credit system whose application conspicuously deviated from its original purport and purpose. Risona entered into the arrangement, which would make a loss to Risona without the foreign tax credit, with the intent to enjoy the avoided tax with other parties sacrificing our government and our people. Thus, the foreign tax credit should not be permitted, because if we did, it would abuse the foreign tax credit system, and fairness of taxation." Most Japanese scholars classify this holding into the category of an anti-avoidance interpretation, because the Court restricted the coverage of the statute providing the foreign tax credit.[27] However, unlike the tax authority that argued the meaning of a statutory word, "payment," the Court made no literal interpretation. We think this shows the characteristic of this approach; that is, an anti-avoidance approach without a statutory base.

Limitation of the approaches, development of tax law

These two approaches extending the power of the tax authority have limitation, which was shown by a Supreme Court case, *Takei v. Suginami District Director*,[28] especially by its concurring opinion. In the case, a wealthy father who operated a major consumer finance company, Takefuji, tried to avoid the huge amount of inheritance tax supposed to be levied on his son, Mr. Takei. The device was an *inter vivos* gift with putting the property and successor out of the Japanese jurisdiction beforehand. To be concrete, (i) Mr. Takei's father transferred his company's appreciated stock to a special Dutch company owned by him and his wife. This significantly increased the value of Dutch company's stock that was an overseas property. (ii) He let his son, Mr. Takei, emigrate and change his address from Japan to Hong Kong where no gift tax is charged. Two and half years later, the gift of the Dutch company's stock was made. Under the Inheritance and Gift Tax Law at that time, when a gift was made (i) of a property that was located outside of the Japanese jurisprudence (overseas property), (ii) to a person who did not have an address in Japan for more than 1 year, it was not subject to the gift tax in Japan. Since the Dutch stock was undoubtedly an overseas property, the place of son's address was at issue. The tax laws do not

27 Kaneko, n.2, p. 132.
28 Supreme Court, Judgement, 18 February 2011, 2111 H.J. 3 [2011].

have the definition of "address", but the term is interpreted as the primary place where someone lives in other laws such as the Civil Law and the Election Law.

Although no anti-avoidance provision covered this case, the tax authority assessed the gift tax, arguing that even though Mr. Takei had stayed in Hong Kong over two thirds of the period from the emigration to his disappearance from Hong Kong that happened one year after the gift, he stayed there just to avoid the tax without the intention to live, which was obvious from the facts that he, a single person, still kept his own room in his father's house and came back there once a month, adjusting the days of stay in Japan so as not to be subject to the Japanese gift tax, while in Hong Kong his place was a hotel equivalent temporary apartment and his job had no substance. This argument can be understood in two ways. First, it was an anti-avoidance factual finding, since the taxpayer's intention to avoid the tax played a significant role in determining his address. Second, the argument was an anti-avoidance interpretation, since the interpretation of "address" was manipulated to nullify the tax avoidance.

The district court held for the taxpayer,[29] but the Tokyo High Court reversed it.[30] Reversing the lower court again, the Supreme Court held for the taxpayer. It confirmed that "address" meant the primary place where someone lived, and stated that Mr. Takei did not have his "address" in Japan at the time of the gift mainly from the facts that he spent over two thirds of the year in Hong Kong even though its purpose was to avoid the tax. The Court placed much emphasis on the taxpayer's objective presence in Hong Kong than his subjective intent to live there. The Court's opinion surely restricted the scope of the two approaches. Note the concurring opinion saying that "The principle of statute-based taxation demands that taxing conditions should be clearly enacted and their text should be literally and strictly interpreted. We cannot permit any special interpretation such as extending or analogical interpretation, interpretation by the applying the abuse of rights doctrine, or any special factual findings without careful consideration in order to nullify tax avoidance and levy tax, unless we can find a clear authority to do so."

During the trial and appeal of this case, the Japanese Diet amended the gift tax residence rule to expand the coverage. Under the new rule, if both the donor and the donee are Japanese citizens, the gift tax cannot be avoided unless the donee establishes a non-Japanese "address" for over 5 years.[31]

However, a more recent case demonstrated the possibility that the new rule was also easily avoided. A pregnant Japanese woman, a Japanese resident, went to the United States, gave birth to a baby and did not let it have Japanese citizenship. Then the baby's grandfather, a Japanese resident, set up a trust fund with his United States treasury securities naming the baby as the beneficiary, which was claimed to be the gift by the tax authority. Whether the baby had "address" in Japan was one of the issues in this case. Since the baby donee was not a Japanese citizen and stayed in the United States mostly during the period from the birth to the appointment as a beneficiary, the baby was not subject to the gift tax when we read the text of the new rule literally. Although the district court held for the taxpayer, Nagoya High Court reversed it,[32] saying that since the baby was 8 months old and under its parent care, his address was supposed to be the same as his parents who had their actual address in Japan.

---

29 Tokyo District Court, Judgement, 23 May 2007, 55 (2) Sho-getsu 267 [2007].
30 Tokyo High Court, Judgement, 23 January 2008, 1283 H.T.119 [2008].
31 Art. 4(1) of the the Former Inheritance and Gift Tax Law. Art. 9(2)-1 of the Current Inheritance and Gift Tax Law.
32 Nagoya High Court, Judgement, 3 April 2013, 60 Sho-getsu (3) 618 (2013).

Later, the Japanese Diet expanded the taxing conditions to cover worldwide gifts by Japanese residents regardless of the citizenship of the donee.[33] It seems to us that these instances of tax avoidance have developed the tax law under the principle of statute-based taxation.

Conclusion

The two approaches used to cope with attempts to avoid tax raise two questions: first, what does "tax avoidance" mean, and second, what should the proper taxing conditions be. Under Japanese law, tax avoidance exists if a transaction avoids satisfying a taxing condition in "particular" way, for example, by way of "unusual legal formulation" according to the major definition of tax avoidance, or by an "improper" way according to the alternative definition. However, one of the approaches, the denial by factual finding in civil law, brings its target transaction, "an attempt of tax avoidance" into the scope of the relevant taxing conditions, and the other approaches, the teleological interpretation of civil law, expands the scope of the relevant taxing conditions to embrace the target transaction. Thus, both methods put the target transaction within the scope of taxing conditions and although the transaction is not deemed to be tax avoidance under the tax law, it is nevertheless subject to tax. This result differs from the application of anti-avoidance provisions, where the target transaction is outside of the scope of taxability, but only deemed to be subject to tax due to the effect of the anti-avoidance provisions.

This distinction poses the first question as to the meaning of tax avoidance in the phrase "an attempt of tax avoidance." Because the attempt results in satisfying taxing conditions, "tax avoidance" here must embody a different concept from those of both the major and alternative definitions. What is it? This question is important because that concept determines the scope of the two approaches; how far they can reach into tax oriented transactions and to what degree can tax planning be active or aggressive? Despite our best efforts, we find no certain boundary in cases or academic theories, not to mention statutes or regulations. We assume other scholars and practitioners have experienced the same. As a legal concept, there may be no such thing as an attempt of tax avoidance. What we can notice or feel is aggressiveness or harmfulness against the treasury. These are no less vague than the improperness in the alternative definition. The two approaches draw a blurry line to extended taxing conditions, or more precisely, the two approaches make the limits of existing taxing conditions vague and loose.

This observation raises the second question about the property of taxing conditions. Can the limit of taxing conditions be blurry despite the principle of statute-based taxation? Are such "soft" taxing conditions acceptable under the Japanese Constitution? Remember the two premises of this constitutional principle: democracy and foreseeability. When taxing conditions become soft and loose, foreseeability suffers. To compensate for this, some kind of an advanced ruling system is necessary.

Our final remark is about Japan's enactment of a GAAR. As in other countries, Japan may enact a GAAR in the near future. Because Japanese courts have already permitted the two approaches in some cases but not in others, it may be better to codify them in order to clarify their application. Our major concern is whether the prospective provision would consist of the three components – deemed taxation, factual finding, and interpretation – like the former German provisions. We think taxation should pursue the existing (not deemed) reality of activities from the perspective of economic substance. Thus, the provision to authorize deemed taxation is unnecessary. The provision would authorize factual findings of taxing conditions and

---

33 Art. 1–4(ii)ro of the Current Inheritance and Gift Tax Law.

teleological interpretation of tax law, both from the perspective or purpose of tax law, not civil law. Business purpose, if it is proper to require, should be prescribed in the provision. Existing anti-avoidance provisions should be totally abolished or strictly limited only for very exceptional cases. The scope of the provision should be unlimited at least logically. All of the economic conducts or attributes could be subject to the provision's scrutiny to determine whether the taxing conditions include them. This provision might be called a "General Anti-Abuse Rule," but it is inappropriate to call it a "General Anti-Avoidance Rule," because it does not distinguish tax avoidance from non-avoidance. If the provision "applies," the transaction is taxed according to its true (not deemed) economic nature, and if the provision does not apply, the same treatment is given. There is no need to define tax avoidance anymore. However, what "the perspective or purpose of tax law" means and how it changes the existing factual finding and interpretation would be a difficult problem for the future.

Finally, from the viewpoint of legal studies, it may be fruitful to examine whether the concept of tax avoidance is valid as an object of social science in Japan, where no statutory or regulatory provision employs the word.[34] Doing research on tax avoidance appears to be like doing extensive research on a shadow.

---

34 T. Okamura, "Sozeikaihi-kenkyu no Igi to Hatten [The Signification and Development of Tax Avoidance Study]", in T. Okamura (eds), *Sozeikaihi-kenkyu no Tenkai to Kadai* [Development and Theme of Tax Avoidance Study] (2015, Minervashobou), 299.

11

THE CONTAINMENT OF CORPORATE TAX AVOIDANCE IN ITALY

Giulio Allevato and Carlo Garbarino

The traditional reluctance to adopt a general anti-avoidance clause

In the Italian tax system, corporate tax avoidance has traditionally been counteracted by means of specific anti-avoidance rules. The Italian legislature has, indeed, traditionally been reluctant towards the enactment of a general anti-avoidance provision – that is, a legal tool whose scope of application, instead of being preventively and precisely defined, is left to a case-by-case evaluation by Tax Authorities and courts.[1] The purpose of such approach was to prevent legal uncertainty in regard to the tax treatment and consequences of business transactions and contracts. Evidence of such reluctance towards the enactment of a general anti-avoidance clause is found, for example, in the preparatory works of the 1970–1973 tax reform: the position was that a general anti-avoidance clause would have significantly increased legal uncertainty and inequality of treatment among taxpayers, because such a clause would have awarded Tax Authorities and courts unacceptably broad discretion.[2]

Such approach persisted in the following decades, despite the strong pressure on the government to adopt more effective measures to counter the rise of aggressive corporate tax planning which Italy, like most of the other OECD countries, had experienced starting from the late 1980s-early 1990s and up to the early 2000s. During this period, various anti-avoidance measures were enacted that focused on specific transactions or arrangements. These rules were more effective compared to those available in the past, but were still limited in their scope of application. Examples of such provisions include the non-deductibility of expenses and costs incurred by Italian enterprises with counterparties located in black-listed jurisdictions, the CFC regulation, and limits on the use of carried forward net operating losses in mergers and acquisitions.

---

1 R. C. Guerra and P. Mastellone, "The Judicial Creation of a General Anti-Avoidance Rule Rooted in the Constitution", 11 *European Taxation* 511–12 (2009); M. Poggioli, "La Corte di Giustizia elabora il concetto di comportamento abusivo in material d'IVA e ne tratteggia le conseguenze sul piano impositivo: epifania di una clausola generale antielusiva di matrice comunitaria?", in *Rivista di Diritto Tributario* (2006), 31; G. Zoppini, *Abuso del diritto e dintorni (ricostruzione critica per lo studio sistematico dell'elusione fiscale)*, in *Rivista di Diritto Tributario* (2005), 808 et seq.; G. Falsitta, *Manuale di diritto tributario, Parte Generale* (Milan: CEDAM, 2005), 202. A. Tomassini, "Elusione ed abuso del diritto nel sistema dell'imposta di registro", 14 *Corriere tributario* 1037 (2012).
2 Poggioli, n.1.

However, during this period, two anti-avoidance provisions were also enacted with a wider, although not general, scope of application: (i) Art. 10 of Law No. 408/1990 and (ii) Art. 37-*bis* of Presidential Decree No. 600/1973 (hereinafter "Art. 37-*bis*"), a provision that in 1997 replaced Art. 10 of Law No. 408/1990.[3] For almost twenty years Art. 37-*bis* was considered the main anti-avoidance provision in the Italian tax system.

Section 1 of Art. 37-*bis* provides that

> acts, facts, and transactions, including those which are interconnected, which lack a sound business purpose, and are aimed at circumventing obligations or prohibitions set out in tax laws, and are designed to obtain tax reductions or refunds that would otherwise be undue, can be disregarded by Tax Authorities.

A requirement for the application of Art. 37-*bis* was that the transactions lacked sound economic reasons and were suitable to circumvent, through manipulation, express tax obligations or prohibitions. Case law and commentators confirmed that the triggering factor for the application of Art. 37-*bis* was the "circumvention" of the relevant tax rules that would have otherwise been applicable to the substance of the arrangement actually implemented by the taxpayers, regardless of the scheme formally put in place by the taxpayers. The distinguishing feature of unlawful tax savings, i.e. tax savings that were not tolerated by the tax system and that Tax Authorities were therefore allowed to disregard, was the existence of circumvention. By contrast, the lack of circumvention characterized those tax saving transactions which were accepted as part of a legitimate tax planning.

The broad definition of avoidance provided by § 1 of Art. 37-*bis* could potentially constitute a general anti-avoidance rule, but the traditional resistance to the adoption of a general statutory anti-avoidance clause manifested itself in § 3 of Art. 37-*bis* providing that § 1 of Art. 37-*bis* applied only to the transactions explicitly listed in § 3. Indeed, according to § 3 of this provision, the scope of application of this rule was limited to the following specific transactions: corporate transformations; mergers and de-mergers; liquidations and contributions of assets in exchange for shares; transfers of business; transfers of receivables; any transactions having as object shares, quotas, notes, and other securities.

Due to the limitation of its scope of application to those transactions listed in § 3, Art. 37-*bis* was generally characterized as a specific anti-avoidance rule, or, at most, as a quasi-general anti-avoidance provision.[4]

Furthermore, before proceeding to an assessment based on such provision, Tax Authorities had to comply with a specific procedure. Specifically, the taxpayer had to receive advance notice of Tax Authorities' intention to apply Art. 37-*bis* to the transaction or arrangement at issue. The taxpayer, therefore, had the right to explain the economic reasons, if any, underlying

---

3 Please note that another provision, included in Art. 10 of Presidential Decree No. 131/1986, has been, in several cases, treated and applied by some tax courts as an anti-avoidance rule with significant effects on the qualification and re-qualification of taxpayers' arrangements for stamp duty purposes. According to this provision, "the stamp duty is applied in accordance to the intrinsic nature and the legal effects of the registered transactions, regardless of the title and form (i.e. the *nomen juris*) of such transactions". However, in large part, the characterization of the provision as an anti-avoidance rule has been rejected by case law and scholarship, mainly because, unlike genuine anti-avoidance rules, it does not allow Tax Authorities to look at the economic substance of the arrangement. Instead, as reported above, it allows Tax Authorities to merely look at the legal effects of the registered transactions. In any case, even if such provision qualified as an anti-avoidance rule, it would be a specific anti-avoidance rule, and not a general anti-avoidance rule, as its scope of application is limited to registration tax and stamp duty.

4 P. Pistone, *Abuso del diritto ed elusione fiscale* (Padua: CEDAM, 1996), 20 et seq.

the transaction or arrangement. If Tax Authorities rejected these reasons, they had to expressly indicate why they did so in the ensuing notice.

The intention not to introduce a general anti-avoidance rule was confirmed in the Explanatory Report to Art. 37-*bis* of Presidential Decree No. 600/1973, which provided that "the first two §s of Art. 37-bis could potentially constitute a general anti-avoidance rule, but (…) it has been provided that its application triggered only when the taxpayer implements one of the transactions listed in § 3". Another, and indirect, confirmation of the Italian legislature's unwillingness to create a general anti-avoidance clause in the Italian tax system can be found in the express provisions according to which, by operation of law, the new transactions types that were added over time to the list of § 3 of Art. 37-*bis* became subject to § 1 only starting from the date the relevant provisions were enacted.

The lack, in the Italian tax system, of a general anti-avoidance measure was expressly confirmed by the Supreme Court in three decisions issued, respectively, in 2000, 2001 and 2002.[5] In these decisions, which concerned so-called "dividend washing" arrangements, the Supreme Court held that tax benefits may be denied only if so provided by a specific tax provision in force at the time a transaction is put in place. Therefore, as the cases in question related to tax years before Art. 37-*bis* or the specific anti-abuse provision in respect of dividend washing operations had been enacted, Tax Authorities were not allowed to re-characterize the arrangements at issue from an anti-avoidance perspective.

For the same reason, the *Corte di Cassazione* (hereinafter the Supreme Court) rejected the argument advanced by Tax Authorities according to which the transactions were void because they were concluded for the purposes of avoiding the application of imperative provisions. Indeed, the pursuit of a tax saving was not regarded *per se* as a violation in the absence of any applicable written rule. Consequently, the position of the Supreme Court appeared, at that time, to have centered around the absence, in the Italian tax system, of a general anti-avoidance rule.

The development of a judicial anti-abuse clause

The 2005 cases and the civil law background for the emergence of an anti-abuse judicial principle

Starting from 2005, the Supreme Court reversed its traditional reluctance to adopt a judge-made anti-avoidance principle and began to acknowledge the existence of a general anti-abuse principle in the Italian legal framework potentially applicable to any type of transactions.

In three decisions, issued within several days at the end of 2005, the Supreme Court held that certain dividend washing and dividend stripping arrangements were void under civil law criteria because these transactions had been put in place only to achieve tax advantages. Therefore, the Supreme Court acknowledged the entitlement of Tax Authorities and tax courts to employ civil law tools in order to declare void a tax-driven arrangement and collect the unpaid taxes, even in the absence of an explicit anti-avoidance provision.

Specifically, in Decisions No. 20398 of 21 October 2005 and No. 22932 of 14 November 2005, the Supreme Court held that two related contracts (the sale and immediate repurchase of shares, respectively, just before and after the dividend distribution date: in the first case, the dates were, in fact, two consecutive days), were void because the two parties did not aim to

---

5 ISC, Decisions No. 3979 of 3 April 2000, No. 11351 of 3 September 2001, No. 3345 of 7 March 2002.

obtain and did not actually obtain any significant economic advantages apart from the tax saving, and, therefore, the transactions lacked a legal cause and/or object.

In Decision No. 20816 of 26 October 2005, which dealt with a dividend stripping arrangement, the Supreme Court position differed slightly. In that case, the Supreme Court held that Tax Authorities were entitled to investigate the actual nature of the commercial contracts to demonstrate the simulated or fraudulent nature of the operation and, therefore, the invalidity of the arrangement.

According to this line of cases, if the contract is only a means to achieve tax benefits, Tax Authorities have the power to disregard contracts or legal arrangements if they lack a legal cause (Decisions No. 20398 and No. 22932) or on the basis of the *fraus legis* doctrine (Decision No. 20186).

This position of the Supreme Court was strongly criticized by commentators, who highlighted how disregarding transactions from a tax law perspective, but also assessing their invalidity from a civil law perspective, constituted a disproportionate remedy capable of generating negative side effects on the freedom of entrepreneurial activities and on the certainty of law. Scholars also highlighted that the use of civil law rules for the purpose of opposing tax avoidance is inconsistent with the very purpose of such civil law rules. Such argument was supported by the consideration that, in drafting the civil code rules on contracts and validity of transactions, the legislators certainly did not conceive any tax ramifications for such rules.[6]

However, for the purposes of our analysis, the most relevant element of such line of decisions was that the Supreme Court held that there was a general anti-abuse principle at the EU level – that is, developed by the Court of Justice of the European Union (hereinafter ECJ).[7] Substantially, the Supreme Court established that, in light of such emerging general anti-avoidance principle, the validity itself, and therefore not just the tax effects but also the civil law effects of certain transactions, should be denied.

The direct applicability of the ECJ's abuse of law doctrine

Less than a year after the 2005 line of decisions, the Supreme Court issued a new series of decisions[8] through which it did not simply mention the anti-abuse doctrine which had been developed at the EU level by the ECJ for over a decade, but affirmed the direct applicability, in the tax field, of a general prohibition of abuse of tax law as specified in the 2006 *Halifax* decision.[9]

---

6 See, in particular, R. Schiavolin, "L'elusione fiscale come abuso del diritto: allo stato dell'arte, più problemi che risoluzioni", in *Elusione fiscale: la nullità civilistica come strumento generale antielusivo. Riflessioni a margine dei recenti orientamenti della Cassazione civile*, 43 il Fisco 1510 (2006).

7 ECJ, Decision of 3 March 1993, Case C-8/92, *General Milks Products v. Hauptzollamt Hamburg-Jonas*; Decision of 12 May 1998, Case C-367/96, *Kefalas and Others v. Elliniko Dimosio*; Decision of 23 March 2000, Case C-373/97, *Dionysios Diamantis v. Elliniko Dimosio and Organismos Ikonomikis Anasinkrotisis*; Decision of 14 December 2000, Case C-110/99; Decision of 12 December 2002, Case C-324/00, *Lankhorst-Hohorst GmbH v. Finanzamt Steinfurt*; Decision of 3 March 2005, Case C-32/03, *I/S Fini H v. Skatteministeriet*.

8 See ISC, Decisions No. 10353 of 5 May 2006; No. 21221 of 29 September 2006: No. 22023 of 13 October 2006; No. 25612 of December 2006; No. 10273 of 4 May 2007. For a comment on decision No. 21221 of 29 September 2006, please see S. Gianoncelli, "Contrasto all'elusione fiscale in materia di imposte sui redditi e divieto comunitario di abuso del diritto", in *Giurisprudenza Italiana* (2008), 1297 et seq.

9 ECJ, 21 February 2006, Case C-255/02, *Halifax plc Leeds Permanent Development Services Ltd. Couty Wide Property Investments Ltd v. Commissioners of Customs and Excise*. See also M. Lang, "Cadbury Schweppes' Line of Case Law From the Member States' Perspective", in R. de la Feria and S. Vogenauer (eds), *Prohibition of Law: A New General Principle of EU Law?* (London: Bloomsbury Publishing, 2011), 442. Such principle was later on affirmed also in ECJ, 21 February 2008, Case C-425/06, *Ministero dell'Economia e delle Finanze v. Part. Service Srl*.

Indeed, in these decisions, unlike the 2005 decisions, the Supreme Court did not employ civil law instruments, but acknowledged the direct applicability, in the Italian tax law system and with no need for any implementation through domestic laws, of the general anti-abuse principle developed by the ECJ according to which "Community legislation cannot be extended to cover abusive practices by economic operators, that is to say transactions carried out not in the *context* of normal commercial operations, but solely for the purpose of wrongfully obtaining advantages provided for by Community law".[10]

According to this judicial trend, before Art. 37-*bis* entered into force, Italian tax law had implicitly acknowledged a principle rooted in EU law and in the ECJ concept of abuse of law, under which taxpayers cannot benefit from tax savings if they enter into transactions exclusively to achieve those tax savings. The Supreme Court emphasized the significance of the introduction of such a general anti-avoidance rule for all fields of taxation.

Indeed, although both the *Halifax* and *Part Service* decisions concerned the EU-harmonized VAT cases, the Supreme Court applied the ECJ's abuse of tax law rule not just in the field of EU-harmonized taxes, but also in relation to non-EU-harmonized taxes, on the basis of the argument that, according to the previous ECJ case law, although direct taxation is a prerogative of the Member States, they shall nevertheless exercise it consistently with the fundamental principles of EU law.[11] As a consequence, a case-law-based general anti-abuse clause had been developed, in spite of the aversion of the Italian legislature towards the introduction of such a provision, discussed previously.

Such decisions were strongly criticized by commentators, mainly because "although the strength of the Supreme Court reasoning is self-evident – due to the supremacy of EU law – when applied to VAT or other areas that have already been the object of harmonization, the situation is not the same when applied to the non-harmonized sector of direct taxation".[12]

Some commentators relied on the Advocate-General Poiares Maduro's Opinion in *Halifax*, in which he noted that the ECJ decisions did not actually imply an extension of the EU prohibition of abuse of law beyond the scope of EU law itself, because this could have the effect of introducing a general anti-abuse principle applicable even when EU law is not at stake.[13] The ECJ accepted this view and held that the rules covered by the anti-abuse principle are "European rules", and not domestic rules.[14] Furthermore, the ECJ highlighted several times that the scope of application of general EU law principles does not extend to domestic situations which have no link with EU law.[15]

10 *Halifax*, n.9, paras 68–9.
11 See ISC, Decisions No. 8772 of 4 April 2008 and No. 25374 of 17 October 2008. See also C. Innamorato, "An Unwritten Anti-abuse Principle in the Italian Tax System", 8 *European Taxation* 449 (2008), et seq; F. Pedrotti, "Il principio giurisprudenziale comunitario di abuso del diritto come strumento di contrasto alle operazioni elusive domestiche: il caso del cd. Dividend stripping (o usufrutto azionario)", 2 *Diritto e Pratica Tributaria Internazionale* 1010 (2008), et seq.
12 A. Fantozzi and G. Mameli, "The Italian Abuse of Law Doctrine for Taxation Purposes", *Bulletin for International Taxation* 445, 447 (August–September 2010).
13 M. Beghin, "Evoluzione e stato della giurisprudenza tributaria: dalla nullità negoziale all'abuso del diritto nel sistema impositivo nazionale", in G. Maisto (ed.), *Abuso del Diritto Tributario, Quaderni della Rivista di Diritto Tributario* (Milan: Giuffrè, 2009), 29; Fantozzi and Mameli, n.12, at 447.
14 C. Sacchetto, "Le libertà fondamentali ed I sistemi fiscali nazionali attraverso la giurisprudenza della Corte di Giustizia UE in materia di imposte dirette", in V. Uckmar (ed.), *La normativa tributaria nella giurisprudenza delle Corti e nella nuova legislature* (Padua: CEDAM, 2007), 45 et seq.
15 See ECJ, Case C-206-94, C-367/97, C-32/03.

The 2008 cases and the claim that a general anti-abuse principle is inherent in the Italian constitution

The criticisms raised in regard to the 2006 decisions eventually induced the Supreme Court to partially modify its anti-abuse doctrine. In three decisions of 2008,[16] indeed, the Supreme Court affirmed that the EU anti-abuse clause could be invoked only in regard to EU-harmonized taxes, such as VAT, while, as far as the non-EU-harmonized taxes are concerned, the source of the anti-abuse principle was rooted in the principles of ability to pay and progressivity set forth in the Constitution.[17] According to the Supreme Court, such rule provides that a taxpayer cannot unduly benefit from arrangements which lack any economically sound reasons for their implementation (except for the tax saving), even if they are not openly in violation of a specific rule.

Therefore, the Supreme Court insisted on arguing that a transaction can qualify as abusive, and therefore can be disregarded for tax purposes. The Court, however, clarified that such general anti-abuse rule directly arises from the constitutional principles of ability to pay and progressivity enshrined in Art. 53 of the Constitution.

The Supreme Court emphasized that the ability to pay is the central principle. Accordingly, the Court found that a taxpayer cannot benefit from undue tax advantages based on the misuse of legal instruments, even if no specific rule is infringed, in the absence of an economic purpose that may justify the transaction. The Supreme Court concluded that its position was aligned with existing statutory anti-avoidance provisions which are, on a case-by-case basis, specific applications of the general anti-abuse principle inherent to the system. It then held that certain dividend washing and dividend stripping transactions were in violation of the general anti-avoidance rule under Art. 53 of the Constitution even if they did not conflict with a specific provision.

From a procedural perspective, the Supreme Court noted that the prohibition of abuse of law as construed by the Court itself could be applied by a judge *ex officio* in every stage of the proceedings, even if the argument was not initially raised by Tax Authorities. This position of the Supreme Court was widely criticized.[18]

The main criticism was that the Supreme Court had acted as a rule-maker and created, on its own, a general anti-avoidance clause in complete disregard of the founding principles of a civil law jurisdiction, such as Italy, which does not consider judicial pronouncements as a source of law. Another criticism was that a constitutional provision, contained in Art. 23, establishes that tax matters can be governed exclusively by law as it provides that "no personal nor economic obligation can be imposed on a citizen if not through a law".[19]

---

16 ISC, Decisions Nos. 30055, 30056 and 30057 of 23 December 2008. See G. Zizzo, "Clausola antielusione e capacità contributiva", 2 *Rassegna tributaria* 489 (2009).

17 Art. 53(1) of the Constitution states that "everybody shall contribute to the public expenses according to their ability to pay".

18 V. Ficari, "Poche luci e tante ombre giurisprudenziali in materia di elusione ed abuso del diritto nelle imposte sui redditi", 13 *Bollettino Tributario* 997 (2009) et seq; Cordeiro Guerra and Mastellone, n.1, at 513; C. Guerra, "Il legislatore nazionale e l'elusione fiscale internazionale", in G. Maisto (ed.), *Elusione ed abuso del diritto tributario. Orientamenti attuali in materia di elusione e abuso del diritto ai fini dell'imposizione tributaria, Quaderni della Rivista di Diritto Tributario* (Milan: Giuffrè, 2009), 221 et seq.

19 As highlighted by Fantozzi and Mameli, n.12 at 448: "What it is not acceptable with regard to the anti-abuse doctrine of the Supreme Court is the fact that it goes beyond asserting the existence of anti-abuse legal interpretation criteria founded on analogy and establishes, *de facto*, a system based on judicial 'law creation' in a civil law system. What is worst, considering the way the system works, is the 'constitutional' abuse of law doctrine, as

Art. 23 of the Italian Constitution has a twofold purpose. On the one hand, Art. 23 implements the "no taxation without representation" principle, by placing mandatory tax rules firmly in the hands of the people's representatives and limiting Government's and administration's intervention in tax matters. On the other hand, Art. 23 grants taxpayers legal certainty as it attributes to legislative language the establishment of legal rights and duties, which can be ascertained by the taxpayer before undertaking economic activities with reasonable certainty.[20]

Therefore, according to this second criticism that is based on Art. 23, the judicial creation of a general anti-abuse clause was in breach of the constitutional principle that the Legislature has the exclusive power to enact tax laws, and gave Tax Authorities an excessive discretion in determining *ex post* the tax treatment of corporate transactions. Accordingly, the judicial anti-abuse clause was claimed to be a violation of taxpayer rights, as it drastically affected their ability to consider in advance the effective tax consequences of their business activities and strategies. Indeed, as a result of such judicial doctrine, Tax Authorities were given, and actually made large use of, the power to consider abusive and therefore disregard potentially any transaction which at the time of its implementation appeared to be lawful, as it did not fall within the scope of application of any codified anti-avoidance rule.

The concern about the lack of certainty of the tax effects of transactions due to a substantially limitless Tax Authorities' and tax courts' power of ex-post recharacterization of transactions carried out by the taxpayers was amplified by the fact that the application of the anti-abuse principle construed by the Supreme Court was not subject to the same procedural mechanism provided for by Art. 37-*bis*. That mechanism was aimed at safeguarding the taxpayer's right to receive notice in advance of the position of Tax Authorities and gave the taxpayer the right to provide a justification to counter their claim.

A further criticism of the creation of a judicial general anti-avoidance rule related to the application of administrative sanctions.[21] In the first place commentators pointed out that administrative sanctions had to be expressly provided by the law, while sanctions applied as a result of the application of the judicial anti-avoidance principle were not.[22] This plainly contrasted with the position of the ECJ, which had remarked that "a finding of abusive practice must not lead to a penalty, for which a clear and unambiguous legal basis would be necessary".[23] Also the Supreme Court in Italy recently confirmed that administrative sanctions are not applicable with regard to abuse of law, despite the opposite position that had been taken by lower courts.

The convergence of the concepts of avoidance and abuse of tax laws

After its 2008 decisions, the Supreme Court continued to assert, in several other decisions, the existence of the general anti-abuse principle and its derivation from the constitutional principle of ability to pay.[24] In these decisions, however, the Supreme Court defined more precisely the

---

it provides Tax Authorities with a mechanism that extends its discretion far beyond that which is constitutionally acceptable".

20 Fantozzi and Mameli, n.12, at 448.
21 R. C. Guerra, "Non applicabilità delle sanzioni amministrative per la violazione del divieto di abuso del diritto", 10 *Corriere Tributario* 771–6 (2009), et seq.
22 According to Art. 25(2) of the Constitution, and Art. 6 (2) of Legislative Decree No. 472 of 18 December 1997, a taxpayer cannot be subjected to penalties for a tax violation if there is uncertainty regarding the objective conditions for the penalty.
23 *Halifax*, n.9, at para. 93.
24 ISC, Decision No. 1465/2009; No. 8481 of 8 April 2009; No. 8487 of 8 April 2009.

main features that transactions were supposed to have in order to be subject to the application of the general anti-abuse principle, the exact scope of the authority to apply the anti-abuse principle, and the consequences in terms of penalties.

According to the definition developed by the Supreme Court,[25] the "abuse of tax laws" consists of "drawing *undue tax benefits* from a *distorted*, albeit not inconsistent with any specific provision, *use of legal instruments* suitable to achieving tax savings, *in the absence of appreciable economic reasons* that may justify the transaction, other than the mere expectation of those tax savings" (emphasis added).

Based on this definition, the Supreme Court has subsequently clarified and delineated the concept of abuse of law, stating that it presupposes "*manipulation*" and "*alteration*" of "*typical nego-tiated agreements*" through "*an unreasonable conduct under normal market conditions*" pursued "*only to achieve such tax result*".[26] The evidence of this must be proven by the Tax Administration, "while the *taxpayer bears the burden to allege the existence of alternative or concurring economic reasons* that may justify transactions to be structured in that way".[27]

Commentators observed that the concept of "abuse of law", as developed by the case law of the Supreme Court, and the concept of "avoidance", as set forth in anti-avoidance legislation (i.e. Art. 37-*bis*) were "converging" and "overlapping" concepts,[28] therefore the former was none other than the latter's "*twin*".[29] In fact, where the concept of abuse of law referred to "a distorted use [...] of legal instruments", Art. 37-*bis* referred to "acts, facts and contracts [...] aiming to circumvent obligations or prohibitions laid down in the legal framework for taxation". Further-more, while the judicial principle made reference to "abuse" in case of "*undue tax benefits*", Art. 37-*bis* mentioned "*tax reductions or refunds otherwise undue*".

The tendency of the judicial concept of "abuse of law" and the legislative concept of "avoid-ance" to converge in practice can be explained by the need to expand the universe of situations that could reasonably be considered to constitute an unlawful behavior, as a reaction to the prior understanding that Art. 37-*bis* and the other specific anti-avoidance rules were applicable only to a restricted range of predefined situations.[30] Commentators also observed that case law shaped the concept of the judicial concept of "abuse of law" essentially by "reusing", "recovering" and "recycling"[31] the distinguishing features of the legislative concept of "avoidance".

The conflation of the legislative concept of "avoidance" into the judicial concept of "abuse of law" however did not extend, in Supreme Court interpretations, to procedural safeguards enshrined in Art. 37-*bis*. Indeed, according to the Supreme Court, the judicial anti-abuse princi-ple could be used to challenge the tax effects of abuse without any of the procedural precautions which were instead set forth for the application of Art. 37-*bis*. Italian tax judges, in fact, would later essentially support the claim by Tax Authorities to apply the judicial principle rather than the anti-avoidance statutory rules, with the result that taxpayers were denied the procedural guarantees offered by the latter rules.[32]

---

25 Italian Supreme Court, Unified Sections, 23 December 2008, Nos. 30055, 30056 and 30057.

26 Italian Supreme Court, Decision No. 21390 of 30 November 2012.

27 Ibid.

28 See D. Deotto, "L'abuso del diritto tributario può essere individuato solo per esclusione", 21 *il Fisco* (2014), 2070–2074.

29 See F. Tundo, "Abuso del diritto ed elusione: un'anomala sovrapposizione", 4 *Corriere Tributario* (2011), 279–291.

30 Dario Deotto, "L'abuso del diritto tributario può essere individuato solo per esclusione", n.28.

31 These terms were introduced by M. Beghin, "L'ammortamento del marchio acquistato a prezzo assertamente abnorme nella Babele dell'abuso del diritto", 15/16 *Bollettino Tributario* (2014), 1191–1197.

32 See Tundo, n.29.

The recent codification of the prohibition of abuse of tax law

To sum up, the Italian tax system was characterized by the simultaneous and utterly ambiguous existence of two rules. On the one hand, a specific anti-avoidance rule contained in Art. 37-*bis* set forth cases of transactions that could be audited and disregarded by the Tax Authorities and required the Tax Authorities to ensure the taxpayers' right to be heard before the issuance of the assessment. On the other hand, a general principle of prohibition of abuse of tax legislation was created by the Supreme Court, but its distinguishing features, scope and procedural safeguards were largely undefined and left to the often fragmented and uncoordinated action of local tax offices and lower tax courts.

This situation eventually led the Italian Parliament to empower the Government to proceed to a review of the current anti-avoidance rules (Law No. 23/2014) to unify them in a codified general anti-abuse clause. According to the Parliament's guidelines contained in Law No. 23/2014, any abusive conduct had to be defined as "misuse of legal instruments suitable to achieving tax savings, even if such conduct is not in conflict with any specific rule". However, the Parliament's guidelines highlighted that the taxpayers have a right to choose between two or more possible transactions which have the same commercial result but which produce different taxable amounts.

More specifically, according to the Parliament's guidelines, the future anti-abuse clause had to be based on the following principles: (a) for a transaction to be characterized as an abuse of tax laws, the purpose of obtaining a tax benefit should be identified as the prevailing reason for implementing that transaction; (b) there can be no abuse when one or more transactions are dictated by "non-marginal non-tax reasons" (i.e. important business reasons).

With the recent enactment of Art. 10-*bis* of the Delegated Decree No. 128/2015 ("Provisions on legal certainty in relations between tax authorities and taxpayers", hereinafter "Delegated Decree for legal certainty"), and the simultaneous repeal of Art. 37-*bis*, the Italian Government has finally codified the rules on the so-called "abuse" of tax law and clarified that the legislative concept of "avoidance" and the judicial concept of "abuse of law" have in fact the same meaning.

Art. 10-*bis* of Delegated Decree for legal certainty (hereinafter Art. 10-*bis*) is entitled "Abuse of law or anti-avoidance rules" and largely inspired by the European Commission Recommendation on aggressive tax planning No. 2012/772/EU of 6 December 2012 (hereinafter "EC Recommendation").[33] This new legislative concept of "abuse of law or anti-avoidance" includes the features of transactions which can be disregarded by Tax Authorities following a mandatory procedure aimed at granting the taxpayers' right to be heard before the issuance of an assessment.

The general concept of "abuse of law or anti-avoidance" is set forth by § 1 of Art. 10-*bis*, according to which "one or more transactions devoid of any economic substance shall constitute abuse of law if, despite the formal observance of the tax rules, they essentially achieve undue tax benefits". Therefore, the finding of evidence for the three following elements is required for transactions to be classified as abusive: (i) the lack of economic substance; (ii) the achievement of undue tax benefits; and (iii) the fact that the undue benefits are essential to the purpose of the transaction.

Lack of economic substance

Art. 10-*bis* § 2(a) provides that "facts, acts and contracts, including if connected together, which are incapable of producing significant effects other than tax benefits shall be considered as

---

33 European Commission Recommendation No. 2012/772/EU of 6 December 2012.

transactions without economic substance", adding, in particular, that "any inconsistencies between the qualification of individual transactions and the legal basis thereof, and non-conformity to normal market logic of the legal instruments used shall constitute evidence of lack of economic substance".

A transaction must be regarded as lacking economic substance when it appears unjustifiable when considered from the standpoint of the normal entrepreneurial logic, or when the acts carried out do not bring any advantage other than tax savings. That is in particular the case when, from a business standpoint, the transaction taken as a whole brings no "economic or legal value added" compared to alternative transactions that are more straightforward on the one side, and more burdensome in terms of taxation on the other.

This requirement follows the model of the anti-abuse clause provided by the EC Recommendation,[34] according to which, the first element in identifying an abuse of tax law is, indeed, the existence of "an artificial arrangement or an artificial series of arrangements".[35]

In light of such link between the newly introduced anti-abuse clause and the EC Recommendation, the latter proved also helpful in providing the criteria to use when investigating whether the arrangements or the series of arrangements implemented by the taxpayers are to be considered as lacking economic substance. The EC Recommendation identifies the following as circumstances that indicate lack of economic substance: (i) inconsistency of one or more stages of the overall conduct with respect to the business and legal aims pursued; (ii) performance, as part of the overall conduct, of one or more stages that cancel each other; (iii) ability to achieve the same economic and legal result by using an alternative legal route; (iv) absence of any impact of the transaction, due to being perfectly "circular", on the economic and legal sphere of the taxpayer.[36]

Undue tax benefits vs. lawful tax savings

As specified under letter b) in § 2 of Art. 10-*bis*, undue tax benefits are "benefits, albeit not immediate, which have been achieved in conflict with the purpose of the tax rules or principles of the tax system".

In this regard, the statement contained in the Explanatory Report to the Delegated Decree for Legal Certainty should be highlighted, namely:

> therefore, there must be a violation of the intent of the rules or general principles of the legal framework and, above all, of the tax rules setting forth the obligations and prohibitions being circumvented. This, in particular, makes it possible to appropriately put forward a case of abuse of law by virtue of the different principles that underpin the taxes not being applied, it being understood that, as held above, the search for the intent and demonstration of the violation thereof must constitute an objective condition that is essential for telling apart the pursuit of lawful tax savings from tax avoidance.

---

34 G. Zizzo, "La nuova nozione di abuso del diritto e le raccomandazioni della Commissione europea", 47 *Corriere Tributario* 4577 (2015); A. Contrino and A. Marcheselli, "Luci e ombre nella struttura dell'abuso fiscale 'riformato'", 37 *Corriere Tributario* 3787 (2015).

35 EC Recommendation, n.33, at paras 4.2 and 4.4.

36 The reference to the economic substance of the transactions is common to most general anti-avoidance clauses introduced by foreign jurisdictions. In particular, see Austria, Germany, France, and the UK. In Austria, Art. 21 of the Tax Code expressly states that "the tax regime applicable to an arrangement is determined on the basis of its economic substance".

Therefore, tax savings may be qualified as unlawful only to the extent that it is possible to find that a tax rule has been avoided, i.e. that the will of the legislature has been "betrayed" through the achievement of tax effects other than those set forth by the legislature itself for a specific transaction. Also this aspect is derived from the EC Recommendation, according to which a tax savings qualifies as undue only "where, regardless of any subjective intentions of the taxpayer, it defeats the object, spirit and purpose of the tax provisions that would otherwise apply".[37]

To better define and limit the scope of the concept of undue tax savings, it is in any case appropriate to also make reference to the provisions laid down in § 4 of Art. 10-*bis*, in which the concept of "lawful tax savings" is codified as follows: "there shall be no prejudice to the taxpayer's freedom of choice between several optional regimes offered by the law and transactions involving a different tax burden". When the taxpayer exercises this right, tax savings are legitimate (i.e. are not undue) and, therefore, abusive conduct may not be invoked before Tax Authorities.

The acknowledgement that the taxpayer is able to choose between two or more possible transactions that have the same commercial result but produce different taxable amounts is common to all major tax systems in the OECD area and was also included in Art. 37-*bis*, so that previous clarifications about that provisions continue to be applicable to Art. 10-*bis*.

In particular, the Report accompanying Art. 37-*bis* clarified that lawful tax savings

> occur when, among various conducts being considered by the tax system as fungible, the taxpayer adopts the less burdensome one from a fiscal standpoint. There will be no circumvention as long as the taxpayer merely chooses between two alternatives that the legal framework makes available to him as a matter of course. A different solution would conflict with a principle common to all the tax systems of developed countries, which allow taxpayers to conduct their business in a fiscally less burdensome manner, and where anti-avoidance rules are only triggered when the abuse of this freedom leads to manipulation, loopholes and gimmicks that – albeit formally compliant – end up distorting the principles of the tax system. Anti-avoidance rules cannot prevent the taxpayer from choosing the less burdensome conduct from a fiscal standpoint from among a number of possible conducts which the system considers as fungible.

That Report observed fungible legal instruments in that context were, for example, "the choice of the type of company to be used, the choice between selling a company and disposing of shareholdings, or a financing system based on own equity or debt, the tax period in which to collect revenues or pay expenses, or even the rate of depreciation, provisions and all other valuation items of the financial statements ... In all these cases, the choice of the least burdensome tax rate is not implicitly prohibited by the system, but it is instead explicitly or implicitly allowed, and no circumvention of any obligations or prohibitions can be put forth."

Non-marginal non-tax reasons and "essential" tax savings

When an unlawful tax benefit is obtained through one or more transactions, the taxpayer's conduct may be qualified as abuse of law – and therefore may be disregarded by Tax Authorities – only to the extent that such tax benefit is "essential". Thus, it becomes vital to understand whether and when the undue tax benefit is considered as "essential" under the operation of Art. 10-*bis*.

---

37 EC Recommendation, n.33, para. 4.5.

Art. 10-*bis* § 3 provides that

> transactions that are justified by valid non-tax and non-marginal reasons, including in regard of the taxpayer's organizational or management structure, pursued for the purpose of the structural or functional improvement of the taxpayer's enterprise or professional activity shall not be considered as abuse of law in any case.

In a shorter summarized version Art. 10-*bis* § 3 provides that "transactions that are justified by valid non-tax reasons and are not marginal, (...) shall not be considered as abuse of law". The undue tax benefits therefore are "essential" only when the "non-tax reasons" (i.e. the business reasons) of the taxpayer's conduct are "*marginal*". By contrast, when the "non-tax reasons" (i.e. the business reasons) of the taxpayer's conduct are "*non-marginal*" (i.e. are important), the tax saving is not considered as "essential" for the purposes of Art. 10-*bis*.

It is a mystery for a reasonable reader of this segment of Art. 10-*bis* to understand why double negations were used instead of simple positive statements. It is rather questionable to define a concept by using a negation: what are exactly the "non-marginal non-tax reasons" referred to by Art. 10-*bis* § 3? It is difficult to say. A different, more readable, version of Art. 10-*bis* § 3 in positive form would have read as follows "transactions that are justified by *valid business reasons* (instead of: valid non-tax reasons) which are *important* (instead of: non-marginal), (...) shall not be considered as abuse of law". In a more simplified positive form: "transactions that are justified by *important valid business reasons* (instead of: non-marginal non-tax reasons) (...) shall not be considered as abuse of law".

In order to better understand the semantically awkward concept of "non-marginal non-tax reasons" it is important to quote a long passage of the Explanatory Report to the Delegated Decree for legal certainty. According to the Report,

> to understand whether non-tax reasons are marginal or otherwise, one should look to the intrinsic value of such reasons with respect to the completion of the examined transaction. In this sense, valid non-marginal non-tax economic reasons only exist if the transaction would not be put in place in their absence. It should, in fact, be proven that the transaction would not be completed in the absence of such reasons.

It is difficult to define a concept or situation by using a counterfactual, i.e. a situation that hypothetically would not have occurred, in an imaginary situation. An evaluation criterion can, however, be drawn from the EC Recommendation, which states that undue tax savings assume the character of essentiality "where any other purpose that is or could be attributed to the arrangement or series of arrangements appears at most negligible, in view of all the circumstances of the case", i.e. when non-tax reasons (business reasons) are insignificant, spurious or otherwise marginal in the specific factual and legal context.

It should be noted that § 3 of Art. 10-*bis* makes reference to "needs pursued for the structural and functional improvement of the taxpayer's business activity". This is, indeed, an important legislative recognition of all those reasons of a restructuring kind that characterize certain corporate transactions, such as, for example, mergers, de-mergers, or transfers of business. The Report observes that "non-marginal non-tax economic reasons shall be understood as reasons that, although not underpinning transactions that create immediate profitability, howsoever meet needs of an organizational kind pursued for the structural and functional improvement of the taxpayer's business activity [...]."

It should be highlighted, finally, that § 9 of Art. 10-*bis* provides that the taxpayer's burden to prove the existence of valid non-tax reasons only operates once Tax Authorities have proven the abusive nature of the conduct, namely the lack of economic substance of the transaction taken as a whole and the undue nature of the tax benefit obtained. This implies that the lack of valid non-tax reasons (i.e. valid business reasons) is rebuttable evidence of the fact that the transaction amounts to tax avoidance/abuse of law, as it should be proved also that the tax benefits are "essential" in the sense defined previously. This is a crucial point: the approach previously adopted by the Tax Administration in applying Art. 37-*bis*, was that the lack of valid non-tax reasons (i.e. valid business reasons) is non-rebuttable evidence of tax avoidance/abuse of law.[38]

Procedural requirements and burden of proof

It is also worth noting that Tax Authorities must comply with strict procedural requirements to apply the newly-codified anti-abuse clause. Specifically, before the notice of assessment is issued, the taxpayer needs to be engaged in a discussion so that it may have the opportunity to illustrate the economic substance underlying the arrangement challenged by Tax Authorities. In addition, with regard to the economic substance criteria and whether there are undue tax benefits derived from a transaction, the burden of proof is on Tax Authorities.[39] Failure to comply with the procedural requirements or with the burden of proof results in the assessment being invalid and void. It is further provided that the tax courts cannot apply the GAAR *ex officio*.

It is, furthermore, important to mention that Tax Authorities can resort to Art. 10-*bis* only in those residual cases in which no specific anti-avoidance rules potentially apply to the arrangements at issue.[40] Taxpayers are also given the opportunity to request a ruling from Tax Authorities to ascertain whether certain transactions constitute an abuse of law. Such request for a ruling can be filed even after the transactions take place, but no later than the deadline to file the tax return for the fiscal year in which the transaction takes place.

The introduction of a cooperative compliance program

In addition to the general anti-abuse clause, the Delegated Decree No. 128/2015 introduced a cooperative compliance program. Such measure is in line with the OECD recommendations[41]

---

38 Contrino and Marcheselli, n.34.

39 This is consistent with the previous regulation under Art. 37-*bis* and also with the approach followed by most foreign jurisdictions.

40 See, for example, Germany, where para. 1 of Section 42 expressly states that "when the conditions for the application of a specific anti-avoidance rule are met, the tax consequences of the transactions at issue are governed exclusively by such specific anti-avoidance provision". Conversely, in Austria there is a stream of case-law according to which the existence of a specific anti-avoidance rule potentially applicable to the transaction at issue does not prevent Tax Authorities from employing the general anti-abuse clause. See VwGH, Decision of 19 January 2005, Case No. 200/13/0176; and Decision of 26 July 2005, Case No. 2001/14/0135.

41 OECD, *Co-Operative Compliance: A Framework. From Enhanced Relationship to Cooperative Compliance* (2013), available at www.oecd-ilibrary.org/docserver/download/2313201e.pdf?expires=1414514965&id=id&accname=oci d177380&checksum=FCAB5DDBA80770F31CAD3655AFDBE1FC; OECD, *Study Into the Role of Tax Intermediaries* (2008), available at www.oecd.org/tax/administration/39882938.pdf. See also J. Owens, "The 'Enhanced Relationship': A Challenge for Revenue Bodies and Taxpayers", *European Taxation* 351 (July 2008).

and other jurisdictions' best practices[42] for the development of a renewed relationship between corporate taxpayers and Tax Authorities aimed at preventing at source tax avoidance.[43]

The introduction of such program was preceded in 2013–2014 by a pilot program open to large corporate taxpayers (i.e. taxpayers with a turnover amounting to over Euro 100 million). Eighty-four corporations applied to the pilot program, but only fourteen of them were selected by the Italian Tax Authorities.[44]

The newly-codified cooperative compliance program is currently open exclusively to those corporations whose revenues amount to at least Euro 10 billion – or whose revenues amount to at least Euro 1 billion and who have filed the request for participation in the pilot project upon invitation by the Italian Tax Authorities – provided that they have adopted an internal tax risk control system (the so-called "Tax Control Framework") within the frame of their corporate governance and internal audit.[45]

Participation in the Cooperative Compliance program may entitle the taxpayer to benefit from various advantages. Among these advantages are: (i) access to an advance exchange with the Tax Authority about those transactions which are more likely to generate tax risks; (ii) an accelerated procedure to obtain an advance ruling by Tax Authorities; (iii) a reduction of the administrative penalties by half and, in any case, not higher than the statutory minimum penalties, and the suspension of the collection of taxes until the assessment becomes definitive, in regard to the transactions on which there has been advance disclosure; (iv) exemption from the duty to provide a guarantee for the payment, by Tax Authorities, of tax refunds, in regard to both direct and indirect taxes.

42 In particular, Australia, the Netherlands, UK and the US have been the leading jurisdictions in developing cooperative compliance programs. For the Australian program, please see Australian Taxation Office for the Commonwealth of Australia, *Large Business and Tax Compliance* (2014), available at www.ato.gov.au/uploaded Files/Content/LB_I/downloads/BUSINESS16985LargebusinessandtaxCompliance.pdf. For the Dutch program, please see The Netherlands Tax and Customs Administration, *Horizontal Monitoring Within the Medium to Very Large Businesses Segment* (30 November 2010), 7–8, available at http://download.belastingdienst.nl/belastingdienst/docs/horizontal_monitoring_very_large_businesses_dv4061z1pleng.pdf; The Netherlands Tax and Customs Administration, *Supervision Large Business in the Netherlands* (2013), available at http://download.belastingdienst.nl/belastingdienst/docs/supervision_large_business_in_netherlands_dv4231z1fdeng.pdf; The Netherlands Tax and Customs Administration, *Guide to Horizontal Monitoring within the SME segment* (2012), available at http://download.belastingdienst.nl/belastingdienst/docs/guide_horiz_monit_dv4071z1pleng.pdf; Committee Horizontal Monitoring Tax and Custom Administration, *Tax Supervision – Made to Measure: Flexible When Possible, Strict When Necessary* (2012), available at www.ifa.nl/Document/Publicaties/Enhanced%20Relationship%20Project/tax_supervision_made_to_measure_tz0151z1fdeng.pdf. See also Chapter 14 of this volume. For the UK program, please see HM Revenue & Customs, *The Framework for a Better Relationship* (2008), available at www.hmrc.gov.uk/budget2008/supplementary.htm. For the US program, please see Internal Revenue Service, *Internal Revenue Manual – 4.51.8 Compliance Assurance Process (CAP) Examinations*, available at www.irs.gov/Businesses/Corporations/Compliance-Assurance-Process.

43 J. Braithwaite, "Large Businesses and the Compliance Model", in V. Braithwaite (ed.), *Taxing Democracy: Understanding Tax Avoidance and Evasion*, Aldershot: Ashgate (2003), 177; V. Braithwaite, "Responsive Regulation and Taxation", 29 *Law and Policy* 3 (2007); K. Murphy, "Moving Towards a More Effective Model of Regulatory Enforcement in the Australian Tax Office", *British Tax Review* (2004), 603–619; G. Allevato, "La 'cooperative compliance' italiana e il progressivo allineamento agli standard internazionali", 41 *Corriere Tributario* 3168 (2016).

44 For more information about the pilot project, see documents available at www.agenziaentrate.gov.it/wps/content/nsilib/nsi/home/cosadevifare/richiedere/regime+di+adempimento+collaborativo/regime+di+adempimento+collaborativo+-+grandi+contribuenti.

45 See Art. 7 of Legislative Decree ("Decreto Legislativo") No. 128 of 5 August 2015.

Conclusion

Italy's experience with the contradictions among corporate anti-avoidance rules represents at its best the difficulties that a civil law system, based on codified rules, may incur in adapting and updating such rules to corporations' behavior in a free-market economy. Corporations have a very dynamic ability to design and implement their arrangements in a way which allows them to take advantage not just of the benefits offered by the system, but also of the gaps and loopholes in the regulatory framework. A civil law system, such as the Italian legal system, traditionally grants legal certainty by codifying its rules. As a consequence, those transactions or arrangements which do not fall within the scope of application of codified rules cannot be considered as void or be disregarded for tax purposes.

The emergence of aggressive tax planning schemes in the last decades by corporations, however, certainly constituted the primary reason for the Supreme Court's push to supplement the codified specific anti-avoidance rules with a case-law-based general anti-avoidance or anti-abuse principle. Such intervention clearly gave rise to a tension between the founding principles of a civil law system and the need to contain and limit corporate tax avoidance. Such tension resulted in an increased complexity in the governance of the Italian tax law system, which, in turn, affected legal certainty for businesses operating in Italy.

After almost ten years, it seems that such a contradictory and destabilizing scenario has been finally ended by the codification of a general anti-avoidance rule, whose unlimited scope of application is balanced by a definition of the main elements an arrangement must contain in order to be considered as abusive and by the establishment of a strict procedure aimed at granting the taxpayers' right to be heard and provide evidence of the business reasons for those transactions before an assessment is eventually issued by Tax Authorities.

The fact that the anti-avoidance general rule has been codified is complemented by the newly introduced cooperative compliance program. Although such program is currently open to a restricted number of corporate taxpayers, it is likely that its scope of application will be extended in the near future.

12

TAX AVOIDANCE ISSUES IN TURKEY

Leyla Ateş

Introduction

Income taxation has been at the centre of tax anti-avoidance and evasion efforts on an international and national level. The OECD Standard for Automatic Exchange of Financial Account Information in Tax Matters and the US domestic legislation of FATCA has shared the common goal of fighting against offshore income tax evasion (OECD 2014). The OECD/G20 Base Erosion and Profit Shifting Project aims to reform the international tax system for curbing corporate income tax avoidance by multinational enterprises (OECD 2013).

Turkey, like many other countries, has taken general and specific anti-avoidance measures to tackle income tax avoidance. The Turkish Tax Procedure Code (TPC) has contained a general anti-avoidance rule in Article 3 since 1980. The Turkish income tax laws have various specific anti-avoidance provisions. In 2006, Turkey introduced new specific anti-avoidance measures, namely transfer pricing (TP) rules, Controlled Foreign Company (CFC) rules, and thin capitalization rules based on clearer and more concrete elements compared to previous rules in the Corporate Income Tax Code to combat multinationals' tax avoidance (Yaltı 2015). In addition, Turkey has introduced withholding tax to the payment to tax havens but since the Council of Ministers has not released the list of tax havens, this measure has not yet been implemented (Yaltı 2015). Most recently, Turkey intends to amend its general anti-avoidance provision to tackle international tax avoidance strategies of multinational enterprises (MNEs) more rigorously in a draft law prepared for the rewriting of a new TPC (TBMM 2016).

Turkey is a developing country. Many countermeasures against tax avoidance of MNEs require complex legislation and significant tax-collection capabilities that make them unused or ineffective for developing countries (UNCTAD 2015). In particular, TP rules and CFC rules are challenging for developing countries to implement and administer, mostly due to inadequate resources and lack of expertise (UNCTAD 2015). Thus, the effective implementation of the new tax anti-avoidance measures in Turkey is dependent to a considerable degree on the capacity of the Turkish tax administration. However, the lack of transparency of the Turkish tax administration problematises any evaluation of its effectiveness by general public and researchers in this respect. This study aims to show the inefficacy of the Turkish tax administrative capacity in implementing the specific anti-avoidance measures of TP and CFC rules at least at the beginning of their main inclusion into the Turkish tax system by examining it against the legal history of presumptive income taxation in Turkey.

"The term presumptive taxation covers a number of procedures under which the 'desired' base for taxation (direct or indirect) is not itself measured but is inferred from some simple indicators which are more easily measured than the base itself" (Ahmad and Stern 1991). Presumptive taxation or, more accurately, 'presumptive *assessment*' (Bird and Wallace 2004) takes advantage of data that are easier for officials to obtain than the information required to determine actual taxable income under the regular income tax rules (Bird and Zolt 2005). It is used mostly to collect tax effectively from the hard-to-tax groups, i.e. small- and medium-sized businesses, individual proprietors, professionals, and farmers (Rajamaran and Singh 1995; Thuronyi 1996) and constitutes an important mechanism for developing countries to overcome weakness in their administration and reduce tax evasion (Bulutoğlu 1995). Although less widespread, developed countries also use presumptive methods to deal with hard-to-tax forms of income. For example, the United States uses presumptive taxation for tip income earned by restaurant servers, standard deduction as a substitute for itemized deductions below a threshold amount, fixed depreciation schedules in lieu of actual measurements of decline in asset value, and the allocation of 30 per cent of business profits to personal services for citizens living abroad (Thomas 2013). Some US scholars have even proposed presumptive taxation of small businesses for filling the tax gap in the US (Thomas 2013; Logue and Vettori 2013).

Presumptive taxation also formed an integral part of Turkish income tax system until 2002. However, Turkey used presumptive assessment not only for income of hard-to-tax groups, but also for annual income tax filers who calculate the tax due as part of the process of filling in the return form and remitting the tax with the form under a self-assessment method, in an effort to curb their income tax avoidance (Bulutoğlu 1997). Its use indicates the Turkish tax administration's difficulty implementing regular income tax laws (Bulutoğlu 1978). It is moreover strongly suggestive of the administration's inefficacy in implementing the new specific anti-avoidance measures, at least when these were initially included in the Turkish tax system in 2006.

Presumptive taxation in early Turkish income tax legislation

Prelude to income taxation

Tax evasion and avoidance has existed as long as tax itself (Evans 2009) and every kind of taxation has evoked its own means of evasion and avoidance as well as anti-evasion and anti-avoidance measures. The jizya tax practice in the Ottoman Empire, predecessor of the Republic of Turkey, is a good example.

The jizya (*cizye*) was an Islamic poll tax paid by non-Muslim adult males and widows possessing the land of their deceased (İnalcık 2000). In classical Islam, jurists set different rates for the poor, middle class and the wealthy. The Ottomans changed these rates in some regions to pre-Ottoman poll-tax levels extant in the conquered countries and levied one fixed rate per household instead of individual payment (İnalcık 1997). In many instances, the Ottomans made agreements with non-Muslim communities in towns or on islands to pay the jizya in a predetermined lump sum for the whole community (*ber vech-i maktu*) (İnalcık 1997; Darling 1996). Although this method guaranteed a stable revenue source for the government, this practice missed newcomers and more importantly caused revenue loss because of fugitives (İnalcık 1997). As a result of collective responsibility, the remaining population was forced to pay for the missing ones, which was as much as three quarters of the population in some cases (İnalcık 2000). In some instances, this collection method ruined an entire village, as was the case in some Balkan Christian villages, or caused mass conversions in various parts of the Balkans (İnalcık 1997).

Similarly Turkish Jews avoided the jizya by expatriating from their village. To afford the expense of defensive war against the Holy League, the Ottoman state levied surtaxes from 1508 to 1515 (Kohen 2007). The city of Salonica where a big Turkish Jewish community lived had a heavy tax share. To avoid a heavy tax burden, a number of taxpayers moved to other Balkan cities, which increased the burden of those remaining, as the sum total payable by the village remained unchanged (Kohen 2007). Some taxpayers left the city before the war tax was levied on them and returned later, claiming that the new war tax could not apply to them since at the time of its proclamation in the midst of the community, they had not resided in Salonica (Kohen 2007). A spiritual leader of the Jewish community firmly pronounced himself against the tax evaders and even expressed a rare opinion that the Jewish leaders could even make an appeal to the state authorities in order to enforce due payments (Kohen 2007).

To fight such a tax evasion, the government employed two methods (İnalcık 1997). First, the government adjusted the register every three years by counting and registering all adult subjects required to pay this tax and removed the names of the fugitives. Second, the government used private tax-farmers (*hâric emînî*) who actively pursued fugitives to collect the poll tax.

The beginning of income taxation dated back to the nineteenth century in Turkey. The Ottoman Empire went through a transformation of the taxation system in the nineteenth century (Şener 1990; Saraçoğlu 2007). The declaration of the 1839 Edict, which represented an internationally sanctioned statement about the new state order (İslamoğlu 2010), initiated the three-and-a-half decades of reform generally referred to as the "Tanzimat" era (Hanioğlu 2008). Taxation was a major area of the reform. The 1839 Edict heralded the abolition of the extant tax-collection method, i.e. the tax-farming system, and an equitable tax system (Hanioğlu 2008; Çakır 2001).

The timar (*tımar*) had been the principal tax-collection method until the seventeenth century in the Ottoman state (Pelin 1945; Hanioğlu 2008). In the timar system, the state apportioned their tax revenues to the Ottoman military and administrators in exchange for services rendered (Quataert 2005). A weak cash economy, an undeveloped central treasury and the soldiery consisting mainly of cavalry rendered the timar system a necessity (İnalcık 2000). The cavalry met its needs in a rural environment, and tithes on grain as the main source of the state revenue were collected and turned into cash in local markets (İnalcık 2000). The timar system was established on and maintained through the information in survey registers (*tahrîr defterleri*) (Barkan 1970). Right after the conquest of a land, the Ottomans conducted surveys enumerating all of the taxable resources of the area (İnalcık 2006). Each surveyor (*tahrîr emînî*) was given a certificate (*berat*) clearly outlining the data collection procedure (İnalcık 2011). By following this procedure, the official counted the households and livestock, population (only tax-paying head of the household and males old enough to serve in the military), measured the land, its fertility, productivity and use and recorded them (Quataert 2005). From the sixteenth century, another tax-collection method, i.e. the tax-farming (*iltizam*) started to replace the timar system because of the state's increasing cash needs (Quataert 2005). In the tax-farming system, the state held auctions at specific times and places for the right to collect the taxes of a district of which the annual value had been already determined by officials (Quataert 2005). In order to centralise government finance (Findley 2006), the Tanzimat government abolished the tax-farming system, and appointed tax collectors (*muhassıl*) together with the officials working under them and the local tax-collection council (*Meclis-i Muhassilîn*) at the beginning of 1840 (Şener 1990; Hanioğlu 2008; Saraçoğlu 2007). The tax collectors' very first assignment was to conduct surveys (*temettüat defterleri*) including name and title of everyone along with their land, property and animals and a yearly profit of merchants and artisans (Pelin 1945). This assignment coincided with the introduction of a new customary tax.

The Ottomans imposed both Islamic or rightful taxes (*tekâlifi şerriye or şerî vergiler*) and customary taxes (*tekâlifi örfiye or örfi vergiler*) (Öncel et al. 2016). Islamic taxes were stipulated by the Islamic law. Customary taxes were levied by the Sultan independently from the religious law and this characteristic is an indication of its local origin (İnalcık 1997). Customary taxes were assessed collectively. They were distributed amongst first communities and then evenly redistributed to the households (Pelin 1945). The Tanzimat government restored Islamic taxes but expended more energy on customary taxes. A bundle of customary taxes was consolidated under a new tax titled "ancemaatin" (Pelin 1945; Shaw 1975; Çakır 2001), which literally means "from the community".[1] As the name suggests (Pelin 1945; Saraçoğlu 2007) the Tanzimat government did not change the collective assessment method. But assessed tax would be distributed on the basis of the new survey registers which took into account taxpayers' land, property, animals and annual profits. The local tax-collection councils were assigned duties in the distribution and collection of the assessed tax (Şener 1996). But the new tax was never strictly enforced since the Ottoman Government did not have the complete information to assess the new tax (Shaw 1975). In fact, in 1838 Sultan Mahmut II ordered cadastral surveys of property values throughout the empire so that subsequent taxes could be assessed according to the ability to pay (Shaw and Shaw 2002). Piecemeal individual wealth and profit surveys were subsequently carried out. However, late in 1858 a Cadastral Department in the Ministry of Finance (*Tahrir-i Emlâk Nezareti*) was organized for the purpose of providing tax officials with a comprehensive inventory of wealth (Shaw and Shaw 2002) and this department started to conduct a completely new survey of land, property and profits (Shaw 1975). Following this development, the collective assessment method was gradually left and an equal-incidence proportional tax on profit (*temettü vergisi*) along with property and land taxes (*emlak ve arazi vergisi*) was introduced (Pelin 1945). This was a prelude to income taxation.

Since then several income tax anti-evasion and anti-avoidance measures have been included in different tax legislation. However, this study limits itself to presumptive taxation in income tax laws. Other measures including general anti-avoidance rules, naming and shaming rules and tax penalties currently regulated under Turkish Tax Procedure Law are not within the scope of this study.

Profit tax legislation

At first, the officials carried out surveys and simultaneously implemented the profit tax along with the land and property taxes in two villages, Bursa and Yanya respectively, under the directives (*talimatlar*) (Sayın 1999). Benefiting from these two pilot projects (Şener 1990), the Ottoman State promulgated a general law on 27 December 1860, called the "Regulation for Surveying Census and Property" (*Tahrir-i Nüfus ve Emlake Dair Nizamname*) and extended surveys to other provinces in 1863 (Sayın 1999). Most tax provisions of the regulation were about land and property taxes. There were only a few provisions for the profit tax and they were vague (Pelin 1945). According to the 1886 revised version of the regulation, the profit tax was levied on merchants, artisans and craftsman according to their profit level. The tax rate was not prescribed by the regulation; instead imperial decrees (*irade-i senniyye*) were referred for determining, increasing or decreasing the rate. Imperial decrees set the rate first at 3 per cent, then at 4 per cent and finally at 5 per cent (Pelin 1945). The regulation authorized local councils to assess income on their best judgement. The local council was constituted of six representatives, two of which were selected by the municipal administration, two by the

1 An-cemaatin. Cemaat means "community". In Ottoman, "an" gave the meaning of "from" to the word it prefixed.

central administration and two from taxpayer representatives. The participation of citizens might have reduced the opportunities for abuse of power in the presumptive tax council (Bulutoğlu 1995). But the law did not define principles the council should have relied on for its assessment and there was no appellate procedure until 1900, i.e. the taxpayer did not have the right to come forward with proper evidence of income (Pelin 1945). The local councils misused their power (Pelin 1945).

The profit tax attained a comprehensive and separate legal ground by means of the Profit Tax Regulation of 1907 (*Temettü Vergisi Nizamnamesi*). Profit tax was levied either as a fixed lump sum (*maktu*) or on a proportional basis (*nisbî*) (Sayın 1999; Pelin 1945). Under the lump-sum method, the regulation established four different groups of taxpayers and determined the taxpayers' tax liability. But a tax council assigned taxpayers to the groups, corresponding to different activities. However, the tax council consisted of only the tax officers. There were no taxpayer representatives in the council at that time. The expressed aim was to ensure accuracy and rapidity of the process (Sayın 1999). But the real reason, considering prior experience, must have been to eliminate malpractice stemming from contacts between taxpayers and tax officers. The proportional method was for businesses and professionals that were not classified under one of those four groups and for contractors and tax-farmers. This method used an objective factor – the value of business place at real estate tax record – to assess the income of taxpayers. Thus, the government employed for the first time the presumptive method based on external signs of wealth (*karine or dış belirtiler usulü*) (Pelin 1945; Bulutoğlu 1971). Three different tax rates, 3 per cent, 5 per cent and 10 per cent, were set corresponding to different activities. Even though the regulation recognized the taxpayer's right of appeal, the profit tax regulation did not produce an equitable and efficient system (Pelin 1945). The exemption of foreign taxpayers from direct taxes as a result of the capitulation – a treaty or unilateral act by which a sovereign state relinquishes jurisdiction within its lands over the subjects of a foreign state (Fawcett 2016) – and the low tax rates were the main reasons behind this failure (Bulutoğlu 1971; Neumark 1946). Besides, at this time determination of groups became a source of corruption. Taxpayers that would normally have been taxed on a proportional basis such as bankers, wholesalers, brokers and manufacturers were included into the lump-sum basis (Pelin 1945).

The last profit tax law was enacted in 13 December 1914. The profit tax was similar to the French 'patente' (Bulutoğlu 1971), a tax on the presumed profits of trade, industry and professions (Kelly and Nick Devas 1999). The amount assessed on an enterprise depended on its type of activity, the value of premises occupied, the number of workers, the types of vehicles, and the turnover (Pelin 1945). The tax had three components: proportional (*nisbî*), additional (*mütehavvil*) or fixed (*maktu*). The proportional and additional bases were for business persons having a place of business. The proportional tax depended on the estimated rental value of the business premises. The classification scheme was divided into six classes for which the businesses to be considered were specified explicitly. Each class was assigned a rate ranging from 5 to 20 per cent. Then an additional lump-sum amount was imposed according to the number of workers and the types of vehicles in the business. The fixed basis was for small and micro enterprises which did not have a place of business. The tax rate ranged from15 kurus to 1,000 kurus depending on the class in which the enterprise was placed in a table. In spite of the advanced profit tax rules, profit tax could not have been an important source of revenue for the state (Bulutoğlu 1971; Pelin 1945).

Revenue tax legislation

The Ottoman Empire entered World War I in 1914 and after the end of the War in 1918, the Turkish War of Independence started in 1919 and continued until the establishment of the Turkish

Republic on 29 October 1923. The first fiscal reform of the Young Republic was the abolition of the tithe – a tax of 1/10 of the produce of the land – in 1925. That also meant the abolition of tax-farming. The share of tithe was up to a quarter of the budget at that time (Pelin 1945). This tax reform aimed to lift the heavy fiscal burden on farmers (Bulutoğlu 1971). Immediately after, the Revenue Tax Law No. 755 (*Kazanç Vergisi Kanunu*) (*Official Gazette*: 14.3.1926, 321) along with general and special consumption taxes (*umumi ve hususi istihlak vergileri*) were introduced in 1926 for transferring tax burden from the agricultural sector to the trade and industry sectors, and workers employed in those businesses. The new revenue tax (*kazanç vergisi*) was imposed separately on income categories of business, self-employment and wages (Bulutoğlu 1971). It was a scheduler income tax system that taxpayers were to determine their gross income and deductible expenses separately for each income type and then to apply the tax rates (see Burns and Krever 1998).

The Law endeavored to tax the actual income (*hakikî kazanç*) by implementing the income tax self-assessment method broadly (Neumark 1946). In other words, the Turkish tax administration generally moved away from presumptive taxation to a self-assessment system which relies on taxpayers' voluntarily compliance with their obligations to register, keep proper records, file correct returns and pay tax on time without the intervention of the tax autorities (Russell 2010). However, the tax administration's capacity was not adequate to carry out such a major system shift (Neumark 1946; Pelin 1945). For that reason, amending laws considerably restricted the self-assessment system first in 1927 and then in 1934 by the re-enacted Revenue Tax Law No. 2395 (*Official Gazette*: 25.3.1934, 2662). Eventually, revenue tax mostly became more of a *patente* tax on the presumed profits of trade, industry and professions similar to the former profit tax. On the other hand, a minimum tax liability (*asgari mükellefiyet*) requirement was imposed on the remaining narrow self-assessed taxpayers group (Bulutoğlu 1971). Self-assessed taxpayers could not declare any amount lower than the minimum tax amount to be calculated based on external signs such as turnover or number of employees (Neumark 1946).

Presumptive taxation in modern Turkish income tax legislation

World War II, even though Turkey pursued the policy of neutrality, increased public expenditure. In order to meet the need for public revenue, Turkey introduced revenue enhancing measures during the War which created a very complex revenue tax system (Bulutoğlu 1971). Thus, a tax reform was needed after the War. Instead of revising the existing revenue tax system, Turkey moved toward modern income taxation in 1949 by introducing two separate tax laws: Personal Income Tax Law or PIT Law (*Gelir Vergisi Kanunu*) for individuals and Corporate Income Tax Law or CIT Law (*Kurumlar Vergisi Kanunu*) for legal persons (companies and other taxable entities). The PIT Law was re-enacted by the Law of 193 (*Official Gazette*: 06.01.1961, 10700) in 1960 and the CIT Law was re-enacted by the Law of 5520 in 2006 (*Official Gazette*: 21.06.2006, 26205). Nevertheless, they continued to follow virtually the same principles.

The new personal income taxation system had two distinct features. First, the income tax was imposed on all income tax categories so the structure of Turkish personal income tax system is now world-wide. The world-wide system considers all income and expenses together to arrive at a single net gain that is subject to tax (Burns and Krever 1998). Second, the PIT Law has defined being actual as one of the basic elements of income in Article 2. The CIT Law has also adopted the same income concept pursuant to Article 2. The principle of actual income requires determining the taxable income upon the taxpayer's income statement based on the actual transactions in the accounting records (Bulutoğlu 1978). In fact, to protect the integrity of the new income tax system in this respect, the parliament passed a separate presumptive tax law called the Artisan Tax Law (*Esnaf Vergisi Kanunu*) along with modern income tax codes in 1949 (Bulutoğlu 1971). This was a lump-sum tax on small businesses, justified by the low-income level and the difficulties of implementing modern income taxation requirements. On the other hand, Turkey has extensively used presumptive tax techniques to support the self-assessment method in an effort to curb widespread tax evasion (Bulutoğlu 1997). This part will examine main presumptive taxation implementation in the PIT and CIT Laws.

Lump-sum taxation

The Artisan Tax Law was abolished after a while. Nonetheless, lump-sum taxation (*götürü usulde vergileme*) for small businesses, professionals and wage earners was integrated into the income tax system by means of the second PIT Law in 1960. The Ministry of Finance divided lump-sum taxpayers into five presumed net earnings brackets for every business and employment type according to the amount of gross income they report (Bulutoğlu 1997). In the beginning, a tax assessment commission (*Takdir Komisyonu*) consisting of some tax officials and representatives from local chambers of commerce or members of locally elected bodies were in charge to establish the presumed values for net income (Bulutoğlu 1978). Taxpayers could alter their brackets by a court decision if not correctly determined but could not appeal against the tax assessment commissions' decision. The Law of 3946 cancelled the tax assessment commission and set up net income amounts for the five earning brackets (*Official Gazette*: 30.12.1993, 21804 *bis*). The lump-sum tax was abolished in 1998 by the law of 4369 (*Official Gazette*: 29.07.1998, 23417).

Average gross profit margin

The PIT Law of 1949 introduced the minimum gross profit margin basis (*asgari kar haddi esası*) in Article 98 and the second PIT Law maintained this concept under the name of average gross profit margin (*ortalama kar haddi esası*) in Article 111. This method was also applied to the corporate income taxpayer pursuant to Article 13(3) of the first CIT Law amended by the Law of 2362 in 1980 (*Official Gazette*: 27.12.1980; 17203). According to average gross profit margin basis, the tax-declared gross profit of a retail business, a manufacturer or a service business could not be explicitly less than average gross profit margin within its lines of business unless taxpayer submitted a justifiable reason for this and the tax administration revealed such a reason by its examination. In such a case, a tax assessment commission (*Takdir Komisyonu*) determined the tax base for the taxpayer. The Ministry of Finance was the authority to decide the lines of business schedules. A special local average gross profit margin assessment commission (*Ortalama Kar Hadleri İl Komisyonu*) consisting of tax officials and taxpayer representatives was in charge of the determination of average gross profit margins for each business activity aligned with the principles set in a regulation promulgated also by the Ministry of Finance (Bulutoğlu 1971).

This basis did not work efficiently for two reasons. First, the tax administration carried the burden of proof. When a taxpayer submitted a justification, the tax administration had to conduct a tax examination and prove that the taxpayers' justification was insufficient. The Turkish tax administration had limited capacity at that time and the number of implementations based on the number of tax examinations occurred was very low (Bulutoğlu 1971). The government wanted to use the average gross profit margin basis as an effective compliance tool so it removed the tax examination requirement in 1964 by the Law of 202 (*Official Gazette*: 28.2.1963, 11343). The tax administration was furnished with the authority to make ex-officio assessment for the difference between the declared amount and the calculated amount based on average margins without further determination of the tax assessment commission. The tax administration still had to invite taxpayers to submit a justification but if submitted, it did not have to prove by an examination that this justification was insufficient. Second, this basis was a cost-based method. Average profit margins were added to the cost price of the product in case of retail businesses and the manufacturers and the operating cost in case of service businesses. The tax administration needed the invoice of sales and purchases to calculate the costs but the size of the unregistered economy in Turkey made this impossible.

A similar mechanism called minimum agricultural income (*asgari zirai kazanç*) was also introduced by the second PIT Law for farmers. However, this basis could not come into practice for a long time since local agricultural income tax assessment commissions (*Zirai Kazanç İl Komisyonu*) had not been set up to develop measures for a presumptive farm produce tax (Bulutoğlu 1978).

In 1980, a new basis purely for service businesses was introduced under the name of minimum gross proceeds (*asgari gayrisafi hasılat esası*) in Article 111 because of difficulties in calculating the profit of service businesses adding average profit margins to the operating cost. Henceforth the tax administration determined the annual gross proceeds minimums for service businesses (Bulutoğlu 1978). If a service business declared a lower amount for annual gross proceeds, the tax administration would take minimum gross proceeds into consideration only after inviting the taxpayer to submit a justification, and typically either the taxpayer did not submit a justification or the tax administration found the justification reason insufficient. Then expenses would be deducted to reach the annual profits.

Average gross profit margin and minimum gross proceeds bases were abolished by the Law of 4108 as of 1 January 1996 (*Official Gazette*: 02.06.1995, 22301). Minimum agricultural income basis was abolished by the Law of 4369, Article 82(3)(n).

Expenditure basis

The PIT Law of 1949 introduced expenditure basis (*gider esası*) in Article 99 and the second PIT Law also maintained the basis in Article 113. Under the expenditure basis, the law used personal expenditures as an external income indicator to determine the tax base. When a taxpayer's expenditures were not commensurate with the tax-declared income in a taxable year and the taxpayer could not explain this excess amount of expenditure based on sources other than income such as wealth, borrowing, and gift the tax administration made *ex-officio* assessment based on the excess amount of expenditure. It was necessary to know the taxpayer's total amount of annual expenditure to process this basis. Thus previous Article 76 and subsequent Article 103 obliged personal income taxpayers to declare those expenditures. Expenditure basis was abolished by the Law of 2995 in 1984 (*Official Gazette*: 27.04.1984, 18384).

Declaration of wealth

The second PIT Law inserted the declaration of wealth (*servet beyanı esası*) amongst revenue safeguard mechanisms in 1960. This method determined the tax base by using wealth accumulation as an external indicator of income. Article 114 required business income, agricultural income and professional income earners who were subject to self-assessed income taxation to declare the elements of wealth enumerated in Article 116. According to Article 115, a taxpayer's annual increases in net wealth shall be commensurate with the income. If the differences between the declared wealth in a year and the previous year exceeded the declared income in this year and the taxpayer could not prove that the income was derived from sources other than the subject of income taxation, the tax administration made ex-officio assessment based on the excess amount of wealth increase. However, the tax administration had to conduct a tax audit on wealth declarations before the additional assessment. Declaration of wealth was also abolished by the Law of 2995 in 1984.

Living standard basis

The parliament introduced a living standard assessment system (*hayat standardı esası*) as Article 116 *bis*. to the second PIT Law in 1982 by the Law of 2772 (*Official Gazette*: 31.12.1982, 17915 *bis*). It was a system of presumptive taxation for business, agricultural and professional income taxpayers that based the tax on specific items of personal expenditures (Kaneti 1987). Article 116 *bis*. enumerated ownership of houses, cars, boats, airplanes, and race horses, employment of personal servants and foreign travel as the indicator of standard of living and determined specific amounts for each indicator. The provision entailed the addition of the amount calculated based on living standard indicators to the base amount specified in the law and then comparison of this amount with the taxpayer' declared income. Under the living standard basis, if the taxpayer declared in a taxable year an amount lower than the total amount of base income and additional income, tax was assessed on presumed income. The tax administration had to assess income based on living standard even if the taxpayer declared loss. However, the taxpayer could appeal providing that his income from other sources was not subject to the income statement.

The parliament amended the living standard basis several times and those amending laws were subject to legal challenge as unconstitutional on various grounds on each occasion (Öden and Akkaya 2001; Solak 2004). In principle, the Turkish Constitutional Court found the living standard basis constitutional and justified this assessment method with the need for a secondary mechanism to support taxation of actual income of taxpayers. According to the Court, the living standard basis was one of the auto-control mechanisms such as average profit margin, minimum gross proceeds, minimum agricultural income, expenditure basis, and wealth declaration. Auto-control mechanisms were needed to arrive at actual income of the taxpayer when the tax administration could not force fully the implementation of documentation requirements for any tax. Thus tax administrations had the means of control other than tax audit. Nonetheless, the Court annulled provisions of the amending laws when the living standard turned from a rebuttable presumption to an irrebuttable presumption. According to the Court, a presumption never prevailed in the case where taxpayers proved their actual income. This precedent of Turkish Constitutional Court is very important because irrebuttable presumptions have been challenged only in limited number of national courts on constitutional grounds (Thuronyi 2004).

The living standard basis was abolished in 1998 by the law of 4369. However, the Law of 4605 created a transition period until 2002 by adding a temporary provision to the PIT Law (*Official Gazette*: 30.11.2000, 26246 *bis*). The Ministry of Finance announced that the continued use of the living standard basis for personal income tax assessment was the result of a significant decline in revenue experienced when the living standard basis was halted (Öden and Akkaya 2001).

An evidence for the Turkish tax administration's incapacity to implement the new specific anti-tax avoidance rules

Turkey introduced new specific anti-avoidance measures comprising TP rules, CFC rules, and thin capitalization rules based on clearer and more concrete elements compared to previous rules in the CIT Law to combat multinationals' tax avoidance in 2006 (Yaltı 2015). It has been recognized that many countermeasures against MNEs' tax avoidance, most prominently TP and CFC rules have been a challenge for developing countries to implement and administer both because they do not have adequate resources and they lack special expertise (UNCTAD 2015). This raises the question of whether the Turkish tax administrative capacity is sufficient to implement the new specific income tax avoidance measures. Unfortunately, the lack of transparency of the Turkish tax administration renders full evaluation of this problematic. Even though the Turkish tax administration has undertaken institutional reforms and improved its information technology infrastructure (Gelir İdaresi Başkanlığı 2013), the details of those capacity-building efforts and their influence in practice is unknown. However, the legal history of presumptive income taxation shows that the capacity of Turkish tax administration was not sufficient to implement the new TP and CFC rules at least in their inclusion in the Turkish tax system.

Tax audit plays a critical role in the administration of tax laws. In fact, it is the major tool for monitoring of taxpayers' noncompliance with regular income tax laws. Tax auditors must carry out intensive examination of taxpayers' books and records to detect whether a taxpayer has fully and correctly assessed and reported their liability and fulfilled other obligations. However, tax audit of self-assessment tax returns is time and resource consuming for the tax administration and burdensome for taxpayers (OECD 2006). Presumptive taxes take advantage of data that are easier for officials to obtain than the information required to determine actual taxable income under the regular income tax rules (Bird and Zolt 2005). They calculate the tax base using easy-to-obtain indicators or other methods, instead of relying on taxpayer self-assessment (Wallace 2002). Thus, presumptive taxation replaces lengthy and costly audits by checking tax evasion at a relatively modest cost even if a considerable administrative effort is still needed to implement presumptive assessment methods properly (World Bank 1991). Since many developing countries have time, skill, and resource weaknesses in their administration, presumptive taxation helps them to overcome these weaknesses (Bulutoğlu 1995). As a result, presumptive taxation has been a pervasive element of the tax systems of most developing countries (Slemrod and Yitzhaki 1994). Nonetheless, presumptive taxes are, by design, approximations of taxes on income and not necessarily reflective of actual income so they raise fairness concerns (Thomas 2013). Moreover, presumptive taxation should serve primarily to bring hard-to-tax groups into the tax net and to encourage participation in the regular tax system. When a presumptive tax regime does not effectively serve this purpose, it may undermine the tax system as a whole and threaten the long-term development of sound tax systems (Bird and Zolt 2005).

As in other developing countries, lump-sum taxation and presumptive methods of assessment have always formed an integral part of Turkish income tax evasion efforts (Bulutoğlu 1997). In the modern era of Turkish income taxation, different methods of presumptive taxation existed simultaneously and side by side. The average gross profit margin remained in force from 1949 to 1996, expenditure basis from 1949 to 1984, wealth declaration from 1960 to 1984, and the standard of living basis from 1982 to 2002. Presumptive taxation had continued uninterrupted until the last implementation of standard of living in 2002. These periods of time indicate that Turkey has long used presumptive taxation broadly to support self-assessment methods. In other words, Turkey expanded the presumptive system instead of expanding the regular tax system. This development of presumptive taxation shows the weakness of Turkish tax administration in implementing regular income tax rules (Bulutoğlu 1978). As a matter of fact, during the following first fiscal year after the abolition of the standard of living basis for income taxation in 1998, the number of business and professional income earners declaring profits decreased from 1.5 million to 1 million with an accompanying loss in revenue (Öden and Akkaya 2001). For that reason, the government extended this basis for personal income tax assessment until 2002. Although the era of presumptive taxation on the basis of standard of living had only come to an end in 2002, the tax authorities had to implement measures to counter sophisticated tax avoidance schemes under TP and CFC rules by 2006 in order to curb continuing MNE avoidance. Such a short interval between 2002 and 2006 poses significant questions as to whether the Turkish tax administration would have been capable of fully and accurately implementing TP and CFC rules at the beginning of their enactment by parliament.

Conclusion

Many income tax anti-avoidance measures require complex legislation and significant tax-collection capabilities. The development of presumptive taxation in the Turkish tax system evidences the inadequacy of the Turkish tax administration the point when the new specific anti-avoidance measures were introduced in 2006, which may have made those countermeasures unused or ineffective for Turkey. Further studies are needed to figure out the current status of the Turkish tax administration, which suggest that the need for transparency in the Turkish tax administration continues to increase.

Bibliography

Ahmad, E. and Stern, N. (1991). *The Theory and Practice of Taxation Reform in Developing Countries.* Cambridge: Cambridge University Press.

Barkan, Ö. L. (1970). "Research on the Ottoman fiscal surveys", in M. A. Cook (ed.), *Studies in the Economic History of the Middle East: From the Rise of Islam to the Present Day.* Oxford: Oxford University Press.

Bird, M. R., and Wallace, S. (2004). "Presumptive taxation of the hard-to-tax", in J. Alm, J. M. Martine-Vazquez and S. Wallace (eds), *Taxing the Hard-to-Tax: Lessons From Theory and Practice.* The Netherlands: Elsevier, 121–58.

Bird, R. and Zolt, E. M. (2005). 'Redistribution via Taxation: The Limited Role of the Personal Income Tax in Developing Countries.' No 0508, *International Tax Program Papers,* International Tax Program, Institute for International Business, Joseph L. Rotman School of Management, University of Toronto.

Bulutoğlu, K. (1971). *Türk vergi sistemi.* İstanbul: Fakülteler matbaası.

Bulutoğlu, K. (1978). *Türk vergi sistemi dersleri.* İstanbul: Ekin.

Bulutoğlu, K. (1995). "Presumptive taxation", in P. Shome (ed.), *Tax Policy Handbook.* Washinton, DC: IMF, 258–62.

Bulutoğlu, K. (1997). "Turkey's struggle for a better tax system", in W. Thirsk (ed.), *Tax Reform in Developing Countries.* Washington, DC: The World Bank.

Burns, L., and Krever, B. (1998). "Individual income tax", in V. Thoronyi (ed.), *Tax Law Design and Drafting,* Vol. 2. Washington, DC: IMF, Ch. 14.

Çakır, C. (2001). *Tanzimat dönemi Osmanlı maliyesi,* 2nd ed. İstanbul: Küre.

Darling, L. T. (1996). *Revenue-Raising and Legitimacy: Tax Collection and Finance Administration in the Ottoman Empire 1560–1660.* Leiden: E. J. Brill.

Evans, C. (2009). "Containing tax avoidance: Anti-avoidance strategies", in J. G. Head and R. Krever (eds), *Tax Reform in the 21st Century: A Volume in Memory of Richard Musgrave.* Alphen aan de Rijn: Kluwer Law International.

Fawcett, L. (2016). *International Relations of the Middle East,* 4th ed. Oxford: Oxford University Press.

Findley, C. V. (2006). 'Osmanlı Siyasal Düşüncesinde Devlet ve Hukuk: İnsan Hakları mı Hukuk Devleti mi?'. In Halil İnalcık-Mehmet Seyitdanhoğlu (eds). *Tanzimat: Değişim Sürecinde Osmanlı İmparatorluğu.* Ankara: Phoenix Yayınevi, 335–46.

Gelir İdaresi Başkanlığı (2013). "EU screening chapter 16: Taxation", 65–74. Available at www.gib.gov.tr/fileadmin/mevzuatek/uluslararasi_mevzuat/cerceve_anlasmalari/Ayrintili_Tarama/LEGAL_FRAMEWORK_TAX_ADMINISTRATION.pdf.

Hanioğlu, Ş. (2008). *A Brief History of Late Ottoman Empire.* Princeton, NJ: Princeton University Press.

İnalcık, H. (1997). *An Economic and Social History of the Ottoman Empire 1300–1600,* Vol. 1. Cambridge: Cambridge University Press.

İnalcık, H. (2000). "Timar", in P. J. Bearman, Th. Bianquis, C. E. Bosworth, E. van Donzel and W. P. Heinrichs, *The Encyclopedia of Islam Volume X T-U,* 502–7.

İnalcık, H. (2011). "Osmanlı'da istatistik metodu kullanıldı m'ı?", in H. İnalcik and Ş. Pamuk (eds), *Data and Statistic in the Ottoman Empire.* İstanbul: Başbakanlık Arşivleri.

Islamoğlu, H. (2010). *Osmanlı İmparatorluğu'nda devlet ve köylü*, 2nd ed. Ankara: İmge.

Kaneti, S. (1987). *Vergi Hukuku*. İstanbul: Fakülteler matbaası.

Kelly, R., and Devas, N. (1999). "Regulation or revenue: Implementing local government business license reform in Kenya", Harvard Development Discussion Paper. Available at www.cid.harvard.edu/hiid/723.pdf

Kohen, E. (2007). *History of the Turkish Jew and Sephardim: Memories of a Past Golden Age*. Lanham: University Press of America.

KPMG (2012). "Global transfer pricing review Israel". Available at www.kpmg.com/Global/en/IssuesAndInsights/ArticlesPublications/Documents/gtps-2012/israel.pdf

Logue, K. D., and Vettori, G. G. (2013). "Narrowing the tax gap through presumptive taxation", Empirical legal studies center, Working paper 10-007. Available at www.law.umich.edu/centersandprograms/lawandeconomics/abstracts/2010/Documents/10-007logue.pdf

Neumark, F. (1946). *Gelir vergisi teori-tarihçe-pratik*. İstanbul: İsmail Akgün matbaası.

Öden, M., and Akkaya, M. (2001). "Hayat standardı esasının anayasaya uygunluğu sorunu", *Ankara Üniversitesi Hukuk Fakültesi Dergisi*, 50(2), 1–35.

"Official Gazette of the Turkish Republic". Available at www.resmigazete.gov.tr/default.aspx

OECD (2006). "Strengthening tax audit capabilities general principles and approaches". Available at www.oecd.org/tax/administration/37589900.pdf.

OECD (2013). *Action Plan on Base Erosion and Profit Shifting*. Paris: OECD Publishing.

OECD (2014). *Standard for Automatic Exchange of Financial Account Information in Tax Matters*. Paris: OECD Publishing.

Öncel, M., Çağan, N., and Kumrulu, A. (2016). *Vergi Hukuku*. Ankara: Turhan Kitabevi.

Pelin, F. (1945). *Finans ilmi ve finansal kanunlar*. İstanbul: İsmail Akgün matbaası.

Quataert, D. (2005). *The Ottoman Empire: 1700–1922*, 2nd ed. New York: Cambridge University Press.

Rajamaran, I., and Singh, K. (1995). *Report on Presumptive Taxation*. New Delhi: National Institute of Public Finance and Policy.

Russell, B. (2010). "Revenue administration: Developing a taxpayer compliance program", IMF. Available at www.imf.org/external/pubs/ft/tnm/2010/tnm1017.pdf

Saban, N. (2014). "What is the being of article 3, B, 1 of the tax procedural law?", in B. Yaltı (ed.), *Preventing Tax Avoidance*. Istanbul: Beta, 169–96.

Saracoğlu, S. (2007). "Letters from Vidin: A study of Ottoman governmentality and politics of local administration 1864–1877". Available at https://etd.ohiolink.edu/ap/10?0::NO:10:P10_ACCESSION_NUM:osu1186601853

Sayın, A.V. (1999). *Tekalif kavaidi*, reprinted version. Ankara: Maliye Bakanlığı.

Şener, A. (1990). *Tanzimat dönemi Osmanlı vergi sistemi*. İstanbul: İşaret.

Shaw, S. J. (1975). "The nineteenth-century Ottoman tax reforms and revenue system", *International Journal of Middle East Studies*, 6(4), 421–59.

Shaw, S. J., and Shaw, E. K. (2002). *History of the Ottoman Empire and Modern Turkey, Volume II: Reform, Revolution, and Republic: The Rise of Modern Turkey 1808–1975*. Cambridge: Cambridge University Press.

Slemrod, J., and Yitzhaki, S. (1994). "Analyzing the standard deduction as a presumptive tax", *International Tax and Public Finance*, 1(1), 25–34.

Solak, İ. (2004). "Türk vergi sisteminde vergi güvenlik önlemleri". Available at https://tez.yok.gov.tr/UlusalTezMerkezi/

TBMM (2016). Available at www.tbmm.gov.tr/develop/owa/tasari_teklif_sd.sorgu_yonlendirme

Thomas, K. D. (2013). "Presumptive collection: A prospect theory approach to increasing small business tax compliance", *Tax Law Review*, 67, 111–67.

Thuronyi, V. (1996). "Presumptive taxation", in V. Thoronyi (ed.), *Tax Law Design and Drafting*, Vol. 1. Washington, DC: IMF, Ch. 12, 6.

Thuronyi, V. (2004). "Presumptive taxation of the hard-to-tax", in J. Alm, J. M. Martine-Vazquez and S. Wallace (eds), *Taxing the Hard-to-Tax: Lessons From Theory and Practice*. The Netherlands: Elsevier, 101–20.

UNCTAD (2015). "Policy action against tax avoidance by MNEs: Existing measures and ongoing discussions". Available at http://unctad.org/en/PublicationChapters/wir2015ch5_Annex_III_en.pdf

Wallace, S. (2002). "Imputed and presumptive taxes: International experiences and lessons for Russia". Available at http://icepp.gsu.edu/files/2015/03/ispwp0203.pdf

World Bank (1991). *Lessons for Tax Reform*. Washington, DC: World Bank Publication.

Yaltı, B. (2015). "Turkey", in Y. Brauner and P. Pistone (eds), *BRICS and the Emergence of International Tax Coordination*. Amsterdam: IBFD Database.

13

TAX AVOIDANCE

The Indian perspective

Tarun Jain

Introduction

As an independent country India has been administering tax laws for about seven decades. Barring the present decade however, tax avoidance as a distinct legislative field has not received the requisite attention and the extant rules have largely been confined to annulling colourable tax avoidance devices. Consequently the Indian judiciary has assumed the role of developing and reinforcing anti-avoidance rules. Largely positioned on the lines of the English jurisprudence on the subject, the traditional judicial response has been vindication of taxpayer's right to mitigate tax liability. Of late an alternate school of judicial thought, which severely condemns an enthused tax avoidance maneuver, seems to be finding feet. The present decade marks a legislative shift with the advent of statutory general anti-avoidance rules. However these rules have still not been implemented and thus the subject of tax avoidance continues to be largely addressed by judicial analysis. On the above lines, this paper draws a reflection of the tax avoidance landscape in India.

Tax laws in India: a legal background

The Constitution of India envisages a federal set-up and provides for distribution of legislative powers (including the taxation subjects)[1] amongst the 'Parliament' (federal legislative institution) and the 'State Legislatures' (provincial legislative institutions). The 'Central Government' (federal executive) and the 'State Governments' (provincial executive) exercise coextensive executive powers over the respective subjects.[2]

Under constitutional stipulations, taxes can be levied only under legislative sanction.[3] Accordingly the Central Government and State Governments administer the tax legislations enacted by the Parliament and State Legislatures respectively on their respective tax subjects which are clearly demarcated[4] under the Constitution. The Parliament administers certain direct taxes i.e.

---

1 Article 246, Constitution of India.
2 Article 73, 162, Ibid.
3 Article 265, Ibid.
4 Seventh Schedule, Constitution of India.

income tax;[5] corporation tax;[6] wealth tax;[7] estate duty;[8] inheritance taxes;[9] and certain indirect taxes i.e. customs duties;[10] excise duties (on manufacture);[11] stamp duties;[12] etc. while the State Legislatures also administer certain direct taxes i.e. land revenue;[13] agricultural income tax;[14] land and building taxes;[15] mineral taxes;[16] professional tax;[17] and certain indirect taxes, i.e. State/local border taxes;[18] electricity tax;[19] sales tax;[20] toll taxes;[21] luxury tax;[22] etc. The taxation subjects not distinctively specified vest with the Parliament[23] such as Service Tax.[24]

The Constitution does not envisage anti-avoidance rules as a distinct legislative subject and as a matter of legislative practice, the anti-avoidance rules are generally a part of the legislation dealing with the principal subject matter of the concerned tax.[25] A survey of laws enacted by the Parliament and the State Legislatures reveals that the Income Tax Act of 1961 carries the most extensive anti-avoidance rules. This Act was enacted by the Parliament and levies[26] both income tax and corporation tax, besides other minor levies such as dividend-distribution tax,[27] fringe-benefits tax,[28] etc. Accordingly the basis for most discussions on anti-avoidance rules is this Act and the judgments dealing with its provisions.[29]

Judicial response to tax avoidance

The common-law principles delineating the distinction between tax planning, tax avoidance and tax evasion have traditionally been applied as a thumb-rule in India, albeit with certain instances of stark deviations which closely parallel the English jurisprudence.[30] The common

---

5 Entry 82, List – I, Seventh Schedule, Constitution of India.
6 Entry 85, Ibid.
7 Entry 86, Ibid.
8 Entry 87, Ibid.
9 Entry 88, Ibid.
10 Entry 83, Ibid.
11 Entry 84, Ibid.
12 Entry 90, Ibid.
13 Entry 45, List – II, Seventh Schedule, Constitution of India.
14 Entry 46, Ibid.
15 Entry 49, Ibid.
16 Entry 50, Ibid.
17 Entry 60, Ibid.
18 Entry 52, Ibid.
19 Entry 53, Ibid.
20 Entry 54, Ibid.
21 Entry 59, Ibid.
22 Entry 62, Ibid.
23 Article 248, Constitution of India.
24 *All India Federation of Tax Practitioners v. Union of India* (2007) 7 SCC 527.
25 See generally, T. P. Oswal and Vikram Vijayaraghavan, "Anti-Avoidance Measures", 22 *National Law School of India Review* 59 (2010).
26 Section 4, Income Tax Act, 1961.
27 Section 115O, Ibid. See also Tarun Jain, "Dividend Distribution Tax: A Rejoinder to 339 ITR (J) 52", 343 *Income Tax Reports (Journal)* 42 (2012).
28 Section 115WA, Ibid.
29 See generally T. Jain, "Taxability of Corporate Gift of Shares", 247 *Current Tax Reporter* (Articles) 53 (2012); T. Jain, "Is Section 206AA unconstitutional? Why Karnataka High Court in Kowsalya Bai Is Wrong?", 349 *Income Tax Reports* (Journal) 74 (2012). It is clarified that the expression "Act" used in this paper refers to the "Income Tax Act, 1961".
30 See generally, Law Commission of India, *Twenty Ninth Report on Proposal to Income Certain Social and Economic Offences in the Indian Penal Code* (1966), 51; S. P. Gupta, "The McDowell Dictum – Vanishing Line Between Tax Avoidance and Tax Evasion", 5 *SCC* (Journal) 15 (2003).

thread of the deviating decisions is the castigation of the subject taxpayer viewing tax avoidance schemes as an abhorrent act.[31] Accordingly, an enquiry into judicial treatment meted out in cases involving tax avoidance maneuvers can be usefully considered in two parts; the first noting the traditional response and the second being an account of those cases which treat tax avoidance as an anathema to the legal system.

The traditional school

The Supreme Court of India, which is the highest court of the country, has time and again held that "what is material in the tax jurisprudence is the evasion of the tax, not the beneficial lawful adjustment thereof",[32] and consistently genuine commercial transactions, even if leading to a reduction in tax liability, have been accepted without demur.[33] Two English decisions, which are prominently noted and continue to be cited even today,[34] can be attributed to be the inspiration for this trend. The first is the often invoked restatement of Rowlett J. in *Cape Brandy Syndicate*[35] that "[i]n a taxing Act one has to look merely at what is clearly said. There is no room for any intendment. There is no equity about a tax. There is no presumption as to a tax. Nothing is to be read in, nothing is to be implied. One can only look fairly at the language used." The second is the opinion of Lord Tomlin in what is now known as the *Duke of Westminster* principle[36] that "every man is entitled if he can to order his affairs so that the tax attaching under the appropriate Acts is less than it otherwise would be". As a consequence, the Indian Courts have traditionally accepted tax mitigation practices.

In *Calcutta Discount Company*[37] the Supreme Court approved the reduction of tax liability at the hands of the taxpayer even though it acknowledged that for the taxpayer the transaction implied "foregoing part of its own profits and at the same time enabling its subsidiary to earn some profits". In view of the Supreme Court "such a course is not impermissible in law" and the tax administration could not take into consideration the market-value by "ignoring the real prices fetched".[38] Earlier in *A. Raman & Co.*[39] the Supreme Court had famously observed that "the law does not oblige a trader to make the maximum profit that he can earn out of his trading transactions" to opine that only the "[I]ncome which accrues to a trader is taxable in his hands: income which he could have, but has not earned, is not made taxable as income accrued to him". Refusing to accede to tax administration's pleas, the Supreme Court went further to declare that "avoidance of tax liability by so arranging commercial affairs that charge of tax is disturbed is not prohibited. ... Effectiveness of the device depends not upon considerations of morality, but on the operation of the Income Tax Act. Legislative injunction in taxing statute may not, except on peril of penalty, be violated, but it may lawfully be circumvented."[40]

The principles of statutory interpretation have also been invoked to the advantage of the taxpayer. Literal interpretation and strict construction of fiscal statute appears to have been the

---

31 Gupta, Ibid.
32 *Commissioner of Income Tax v. Sarabhai Holdings Pvt. Ltd.* (2009) 1 SCC 28.
33 *Commissioner of Income Tax v. Walfort Share and Stock Brokers Pvt. Ltd.* (2010) 8 SCC 137.
34 *Shabina Abraham v. Collector of Central Excise* (2015) 10 SCC 770.
35 *Cape Brandy Syndicate v. Inland Revenue* [1921] 1 KB 64. Cited with approval, *inter alia*, in *Ranbaxy Laboratories Ltd. v. Union of India* (2011) 10 SCC 292; *Commissioner of Central Excise v. Acer India Ltd.* (2004) 8 SCC 173.
36 *Duke of Westminster v. Commissioners of Inland Revenue* (1936) AC 1 (HL), quoting Lord Cairns.
37 *Commissioner of Income Tax v. Calcutta Discount Co. Ltd.* (1974) 3 SCC 260.
38 Ibid., 265.
39 *Commissioner of Income Tax v. A. Raman & Co.* (1968) 67 ITR 11 (SC).
40 Ibid., at para 9.

norm[41] and refusal of the courts to supply *causus omissus*[42] has led to the evolution of the principle that "[i]n interpreting a fiscal statute, the court cannot proceed to make good deficiencies if there be any: the court must interpret the statute as it stands and in case of doubt in a manner favourable to the taxpayer."[43] The benefit of ambiguity in a fiscal statute is to be extended to the taxpayer as "in each case the Court must take the taxing statute as it stands, subject to all its imperfection: if the transaction does not fairly fall within the letter of the law, the Court will not seek to put a strained construction to bring it within the law."[44]

Further, applying the rules of evidence that "the burden of proving any form of *mala fide* lies on the shoulders of the one alleging it" to tax cases,[45] the Supreme Court has constantly reminded the tax administration that the onus to impeach the tax treatment claimed by the taxpayer rests on the tax administration. In *Aggarwal Industries*[46] the Supreme Court opined that "a mere suspicion upon the correctness" is not sufficient to reject the case of the taxpayer as "the doubt held by the officer concerned has to be based on some material evidence and is not to be formed on a mere suspicion or speculation". Earlier in *A. V. Fernandez*[47] it was held that "no tax can be imposed by inference or by analogy or by trying to probe into the intentions of the legislature and by considering what was the substance of the matter."

Considerable importance has also been attached to the "doctrine of commercial expediency" which requires the state-of-affairs to be judged from a business-prudence perspective.[48] For illustration, the Supreme Court has held that reasonableness of the expenditure incurred on litigation,[49] grant of loan to sister companies,[50] etc. are areas where the tax administration cannot superimpose its views so as to revisit the transactions thereby increasing the tax liability. On the other hands, while the corporate identify of a taxpayer is generally respected,[51] it is nonetheless settled that "the Court is entitled to lift the mask of corporate entity if the corporation is used for tax evasion, or to circumvent tax obligation or to perpetuate a fraud"[52] and the veil can be lifted "to pay regard to the economic realities behind the legal facade".[53] Thus the need to deal with "the realities, and not devices and subterfuges" has been acknowledged and still a legal

---

41 *State of Bombay v. Automobile & Agricultural Industries Corporation* (1961) 12 STC 122 (SC); *Commissioner of Wealth Tax v. Ellis Bridge Gymkhana* (1998) 1 SCC 384; Law Commission of India, *One Hundred and Fifteenth Report on Tax Courts* (1986).
42 *Commissioner of Income Tax v. B.C. Srinivasa Setty* (1981) 128 ITR 294 (SC); *Commissioner of Central Excise v. Larsen & Toubro Ltd.* (2016) 1 SCC 170.
43 *Mathuram Agrawal v. State of M.P.* (1999) 8 SCC 667 which follows *Russell (Inspector of Taxes) v. Scott* (1948) 2 All ER 1 holding that "the subject is not to be taxed unless the words of the taxing statute unambiguously impose the tax on him". See also *Commissioner of Income Tax v. Karamchand Premchand Ltd.* (1960) 40 ITR 106 (SC).
44 *His Highness Yeshwant Rao Ghorpade v. Commissioner of Wealth Tax* (1966) 61 ITR 444 (SC). See also *Commissioner of Income Tax v. Vadilal Lallubhai* (1973) 3 SCC 17.
45 *Uniworth Textiles Ltd. v. Commissioner of Central Excise* (2013) 9 SCC 753.
46 *Commissioner of Customs v. Aggarwal Industries* (2012) 1 SCC 186.
47 *A. V. Fernandez v. State of Kerala* AIR 1957 SC 657. See also *Commissioner of Income Tax v. B.M. Kharwar* (1969) 72 ITR 603 (SC) which observes similarly.
48 *Shahzada Nand & Sons. v. Commissioner of Income Tax* (1977) 3 SCC 432.
49 *Commissioner of Income Tax v. Dhanrajgiri Raja Narasingirji* (1973) 91 ITR 544 (SC) observing "It is not open to the Department to prescribe what expenditure an assessee should incur and in what circumstances he should incur that expenditure. Every businessman knows his interest best."
50 *S.A. Builders Ltd. v. Commissioner of Income Tax* (2007) 288 ITR 1 (SC); *Hero Cycles (P) Ltd. v. Commissioner of Income Tax* (2016) 379 ITR 347 (SC).
51 *Vodafone International Holdings BV v. Union of India* (2012) 6 SCC 613.
52 *Union of India v. Playworld Electronics Pvt. Ltd.* (1989) 3 SCC 181.
53 *Commissioner of Income Tax v. Sri Meenakshi Mills Ltd.* (1967) 63 ITR 609 (SC).

declaration has been made that "the vision cannot be permitted to be blurred by the blinkers of colourable devices and dubious methods".[54]

The alternate school of judicial opinion

Despite an overwhelming reiteration of the common-law principle that "there is no morality in tax"[55] there exists another school of judicial opinion. It is observed that "it is the obligation of every citizen to pay the taxes honestly without resorting to subterfuges".[56] The Supreme Court in *Juggi Lal*[57] rejected the defence of the taxpayer that "mere intention on the part of the assessee to evade income-tax will not nullify an otherwise lawful transaction" to hold a sham transaction "stage-managed merely with a view to evade income-tax" could not be sustained. Similarly in *Phoenix International*[58] the Supreme Court observed that "[w]hen there is an allegation of subterfuge, the court has to examine the circumstances surrounding the import to ascertain whether the importer had entered into fictitious arrangement". A number of legislative interventions to prevent tax evasion have also been sustained for similar reasons by the Supreme Court.[59]

The real impetus to the alternate school was the moralistic 'sermon'[60] of Chinnappa Reddy J. in *McDowell*.[61] Four of the five judges of the Supreme Court in this case acknowledged that "tax planning may be legitimate provided it is within the framework of law". They however, caveated the declaration with the observation that "[c]olourable devices cannot be part of tax planning and it is wrong to encourage or entertain the belief that it is honourable to avoid the payment of tax by resorting to dubious methods. It is the obligation of every citizen to pay the taxes honestly without resorting to subterfuges."[62] Chinnappa Reddy J. as the fifth judge in *McDowell*[63] went beyond. He described tax avoidance as "the art of dodging tax without breaking the law". Enumerating the factors which he perceived as the "evil consequences" of tax avoidance, he observed that "[i]t is neither fair nor desirable to expect the legislature to intervene and take care of every device and scheme to avoid taxation. It is up to the Court to take stock to determine the nature of the new and sophisticated legal devices to avoid tax and consider whether the situation created by the devices could be related to the existing legislation with the aid of 'emerging' techniques of interpretation."[64]

Even though his views were not immediately accepted by the Supreme Court,[65] the views of Chinnappa Reddy J. were a watershed moment in the judicial thought on the subject with severe repercussions. Relying on the views of Chinnappa Reddy J., tax administration doggedly,

---

54 *Kirti Chand Tarawati Charitable Trust v. Director of Income Tax* (1998) 232 ITR 11 (Del).
55 *T.A. Qureshi v. Commissioner of Income Tax* (2007) 2 SCC 759; *R.K. Garg v. Union of India* (1981) 4 SCC 675.
56 *Playworld Electronics Pvt. Ltd.*, see n.52.
57 *Juggi Lal Kamlapat v. Commissioner of Income Tax* (1969) 73 ITR 702 (SC). See also *Lachminarayan Madan Lal v. Commissioner of Income Tax* (1973) 3 SCC 76 which holds similarly.
58 *Commissioner of Customs v. Phoenix International Ltd.* (2007) 10 SCC 114.
59 For illustration, see *State of Uttar Pradesh v. Mohan Meakin Breweries Ltd.* (2011) 13 SCC 588; *Union of India v. M.V. Valliappan* (1999) 6 SCC 259.
60 *Arvind Narottam*, see n.65.
61 *McDowell & Co. Ltd. v. Commercial Tax Officer* (1985) 3 SCC 230.
62 Ibid., 254.
63 Ibid., 233.
64 Ibid., 243.
65 *Commissioner of Wealth Tax v. Arvind Narottam* (1988) 4 SCC 113 reflecting upon the woeful disconnect between the *McDowell* 'sermon' to disregard tax avoidance with the ground reality.

though unsuccessfully, pursued the vindication of its attempts to counter tax avoidance before the High Courts[66] which held that his views did not lay down that every attempt at tax planning is illegitimate and must be ignored. Not disheartened, in *Azadi*[67] the tax administration contended before the Supreme Court that "*McDowell* has changed the concept of fiscal jurisprudence in this country and any tax planning which is intended to and results in avoidance of tax must be struck down by the Court". However even the Supreme Court distanced itself from the "radical thinking" of Chinnappa Reddy J. declaring it to be his views alone and not the law declared by the Supreme Court.[68]

Subsequently, in *Walfort Share*[69] the Supreme Court held the *McDowell*[70] dictum inapplicable to a case of the taxpayer earning tax-free income based on statutory provisions as it was not a case of "abuse of law" and even if "the transaction was pre-planned there is nothing to impeach the genuineness of the transaction".[71] Unperturbed, in *Vodafone*[72] the tax administration specifically requested the Supreme Court to reject the *Azadi*[73] conclusion and vindicate the view of Chinnappa Reddy J. in *McDowell*.[74] The Supreme Court in *Vodafone* did consider the request but only to conclude that not "all tax planning is illegal/illegitimate/impermissible"; and the views are to be read as "only in the context of artificial and colourable devices".[75]

The Supreme Court in *Vodafone*, however, restated the judicial tolerance limits to declare that "the Revenue may invoke the 'substance over form' principle or 'piercing the corporate veil' test only after it is able to establish on the basis of the facts and circumstances surrounding the transaction that the impugned transaction is a sham or tax avoidant."[76] The Supreme Court particularly acknowledged round-tripping structures as deserving cases for invoking "doctrine of fiscal nullity"[77] and discarding their legal form. Further, in *Vodafone* the Supreme Court propounded a new test, i.e. the "look at" test whereby the tax administration must "ascertain the legal nature of the transaction and while doing so it has to look at the entire transaction as a whole and not to adopt a dissecting approach."[78] The Supreme Court further implored the need to ascertain the "dominant purpose" and the "business purpose" of the transaction to determine whether the transaction is a "colourable or artificial device".

Reading the decisions in *Azadi*[79] and *Vodafone*[80] together, the legal position as it stands today is that the views of Chinnappa Reddy J. may no longer be relevant to determine the acceptability of the tax treatment proposed by the taxpayer. These decisions also vindicate the *Duke of Westminster*

---

66 For illustration, see *Banyan and Berry v. Commissioner of Income-Tax* (1996) 222 ITR 831 (Guj); *Commissioner of Income Tax v. Modest Enterprises Ltd.* (1994) 207 ITR 618 (Cal); *Commissioner of Income Tax v. Nandkishore Sakarlal* (1994) 208 ITR 14 (Guj); *Bhaktimala Beedi Factory v. Commissioner of Income Tax* (1996) 219 ITR 6 (AP).

67 *Union of India v. Azadi Bachao Andolan* (2004) 10 SCC 1.

68 Ibid., 56.

69 See n.33. See also *Commissioner of Income Tax v. Sivakasi Match Exporting Company* (1964) 53 ITR 204 (SC) which opines similarly.

70 See n.61.

71 See n.33 at 153.

72 See n.51.

73 See n.67.

74 See n.61.

75 See n.51 at 668.

76 Ibid., 670.

77 Ibid.

78 Ibid.

79 See n.67.

80 See n.51.

principle[81] and its continuing relevance to determine such disputes. However the decision in *Vodafone* has stirred the waters seemingly settled by *Azadi*.[82] As a knee-jerk reaction[83] to the decision in *Vodafone*, the Government of India introduced ominous "General Anti-Avoidance Rules" (GAAR) in the income tax legislation, as discussed in the later part.

The developments post *Vodafone*[84] reflect an emboldened tax administration which has sought to extrapolate a hidden colourable device in almost every tax avoidance dispute to allege abuse, though with mixed results. In an ultimately unsuccessful effort, the tax administration urged the Gujarat High Court in *Vodafone Essar*[85] to reject a scheme of amalgamation of two companies. It was contended by the tax administration that the scheme was intended to avoid payment of tax which would potentially be payable if assets of one were sold to the other company instead of carrying out the amalgamation. It was urged that the scheme of amalgamation "is nothing but a device and a conduit having the sole purpose of avoiding and evading taxes including income tax, stamp duty, registration charges and VAT."[86] Similar was the outcome of a case before the Andhra Pradesh High Court in *Sanofi*[87] where claim for capital gains tax in India on account of sale of shares of a French Company held outside India was rejected notwithstanding the fervent plea of the tax administration alleging tax avoidance.[88]

The tax administration, however, received a favourable outcome from the Delhi High Court in the case of *Shiv Raj*.[89] In this case the taxpayer was the erstwhile owner who sold his entire manufacturing facility against sale consideration and also received a non-compete fee from the buyer. The taxpayer claimed immunity from taxes, citing the settled law that non-compete fee is not taxable for the relevant period in dispute. Having unsuccessfully claimed before the Tax Tribunal that the non-compete was a "smokescreen" to avoid tax liability on a part of sale consideration which was artificially broken up and termed as non-compete, the tax administration appealed to the High Court. Obliging the tax administration, the High Court opined that there were "surrounding and corroborating circumstances which must not be ignored" and took note of the fact that the non-compete fee was more than ten times the sale consideration, concluding that the "figure *per se* does not appear to be a realistic payment".[90]

For our discussion it is critical to note that the High Court in this case redrew the conceptual boundaries to opine that there exist four concepts i.e. "tax mitigation, tax evasion, acceptable tax avoidance and abusive tax avoidance", each of which "involves an element of tax planning" but it is the "nature and character of the planning and its nexus with the transaction" which is decisive to distinguish these concepts.[91] The High Court approved the first and third categories acknowledging the "taxpayers' rights to arrange ones affairs within the confines of law" provided

---

81 See n.36.
82 For illustration, see T. Jain, "How Vodafone Has Overruled Azadi Bachao Andolan Decision", 250 *Current Tax Reporter* (Articles) 8 (2012); T. N. Pandey, "McDowell Decision Still Relevant – Says the Supreme Court in Vodafone's Decision", 341 *Income Tax Reports* (Journal) 34 (2012).
83 Memorandum to the Finance Bill, 2012 acknowledges the variance between judicial decisions as the prime impetus to introduction of GAAR. (2012) 342 ITR (St.) 234 at 282.
84 See n.51.
85 *Vodafone Essar Gujarat Ltd. v. Department of Income Tax* 2012 SCC Online 4141 (Guj).
86 The Supreme Court also did not interfere with this decision. *Department of Income Tax v. Vodafone Essar Gujarat Ltd.* (2015) 373 ITR 525 (SC).
87 *Sanofi Pasteur Holding SA v. Department of Revenue* (2013) 354 ITR 316 (AP).
88 This case is pending consideration in the Supreme Court as Civil Appeal No. 8031-8033/2015.
89 *Commissioner of Income Tax v. Shiv Raj Gupta* (2015) 372 ITR 337 (Del).
90 Ibid., para 22.
91 Ibid., paras 42–48.

the choice of the taxpayer is a real event and not a colourable device. Severely castigating the cases falling in the second and fourth categories, the High Court declared impermissible all instances of "willful violation or circumvention of applicable tax laws to minimize tax liability". Instead of laying down an objective test, as to what constitutes the willful transgression of the dotted lines, the High Court held that such assessment required a case-to-case examination.[92] In view of the author, this decision completely subjugates all attempts to elevate the conceptual foundations of tax avoidance in an objective manner divorced from the engrossing fact-pattern of a case. Perhaps this is the inevitable consequence of the legislature's refusal to define the anti-avoidance rules and relegating its responsibility to the judiciary.

On a factual matrix, the decision in *Shiv Raj* clearly reflects the legal position in a state of flux where "colourable schemes" can be cited as a reason to distinguish and deviate from precedents. It is additionally intriguing that in this case the High Court revisited the "look at" test propounded in *Vodafone*. The Supreme Court had evolved and applied this test to conclude that the tax administration was precluded from examining a part of the transaction and allege abuse. The High Court has concluded that this test obliges the Court to ascertain the intention of the parties by collectively examining the sale and non-complete agreements. On such basis the High Court has rejected construing the two agreements independently as doing it "would be to ignore reality, insularize ourselves and treat sham and deceit at a true and real event" and opines that "in doing so, we are following the ratio and reasoning" in *Vodafone*.[93] In view of this author, the ratio of *Vodafone* has been turned on its head in *Shiv Raj*.

Additionally, the High Court in *Shiv Raj* has concluded that the true ratio of *Vodafone* "negates and disqualifies colourable device, deceit and sham as a legitimate and acceptable tax event". In the view of the High Court these "terms have some-what ethical and casuistical connotations and are the elective test for differentiating tax planning from abusive tax avoidance".[94] Thus clearly *Vodafone* has been interpreted to mean not a step further to the *Duke of Westminster* principle or the decision in *A. Raman & Co.*[95] but instead is taken as a step back towards the view of Chinnappa Reddy J. in *McDowell*[96] in as much as moralistic attributes are sewn in as relevant factors for adjudging validity of tax avoidance maneuvers.

The appeal of the taxpayer against *Shiv Raj* decision is pending consideration in the Supreme Court.[97] Thus a final word on the subject is awaited. However the aforesaid discussion clearly establishes the influence of an alternate judicial school on the legal position of tax avoidance in India. Three decades of adjudication and unanimous decisions of the Supreme Court *inter alia* in *Arvind Narottam*;[98] *Azadi*;[99] *Walfort Share*;[100] and *Vodafone*[101] have failed to control the *sui generis* thoughts of Chinnappa Reddy J. This has been to the detriment of the taxpayer and the legal world alike[102] as it considerably muddles the application of rule of literal construction of fiscal laws. Consequently the judicial opinion relating to tax avoidance appears to be precariously settled in India and is continuously under a scanner with each passing judgment on the subject.

92 Ibid., para 43.
93 Ibid., para 63.
94 Ibid., para 41.
95 See n.39.
96 See n.62.
97 Special Leave Petition (Civil) No. 25392/2015. Notice issued on 9 November 2015.
98 See n.64.
99 See n.66.
100 See n.33.
101 See n.51.
102 Gupta, n.30.

This leaves both the taxpayer and the tax administration without reasonable certainty as to the application and level of engagement of the judicially evolved tests to resolve tax disputes.

Conclusion on the judicial approach

Fortunately or unfortunately the deviations in the traditional outlook, as noted previously, are neither too few to be summarily dismissed from the list of relevant considerations in the study of the subject nor are unyielding to have attained the stature of the mainstream discourse on tax avoidance.[103] The formalistic and traditional judicial response to tax avoidance schemes, therefore, is neither a thing of the past nor the only dominant view in determining the sustainability of these schemes.[104] As a student of the subject, therefore, one is required to keep oneself abreast with the parallel responses perpetually being unsure of the approach which would be applied in the next tax avoidance case.[105]

The next section reveals that the Parliament has intervened to institute both specific and general anti-avoidance rules. SAARs have to a large extent, primarily by overcoming specific precedents, curtailed the scope for alternative tax treatment claimed by the taxpayers. GAARs, however, are hotly decried and are continuously deferred as they remain embroiled in the debate over their effective and impartial implementation. Even otherwise, the very fact that GAARs involve a subjective reappraisal of taxpayer's conduct and in any case a GAAR determination is also subject to judicial review, the fate of the taxpayer appears to be tied to wavering judicial opinion which would continue to remain so in the absence of a categorical decision of a larger bench of the Supreme Court. Given that a larger bench is constituted upon a formal request by the incumbent judges of the Supreme Court in a pending dispute and such requests are not out-of-routine, it may be a while before the judicial opinion on the subject is settled.

Legislative response to tax avoidance

Tax avoidance has been on the legislative agenda, albeit with varying priority. The initial six decades of independent India reflect a legislative choice of "Specific Anti Avoidance Rules" (SAARs).[106] Grappling with specific issues, the Parliament enacted measures to counter tax avoidance on account of associations; partnership firms; corporate dividends; 'zero-tax' companies; 'Hindu-Undivided Families' (HUF); family partition; 'benami transactions' (i.e. surrogate ownership cases); varying accounting and tax years; 'Non-Ordinary Residents'; agricultural income; cash economy; etc.[107]

It was only in 2001 that the Parliament took the leap of enacting extensive anti-avoidance provisions in the form of transfer-pricing rules.[108] Initially confined to international transactions, the transfer-pricing rules were extended to domestic transactions[109] in 2012 to principally cover

---

103 Law Commission of India, n.41, *inter alia* acknowledged the varying dimensions of the tax avoidance debate.

104 J. S. H. Kapadia, "Taxation and Economic Reforms", 6 *SCC* (Journal) 13 (2004) suggests that the debate on tax avoidance also arises on account of mixed application of commercial and legal concepts.

105 For illustration, see *Commissioner of Income Tax v. Abhinandan Investment Ltd.* 2015 SCC Online Del 13523.

106 See generally, J. S. Ranganathan, "Indian Income Tax Law – Five Decades", 1 *Law Weekly* (Journal) 17 (2002) for an account of specific legislative action to counter tax evasion.

107 Ibid.

108 Currently under Sections 92–92F, Income Tax Act, 1961.

109 Sections 92D, 92E, Ibid.

transactions with related-entities enjoying tax benefits.[110] These rules are implemented through the aid of specialized officers.[111] Recently the law has been amended to install safeguards in the form of 'safe harbour' rules[112] and 'advance pricing agreements'.[113] The transfer-pricing rules form part of Chapter X of the Act which is christened as 'special provisions relating to avoidance of tax' and covers other SAARs dealing with securities transactions,[114] transactions with Non-Residents,[115] tax havens[116] etc. These rules have been revised time and again to catch up with the international trends and fill up the loopholes pointed out by the courts. Tax on book profits on companies with zero or negligible net profits[117] has also been branded[118] as a tax avoidance measure. The Act additionally carries SAARs targeting tax avoidance devices peculiar to India such as cases involving 'transfer of income when there is no transfer of assets';[119] 'revocable transfer of assets';[120] avoidance of tax by transfer of income to the benefit of spouse, minor child[121] or other associated persons;[122] etc. is also countered by SAAR under the Act. Judicial rulings construed as accommodating tax avoidance on buy-back of shares[123] have also been legislatively overruled by another SAAR.[124]

In an attempt to overhaul the Act, the Government of India proposed a draft 'Direct Taxes Code, 2010'.[125] This draft principally established the policy choice of the Government to provide stringent 'General Anti-Avoidance Rules' (GAARs) besides making substantial additions to the existing SAARs. It was proposed that any transaction could be declared an "impermissible avoidance arrangement" and its consequences could be determined, *inter alia*, by "disregarding, combining or recharacterising any step in, or a part or whole of" the transaction treating the transaction "as if it had not been entered into or carried out"; "disregarding any accommodating party"; relocating receipts/expenses amongst the parties; or recharacterising the nature of the receipt/expense and even of equity and debt.[126] The draft Code also carried provisions to impose 'Branch Profits Tax'[127] and levy of tax on income attributable to 'controlled foreign corporations'[128] (CFCs).

Mincing no words, the Government of India in a Discussion Paper accompanying the draft Code[129] justified these provisions as countering "severe erosion of the tax base" and "serv[ing] as

---

110 Covered under "specified domestic transaction" defined in Section 92BA, Ibid.
111 'Transfer Pricing Officer', Section 92CA, Ibid.
112 Section 92CB, Ibid.
113 Section 92CC, Ibid.
114 Section 94, Ibid.
115 Section 93, Ibid.
116 Section 94A, Ibid.
117 Chapter XII-B, Income Tax Act, 1961 titled "special provisions relating to certain companies".
118 *Apollo Tyres Ltd. v. Commissioner of Income Tax* (2002) 9 SCC 1.
119 Section 60, Income Tax Act, 1961.
120 Section 61, Ibid.
121 Section 64, Ibid.
122 Section 65, Ibid.
123 For illustration, see *In Re. Dana Corporation* 321 ITR 178 (AAR).
124 Section 115QA, Income Tax Act, 1961.
125 (2010) 326 ITR (St.) 41. Part F of the Code dealt with provisions relating to 'Prevention of Abuse of the Code'.
126 Section 123, Direct Taxes Code, 2010.
127 Section 111, Direct Taxes Code, 2010 made every foreign company liable to tax in India on "the income attributable, directly or indirectly, to the permanent establishment or an immovable property situated in India".
128 Section 58(2)(u) read with Twentieth Schedule, Direct Taxes Code, 2010. CFC under the Code was defined as a foreign unlisted company controlled by Indian Residents "not engaged in any active trade or business" having income beyond the stipulated threshold and resident of another country with lower tax rate.
129 Available at www.prsindia.org/uploads/media/DTC%20Bill/Discussion%20Paper.pdf (accessed 1 February 2016).

a deterrent against such practices".[130] Acknowledging yet unyielding to the protests against these measures, in its Second Discussion Paper the Government reiterated that "a statutory GAAR can act as an effective deterrent and compliance tool against tax avoidance in an environment of moderate tax rates."[131] A Parliamentary Committee which evaluated the nuances of the draft Code recommended introduction of safeguards, *inter alia* to ensure that the "provisions to deter tax avoidance should not end up penalizing taxpayers, who have genuine reasons for entering into a bonafide transaction" and vouchsafe against the possibility that the draft does "not lead to any fiscal uncertainty or ambiguity".[132]

The Government of India instead went ahead in 2012 to introduce GAAR in an expanded form in the Income Tax Act 1961, presumably in the wake of the *Vodafone*[133] decision.[134] These rules[135] provide that an arrangement whose main purpose or one of the main purposes is to obtain a tax benefit and which also satisfies at least one of the four tests, can be declared as an 'impermissible avoidance arrangements'. The four tests are[136] that the arrangement (a) creates rights and obligations not at arm's length; (b) results in misuse or abuse of provisions of the Act; (c) lacks or is deemed to lack 'commercial substance'; or (d) is carried out in a manner, which is normally not employed for bonafide purpose. The Act was amended to legislatively enact the substance-over-form test where it is provided that "an arrangement shall be deemed to lack commercial substance if the substance or effect of the arrangement as a whole, is inconsistent with, or differs significantly from, the form of its individual steps or a part".[137] Additionally, specific instances have been declared as deemed to be lacking commercial substance. These are where the transactions "involve or include (i) round trip financing; (ii) an accommodating party; (iii) elements that have effect of offsetting or cancelling each other; or (iv) a transaction which is conducted through one or more persons and disguises the value, location, source, ownership or control of funds which is the subject matter of such transaction".[138]

It appears that the idea underlying GAAR is to reconstruct transaction(/s) intended to avoid tax by, *inter alia*, disregarding their form and structure. While providing detailed illustration of what instances/structures do not constitute 'commercial substance',[139] the tax administration has also been empowered[140] to disregard the transaction[141] or make amends by "disregarding, combining or recharacterising any step in, or a part or whole of, the impermissible avoidance arrangement".[142] In no uncertain terms, it is stipulated that "if an arrangement is declared to be an impermissible avoidance arrangement, then the consequences, in relation to tax, of the arrangement, including denial of tax benefit or a benefit under a tax treaty, shall be determined,

---

130 Ibid., paras 24.1 to 24.3. See Mathews P. George and Pankhuri Agarwal, "Use of Corporate Vehicles for Tax Planning: The Vodafone Case and Direct Taxes Code", 3 *NLUD Student Law Journal* 201 (2010) who argue that the Direct Taxes Code virtually rules out continued use of corporate entities for tax planning.

131 Available at www.prsindia.org/uploads/media/DTC_%20RevisedDiscussionPaper_%20June%202010.pdf (accessed 1 February 2016).

132 (2012) 342 ITR (St.) 305.

133 See n.51.

134 See n.83.

135 Section 95, Income Tax Act, 1961 providing for 'applicability of General Anti-Avoidance Rule'.

136 Section 96, Income Tax Act, 1961 defining 'impermissible avoidance agreement'.

137 Section 97(1)(a), Income Tax Act, 1961.

138 Section 97(1)(b), Ibid.

139 Section 97, Income Tax Act, 1961 defining 'arrangement to lack commercial substance'.

140 Section 98, Income Tax Act, 1961 providing 'Consequences of impermissible avoidance agreement'.

141 Section 98(1)(b), Income Tax Act, 1961.

142 Section 98(1)(a), Ibid.

in such manner as is deemed appropriate, in the circumstances of the case."[143] The 'tax benefit', entitlement or availment of which may trigger GAAR, has also been defined very widely to cover any reduction/avoidance/deferral of tax, either on account of a tax treaty or otherwise; increase in tax refund, either on account of a tax treaty or otherwise; a reduction in total income; or an increase in loss.[144]

The rules further provide that in such cases "(i) any equity may be treated as debt or vice versa; (ii) any accrual, or receipt, of a capital nature may be treated as of revenue nature or vice versa; or (iii) any expenditure, deduction, relief or rebate may be recharacterised."[145] To deal with instances involving multiple parties it has been provided that the transaction may be re-determined by the tax administration by "disregarding any accommodating party or treating any accommodating party and any other party as one and the same person",[146] or "deeming persons who are connected persons in relation to each other to be one and the same person for the purposes of determining tax treatment of any amount"[147] or by "reallocating amongst the parties to the arrangement (i) any accrual, or receipt, of a capital or revenue nature; or (ii) any expenditure, deduction, relief or rebate".[148] In fact the tax administration has now been given statutory power to lift the corporate veil.[149]

Enacted in 2012, GAAR was originally made applicable from April, 2013 and draft guidelines were published[150] clarifying their ground-level implementation. However there was a widespread public outcry.[151] GAAR were even touted as impinging upon the 'rule of law' regime guaranteed under the Indian Constitution.[152] Consequently its application was deferred and an Expert Committee was constituted "to receive comments from stakeholders and the general public on the draft GAAR guidelines" and "vet and rework the guidelines based on the feedback".[153]

The Expert Committee Report[154] acknowledged the need for GAAR to "serve as a deterrent"[155] against tax avoidance practices but suggested their deferral by three years "on administrative grounds" and particularly to ensure "intensive training of tax officers".[156] Significant dilution of GAAR's scope was also proposed such that "only arrangements which have the main purpose (and not one of the main purposes) of obtaining tax benefit should be covered under GAAR".[157] Simultaneously a new definition of 'commercial substance' and other factors

143 Section 98(1), Ibid.
144 Section 102(10), Ibid.
145 Section 98(2), Ibid.
146 Section 98(1)(c), Ibid.
147 Section 98(1)(d), Ibid.
148 Section 98(1)(e), Ibid.
149 Section 98(1)(g), Ibid.
150 (2012) 251 CTR (Statutes) 198.
151 See generally A. K. Sharma, "International Tax Avoidance Issues: An Analysis of Indian Law and Policy", 42 *Intertax* 807 (2014); ICRIER, *India's Investment Climate: Addressing Concerns About Tax Policy* (2014), Available at http://icrier.org/ICRIER_Wadhwani/Index_files/India%27s_Investment_Climate.pdf.
152 See generally T. Jain, "GAAR and 'Rule of Law': Mutually Incompatible?", 43 *Chartered Accountant Practice Journal* 424 (2013); B. M. Sagar and Punya Varma, "GAAR in India: Constitutionality of the Proposed Taxation Regime", 2 *NLUD Student Law Journal* 94 (2013) for a detailed legal account of these concerns.
153 See n.154 at 9.
154 (2012) 348 ITR (St.) 1.
155 Ibid., para 2. See also T. Jain, "'GAAR' and Corporate Governance: Will the Stick Do the Trick?", 1:6 *Journal on Governance, National Law University, Jodhpur* 629–74 (2012).
156 Ibid., para 3.13.
157 Ibid., para 3.2.

were suggested to "be taken into account in forming a holistic assessment to determine whether an arrangement lacks commercial substance".[158] To ensure that any and every transaction does not trigger a GAAR analysis, the Expert Committee recommended detailed guidelines on formation and working of an "Approval Panel" comprising of senior tax officials and independent experts upon whose approval alone further proceedings would be initiated.[159] The Expert Committee also recommended grand-fathering provisions to protect past transactions;[160] excluding tax treaty cases from coverage of GAAR;[161] etc. and dilution of GAAR in a manner such that "(1) Tax mitigation should be distinguished from tax avoidance before invoking GAAR; (2) An illustrative list of tax mitigation or a negative list for the purposes of invoking GAAR should be specified; and (3) The overarching principle should be that GAAR is to be applicable only in cases of abusive, contrived and artificial arrangements."[162] A large part of the recommendations of the Expert Committee were accepted by the Government and the GAAR provisions were amended and it was provided that the GAAR provisions would apply from April 2016.[163] Subsequently the application of GAAR has further been deferred[164] and as per current law GAAR would be prospective in its application to cover transactions undertaken from April 2017.[165]

In the year 2015 the Government enacted a stringent law "to deal with the problem of the Black money that is undisclosed foreign income and assets".[166] This law, *inter alia*, targets tax evasion and in particular, foreign parking of unaccounted income[167] by providing stringent punishment for under-reporting and non-disclosure of foreign income and assets.[168] The Act was further amended to replace the corporate residence test from 'the whole of control and management of the company' in India for the entire year to 'Place of Effective Management' ('POEM') in India to counter tax avoidance "by simply holding a board meeting outside India".[169] However on account of practical issues,[170] POEM concept is proposed for a year's deferral up to April 2017.[171]

The year 2016 was witness to further amendments in the Act towards countering tax avoidance.[172] Taking cue from OECD's Base Erosion and Profit Shifting Project (BEPS), three significant changes were carried out in the Act namely (a) 'Equalisation Levy'; (b) Country-by-Country Reporting Rules; and (c) taxation of proceeds from exploitation of Patents.[173] On the first count, India emulated the OECD Report on BEPS Action Plan 1 by imposing a withholding tax on "consideration received for online advertisement" earned by foreign e-commerce

---

158 Ibid., para 3.3.
159 Ibid., para 3.10.
160 Ibid., para 3.14.
161 Ibid., para 3.16.
162 Ibid., para 3.11.
163 Section 95, Income Tax Act, 1962, as amended by Finance Act, 2013.
164 Section 95(2), Income Tax Act, 1962, as amended by Finance Act, 2015.
165 Finance Minister Speech presenting the Budget for Financial Year 2015–16; (2015) 371 ITR (St.) 97 at 119. See also Finance Minister Speech presenting the Budget for Financial Year 2016–17; (2016) 381 ITR (St.) 9 at 32.
166 Preamble, "The Black Money (Undisclosed Foreign Income and Assets) and Imposition of Tax Act, 2015" which came into effect from April 2016.
167 Government of India Press Release, Introduction of Undisclosed Foreign Income and Assets (Imposition of Tax) Bill, 2015 (20 March, 2015).
168 Chapters IV and V provide for penalties and offences respectively for failure to carry out the obligations under the law.
169 Section 6(3) of the Act, as amended by Finance Act, 2015.
170 Memorandum explaining the provisions of Finance Bill, 2016, (2016) 381 ITR (St.) 241 at 273.
171 Section 4, Finance Act, 2016.
172 Finance Act, 2016, Ibid.
173 Memorandum, see n.170.

companies from Indian residents.[174] Indian residents paying for such services have been made responsible[175] for ensuring collection and remission of the levy and are liable for other compliances under law.[176] On the second count, detailed rules have been adopted[177] on the lines of the template provided in the OECD BEPS report on Action Plan 13 whereby international groups having related Indian-entities are required to report on various aspects i.e. "aggregate information in respect of revenue, profit and loss before Income-tax, amount of Income-tax paid and accrued, details of capital, accumulated earnings, number of employees, tangible assets other than cash or cash equivalent in respect of each country or territory along with details of each constituent's residential status, nature and detail of main business activity and any other information as may be prescribed."[178] For this purpose, the international consensus on threshold of consolidated revenues of the preceding year of the group (based on consolidated financial statement) of 750 million Euros in local currency has also been adopted.[179] On the third count India has accepted the OECD BEPS Report on Action Plan 5's recommendation on the "the nexus approach which prescribes that income arising from exploitation of Intellectual property (IP) should be attributed and taxed in the jurisdiction where substantial research & development (R&D) activities are undertaken rather than the jurisdiction of legal ownership only."[180] Accordingly a new provision is adopted[181] to tax at gross-basis on royalty earned on a patent developed and registered in India. However the tax rate is moderate with a view "to encourage indigenous research & development activities".[182] A few other minor amendments are carried out in the Act towards countering specific avoidance devices. Thus there is significant legislative movement on legislative landscape relating to action against tax avoidance in the present decade.

Conclusion

An appraisal of the anti-avoidance landscape in India largely reveals a reactionary legislative attitude. Most SAARs have been enacted in response to judicial affirmation of the taxpayers' attempt to tax mitigation. A noted jurist was constrained to observe that "ceaseless spate of amendments" are made on account of the "unending competition in ingenuity between the tax-gatherer and tax-evader" which "has rendered the taxation statutes increasingly complicated".[183] Simultaneously, various devices for tax avoidance having "been neutralized by the statute", especially the SAARs, the "liability to tax has broadened from legislative supersession of precedent after precedent".[184] The recent enactment of GAAR as a response to fallacies pointed out, *inter alia*, in *Vodafone*[185] reaffirms this conclusion. The executive's apathy in consistently enforcing anti-avoidance rules, largely on account of varying political agenda,[186] gives further impetus to

174 Speech of the Finance Minister presenting the Finance Bill, 2016; (2016) 381 ITR (St.) 9 at 34.
175 Section 163, Finance Act, 2016 effective from 1 June, 2016.
176 Chapter VIII, Finance Act, 2016.
177 Section 92D(4) read with Section 286 inserted in Income Tax Act, 1962 by Finance Act, 2016 effective from April 2017.
178 Section 286(3), Income Tax Act, 1961. See also Memorandum, see n.170 at 288.
179 Memorandum, see n.170.
180 Memorandum, Ibid., 260.
181 Section 115BBF inserted in Income Tax Act, 1962 by Finance Act, 2016 effective from April 2017.
182 Memorandum, see n.170.
183 Jamshedjii Kanga and Nani Palkhivala, *The Law and Practice of Income Tax*, 8th ed. (1990), 19–20.
184 Ibid.
185 See n.51.
186 For illustration, see *Jagati Publication Ltd. v. President, Income Tax Appellate Tribunal* (2015) 377 ITR 31 (Bom).

this trend which has resulted in a stifled and wavering judicial discourse on tax avoidance with varying and acutely subjective consideration of tax avoidance disputes.[187]

Perhaps even GAAR is not the final answer to a tumultuous tide of tax avoidance disputes. A categorical decision of a larger bench of the Supreme Court laying down specific parameters for appraisal of a tax avoidance dispute, laid out after due consideration of all past precedents, appears to be a far superior solution as it would serve as an objective and guiding beacon for the dispute resolution and also guard against deviating judicial view. Till such time, while an inquiry on anti-avoidance law in India may legitimately begin with the assessment of legislative rules, one is invariably required to traverse through the wavering jurisprudence for a final word on the subject.

187 For illustration, see *Shiv Raj Gupta* (see n.89); *Aditya Birla Nuvo Ltd. v. Director of Income Tax* (2011) 342 ITR 308 (Bom); *Abhinandan Investment Ltd.*, see n.105.

14

SECURING TAX COMPLIANCE WITH COLLABORATION

The case of *cooperative compliance* in Denmark

Karen Boll

Introduction

All national tax administrations have challenges with figuring out how best and most cost-efficiently to regulate the corporations in their jurisdiction. Probably no one disputes that it happens that corporations use the tax regime in their jurisdictions – within the 'letter of the law' – to their own advantage to reduce the amount of taxes that are payable and that there is a void of 'grey-zones' that may be interpreted variedly. One could imagine that the regulation of large corporate taxpayers from the national tax administrations vary due to national legislation and different jurisdictions; yet, this is not always the case. Rather a significant number of tax administrations in Western democracies have adopted similar approaches to regulating the corporations. One example of such homogeneity is the organisation of the regulation of certain large corporate taxpayers. When regulating these, tax compliance is secured by creating increased trust, dialogue and collaboration between the tax administrations and the large corporate taxpayers. Broadly speaking, this approach is termed *cooperative compliance* (or previously *enhanced relationship*) because tax compliance is nurtured and promoted voluntarily in a proactive alliance between corporations, other stakeholders and the national tax administrations.

Several scholars have analysed national experiences with cooperative compliance programs (Burton 2007; Dabner and Burton 2009; Owens 2013; Vella et al. 2010). This literature agrees that there are challenges with implementing and using cooperative compliance. This relates, for instance, to how cooperative compliance requires that tax officials work in new ways, how cooperative compliance requires that a 'partnership' must be created between the participating large corporate taxpayers and the tax administrations, and lastly what are the challenges in documenting the effects and outcomes of the program. While the existing literature thoroughly has described many of these challenges connected to adopting cooperative compliance, the actual spread of cooperative compliance throughout the various national tax administrations and across national borders has been largely taken for granted. In this chapter, I suggest using institutional theory (DiMaggio and Powell 1991; Meyer and Rowan 1977; Zald and Lounsbury 2010) to analyse the spreading of the program and to understand the caveats connected to copying a rather standardised institutional form.

To go into detail with what happens when a standardised institutional form is spread and adopted in a new institutional context the chapter reports a case study of the Danish Tax and

Customs Administration. In this administrative setting, a program of cooperative compliance, called *Tax Governance*, has been implemented and used in practice. The program builds on a dialogue-based collaboration between this administration and a selection of the largest corporate taxpayers in Denmark. The methodology used to study the case is qualitative and builds on interviews with the Danish tax officials who have first-hand experience with the approach. Using institutional theory, I show that the program in Denmark is a close copy of what has been done elsewhere in other countries and that the program has been adopted because it provides legitimacy to the Danish Tax and Customs Administration. Furthermore, I show that the Danish tax administration has severe challenges in accounting for the outcomes of the program. These findings are interesting because they show the outspoken isomorphism at play in the field and they show that a tax administration 'dares' copy a program whose outcomes are difficult to account for with traditional means. The chapter's conclusion lifts the gaze from the specific Danish case and discusses what we can learn about cooperative compliance as a global phenomenon that has been spread to a vast number of Western tax administrations.

Cooperative compliance

The cooperative compliance approach is thoroughly described in the report "IFA Initiative on the Enhanced Relationship. Key Issues Report" published by the *International Fiscal Association* (2012). Here we can read that cooperative compliance is a proactive program or approach in which tax compliance is created based on trust and dialogue between a tax administration and a taxpayer. Looking broadly at the approach, cooperative compliance stands in contrast to what we know as more traditional coercive and reactive enforcement. In this approach, tax administrations command taxpayers to follow rules and control their activities. In the proactive and cooperative compliance approach, tax administrations seek to create positive and trust-full relationships with taxpayers. The tax administrations pursue to behave predictably and provide certainty regarding taxpayers' arrangements and future plans. Within the cooperative compliance approach the aim is to use increased levels of guidance and services to secure tax compliance pre-emptively. Most often, cooperative compliance initiatives are targeted at large corporate taxpayers. These are typically responsible for huge amounts of corporate taxes, employ large staff, and have professional tax units.

According to the research article "The concept of cooperative compliance" (Enden and Bronzewska 2014), cooperative compliance originates from the 'enhanced relationship' initiative started in the Netherlands around 2005. The *enhanced relationship* approach was rebranded as *cooperative compliance* around 2013. Around the same time, the OECD blueprinted the approach by providing reports with practical guidance as to how to enhance the relationships with selected taxpayers, how to engage these and how to conduct cooperative compliance (OECD 2013a, 2013b). The OECD stated that cooperative compliance is an effective and efficient way of creating tax compliance. Since these experiences grew, several countries have followed. Today it is common that countries have some form of a cooperative compliance program that targets their large corporate taxpayers. The United States has implemented what is called the Compliance Assurance Process (CAP) which is an example of an enhanced relationship between large corporate taxpayers and the Inland Revenue Service. In Australia, the enhanced relationship ideas are represented in the Annual Compliance Arrangement (ACA) initiative which is a scheme for large businesses to manage their compliance relationships with the Australian Tax Office in an open and transparent way (Enden and Bronzewska 2014). These and other national experiences have been described in the literature (Burton 2007; Dabner and Burton 2009; Enden and Bronzewska 2014; Vella et al. 2010).

Looking at these different national experiences of cooperative compliance, a number of characteristics emerge. As noted previously, it is an initiative that is targeted at large corporate taxpayers. Often these are invited to participate by the public tax administrations or, alternatively, they can apply to be part of a cooperative compliance program. It is thus an initiative that is only available to certain taxpayers. It is also an initiative in which the public tax administrations take care to provide extended guidance, service, and provide clear and quick answers to the participating large corporations to make sure that their arrangements, reporting and assessments are correct up front. An effect of this is that the participating corporations can expect less of the classic reactive command and control enforcement which they would normally be exposed to. As the report "IFA Initiative on the enhanced relationship" writes: "The end result of the successful introduction of an ER (Enhanced Relationship) program is that there are TPs (Tax-payers) with ER benefits and TPs without ER benefits, subject to more stringent checks" (IFA 2012). Lastly, what characterises the program is that it is seen as a cost-efficient way of securing tax compliance and preventing future tax avoidance because resources are targeted high up in organizations. In these organisations even small errors may have large impacts, and performing reactive control and inspections is a resource- and time-demanding exercise for both tax administrations and taxpayers.

In Denmark, which is relatively a tiny player among the various national tax administrations, cooperative compliance initiatives were first adopted in 2009 and have since been consolidated as a central part of the compliance initiatives towards large corporate taxpayers. The Danish Tax and Customs Administration calls the Danish initiative "Tax Governance". The administration has listed the 150 largest corporate taxpayers in Denmark and from these approximately 30 corporations participate in the program. These invited participants are all perceived to have high levels of compliance when entering the program as this is a prerequisite for participating. The Tax Governance program is publicly described on the tax administration's webpage. Here it can be read that the program is voluntary and that it is a dialogue-based initiative that is aimed proactively at securing tax compliance in a collaborative fashion. Within the Danish Tax and Customs Administration, Tax Governance is a high profile program, yet it is important to note that it only constitutes a smaller part of the general inspection and control of large corporations' arrangements and taxation practices. It is still the majority of the large corporations in Denmark who experience the tax administration's regular procedures which are based on direct enforcement, control and sanctions.

Theories on cooperative compliance

According to the academic literature on cooperative compliance, this program is facing three major challenges. First, it is not easy to change working practices within the national tax administrations that has often mostly been based on mistrust and on repressive and reactive audits. Working with a cooperative compliance program implies that tax officials must be open, service-minded and trustful. Such an attitude can be difficult to cultivate in a traditional 'control and command' organisation (Enden and Bronzewska 2014: 571). Second, intuitively it seems reasonable to have a partnership around securing compliance and prevent potential future tax avoidance. Yet, experiences have shown that there is a problem of an actual 'absence of a common interest'. This absence is rooted in the fact that the participating tax administrations and the large corporations have different goals: to maximize government revenue and to minimize it, respectively. As it is noted in the literature, there is often no 'correct' amount of taxes to be paid or a 'clear cut' interpretation of the tax rules and regulation. Rather, much depends on an inherent ambiguity in the laws and regulations that can be read and interpreted differently

(Dabner and Burton 2009: 318). Lastly, while the program does help to improve the relationships between many large corporate taxpayers and tax administrations, the program is less clear on the extent to which is succeeds in getting the corporate taxpayers to be more accepting of anti-avoidance legislation and hence, making them engage less in (negative) tax avoidance practices (Vella et al. 2010: 136). In other words, it is difficult to assess and evaluate the actual impact or outcomes of the approach.

While the existing literature has described in detail many of these challenges connected to using a cooperative compliance program, the spread of cooperative compliance throughout various national tax administrations and across national borders has been largely taken for granted. It is noteworthy that this intense spread and adoption of the program has not been analysed, or theorised. It is just taken as a matter of fact. In relation to this lack of analytical focus, my aim in this chapter is to explore the mechanisms in the spread of the cooperative compliance program and to look at the consequences this may have for the day-to-day work with the program. I suggest, that the copying and adoption of the cooperative compliance program is best described with institutional theory (DiMaggio and Powell 1991; Meyer and Rowan 1977).

Institutional theory

The key question that has driven and drives institutional theory is what makes organisations so strikingly similar (DiMaggio and Powell 1991). If we look around at different organisations, or in this case if we look at different forms of regulation strategies, then we see that they resemble each other. Institutional theory has for years been interested in explaining and understanding this convergence and homogeneity in forms. This, indeed, is also why this theoretical framing has been selected to analyse the Danish case. Next, I introduce some of the key concepts within institutional theory; these concepts will later be used to analyse the adoption of the program in Denmark.

DiMaggio and Powell present the concept of *institutional isomorphism*. This concept denotes a process whereby organisations adapt to what they believe society expects from them. Central to this argument is that the adoption happens in relation to the environment, e.g. society. To specify this adoption to the environment, DiMaggio and Powell describe three forms of isomorphic pressures: *Coercive pressure* where homogeneity is explained with reference to demands from politics and the state; *Mimetic pressure* where homogeneity is explained by reference to how peers imitate (successful) peers in situations with uncertainty; and *Normative pressure* where homogeneity in forms emerges due to the fact that similar professions have similar training and often encourage connected courses of action (Boxenbaum and Jonsson 2008; DiMaggio and Powell 1991). What unites these forms of isomorphism is that they all relate to structures 'outside' the organisation: either above from the state or horizontally from other organisations or peers. In brief, homogeneity emerges as a response to the pressures in the environment.

Meyer and Rowan connect DiMaggio and Powell's ideas about isomorphism to the concept of *legitimacy*. Meyer and Rowan add that organisations are driven to incorporate practices and procedures defined by prevailing rationalized concepts of what works in other organizations (a form of mimetic pressure) because this creates legitimacy. Examples of this are when it becomes 'comme-il-faut' for organisations to have *human resource departments*, to have *environmental policies*, to make *risk assessments* or to have *Research and Development departments*. Looking at the adoption and spread of such institutional forms, Meyer and Rowan write that copying these from others increases an organisation's legitimacy. It does so because these forms are considered proper, adequate, rational and necessary for the running of a modern organisation (Meyer and Rowan 1977). This, indeed, is expressed by public opinion, central constituents, the educational system or by laws and courts. Together this creates a common understanding of the rational structural forms that organisations must adopt in order to operate in a modern society.

In 2010, Zald and Lounsbury – who are also key figures within institutional theory – challenge Meyer and Rowans' thesis from 1977 about legitimacy. Zald and Lounsbury write that Meyer and Rowan's approach to legitimacy points in the direction of a passive acceptance of new forms (Zald and Lounsbury 2010: 963). In contrast to this, Zald and Lounsbury argue that the dynamics in a society (and the spread and adoption of new institutional forms) are fundamentally shaped by various *command posts*. With the notion of command posts they refer to traditional centres of societal power that regulate, oversee and maintain social order (ibid. 964). What they add to the thinking about homogeneity in form is that this is shaped by strong power posts; these command posts are central to study because these are the key to the shaping of international policy and regulation.

While the copying and incorporation of popular institutional forms can be seen as a positive feature that adds value in terms of legitimacy, Meyer and Rowan also emphasise that copying has a 'Janus-face'. Organisations that incorporate prevailing forms, they say, often do so "independent of the immediate efficiency of the acquired practices and procedures" (Meyer and Rowan 1977: 340). Their argument is that conformity to (external) institutionalised forms often actually conflicts with (internal) efficiency criteria. In line with this, DiMaggio and Powell say that when a new institutional form or an innovation spreads and is adopted in new settings a threshold is often reached, beyond which it provides legitimacy rather than improving performance. Perhaps, then, it is not necessarily rational to adopt new institutional forms if the aim is to improve performance. But, because the new institutional forms are 'normatively sanctioned', that is accepted by the general society they can provide external legitimacy even when they do not increase internal efficiency.

My aim in the analysis is to explore these theoretical insights from institutional theory in relation to the cooperative compliance program. If we follow institutional theory and accept that the cooperative compliance program is an institutional form which is considered proper, adequate, and rational for the running of a modern tax administration, then this fundament provides some theoretical expectations about this new form. Following institutional theory, I may assume that the Danish Tax and Customs Administration has adopted the cooperative compliance program as a response to what happens in its environment and as a means to create legitimacy. Also, I may assume that the program is not necessarily a guarantee of increase in outcome. Playing with these theoretical assumptions in relation to the case is interesting because it enables exploration of the Danish Tax and Customs Administration's work with the cooperative compliance program. Further, the analysis informs us about the mechanisms in the copying and spreading of the cooperative compliance program throughout and across national borders.

The qualitative data from Denmark

As noted in the introduction, the chapter builds on a carefully selected case of cooperative compliance in Denmark. Many public tax administrations have moved from a command and control approach to taxpayers to a more accommodating and servicing approach where tax compliance is sought to be accomplished by having increased dialogue. While some may perceive this as a as general trend of cooperative compliance, this is not what I perceive as such in this analysis. Rather, as the introduction and the analysis will show, cooperative compliance indicate adherence to a quite specific set of activities and it goes deeper than merely *more service, more dialogue* and *less command and control*. When I state that the case is 'carefully selected' it refers to its fit with and use of the key ideas in cooperative compliance.

In 2015, I contacted the Danish Tax and Customs Administration to hear if I could interview employees working with the Tax Governance program. I was granted permission to do this and I was allowed to get access to a number of internal documents which are not public. These documents are a project description, two evaluations, and various work templates. The documents describe the internal guidelines to the work and provide internal evaluations of the program. Concerning the interviews, I conducted 11 in-depth interviews. These interviews cover the senior management level which takes the strategic decisions concerning the Tax Governance program and it cover the employees working with Tax Governance on a daily basis – called TG managers. All interviews have been transcribed. The sorting of the material for this analysis has primarily focussed on how the interviewees describe the copying and spreading of the program, and how the interviewees describe the measurement and efficiency of the program.

The strength of the material – including both the interviews and the internal documents – is that it provides detailed insights into these issues and especially into how the tax officials perceive and handle the Tax Governance work. Such detailed knowledge about the management and daily running of a cooperative compliance program has not previously been presented in the academic literature. A caveat to the data and the analysis is that the material only represents the tax administration's point of view. While it would be relevant in future research to supplement the data with the participating large corporate taxpayers' perspectives, this has not been the purpose in this analysis. Rather, the purpose is to use the unique access to the tax officials' point of view to gain knowledge about their stances and work.

The cooperative compliance program in Denmark

Concerning the adoption of the cooperative compliance program in Denmark, the managers explain that the Tax Governance program is built on the same principles that have been applied in the first Dutch experience with *enhanced relationships*. Furthermore, they emphasize that the program is inspired and further developed based on the OECD's best practice and guidelines concerning cooperative compliance:

> We've built our initiative on the experiences from the Netherlands. And then, the OECD took up the idea and came with several recommendations concerning how tax administrations may best – or most rationally – approach large corporations. They [the OECD] argued that there should not be a relationship of a 'clash of interests', but that we should work to get a common agreement. This was suggested instead of the traditional control framework. And then, we kind of 'caught' that idea and have been working a lot with it.
>
> *Senior manager, SKAT*[1]

And further:

> It is not just the Netherlands that we're inspired by. It is also Ireland, they are working a lot with this. And we've also sought some inspiration from the UK. Yet, the UK approach to the taxpayers is slightly different – they need some more contractual requirements, than us – so compared to them, we do it a bit differently.
>
> *Senior manager, SKAT*

---

1 Danish expression for "The Danish Tax and Customs Administration".

In addition to this, the managers comment on experiences in Finland, Sweden, Norway and Australia. These they are either inspired by or they keep an eye on their programs to monitor what these tax administrations are doing.

Looking at the ideas in the Danish Tax Governance program, it also mirrors the official or normatively sanctioned version of what cooperative compliance is as defined by the International Fiscal Association (IFA). IFA describes the enhanced relationship (i.e. cooperative compliance programs) as having the following characteristics. It is voluntary; there are no legal obligations to enter the program. It is 'low risk' corporations that are invited to participate and the program is therefore only available to some (already compliant) taxpayers. It is necessary to have strong commitment from both parties in being open to the discussion of tax arrangements and to mutual understanding of each other's needs. There should be trust between the parties so that taxpayers can present future arrangements and get the tax administration to carry out a risk assessment of these arrangements and to provide clarity concerning their view on these arrangements. The program must ensure that the participating taxpayers have their tax matters resolved quickly, quietly, fairly and with finality (see; IFA 2012: 6 ff). The Danish case is exemplary because it holds all these core characteristics.

The previous citations demonstrate that the Danish program to a great extent is a close copy of what has been done elsewhere, e.g. in the Netherlands, UK, Ireland and Australia. Indeed, the Danish case mirrors the core elements of cooperative compliance as described by IFA. Like IFA, the Danish program "is voluntary", targets "low risk large corporations" and builds on "strong commitment for both parties". The Danish program has obviously been influenced by the international circulation of ideas on cooperative compliance. Recalling Zald and Lounsbury's concept of 'command posts', both the OECD and the IFA function as powerful command posts. These centres of societal power strongly influence how the regulation is developed in various countries because they are referred to and followed by various national tax administrations.

Relating these empirical insights further to institutional theory, I will also argue that it is reasonable to use the concepts of *coercive* and *mimetic isomorphism* (DiMaggio and Powell 1991: 69ff) to describe the copying of the program. Coercive isomorphism emphasises that homogeneity is explained with reference to political/state mandates or by pressure from other societal organisations. This coercive pressure is no doubt linked to the pressure exercised by the 'command posts' described previously. Hence, there is a strong form of coercive isomorphism at play because these international organisations exert a pressure on the tax administrations towards adopting the program. At least this is what the case from Denmark shows.[2] Importantly, this pressure is not in any way a direct 'imposition', but an indirect push and encouragement towards adapting an apparent new and cost-effective regulation.

Looking at mimetic isomorphism, this describes a situation in which an organization experiences some form of uncertainty, and to cope with this uncertainty it models other organisations' solutions. As DiMaggio and Powell write there are advantages of this mimetic behaviour; copying others yield a viable solution with little expense (ibid., 69). It is reasonable to assume that the Danish Tax and Customs Administration has been in a situation of uncertainty concerning how they should regulate large corporations in Denmark. This uncertainty stems primarily from the fact that the traditional 'command and control' approach was under pressure because it was a very resource-demanding approach to use in a situation where cost-cutting was in focus. The

---

2 While this chapter underscores the homogeneity in adopting cooperative compliance, it should also be emphasised that there are countries such as Belgium and Germany, and also Sweden, where the program has either not been used or – as in the case of Sweden – has been stopped.

uncertainty that the Danish tax administration experienced was linked to the question of how it could reform its regulations and make them more efficient and 'up-to-date'. In this situation, copying others who were successful was a sensible solution. While I am not aware of the specific reasons for the incorporation of the cooperative compliance program in other countries, it seems reasonable to assume that in the Danish case mimetic isomorphism was at play.

Gaining legitimacy

Continuing to follow institutional theory, I would also expect that a central reason for the adoption of the cooperative compliance program in Denmark is that the Danish Tax and Customs Administration seeks legitimacy. The institutional theory states that organisations are driven to incorporate prevailing rationalised practices and procedures because this increases their legitimacy (Meyer and Rowan 1977: 340). The legitimacy refers to how the organisation's audience (that is, the taxpayers and the political system) perceives the actions of the organisation as desirable, proper or consistent with existing norms, values and beliefs (e.g. Suchman 1995: 574).

One of the central internal reasons for the uptake of the cooperative compliance program was that the Danish Tax and Customs Administration in general have had (and has) a strategy of providing service and guidance to 'co-players' rather than providing inspection and control. The philosophy of the cooperative compliance program fits this existing strategy of how the tax administration creates tax compliance among this segment of taxpayers. Another reason for the uptake of the program – as explained by the interviewees – was that it fitted the ambition of doing more 'proactive' work in contrast to 'reactive' audits. It is costly to conduct reactive audits – both for the tax administration and for the involved taxpayers. Therefore, a general strategy in the Danish Tax and Customs Administration has been to increase the number of proactive initiatives whereby taxpayers are informed and guided about rules and regulations before they submit their tax accounts or before they take decisions with a taxation impact. The aim is to get more correct registration, filing, lodging, reporting and payment of tax obligations. If this is achieved pre-emptively by assisting the taxpayers, fewer resources are needed for the reactive audits. The cooperative compliance program fits this overall strategy neatly.

In addition to the previously mentioned elements, the interviewees also pointed out, as a reason for starting up the Tax Governance program that the politicians wished to turn Denmark into a country with good conditions for industry:

> If we can create this sensible dialogue with large corporations, this is clearly preferable. And well, now we have a 'right wing' government, but also when we had the 'left wing' government. Then all these politicians – from both sides – wished to create good conditions for industry.
>
> *TG manager, SKAT*

Hence, the initiative is also used as an element in a strategy of turning Denmark into a country with favourable conditions for large corporations.

Looking at the previous explanations, the question is to what extent this can be interpreted as a search for legitimacy. Meyer and Rowan state that legitimacy occurs when an organisation adopts 'proper', 'adequate', 'rational' and even 'necessary' organisational forms. I suggest that the entire discourse around the Tax Governance program and its start-up circulates precisely around how the program is rational to adopt as it fits existing strategies and how it is an adequate solution to the regulation of large corporate taxpayers. It is a solution that has been sanctioned by other countries, by authoritative voices such as the IFT and the OECD, and by the Danish politicians. The program does indeed closely resemble a necessary form to take up for the tax administration to act like a rational and a resource-conserving administration. Hence, it seems highly plausible that the adoption and incorporation of the Tax Governance program has to do with how the tax administration becomes legitimate in the eyes of the taxpayers and the politicians. The simultaneous adoption of the program not just in Denmark, but in several countries, thus not only creates homogeneity concerning the structural forms used to regulate large corporations, but it also provides legitimacy to the organisations that take up and use the form.

Efficiency in the day-to-day technical work

As indicated in the theory section, institutional theory argues that while organisations increase their legitimacy by incorporating sanctioned forms and practices, there is no guarantee that the newly incorporated forms and practices are efficient; that is, that they have an outcome proportional to the resources invested in the work. Quite the contrary, these may be copied and used regardless of their immediate efficiency. What is interesting to explore is how this theoretical assertion fits the Danish case. To discuss the outcomes of the Tax Governance program, the following paragraphs will go into detail with the day-to-day work implied in the program and how the outcomes of the program are accounted for.

As noted previously, around 30 large corporate taxpayers participate in the Danish Tax Governance program. The basic nature of the program is to have a continuous dialogue with these large corporations. This dialogue should pre-emptively secure that the corporations' tax arrangements and plans stay truthful to the legal obligation. To initiate and maintain this dialogue, each corporation has a Tax Governance manager and a team of Tax Governance specialists assigned to it. Often, the Tax Governance manager is a specialist in corporate taxes, while the Tax Governance specialists are experts in transfer pricing, VAT, duties, income taxes or other relevant areas. The Tax Governance manager is the main contact person for a participating corporation. If, for instance, a corporation needs to get the tax administration's viewpoint on some future arrangements or if the corporation needs some kind of tax related case work to be sorted, the Tax Governance manager is contacted. The Tax Governance managers can handle this themselves when the question concerns their area of expertise, or the Tax Governance managers can contact one of the affiliated Tax Governance specialists. This continuous dialogue has two main elements, first, quick replies to the corporations concerning pressing questions and, second, provision of clarity concerning the tax administration's view on larger arrangements and future plans of the corporations.[3] Next, these are detailed in turn.

Quick responses to pressing questions and provision of certainty

Several of the interviewees mention as one core advantage of participating in the program that when the corporations have specific questions, then the Tax Governance manager and the Tax Governance specialists will try to provide quick responses and try to handle the case quickly. One explains that: "It is the set-up in Tax Governance that we will reply as quickly as it is feasible. You know, things shouldn't be lying around for months, or for half a year. We need to take

---

3 The Tax Governance work in Denmark has one emergent additional element to it; namely the development of systems for monitoring the large corporations' 'self-control/monitoring'. The focus on this has not been incorporated in this article as the initiatives to develop these systems were only in the making and new to many of the interviewed tax officials.

up problems and questions as quick as possible. It is a key to this." (TG manager, SKAT) Another one says: "Compared to the 'normal' large corporations, we offer quicker answers and a higher average level of competence." (TG manager, SKAT) As an example, one interviewee explains that a normal case work to get a certificate concerning national taxation takes approximately three weeks or more, whereas a corporation in the program obtains it within two days.

The interviewees also explain that another key element in the Tax Governance program is that often large corporations have questions and uncertainties concerning their long-term arrangements and plans. This can, for instance, be acquisitions, change of owners, selling off parts of the company, displacement of activities from country to country, mergers etc. In these cases, it is key that the corporations present these future arrangement and plans, and that the Tax Governance manager or the Tax Governance specialists provide certainty about how the tax administration sees these dispositions in relation to taxation issues. Does the tax administration basically agree that this is a right arrangement/action in relation to taxation issues, or does the tax administration perceive the arrangement/action as dubious in relation to the calculations and the impact on taxation? Many of these issues are either grey areas or open for interpretation.

To have an indication of certainty concerning such future matters and their taxation consequences can be of great value to the corporations. 'Wrong' dispositions may be costly and resource-demanding to change. In relation to this, the advantage is that divergences and disagreements concerning future dispositions are dealt with 'up front'. One Tax Governance manager explains, for instance, that his contact corporation was going into a process of handling a large merger. This Tax Governance manager was involved from the start – meaning that he participated in meetings and was handed relevant documentation – to provide the tax administration's viewpoints on the merger and secure as best as possible that the tax administration could accept the negotiated arrangements (TG manager, SKAT). Talking to another Tax Governance manager he explains that he had an example of a corporation that wanted to discuss some future tax arrangements with him – arrangements that included a 500 million DKK transaction which was a bit unclear. He explains that he told the corporation that the transaction would most likely not be accepted by the tax administration. As a result, the corporation did not proceed with the transaction.

Importantly, the responses and the feedback that are provided in these dialogues are not what in Danish are called "Bindende svar", a term that may be translated as *compulsory responses*. Compulsory responses are conclusive or enforceable responses (derived from the tax laws) that show how the tax administration must act or respond to certain arrangements. These have a legal obligation connected to them and a taxpayer must pay to obtain such a compulsory response. The responses and the dialogue that the Tax Governance employees provide and engage in do not have the legal aspect which the compulsory responses have. It is 'only' guidelines or 'soft law'. However, it is indeed guidelines which the Tax Governance employees perceive as being as close as possible to what the tax administration would also provide as a compulsory response. What is also important in relation to this is that while the chances for a reactive audit of the participating corporations' dispositions are reduced after this dialogue-process and while the corporations can be more certain about the rightfulness of their actions, it does not rule out the possibility for a reactive audit. If something appears to be wrong, the tax administration always has an authority to conduct a regular audit or a random spot check.

Measuring outcomes of the tax governance program

When the basic nature of the Tax Governance work is to have a continuous dialogue, the challenge is to measure the outcomes of this work; what is actually the outcome of the dialogue and discussions? On a very basic level, the *outputs* of the work can be listed. It can be listed how many meetings the Tax Governance employees participate in and how many questions – and perhaps how fast – the Tax Governance employees had answered. This, however, tells nothing about the *outcomes* of the program. What kind of impact does it have on the participating large corporations' tax compliance levels? Asked about how this is measured, one of the Tax Governance managers bluntly asked me if I wanted a brief answer. The brief answer was, essentially, that the tax administration is *not* measuring this, and that the tax administration does *not* know how to measure the impact and outcomes of the Tax Governance work (TG manager, SKAT).

The reason why the outcomes of the Tax Governance program are so difficult to account for is that the dialogue and the discussion is not something that can be calculated or made easily quantifiable. One Tax Governance manager explains the outcomes of his own work by imagining that if he was *not* working as a Tax Governance manager, then 'his' corporation would most likely have realized many more wrong or borderline arrangements. Then the tax administration would have needed to spend resources on subsequent reactive audits and regulations. These regulations would probably have resulted in large revenue regulations in the favour of the tax administration and a large 'outcome' could be accounted for. Looking, in contrast, at the outcomes of his present Tax Governance work, he comments that he cannot really document revenue-wise what his activities add. He knows that the corporation he works with has changed its plans due to his feedback, but this cannot be documented in any 'numbers' or 'revenue' (TG manager, SKAT). The point is that many of the Tax Governance managers and the Tax Governance specialist may have continuous meetings, provide much feedback and interact with the corporations, yet how this precisely influences the decision and arrangements of the corporations is extremely difficult to document and to measure.

Reflecting on these challenges, one of the Tax Governance managers explains that it is important to understand that there are goals within the Tax Governance program beyond merely measurable revenue or corrections:

> Of course we could have wished to have a better knowledge-basis for this work. It was and is still very difficult to know which parameters we should influence and support to get the 'right' behaviour in the corporations. And it is difficult to know what to do to get a long lasting (positive) effect, because this is not about numbers. It is about relations, it is about the way we act. That can be difficult to measure. I think that is very difficult to measure.
>
> *Senior manager, SKAT*

Summing up the above, a dilemma emerges. The Danish Tax and Customs Administration invests considerable resources in the Tax Governance program. It takes resources first to connect senior and highly knowledgeable Tax Governance managers and Tax Governance specialists to the participating corporations and, second, to get them to engage in continuous dialogue and provide quick responses to the corporations. When investing such resources, it is reasonable to assume that an outcome can be accounted for. Here, however, the dilemma emerges because the Tax Governance managers cannot account for outcomes in the usual quantitative and numeric ways. Instead, they argue that in the long run the program facilitates the establishment of sound *relations* between the large corporate taxpayers and the tax administration, and that the continuous dialogue increases the chances that more tax arrangements and plans are carried out in agreement with the tax administration's interpretations of the tax rules and regulations.

Relating these empirical findings back to institutional theory, DiMaggio and Powell say, that a threshold may be reached beyond which the adoption of a new institutional form provides legitimacy rather than improves performance. Now, because the Danish Tax and Customs Administration cannot account for the outcomes of the Tax Governance program in a quantitative way, I can conclude that my case conforms to the theoretical predictions. Yet, this interpretation is not correct because the Tax Governance program may indeed create outcomes and improve the (tax compliant) performance of the large corporations, but it is just not possible to document this in the usual fashion. What this shows is not so much that institutional theory is 'wrong' or 'misleading', but rather how difficult it is to operate *in practice* with a clear concept of efficiency or outcomes. This is difficult because it is inherently challenging to define these concepts when the character of the work is dialogue, relations and discussions. This challenge is not really addressed in institutional theory where it seems to be taken for granted that performance, efficiency and outcomes can be accounted for unambiguously. This, indeed, may not always be the case.

Conclusion

This chapter started out with a puzzle concerning the significant number of tax administrations in Western democracies that have adopted a rather similar approach to the organisation of the regulation of their large corporate taxpayers. We see that when tax administrations want to secure tax compliance and want to prevent large corporations engaging in tax avoidance then some form of a cooperative compliance initiative or program is often embarked on. As described, this trend can be detected in the Netherlands, the UK, Australia, and the US – and according to the interviewees, also in Sweden, Finland and Ireland. To understand this spread, the chapter goes into detail with one case; the adoption of a cooperative compliance program in Denmark. While a single regional/local case may seem insufficient for understanding the spread of the program, due to the richness of detail in this specific case, it provides a unique point for investigating precisely the rationales for why and how the program was adopted. In this chapter, I suggested using institutional theory (DiMaggio and Powell 1991; Meyer and Rowan 1977; Zald and Lounsbury 2010) to analyse the cooperative compliance program and to understand some of the caveats related to copying such an institutionalized form.

If my argument has been persuasive, we must conclude that The Danish Tax Governance programme is a close copy of what has been done elsewhere and that this tax administration has a hard time accounting for the program's outcomes. A number of powerful 'command posts' have driven the spread of the programme and the adoption of the programme has been closely linked to a search for legitimacy. The Danish Tax and Customs Administration has experienced direct and indirect coercive pressures from, respectively, politicians and authoritative organisations such as the OECD and IFA. In a situation where new methods were called for, the Danish Tax and Customs Administration mimetically adopted a form that functioned well in other tax agencies. A number of challenges remain in accounting for outcomes, but they are not so much about a lack of outcomes, as a lack of possible ways to measure the outcomes. As pointed out in the chapter, this finding suggests a new direction for inquiry into how academics may conceptualise efficiency and outcomes within institutional theory.

Whereas the theoretical caveat discussed previously may be central to a (smaller) academic audience, the chapter's broader findings have profound implications for tax practitioners. To them, the chapter may be illustrative in a situation where they need to choose to copy and adopt a 'standardised' regulation program. The cooperative compliance program is a pre-defined package that circulates and it may be characterised as a somewhat 'fashionable' solution that is highly promoted as an effective and efficient program that grants legitimacy to the tax administrations. In practice, however, this chapter shows that it may not be that easy to account for the effectiveness and efficiency of the program. This questions to what extend the program may continue to be a legitimate program for regulating large corporate taxpayers. Such considerations, I suggest, should be on the top of the mind when any tax administration decides to implement any of the current 'fads and fashions' programs promoted by the OECD, IFA or other authoritative 'command posts' within the tax field.

References

Boxenbaum, E., and Jonsson, S. (2008). "Isomorphim, diffusion and decoupling", in R. Greenwood, C. Oliver, R. Suddaby and K. Sahlin-Andersson (eds), *The SAGE Handbook of Organizational Institutionalism*. Los Angeles, CA; London: SAGE, 78–98.

Burton, M. (2007). "Responsive regulation and the uncertainty of tax law – Time to reconsider the commissioner's model of cooperative compliance?" *eJournal of Tax Research*, 5(1), 71–104.

Dabner, J., and Burton, M. (2009). "Lessons for tax administrators in adopting the OECD's 'enhanced relationship' model: Australia's and New Zealand's experiences", *Bulletin for International Taxation*, 63(7), 316–26.

DiMaggio, P., and Powell, W.W. (1991). "The iron cage revisited: Institutional isomorphism and collective rationality in organizational fields", in W.W. Powell and P. DiMaggio (eds), *The New Institutionalism in Organizational Analysis*. Chicago: University of Chicago Press, 63–82.

Enden, E. v. d., and Bronzewska, K. (2014). "The concept of cooperative compliance", *Bulletin for International Taxation*, 68(10).

IFA. (2012). "IFA initiative on the enhanced relationship". Available at International Fiscal Association.

Meyer, J.W., and Rowan, B. (1977). "Institutionalized organizations: Formal structure as myth and ceremony". *American Journal of Sociology*, 83(2), 340–63.

OECD (2013a). *Co-Operative Compliance: A Framework. From Enhanced Relationship to Co-Operative Compliance*. Paris: OECD Publishing.

OECD (2013b). *Together for Better Outcomes: Engaging and Involving SME Taxpayers and Stakeholder. Forum on Tax Administration Compliance Sub-Group*. Paris: OECD Publishing.

Owens, J. (2013). "The role of the enhanced relationship in the current crisis", *International Taxation*, 8 (April), 422–7.

Suchman, M. C. (1995). "Managing legitimacy: Strategic and institutional approaches". *The Academy of Management Review*, 20(3), 571–610.

Vella, J., Freedman, J., and Loomer, G. (2010). "Analyzing the enhanced relationship between corporate taxpayers and revenue authorities: A UK case study", In J. Dalton and M. E. Gangi (eds.), *The IRS Research Bulletin: Proceedings of the 2009 IRS Research Conference*. Washington, DC, Internal Revenue Service, 103–51.

Zald, M. N., and Lounsbury, M. (2010). "The wizards of Oz: Towards an institutional approach to elites, expertise and command posts". *Organization Studies*, 31(7), 963–96.

15

CORPORATE TAX EVASION AND AVOIDANCE IN DEVELOPING COUNTRIES

Bodo Knoll, Nadine Riedel, Farzaneh Shamsfakhr, and Kristina Strohmaier

Introduction

Recent years have seen a rising academic and political interest in the link between taxation and economic prosperity of developing economies and emerging markets. Mascagni et al. (2014: 4) attribute this observed prominence to factors such as the "potential benefits of taxation for state building; long-term independence from foreign assistance; and the acute financial needs of developing countries". Most developing and emerging countries struggle with small tax-to-GDP ratios, often well below 20%, which contrasts OECD countries with tax-to-GDP ratios of 30 to 40% IMF (2011). In a recent paper, Besley and Persson (2013: 2) state that "tax lies at the heart of state development" and that the central question is how governments in developing countries "can go from raising about 10% of GDP in taxes to raising around 40%".

While answering this question has remained elusive, there is some agreement that addressing tax enforcement problems and the prevalence of tax evasion and avoidance in poorer countries is of key importance (see e.g. Easterly and Rebelo (1993); Gordon and Li (2009)). The academic literature on tax evasion and avoidance in developing economies is still small though. Most importantly, limited access to high-quality (micro) data has largely prevented a sound assessment of the size and determinants of evasion and avoidance behaviour in developing countries. The aim of this chapter is to provide a brief review of the existing literature on the topic. We will moreover present our own empirical estimates on tax avoidance activities of multinational corporations in developing countries based on rich firm-level data.

Literature review

The aim of the literature review is to critically discuss existing empirical approaches to quantify the scope of tax evasion and avoidance behaviour in the developing world. In doing so, we distinguish between the domestic component of tax evasion and avoidance in developing economies (mostly, operations in the shadow economy) and international tax evasion and avoidance activities through income transfers to low-tax or no-tax countries. The second part of the literature review briefly sketches empirical evidence on the determinants of tax evasion and avoidance behaviour.

Quantifying tax evasion and avoidance in the developing world

Domestic component

Existing attempts to quantify the domestic component of tax evasion and avoidance mainly rely on macro data. The most common approaches make use of macro indicator variables like monetary and physical input demand to determine the overall size of non-recorded transactions.[1]

A widely used approach is the currency demand method (see e.g. Cagan (1958), Gutmann (1977), Tanzi (1983)). The idea behind the currency demand approach is that activities in the shadow economy involve cash payments in order to avoid leaving traces that could lead to detection by tax authorities. Thus, the approach quantifies an "excess cash" demand beyond the cash demand that can be explained by transactions in the official economy and exploits this estimate to derive a measure for the size of the shadow economy. The estimation approach crucially hinges on the assumption that the degree to which activities are shifted into the unofficial sector is a function of the tax burden and the complexity of the tax system and that this becomes visible in changes for cash demand. As this may not hold true, the approach has been subject to criticism in the literature, see e.g. OECD (2002a, 2002b) and Fuest and Riedel (2009). One particular shortcoming with respect to developing countries is that transactions in the shadow economy are often undertaken in US dollars rather than the national currency, which obviously further reduces the suitability of the approach.

A second prominent method for estimating the shadow economy based on macro indicators is the physical input method (see Kaufman and Kaliberda (1996) for the seminal work). The idea behind this approach is that electric power consumption is a good indicator for overall economic activity (as the electricity to GDP elasticity is estimated to be close to 1). An estimate for the shadow economy is then derived by using electricity consumption as a proxy for the overall economy and subtracting an estimate for official GDP. This approach, too, has received critical reviews, mainly since not all shadow economy activities require a considerable amount of electricity and technical progress has made the use of electricity more efficient in both the official and unofficial economy (see Fuest and Riedel (2009)).[2]

Beyond the conceptual problems previously stressed, estimates of the shadow economy based on macro indicators have turned out to be rather sensitive to minor sample adjustments or changes in the estimation approach, which further reduces their credibility. Furthermore, note that the shadow economy also comprises illegal activities (especially in developing countries), which would be stopped if detected and hence would not yield additional tax revenues. Moreover, not all activities in the shadow economy are taxable as individuals might reduce the scope of activities or stop them altogether when they become subject to tax costs.

1 Note that this section heavily draws on Fuest and Riedel (2009).
2 Some authors (e.g. Schneider (2005)) have used the so-called "Multiple Indicator Multiple Cause" (MIMIC) approach to quantify the size of the shadow economy. The MIMIC approach is a structural equation model that captures the statistical relationship between a latent (unobservable) variable (here: the shadow economy) and manifested (observed) variables. Schneider (2005) employs the share of direct and indirect taxation in GDP, the burden of state regulation and state interference, the unemployment quota and GDP per capita as causal variables that explain the size of the shadow economy. To relate the index to real variables like GDP one must estimate (or otherwise obtain) the size of the shadow economy for a 'base year'. The size of the shadow economy for all other years can then be extrapolated from the index. Therefore, the level of the shadow economy is not derived from the MIMIC model, but only the change of the time path (see Breusch (2005); OECD (2002a, 2002b)). Thus, a quantification of the shadow economy based on the MIMIC model relies on the validity of the reference value, which is often an estimate based on the currency demand or physical input method described above. See e.g. Schneider (2005) or Fuest and Riedel (2009) for a more detailed description of the MIMIC approach.

Additionally, there have been some attempts to quantify tax evasion and avoidance activities in developing countries with macro accounting approaches that identify tax gaps by comparing data from national and financial accounts. The underlying idea is that discrepancies in these accounts can plausibly only be explained by tax evasion and avoidance behaviour. In contrast to the money demand approaches and the physical input demand approaches previously described, the macro accounting methods aim at determining tax gaps for specific tax instruments (rather than quantifying the overall size of the shadow economy). Tax gaps determined by such accounting methods are much less controversial than the shadow economy estimates previously described. They nevertheless also suffer from some shortcomings. Most importantly, discrepancies between accounting figures may also have statistical reasons or reflect insufficient data quality, which may confound the estimates.

These shortcomings may give preference to determining tax evasion and avoidance based on micro methods (see e.g. Slemrod and Yitzhaki (2002)) which exploit data on individual taxpayers and either rely on surveys or on information retrieved from tax audits.

Survey methods are not widely used, especially not in developing countries (see e.g. Fuest and Riedel (2009)). Exceptions include La Porta and Shleifer (2008) and De Paula and Scheinkman (2011). De Paula and Scheinkman (2011) analyze a survey of small entrepreneurs in Brazil and find that only 13% of these entrepreneurs are registered with the tax authority. La Porta and Shleifer (2008) exploit survey data in which business leaders (from registered firms) in various countries are asked to estimate the scope of the informal economy in their home country. Obviously, this measure offers a rough estimate of the informal economy only since it is based on personal experience and anecdotal evidence. Survey-based assessments of respondents' own evasion activities have to be interpreted even more carefully as taxpayers likely underreport evasion activities out of shame or fear of being detected by public authorities.

Besides the survey method, tax authorities use tax audit methods to determine (part of) their national tax gap. Ideally, such a tax gap investigation is based on a random and controlled sampling process. The sampled taxpayers are then surveyed by the tax authority, which carries out a detailed risk assessment with respect to the taxpayers' evasion activities. Since the tax authorities do not necessarily observe all concealed income, a 'controllable' tax gap rather than a 'true' tax gap is identified by that procedure (see Fuest and Riedel (2009)). Moreover, due to the high quality of tax return data and the experimental nature of random audits, audit approaches are widely considered to be the 'gold standard' when determining tax gaps and have been especially popular for studying income tax evasion. Kleven et al. (2011) e.g. employ this method to analyze income tax evasion in Denmark. For developing countries, a lack of appropriate data has prevented according estimates so far. Note moreover, that audit-based estimates are restricted to tax evasion and avoidance by taxpayers who are registered with the tax authorities. Hence, the approach does not allow investigating shadow economy activities of non-registered taxpayers, which likely make up the bulk of evaders in developing countries.

Concluding, using macro approaches to determine the size of 'domestic' tax avoidance and evasion has the advantage of relying on readily available data (for countries in the developing world of sometimes poor quality though) but suffer from a number of non-trivial conceptual shortcomings. Micro approaches, in turn, are likely to deliver more informative and reliable estimates but require rich individual-level data, which is only slowly becoming available to researchers for countries in the developing world. Pinning down the size of tax evasion and tax avoidance in developing economies, beyond the numerous anecdotes and rough estimates, has thus proved difficult so far.

International component

In the following, we will turn to studies that quantify the international component of tax evasion and avoidance. Tax revenue losses of developing countries through international income relocation are mainly related to two channels: first, corporate profit-shifting activity to low-tax countries (e.g. achieved through the relocation of immaterial assets to tax haven economies) and second, the evasion of capital income taxes by residents through offshore wealth holdings.

The last years have seen the emergence of a flourishing literature studying income shifting to low-tax countries by multinational corporations. For developing countries, the topic is of high relevance as the corporate income tax is a very important revenue source for developing economies, accounting for over 17% of total tax paid, compared to only around 10% in the OECD (see e.g. Sabirianova Peter et al. (2010) and IMF (2011)). This makes enhanced corporate income tax compliance one key aim of revenue collection in the developing world, especially with respect to larger multinational entities, which belong to the main revenue contributors.

Most of the existing academic literature that aims to quantify multinational income shifting from high-tax to low-tax countries pursues an indirect approach and assesses the sensitivity of firms' reported pre-tax profits to changes in the host country's corporate tax rates (or the corporate tax rate differential to other group affiliates respectively). Papers consistently report negative semi-elasticities, which are interpreted as evidence in favour of income-shifting behaviour and are used to quantify income volumes transferred to low-tax countries. The literature has recently been reviewed by Dharmapala (2014) and Heckemeyer and Overesch (2013). Heckemeyer and Overesch (2013), moreover, conduct a meta-analysis based on 238 primary estimates sampled from 25 empirical studies on the tax sensitivity of reported multinational parent or subsidiary profits. Their analysis yields a consensus estimate of 0.8, implying that an increase in the corporate tax rate by 10 percentage points lowers multinational affiliates' reported pre-tax profits by 8% (which are presumed to be shifted to lower-tax entities within the group).

A number of papers moreover tested for international income relocation by multinational firms through specific profit-shifting channels. Using rich data on extra- and intra-firm trade (linked to company-level data), Clausing (2003), Cristea and Nguyen (2016), Davies et al. (2017), for example, show that multinational corporations systematically distort intra-firm transfer prices to relocate income from high-tax to low-tax entities. Specifically, they report systematic adjustments in intra-firm relative to inter-firm pricing in response to changes in host country tax rates that are consistent with income shifting activities. Buettner and Wamser (2013) and Egger et al. (2014) moreover present evidence that multinational firms relocate income to low-tax affiliates by distorting the debt-equity structure, namely by endowing low-tax affiliates with equity, which then lend to high-tax entities within the group and strip off the associated interest income. Both papers present evidence for significantly positive responses of internal debt holdings to corporate tax rate changes, which are consistent with debt-shifting behaviour.

Using rich data on patent applications linked to firm-level information, Karkinsky and Riedel (2012) and Griffith et al. (2014) moreover show that multinational firms distort the location of valuable and mobile patents towards low-tax entities to relocate income to these affiliates.

A striking feature of this literature, however, is that the existing evidence is largely restricted to economies in the industrialized world. It is not clear whether these estimates carry over to developing countries. Specifically, as tax administration resources and capacity are perceived to be considerably lower in developing economies, these countries may be even more prone to outward profit shifting from their borders than countries in the developed world. Along these lines, the only two papers on profit shifting from developing economies that we are aware of indeed suggest multinational income shifting to be a quantitatively relevant phenomenon in the developing world. Fuest et al. (2011) examine debt shifting in developing countries based on rich firm-level data for multinationals headquartered in Germany. Their empirical results show that, in line with debt-shifting activities, affiliates' internal debt ratios are positively affected by the corporate tax rate differential between the host country tax rate and the lowest tax rate within the multinational group. This sensitivity is larger for affiliates in developing countries relative to their counterparts in developed economies. Quantitatively, a 10 percentage point increase in a developing host country's tax rate is estimated to increase internal debt ratios by 2.75 percentage points, compared to 1.10 percentage point in developed countries.

Along the same lines, a recent paper by Crivelli et al. (2016) provides evidence on tax 'base' spillovers in developing countries, estimating the impact of one country's corporate tax policy on the corporate tax bases of neighboring economies. In doing so, they distinguish between tax base effects related to real capital flows and tax base effects related to the shifting of paper profits. They propose to separate the two channels by assessing the responsiveness of country-level corporate tax bases to corporate tax rates of neighbors, firstly calculated as GDP-weighted averages and secondly calculated as 'tax-haven' weighted averages, i.e. unweighted averages of the corporate tax rates of neighboring countries that appear on standard tax haven lists. The authors argue that observing spillovers with the GDP-weighted average tax rates provides evidence for the 'real activity' channel and observing spillovers with the haven-averages provides evidence for the profit-shifting channel. The authors' findings point to significant spillover effects, with quantitatively larger estimates for non-OECD countries (comprising emerging markets and developing countries mostly), particularly if haven-weighted average tax rates are used as regressors. This may be interpreted as evidence for quantitatively relevant multinational profit shifting in the developing world.

While corporate income shifting to low-tax countries is increasingly studied in a dynamic sub-strand of the literature, somewhat less attention has been given to the quantification of international tax evasion of individual taxpayers through offshore wealth holdings. One exception is the seminal work by Zucman (2013) who estimates global wealth holdings in tax haven economies. Based on Swiss data, Zucman (2013) employs the anomalies in the portfolio data of countries, caused by inconsistencies between cross-border portfolio liabilities and assets, received and paid cross-border dividends and interest, purchased and sold securities by offshore account holders as well as discrepancies in transfers of funds to tax havens at the global level, to approximate the financial wealth held by households through tax havens worldwide. Zucman (2013) finds that around 8% of the global financial wealth of households is held in tax havens, three-quarters of which goes unrecorded. He moreover documents that the most part of individual offshore assets is related to owners in rich countries (especially in Europe and in the United States), while only 30% of all foreign wealth belongs to developing and emerging economies (about 10% for oil exporters and 20% for non-oil developing countries).

For the sake of completeness finally note that there are a number of estimates for the tax revenue loss of developing countries through outward multinational profit shifting and tax haven wealth holdings conducted by NGOs. Much of this work relies on very strong empirical identification assumptions though, which likely lead to a substantial (upward) bias in the estimates (see e.g. Fuest and Riedel (2009)).

Determinants of tax avoidance and evasion

The following section will briefly discuss determinants of tax evasion and avoidance decisions identified in the (empirical) economic literature. A recent paper by Waseem (2015) uses rich data for Pakistan to show that income tax rates significantly impact the evasion decision of taxpayers.

Using a non-anticipated tax reform that retroactively changed the tax rates faced by a subgroup of Pakistani taxpayers by the end of the tax year, he finds strong adjustments in reported taxable income relative to a control group of non-affected taxpayers. Since the reform was announced by the end of the tax year only, individuals hardly had any chance for adjusting their reported income along the real activity margin and the strong observed adjustments in reported taxable income is hence largely attributable to evasion activities. The paper thus suggests that taxpayers in developing countries can evade taxes and move into informality rather easily, hence significantly limiting the ability of governments to collect tax revenues.

Many recent empirical studies moreover focus on the role of authorities' deterrence instruments, namely audits and fines (see e.g. Allingham and Sandmo (1972) for the standard theoretical model), in limiting evasion activities. Most of the existing research in this area is based on taxpayer surveys and laboratory experiments (Torgler (2002); Alm and McClellan (2012)). Both have been criticized, the former because of obvious incentives to misreport evasion activities in answers to survey questions and the latter for a lack of generalizability (see e.g. Gangl et al. (2014)). Thus, the literature has recently turned to controlled field experiments, where audit propensities or expected fines are adjusted in the field (see e.g. Blumenthal et al. (2001), Slemrod et al. (2001) and Kleven et al. (2011)).

In an experimental study implemented in collaboration with the Danish tax authorities, Kleven et al. (2011) find that exogenously raising perceived audit propensities of individuals' personal income tax returns (by sending out letters to taxpayers stating different audit probabilities) significantly increases subsequent income reporting of the taxpayers. Along the same lines, taxpayers randomly selected for audits report higher income in later years. Broadly similar results are reported by Slemrod et al. (2001) and Hasseldine et al. (2007).[3]

While most studies find positive effects of deterrence instruments, there is still a controversy about the effect of messages that appeal to moral considerations, and those reflecting the use of public monies by the government (see e.g. Blumenthal et al. (2001), Torgler (2002, 2004), Dell'Anno (2009), Fellner et al. (2013)). A large literature moreover stresses that decision-making processes of taxpayers are affected by social interactions (e.g. Kim (2003), Fortin et al. (2007), Eisenhauer (2008), Dell'Anno (2009), Traxler (2010)). The vast majority of this literature is restricted to developed economies though. Among the few exceptions, Castro and Scartascini (2015) examine individual taxpayers' compliance in a large field experiment in Argentina. They report that compliance significantly increases with stricter deterrence, while no effect of moral appeals is found.

Finally, the literature has stressed that the role of third-party reporting to verify taxpayer self-reports is critical for tax enforcement (see Kleven et al. (2011) for the seminal work). However, Carrillo et al. (2017) show that there may be limits to the effectiveness of third-party information in developing countries if taxpayers can easily substitute misreporting to less verifiable margins. The authors provide strong empirical evidence for substitution behaviour by exploiting a natural experiment and rich tax return data for Ecuador. Specifically, they show that when firms are notified by the tax authority about detected revenue discrepancies on previously filed corporate income tax returns they increase reported revenues, matching the third-party estimate

---

3 Additionally, sending out letters manipulating audit propensities may not allow to isolate audit effects, as the letters could be perceived as unfriendly, causing a reluctant reaction from taxpayers because of the unfriendly communication and not just due to deterrence itself (see e.g. Gangl et al. (2014)). The literature has moreover stressed that the effect of deterrence instruments on income reporting may in fact be ambiguous as deterrence instruments may crowd out the intrinsic motivation of paying taxes (see e.g. Feld and Frey (2002), Torgler (2002), Kirchler et al. (2008), Gangl et al. (2014)).

when provided. Firms also increase reported costs though, by 96 cents for every dollar of revenue adjustment, consequently resulting in only minor increases in total tax collection.

Best et al. (2015) moreover emphasize the role of the structure of the tax system in raising income reporting. Specifically, the authors assess Pakistani firms' tax evasion under profit and turnover taxation over 2006–2010. Their bunching estimates show that turnover taxes reduce tax evasion by 60–70% of all corporate income, compared to profit taxes. They estimate that switching from profit taxation to turnover taxation increases corporate tax revenues by 74%, without reducing aggregate after-tax profits, making turnover taxes a viable policy instruments in low-enforcement environments.

Along similar lines, Fuest and Riedel (2009) discuss the role of tax expenditures which are extensively granted in many developing countries, e.g. in the form of tax credits, exemptions, exclusions, deferrals and allowances. The authors stress that these expenditures can be a possible source for tax avoidance and tax evasion, especially in the context of emerging countries where due to a lack of appropriate fiscal transparency and political accountability, tax expenditures are less visible and difficult to control. This may increase the scope for corruptive behaviour of tax administrators and raise lobbying behaviour of interest groups. However, tax expenditures policies can obviously, on the other hand, also benefit countries, e.g. by allowing them to discriminate tax rates between taxpayers that differ in international mobility or are more or less prone to engage in avoidance and evasion.

Finally, countries have introduced measures to hedge against multinational tax avoidance activities. For example many countries around the world introduced anti profit-shifting legislation designed to limit income shifting from their borders to lower-tax countries. Büttner et al. (2012) and Blouin et al. (2014) assess the role of thin-capitalization rules, which limit the scope of interest deductions from the corporate tax base if the firm's (internal) debt-to-equity rate is considered to be excessive. The authors report that thin-capitalization rules decrease the incentive to use internal debt for tax planning by multinationals (but at the same time imply higher external debt holdings of multinational affiliates).

Ruf and Weichenrieder (2012, 2013) and Egger et al. (2015) moreover determine the effectiveness of so-called controlled foreign company (CFC) laws in limiting profit-shifting behaviour. CFC laws make income from passive sources (e.g. interest or royalties) earned in tax havens taxable at the multinational firm's parent location. Therefore, these rules reduce incentives to shift income to low-tax entities. In line with this notion, existing papers report a reduction (increase) in passive and active investment holdings at low-tax locations in response to a tightening (loosening) of CFC legislations in the parent's host country.

Finally, Lohse and Riedel (2012) and Beer and Loeprick (2015) present evidence suggesting that profit-shifting activities within multinational entities have been effectively curbed by the introduction and tightening of so-called transfer pricing legislations, which require multinational firms to document that their transfer prices adhere to the arm's length principle (based on pre-determined methods).

In general, all cited studies on governments' anti profit-shifting instruments, however, focus on the developed world. Evidence on the effectiveness of the measures in diminishing income shifting from developing countries is to the best of our knowledge, in turn, still missing.

Moreover, to fight the evasion of capital income taxes through offshore wealth holdings, policy makers have put great faith in information exchange agreements, presuming that they raise detection probabilities and facilitate the prosecution of tax evasion. During the financial crisis, G20 countries e.g. compelled tax havens to sign bilateral treaties providing for exchange of bank information under the threat of economic sanctions. Policymakers have celebrated this global initiative as the end of bank secrecy (see Johannesen and Zucman (2014)). The empirical evidence, however, challenges the presumption that such agreements are effective in limiting offshore wealth holdings. A recent paper by Johannesen and Zucman (2014) finds only a moderate effect of information exchange treaties on deposits in tax havens, indicating that individuals, instead of repatriating deposits, choose to relocate their assets to tax havens not covered by the agreements. This may relate to the fact that, under the G20 provision, tax havens had to sign 12 bilateral treaties only to be whitelisted (many havens have signed contracts with other havens to meet this requirement). Moreover, some taxpayers may not have adjusted their perceived detection probability and hence continued holding their deposits in the tax havens. If information is not exchanged automatically but upon request (as implemented in most tax treaties), agreements are moreover of limited use for tax authorities without prior knowledge about potential tax evaders.

A second prominent strategy to address tax evasion through offshore wealth holdings are tax amnesties or voluntary disclosure programs under which taxpayers can bring their assets home without being prosecuted. Langenmayr (2017) shows theoretically and empirically that permanent voluntary disclosure programs increase tax evasion (as individuals anticipate that they can bring their money back in the future). Governments may nevertheless benefit from these programs as they may lead to higher tax revenues if fining taxpayers is associated with high administrative costs.[4]

Empirical analysis – responses of pre-tax profitability to corporate tax rate changes

As previously described, evidence on tax evasion and avoidance in developing countries is scarce. In the following, we will make use of rich firm-level data to empirically assess corporate income shifting from developing countries and emerging economies.

Data

The empirical analysis relies on the Orbis database provided by Bureau van Dijk (version: August 2014, including middle, large and very large firms). The data offers rich accounting and ownership information on companies worldwide between 2004 and 2013. Since the aim of this section is to assess tax-motivated international income shifting by multinational firms in emerging markets and developing countries, we restrict the data to firms in middle and lower income countries (following the World Bank classification) and to multinational entities, defined as firms that are either majority-owned by a firm in a foreign country or have at least one majority-owned subsidiary in a foreign country.[5] A distribution of firms and observations across countries is presented in Table 15.1. In total, the sample comprises information on 19,582 firms and 55,544 firm-years in 38 countries. Please see Table 15.1 for the country distribution. The analysis draws on panel data for the years 2004 to 2013. Note that our version of the database

---

4   The prior literature noted that short-run programs may be ineffective in raising tax revenues as the existence of temporary amnesties deteriorates credible announcements of stricter enforcement in future periods (see Stella (1991) for a theoretical model and Alm and Beck (1993) for empirical evidence).

5   Note that, while accounting data in Orbis is available in panel format, ownership information has a cross-sectional dimension and is available for the last reported date only. We hence assume that firms that belonged to multinational entities in 2013 did so over the whole sample period. Following this strategy, we might misclassify some national firm-years as multinational firm-years. As national firms plausibly have no or only very limited options to engage in international income shifting, our estimates are hence a lower bound to the true effect.

Table 15.1 Country Statistics – Firm-Years per Country

Argentina	295
Bosnia and Herzegovina	2,864
Bangladesh	19
Brazil	578
Botswana	7
Cote d'Ivoire	9
Chile	16
China	10,695
Colombia	17
Dominican Republic	1
Ecuador	7
Fiji	15
Guatemala	1
Indonesia	11
India	369
Jordan	2
Kazakhstan	27
Sri Lanka	35
Moldova	14
Macedonia	141
Mauritius	2
Mexico	306
Malaysia	1,087
Nicaragua	2
Panama	1
Peru	26
Philippines	151
Paraguay	4
Serbia	6,547
Russian Federation	21,336
Thailand	1,093
Turkey	35
Trinidad and Tobago	1
Tanzania	2
Ukraine	9,407
Uruguay	3
Vietnam	416
South Africa	2
Sum	55,544

Notes: The table displays the firm-year observations per country.

comprises middle and large companies in the developing world only and that sample coverage moreover varies widely across countries, implying that our results – while offering insights in the avoidance and evasion behaviour of firms in developing countries – may not allow to draw conclusions on profit shifting in the population of firms in the developing world.

Table 15.2 presents descriptive statistics for our sample firms. On average, the firms in our sample are subject to a corporate tax rate of 22.5%, varying between 0% and 36.6%. The average firm moreover has around 19.8 million US dollars in total assets, employs 212 employees

Table 15.2 Descriptive Statistics

Variable	No. of Obs.	Mean	Std. Dev.	Min	Max
Corporate Tax Rate	55,544	.2251	.0656	0	.3659
Total Assets (in Tsd. US Dollars)	55,544	19,810.27	30,795.86	3	162,671
Employment	55,544	211.6913	297.1686	1	1635
Pre-tax Profit	55,544	2509.609	6285.246	1	162,851
Pre-tax Profitability	55,544	.1496	.1855	6.73e – 06	2
GDPpC	55,544	4212.915	1939.916	453.1125	14,143.93
GDP Growth	55,544	5.6361	4.6692	-14.8	14.195
GDP	55,544	1.03e+12	1.18e+12	3.01e+09	4.56e+12
WB Corruption Index	55,544	29.6049	13.1912	8.7805	91.3876
WB Political Stability	55,544	27.179	10.9637	.9615	88.1517
Tax Administration Staff	55,544	.8917	.3714	.0260	1.3184

Notes: Corporate tax rate stands for the statutory corporate tax rate in the firm's host country and was drawn from publications in the corporate tax guides of KPMG. Total assets and Employment depict the total assets (in thousands of US dollars) and the number of employees downloaded from Bureau van Dijk's Orbis data base in August 2014 (middle, large, very large firms). Pre-tax Profit and Pre-tax Profitability stand for the pre-tax profits of firms and its pre-tax profitability defined as pre-tax profits over total assets and are equally drawn from Bureau van Dijk's Orbis database. GDPpC, GDP Growth and GDP depict the gross domestic income per capita, the growth rate of gross domestic income and overall gross domestic income and are drawn from the World Bank's World Development Indicators. WB Corruption Index and WB Political stability furthermore stand for the World Bank's corruption and political stability index and are taken from the World Bank's governance database. Finally, Tax Administration Staff depict the number of tax administrators per 1,000 inhabitants and was provided by US aid.

and earns about 2.5 million US dollars in pre-tax profits. The average pre-tax profitability is 15%. Note that the baseline analysis ignores firms with negative pre-tax profits. In doing so, we follow much of the previous literature, which restricts its view to profitable firms, arguing that international profit-shifting incentives are most pronounced for this subgroup. We will expand our sample by loss-making firms in a robustness check. To avoid results driven by outliers and in order to reduce measurement error, we furthermore drop firm-year observations with a pre-tax profitability beyond 200%. Table 15.2 presents descriptive statistics for further host country characteristics, namely GDP per capita, GDP, GDP growth, the World Bank's corruption and political stability index (drawn from the World Development Indicators database and the World Bank's governance data respectively). Finally, tax administration staff is the number of tax administrators per one thousand inhabitants, provided in panel format by USAID.

Empirical model

We rely on an indirect approach to ferret out the scope of corporate tax avoidance in the developing world. Namely, we follow much of the previous research (see e.g. Dharmapala (2014)) that assesses multinational income shifting to low-tax countries by testing for a causal effect of host country corporate tax rates (or the corporate tax rate differential to other entities within the same group) on firms' reported pre-tax profits. As pre-tax profits is a comprehensive measure for the aggregate corporate tax base, the approach captures corporate profit shifting through different channels, comprising the distortion of intra-firm transfer prices as well as intra-firm debt shifting and the strategic location of intangible assets at low-tax affiliates. Note that many of these income shifting strategies remain within the boundary of the law and hence reflect avoidance rather than evasion behaviour, although the line between the two concepts is certainly blurry. Formally, we estimate a model of the following form

$$PBT_{it} = \alpha + \beta \tau_{it} + \gamma X_{it} + \theta_i + \rho_t + \epsilon_{it}$$

where PBT_{it} represents the pre-tax profit of firm i at time t. τ_{it} captures the host country's corporate tax rate, X_{it} is a vector of control variables, comprising firm characteristics, namely the input factors into the production process (total assets and the number of employees), and the host country characteristics, namely GDP, GDP per capita, GDP growth, the corruption indicators and proxy variables for tax authority staffing described previously. The empirical model furthermore includes a full set of firm fixed effects and year fixed effects to filter out time constant heterogeneity in reported pre-tax profits across firms and common shocks to the corporate tax base over time. Finally, we assess the robustness of our findings to clustering at different levels. The main specifications allow for clustering at the country-year level. In robustness checks, we also assess the sensitivity to clustering at the firm and 2-digit industry levels respectively. Moreover note that since changes in corporate taxes impose a common shock to firms in the same country, clustering at the country level may appear warranted, but is tempered with the concern of a less than reasonable number of clusters in the context of our study. We thus follow Bertrand et al. (2004) and Cameron et al. (2011) and present robustness checks, which account for two-way clustering of errors at the country-year and firm level.

Empirical results

The empirical results presented in Table 15.3 indeed point to a negative correlation between firms' pre-tax profits and host country corporate tax rates. Specification (1) regresses reported pre-tax profits on total assets and the number of employees, the country controls described in the notes of Table 15.2 and a full set of firm and year fixed effects. In line with previous research, we find a negative and statistically significant effect of corporate tax rate changes on the pre-tax profit reported by multinational firms. The semi-elasticity amounts to -1.7, suggesting that an increase in the corporate tax rate by 1 percentage point lowers the reported pre-tax profits by around 1.7%. Note that the estimate tends to be larger than prior findings for developed economies. As described in the literature review, Heckemeyer and Overesch (2013) report a consensus estimate of -0.8, which amounts to about half the size of our estimate. This qualitative and quantitative finding is robust to controlling for industry-year fixed effects (at the 1-digit level), see specification (2). As the sample is dominated by firms in China, Russia and Ukraine, we furthermore assess the sensitivity of our findings to excluding corporations from these countries in specifications (3)–(5). The coefficient estimates for the tax rate variable are strikingly robust to these sample adjustments. Excluding China and Russia increases the coefficient estimate for the corporate tax rate variable, suggesting that a 1 percentage point rise in the tax rate lowers the reported pre-tax profit by around 2%.

Specifications (1) and (2) of Table 15.4 furthermore reestimate the baseline model in column (2) of Table 15.3, accounting for clustering at the firm and two-digit industry levels respectively. The model in Column (3) moreover accounts for two-way clustering at the firm and country-year level. These modifications do not affect the significance of our results.

Table 15.3 Baseline Results

	(1)	*(2)*	*(3)*	*(4)*	*(5)*
Corporate Tax	−1.678★★★	−1.622★★★	−1.913★★★	−1.565★★★	−2.064★★★
Rate	(0.403)	(0.443)	(0.460)	(0.344)	(0.436)
Log Total Assets	0.652★★★	0.649★★★	0.640★★★	0.706★★★	0.627★★★
	(0.0194)	(0.0191)	(0.0191)	(0.0197)	(0.0198)
Log Employment	0.262★★★	0.274★★★	0.274★★★	0.192★★★	0.313★★★
	(0.0299)	(0.0280)	(0.0307)	(0.0180)	(0.0313)
Log GDPpC	1.471	0.974	1.837	2.498★★	2.853★★
	(1.415)	(1.562)	(1.581)	(1.014)	(1.180)
GDP Growth	−0.00483	−0.00423	−0.00348	−0.000444	0.0153
	(0.00411)	(0.00448)	(0.00551)	(0.00344)	(0.0104)
Log GDP	−1.092	−0.696	−1.380	−2.498★★★	−2.450★★
	(1.334)	(1.483)	(1.334)	(0.932)	(1.119)
WB Corruption	−0.0175★★★	−0.0164★★★	−0.0177★★★	−0.00571	−0.0134★★★
Index	(0.00394)	(0.00430)	(0.00443)	(0.00375)	(0.00382)
WB Political	−0.00111	−0.00140	−0.00177	−0.00645★★	0.000210
Stability	(0.00311)	(0.00342)	(0.00374)	(0.00272)	(0.00328)
Tax	−0.191	−0.0953	−0.694★★★	0.229	0.0196
Administration	(0.125)	(0.153)	(0.240)	(0.151)	(0.143)
Staff					
Sample	All	All	No CN	No RU	No UA
Firm Fixed	Yes	Yes	Yes	Yes	Yes
Effects					
Year Fixed	Yes	Yes	Yes	Yes	Yes
Effects					
Clustering	Ctry–Year	Ctry–Year	Ctry–Year	Ctry–Year	Ctry–Year
Industry–Year FE		Yes			
N	55,544	54,942	44,741	33,606	45,535

Notes: ★, ★★, ★★★ indicate significance at the 10%, 5%, 1% level. The observational unit in all regressions is multinational firm i at time t. The dependent variable is the natural log of pre-tax profits throughout all specifications. For a definition of the control variables, see the notes to Table 1. All specifications account for clustering at the country-year level and include a full set of firm and year fixed effects. Specification (2) moreover includes a full set of industry year fixed effects at the 1-digit level. "No CN", "No RU" and "No UA" moreover indicates that China, Russia and the Ukraine were excluded from the regression respectively.

Specification (4) reestimates the baseline model using the pre-tax profitability of firms (defined as pre-tax profits over total assets) as the dependent variable. Again, the results point to a quantitatively important effect, suggesting that an increase in the corporate tax rate by 10 percentage points lowers the pre-tax profitability of firms by around 1 percentage point, or 6.6% evaluated at the sample mean. Specification (5) reruns the same model (with pre-tax profitability as dependent variable) augmenting the sample by loss-making firms. In line with intuition, this lowers the coefficient estimate for the corporate tax rate variable and renders it statistically not different from zero, which is in line with the presumption that loss-making firms have less incentives to shift income from high-tax to low-tax countries (as the loss-making affiliates become 'tax-havens' within the group which changes tax-motivated income shifting incentives).

Table 15.4 Robustness Checks

Dependent Variable	(1) Log Profit	(2) Log Profit	(3) Log Profit	(4) Profitability	(5) Profitability	(6) Log Profit	(7) Log Profit
Corporate Tax Rate	-1.622***	-1.622***	-1.622***	-0.0982***	-0.0635	-2.126***	-0.954
	(0.343)	(0.322)	(0.494)	(0.0314)	(0.0761)	(0.516)	(0.613)
Log Total Assets	0.649***	0.649***	0.649***			0.728***	0.645***
	(0.0147)	(0.0333)	(0.0214)			(0.0398)	(0.0230)
Log Employment	0.274***	0.274***	0.274***	0.00717**	0.0196***	0.248***	0.278***
	(0.0170)	(0.0225)	(0.0300)	(0.00301)	(0.00292)	(0.0393)	(0.0343)
Log GDPpC	0.974	0.974	0.974	-0.0779	0.144	1.755	-1.323
	(1.198)	(1.573)	(1.745)	(0.132)	(0.213)	(1.406)	(3.592)
GDP Growth	-0.00423	-0.00423	-0.00423	-0.000793**	0.00138*	0.000915	-0.00250
	(0.00314)	(0.00390)	(0.00472)	(0.000378)	(0.000798)	(0.00487)	(0.00519)
Log GDP	-0.696	-0.696	-0.696	0.0821	-0.156	-1.530	0.747
	(1.085)	(1.543)	(1.641)	(0.126)	(0.196)	(1.327)	(3.230)
TPI Corruption Index	-0.0164***	-0.0164***	-0.0164***	-0.00136***	0.000407	-0.0137**	-0.0106**
	(0.00252)	(0.00283)	(0.00456)	(0.000340)	(0.000672)	(0.00536)	(0.00475)
Polstability Stability	-0.00140	-0.00140	-0.00140	0.0000477	-0.000916	-0.00543	0.000862
	(0.00226)	(0.00261)	(0.00363)	(0.000241)	(0.000568)	(0.00372)	(0.00448)
Tax Administration Staff	-0.0953	-0.0953	-0.0953	-0.0308**	-0.00972	-0.0776	-0.0425
	(0.111)	(0.142)	(0.164)	(0.0141)	(0.0211)	(0.149)	(0.275)
Sample	All	All	All	All	Incl. Loss Mak.	Large Firms	Small Firms
Firm Fixed Effects	Yes	Yes	Yes	Yes	Yes	Yes	Yes
Industry–Year Fixed Effects	Yes	Yes	Yes	Yes	Yes	Yes	Yes
Clustering	Firm	Industry	Two–Way	Ctry–Year	Ctry–Year	Ctry–Year	Ctry–Year
N	54,942	54,942	49,076	54,551	75,942	27,402	27,540

Notes: *, **, *** indicate significance at the 10%, 5%, 1% level. The observational unit in all regressions is multinational firm i at time t. The dependent variable is the natural log of pre-tax profits in Specifications (1)–(3) and (6)–(7) and pre-tax profitability in Specifications (4) and (5). For a definition of the control variables, see the notes to Table 1. The specifications account for clustering at the country-year level ('Ctry–Year'), firm ('firm') and industry ('industry') level. In Specification (3), we implement two-way clustering at the ctry-year and firm level. All specifications include a full set of firm and year fixed effects.

Finally, the specifications in columns (6) and (7) follow the notion that profit-shifting incentives and costs vary across firms. Specifically, a number of recent papers claim that firm size is a major predictor of the scope of multinational profit-shifting activities. Davies et al. (2017) e.g. find that significant tax-motivated mispricing of intra-firm trade is largely restricted to a few hundred very large firms in France. Evidence along the same lines is reported in Egger et al. (2015). Following these studies, we reestimate the link between corporate tax rates and reported pre-tax profits in subsamples of large and small firms (determined as firms with above and below average total assets). In line with the prior evidence, we find that reported pre-tax profits of large multinational firms react more sensitively to changes in the corporate tax rate than reported pre-tax profits of smaller entities. In the large-firm sample, the semi-elasticity is -2.1, while in the small-firm sample it amounts to a statistically insignificant semi-elasticity of -1.0. The findings hence suggest that, conditional on real activity, larger firms respond to a corporate tax rate increase by 10 percentage points with a reduction in their reported taxable income by 21% (presumed to be transferred to other lower-tax affiliates within the multinational group by means of transfer pricing, debt shifting or the strategic location of intangible assets). Note that, since developing countries often grant special tax incentives to multinational firms, our estimates may be affected by measurement error. Specifically, observed changes in statutory corporate tax rates may exceed changes in actual corporate tax rates of multinational firms, implying that the previous estimate is a lower bound to the true effect.

Conclusion

The aim of this chapter was to review the literature on tax evasion and avoidance in the developing world. The topic is of high importance as developing countries struggle with low tax-to-GDP ratios and hence lack resources for the provision of public goods and services. Tax noncompliance moreover not only hampers revenue collection but also undermines the fairness of the tax system. Furthermore, Feldman and Slemrod (2007: 327) stress that noncompliance in the form of tax evasion and avoidance "also imposes economic costs because taxpayers expend resources to facilitate evasion and the tax agency expends resources to contain it".

The academic literature that quantifies tax evasion and avoidance activities in the developing world (beyond the wide array of anecdotal evidence) has, in turn, struggled with a lack of appropriate micro data that allows for a rigorous assessment. Specifically, while avoidance and evasion activities are difficult to identify in any setting, since taxpayers try to hide these activities from the public and from authorities, the majority of existing approaches has drawn on aggregate indicators and used strategies that built on strong (and non-testable) identification assumptions. The approaches have hence been subject to criticism and it appears fair to say that they provide rough estimates at best.

High-quality microeconomic data (e.g. tax audit data on corporate tax returns) offers a more promising road to quantify the size of the tax gap in the developing world and to assess its determinants. Such data is slowly becoming available to researchers. A number of papers have presented convincing micro-data evidence suggesting a link between corporate tax rates and taxpayers' evasion practices (Waseem (2015)) or questioning the effectiveness of third-party reporting in limiting tax evasion in developing countries (Carrillo et al. (2014)). In this chapter, we also present micro-evidence on tax-motivated multinational income shifting from the developing world. More research along these lines is needed to increase our understanding of the scope and determinants of evasion and avoidance behaviour in the developing world and to learn about the effectiveness of countermeasures.

References

Allingham, M. G., and Sandmo, A. (1972). "Income tax evasion: A theoretical analysis", *Journal of Public Economics*, 1, 323–38.

Alm, J., and Beck, W. (1993). "Tax amnesties and compliance in the long run: A time series analysis", *National Tax Journal*, 46(1), 53–60.

Alm, J., and McClellan, C. (2012). "Tax morale and tax compliance from a firm's perspective", *Kyklos*, 65(1), 1–17.

Bayer, R. C. (2006). "A contest with the taxman – the impact of tax rates on tax evasion and wastefully invested resources", *European Economic Review*, 50(5), 1071–104.

Beer, S., and Loeprick, J. (2015). "Profit shifting: Drivers of transfer (Mis)pricing and the potential of countermeasures", *International Tax and Public Finance*, 22(3), 426–51.

Bertrand, M., Duflo, E., and Mullainathan, S. (2004). "How much should we trust differences-in-differences estimates?", *Quarterly Journal of Economics*, 119(1), 249–75.

Besley, T. J., and Persson, T. (2013). "Taxation and development", *Handbook of Public Economics*, 5, 51–110.

Best, M. C., Brockmeyer, A., Kleven, H. J., Spinnewijn, J., and Waseem, M. (2015). "Production versus revenue efficiency with limited tax capacity: Theory and evidence from Pakistan", *Journal of Political Economy*, 123(6), 1311–55.

Blouin, J. L., Huizinga, H., Laeven, L., and Nicodème, G. (2014). "Thin capitalization rules and multinational firm capital structure", IMF Working Paper No. 14.

Blumenthal, M., Christian, C., and Slemrod, J. (2001). "Do normative appeals affect tax compliance? Evidence from a controlled experiment in Minnesota", *National Tax Journal*, 54, 125–36.

Breusch, T. (2005). "Estimating underground economic activity using MIMIC models", Econometrics 0507003, EconWPA.

Buettner, T., and Wamser, G. (2013). "Internal debt and multinational profit shifting: Empirical evidence from firm-level panel data", *National Tax Journal*, 66(1), 63–95.

Büttner, T., Schreiber, U., Overesch, M., and Wamser, G. (2012). "The impact of thin-capitalization rules on multinationals", *Journal of Public Economics*, 96(11–12), 930–8.

Cagan, P. (1958). "The demand for currency relative to the total money supply", *Journal of Political Economy*, 66(3), 302–28.

Cameron, A. C., Gelbach, J. B., and Miller, D. L. (2011). "Robust inference with multiway clustering", *Journal of Business & Economic Statistics*, 29(2), 238–49.

Carrillo, P., Pomeranz, D., and Singhal, M. 2017. "Dodging the taxman: Firm misreporting and limits to tax enforcement", *American Economic Journal: Applied Economics*, 9(2), 144–64.

Castro, L., and Scartascini, C. (2015). "Tax compliance and enforcement in the pampas evidence from a field experiment", *Journal of Economic Behavior & Organization*, 116, 65–82.

Clausing, K. A. (2003). "Tax-motivated transfer pricing and US intrafirm trade prices", *Journal of Public Economics*, 87, 2207–23.

Cowell, F. A., and Gordon, J. P. F. (1988). "Unwillingness to pay: Tax evasion and public good provision", *Journal of Public Economics*, 36(3), 305–21.

Cristea, A. D., and Nguyen, D.X. (2016). "Transfer Pricing by Multinational Firms: New Evidence from Foreign Firm Ownerships", *American Economic Journal: Economic Policy*, 8(3), 170–202.

Crivelli, E., de Mooij, R.A., and Keen, M. (2016). "Base erosion, profit shifting and developing countries", *FinanzArchiv: Public Finance Analysis*, 72(3), 268–301.

Davies, R. B., Martin, J., Parenti, M., and Toubal, F. (2017). "Knocking on tax haven's door: Multinational firms and transfer pricing", *Review of Economics and Statistics*, forthcoming.

De Paula, Á., and Scheinkman, J.A. (2011). "The informal sector: An equilibrium model and some empirical evidence from Brazil", *Review of Income and Wealth*, 57, S8–S26.

Dell'Anno, R. (2009). "Tax evasion, tax morale and policy maker's effectiveness", *Journal of Socio-Economics*, 38(6), 988–97.

Dharmapala, D. (2014). "What do we know about base erosion and profit shifting? A review of the empirical literature", *Fiscal Studies*, 35, 421–48.

Easterly, W., and Rebelo, S. (1993). "Marginal income tax rates and economic growth in developing countries", *European Economic Review*, 37(2), 409–17.

Egger, P., Keuschnigg, C., Merlo, V., and Wamser, G. (2014). "Corporate taxes and internal borrowing within multinational firms", *American Economic Journal: Economic Policy*, 6(2), 54–93.

Egger, P., Merlo, V., and Wamser, G. (2015). "Unobserved tax avoidance and the tax elasticity of FDI", *Journal of Economic Behavior & Organization*, 108(2014), 1–18.

Eisenhauer, J. G. (2008). "Ethical preferences, risk aversion, and taxpayer behavior", *Journal of Socio-Economics*, 37, 45–63.

Feld, L. P., and Frey, B. S. (2002). "Trust breeds trust: How taxpayers are treated", *Economics of Governance*, 3(2), 87–99.

Feldman, N., and Slemrod, J. (2007). "Estimating tax noncompliance with evidence from unaudited tax returns", *Economic Journal*, 117(518), 327–52.

Fellner, G., Sausgruber, R., and Traxler, C. (2013). "Testing enforcement strategies in the field: Threat, moral appeal and social information", *Journal of the European Economic Association*, 11(3), 634–60.

Fortin, B., Lacroix, G., and Villeval, M. C. (2007). "Tax evasion and social interactions", *Journal of Public Economics*, 91(11–12), 2089–112.

Fuest, C., Hebous, S., and Riedel, N. (2011). "International debt shifting and multinational firms in developing economies", *Economics Letters*, 113(2), 135–8.

Fuest, C., and Riedel, N. (2009). "Tax evasion, tax avoidance and tax expenditures in developing countries", Working Papers, Oxford University Centre for Business Taxation.

Gangl, K., Torgler, B., Kirchler, E., and Hofmann, E. (2014). "Effects of supervision on tax compliance: Evidence from a field experiment in Austria", *Economics Letters*, 123(3), 378–82.

Gordon, J. P. (1989). "Individual morality and reputation costs as deterrents to tax evasion", *European Economic Review*, 33(4), 797–805.

Gordon, R., and Li, W. (2009). "Tax structures in developing countries: Many puzzles and a possible explanation", *Journal of Public Economics*, 93(7–8), 855–66.

Griffith, R., Miller, H., and O'Connell, M. (2014). "Ownership of intellectual property and corporate taxation", *Journal of Public Economics*, 112, 12–23.

Gutmann, P. (1977). "The subterranean economy", *Financial Analyst Journal*, 34(1), 24–7.

Hasseldine, J., Hite, P., Simon, J., and Toumi, M. (2007). "Persuasive communication: Tax compliance enforcement strategies for sole proprietors", *Contemporary Accounting Research*, 24(1), 171–94.

Heckemeyer, J. H., and Overesch, M. (2013). "Multinationals' profit response to tax differentials: Effect size and shifting channels", ZEW Discussion Papers 13-045.

International Monetary Fund (2011). "Revenue mobilization in developing countries". Available at www.imf.org/external/np/pp/eng/2011/030811.pdf

Johannesen, N., and Zucman, G. (2014). "The end of bank secrecy? An evaluation of the G20 tax haven crackdown", *American Economic Journal: Economic Policy*, 6(1), 65–91.

Karkinsky, T., and Riedel, N. (2012). "Corporate taxation and the choice of patent location within multinational firms", *Journal of International Economics*, 88(1), 176–85.

Kaufmann, D., and Kaliberda, A. (1996). "Integrating the unofficial economy into the dynamics of postsocialist economies: A framework of analysis and evidence", Policy Research Working Paper Series 1691, The World Bank.

Kim, Y. (2003). "Income distribution and equilibrium multiplicity in a stigma-based model of tax evasion", *Journal of Public Economics*, 87(9), 1591–616.

Kirchler, E., Hoelzl, E., and Wahl, I. (2008). "Enforced versus voluntary tax compliance: The 'slippery slope' framework", *Journal of Economic Psychology*, 29(2), 210–25.

Kleven, H. J., Knudsen, M. B., Kreiner, C. T., Pedersen, S., and Saez, E. (2011). "Unwilling or unable to cheat? Evidence from a tax audit experiment in Denmark", *Econometrica*, 79(3), 651–92.

La Porta, R., and Shleifer, A. (2008). "The unofficial economy and economic development", *Brookings Papers on Economic Activity*, 2008, 275–352.

Langenmayr, D. (2017). "Voluntary disclosure of evaded taxes – increasing revenue, or increasing incentives to evade?", *Journal of Public Economics*, 151, 110–25.

Lohse, T., and Riedel, N. (2012). "The impact of transfer pricing regulations on profit shifting within European multinationals", FZID Discussion Papers 61-2012, University of Hohenheim, Center for Research on Innovation and Services (FZID).

Mascagni, G., Moore, M., and McCluskey, R. (2014). "Tax revenue mobilisation in developing countries: Issues and challenges", European Parliament, EXPO/B/DEVE/2013/35, April.

Myles, G. D., and Naylor, R. A. (1996). "A model of tax evasion with group conformity and social customs", *European Journal of Political Economy*, 12(1), 49–66.

OECD (2002a). Measuring the Non-Observed Economy – A Handbook. Paris: OECD.

OECD (2002b). "Measuring the non-observed economy", Statistics-Brief No. 5, November.

Ruf, M., and Weichenrieder, A. (2012). "The taxation of passive foreign investment – lessons from German experience", *Canadian Journal of Economics*, 45(4), 1504–28.

Ruf, M., and Weichenrieder, A. (2013). "CFC legislation, passive assets and the impact of the ECJ's Cadbury-Schweppes decision", CESifo Working Paper Series 4461.

Sabirianova Peter, K., Buttrick, S., and Duncan, D. (2010). "Global reform of personal income taxation, 1981–2005: Evidence from 189 countries", *National Tax Journal*, 63(3), 447–78.

Schneider, F. (2005). "Shadow economies of 145 countries all over the world: What do we really know?", *European Journal of Political Economy*, 21(3), 598–642.

Slemrod, J., Blumenthal, M., and Charles, C. (2001). "Taxpayer response to an increased probability of audit: Evidence from a controlled experiment in Minnesota", *Journal of Public Economics*, 79, 455–83.

Slemrod, J., and Yitzhaki, S. (2002). "Tax avoidance, evasion and administration", in A. J. Auerbach and M. Feldstein (eds), *Handbook of Public Economics*, Vol. 3, 1st ed., Ch. 22, 1423–70.

Stella, P. (1991). "An economic analysis of tax amnesties", *Journal of Public Economics*, 46, 383–400.

Tanzi, V. (1983). "The underground economy in the United States: Annual estimates, 1930–1980", *IMF Staff Papers*, 30(2), 283–305.

Torgler, B. (2002). "Speaking to theorists and searching for facts: Tax morale and tax compliance in experiments", *Journal of Economic Surveys*, 16, 657–84.

Torgler, B. (2003). "Tax morale, rule-governed behaviour and trust", *Economics of Governance*, 14(2), 119–40.

Torgler, B. (2004). "Moral suasion: An alternative tax policy strategy? Evidence from a controlled field experiment in Switzerland", *Economics of Governance*, 5(3), 235–53.

Traxler, C. (2010). "Social norms and conditional cooperative taxpayers", *European Journal of Political Economy*, 26(1), 89–103.

Waseem, M. (2015). "Taxes, informality and income shifting: Evidence from a recent Pakistani tax reform", Available at SSRN: https://ssrn.com/abstract=2803919

Zucman, G. (2013). "The missing wealth of nations: Are Europe and the U.S. net debtors or net creditors?", *Quarterly Journal of Economics*, 128(3), 1321–64.

16

TRADE MISINVOICING

Volker Nitsch

Introduction

A common and frequent feature of many fraudulent acts is the misdeclaration of economic activities. Income and earnings from illegal businesses, for instance, typically remain unreported to fiscal authorities in order to hide such operations. Expenditures eligible for public fund reimbursement, in contrast, may be overstated to increase transfer revenues. In general, publicly recorded activities may be misreported for a broad range of potential reasons.

Declarations of cross-border trade transactions are not exempt from such misbehavior. Similar to other cases of false reporting, criminal traders face incentives to fake data entries in customs declarations and other official documents for various reasons and along almost every dimension. For instance, the quantity and the value of a shipment may be manipulated to either reduce the payment of customs duties (underinvoicing) or to better take advantage of export subsidies (overinvoicing); a misclassification of products or a misdeclaration of the final destination of a shipment may allow circumventing trade restrictions. Overall, the accuracy of international trade statistics is likely to be compromised, to an unknown degree, by fake transactions.

Misreporting of economic activities is far from being a new phenomenon. It has also been analyzed extensively, especially by statistical offices seeking to produce more reliable statistics. Still, despite the ongoing interest in identifying and correcting for misreporting, misinvoicing of international trade transactions seems to have recently attracted growing attention, for at least three reasons. First, international trade typically accounts for an increasing share of a country's GDP. As trade has become relatively more important, there has also been a growing interest in the precision of the measurement of trade activities.[1] Second, in contrast to other forms of misbehavior, misinvoicing of international trade transactions seems to be, in principle, more easily to detect because of the existence of mirror statistics. Since every cross-border shipment is recorded independently by two separate authorities, at the time of leaving the source country as an export and at the time of arriving in the destination country as an import, any discrepancy

---

1 For instance, when in 2003 the United Kingdom's Office for National Statistics made corrections to trade figures for VAT fraud, real GDP growth for previous years was lowered by up to 0.2 percentage points. Ruffles et al. (2003) provide a more detailed description.

between corresponding data entries may provide a direct indication of misreporting. Finally, it has been argued that trade misinvoicing is a major conduit to move capital unrecorded out of a country. Observed evidence of misinvoicing may therefore serve as a reasonable benchmark estimate of the magnitude of illicit financial flows.

In this chapter, instead of reviewing the literature extensively, I discuss selected issues in the analysis of trade misinvoicing. The remainder of this chapter is structured as follows. In the next section, I examine various motives for the misdeclaration of trade activities. Specifically, it is argued that the broad range of incentives to fake customs declarations provides an important challenge for the empirical assessment of the extent of trade misinvoicing. Consequently, the section after that analyzes the costs and benefits of different empirical approaches to quantify trade misinvoicing, followed by a review of the accuracy and reliability of estimation results that are reported in the literature. Finally, there is a brief conclusion.

Motives

For traders, it may be attractive to manipulate official trade documents along various lines and for various reasons. While individual motives to fake invoices are probably highly diverse, often depending on circumstances, general incentives to misreport trade activities are directly related to a country's trade and fiscal policies. Trade restrictions, for instance, provide an incentive to hide trade activities; trade subsidies, in contrast, imply an incentive to inflate trade values.

Measured by their impact on a country's national trade statistics, then, four types of trade misinvoicing can be distinguished: overinvoicing of exports, underinvoicing of exports, over-invoicing of imports, and underinvoicing of imports. Each type of misinvoicing is observed in practice and documented by both anecdotal evidence and empirical findings.

Export overinvoicing, for instance, is a frequent phenomenon in countries which seek to promote exports by offering tax incentives. Celâsun and Rodrik (1989a, 1989b) provide a detailed account of this form of misbehavior for Turkey. In the early 1980s, a comprehensive package of policy measures was introduced that was explicitly oriented toward encouraging manufactured exports; these measures included export tax rebates, subsidized export credits, and preferential allotment of foreign exchange and duty-free imports. To take advantage of these subsidies, "Turkish entrepreneurs, never too shy in exploiting arbitrage opportunities" (Celâsun and Rodrik, 1989b: 723), changed their invoicing practices; exporters substantially overinvoiced shipments or simply declared exports where none had in fact taken place. Celâsun and Rodrik (1989a: 207) conclude that "a non-negligible share of the increase in exports after 1980 turns out to have been the result of a statistical fiction."

Another form of misinvoicing, underinvoicing of exports, allows fraudulent traders to evade export restrictions. At an extreme, it may be attractive for traders not only to report reduced trade values but also to manipulate official trade documents at even greater scale. Sanctions of countries, for instance, may be circumvented by a misdeclaration of the final destination of a shipment (thereby adding further distortions to a country's trade statistics by effectively overin-voicing its exports to other destinations); export bans on specific products may be bypassed by a misdeclaration of the product category. Fisman and Wei (2009) provide an illustrative exam-ple for this type of misreporting by examining trade for a specific product category, cultural objects, for which exports are often prohibited without permission. Specifically, Fisman and Wei (2009: 83) argue that for this product there is a "stark difference in legality of shipments between importing and exporting countries." Analyzing mirror trade statistics, they find that the observed gap in reported trade figures is highly correlated with corruption levels of exporting countries, with particularly strong effects for artifact-rich countries.

Import overinvoicing is typically observed in product categories with low or zero import tariffs. In practice, fake imports appear in international trade statistics for at least two reasons. First, a large import bill allows producers to lower their domestic profits (which are then subject to lower taxation). Since this strategy comes at the cost of inflated tariff payments, however, the approach only seems reasonable for products which are largely exempt from taxes. Second, overreporting of imports is a direct consequence of misclassification. If imported goods are not declared under the appropriate tariff heading (e.g., in order to evade trade taxes by classifying high-taxed goods as zero-taxed products), imports in the product category that is mistakenly reported in the customs declaration are effectively overreported. Chalendard et al. (2016) document this fraudulent behavior for Madagascar. Noting that the importation of fertilizers, books and some cereals is exempt from tariff and VAT in Madagascar, they find that the import value for these products indeed significantly exceeds the corresponding export value. Overall, their estimates suggest that customs fraud reduced non-oil customs revenues (duties and import value-added tax) in Madagascar by at least 30 percent in 2014, with tariff misclassification (and, consequently, import overinvoicing) accounting for slightly less than one half of these losses.

Finally, the opposite strategy of manipulating customs declarations at the time of arrival, underinvoicing of imports, is probably the most prominent form of trade misreporting, mainly because of its immediate benefits. Since customs duties are typically determined based on the declared value of the article, which may be difficult to verify in practice, undervaluation directly reduces tax payments. Yang (2008) provides an illustrative example that highlights tax evasion behavior of importers. When Philippine customs increased enforcement by hiring private firms to conduct preshipment inspection of imports from a subset of countries, imports from treatment countries shifted to an alternative duty-avoidance method: shipping via duty-exempt export processing zones.

In view of these alternative motives and methods to manipulate customs declarations, it seems difficult to identify a predominant type of misreporting. Country studies suggest that the incentives to fake trade declarations often depend on specific circumstances and, therefore, vary sizably both across countries and over time; these studies typically put strong emphasis on a specific form of misreporting that seems to be particularly relevant for the episode that is analyzed. Still, the findings in Chalendard et al. (2016) and Yang (2008) indicate that underinvoicing of imports to evade payment of import taxes is a frequent and widely used practice of trade misinvoicing.

As a consequence of the diversity in misinvoicing behavior, a general focus on the capital flight motives of trade misreporting seems misguided. Approaches that automatically attribute instances of import overinvoicing and export underinvoicing to illicit financial outflows ignore other (potentially more relevant) motives of traders for this type of misbehavior. More notably, the analysis of import overinvoicing and export underinvoicing covers only a fraction of a country's total trade misinvoicing. Overall, the extent to which intentions to move capital unrecorded out of the country indeed determine trade misinvoicing behavior in practice is unknown. The special interest in trade misinvoicing when quantifying illicit financial flows is mainly motivated by the idea that faking trade declarations is a main conduit for the illicit movement of capital. Beja Jr. (2005: 63), for instance, claims that "trade misinvoicing may be the least risky technique for capital flight."

Empirics

In the literature, various empirical approaches are applied to quantify the extent of trade misinvoicing. While each method has specific strengths and weaknesses, discussed in more detail later, all quantitative results are subject to an important qualification, as not all fraudulent trade activities are taken into account in the analysis.[2] More specifically, the empirical identification of trade misinvoicing practices crucially depends on two features of a trade transaction. First, the transaction has to be recorded somewhere. Trade activities which remain hidden completely from public authorities, often labeled as smuggling, are not considered in the analysis of trade misinvoicing. Second, the trade declaration should have at least some correct entries. For instance, trade misinvoicing is difficult to identify from mirror statistics when the same details are misreported in both the exporting and the importing country. Similarly, a transaction is less suspicious of mispricing when both the value and volume of the transaction are misreported. Overall, given that only an unknown fraction of all misreported trade activities is identified from official statistics, the accuracy of trade misinvoicing estimates also is unknown.

Apart from this general source of uncertainty, estimates of trade misinvoicing are highly sensitive to the type and quality of data that is analyzed. Misinvoicing practices are, in principle, best identified by examining information from individual trade declarations. This highly disaggregated transaction-level data, however, is only rarely available to researchers, especially for the broad range of countries for which data is needed in order to provide a meaningful empirical analysis. Given the lack of data, misinvoicing behavior is often identified from more aggregate trade information which introduces at least two types of problems. First, at a more aggregate level, discrepancies in mirror trade statistics from misinvoiced trade transactions may cancel each other out. At an extreme, a country's reported trade with the rest of the world can be perfectly identical to the corresponding figure of the rest of the world's trade with the country (which would imply that there is no evidence of trade misinvoicing), although there are possibly large differences in mirror trade statistics with individual partners. Second, for the analysis of aggregate data, the set of assumptions that is used for the identification of misinvoicing practices typically becomes even more restrictive (and debatable). In view of these difficulties, estimates of the extent of trade misinvoicing activities often seem to lack any substantive meaning.

Mirror trade statistics

The most prominent method to identify trade misinvoicing is to compare the reported value of a trade transaction in a country with the corresponding entry in the mirror statistics of the partner country. Implicitly, it is assumed that traders have an incentive to misdeclare on only one side of a transaction, while the data entry on the opposite side of the transaction is correct. The difference between the flawed and the correct declaration of a transaction is then interpreted as misinvoicing.

Although this approach seems to be generally intuitive, there are, in practice, a number of critical issues, each having the potential to seriously affect (and possibly distort) quantitative results. As is well known, for instance, discrepancies in mirror trade statistics do not necessarily provide evidence of misinvoicing, but often arise for legitimate statistical reasons, ranging from conceptual differences in the valuation of exports and imports to the redirection of shipments while en route; Nitsch (2012) provides a more comprehensive discussion. To the extent that these factors are not properly taken into consideration in the empirical analysis of mirror trade statistics, estimates of trade misinvoicing are misspecified. Moreover, the often-used practice of applying a plain correction factor to adjust matched export and import values for their different statistical treatment of freight and insurance costs introduces additional distortions; see Nitsch (2015).

---

2   Missing some activities in the analysis does not automatically imply that reported results of trade misinvoicing are a lower bound estimate of misinvoicing activities; observed misinvoicing may still be overestimated.

Another source of concern is the assumption that misinvoicing of trade activities is limited to only one side of a transaction. Fisman and Wei (2009) convincingly make this case for a specific product category, cultural property and antiques. For these goods, traders often face strict export restrictions, with many countries prohibiting the export of cultural objects, while zero import tariffs and the risk of forfeiture (in case of improper declaration) imply strong incentives to truthfully report shipments upon entry. For other goods, however, the difference in reporting incentives between source and destination countries may be less pronounced. At a more aggregate level, it has become common practice to analyze a country's trade only with developed countries, arguing that the trade statistics of these countries are generally more accurate than those in developing countries.[3] While this assumption seems plausible, trade flows between developing countries are not ignored in the analysis, but observed discrepancies in mirror statistics with developed countries are simply scaled up for a country's overall trade; see, for instance, Beja Jr. (2005). Accordingly, observed evidence of misreporting is hypothesized to affect all partners alike, proportional to the partner's share in a country's total trade.

A key concern for the analysis of mirror trade statistics is the common unavailability of transaction-level trade data. In principle, misinvoicing can be identified only if the export and import declarations of a transaction are compared and, therefore, the corresponding entries in mirror trade statistics are successfully matched.[4] Once an inconsistency is detected, it may be possible to figure out the likely reason for the difference in the declarations (allowing for reasonable interpretation of this finding). Any analysis of aggregate trade data, in contrast, produces, by definition, unreliable results, with quantitative outcomes being potentially distorted in either direction. At aggregate levels, for instance, a misclassification of a trade transaction, when a product is reported under different tariff headings in the export and import declarations, may imply a double counting of misinvoicing practices, thereby inflating the overall estimate. Alternatively, the empirical assessment of trade misinvoicing is biased downwards when different types of misinvoicing (that is, overinvoicing in one transaction and underinvoicing in another transaction) simply cancel each other out.

Abnormal prices

Another promising approach to identify trade misinvoicing practices is the analysis of reported unit values in trade declarations. For any given transaction, the manipulation of either trade values or trade quantities (but not both) implies a deviation of the observed unit value from its true value. Consequently, substantial deviations in unit values (i.e., outliers) may be indicative of misinvoicing behavior. Nitsch (2017) provides a more detailed discussion.

Estimates

Global estimates

The most comprehensive assessment of trade misinvoicing practices of countries around the world is provided by the Washington, DC-based advisory organization Global Financial Integrity (GFI), which regularly publishes a report in which various techniques are applied, including

---

3 Potential explanations for this claim range from a better quality of the national statistical service to smaller incentives for a misdeclaration of trade activities.

4 As a result, it is not sufficient to get access to transaction-level trade data from one country (which is typically highly restricted), but the matching procedure requires access to similar data for at least one other country.

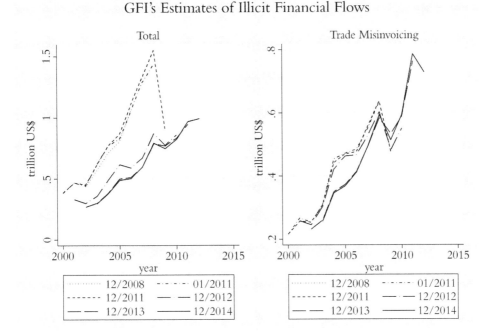

Figure 16.1 Estimates of illicit financial flows.

an empirical analysis of trade misinvoicing, to quantify the magnitude of illicit financial flows from developing countries. GFI's estimates forcefully illustrate the difficulties of applying a very general approach on aggregate trade data to quantify trade misinvoicing.

For instance, for a detailed assessment of quantitative results, it is essential that the estimation outcomes turn out to be reasonably robust. GFI's estimates of illicit financial flows, however, display considerable variation, both across countries and over time, such that a reliable interpretation of the empirical findings seems difficult.

Figure 16.1 examines the stability of GFI's aggregate annual estimates of illicit financial flows from developing countries over time. The plot on the left of Figure 16.1 presents GFI's headline figures of total illicit flows, while that on the right plots the corresponding estimates of illicit financial flows due to trade mispricing. As shown, there seems to be a clear pattern. Typically, illicit financial flows have tended to sizably increase over the sample period; according to GFI's projections, illicit financial flows are estimated to have risen, on average, by about 70 percent over the previous five years. At the same time, however, estimates at the beginning of the sample period have been consistently revised downwards. For instance, the total estimate of illicit financial flows from developing countries in 2003 has been cut by about one half, from 569 billion US dollars in Kar and Cartwright-Smith (2008) to 297 billion US dollars in Kar and Spanjers (2014).[5] In sum, the latest estimate of the annual amount of unrecorded money shifting out of developing

---

5 The majority of this decline is explained by GFI's shift from the World Bank residual method (CED) to the hot money (narrow) approach (HMN). Kar and Freitas (2012, Table 4) compare the estimation results for different methods directly; they report that the change in methodologies has lowered their estimate of illicit financial flows in 2003 from 617 billion US dollars to 359 billion US dollars. Since then, the estimate has been further reduced by 17 percent.

countries has remained relatively stable at around 1 trillion US dollars since GFI's first publication in 2008.

Table 16.1 examines the stability in GFI's estimates for individual countries. GFI has revised the methodology for the estimation of trade misinvoicing, for a selected group of countries, from a country-world comparison to a country-by-country comparison of mirror trade statistics. In addition, trade data has been adjusted for re-exports through Hong Kong.

Table 16.1 confronts the country estimates of illicit financial flows from Kar and Freitas (2012) with the corresponding new estimates from Kar and Spanjers (2014). The shift to a new methodology has, in most cases, dramatic effects on the quantitative estimates for individual countries. At one extreme, illicit outflows from the Russian Federation, which were initially estimated to amount to about 7 billion US dollars in 2009, are now estimated to amount to 123 billion US dollars in 2009, an increase by a factor of 20. At another extreme, the initial estimate of illicit financial outflows from China has been reduced by about 200 billion US

Table 16.1 Estimates of Trade Misinvoicing by Country

	Country-World comparison		Country-by-Country comparison		Difference	
	2009	*Yearly average, 2001–10*	*2009*	*Yearly average, 2003–12*	*2009*	*Yearly averages*
	mn. US$	*mn. US$*	*mn. US$*	*mn. US$*	*%*	*%*
Armenia, Republic of	1,071	523	832	735	-22.3	40.5
Aruba	1,829	2,351	8,034	8,237	339.3	250.4
Belarus	.	.	7,569	8,404	.	.
Brazil	5,795	2,437	21,977	20,549	279.2	743.2
Bulgaria	526	477	886	1,498	68.4	214.0
Chile	939	1,751	3,303	3,957	251.8	126.0
China, P.R.: Mainland	294,726	264,265	98,528	105,726	-66.6	-60.0
Cote d'Ivoire	506	579	1,177	2,297	132.6	296.7
India	0	11,999	28,723	43,495	n.a.	262.5
Indonesia	8,586	9,425	17,576	16,897	104.7	79.3
Latvia	0	563	2,093	2,370	n.a.	321.0
Lithuania	1,239	653	981	2,085	-20.8	219.3
Malaysia	25,172	22,766	29,245	32,057	16.2	40.8
Paraguay	1,447	681	2,882	3,586	99.2	426.6
Philippines	8,292	12,807	5,637	7,783	-32.0	-39.2
Russian Federation*	6,876	7,835	123,065	90,357	1,689.8	1,053.2
Thailand	8,406	5,938	14,755	15,966	75.5	168.9
Togo	200	194	4,250	1,823	2,025.0	839.7
Zambia	206	486	1,977	2,547	859.7	424.1

Note: * Kar and Spanjers (2014, Table 1) do not indicate the Russian Federation as a developing country that reports bilateral trade to all advanced economies. However, they follow Kar and LeBlanc (2013) in reporting results based on a country-by-country comparison.

Source: Estimates of trade misinvoicing based on a country-world comparison are obtained from Kar and Freitas (2012: Table 7). Estimates of trade misinvoicing based on a country-by-country comparison are obtained from Kar and Spanjers (2014: Table 4).

dollars. Overall, the downward correction of the estimate of trade misinvoicing for China has been more than matched by a measurable upward adjustment for a few other countries, most notably Russia and India, raising serious questions about the robustness and reliability of the country-level estimates.

Since GFI applies the modified empirical approach to only a selected group of countries, the country estimates of illicit financial flows due to trade misinvoicing are effectively derived from different methodologies. GFI justifies this mix of methodologies by arguing that results derived from the country-world comparison of mirror trade statistics understate outflows as a country's outflows to one partner would cancel out with inflows from another country. In similar fashion, however, a country-by-country comparison may overstate a country's outflows when only (one-sided) errors in mirror trade statistics indicating capital outflows are considered. Specifically, since exports for which the final destination is unknown at the time of shipment typically cause offsetting errors in trade statistics, a country-by-country comparison which ignores one component of the transaction artificially inflates estimates of illicit financial flows due to trade misinvoicing.[6]

Moving forward

In view of the shortcomings of GFI's approach to quantify illicit financial flows from developing countries, it seems useful to highlight possible methodological improvements that may help to generate more reliable estimates. Obviously, there is no first-best solution, given the limitations of available information and data; illicit flows are, by their very nature, difficult to identify. Still, a key precondition for the estimation of illicit financial flows due to trade misinvoicing and, more generally, a proper interpretation of observed discrepancies in international trade statistics is to take a more nuanced approach that goes beyond the routine analysis of aggregate trade flows and takes more details of pairwise trade relationships into account. In particular, I suggest proceeding along three lines.

First, there is a strong need for more micro evidence about procedures using misinvoiced trade transactions to move capital unrecorded out of a country. For one thing, evidence obtained "from the field" may provide insights on the overall relevance of trade misinvoicing. Since there is a broad range of methods available to move funds illegally across national borders, including the smuggling of cash, any quantitative estimate of a country's illicit financial flows crucially depends on the assumption about the relative importance of trade misinvoicing – an aspect about which relatively little is known. In addition, anecdotal evidence may provide useful details for an informed assessment of observed discrepancies in trade statistics. For instance, it seems reasonable to assume that most of a country's illicit financial flows are destined to a small number of

---

6 To illustrate the problem, consider a shipment from a developing country to the European Union. Assume that the container is directed to the port of Antwerp in Belgium but that the goods are intended to be sold throughout the European Union, with the final destination being determined only when the container is already en route. In the trade statistics of the developing country, this transaction will be recorded as an export to Belgium without a corresponding entry in the Belgian trade statistics (because the goods are immediately transshipped), while the European Union countries report an import from the developing country without a corresponding entry in the developing country's trade statistics. In a country-world comparison, these (factitious) findings of export over-invoicing (to Belgium) and export underinvoicing (to other European Union countries) would cancel out. In a country-by-country comparison, observed export underinvoicing may be interpreted as evidence of an illicit financial outflow.

countries. Consequently, differences in matched trade statistics with other countries are unlikely to reflect illicit financial flows.

Second, it may be useful to restrict the empirical analysis. A limited sample does not only allow a more detailed analysis of misinvoicing behavior, instead of automatically attributing any discrepancy in bilateral trade statistics to illicit financial flows, but also yields, in most cases, empirical results of sufficient accuracy. For instance, for the quantification of illicit financial flows at a global scale, it seems suitable to focus on a few large countries that account for the overwhelming majority of illicit outflows. At the country level, the analysis may be centered on a few selected partner countries that turn out to be the main destinations for the country's illicit flows. Ferrantino et al. (2012) provide an interesting example of a detailed assessment of the US–China trade data discrepancy.

Third, to the extent that institutional knowledge about practices of trade misinvoicing is missing, a systematic analysis of observed differences in matched partner trade statistics is helpful, especially for trade data at the product level. By identifying any systematic variation in discrepancies across products and countries, this analysis allows correcting for alternative sources of disparities in pairwise trade statistics; see, for example, Berger and Nitsch (2012) for an application.

Conclusion

In recent years, there has been a growing interest in the understanding of trade misinvoicing practices, both among policymakers and economists. This paper discusses selected issues in the analysis of trade misinvoicing. Examining various motives for the misdeclaration of trade activities, it is argued that the broad range of incentives to fake customs declarations provides an important challenge for the empirical assessment of the extent of trade misinvoicing. After analyzing the costs and benefits of different empirical approaches to quantify trade misinvoicing, the accuracy and reliability of estimation results reported in the literature are reviewed.

Acknowledgements

This chapter is closely related to, and draws extensively on, my earlier works "Trillion Dollar Estimate: Illicit Financial Flows from Developing Countries" and "Trade Misinvoicing in Developing Countries," commissioned by the Center for Global Development. I am grateful to Vijaya Ramachandran for encouragement.

References

Beja Jr., E. L. (2005). "Capital flight: Meanings and measures", in G. A. Epstein (ed.), *Capital Flight and Capital Controls in Developing Countries*. Cheltenham: Edward Elgar.

Berger, H., and Nitsch, V. (2012). "Gotcha! A profile of smuggling in international trade", in C. C. Storti and P. De Grauwe (eds), *Illicit Trade and the Global Economy*. Cambridge, MA: MIT Press.

Bhagwati, J. (1964). "On the underinvoicing of imports", *Bulletin of the Oxford University Institute of Economics and Statistics*, 26 (August), 389–97.

Celâsun, M., and Rodrik, D. (1989a). "Turkish experience with debt: Macroeconomic policy and performance", in J. D. Sachs (ed.), *Developing Country Debt and the World Economy*. Chicago: University of Chicago Press.

Celâsun, M., and Rodrik, D. (1989b). "Debt, adjustment, and growth: Turkey", in J. D. Sachs and S. M. Collins (eds), *Developing Country Debt and Economic Performance: Country Studies*. Chicago: University of Chicago Press.

Chalendard, C., Raballand, G., and Rakotoarisoa, A. (2016). "The use of detailed statistical data in customs reform: The case of Madagascar", World Bank Policy Research Working Paper 7625.

Ferrantino, M. J., Liu, X., and Wang, Z. (2012). "Evasion behaviors of exporters and importers: Evidence from the U.S.-China trade data discrepancy", *Journal of International Economics*, 86 (January), 141–57.

Fisman, R., and Wei, S-J. (2009). "The smuggling of art, and the art of smuggling: Uncovering the illicit trade in cultural property and antiques", *American Economic Journal: Applied Economics*, 1 (July), 82–96.

High Level Panel on Illicit Financial Flows from Africa (2015). "Illicit financial flow", Report commissioned by the AU/ECA Conference of Ministers of Finance, Planning and Economic Development. Available at www.uneca.org/publications/illicit-financial-flows.

Kar, D., and Cartwright-Smith, D. (2008). *Illicit Financial Flows From Developing Countries: 2002–2006.* Washington, DC: Global Financial Integrity.

Kar, D., and Freitas, S. (2012). *Illicit Financial Flows From Developing Countries: 2001–2010.* Washington, DC: Global Financial Integrity.

Kar, D., and LeBlanc, B. (2013). *Illicit Financial Flows From Developing Countries: 2002–2011.* Washington, DC: Global Financial Integrity.

Kar, D., and Spanjers, J. (2014). *Illicit Financial Flows From Developing Countries: 2003–2012,* Washington, DC: Global Financial Integrity.

Kessler, M., and Borst, N. (2013). "Did China really lose $3.75 trillion in illicit financial flows?", *China Economic Watch*, Peterson Institution for International Economics, 10 January. Available at http://blogs.piie.com/china/?p=2194.

Nitsch, V. (2012). "Trade mispricing and illicit flows," in P. Reuter (ed.), *Draining Development? Controlling Flows of Illicit Funds From Developing Countries.* Washington, DC: The World Bank, pp. 309–34.

Nitsch, V. (2015). "Trillion dollar estimate: Illicit financial flows from developing countries", Darmstadt University of Technology Discussion Paper #227.

Nitsch, V. (2017). "Trade misinvoicing in developing countries", CGD Policy Paper #103.

Ruffles, D., Tily, G., Caplan, D., and Tudor, S. (2003). "VAT missing trader intra-community fraud: The effect on balance of payments statistics and UK national accounts", *Economic Trends*, 597 (August), 58–70.

United Nations. (2013). *International Merchandise Trade Statistics: Compiler Manual, Revision 1.* New York: United Nations.

Yang, D. (2008). "Can enforcement backfire? Crime displacement in the context of customs reform in the Philippines", *Review of Economics and Statistics*, 90 (February), 1–14.

17

TAX AVOIDANCE AND GLOBAL WEALTH CHAINS

Leonard Seabrooke and Duncan Wigan

Introduction

Global Value Chains (GVC) analyses have addressed the cross-border dispersal of production activities by multinational corporations. Firms have sought market dominance through access to geographically particular advantages in terms of, amongst others, proximity to customers, specific technological inputs, know-how and, of course, lower labour costs. Stephen Roach of Morgan Stanley summarised this multi-faceted process by noting that an 'unrelenting ... search for new efficiencies ... by extract[ing] product from relatively low-wage workers in the developing world has become an increasingly urgent survival tactic for companies in the developed economies' (2003: 5–6). Analyses under the banner of GVC and Global Production Networks (GPN) have engaged the transcendence of the multi-national and vertical corporation with branches competing in foreign markets as discrete and relatively freestanding entities. As the pressure of shareholder value has increased firms have pursued, 'industrial organization strategies that shift labour and physical assets outside the legal boundaries of the firm' (Schwartz 2016: 228). The contemporary multinational corporation (MNC) produces and exchanges via inter- and intra-corporate chains and networks with units fulfilling specific functions in and across now only ostensibly national political economies (Bair 2005; Desai 2008; Gereffi 1994; Henderson 2002; Gereffi et al. 2005; Kaplinsky 2010; Yeung 2009). This has been considered a central hallmark of economic globalization.

In this context GVC and GPN analyses have made considerable strides forward and become omnipotent in various social science disciplines, effectively capturing the prominence of fluidity and flexibility in characterizing the operations of the multinational corporation. These approaches have pushed policy makers and the academy to produce an effective comprehension of the evolving spaces and institutional forms of trade and commodity production, and allow for the tracking of more fluid and mobile processes of value creation and realisation. International Political Economy (IPE) has been one discipline in the lead here, fortifying its claim to policy and real world relevance (Gereffi et al. 2005; Neilson and Yeung 2014). Beyond IPE, these developments have led to a host of varied approaches to global economic activities and the processes through which these unfold, drawing attention to their spatial, jurisdictional, political and regulatory content and implications (Castells 1996; Held et al. 1999; Luo et al. 2012; Ruggie 1993; Sassen 1996; Walker 1989). As a consequence, research from a number of disciplines has pointed to the need to develop new conceptions of the corporate form, territoriality and borders when engaging evolution in production's spaces and time, and ostensible national bases (Agnew; 1999; Cameron and Palan 2004; Coates and Rafferty 2007; Deleuze and Guattari 1987; Desai 2008; Harvey 1982; Hudson 2000; Palan 1998; Ruggie 1993; Scott 1998; Wai 2002, 2008).

In tandem with these processes, and in similar ways, finance has grown in size, significance and fluidity. Financial market size dwarfs global GDP, and the ability to shift assets, liabilities, costs and profits across what are now only formally nationally demarcated economies (Bryan 1995; Wigan 2009), is increasingly pronounced. These integrated phenomena have had a singular consequence; a disjuncture, or nigh on divorce, between nationally circumscribed regulatory and fiscal systems on one hand, and mobile and fluid finance and production on the other. In many ways national spaces and the jurisdictional order built upon them have been transcended by the evolution in international capital. As a consequence, the conceptual tools that jurisdictional orders rest upon are no longer fit for task with stark implications for regulatory traction. Financial mobility, fluidity and fungibility – the capacity to switch form, legal character and geographic attachment – have raised the prospect of an entrenched divide between where value is created and the jurisdictional and social distribution of profits and wealth (Bryan et al. 2017). The division applies as equally to ownership and profit claims on large corporations as to the wealth preservation strategies of elites (Piketty 2014; Santos 2018; Zucman 2015). The divide is constructed, policed and reinforced through a wide range of products from those that can easily be obtained off the shelf, such as shell companies (Findley et al. 2013), to those that are tailor made to client specifications or risk appetites. The latter include complex structured financial products in the shadow banking system (Bryan et al. 2016).

This chapter pushes forward on a theoretical framework to capture these processes and changes, integrating the analysis of what we call 'Global Wealth Chains' (Seabrooke and Wigan 2017) with a focus on tax avoidance strategies employed by corporations and individuals. We define Global Wealth Chains (GWCs) as the transacted forms of capital operating multi-jurisdictionally for the purposes of wealth creation and protection. The chapter proposes a simple framework to deploy in disaggregating and specifying types of GWC and the dynamics that play out within them (see Seabrooke and Wigan, 2014 for an early provocation to this argument). The framework we elaborate is an open invitation for further interrogation and collaboration in developing our understanding of how international capital is evolving, and to those interested in redressing the various inequalities that arise from this evolution and the widely noted growing disjuncture between value creation and wealth appropriation and allocation.

GWCs have pervasive and often overtly negative effects. In so much as many GVC analyses have increasingly departed from a focus on entrenched inequalities and unequal exchange to attempt to identify opportunities at the micro-level for firms in developing countries to upgrade and learn from value chain participation, our GWC framework is the 'yin' to the GVC 'yang'. Where GVC analyses focus on opportunity, the GWC framework points to obstacles and opacity. Relatedly, GVC research has on the whole neglected links between value chains and financial and legal innovations created by firms, lawyers and investors (but see Coe et al. 2014; IGLP 2016; Milberg 2008; Williams 2000). The management of assets through GWCs can define competitive outcomes between firms and exacerbate global inequalities in circumscribing who gets the wealth arising from globalizing economic activities. Relative capacity to construct and deploy GWCs effects the developmental prospects of countries and determines on which shoulders an increasing fiscal burden rests (Seabrooke and Wigan 2014). This chapter contributes to efforts to track the evolution of the relations between states and markets, trace the evolution of forms of international capital, invite work from multiple theoretical sources, including value theoretical approaches to the global economy, and nourish on-going yet fragile multilateral and unilateral efforts to redress the disjuncture between value creation and wealth distribution (OECD 2015). We push forward on the project of GVC analysis; namely the identification of that which obstructs progress and how to upgrade, develop, and 'compete' in the world economy, and, in doing, ameliorate extenuated inequalities.

In building our framework, we draw on a variety of sources including literature on finance and law in Institutional Economics (Bryan et al. 2016; Commons 1924, 1934; Finnerty 1988; Merton 1995; Morgan 2016; Wigan 2013), as noted above, in Economic Geography and International Political Economy on GVCs, and in Economic Sociology on relations within networks that define market dynamics. We pinpoint three drivers of how Global Wealth Chains evolve and are constructed. Mirroring the seminal work of Gereffi et al. (2005), the chapter specifies five forms of GWC; market, modular, relational, captive and hierarchy. For tax avoidance the forms are united by constructed ambiguity via which how much tax is due where, when and on what is made nebulous. We illustrate the forms of GWC with a consideration of a range of assets used to achieve tax avoidance and open to a GWC analysis. The chapter provides some necessarily somewhat perfunctory cases in demonstration.

Key to our focus here on tax avoidance and GWCs is the identification by J.C. Sharman of, 'a common thread running through many manifestations of the offshore phenomenon: the pursuit of a calculated ambiguity'. This refers to the ability to give, 'diametrically opposed but legally valid answers when responding to the same question from different audiences' (2010: 2). Firms and elites purposively navigate between tax categories, legal identities, temporal certainties and spatial specificity to create multiple ambiguities. These ambiguities may be jurisdictional, when which national tax authority has the right to impose a tax charge is at stake. For instance, one national tax authority may deem a corporate subsidiary a 'permanent establishment' in its place of business while another determines that the nature of the subsidiary's operations are more fleeting and not substantive and therefore the entity is not subject to a tax charge where it is operating. Alternatively the ambiguity may concern purely fiscal regulation, where it is unclear if a particular form of operation is subject to a particular tax. In terms of space, the ambiguity will concern where an activity is taking place. The taxpayer or transaction may appear to one tax authority as occurring in one place while a second is of the opinion that the activity is taking place somewhere else. It may be that the activity or transaction is understood to be occurring elsewhere and is effectively occurring nowhere for tax authority and taxation purposes (Murphy 2009). Time is also up for grabs. Ambiguity here may be about the duration of a transaction, with short term transactions attracting higher tax charges than long term. Often the existence or level of a tax exposure is a function of the identity of the taxpayer or transaction. Finance and financial engineering are used to blur the identity of a transaction or series of transactions so tax authorities become uncertain of exactly what a tax charge is addressing. The examples briefly described in the next section illustrate these ambiguities and the central role of 'calculated ambiguity' in tax avoidance.

Routes and roots to GWCs and tax avoidance

We provide a simple mechanism to disentangle types of GWC prevalent in the contemporary world economy. GWCs refract on-going challenges to common understandings of state-market relationships and force us to confront the specificity of globalizing capital. This chapter provides a means of categorizing and specifying GWCs as ideal types. Of course, our invitation is to engage with, interrogate and dismantle these ideal types and augment or reconstruct them as fit. Our aim here is to provide analytical tools to understand how capital is transacted multi-jurisdictionally, understand the drivers of these processes, and gain insight into the various forms they take. Work on value chains is instrumental in identifying processes in market; work on finance and law highlights the institutional basis of wealth chains and drivers of product supply; and Economic Sociology illuminates how actors select particular products and what relations and network forms prompt them to do so. We use this work to identify the following:

1   Power asymmetries and related degrees of transaction complexity between suppliers and clients;
2   Incentives for innovation in finance and law through institutional forms, including the drive to specialize and diversify;
3   The reasons why markets segment according to the status of the client and supplier, and what relationships reinforce wealth chains in particular ways.

In providing a theory of the governance of GWCs a key target is an understanding of the governance structure surrounding the various wealth chains that we identify and invite others to locate. This chapter proposes the integration of work on the 'offshore world' with the insights referred to in the previous section on GVCs, finance and law, and Economic Sociology to generate a typology of GWCs. Drawing directly from the established typology on global value chains provided by Gereffi, Humphrey and Sturgeon, between 'pure' markets and hierarchies within firms there are network relationships characterized as modular, relational, and captive (Gereffi et al. 2005: 83–4). Market value chains refer to when information is easily communicated and transactions are arms-length and governed with low or no levels of overt coordination. Modular value chains encapsulate the provision of products to a customer's specification but with generic machinery. Relational value chains involve complex interactions and high levels of specificity in what is being supplied. Captive value chains depict when small suppliers are dependent on larger suppliers. Hierarchy value chains display high levels of managerial control and are variously vertically or tightly integrated.

We adapt these five types of governing value chains to Global Wealth Chains. The types are analytical. As noted, and as with all ideal types, our types of governance for GWCs are constructed for the purpose of learning and should be broken down and recomposed where appropriate. Moreover, these five types are not hermetically sealed. They interact and are often integrated in articulating GWCs across space and time. Wealth chains morph, particularly under the pressure of regulatory innovation and intervention. The types of governance in Global Wealth Chains are as follows:

1   *Market* wealth chains are where linkages occur through arms-length relationships with low complexity in established legal regimes. Products can be accessed from multiple suppliers who compete on price, capacity and reputational capital.
2   *Modular* wealth chains offer more bespoke services and products within well-established financial and legal environments that restrict supplier and client flexibility. Products involve complex information but can be exchanged with little explicit coordination. Bespoke suppliers are commonly associated with a lead supplier.
3   *Relational* wealth chains involve the exchange of complex tacit information, requiring high levels of explicit coordination. Strong trust relationships managed by prestige and status interactions make switching costs high and are often interpersonal.
4   *Captive* wealth chains occur when lead suppliers dominate smaller suppliers by dominating the legal apparatus and financial technology. Clients' options are limited by the scope of what can be provided by small suppliers and, in turn, lead suppliers.

5   *Hierarchy* wealth chains are tightly or vertically integrated. A high degree of control is exer-
    cised by senior management, such as the chief financial officer. Clients and suppliers are
    highly integrated and coordinate on complex transactions.

Figure 17.1 illustrates these five types. It identifies the lead suppliers of financial products and
services, the secondary suppliers (whether bespoke, relational or new businesses seeking market
share), the clients and the basic relationships in the transfer and transformation of capital from its
source and original form to facilitate wealth creation, appropriation or reallocation. The capital
movement, or construed movement, is of course circular and wealth returns to the client. Global
Wealth Chain analyses denote the flow of capital from source through wealth creation, protection and appropriation mechanisms, and back again. Coordination in these different GWCs and
amidst these related forms of governance becomes more complex and explicit as we move from
the left to the right of the diagram.

Our typology of Global Wealth Chains is an adaptation of Gereffi et al.'s (2005) typology, but
contains significant differences. These scholars provide a theory of value chain governance based
on three variables: the complexity of information required to sustain transactions; the ability to
codify transactions; and the capabilities of suppliers to meet the requirements of the transaction (Gereffi et al. 2005: 85). These are apposite for value chains because they enable the identification of transaction complexity, efficiency of process and capacities for delivery. However,
as much of the activity of GWCs is explicitly intended to avoid codification, the focus on
codification, as means of distinguishing wealth chains, is less appropriate than a focus on regulatory liability. The value of a wealth chain to suppliers and clients most often is a function of
minimizing the chances of regulatory intervention. Capabilities for those supplying products
and services is less about the ability to meet the requirements of the transaction and more about
the ability to fend off challenges and cope with uncertainty in regard to the legal or regulatory

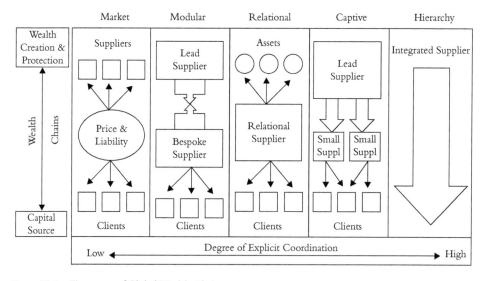

Figure 17.1   Five types of Global Wealth Chain governance.

Source: Seabrooke and Wigan 2017, adapted from Gereffi et al. 2005: 89.

status of the transaction. These considerations lead to the following factors in a theory of Global Wealth Chain governance:

1   The complexity of information and knowledge transfer with regard to the product or service being provided by the supplier to meet the client's requirements;
2   The regulatory liability involved in transactions and the ease of often multi-jurisdictional regulatory intervention;
3   The capabilities of suppliers to create solutions to mitigate challenges to the status of the product or service by regulators.

These three variables explain a great deal of the variation in the governance of Global Wealth Chains, and provide a basis for explaining differences in function and form. Form and function are up of grabs when the environment is conditioned by 'calculated ambiguity'. As noted previously, Sharman (2010: 2) identifies 'a common thread running through many manifestations of the offshore phenomenon: the pursuit of a calculated ambiguity'. We add that 'calculated ambiguity' is a common thread linking many of the institutions and transactions in the GWCs. These variables also prompt us to think of GWCs as comprising not only buyers and suppliers or clients and suppliers, but also regulators. Figure 17.2 provides a series of illustrations on information asymmetries between suppliers, clients, and regulators in the governance of GWCs. The length of a line between any two points represents how opaque information is between these actors. Information asymmetry provides a source of innovation and a shield against regulatory intervention.

Regarding illustration (a), 'Market', in Figure 17.2, an example is a standard 'off the shelf' offshore shell company established in Panama, Lichtenstein, Delaware or the British Virgin Islands. The client and supplier both have a clear vision of that being provided by the product and required information about both parties. In many cases the supplier has (and has purposively

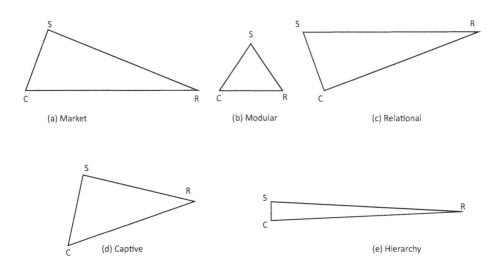

Figure 17.2   Information asymmetries in the governance of Global Wealth Chains.
(Key: S=Supplier, C=Client, R=Regulator)
Source: Seabrooke and Wigan 2017: 14.

contrived to have) little information regarding who the client actually is (see Findley et al. 2013). The key information asymmetry is between the client and the regulator. Secrecy, legal tradition, and creative compliance and non-compliance with international rules ensure this is the case. The distance between the supplier and the regulator is less than between the client and the regulator because that is the main point of such tax avoidance and evasion operations – to place the supplier between the regulator and client and to hide the real identity of the client. Layers of nominal owners can assist in this. As such the supplier acts as a buffer between the client and regulator, as allowed for by law that permits pervasive offshore activity. As both LuxLeaks and the Panama Papers recently and clearly demonstrate (Obermayer and Obermaier 2016), the main way of being discovered within this GWC is via a whistleblower that has and decides to share a list of clients, often at considerable personal risk and cost. However, contract specifications, 'flee clauses', that oblige a supplier to relocate titles or assets subject to regulatory intervention, or intervention visible on the horizon, can allow the supplier to fend off challenges.

Information asymmetries are less in the Modular form shown in illustration (b) in Figure 17.2, as this is an actively regulated market with clear anti-money laundering legislation and reporting requirements on the source of income. In some part, this is because Modular forms of GWCs are more popular, as with expatriate communities, and easier to trace. For instance, an expatriate who holds an offshore account can use this product to avoid taxes, but there is quite a lot of information known between the client, the supplier (HSBC, for example), and the regulator, whether they are authorities in an offshore jurisdiction or authorities in the country of the client's origin or residence (de Carvalho and Seabrooke 2016). Given the lack of information asymmetries here the lack of forward moving regulation on these GWCs is a function of a lack of political will rather than absent capacity. However, there has been a lot of momentum from U.S. authorities to plug some of the fiscal leaks created by Modular wealth chains (Palan and Wigan 2014).

In Relational wealth chains, depicted in illustration (c) in Figure 17.2, the greatest information asymmetry is between the supplier and the regulator, since the point of the relationship between the supplier and the client is to ensure that the client's assets cannot be touched by the regulator, even if the client comes under scrutiny. An example here is specialists providing family wealth management to the very wealthy, who specialise in managing wealth across generations within families, deploying strategies so that even if a family member is in trouble with the regulator the wealth is still protected (Harrington 2016; Santos 2018).

The Captive form, in illustration (d) in Figure 17.2, shows greater information asymmetries than in the Modular form but also less than in the other forms. This is again a function of the size and scale of activity that is linked back to residence or origin jurisdictions where Regulators can attempt to keep an eye on what is going on. An example here is the relationship between Ernst & Young (the supplier) and a firm (the client) over the best strategies to avoid and minimize corporate taxes. Regulators have clear information on how this takes place and the likely revenue lost, and the client and Supplier have clear lines of communication to share information on their needs. The regulator is a little more distant from the client than from the supplier, since a large part of the service provided by the supplier is to provide professional and legal reasons to Regulators for the client's activities. The supplier's multi-jurisdictional and cross-disciplinary expertise (accounting, law, tax, supply chain management) is a valuable asset in avoiding regulatory interventions (Christensen 2018). Indeed, large suppliers, such as global professional services firms, have a geographic scope of perspective and operation, and corresponding global knowledge resources that by definition outrun the capacities of regulators, perhaps with the partial exception of the United States, which through the Foreign Account Tax Compliance Act has demonstrated a rare extraterritorial reach (Grinberg 2012).

Finally, the Hierarchy form, in illustration (e) in Figure 17.2, shows a short distance and low information asymmetries between the supplier and the client while clear and significant information asymmetries between the client and the regulator and the supplier and the regulator are apparent. A key reason here is that relations between the client and supplier are often 'in house', reducing information asymmetries. A dominant market position and shared strong capacities mean that the pace of financial and legal innovation can be enhanced, supported by superior information sharing. Innovation seeks to obscure information going to the regulator or place a product beyond the regulatory radar where the product is simply not understood, or not known to exist by the regulator. An example here has been Apple's tax planning, or structured finance solutions provided by Barclays and Deutsche Bank to major hedge fund clients (Bryan et al. 2016; Seabrooke and Wigan 2014).

Note here that only the Modular form of governance is characterized by low capabilities in terms of being able to mitigate uncertainty, and also that this type and the Captive type are the only forms of governance where regulatory liability is high. This can be explained by a strong regulatory focus on large institutions that regulators can monitor or attempt to monitor, compared to the Market and Relational types that rely on contracts or carefully managed trust relationships as the key means of completing transactions without passing through traditional financial intermediaries. Products in the Hierarchy form are able to provide comprehensive mechanisms of mitigation that mix conventional and shadow banking with products and services in offshore jurisdictions to minimize tax exposures and valorize opportunities at the boundaries between jurisdictions. Complexity is a weapon here.

We also note that the degree of explicit coordination increases are we move through the forms of wealth chain. Ordering a shell company can be done from the online Market without unnecessary fuss. Clients engaging in Modular forms of governance will only receive a private banker who can assist them with international taxation issues once they have invested £250,000 (de Carvalho and Seabrooke 2016). Families dealing with trust and estate planners or asset protection trusts have more significant sums to pay for highly customized services (Harrington 2016). Clients and suppliers in Captive markets engage in a range of complex transactions to create wealth chains and rely heavily on professionals and experts from firms such as KPMG, Ernst & Young and the like. These professionals have a strong interest in maintaining their expert community by limiting the terms of debate over what can be governed (Seabrooke and Tsingou 2014; Seabrooke and Henriksen 2017), and activist challenges to them are forced to address them on their own terms (Seabrooke and Wigan 2013, 2015, 2016). Those engaged in the Hierarchy form have extremely complex systems of governance to ensure that transfer pricing and tax avoidance and evasion cannot be sufficiently traced by regulators.

Assets for tax avoidance in global wealth chains

Global Wealth Chain analyses can be applied to a host of economic processes characteristic of the contemporary world economy. The GWC approach should be used to augment the huge range of cases that the Global Value Chain approach has inspired. One approach for GWCs is to explore a range of asset types, with assets being also relational, and not necessarily strictly economic and transferable as in the commodity form. This section provides examples of assets that are deployed in global wealth chains (see also Seabrooke and Wigan 2018).

Here we might consider the supply of legal opinion by small number of UK Queen's Counsel to shield declared tax positions from regulator intervention, a Relational-Market chain asset available to those with a deep pocket. A 'Queen's Counsel' or 'QC' is a barrister at the top of his or her trade who has been endorsed by the state as pre-eminent within the profession. The status of a QC is high and provides a basis for the charging of exceptionally high fees for advice given. A QC's opinion is the most authoritative legal advice in England and Wales. Legal opinion shields tax positions from regulatory intervention by exploiting the potential bifurcation between legal argument and forensic outcome. Queen's Counsel are well-positioned to offer this bifurcation with significant authority, which is difficult to challenge. Legal opinion reflects a kind of 'virtual offshore', where the offshore space is defined in legal argument and yields potentially huge tax savings. The exploration of legal opinion on GWCs also gives rise to an opportunity to recognise tax avoidance as a form of 'risk mining'. The magnitude, and audacity of resulting tax savings are a function of how far the client and supplier are willing to climb the high wire of risk and return. At the extreme end of the deliberately false legal opinion, the key information asymmetry in these Relational-Market chains is with regard to the fact that the risk mining is occurring at all, since it will be expected to fail on challenge from the tax authority. Importantly, many positions taken on the basis of a supporting legal opinion are never challenged by the tax authority (Quentin 2018).

An example is Amazon's former UK corporate tax structuring. The structuring relied on a separation of the functions of Amazon's UK business into the actual contractual selling, which was done by a Luxembourg entity, and auxiliary functions performed by a UK entity, which were arguably not substantive enough to generate a taxable presence in the UK over the activities of the Luxembourg entity where profits were being booked. This arrangement could lead to the legally condoned avoidance of UK corporation tax, and was no doubt endorsed prior to implementation by advice to that effect. The robustness of this opinion would rely on keeping the auxiliary and sales functions substantively separate. However, the activities were in reality not kept separate at all, and subsequently it was found that the argued for separation of functions was entirely fictitious. However, this finding occurred in non tax related litigation and consequently did not affect the outcome with regard to Amazon's contributions to the UK exchequer (ibid.)

Perhaps the most pervasive asset deployed in international tax planning is the system of bilateral tax treaties, which effectively form a super tax light highway for firms operating internationally (Hearson 2018). The relationship between multinational companies' value chains and their increasingly hierarchical wealth chains is changing, and the role played by tax treaties in this process in critical. Around 3,000 tax treaties limit the extent to which the transactions at each stage of the chain can be taxed in the countries between which the earnings flow. Double tax treaties govern the division of taxation rights over cross-border activities between the resident country of the taxpayer and the source country where economic activity takes place. In particular, they often prevent the host country from imposing tax on investor profits, cross-border income flows, and/or capital gains. Earlier multinational tax strategies involved the creation of wealth chains that were increasingly detached from the corresponding value chains in order to obtain tax benefits. More recent approaches restructure the real activities in value chains around the desired wealth chains, including the availability of tax treaties. Advisory firms commonly sell services such as 'tax efficient supply chain management' operating what are in effect Modular wealth chains. Increasing integration of value and wealth chains has led to a change in the type of supplier needed, since these complex structures require a depth, breadth and geographical reach of expertise that can only be provided by the 'Big 4' professional services firms. Certain states specialise in the supply of a tax treaty network replete with advantageous positions. This is an area where regulators from different states, and international organizations, will be in conflict, with developing country regulators distanced by a lack of capacity and a legal framework biased to developed country interests. The role of jurisdictions such Mauritius and the Netherlands as 'treaty hubs' in Global Wealth Chains is important here as are the implications of the tax treaty network for developing countries.

An example is the case of Zambia Sugar, a Zambian subsidiary of Associated British Foods (ABF). In this case, the Zambian firm took a loan from a UK-based bank via an Irish intermediary, also part of ABF, to take advantage of the zero rate of withholding taxes on interest payments specified by the Zambia-Ireland treaty, instead of the 10 percent prescribed by the Zambia-UK tax treaty. Even more perverse is the case of the India-Mauritius tax treaty, which had the effect of making Mauritius the main source of foreign investment into India, at least by legal artifice, because Indian domestic investors took advantage of the treaty provision preventing India from taxing capital gains made by Mauritian investors in India. This is the case despite that these 'Mauritian investors' are more than likely to be merely tax avoidance vehicles established by Indian investors (ibid.). Notably, both these treaties have now been amended to prevent such avoidance, partly in consequence of the attention shone on these examples in wake of civil society investigations and campaigns. Many other treaties have not attracted similar attention or been amended. The now infamous tax structures of Google, Apple, Amazon and Starbucks, for example, rely for their efficacy on tax treaties between the countries implicated in the stucturing.

Art is increasingly a clear counterpoint to financial wealth. Since 2000 the market for high value art has witnessed growth of 600 percent, reaching a total value of $1 trillion. While auction prices are known, approximately 70 percent of the market operates privately and no data on sales and prices are available. Further, a 'true value' is difficult to ascertain. This valuation difficulty is the distinctive feature of this asset when deployed in Global Wealth Chains, leaving lots of room for price fixing, tax avoidance, and money laundering. Suppliers include auction houses, private galleries and specialised storage facilities such as the Geneva Freeport, which shields the asset behind a veil of secrecy and Switzerland's network of tax treaties. Close relationships between suppliers and clients ensure effective coordination, placing this asset in the Relational wealth chain type where status and prestige are decisive. Here the regulator in multijurisdictional space is not unified, with regulators split between criminal activity, such as INTERPOL, and transgovernmental groups working on tax evasion, avoidance and money laundering issues. Fragmentation inhibits regulatory traction in these markets. Notably, since there is no income stream attached to the asset, ownership is predicated on the increasing inequality in art prices (Helgadottír, 2018).

A great deal of valuable art disappears from view once it is bought and is never displayed, even in private homes. Instead, it is kept in specialized storage facilities called 'freeports,' which offer a host of exemptions that may include no transaction, capital gains, value added or inheritance tax. These facilities coalesce around major centres of wealth, such as Luxembourg, Monaco, Paris, Dubai, Singapore, Beijing and Shanghai. Most of the assets kept in freeports are likely acquired legally, yet illicit art has been discovered in freeports. In 2003, hundreds of antiques, including mummies, sarcophagi and statues, all of which had been stolen from excavation sites in Egypt, were traced back to the Geneva Freeport. Such scandals are, however, the exception rather than the rule. The main issue is the legal use of art for tax planning purposes in an environment that is not legible to the tax authorities (ibid.). As a recent report explains,

> The purpose behind such corporate maneuvers nearly always involves opacity: to ensure that no one knows who the sellers might be, or what other art they might own. "The tax laws in art make it basically legal to not pay taxes on art. If you're a serious art buyer, you just get a good tax accountant," former New York-based art consultant Beth Fiore tells Hopes & Fears. "If you show newly purchased works in certain museums then you never have to pay taxes on it." Edward Winkleman of Winkleman Gallery maintains that his gallery keeps fastidious records of all transactions and pays

taxes even on cash sales. But he admits that, "the state generally wouldn't question what is reported." He also tells us that individual sales don't need to be reported, only the totals for each quarter. Hypothetically, someone could buy millions of dollars worth of art without the IRS knowing, and then later sell those works for a "legitimate" profit that looks clean on taxes.

Salmon and Fusion.net 2016 quoted in Helgadottír, 2018

Traditional currency systems have a central authority who issues currency, regulates it and guarantees the legal tender (Burgos and Hen 2018). In the cryptocurrency world, there is no central authority. Rather, complex and machine-intensive computational proofs to authenticate and record the transaction are required to verify the transaction. For cryptocurrencies to work, one does not have to trust a bank or any other person or institution. One must simply trust the code or, more precisely, the cryptographic algorithm. The transaction and verification is achieved by 'miners' with a computer and through peer-to-peer networks. When miners first validate a transaction they are rewarded with a set of coins issued by the system. Cryptocurrencies, such as those supplied by Bitcoin and Ripple, are both an investment asset and money system used by High Net Worth Individuals (HNWIs). These clients face the problem of wealth storage, accumulation and transfer. HNWIs may buy physical assets such as art or gold because they don't trust the central bank or buy foreign property to shield wealth from an intrusive home government. They may also buy cryptocurrency. Cryptocurrency opens up channels for quasi-anonymous wealth movements and investment, away from the eyes of multijurisdictional regulators. The expansion of this pure market chain is rapid and ongoing. Bitcoin, Ripple and other blockchain-based systems may provide a way for instantaneous global money laundering, tax avoidance and evasion.

More prosaic perhaps are the investor operations around public utilities. Productionist conceptions of firm activity miss the point that firms are now integrated financial and productive assets and are consequently articulated in global wealth chains, as well as value chains (Leaver 2018). Investors conceive of the firm as an aggregate of separable assets, so that wealth is extracted both from underlying productive activities and also from forms of financial engineering. In the case of UK water companies, the response to regulatory price-setting has been to innovate around law and accounting arrangements to maximise cash extraction and private wealth appropriation. In the case of the multinational French firm Veolia, the provision of water and waste services provide the secure income stream through which debt-loaded subsidiaries remit returns back to the French parent. Asset revaluations, inter-company debt and special dividends are used to corral a greater share of wealth within the corporate network and evict the claims of the UK state.

This example illustrates how the firm has become a conduit between debt markets and investor returns and a source of collateral to back extended chains of financial engineering. Public utilities are particularly attractive as a conduit asset because of their security and the predictability of their income streams The governance of these global wealth chains is a hybrid of the Captive and Hierarchy types – the regulator is close during the price setting phase, but kept at a distance as client and supplier co-ordinate tightly to seek extractive opportunities from the new regulatory arrangements and are separated only by legal boundaries between related corporate entities. Intervention would therefore require not only changes in domestic regulation but also multilateral coordination.

The case of Veolia Water UK is one of financial engineering, specifically the use of inter-company debt and special dividends to move wealth around within an international corporate structure. This financial engineering in this particular example began in 2010 when Veolia Water

UK revalued its assets from historic cost methods to fair value methods, following accounting rule FRS15. This had a profound effect on the balance sheet as Veolia Water UK PLC revised the value of some of its tangible assets up by a little under £440m, which, through the double entry effect, directly increased shareholder funds on the liability side by the same amount. Even though this innocuous accounting exercise had added multiples of millions of pounds to its shareholder funds, this was still only a paper gain. To access that new asset value created there needed to be a way of liquefying those assets and then extracting value from them. To do this Veolia Water UK PLC was loaded with a little over £320m of inter-company long term and short term debt. This created an asset (£320m cash from the loan) and a liability (the £320m which had to be paid back to the parent). The cash from that debt was then used to finance an equivalent equity dividend payment of a little over £320m back up the structure to the French parent. The £320m disappeared from the asset side and an identical reduction had to be booked to the liability side – the obligation to repay remained, so equity was reduced by £320m. The use of inter-company debt and special dividends gave Veolia two main benefits: the higher interest payments resulted in a lower post-interest profit, which reduced their tax burden; the inter-group interest then became a second form of extraction from the UK subsidiary to the French parent, allowing the French parent to increase its own dividend payout to €735.6m in 2010 from €434m in 2009 – a sum unerringly similar to the special dividend paid to it by its UK subsidiary. This financial manoeuvre helped limit the claims of the State on the surpluses of this UK subsidiary, surpluses effectively underwritten by the regulator, and which could have been redirected into socially useful capital investment (Leaver 2018).

Conclusion

Our aim in this chapter has been to provide an original theoretical framework for understanding how Global Wealth Chains are articulated and governed and are deployed for tax avoidance purpuses. We argue that an analysis of GWCs is essential for understanding the integration of production and finance. As noted above, GWCs are the yin to the yang of GVCs. Many value chains, which do have the potential to reduce information asymmetries, enhance development and redress expanded inequalities, exist alongside wealth chains that operate multijurisdictionally to protect and create wealth. Here we argue that GWCs can be understood by the complexity of transactions, the regulatory liability implied, and the capacities of suppliers to provide certain kinds of financial instruments. We have outlined how GWCs can be seen in five types: Market, Modular, Relational, Captive, and Hierarchy. These types are often mixed as firms, groups, and individuals engage in innovative forms of multijurisdictional wealth protection and creation. Future research can use these types to investigate and reflect on how GWCs are articulated, including locating what kinds of actors and organizations are involved and what kind of processes permit the existence of GWCs. We suggest that analyses of GWCs are essential for understanding not only how finance is changing but also core changes in long assumed characteristics of the world economy.

Wealth chains are pervasive, systemic and significant. Their construction, operation, maintenance, consequences and regulation all require sustained analysis. First, there is a need to establish taxonomies of wealth chains and specify, via thick descriptions, the role of wealth chains in the evolution of tax avoidance. Here, we should identify how far financial innovations, such as derivatives, characterize transfers through wealth chains and what role offshore jurisdictions play in asset transfer and transformation. Second, there is a need for a clearer picture of how wealth chains have an impact on developed and developing countries alike in different regions of the world. Of particular interest are the apparent irreconcilable interests of developing countries that host wealth chains as a developmental strategy and developing countries that are detrimentally impacted by wealth chains. Third, as policy innovation accelerates there is a need to evaluate the traction and distributive consequences of regulation in areas as diverse as money-laundering, corporate reporting and shadow banking. More broadly, there is an urgent requirement to account for the impact of Global Wealth Chains on how we conceive central elements of the agenda of the tradition we work in, namely International Political Economy. This necessarily includes rethinking our understanding of how to measure global capital flows, as well as our conceptions of the MNC, state formation, professions, expert networks, the links between wealth chains and value chains, and the sources of inequality in an increasingly unequal world.

Bibliography

Agnew, J. (1999). 'Mapping political power beyond state boundaries', *Millenium*, 28, 499–521.
Bair, J. (2005). 'Global capitalism and commodity chains: Looking back, going forward', *Competition & Change*, 9(2), 153–180.
Bryan, D. (1995). *Chase Across the Globe: International Accumulation and the Contradictions for Nation States.* Boulder, CO: Westview Press.
Bryan, D., Rafferty, M., and Wigan, D. (2016). 'Politics, time and space in the era of shadow banking', *Review of International Political Economy*. doi:http://dx.doi.org/10.1080/09692290.2016.1139618.
Bryan, D., Rafferty, M., and Wigan, D. (2017). 'Capital unchained: Finance, intangible assets and the double life of capital in the offshore world', *Review of International Political Economy*, 24(1), 56–86.
Burgos, M., and Hen, M. (2018). 'Cryptocurrencies', in L. Seabrooke and D. Wigan (eds.), *Global Wealth Chains: Governing Assets in the World Economy*. Oxford: Oxford University Press.
Cameron, A., and Palan, R. (2004). *The Imagined Economies of Globalisation*. London: Sage.
Castells, M. (1996). *The Rise of the Network Society*. Oxford: Blackwell.
Christensen, R.C. (2018). 'Professional Competition in the Battle for Corporate Wealth Chain Transparency', in L. Seabrooke and D. Wigan (eds), *Global Wealth Chains: Governing Assets in the World Economy*. Oxford: Oxford University Press.
Coates, N., and Rafferty, M. (2007). 'Offshore financial centres, hot money and hedge funds: A network analysis of international capital flows', in L. Assassi, A. Nesvetailova and D. Wigan (eds), *Global Finance in the New Century: Beyond Deregulation*. Basingstoke: Palgrave Macmillan.
Coe, N., Lai, K., and Wójcik, D. (2014). 'Integrating finance into global production networks', *Regional Studies*, 48(5), 761–77.
Commons, J. (1924). *The Legal Foundations of Capitalism*. New York: Macmillan Company.
Commons, J. (1934). *Institutional Economics: Its Place in Political Economy*. Madison, WI: University of Wisconsin Press.
de Carvalho, B. and L. Seabrooke (2016) 'Expatriates in Global Wealth Chains', NUPI Policy Brief 16-6, Norwegian Institute of International Affairs.
Deleuze, G., and Guattari, F. (1987). *A Thousand Plateaus: Capitalism and Schizophrenia*. Minneapolis, MN: Minnesota University Press.
Desai, M. (2008). 'The decentering of the global firm', Working Paper 09–054, Harvard Business School.
Findley, M. G., Nielson, D. L., and Sharman, J. (2013). *Global Shell Games*. Cambridge: Cambridge University Press.
Finnerty, J. D. (1988). 'Financial innovation in corporate finance: An overview', *Financial Management*, 17(4), 14–33.
Gereffi, G. (1994). 'The organisation of buyer-driven global commodity chains: How US retailers shape overseas production networks', in G. Gereffi and M. Korzeniewicz (eds.), *Commodity Chains and Global Capitalism*. Westport, CT: Praeger.
Gereffi, G., Humphrey, J., and Sturgeon, T. (2005). 'The governance of global value chains', *Review of International Political Economy*, 12(1), 78–104.
Grinberg, I. (2012). 'Beyond FATCA: An evolutionary moment for the international tax system', Georgetown Law the Scholarly Commons: Georgetown Law Library, Georgetown Law Faculty Working Papers, Paper 160. Available at http://scholarship.law.georgetown.edu/fwps_papers/160
Harrington, B. (2016) *Capital without Borders: Wealth Managers and the One Percent*. Cambridge: Harvard University Press.

Harvey, D. (1982). *The Limits to Capital*. Oxford: Basil Blackwell.

Hearson, M. (2018). 'Treaties', in L. Seabrooke and D. Wigan (eds.), *Global Wealth Chains: Governing Assets in the World Economy*. Oxford: Oxford University Press.

Held, D., McGrew, A., Goldblatt, D., and Perraton, J. (1999). *Global Transformations: Politics, Economics, Culture*. Cambridge: Polity Press.

Helgadottír, O. (2018). 'Gauguin Goes to Freeport: Art and Global Wealth Chains', in L. Seabrooke and D. Wigan (eds), *Global Wealth Chains: Governing Assets in the World Economy*. Oxford: Oxford University Press.

Henderson, J. (2002). 'Globalisation on the ground: Global production networks, competition, regulation and economic development', Centre on Regulation and Competition (CRC) Working papers 30605, University of Manchester, Institute for Development Policy and Management (IDPM).

Hudson, A. (2000). 'Offshoreness, globalization an sovereignty: A postmodern geo-political economy?', *Transactions of the Institute of British Geography*, 25, 269–83.

IGLP Law and Global Production Working Group (2016). 'The role of law in global value chains: A research manifesto', *London Review of International Law*, 1 of 23. Available at http://wrap.warwick.ac.uk/77628/1/WRAP_1571663-la-290216-lond._rev._int._law-2016--lril-lrw003.pdf.

Kaplinsky, R. (2010). 'The role of standards in global value chains', World Bank Policy Research Working Paper Series 5396. Available at SSRN: http://ssrn.com/abstract=1653682.

Leaver, A. (2018). 'Public utilities', in L. Seabrooke and D. Wigan (eds), *Global Wealth Chains: Governing Assets in the World Economy*. Oxford: Oxford University Press.

Luo, J., Baldwin, C., Whitney, D., and Magee, C. (2012). 'The architecture of transaction networks: A comparative analysis of hierarchy in two sectors', *Industrial and Corporate Change*, 21(6), 1307–35.

Merton, R. C. (1995). 'Financial innovation and the management and regulation of financial institutions', *Journal of Banking & Finance*, 19, 461–81.

Milberg, W. (2008). 'Shifting sources and uses of profits: Sustaining US financialization with global value chains', *Economy and Society*, 37(3), 420–51.

Morgan, J. (ed.) (2016). *What Is Neoclassical Economics? Debating the Origins, Meaning and Significance*. London; New York: Routledge.

Murphy, R. (2009). 'Defining the secrecy world: Rethinking the language of "Offshore" tax justice network'. Available at www.financialsecrecyindex.com/PDF/SecrecyWorld.PDF.

Neilson, J., and Yeung, H. (2014). 'Global value chains and global production networks in the changing international political economy: An introduction', *Review of International Political Economy*, 21(1), 1–8.

Obermayer, B., and Obermaier, F. (2016). *The Panama Paper: Breaking the Story on How the Rich and Powerful Hide Their Money*. Cologne: Oneworld Publications.

OECD (2015). *BEPS 2015 Final Reports*. Paris: OECD. Available at www.oecd.org/tax/beps-2015-final-reports.htm [Accessed 15 January 2016]

Palan, R. (1998). 'Trying to have your cake and eating it: How and why the state system has created offshore', *International Studies Quarterly*, 42, 625–44.

Palan, R., and Wigan, D. (2014). 'Tackling tax havens in the US and EU: A strategy of not in my backyard (NIMBY)', *Global Policy*, 5(3), 334–43.

Piketty, T. (2014). *Capital in the Twenty-First Century*. Cambridge, MA: Harvard University Press.

Quentin, D. (2018). 'Legal Opinion as an Assets', in L. Seabrooke and D. Wigan (eds), *Global Wealth Chains: Governing Assets in the World Economy*. Oxford: Oxford University Press.

Roach, S. (2003). 'Outsourcing, protectionism, and the global labor arbitrage', *Morgan Stanley Special Economic Study*. November 11, 2013, 1–16.

Ruggie, J. (1993). 'Territoriality and beyond: Problematizing modernity in international relations', *International Organization*, 47(1), 139–74.

Salmon, A., and Fusion.net (2016). 'Panama papers show how the very rich use art to get richer'. Available at http://fusion.net/story/288515/panama-papers-leak-art-market/

Santos, M. (2018). 'Keeping it in the family; keeping it in the bank: intergenerational relational work in the wealth management sector', in L. Seabrooke and D. Wigan (eds), *Global Wealth Chains: Governing Assets in the World Economy*. Oxford: Oxford University Press.

Sassen, S. (1996). 'Cities and communities in the global economy', *American Behavioral Scientist*, 39(5), 629–39.

Schwartz, H. M. (2016). 'Wealth and secular stagnation: The role of industrial organization and intellectual property rights', *The Russell Sage Journal of the Social Sciences*, 2(6), 226–49.

Scott, J. (1998). *Seeing Like a State: How Certain Schemes to Improve the Human Condition Have Failed*. New Haven, CT: Yale University Press.

Seabrooke, L. and L.F. Henriksen (eds). (2017) *Professional Networks in Transnational Governance*. Cambridge: Cambridge University Press.

Seabrooke, L., and Tsingou, E. (2014). 'Distinctions, affiliations, and professional knowledge in financial reform expert groups', *Journal of European Public Policy*, 21(3), 389–407.

Seabrooke, L., and Wigan, D. (2013). 'Emergent entrepreneurs in transnational advocacy networks: Professional mobilization in the fight for global tax justice', GREEN Working Paper No. 41, Centre for the Study of Globalisation and Regionalisation, University of Warwick.

Seabrooke, L., and Wigan, D. (2014). 'Global wealth chains in the international political economy', *Review of International Political Economy*, 21(1), 257–63.

Seabrooke, L., and Wigan, D. (2015). 'How activists use benchmarks: Reformist and revolutionary benchmarks for global economic justice', *Review of International Studies*, 41(5), 887–904.

Seabrooke, L., and Wigan, D. (2016). 'Powering ideas through expertise: Switchmen in global tax battles', Special Issue on 'Ideas, power, and public policy', *Journal of European Public Policy*, 23(3), 357–74.

Seabrooke, L., and Wigan, D. (2017). 'Global wealth chains', *Review of International Political Economy*, 24(1), 1–29.

Seabrooke, L. and D. Wigan (eds) (2018). *Global Wealth Chains: Governing Assets in the World Economy*. Oxford: Oxford University Press.

Sharman, J. C. (2010). 'Offshore and the new international political economy', *Review of International Political Economy*, 17(1), 1–19.

Wai, R. (2002). 'Transnational liftoff and juridicial touchdown: The regulatory function of private international law in an era of globalization', *Columbia Journal of Transnational Law*, 40(2), 209–74.

Wai, R. (2008). 'The interlegality of transnational private law', *Law and Contemporary Problems*, 71, 107–27.

Walker, R. (1989). 'A requiem for corporate geography: New directions in industrial organization, the production of place and the uneven development', *Geografiska Annaler*, 71B(1), 43–68.

Wigan, D. (2009). 'Financialisation and derivatives: Constructing an artifice of indifference', *Competition and Change*, 13(2), 159–74.

Wigan, D. (2013). 'Financial derivatives: Fiscal weapons of mass destruction?', *Politik*, 16(4), 18–25.

Williams, K. (2000). 'From shareholder value to present-day capitalism', *Economy and Society*, 29(1), 1–12.

Yeung, H. (2009). 'Regional development and the competitive dynamics of global production networks: An East Asian perspective', *Regional Studies*, 43(3), 325–51.

Zucman, G. (2015). *The Hidden Wealth of Nations: The Scourge of Tax Havens*. Chicago: University of Chicago Press.

18

ARRESTED DEVELOPMENT IN AFRICA'S GLOBAL WEALTH CHAINS

Accountability and hierarchy among 'tax havens'

Attiya Waris and Leonard Seabrooke

Improving global value chains has been heralded by academics, civil society and international economic organizations as a key way to upgrade African economies. There has been far less emphasis on upgrading financial institutions, or on the role of aggressive tax planning and tax avoidance that is important in how firms profit from their value chains. In global value chains research finance is generally tied to a defined development paradigm, such as microfinance. This chapter examines attempts by different African states to develop international financial centers as hubs for global wealth chains. There are many domestic and international obstacles in doing so, including reputational problems in demonstrating reliable domestic elites, intrastate and interstate conflicts, and lack of infrastructure, market and technology access. While there is a long history of states creating international financial centers in advanced economies and off-shore jurisdictions, this requires accountable elites and/or for the state to have a sufficient place in the hierarchy of international decision-making regimes for finance. Such jurisdictions have not, until recently, been punished internationally for offering aggressive tax planning services. In the African case the perceived absence of elite accountability and poor positioning in interstate hierarchies makes it difficult for African financial institutions to act as leaders in connecting local, regional and global capital. This chapter discusses how African attempts to create complex global wealth chains, through the establishment of international financial centers, can be characterized as a case of arrested development.

Introduction

Global value chains can assist development, facilitate information flows between suppliers and producers, and generate positive growth for advanced and developing economies alike. This has been the popular view of global value chains (GVCs) in academic research and, more recently, the standpoint of the international economic organizations, like the OECD and the World Bank (Gereffi 2014; OECD 2015; Taglioni and Winkler 2014), where GVCs are generally viewed as a means for progressive economic development. The most positive example in the public imagination is Fair Trade coffee, where well-governed value chains can ensure a good return to farmers and a clean conscience to consumers. As many have commented, GVCs do not always lead to genuine development, including the 'latte revolution' (Daviron and Ponte 2005). Rather than producing 'factory Africa' many GVCs do not lead to industrial upgrading and knowledge transfers, and African firms commonly stay as second- or third-tier partners within a value chain, taking orders from above (Gibbon and Ponte 2005; Haakonsson 2009; Farole and Winkler 2014). This critical view of GVCs contains an implicit argument that African production networks are enmeshed in an international hierarchy where the chance of African firms being leaders within chains is minimal. This chapter suggests that hierarchy can also be seen in Africa's engagement with global wealth chains. This chapter contributes to this volume through an analysis of global wealth chains (GWCs), which seeks to understand how different types of financial relationships are governed across jurisdictions, and to unpick the relationships between lead financial institutions, those supplying capital, clients, and regulators.

In the African context GWCs are important as they are the means through which trade and investment are facilitated, as well as taxes paid or avoided. Multinational corporations (MNCs) can minimize, avoid or evade taxes, exploit tax policies and divert financial and other geographically mobile capital, income and profits through nodes such as offshore financial centers, tax havens, and secrecy jurisdictions. These actions induce potential distortions in the patterns of trade and investment that form the linkages or chains within the wealth chains and reduce global welfare by eroding national tax bases of other countries. Knock-on effects include altering the structure of tax base (by shifting part of the tax burden from mobile to relatively immobile factors and from income to consumption) and hampering the application of progressive tax rates and the achievement of redistributive goals in the states from which the wealth is moved. As a result, GWCs can boost fiscal revenues but also deplete them. As such, there is a shared fiscal concern between the growing literature on wealth chains and the much earlier research on 'state capacity' in Africa (Migdal 1988), including what institutional foundations are necessary to permit economic prosperity (Bates 1989).

GWCs that assist tax avoidance and evasion inhibit development in various ways. Developing countries can fail to benefit from the activities of MNCs within their jurisdiction when the maintenance or construction of the domestic tax base is impeded, and when they suffer from either illicit or volatile capital flows beyond their control and the regulatory reach of the principal global financial centers. Pressure of this sort can result in changes in tax structures into which many countries may be forced, by virtue of the spillover effects of changes in the tax bases, even though a more desirable result could have been achieved through intensifying international co-operation of all jurisdictions. In light of the previous statement, it has been estimated that $11 trillion of private and corporate wealth resides in 'secrecy' jurisdictions, and that up to half of the world's capital passes through offshore financial centers, secrecy jurisdictions and tax havens (Henry 2012). The tax loss to developing countries, as a result of the extensive use of these jurisdictions, at least matches the funding required to meet the Millennium Development Goals (Fröburg and Waris 2011).

Léonce Ndikumana and James Boyce (2011) estimated capital flight from 33 African countries at an accumulated $735bn during 1970–2008, worth $944bn at conservative interest rates; this number happens to tally closely with industry estimates of the holdings of African High Net Worth Individuals at $800–1,000bn. Most of this capital flight escaped offshore, and stayed offshore. Compare these numbers to the estimated external debts for these countries of 'just' $177bn in 2008 – suggesting that Africa was a net creditor to the world of $767bn (see also Ajayi and Ndikumana 2015). The trouble is, of course, that the assets are in the hands of a small, wealthy African elite, while the broader African populations are impacted via reduced health, education and infrastructure – or higher taxes shoulder the liabilities (Fröburg and Waris 2011).

The upshot here is that developing GWCs are not only an opportunity for those in the financial sector, but also a source of potential fiscal revenue that can boost state capacity and assist economic development. We see GWCs as being neither good nor bad but wish to examine what types are supported in African states. We know much less about the multi-jurisdictional links between clients and suppliers in the African financial sector, or what we refer to as African GWCs. This chapter aims to begin filling this gap (see also earlier work by Styger et al. 1999). Identifying these links is important in understanding what techniques are used in aggressive tax planning and tax avoidance. Improving our information about GWCs is important in combating fiscal leaks and enabling governments to help their societies.

Seabrooke and Wigan (2017; see also their chapter in this volume) define global wealth chains as 'transacted forms of capital operating multi-jurisdictionally for the purposes of wealth creation and protection'. GWCs differ in the complexity of transactions and information asymmetries between clients, suppliers and regulators. We suggest that African attempts to develop complex financial institutions that integrate local regional and global capital are constrained by perception of accountable elites and an insufficient place in the hierarchy of states that govern international finance. Rather than encouraging the development of international financial centers (IFCs), external pressures on African states have led to an increasing role of international economic organizations as intermediaries for financial flows (Lavelle 1999) or for less complex financial systems, typically microfinance (Buckley 1997). While the international political economy has a long history of states creating IFCs in advanced economies and offshore, this option is not necessarily still open to all states globally as well as specifically to developing or African states. This chapter discusses the importance of indigenous innovations in the creation of simple local to regional and global wealth chains, as well as how attempts to create more complex local to regional and then global wealth chains utilizing IFCs are blocked for political, social as well as economic reasons. In short, those building international financial services exist in a 'neo-imperial' space that is full of contradictions and hypocrisy (Boussebaa and Morgan 2014). While it may be very well for the United States and northwestern European nations to offer aggressive tax planning services that facilitate tax avoidance, such practices are not encouraged for African economies.

GWCs can be categorized in a variety of ways, depending on the complexity of the transactions and the types of relationships between suppliers, clients and regulators. According to the GWCs framework, there are five types of wealth chains that mirror the established types in GVCs literature (Gereffi et al. 2005). Figure 18.1 reproduces the five types from Seabrooke and Wigan (2017), defined as the Market, Modular, Relational, Captive, and Hierarchy wealth chains. *Market* wealth chains form through arm's-length relationships with low complexity in established legal regimes. *Modular* wealth chains offer bespoke services and products within well-established financial and legal environments that restrict the supplier and client flexibility. Products involve complex information but can be exchanged with little explicit coordination and within established institutional frameworks. *Relational* wealth chains involve the exchange of complex tacit information, requiring high levels of explicit coordination and often rely on trust networks. *Captive* wealth chains exist where lead suppliers control smaller suppliers by dominating the legal apparatus and financial technology. Finally, the *Hierarchy* wealth chains are vertically integrated and highly complex entities, with a high degree of control exercised by senior management. These five types of GWCs are often mixed in practice, and the development of this classification as an analytic device intends to highlight how wealth is created and protected in a variety of ways across jurisdictions.

A key aspect of the work on GWCs that strongly differs from GVCs is the ability to codify transactions. In the GVCs framework coding information on transactions along the value chain

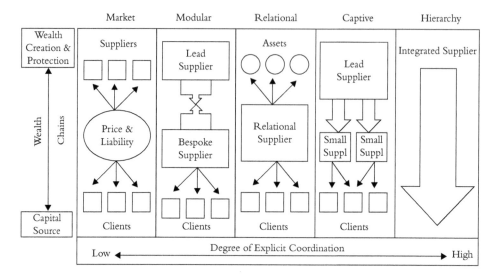

Figure 18.1 Five global wealth chain governance types.

Source: Seabrooke and Wigan 2017: 12, adapted from Gereffi et al. 2005: 89.

is an important aim for efficiency, knowledge sharing and development. In GWCs much of the activity is concerned with limiting access to information on who is transacting what, and in what financial form. As such, the GWCs framework focuses on *regulatory liability* – the chance of getting in trouble with multi-jurisdictional regulators – and specifies the types of information asymmetries involved in different wealth chains. Market wealth chains are characterized by arm's-length relationships between clients and suppliers, and especially regulators. Those selling 'off-the-shelf' shell companies often know little about their clients, and mainly so regulators know even less about them. Relational wealth chains, such as family trusts, are built on complex schemes to protect the identity and assets of clients, even if the suppliers are well-known and are integrated in political and professional networks. Hierarchy wealth chains are highly complex and integrated, providing financial innovations that outstrip regulators' capacity to detect exactly what transactions are taking place (as has been the case with Apple; see Seabrooke and Wigan 2014). However, in the Modular and Captive wealth chains there is a lot of information about what is going on between clients, suppliers, and regulators. Authorities have information on what may constitute tax avoidance and evasion but often do not prosecute. The failure to clamp down on 'expat' finance schemes operating in Jersey for major financial institutions such as HSBC and Lloyd's is but one example (De Carvalho and Seabrooke 2016). In these Modular and Captive examples we have an important element – state permissiveness. Such permissiveness is conditioned not only by what practices domestic elites are willing to sweep under the carpet and ignore, but also by other states and elites' perceptions of how important the country is to the international financial governance. A bold international financial center requires a widespread perception that reliable elites are present and the state has a sufficient place in the hierarchy of states in the international political economy.

The GWCs framework helps us to identify what kind of relationship the state can have with international capital, as well as what the international system will accept or reject. State permissiveness in offshore finance has long been noted as important in the 'commercialization of sovereignty' (Palan 2003). Such permissiveness not only is an attribute of actors in the international political economy but also is a characteristic of the system. Some states are permitted to pursue complex financial sectors with aggressive tax optimization schemes, while others are not. Whether or not they are permitted to do so depends on the character of elites in the state involved, and also how states are placed in hierarchies of decision-making in international regimes, such as those for international financial and fiscal governance. As such, the development of an IFC depends on two key perceptions from policy elites in the international political economy. The first is that domestic elites are accountable to a recognized authority so that financial operations are not reduced to facilitating corruption and illicit money flows. The second is that the government is integrated into international decision-making and has an adequate place in the international hierarchy. In short, the formula is as follows:

Sufficient Accountability + *Sufficient Hierarchy* = *Prosperous International Financial Center*

Here we have the issues of accountability and hierarchy. Historically, international financial centers needed to have only one of these conditions to prosper. Many of the smaller jurisdictions that provide offshore financial services have reliable elites but only proxy influence within international hierarchies, mainly through former colonial powers. Typical examples are Barbados or Curacao. Other jurisdictions have used their place in international hierarchies to set up an international financial center, even if their domestic elites could not demonstrate accountability. Tax havens in the heart of Europe, such as Luxembourg and Switzerland immediately come to mind. We suggest that in the realm of international financial centers, a latecomer aspiring to develop and prosper must satisfy both criteria and, moreover, ensure that an international financial center contributes to tax revenues of the domestic economy.

The accountability of local elites is especially prominent in the African context. Since 1995, the corruption index compiled by Transparency International has featured African countries as the most corrupt in the world. The focus on corruption of the domestic political elites must be placed in the context of what global wealth chains can provide. Corruption estimates do not recognize that the international fiscal framework is a contributing factor (Otusanya 2011a), especially in allowing for the existence of transitory and end nodes within opaque systems, such as Mauritius and Seychelles, as well as other tax havens that allow corrupt elites to hide illicitly gotten gains (Cobham 2014). It has been estimated that West Africa's political elites hold between $700bn to $800bn in offshore accounts (Baker 2005). Boston Consulting Group (2011: 3) and Gabriel Zucman (2015: 53) suggest that a third of African wealth is held offshore. According to the World Bank's StAR Initiative report, Muammar Qaddafi's wealth allegedly included assets in the United States (estimated at $37bn), United Kingdom (£12bn), the Netherlands ($2.1bn), Austria ($1.8bn), Sweden ($1.6bn) and Switzerland ($416 million) (Ndikumana and Boyce 2012). Interestingly, in the case of Hosni Mubarak, Switzerland immediately froze the money sent illicitly out of Egypt in the days leading to the overthrow of his government. What remains of concern, however, is that the Swiss banks obtained the funds and simply rejected the transfer (World Bank 2015; see also van der Does de Willebois et al. 2011).

A further point here is that demonstrating the accountability of individuals is a fundamental norm in world politics (Kim and Sharman 2014), while the perception of jurisdictional control is tied to the national level rather than the usage of the global systems by individuals. Much of the politics here is linked to the perception of corruption and accountability. A seemingly superficial but important study of email scams is an illustrative example. A Microsoft-based study of email scams notes that those seeking to obtain bank account information from the gullible describe the source of the funds as being from Nigeria (51%), or Cote d'Ivoire, Ghana, Senegal or other West Africa countries (34%) (Herley 2012: 11). The reason why con artists mention Nigeria is because they don't want to spend time and effort in concocting a unique plausible story for each potential victim. Instead, they rely on the basic beliefs among those targeted about places that are likely to have elite politicians, or royal family members, in desperate need of a highly unusual financial transaction. While there is indeed strong evidence that Nigerian elites engage in complex illicit financial schemes to evade taxes, sometimes with the assistance of MNCs (Otusanya 2011b), the broader perception problem remains. In short, African economies seeking to build complex financial systems suffer from actual corruption problems as well as significant perception problems. Credibly demonstrating accountability is difficult.

Improving a country's position within international hierarchy is even harder. Hierarchy has been a popular theme in recent years in International Relations and International Political Economy (Cooley 2003; Cooley 2005; Donnelly 2006; Hobson and Sharman 2005; Lake 2009). Lake notes how social contracts are formed between dominant and subordinate members and highlights that because sovereignty is negotiated, international relations are not a uniform piece of cloth, but a rich tapestry of varying shades, hues, and patterns (Lake 2009: 175). Other work on hierarchy has stressed the importance of difference and self-differentiation among the units of the international system. The basic insight from this literature is that the attempts by the states to create value and wealth chains exist within constructed hierarchical orders rather than under conditions of the rational incentives of atomized states (Keene 2007). In short, hierarchy matters in what states are allowed to do. States that do not have a sufficient place in international hierarchy will find it difficult to influence international regimes and transnational rule-making. We suggest that African attempts at creating complex wealth chains are inhibited by an insufficient place in international hierarchy. While European 'tax havens' can host international institutions such as the Bank for International Settlements or the European Court of Justice to affirm their place in the hierarchy for international financial governance, African states have no such possibility. Indeed, we suggest that research on tax avoidance must take perceptions of accountability and hierarchy into account. Policy discussions about eliminating tax avoidance do not take place on a level playing field, and such perceptions are important in understanding what are sensible policy options for international organizations, advanced economies, and developing economies (see Chaikin and Sharman 2009).

This chapter proceeds as follows: (i) we discuss how states have historically pursued building complex GWCs as an explicit strategy, drawing on the accountability of their elite and position within international hierarchy; (ii) we then locate African states among the types of GWCs and potential lead supplier relationships; (iii) we discuss African attempts at creating IFCs, including 'tax havens', and what restrictions they are facing in developing them. We then reflect on our concepts of hierarchy and dependence and discuss how analyzing the attempts to create GWCs helps us understand a broader structural dynamics in the international political economy.

Financial centers as state-building

The prerequisites for creating financial centers include the presence of foreign investment opportunity, low to no foreign corporation tax rate; collaboration with other financial centers, and a demonstrated capacity for a strong regulatory and legislative framework. An international financial center must have high concentration of banking activities such as financing foreign trade by issuing credit for imports, currency exchange, foreign exchange (FOREX) trading, transferring funds across political boundaries (foreign currency deposits), foreign borrowing and lending as well as foreign investment. An international financial center is often a city which facilitates the flow of domestic capital to the outside world or a city, which due to its location and facilities serves as a foreign lending and trading center for foreign currencies. It is typically a place that, due to its favorable tax laws and banking regulations, acts as a haven for foreign lending and borrowing. IFCs require adequate state supervision (permissive, and not invasive), a skilled workforce, frameworks for dealing with insolvency and bankruptcy, credit information mechanisms, and adherence to international governance regimes.

States create financial centers to attract capital and export capital in particular forms. Historical examples are London, Amsterdam and New York (Germain 1997; Cassis 2006), with New York as recently as the early 1980s creating an International Banking Facility that explicitly sought to undercut other financial markets (Seabrooke 2001: 111; Picciotto 2012: 95). In the postwar period the emergence of a new era of global finance included not only the establishment of the Bretton Woods institutions but also aggressive strategies from OECD states and their former colonies to capture a share of an ever expanding international private market for capital (Helleiner 1995). Within the OECD, and especially in the UK, the desire to increase market share in international finance led to the creation of the Euromarkets as an implicit state policy (Burn 1999), as well as exploiting British dependencies as locations to permit offshore capital to find a home (Palan 2003). Some of them emerged from strong trading activities, such as Hong Kong (Schenk 2007), while others were created to lessen imperial dependence and provide financial services offering low tax rates and, in many cases, anonymity. The Bahamas, British Virgin Islands, the Cayman Islands, Guernsey, and Jersey offer prominent examples, as well as Dutch dependencies such as Aruba and Curacao. These territories have 'commercialized' their sovereignty (Palan 2003), and they use international law to protect their right to arbitrage to the benefit of international financiers (Hudson 1998). In the GWCs scheme they are commonly a host to Market and Relational forms within wealth chains, where simple shell companies or trust-based tax evasion networks are prominent. The broader term for these types of economies is, of course, 'tax havens'.

In the early 2000s there was a crackdown on tax havens from the OECD, including the development of a 'blacklist' of harmful tax competitors (excluding the OECD's own tax havens) (Sharman 2006; Vlcek 2008), and the eventual development of a 'whitelist' of jurisdictions that had signed at least a dozen Tax Information Exchange Agreements by the end of 2012. The hypocrisy of the OECD initiative was clear to all concerned – that 'tax havens' outside of the OECD should be deemed as harmful to competition while those within the OECD are simply providing services to improve competitiveness and tax efficiency (Kyle 2006; Sharman 2006). This is still a common argument from OECD-based tax experts and officials seeking to fend off reforms to tax havens within the OECD membership (Seabrooke and Wigan 2016). Another way of understanding this hypocrisy is through hierarchy, where what is bad for many is permissible for some. This is especially the case among tax havens such as Switzerland that make historical claims to why their financial sector is so complex, secretive, and unique. Latecomers find it much harder to make these claims.

In the African context the development of the offshore financial centers and IFCs has been tied to simple Market GWC operations, such as the selling of shell companies or, ideally, tied to the industrial production by being married to Export Processing Zones (EPZs). Examples can be found in Djibouti, Liberia, Mauritius, the Seychelles, and Tangiers (Styger et al. 1999; Vlcek 2006), as we discuss next. A key challenge for the upgrading of these financial centers is that MNCs active in Africa have little interest in developing them (Palan et al. 2010: 175), while locally developed services face the international accountability and hierarchy issues previously outlined. We suggest that there may be a strong element of path dependency in how states view new entrants with financial centers. Mosley's (2003) work on who can invest where discusses 'OECD', 'Emerging', and 'Frontier' types of economies and how sovereign bond traders evaluate them. A more recent way of describing the effects of evaluation within closed systems is 'performativity', where the onlookers induce what they seek to find in what they are observing. For

African GWCs the onlookers, including private capital, international organizations, and NGOs, focus on the assistance from the international organizations or the grassroots microfinance initiatives (Lavelle 1999; Henriksen 2013). Indeed, these are the kinds of wealth chains that are actively encouraged, including the creation of the best international practices for microfinance (McKeen-Edwards and Porter 2014: 137). We suggest that while this is certainly a positive state of affairs, the focus on African finance affirms these simpler forms while accountability and hierarchy problems inhibit the development of more complex forms of wealth chains.

Africa's place in the global governance of wealth chains

Latecomers to the world of international financial centers and the offshore capital need to show conformity with international standards, even when the bearers of those standards often fail themselves. Here Bill Vlcek's (2012) notion that we can see a new 'financial governmernality', through demonstration of self-discipline and self-monitoring that conforms to international standards, is useful. African attempts to create more complex GWCs are constrained by accountability and hierarchy problems, while those higher in the hierarchy do not suffer severe accountability issues in international financial governance. A look at Tax Justice Network's Financial Secrecy Index confirms this.

Table 18.1 presents the top 30 jurisdictions of the top 92 ranked by the Financial Secrecy Index. The FSI is composed from an evaluation of a country's laws and regulations on financial secrecy, its involvement in tax treaties, and applies a 'Global Scale Weight' for the size of the country in global financial services (Cobham et al. 2015). The secrecy assessment is based on whether it is possible to access information on beneficial owners, whether country-by-country reporting is required, whether anti-money-laundering regulations are in place, the use of tax identifiers, and whether the country has a capacity to automatically exchange information. While some of these measures are controversial (see Seabrooke and Wigan 2015: 899–900), they are also now widely accepted by the activist community and also by some international organizations. As it can be seen from Table 18.1, African countries, with the exception of Mauritius, are absent from the top 30, with Liberia ranked 33rd, Ghana 48th, South Africa 61st, and the Seychelles 72nd. So while Transparency International's corruption index lists most African countries in the top quintile, they are not obvious places to store or hide money, whereas many jurisdictions within the OECD specialize in providing complex financial services that facilitate tax avoidance and evasion.

Table 18.1 Top 30 Jurisdictions in Tax Justice Network's Financial Secrecy Index, 2015

1. Switzerland	12. Japan	23. Mauritius
2. Hong Kong	13. Panama	24. Austria
3. USA	14. Marshall Islands	25. Bahamas
4. Singapore	15. United Kingdom	26. Brazil
5. Cayman Islands	16. Jersey	27. Malta
6. Luxembourg	17. Guernsey	28. Uruguay
7. Lebanon	18. Malaysia (Labuan)	29. Canada
8. Germany	19. Turkey	30. Russia
9. Bahrain	20. China	
10. United Arab Emirates (Dubai)	21. British Virgin Islands	
11. Macao	22. Barbados	

Source: www.financialsecrecyindex.com/introduction/fsi-2015-results.

Another measure of secrecy and corruption can be found in a recent study by Findley et al. (2013). They tested nearly 4,000 service-selling companies, to see whether or not they would comply with international law and international crime and terrorism regulations when requested to establish, for payment, an untraceable company. They found through the testing process that tax havens were extraordinarily compliant, with the Cayman Islands (100% compliance), Jersey (100%), Luxembourg (86%) and the Seychelles (82%) scoring high in their adherence to the rules. This was in a marked contrast with the 'great powers' at the top of the hierarchy in international financial governance, with the USA (25% compliant), UK (51%), Germany (50%), China (22%), Brazil (60%), Russia (71%), and Switzerland (55%) demonstrating low or middling compliance. Findley et al. (2013) have found that African states presented a mixed picture of compliance, ranging from low in Kenya (16%), Nigeria (17%), and Ghana (21%), to high in South Africa (77%), Libya (100%), and Algeria (100%). According to their report, the easiest place in the world to obtain a false ID and a company was Delaware (6% compliant).

We suggest that African economies can be considered source nodes of GVCs and GWCs due to the case of arrested development in creating more complex financial systems. Historically the GVCs have been conducting the flow outwards from most African countries to the rest of the world, with African states being a source in the value chain, especially for raw materials including minerals as well as agricultural produce. It comes as no surprise, then, that GWCs similarly place African states at the point of the source node in the wealth chain. The most recently formed Africa state Southern Sudan had an unprecedented $1.89bn portfolio investment trade with Bermuda in 2012, placing it securely as a source node (IMF CDIS 2013).

In general, there is a clear distinction to be made between direct investments among African economies that support productive enterprises versus the use of tax havens. Figures 18.2 and 18.3, contrast the outward direct investments and the outward portfolio investments from a selection of African economies in 2012. The data is derived from the IMF Direct Investment (CDIS) and Portfolio Investment (CPIS) databases. Figure 18.2 clearly shows flows of investment between major African economies and to sub-Saharan states. The picture in Figure 18.3 is radically different, with portfolio investment flowing heavily to Bermuda, Ireland, Luxembourg, Mauritius, the United Kingdom, and the United States.

The types of GWCs commonly found on the African continent concentrate around the Market, Relational, and Captive chains. Market chains are those based around simple service provision, including the sale of shell companies, for example. Relational wealth chains are based around trust relationships, including High Net Worth Individuals finding means to avoid tax and send their wealth abroad (as noted previously). Captive wealth chains can be seen in the concentration of more complex financial services around a handful of players, such as the Standard Bank Group and what was formerly ABSA and now, tellingly, is Barclays Africa Group. A few African countries such as Kenya, South Africa and Nigeria, as middle income countries, developing their own multinationals at the regional level, are currently struggling to develop more indigenously based complex financial services, and especially those that would be fiscally responsible.

Struggles by African states to develop complex forms of wealth chains are hindered by several key internal and external challenges. They include not only the characteristics mentioned in the previous section, but also conflicts and wars and ethnic influences in the economy. The lack of stability resulting from intra and interstate conflicts within the African continent affect not only an individual state but most of its regional neighbors. The result destabilizes the economy and is often based on ethnicity-based allegiances that are reflected in the economy, which inflates the distrust of investors globally, including negative perceptions of accountability of policy elites. In addition, the low levels of capacity and experience within the source nodes of African states

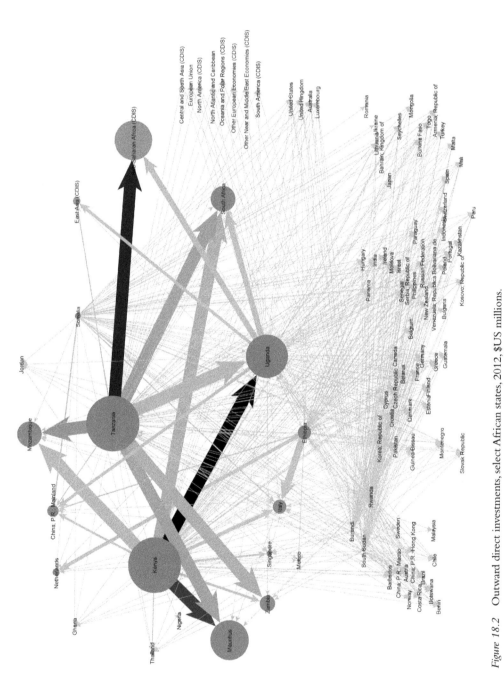

Figure 18.2 Outward direct investments, select African states, 2012, $US millions.

Source: IMF CDIS data.

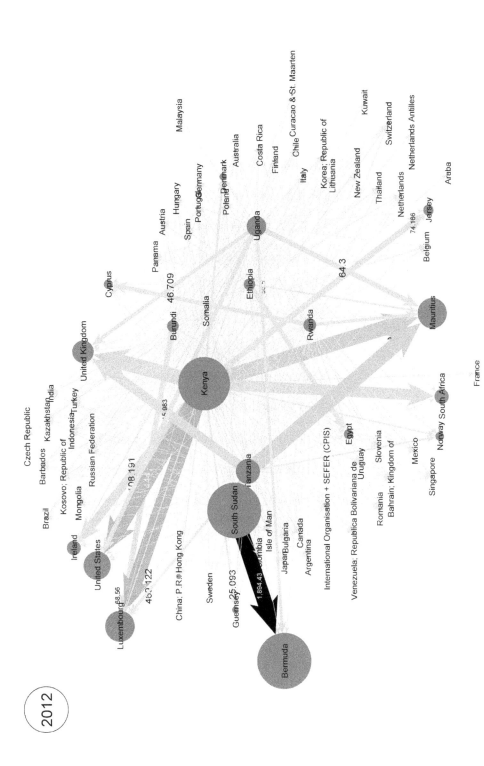

Figure 18.3 Portfolio investments, selected African states, 2012, $US millions.

Source: IMF CPIS data.

mean that the chances of African financial institutions to become lead suppliers in a multi-jurisdictional context are slim.

African attempts at international financial centers

Most of the international policy attention in reforming African financial systems has focused on resolving the accountability problems, and especially on dealing with perceptions of African finance as corrupt, illicit, or embroiled in tax havens. In June 2009, the World Bank organized its first senior-level global forum on the Stolen Asset Recovery and Development, and pledged to help return the money to the countries of origin. This followed a meeting of G20 heads of state in April 2009, which has declared that the era of banking secrecy is over. In 2010, under pressure from civil society and member states of the G8, the OECD created lists of the states that fall under the secrecy jurisdiction/tax haven definition. More specifically, the white, grey, and black lists have been created to identify less secret versus more secret jurisdictions, as requested by the G8. A working group was set up which included two African states: Mauritius and the Seychelles. The group has developed a model exchange of information agreement (TIEA), and the OECD demanded that any state wishing to be moved upwards or struck off the list would have to sign a minimum of 12 of these agreements with other states. Predominantly, those states that appeared in these lists as tax havens/secrecy jurisdictions, as well as those with the IFCs, swiftly signed these TIEAs in order to get the required 12 agreements to be taken off the black list.[1] As a result, well over a third of these are with other tax havens or with tiny jurisdictions such as Greenland, Andorra and the Faroe Islands (Sharman 2013). Of the over 200 TIEAs signed, just four were with or between African countries, Liberia, South Africa, the Seychelles and Ghana. Apart from Ghana, which has only signed one TIEA with Liberia, the other three countries are considered either to be a tax haven/secrecy jurisdiction) or have an IFC and have signed multiple agreements but only with other secrecy jurisdictions.[2] These include agreements signed by South Africa with the Bahamas and Bermuda; the Seychelles with Greenland, the Faroe Islands, Finland, Iceland, Denmark, Norway and Sweden; and Liberia with Ghana, Denmark, Sweden, Norway, Faroe Islands, Greenland, Iceland, Finland, United Kingdom, the Netherlands and Australia.[3]

Collective intergovernmental efforts have also aimed to address illicit capital flows and corruption problems. The African Tax Administrators Forum (www.aftatax.org), created in 2010 on the initiative of the revenue authority officials, is working on facilitation of joint audits on cases of potential illicit flows between African states. The Forum has developed a model of information exchange between revenue authorities. In 2011, the African Commission on Human and Peoples' Rights (www.achpr.org) passed a resolution stating that illicit capital flows were affecting the development of African continent and the ability of African states to protect human rights. In 2014, the Tana Forum of African Heads of States (www.tanaforum.org) held their 3rd session on Illicit Financial Flows and Their Effect on Peace and Security in Africa. Most recently, the African Union released a report by the Thabo Mbeki Special Panel on Illicit Financial Flows (www.uneca.org/iff) in 2015 reflecting on the urgency in dealing with this problem.

1 Tax Information Exchange Agreements (TIEAs), available at www.oecd.org/ctp/exchange-of-tax-information/taxinformationexchangeagreementstieas.htm [accessed 10 January 2015].
2 OECD: Countering Offshore Tax Evasion, 25 May 2011. Available at https://www.oecd.org/ctp/harmful/43775845.pdf [accessed 2 July 2017].
3 Tax Information Exchange Agreements (TIEAs), available at www.oecd.org/ctp/exchange-of-tax-information/taxinformationexchangeagreementstieas.htm [accessed 10 January 2015].

This international change has found support in numerous academic, government as well as civil society publications pointing to the fact that illicit financial flows take place through tax havens.[4] Recent cases include the SAB Miller report, which showed that a retail shop right next to the SAB Miller factory in Accra was paying more tax than the factory itself (ActionAid 2010). In addition, most of the money looted or stolen from developing countries by African leaders has found its way into secret bank accounts in some IFCs in developed countries, with examples including Hosni Mubarak (Egypt) who has accounts in Switzerland, Sani Abacha (Nigeria) who allegedly had accounts in both the UK and Switzerland, and Mobutu Sese Seko (Democratic Republic of Congo) with accounts across Europe. (Oxfam 2000; Sikka 2003; US Senate Subcommittee on Investigations 2005, 2010; Tax Justice Network 2005; AAPPG 2006; Otusanya 2011b; Leaman and Waris 2013).

So why are African states going against the flow and still trying to set up the IFCs? Various African countries have continued to move in the direction of granting wide sweeping tax exemptions for foreign direct investment as well as establishing the IFCs. In Kenya, for example, it has been argued that an IFC is being created to attract foreign investment and boost the financial services industry, with the hope that this will trigger spillover effects into other sectors, and ultimately have positive repercussions for economic growth and development.[5] The aim is to develop IFCs as nodes for GWCs where African suppliers can reap the rewards from providing complex financial services, rather than serving as source or transit points.

Existing IFCs within the African continent

IFCs on the African mainland (i.e. excluding Mauritius and the Seychelles) either have been recently established or are still in the planning phase, apart from the ones in Morocco, Djibouti and Liberia. Different countries have chosen different IFC models. In Morocco, Tangiers offers a tax-free environment via the Tangier Exportation Free Zone. Considered an 'offshore center' by the IMF, the Zone was described by Deloitte (2013) as an offshore financial center open to all international banks and financial establishments. Although the corporate tax rate is on a par with countries not classified as tax havens, companies are subject to tax 'only on income generated from activities carried out in Morocco'. Holding company regulations allow for a corporate tax rate of $500 per year for 15 years and a tax exemption on dividend distributions and the repatriation of profit.[6]

In Seychelles it is estimated that 11% of the island's GDP is generated from ring-fenced financial services. These services include the classic mix of banking secrecy, company re-domiciliation, protected shell companies, tax exemptions, absence of financial reporting requirements and a lack of disclosure concerning beneficial owners and company ownership, including shareholders, directors, trusts and other critical details. Shell companies can be established within a day. Registration fees are between $100 and $1000 per annum thereafter. Banks even provide 'account signatory' services that allow foreign clients to benefit from enhanced secrecy. The International Business Companies Act 1994 allows companies to operate completely tax-free provided the foreign entities do not conduct economic activities in Seychelles or own real estate. International business company (IBC) benefits also include air and vessel services. According to Fidelity Corporate Services, an offshore agent in Seychelles: 'This means that you can have your

---

4 Froburg and Waris, *Bringing Back the Billions*; ActionAid SAB Miller report; Boyce and Ndikumana, Resolution of African Commission.
5 Interview 1, Treasury Official Kenya.
6 Interview 2, Somaliland businessman, Hargeysa, Somaliland (28 March 2014).

IBC registered in Seychelles with an authorized capital of a hundred million dollars and still pay the same government fee of $100.' Since 1994, the Seychelles have registered 30,000 IBCs, with 600 new entities being created each month.

Djibouti has been operating as a free port since 1949. The Djibouti Free zone – in the process of development – allows for company re-domiciliation, tax breaks, five- to ten-year licensing exemptions, among other perks, and will serve as a transshipment center. Situated at the strategic point between Europe, Africa and the Middle East, Djibouti provides foreign companies with port infrastructure, offshore services as well as export-oriented goods via entities with the title of Export Processing Company. Djibouti's services render the country one of few African countries that serve as regional offshore finance centers, characterized by relatively developed infrastructure and a range of geographically specific services. It also houses companies that operate in Somaliland where, because of the lack of state recognition, laws remain unsettled, and, as a result, flows of money moving into the region are registered as Djibouti-based. Barclays Bank attempted to stop transfers of money to this market, and it is alleged that this was an attempt to abuse its dominant position in the African market.[7]

In the late 1940s, Liberia developed a flag state to provide corporate and maritime tax haven services, specifically to vessel owners and operators. It was developed under the wing of Standard Oil, arguably the largest oil corporation at the time. Liberia's registry, administered by a private corporation based in the US, currently hosts 10% of the global fleet – including 1,049 German vessels and 509 oil rigs – representing almost ten times the share of the US. The government does not tax profits and collects fees that rise to several hundreds of dollars per company each year. Offering many of the same services as leading secrecy jurisdictions, Liberia's maritime registry supplied between 40 and 70 per cent of the government's official revenue between 1997 and 2003.[8]

Emerging tax havens

The question then arises whether it can be said that there are already offshore centers in place in Africa. Furthermore, since the world is slowly being pushed away from offshore centers and tax havens with a growing international outcry against not only the existence of tax havens and offshore centers but also the practice of granting of tax exemptions and incentives, the question is why is the opposite taking place in Africa. Botswana has attempted to set up a center in 2003, which is now perceived as not being successful. In Ghana, there was an attempt to set up an offshore center in 2008, while Kenya since 2010 has been in discussions of legislation that would enable it to set up an IFC (Waris 2014) This addition of a transitory or an end node within the global wealth chain is a cause for concern for the existing players, private stakeholders as well as states. When the control of a source, a transitionary and an end node are all within a state or a region, the links are being weakened or broken off with other nodes in other parts of the world, not only threatening the existing system of nodes and their linkages, but also destabilising other economies which previously served as a transitory or an end node. The source node usually remains stable. The result is that the linkages and nodes within GWCs are now unstable, under a threat and also in a flux.

---

7 C. Provost, 'Row as Barclays Promotes Tax Havens as "Gateway for Investment" in Africa', *The Guardian* (20 November 2013), available at www.theguardian.com/global-development/2013/nov/20/barclays-bank-tax-havens-africa-mauritius-offshore [accessed 1 April 2104].

8 K. Sharife, 'Liberia, Flags of Convenience and Corporate Capitalism', *Pambazuka News* (21 October 2010), 501, available at www.pambazuka.net/en/category.php/features/67971.

Botswana has had an IFC in place since 2003, but has not managed to emerge as a significant player in the global market for financial services, although it does occupy an important space at the regional level. It was structured after the Irish model: a low corporate tax rate, no capital gains tax, a wide network of tax treaties, including those with secrecy jurisdictions, but no special arrangements for formation and registration of corporate entities. This model has traditionally attracted tax evasion and avoidance flows. It facilitates the easy transfer and repatriation of funds to avoid withholding and capital gains tax, thus earning the moniker of 'Switzerland of Africa' in an article by the Harvard International Review in 2010.[9]

Gambia is putting in place a model similar to that of Mauritius or the Seychelles, by offering a new online corporate registry with quick and cheap incorporation of secretive companies and trusts. This model has typically attracted flows from individuals looking to launder illicit funds. At the same time, in Ghana the announcements that the government is planning to create an IFC in Accra with the support of Barclays Bank has generated concerns, both locally and from the international community, particularly the OECD. Eventually, the parliament decided to put the plan on hold in 2008, before it was implemented.

In Kenya, authorities' efforts to turn Nairobi into a major regional financial center are currently underway. The Vision 2030 Development Plan of Kenya has identified the IFC as the flagship project within its development plan, which will be the vehicle by which all other issues set out in its development agenda will be financed. The country is a particularly interesting case study, as it is an important regional power and a large market; many multinational corporations, such as Google, IBM and Coca Cola, have set up their Africa-wide regional headquarters in Nairobi. Strengthening the country's financial markets is a natural step, if the country wants to preserve its regional role and compete with other regional IFCs such as Johannesburg, Mauritius and the Seychelles.

While the establishment of an IFC could have positive effects for an economy and help the state retain and draw foreign investment, academics, policy makers and advocates have expressed doubts. An IFC could facilitate the flow of capital out of the country through tax evasion and avoidance, thus undermining the tax base, and draw illicit capital from the rest of the region. Such concerns are heightened by a number of factors: the country's vulnerability to corruption, poor compliance with international anti-money-laundering standards, proximity to conflict-ridden, or fragile resource-rich countries, exposure to trafficking and smuggling (small arms, minerals and poached wildlife) and, more recently, the exposure to terrorism.

In addition, there is the issue of the legislative framework that guides the creation of an IFC. In all the models there is inevitably the need for special laws to be put into place to guide the workings of the IFC. However, in those countries in the developing world where existing judiciaries and parliaments move slowly, the political process can halt the progress of the creation of an IFC, – as is evidenced by the now a five-year long process of setting up an IFC in Kenya which has not yet reached fruition. Many judiciaries also have limited commercial training and resolving difficulties will inevitably be slow. Politically, judiciaries maintain a very strong control on their functions. Recently, Kenya's Chief Justice has announced creation of a dispute resolution arm within the commercial wing of the judiciary, potentially in response to the possibility of the establishment of an IFC which may require a special judiciary dedicated to resolving any IFC-related disputes, as seen in Qatar and the UAE.

However, this does not mean that no other countries offer tax breaks for investors. Countries in both the anglophone and the francophone Africa have sweeping provisions for foreign direct

---

9   Hilaire Avril, "Africa: Emerging trend towards establishing offshore tax havens." Available at www.ipsnews. net/2011/08/africa-emerging-trend-towards-establishing-offshore-tax-havens/

investment in the form of special economic zones. This includes, but is not limited to, countries like Kenya, Rwanda, Nigeria, Ghana and South Africa. The issue that remains unclear is how to explain these attempts within the African continent to set up areas of preferential taxation when the rest of the world is tightening its legislation. The opinions presented in the interviews conducted with the officials in Kenya, Rwanda, Puntland and Nigeria, differed. In many cases the officials did not clearly articulate the effect of IFCs on their own countries. However, once the arguments on both sides were presented to them, they quickly grew concerned. The Nigerian Commissioner of Economy[10] responded in a patriotic manner, stating that all potential methods of improving his country's economy would be utilized as much as possible to improve the situation in his country. The President of Puntland reacted by immediately stating that the creation of an IFC would harm the continent by focusing finances in one part and thus potentially causing collapse of neighboring economies.[11] The Rwandan Director of Health Finance in the Ministry of Health stated that all provisions within the East African Community (EAC) must be compliant with the EAC requirements and that this would require agreement with all member states.[12]

Concerns should, however, be put in perspective. For instance, developing countries like Kenya and Ghana already have a significant corruption problem, and it is not clear whether corruption would increase, should such a location fulfill its aspirations of becoming an IFC. Similarly, as the case of Botswana demonstrates, it is unlikely that criminals or legitimate clients from Africa or elsewhere will be rushing to transfer their money out of well-established financial centers such as London or Zurich, into a less well-regulated, politically unstable city in an ethnically divided state. The key is, rather, to understand whether having in place an IFC would be good or bad for sustainable development.

Conclusion

In order for African states to have financial institutions that facilitate international capital flows they need to give regulatory authorities a greater oversight over the issues of fiscal sustainability, preventing tax avoidance and evasion. The barriers to development of Captive and Modular wealth chains in Africa is a combination of insufficiently strong lead firms and an international environment that rejects the notion of offshore finance in Africa other than in 'tax haven' microstates.

Global wealth chains provide the means for capital to be transacted in ways that can create and protect wealth and fund development goals. In contrast to global value chains, which are encouraged as pro-development and enhancing transparency, wealth chains rely on an opaque network of financial practices and jurisdictional protections that are firmly enmeshed in the structure of financial capitalism, including its privileges and biases. This chapter examined how African states have attempted to integrate themselves into global wealth chains. We suggest that wealth chains differ not only in complexity but also in their location within the international politico-economic hierarchies. Some jurisdictions are permitted to host and develop complex methods of storing wealth for elites, while others are prevented from doing so. We examined African attempts to create complex wealth chains through the establishment of the financial centers, and discussed the reasons for why African global wealth chains are restricted to the

10 Interview 3 Former Chair, Economic Commission of Nigeria Nuru Ribadu 27 April 2014, Addis Ababa, Ethiopia.
11 Interview 4, President of Puntland, Abdul Weli 27 April 2014, Addis Ababa, Ethiopia.
12 Interview 5, Ag Director Health Finance, Ministry of Health, 29 April 2014, Nairobi Kigali. EAC includes Burundi, Kenya, Rwanda, South Sudan, Tanzania, and Uganda.

forms that reflect and reinforce their dependency in the world economy. In short, we suggest that international perceptions of accountability and hierarchy matters for how global wealth chains can be structures, and who is permitted to create them. Which economies are allowed to engage in aggressive tax planning and provide tax avoidance services is determined in large part by accountability and hierarchy, and not only by the capacity.

The message coming out from Africa could almost be regarded as schizophrenic. On the one hand, the regional response is to prevent illicit capital flows, while the states within the continent seem to be repeatedly attempting to set up tax-free zones in the form of tax havens, financial centers or offshore centers, in addition to continuing to grant tax incentives and exemptions. These are not just mixed messages being received globally, but contradictions that further impede the stability of the continent. However, it is clear that international tax rules must be developed as a coherent body of the law applicable and enforceable worldwide. If this is not done consistently, where a set of laws is dismantled the users of these structures will simply push to have it re-constructed in another, less regulated and more opaque jurisdiction.

References

AAPPG (2006). 'The other side of the coin: The UK and corruption in Africa', a report by the Africa All Party Parliamentary Group, March.

ActionAid (2010). *Calling Time on Tax Avoidance*. London: ActionAid.

Ajayi, S. I., and Ndikumana, L. (2015). *Capital Flight From Africa: Causes, Effects, and Policy Issues*. New York: Oxford University Press.

Amutabi, M. N. (2006). *The NGO Factor in Africa: The Case of Arrested Development in Kenya*. London: Routledge.

Baker, R. (2005). *Capitalism's Achilles Heel: Dirty Money and How to Renew the Free-Market System*. London: Wiley.

Barrientos, S., Knorringa, P., Evers, B., Visser, M., and Opondo, M. (2015). 'Shifting regional dynamics of global value chains: Implications for economic and social upgrading in African horticulture', *Environment and Planning A* 48(7), 1266–1283.

Bates, R. H. (1989). *Beyond the Miracle of the Market: The Institutional Foundations of Agrarian Development in Kenya*. Cambridge: Cambridge University Press.

Boston Consulting Group (2011). 'Global wealth 2011: Shaping a new tomorrow'. Available at http://piketty.pse.ens.fr/ les/BCG2011.pdf [Accessed 11 January 2016]

Boussebaa, M., and Morgan, G. (2014). 'Pushing the frontiers of critical international business studies: The multinational as a neo-imperial space', *Critical Perspectives on International Business*, 10(1/2), 96–106.

Buckley, G. (1997). 'Microfinance in Africa: Is it either the problem or the solution?', *World Development*, 25(7), 1081–93.

Burn, G. (1999). 'The state, the city, and the euromarkets', *Review of International Political Economy*, 6(2), 225–61.

Cassis, Y. (2006). *Capitals of Capital: The Rise and Fall of International Financial Centres 1780–2005*. Cambridge: Cambridge University Press.

Chaikin, D., and Sharman, J. C. (2009). *Corruption and Money Laundering: A Symbiotic Relationship*. Basingstoke: Palgrave.

Cobham, A. (2014). 'The impacts of illicit financial flows on peace and security in Africa, study for TANA high-level forum on security in Africa 2014', London. Available at www.tanaforum.org//illicit_nancial_ows_con ict_ and_security_in_africa_ nal.pdf [Accessed 11 January 2016]

Cobham, A., Janský, P., and Meinzer, M. (2015). 'The financial secrecy index: Shedding new light on the geography of secrecy', *Economic Geography*, 91(3), 281–303.

The Competition of International Financial Centres and the Role of Law Douglas W. Arner★ Director, Asian Institute of International Financial Law (www.AIIFL.com), Director, LLM (Corporate & Financial Law) Programme, and Associate Professor, Faculty of Law, University of Hong Kong.

Cooley, A. (2003). 'Thinking rationally about hierarchy and global governance', *Review of International Political Economy*, 10(4), 672–84.

Cooley, A. (2005). *Logics of Hierarchy: The Organization of Empires, States and Military Occupations.* Ithaca, NY: Cornell University Press.

Daviron, B., and Ponte, S. (2005). *The Coffee Paradox: Global Markets, Commodity Trade and the Elusive Promise of Development.* London: Zed Books.

de Carvalho, B., and Seabrooke, L. (2016). 'Expatriates in global wealth chains', NUPI Policy Brief 6, NUPI: Oslo.

Desai, M. C., Foley, C. F., and Hines, J. R. (2005). 'Foreign direct investment and the domestic capital stock', NBER Working Paper 11075, January.

Deloitte (2013). *Middle East Tax Handbook: Spotlight on Tax.* Available at https://www2.deloitte.com/content/dam/Deloitte/xe/Documents/tax/me_tax_handbook_2013.pdf

Donnelly, J. (2006). 'Sovereign inequalities and hierarchy in anarchy: American power and international society', *European Journal of International Relations*, 12(2), 139–70.

EFCC Report (2006). 'Africa loses $148b yearly to corruption'. Available at www.efccnigeria.org/index.php?option=com_content&task=view&id=811&Itemid=2 [Accessed 21 February]

Farole, T., and Winkler, D. (2014). *Making Foreign Direct Investment Work for Sub-Saharan Africa: Local Spillovers and Competitiveness in Global Value Chains.* Washington, DC: World Bank.

Findley, M. G., Nielson, D. L., and Sharman, J. C. (2013). *Global Shell Games: Experiments in Transnational Relations, Crime, and Terrorism.* Cambridge: Cambridge University Press.

Fröburg, K., and Waris, A. (2011). *Bringing the Billions Back – How Africa and Europe Can End Illicit Capital Flight.* Stockholm: Forum Syd förlag.

Gereffi, G. (2014). 'Global value chains in a post-Washington consensus world', *Review of International Political Economy*, 21(1), 9–37.

Gereffi, G., Humphrey, J., and Sturgeon, T. (2005). 'The governance of global value chains', *Review of International Political Economy*, 12(1), 78–104.

Germain, R. (1997). *The International Organization of Credit.* Cambridge: Cambridge University Press.

Gibbon, P., and Ponte, S. (2005). *Trading Down: Africa, Value Chains, and the Global Economy.* Philadelphia, PA: Temple University Press.

Haakonsson, S. J. (2009). 'Learning by importing in global value chains: Upgrading and South-South strategies in the Ugandan pharmaceutical industry', *Development Southern Africa*, 26(3), 499–516.

Halperin, S., and Palan, R. (eds) (2015). *Legacies of Empire: Imperial Roots of the Contemporary Global Order.* Cambridge: Cambridge University Press.

Hampton, M. P., and Christensen, J. (2011). 'Looking for plan B: What next for island hosts of offshore finance?', *The Round Table*, 100(413), 169–81.

Helleiner, E. (1995). 'Explaining the globalization of financial markets: Bringing states back in', *Review of International Political Economy*, 2(2), 315–41.

Henriksen, L. F. (2013). 'Performativity and the politics of equipping for calculation', *International Political Sociology*, 7(4), 406–25.

Henry, J. (2012). 'The price of offshore revisited', *Chesham: Tax Justice Network.* Available at www.taxjustice.net/cms/upload/pdf/Price_of_Offshore_Revisited_120722.pdf

Herley, C. (2012). 'Why do Nigerian Scammers say they are from Nigeria?', paper presented at the Workshop on the Economics of Informational Security, Berlin, 15–26 June. Available at http://weis2012.econinfosec.org/papers/Herley_WEIS2012.pdf

Hickey, S. (2012). 'Beyond "poverty reduction through good governance": The new political economy of development in Africa', *New Political Economy*, 17(5), 683–90.

Hobson, J. M., and Sharman, J. C. (2005). 'The enduring place of hierarchy in world politics: Tracing the social logics of hierarchy and political change', *European Journal of International Relations*, 11(1), 63–98.

Hudson, A. C. (1998). 'Reshaping the regulatory landscape: Border skirmishes around the Bahamas and Cayman offshore financial centres', *Review of International Political Economy*, 5(3), 534–64.

IMF CDIS (2013). International Monetary Fund Coordinated Direct Investment Survey (CDIS). Available at http://data.imf.org/?sk=40313609-F037-48C1-84B1-E1F1CE54D6D5.

Keene, E. (2007). 'A case study of the construction of international hierarchy: British treaty-making against the slave trade in the early nineteenth century', *International Organization*, 61(2), 311–39.

Kim, H. J., and Sharman, J. C. (2014). 'Accounts and accountability: Corruption, human rights, and individual accountability norms', *International Organization*, 68(2), 417–48.

Kyle, G. (2006). 'Civilizing tax havens: The OECD and the harmful tax practices initiative', in B. Bowden and L. Seabrooke (eds), *Global Standards of Market Civilization.* London: Routledge, 161–74.

Lake, D. A. (2009). *Hierarchy in International Relations.* Ithaca, NY: Cornell University Press.

Lavelle, K. C. (1999). 'International financial institutions and emerging capital markets in Africa', *Review of International Political Economy*, 6(2), 200–24.

Leaman, J. and Waris, A. (2013). 'Why tax justice matters in global economic development', in Leaman, J. and Waris, A. (eds.), *Tax Justice and the Political Economy of Global Capitalism, 1945 to the Present*. Oxford: Berghahn, pp. 1–16.

McKeen-Edwards, H., and Porter, T. (2014). 'The role of private finance in global governance', in M. Moschella and C. Weaver (eds), *Handbook of Global Economic Governance*. London: Routledge, 129–92.

Meessen, K. M., Bungerberg, M., and Puttler, A. (2009). *Economic Law as an Economic Good: Its Rule Function and Its Tool Function in the Competition of Systems*. Munich, Sellier: European Law Publishers.

Migdal, J. S. (1988). *Strong Societies and Weak States: State-Society Relations and State Capacities in the Third World*. Princeton, NJ: Princeton University Press.

Mosley, L. (2003). *Global Capital and National Governments*. Cambridge: Cambridge University Press.

Ndikumana, L., and Boyce, J. (2011). *Africa's Odious Debt: How Foreign Loans and Capital Flight Bled a Continent*. London: Zed Books.

Ndikumana, L., and Boyce, J. (2012). 'Capital flight from North African countries', PERI Research Report, University of Massachusetts at Amherst, October.

Organisation for Economic Co-Operation and Development (2015). 'The participation of developing countries in global value chains: Implications for trade and trade-related policies', Summary Paper, Paris: OECD.

Otusanya, O. J. (2011a). 'Corruption as an obstacle to development in developing countries: A review of literature', *Journal of Money Laundering Control*, 14(4), 387–422.

Otusanya, O. J. (2011b). 'The role of multinational companies in tax evasion and tax avoidance: The case of Nigeria', *Critical Perspectives on Accounting*, 22(3), 316–32.

Oxfam (2000). *Tax Havens: Realising the Hidden Billions for Poverty Eradication*. London: Oxfam.

Palan, R. (2003). *The Offshore World: Sovereign Markets, Virtual Places, and Nomad Millionaires*. Ithaca, NY: Cornell University Press.

Palan, R., Murphy, R., and Chavagneux, C. (2010). *Tax Havens: How Globalization Really Works*. Ithaca, NY: Cornell University Press.

Picciotto, S. (2012). *Regulating Global Corporate Capitalism*. Cambridge: Cambridge University Press.

Pitluck, A. Z. (2011). 'Distributed execution in illiquid times: An alternative explanation of trading in stock markets', *Economy and Society*, 40(1), 26–55.

Riisgaard, L. (2009). 'Global value chains, labor organization and private social standards: Lessons from East African cut flower industries', *World Development*, 37(2), 326–40.

Royal African Society (2005). 'A message to world leaders: What about the damages we do to Africa?', *Africa Focus Bulletin*, 13 July. Available at www.africafocus.org/docs05/ras0507.php [Accessed 26 April 2008]

Schenk, C. R. (2007). 'The rise of Hong Kong and Tokyo as international financial centres after 1950', in P. L. Cottrell, E. Lange and U. Olsson (eds), *Centres and Peripheries in Banking: The Historical Development of Financial Markets*. Abingdon: Ashgate, 81–110.

Seabrooke, L. (2001). *US Power in International Finance*. Basingstoke: Palgrave Macmillan.

Seabrooke, L., and Wigan, D. (2014). 'Global wealth chains in the international political economy', *Review of International Political Economy*, 21(1), 257–63.

Seabrooke, L., and Wigan, D. (2015). 'How activists use benchmarks: Reformist and revolutionary benchmarks for global economic justice', *Review of International Studies*, 41(5), 887–904.

Seabrooke, L., and Wigan, D. (2016). 'Powering ideas through expertise: Professionals in global tax battles', *Journal of European Public Policy*, 23(3), 357–74.

Seabrooke, L., and Wigan, D. (2017). 'The governance of global wealth chain', *Review of International Political Economy* 24(1), 1–29.

Sennholz-Weinhardt, B. (2014). 'Regulatory competition as a social fact: Constructing and contesting the threat of hedge fund managers' relocation from Britain', *Review of International Political Economy*, 21(6), 1240–74.

Sharman, J. C. (2006). *Havens in a Storm: The Struggle for Global Tax Regulation*. Ithaca, NY: Cornell University Press.

Sharman, J. C. (2009). 'The bark is the bite: International organizations and blacklisting', *Review of International Political Economy*, 16(4), 573–96.

Sharman, J. C. (2013). 'International hierarchy and contemporary imperial governance: A tale of three kingdoms', *European Journal of International Relations*, 19, 189–207.

Sikka, P. (2003). 'The role of offshore financial centers in globalisation', *Accounting Forum*, 27(4), 365–99.

Styger, P., Jhurani, S. H., and Schimming-Chase, E. (1999). 'Offshore finance in Southern Africa', in M. P. Hampton and J. Abbott (eds), *Offshore Finance Centers and Tax Havens*. Basingstoke: Palgrave Macmillan, 230–47.

Taglioni, D., and Winkler, D. (2014). 'Making global value chains work for development', *Economic Premise*, 143 (May), 1–10.

Tax Justice Network (2005). 'Tax us if you can', a TJN Briefing Paper, September.

Tax Justice Network (2015). *Financial Secrecy Index: Narrative Report on Botswana*. London: TJN. Available at www.financialsecrecyindex.com/PDF/Botswana.pdf [Accessed 15 January 2016]

Thomson Reuters Foundation. (2013). 'Chic Nairobi throbs to the beat of dirty money', 10 December. Available at www.trust.org/item/20131209150854-1kirf/

US Senate Subcommittee on Investigations (2005). 'The role of professional firms in the US tax shelter industry', Committee on Foreign Relations United States Senate, US Government Printing Office, Washington, DC, 13 April.

US Senate Subcommittee on Investigations (2010). 'Keeping foreign corruption out of the United States: Four case histories', PSI Staff Report, April, US General Accounting Office, Washington, DC.

van der Does de Willebois, E., Halter, E., Harrison, R. A., and Park, J. W. (2011). *The Puppet Masters: How the Corrupt Use Legal Structures to Hide their Stolen Assets and What to do About It*. Washington, DC: World Bank.

Vlcek, W. (2006). 'Small states and the challenge of sovereignty: Commonwealth Caribbean offshore financial centers and tax competition', doctoral dissertation, London School of Economics.

Vlcek, W. (2008). *Offshore Finance and Small States: Sovereignty, Size and Money*. Basingstoke: Palgrave Macmillan.

Vlcek, W. (2012). 'Power and the practice of security to govern global finance', *Review of International Political Economy*, 19(4), 639–62.

Waris (2014). 'The creation of international financial centres in Africa: The case of Kenya', Bergen. U4B Brief.

World Bank (2015). 'Stolen assets recovery initiative'. Available at https://star.worldbank.org/corruption-cases/node/18511

Zucman, G. (2015). *The Hidden Wealth of Nations*. Chicago: University of Chicago.

PART IV

Tax avoidance in an individual decision

19

INDIVIDUAL ATTITUDES AND SOCIAL REPRESENTATIONS OF TAXATION, TAX AVOIDANCE AND TAX EVASION

Matthias Kasper, Jerome Olsen, Christoph Kogler,
Jennifer Stark and Erich Kirchler

> The avoidance of taxes is the only intellectual pursuit that still carries any reward.
> John Maynard Keynes[1]

Introduction

Conservative estimates indicate that tax avoidance accounts for annual losses of 100 to 240 billion USD in global corporate income taxes (OECD 2015). Against this background, various policy initiatives seek to impede multinationals' aggressive tax planning. Traditionally, these initiatives relied mainly on a command and control approach and advocated tighter laws and stricter sanctions for non-compliance (Allingham and Sandmo 1972). This approach, however, has significant drawbacks, because tax avoidance is not necessarily illegal. And while enacting and implementing tax law reform usually takes years, multinational corporations as well as wealthy individuals quickly adopt new strategies that shield their income from taxation.

Tax avoidance schemes often exploit differences between national tax laws. Therefore, national initiatives to fight tax avoidance are increasingly embedded in international efforts. The OECD/G20 BEPS project, for instance, aims to introduce new standards in international taxation. These include, among others, global models for automatic exchange of information and legal harmonization. The OECD defines tax avoidance as "the arrangement of a taxpayer's affairs that is intended to reduce his tax liability and that although the arrangement could be strictly legal it is usually in contradiction with the intent of the law it purports to follow" (OECD, Glossary of Tax Terms).[2] But given the legal nature of many tax planning schemes, capacity building and traditional deterrence measures based on command and control regulation might not be sufficient to fight base erosion and profit shifting.

Apart from its economic effects, tax avoidance has significant psychological implications. While multinational corporations shift their profits to low tax jurisdictions in order to reduce their tax

---

1 As quoted in *A Dictionary of Scientific Quotations* (1977) by A. L. MacKay, p. 140.
2 Available at www.oecd.org/ctp/glossaryoftaxterms.htm

payments, most individual taxpayers have few opportunities to save on taxes. As a consequence, average taxpayers bear a greater share of the tax burden than international firms or the mobile group of high net worth individuals. This likely affects the tax compliance behaviour of the cooperative majority, as unequal opportunities to reduce ones' tax liability are perceived as unfair. Psychological research, for example indicates that unfair treatment undermines the willingness to comply (Barth et al. 2013). On the other hand, perceived distributional fairness through progressive taxation increases well-being if taxpayers are satisfied with the provision of public goods (Oishi et al. 2012). However, the provision of public goods is threatened by aggressive tax planning practices.

At the same time, global inequality rises. As developing countries rely heavily on revenues from direct taxes such as corporate income tax, they are particularly affected by multinationals' tax avoidance activities. And because they often lack capacities to protect their tax bases, developing countries are more vulnerable to aggressive tax planning. This exacerbates inequality between developed and developing countries and threatens economic growth. On the other hand, with tax avoidance intensifying inequality within societies, the debate over the role of taxes in protecting social stability gains momentum.

This development is reflected in the growing public interest in multinationals' tax planning activities. Many people perceive tax avoidance as unfair and morally wrong, so that corporate and wealthy individual taxpayers are confronted with growing social pressure to pay their fair share. In the UK, for instance, anti-tax avoidance protesters repeatedly targeted the aggressive tax planning schemes of multinational corporations such as Starbucks, Google or Amazon. Consequently, many firms are concerned with reputational risks related to their tax planning strategies. But while some empirical evidence indicates that public scrutiny reduces firms tax avoidance behaviour (Dyreng et al. 2016), other findings suggest that corporate social responsibility activities, which are often used to promote the public reputation of a firm, are positively correlated with investments in tax lobbying activities but negatively related to corporate tax payments (Davis et al. 2016).

In this chapter we discuss the socio-psychological dimension of tax avoidance and evasion behaviour. Specifically, we analyse the role of social norms and taxpayers' attitudes towards tax non-compliance because little is known about taxpayers' perceptions of different opportunities to save on taxes. We moreover investigate the perceptions and social acceptance of different types of taxpayers. As deterrence alone is apparently not sufficiently effective in reducing aggressive tax planning, a better understanding of the motives that drive taxpayer behaviour as well as the social norms underlying taxpayers' compliance decisions is needed in order to foster a high degree of tax compliance. In addressing these issues, we add to the understanding of factors that shape attitudes and social norms to pay taxes honestly.

This chapter is structured as follows. First, we describe the concept of social representations and introduce a method to define and evaluate social phenomena such as tax avoidance. Second, we discuss how fairness perceptions shape the social representations of tax avoidance, tax evasion and tax flight. Third, we present an empirical study on the social representations of taxes and the images of different types of taxpayers. Fourth, we present new and unpublished data on taxpayers' social representations of typical taxpayers, honest taxpayers, tax avoiders and tax evaders. Fifth, we discuss methods to promote tax compliance such as increasing perceptions of fairness and strengthening social norms.

Taxpayer behaviour and social representations

Individuals' beliefs, feelings and attitudes shape their perceptions of taxes (Kirchler, 2007). However, taxpayer behaviour is not exclusively driven by individual perceptions. As taxes are social phenomena, collective attitudes and shared social norms affect compliance behaviour. In order to understand taxpayers' compliance decisions, it is thus necessary to analyse the dynamics between individuals and their social environment. Corporate tax planning, for instance, increases a firm's competitiveness and shareholder wealth. On the other hand, it erodes public revenues. This, in turn, might be perceived as unfair and thus undermine individuals' willingness to comply.

Social representation theory offers a theoretical framework to identify the social concepts that underlie individuals' perceptions of taxes. Values, attitudes, ideas, knowledge and practices that are shared within groups facilitate a collective understanding. These social representations can refer to concrete objects such as paintings or to abstract phenomena such as taxes. Social representations develop through discourse and group interaction. They alleviate social exchange and facilitate communication. Hence, they enable individuals to understand social objects and to orient themselves in their environment (Moscovici 1973, 1976).

The development of social representations involves two cognitive processes: anchoring and objectification. Anchoring is an ordering process that categorizes and classifies information (el Sehity and Kirchler 2006; Stark et al. 2017). Novel information about a social object is integrated into existing knowledge. This process conventionalises new information and changes preexisting knowledge (Wagner et al. 1999). While anchoring orders and familiarizes a social object, objectification transforms an abstract phenomenon into a concrete and specific form (el Sehity and Kirchler 2006; Stark et al. 2017). Terms, metaphors, symbols or images develop which typify the social object (Wagner et al. 1999).

Even though social representations consist of complex psychological content such as attitudes, feelings, values, ideals, traditions and attributions, they are clearly structured. Two organizational areas can be distinguished, namely the central core and the periphery (Abric 1984). The central core is the heart of the representation. It comprises the terms, names, metaphors and emotions that are immediately and frequently associated with a social object (Abric 1994), thereby defining the meaning of the object. They are normative and form a stable unit that is resistant to situational changes. Furthermore, they organize all other elements and thereby determine the meaning of the peripheral elements (Wagner et al. 1996). While core elements illustrate shared knowledge of a group, peripheral elements reflect the individual content of a social representation. Stemming from individual experiences, they are more loosely tied and less frequently associated with a social object. In different social contexts, their meaning and relationships to each other as well as to the core elements can change. This flexibility serves to specify and corroborate the core in a given context, to adjust to temporal developments and to protect the core by positioning new elements and attributes in the periphery (Wagner et al. 1996).

Social representations can be investigated by a multitude of methods (el Sehity and Kirchler 2006; Stark et al. 2017; Wagner et al. 1999) ranging from experiments, interviews, questionnaires to observations in the field. Free association tasks and Peabody's (1985) semantic differential constitute two popular approaches to investigate social representations because they are implicit and allow gathering qualitative as well as quantitative data.

In free association tasks people are presented with a stimulus word and asked to write down all thoughts and notions that come to their mind. The elicited associations comprise information about individuals' beliefs, thoughts and feelings with regard to the respective social object (Nelson et al. 2000; Vergès 1992). This method provides a great amount of freedom of expression, since individuals are not led into a predetermined direction by structured questions (Gangl et al. 2012). Additionally, participants have to evaluate their associations as positive, neutral or negative. The analysis offers insight into the content as well as organization and structure of the social representation, and core and peripheral elements can be identified (Vergès 1992). Finally, this method allows assessing the valence of a given social object (De Rosa 1995).

Originally developed to assess characterizations of nations, Peabody's (1985) semantic differential represents another popular method to explore social objects. It consists of 32 bipolar pairs of adjectives that are organized in tandems of two adjective pairs which allow the disentanglement of their descriptive and evaluative component. In order to illustrate the underlying rationale, we present an example tandem and explain how the descriptive component is separated from the evaluative component: Let us assume that a person named Joe is judged *thrifty* in the contrast of *extravagant* (-) vs. *thrifty* (+). *Thrifty* is a desirable attitude or behaviour and thus entails the evaluative positive aspect in this contrast. Therefore, the judgement of Joe being *thrifty* tells us "Joe is good". However, on a descriptive level it also implies that "Joe tends not to spend money". Based on this information we are left with the question whether the judgement of Joe should be understood as an evaluative or a descriptive one. Peabody (1967, 1985) proposes to disentangle this information by pairing a trait contrast that entails opposite evaluative and descriptive aspects. For instance, *extravagant* (-) vs. *thrifty* (+) (contrast a) is paired with a second contrast that reverses the evaluative aspect, but is similar with regard to the descriptive aspect, *generous* (+) vs. *stingy* (-) (contrast b) in this case. Both contrasts are measured on a scale from -3 to +3. Thus, one can compute the evaluative score $E = \frac{1}{2} (a + b)$, while the descriptive score is defined as $D = \frac{1}{2} (a - b)$. The analyses of these ratings give insight into how the stimulus, that is the social object, is described and evaluated.

In a nutshell, social representations are opinions, ideas and beliefs that are shared among members of groups (Moscovici 1981, 1984). They shape attitudes and thus affect behaviour. Analysing social representations therefore adds to the understanding of taxpayers' perceptions of non-compliance.

Fairness perceptions of tax avoidance, tax evasion and tax flight

Few people like paying taxes, but while most taxpayers have little opportunity to reduce their tax burden, business owners, for instance, might under-declare income or over-deduct expenses to increase their profits. Wealthy individuals, on the other hand, often move to low tax jurisdictions in order to pay less tax and multinational corporations use tax planning strategies that reduce their tax liabilities. Many taxpayers therefore believe that the tax burden is mostly born by the "ordinary people" (Kinsey 1984).

In order to gain a better understanding of the socio-psychological dimension of tax compliance behaviour it is important to investigate the social acceptance of different forms to save on taxes. Specifically, it is crucial to understand how taxpayers' efforts to avoid paying taxes affect fairness perceptions. The common economic effect of different attempts to reduce tax payments is a decline in public revenues. This is crucial as fairness in taxation is key in alleviating global inequality. However, not all means to reduce ones' tax burden are equally legal and it is often difficult to draw the line between legal tax avoidance and illegal tax evasion. Generally, employed taxpayers have relatively little opportunities to minimize their tax payments compared to business owners or corporations. This is often perceived as unfair, potentially undermines tax morale and might ultimately reduce taxpayers' intentions to comply. Therefore, fairness considerations are a key element in the debate on more efficient tax policies (cf. Wenzel 2003).

Kirchler et al. (2003) surveyed fiscal officers, business students, business lawyers and small business owners in order to investigate their social representations of different strategies to save on taxes: tax avoidance, tax evasion and tax flight. In this study, participants were confronted with tax avoidance referring to legal actions that reduce tax payments such as the exploitation of tax-loopholes. Tax evasion, on the other hand, represented illegal activities, for instance the under-declaration of income or the over-deduction of expenses, whereas tax flight described legal, tax-driven business relocation decisions.

When considering economic implications exclusively, tax avoidance, tax evasion and tax flight should not be perceived differently. From a psychological perspective, however, the authors expected to find disparities in the social representations of these actions. Therefore, they assumed that tax avoidance, tax evasion and tax flight are perceived differently and unequally fair. As tax evasion implies breaking the law, Kirchler et al. (2003) conjectured that it would be seen as the least fair option to reduce ones' tax liability. Tax flight, on the other hand, is no criminal offense but violates the spirit of the law. Moreover, only few and potentially rather wealthy individuals have the opportunity to relocate their business activities only for tax purposes. This is why the authors expected tax flight to be perceived as less fair than tax avoidance, yet not as unfair as tax evasion. Tax avoidance, a legal means to save on taxes, was assumed to be rated as the least unfair of all three options.

In addition to fairness considerations, the study addressed the effects of tax knowledge on the evaluation of different tax planning strategies. The effects of knowledge about taxes on compliance behaviour are discussed controversially in the literature. While Groenland and van Veldhoven (1983) report that sound tax knowledge reduces compliance, Kirchler and Maciejovsky (2001) observed low tax compliance especially among study participants with little knowledge about taxes. A study by Eriksen and Fallan (1996) found that participants who gained tax knowledge considered the tax system in general as fairer and perceived their own as well as other people's tax evasion activities to be more serious. In the light of these findings, Kirchler et al. (2003) hypothesized that tax knowledge triggers different perceptions of tax avoidance and tax evasion: they expected that profound tax knowledge had positive effects on the fairness evaluation of tax avoidance, whereas they predicted opposite effects for tax evasion. Finally, they investigated the effects of opportunities to evade on intended tax compliance. In many cases business owners have more opportunities to reduce their tax payments than employed taxpayers. Therefore, the authors hypothesized that small business owners exhibit less intentions to comply than employed taxpayers.

The overall sample in the respective study comprised 252 fiscal officers, business students, business lawyers and small business owners from east Austria. All participants were randomly confronted with one fictitious scenario describing a person engaged in tax avoidance, tax evasion or tax flight. After reading the scenario subjects were instructed to produce spontaneous associations to the activities described in the text and to evaluate them as positive, neutral or negative. Moreover, participants were asked to rank the perceived fairness of tax avoidance, tax evasion and tax flight, as well as to complete a multiple-choice test on tax knowledge. Subjects who were assigned to a tax evasion scenario were also instructed to indicate how likely they expected the person described in the study to declare her taxes honestly.

To detect differences in subjects' perceptions of tax avoidance, tax evasion and tax flight, the authors first analysed the immediate associations after having read the scenario. While tax avoidance was often associated with the terms *legal, intentions to save taxes, cleverness* and *a good idea*, tax evasion was associated with notions such as *illegal, fraud, criminal prosecution, risk* and *black money*. Tax flight, on the other hand, was associated with *intentions to save taxes, lower taxes abroad* and *double tax agreement*. The findings indicate that participants clearly distinguished between different activities to save on taxes. In the second step, all associations were regrouped into a broad set of categories that had been identified by a group of experts. These categories were, for instance, *intentional tax evasion, personal advantage* and *risk tendency*. Based on this classification the authors conducted a correspondence analysis which revealed that the legality and morality factors accounted for a significant share of the variance in the data. While tax avoidance was considered to be legal and moral alike, tax evasion was seen as illegal and immoral, whereas tax flight was perceived to be legal and immoral.

In a third step, the authors analysed participants' evaluations of tax avoidance, tax evasion and tax flight. The results indicate that the strongest negative associations were elicited in the tax evasion condition and the most positive associations in the tax avoidance condition. Overall, tax flight was perceived as rather neutral. Moreover, participants were asked to indicate the subjective fairness of different means to reduce ones' tax liability. In all employment groups tax evasion was considered to be the least fair, while tax avoidance was seen as the fairest way to save on taxes. As depicted in Figure 19.1, fiscal officers found all forms of tax reduction significantly less fair than other participants and business owners perceived tax flight fairer than other employment groups.

In addition to these findings, Kirchler et al. (2003) observed significant disparities in tax knowledge between different professions. Fiscal officers were more knowledgeable than business students and business lawyers. Interestingly, business owners scored the lowest on tax knowledge. In contrast to their hypothesis, the authors did not find a correlation between tax knowledge and perceived fairness of tax avoidance or tax evasion. However, business owners as well as business lawyers with a sound understanding of taxes perceived tax avoidance fairer than other groups. Fiscal officers, on the other hand, who scored high on tax knowledge, perceived tax evasion less fair than their colleagues with less tax knowledge. Finally, the authors did not observe

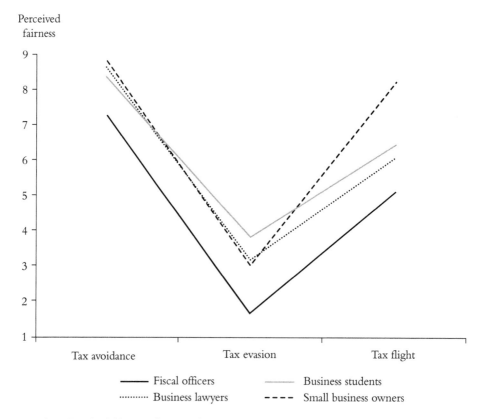

Figure 19.1 Perceived fairness of tax avoidance, tax evasion and tax flight among fiscal officers, business students, business lawyers and small business owners.

Source: Kirchler et al. 2003: 548.

any differences in intended tax compliance between the participants in different occupational groups who were assigned to the tax evasion treatment.

The findings from Kirchler et al. (2003) suggest that tax avoidance, tax evasion and tax flight are perceived differently, and that knowledge about taxes differs between employment groups. The discrimination between different activities to reduce ones' tax liability were based on legal as well as moral considerations and depended on personal affectedness, experience, occupational status and knowledge about taxes. Generally, legal forms to save on taxes were deemed more acceptable than illegal forms. And as many taxpayers considered saving on taxes to be a key motive for all actions that reduce ones' tax liability, the authors suggest that taxpayers should be informed in greater detail about their options to legally avoid paying taxes in order to strengthen their tax morale and to prevent illegal tax evasion. On a more general level, however, the findings indicate that tax policy reform should not only target tax planning schemes that have significant revenue effects, but also aim at those practices that are perceived as highly unfair by the majority of taxpayers.

Social representations of typical taxpayers, honest taxpayers and tax evaders

In order to gain a more nuanced understanding on the determinants of tax compliance behaviour Kirchler (1998) investigated social representations of taxes among five occupational groups: blue- and white-collar workers, civil servants, entrepreneurs and students. From a practical perspective, entrepreneurs are more likely to evade taxes than employees, because they have more discretion in the design of their tax returns. Informal labour, on the other hand, is usually more common among blue-collar workers. Consequently, they might find it relatively easy to under-declare income in order to avoid paying income tax and VAT. But while one might easily conjecture that opportunity makes a thief, the social representations of taxes may differ between professional groups, so that some groups of taxpayers feel more obliged to pay their taxes honestly than others.

Kirchler (1998) surveyed five different employment groups to identify potential disparities in their social representations of taxes. A sample of 171 Austrian residents completed a two-part questionnaire. First, applying a free association task, participants were asked to list all their spontaneous thoughts on *taxes*, to number them by order of production and to evaluate them as positive, neutral or negative. Second, participants were presented with Peabody's (1985) semantic differential, comprising 32 adjective pairs, and asked to judge *typical taxpayers*, *honest taxpayers* and *tax evaders* according to the tandems.

Overall, 1,003 free associations were produced, of which 547 were different words. The associations were categorized by two independent raters and then assigned to one of 25 categories, with an interrater agreement of 92%. A correspondence analysis revealed that when confronted with the stimulus *taxes*, entrepreneurs think of punishment and demotivation, public constraint, as well as a lack of transparency in tax law and the use of tax revenues. They perceive taxes as pressuring and impeding to their work. Furthermore, they find the administration of taxes too complex. Entrepreneurs must pay taxes out of their own pocket. Thus, they describe taxes as a form of punishment and a loss of personal freedom. According to Brehm (1966), real or perceived loss of freedom leads to reactance and individuals attempt to re-establish control by non-compliant behavior. Blue-collar workers, on the other hand, criticize the government and politicians. They accuse them of using taxes strategically and being responsible for the public deficit. Nevertheless, blue-collar workers are aware of the role of taxes in financing public goods. White-collar workers often think of social security and public welfare, but also

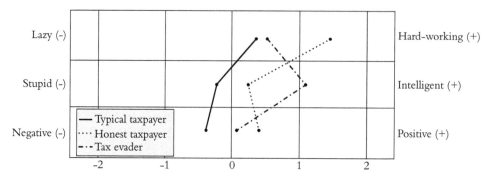

Figure 19.2   Mean judgements of typical taxpayers, honest taxpayers and tax evaders.
Source: Data is from Kirchler 1998.

perceive taxes as a necessary burden and a financial loss. Civil servants, on the other hand, are aware of the importance of taxes in redistributing wealth and establishing social justice. They are concerned about tax avoiders and evaders, who maximize their income but still profit from public goods. Students, finally, note abstract theoretical and technical concepts and mention names of politicians and fictional or comic characters. These results go in line with exchange theories. Blue-collar workers, white-collar workers and civil servants, who receive an already tax-deducted net income, mention public goods, welfare, social security and justice, and seem to associate taxes with exchange relationships. They pay their taxes and in exchange receive access to public goods.

In line with Peabody (1985), Kirchler (1998) analysed judgements on *typical taxpayers, honest taxpayers* and *tax evaders* and disentangled descriptive and evaluative aspects. The descriptions and evaluations of the three groups differed significantly. Tax evaders were described and evaluated rather positively, as highly intelligent and hard-working. Typical taxpayers were evaluated most negatively, as lazy and rather stupid, whereas honest taxpayers were evaluated most positively as hard-working and intelligent (see Figure 19.2). These descriptions and evaluations suggest that tax evasion was not perceived as a crime, but rather as a game played by intelligent people. While the social representations of all five employment groups differ regarding their content, all groups had equally negative attitudes towards taxes and did not regard tax evasion as a crime.

Tax avoidance: A recent study on social representations of different taxpayers

In order to investigate possible changes in the perception and evaluation of different types of taxpayers, we replicated Kirchler's (1998) study and added tax avoiders, an additional type of taxpayers. We incorporated tax avoiders because tax avoidance recently gained a lot of attention in the media and investigating social representations offers the possibility to identify how tax avoiders are perceived in comparison to other types of taxpayers. Similar to the original study, participants had to fill in a questionnaire measuring attitudes towards different types of taxpayers: (1) typical taxpayers, (2) honest taxpayers, (3) tax avoiders and (4) tax evaders. The study was based on a within-subject-repeated-measures design and the questionnaire was fully permutated and randomly administered in one of 24 possible orders.

Using convenience sampling, data from 235 individuals in Austria was collected. The median age of the sample was 33 (interquartile range = 21.75). Gender was equally distributed with 55.1% females. A share of 3.1% participants indicated compulsory school as highest education, while 50.0% of the sample stated to have finished high school or vocational education and another 46.9% indicated to hold a university degree. The majority (80.0%) were employed taxpayers, while 13.6% were self-employed. The remaining samples were either unemployed (0.5%), retired (2.3%) or students (3.6%). With respect to income most participants (72.2%) stated to earn a net income between €1.001 and €2.500. Data was collected between fall 2014 and winter 2015. The questionnaire was administered in paper-pencil form (81.3%) and online (18.7%). It took about 15 minutes to complete the questionnaire. Participation was voluntary and no monetary incentives were provided. In case of missing values, the pairwise deletion method was used in order to maximize the sample size for each analysis.

Attitudes towards the different types of taxpayers were measured applying Peabody's (1967, 1985) semantic differentials that consist of 32 adjective pairs, which allow the disentanglement of evaluative and descriptive aspects of participants' judgement. Therefore, for each domain of interest two pairs of adjectives (tandems) were used in a semantic differential. The analysis focuses on the descriptive aspects of each of the 15 tandems listed in the first and second column of Table 19.1. Additionally, two trait evaluations (*lazy* vs. *hard-working*, and *stupid* vs. *intelligent*) were assessed. All 32 resulting trait contrasts were used to compute one mean evaluation.

As indicated in Figure 19.3, on the aggregated level all types of taxpayers were evaluated as positive rather than negative. Tax evaders received the lowest, yet overall neutral score ($M = 0.05$). However, in relative terms, there are substantial differences between the types of taxpayers. Interestingly, honest taxpayers ($M = 0.52$) were not evaluated as the most positive, but were seen equally positive (in terms of statistical significance) as tax avoiders ($M = 0.60$). Typical taxpayers ($M = 0.20$), on the other hand, were evaluated more positive than tax evaders, but less positive than honest taxpayers and tax avoiders. Compared with Kirchler's (1998) finding, it is worth noting that tax evaders are not evaluated more positively than typical taxpayers anymore, as representations of both are rather neutral. However, tax avoiders are perceived as very similar to honest taxpayers and overall, both are perceived as clearly positive.

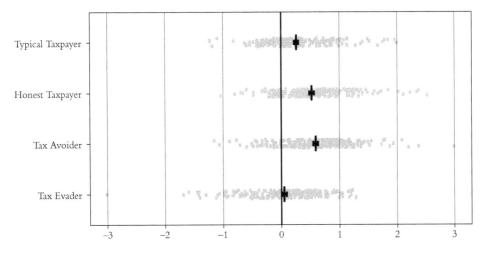

Figure 19.3 Mean overall judgements of typical taxpayers, honest taxpayers, tax avoiders and tax evaders.

We calculated a one-way repeated-measures ANOVA[3] with the four types of taxpayers as within subject factors and the judgements as dependent variable for each tandem (15 in total) or trait evaluation (two in total plus the overall evaluation score. The results for each contrast are depicted in the last column of Table 19.1. The effects sizes for the significant effects vary considerably between $\eta^2_p = 0.01$ and $\eta^2_p = 0.49$, which correspond to the more commonly used Cohen's d from $d = 0.20$ to $d = 1.96$. We refer to results in the text that have effect sizes of $\eta^2_p \geq .13$ in descending order, which correspond to large effects with considerable practical relevance (see Figure 19.4). Detailed statistics and the remainder of results can be found in Table 19.1.

Four tandems show similar patterns with clear differences between typical and honest taxpayers on the one hand and tax avoiders and evaders on the other hand. In fact, the strongest effect was found for uncooperative and independent vs. cooperative and confirming (contrast 12). Here, all four types of taxpayers differ significantly from each other. Honest taxpayers ($M = 0.86$) are described as being the most cooperative and confirming ones, followed by typical taxpayers ($M = 0.56$). On the other hand, tax avoiders ($M = -0.57$) are characterized as uncooperative and independent, yet less so than tax evaders ($M = -1.29$). The same pattern of results holds true for conceited and self-confident vs. modest and unassured (contrast 11) with honest taxpayers ($M = 0.62$) and typical taxpayers ($M = 0.34$) attributed as modest and unassured, whereas tax avoiders ($M = -0.77$) and tax evaders ($M = -1.42$) are both regarded as rather conceited and self-confident. With respect to aggressive and forceful vs. peaceful and passive (contrast 10), honest taxpayers ($M = 0.71$) and typical taxpayers ($M = 0.47$) are described as peaceful and passive, while tax avoiders ($M = -0.45$) and tax evaders ($M = -0.93$) are seen as aggressive and forceful. Concerning the contrast rash and bold vs. cautious and timid (contrast 8), all four types differ significantly from each other. Honest taxpayers ($M = 1.00$), typical taxpayers ($M = 0.76$) and tax avoiders ($M = 0.19$) are regarded as cautious and timid, while tax evaders ($M = -0.69$) are described as rash and bold.

Subsequently, we identify one tandem where tax avoiders ($M = 0.98$) and tax evaders ($M = 1.08$) are described as clearly firm and severe (contrast 5), whereas no clear description becomes evident for typical taxpayers ($M = -0.01$) and honest taxpayers ($M = -0.05$). With regard to agitated and forceful vs. calm and inactive (contrast 9), all types differ significantly from each other and again we find a pattern of results where typical and honest taxpayers are described different from tax evaders and avoiders. Honest taxpayers ($M = 0.51$) and typical taxpayers ($M = 0.33$) are attributed as calm and inactive, whereas tax avoiders ($M = -0.26$) and tax evaders ($M = -0.58$) are seen as agitated and active.

Contrast 7 reveals a similar differentiation between typical and honest taxpayers on one side and tax evaders and avoiders on the other. Tax avoiders ($M = 0.79$) and tax evaders ($M = 0.94$) are described as relatively selective and choosy. Typical taxpayers, on the other hand, are described in the same direction, but to a significantly lesser extent ($M = 0.13$). Honest taxpayers ($M = -0.12$) are regarded as mildly undiscriminating and broad-minded. The same pattern of results can be found for gullible and trusting vs. skeptical and distrustful (contrast 4). Tax avoiders ($M = 0.92$) and tax evaders ($M = 0.97$) are described as significantly more skeptical and distrustful than typical taxpayers ($M = 0.15$). Honest taxpayers ($M = -0.14$), on the contrary, are seen as gullible and trusting.

---

3 In all models Mauchly's test of sphericity was violated, thus the degrees of freedom were corrected using the Greenhouse-Geiser estimation method.

Table 19.1 Mean description scores of *typical taxpayers*, *honest taxpayers*, *tax avoiders* and *tax evaders*

Descriptive contrasts		*Types of taxpayers*				
A expressed by negative value	*B* expressed by positive value	*Typical*	*Honest*	*Avoider*	*Evader*	*ANOVA results*
1a. Extravagant (–) b. Generous (+)	Thrifty (+) Stingy (–)	0.42[a]	0.32[a]	1.21[b]	0.53[a]	$F(2.4, 538.6) = 30.2$, $p < .001$, $\eta^2_p = 0.12$
2a. Impulsive (–) b. Spontaneous (+)	Self-controlled (+) Inhibited (–)	0.33[a]	0.64[b]	0.33[a]	-0.31[c]	$F(2.6, 573.0) = 37.8$, $p < .001$, $\eta^2_p = 0.15$
3a. Frivolous (–) b. Gay (+)	Serious (+) Grim (–)	0.31	0.36	0.37	0.30	$F(2.6, 559.9) = 0.4$, $p = .721$, $\eta^2_p = 0.00$
4a. Gullible (–) b. Trusting (+)	Skeptical (+) Distrustful (–)	0.15[a]	-0.14[b]	0.92[c]	0.97[c]	$F(2.6, 566.0) = 53.6$, $p < .001$, $\eta^2_p = 0.20$
5a. Lax (–) b. Lenient (+)	Firm (+) Severe (–)	-0.01[a]	-0.05[a]	0.98[b]	1.08[b]	$F(2.5, 539.7) = 91.1$, $p < .001$, $\eta^2_p = 0.30$
6a. Vacillating (–) b. Flexible (+)	Persistent (+) Inflexible (–)	0.26[a]	0.30[ab]	0.50[b]	0.45[ab]	$F(2.7, 574.6) = 3.1$, $p = .032$, $\eta^2_p = 0.01$
7a. Undiscriminating (-) b. Broad-minded (+)	Selective (+) Choosy (–)	0.13[a]	-0.12[b]	0.79[c]	0.94[c]	$F(2.5, 545.9) = 63.1$, $p < .001$, $\eta^2_p = 0.23$
8a. Rash (–) b. Bold (+)	Cautious (+) Timid (–)	0.76[a]	1.00[b]	0.19[c]	-0.69[d]	$F(2.7, 589.2) = 98.8$, $p < .001$, $\eta^2_p = 0.31$
9a. Agitated (–) b. Active (+)	Calm (+) Inactive (–)	0.33[a]	0.51[b]	-0.26[c]	-0.58[d]	$F(2.6, 570.4) = 71.5$, $p < .001$, $\eta^2_p = 0.25$
10a. Aggressive (–) b. Forceful (+)	Peaceful (+) Passive (–)	0.47[a]	0.71[b]	-0.45[c]	-0.93[d]	$F(2.4, 520.1) = 144.5$, $p < .001$, $\eta^2_p = 0.40$
11a. Conceited (–) b. Self-confident (+)	Modest (+) Unassured (–)	0.34[a]	0.62[b]	-0.77[c]	-1.42[d]	$F(2.7, 595.6) = 204.5$, $p < .001$, $\eta^2_p = 0.48$
12a. Uncooperative (–) b. Independent (+)	Cooperative (+) Confirming (–)	0.56[a]	0.86[b]	-0.57[c]	-1.29[d]	$F(2.2, 471.8) = 207.5$, $p < .001$, $\eta^2_p = 0.49$
13a. Tactless (–) b. Frank (+)	Tactful (+) Devious (–)	0.08	0.05	-0.11	0.00	$F(2.8, 613.1) = 2.6$, $p = .053$, $\eta^2_p = 0.01$
14a. Impractical (–) b. Idealistic (+)	Practical (+) Opportunistic (–)	0.25[a]	0.13[a]	0.59[b]	0.27[a]	$F(2.4, 532.1) = 8.9$, $p < .001$, $\eta^2_p = 0.04$
15a. Deplorable (–) b. Likeable (+)	Admirable (+) Not likeable (–)	-0.13[a]	-0.17[a]	0.22[b]	0.11[b]	$F(2.7, 607.3) = 15.0$, $p < .001$, $\eta^2_p = 0.06$
16a. Lazy (–)	Hard-working (+)	0.84[a]	1.07[a]	1.00[a]	0.30[b]	$F(2.6, 578.2) = 16.7$, $p < .001$, $\eta^2_p = 0.07$
17a. Stupid (–)	Intelligent (+)	0.20[a]	0.33[a]	1.40[b]	0.72[c]	$F(2.4, 522.8) = 38.5$, $p < .001$, $\eta^2_p = 0.15$
Mean of all 32 evaluations		0.26[a]	0.52[b]	0.60[b]	0.05[c]	$F(2.4, 531.5) = 44.2$, $p < .001$, $\eta^2_p = 0.16$

Note. The descriptive scores were computed by inversing the score of every second contrast of a tandem before taking the mean, which disentangles the evaluative aspect of the tandem and reveals the descriptive component. Cells with differing superscripts in one line indicate significant differences ($p < .05$) based on post-hoc analyses (Bonferroni method).

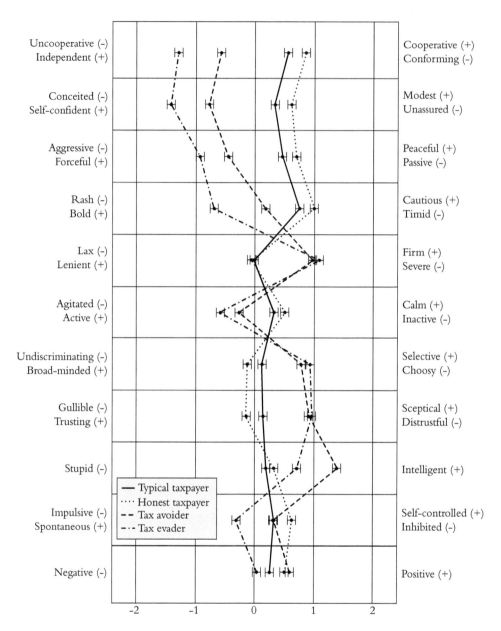

Figure 19.4 Mean descriptions of typical taxpayers, honest taxpayers, tax avoiders and tax evaders for selected contrasts.

The evaluation on the single dimension stupid vs. intelligent reveals an interesting result. While typical ($M = 0.20$) and honest taxpayers ($M = 0.33$) are judged as mildly intelligent (contrast 17), tax evaders are seen as significantly more intelligent ($M = 0.72$). However, tax avoiders are judged as most intelligent ($M = 1.40$).

With regard to the tandem impulsive and spontaneous vs. self-controlled and inhibited (contrast 2), typical taxpayers ($M = 0.33$), honest taxpayers ($M = 0.64$) and tax avoiders ($M = 0.33$)

are described as more self-controlled and inhibited than tax evaders, who are described as impulsive and spontaneous ($M = -0.31$), with both honest taxpayers and evaders differing significantly from all other types.

Discussion

Multinational corporations minimize their tax payments to increase their competitiveness. But while corporate tax planning aims at increasing shareholder value, it also threatens public revenues. As a consequence, international efforts are taken to reduce base erosion and profit shifting. Fighting tax avoidance is difficult, however, because many corporate structures that shield firms' income from taxation violate the spirit rather than the letter of the law. The vast majority of taxpayers, on the other hand, has only few opportunities to save on taxes and perceives multinationals' tax avoidance as unfair. As a result, public pressure rises and corporations are increasingly expected to pay their fair share. This elevates the reputational risk of firms' tax planning. Although empirical findings on the effects of reputational risk on compliance behaviour are ambiguous, corporations' efforts to exploit legal loopholes to save on taxes likely affect the compliance behaviour of the cooperative majority. Perceived injustice, for instance, might undermine tax morale and thus increase individuals' propensity to evade taxes.

However, as the public opinion also affects corporate behaviour, a better understanding of the socio-psychological dimension of tax avoidance is much needed in order to establish a high degree of tax compliance. Analysing the social representations of taxes provides insights into the motives for tax compliance behaviour. According to Kirchler et al. (2003) taxpayers evaluate tax avoidance, tax evasion and tax flight along the dimensions legality and morality. While tax avoidance is perceived as legal and moral, tax flight is seen as legal and immoral, whereas tax evasion is regarded as illegal and immoral alike. Accordingly, taxpayers find tax evasion less fair than tax flight and tax avoidance. Regarding the tax knowledge of different occupational groups, the results from Kirchler et al. (2003) indicate that small business owners score significantly lower on tax literacy than other study participants such as fiscal officers or business students. As tax knowledge is apparently correlated with the acceptance of taxes, this finding contributes to the understanding of low observed compliance rates among small firms.

Other findings (Kirchler 1998) suggest that individuals' experiences with paying taxes and the characteristics of their working environment, such as the opportunity to report income from self-employment, shape the social representations of taxes. Interestingly, typical taxpayers have a rather poor image compared to other groups of taxpayers. While tax evaders were evaluated more positively than typical taxpayers in an older study, recent data suggests that this order has turned around. However, our results show that tax avoiders are evaluated more positively than typical taxpayers and tax evaders. Altogether, these results indicate that cheating on taxes is not necessarily perceived as a crime, but rather as a game played by smart people. Tax policies that aim at increasing compliance should thus not only diminish the opportunities to evade or evade taxes, but also highlight the negative social effects of tax avoidance.

Overall, socio-psychological findings indicate that considering the social determinants of compliance behaviour adds to the understanding of tax avoidance. Since not all strategies to save on taxes are perceived as equally unfair, the legal nature of many tax avoidance schemes might be used to justify tax avoidance. One could argue that as long as it is legal, it cannot be morally wrong to avoid paying taxes. While the legal distinction between tax evasion and tax avoidance is often difficult, tax avoidance appears to be more socially accepted. It is therefore necessary to tackle the social acceptance of tax avoidance in order to establish a social and reputational disincentive for profit shifting activities. The findings of Kirchler et al. (2003) suggest that legal and moral considerations do not overlap regarding the categorization of different forms to save on taxes. While the legal perspective can be addressed by stricter laws, more international coordination and capacity building, the moral perspective results from the dynamics between personal and social factors. It is thus important to understand taxpayers' attitudes and social norms in order to increase compliance.

Socio-psychological research identified several measures to fight avoidance and to establish norms of high tax compliance: (1) The positive impact of effective tax systems must be highlighted and communicated more efficiently just as benefits from public goods have to be made more salient. (2) Negative effects of tax avoidance on public revenues and the provision of public goods and services have to be addressed in public. (3) Successful efforts to fight multinationals' tax planning activities have to be visible for average taxpayers, in order to emphasize that also MNEs have to pay their fair share. (4) Tax compliance should be facilitated through education, easy access to information, the provision of taxpayer services and by clearly indicating the potential and legal boundaries of different methods to save on taxes.

Acknowledgement

The authors gratefully acknowledge financial support by the Austrian National Bank (OeNB) Anniversary Fund: 16042.

Literature

Abric, J. C. (1984). 'A theoretical and experimental approach to the study of social representations in a situation of interaction', in R. Farr and S. Moscovici (eds.), *Social Representations*. Cambridge: Cambridge University Press, 223–50.

Abric, J. C. (1994). *Practiques sociales et representations*. Paris: PUF.

Allingham, M., and Sandmo, A. (1972). 'Income tax evasion: A theoretical analysis', *Journal of Public Economics*, 1(3–4), 323–38.

Barth, E., Cappelen, A. W., and Ognedal, T. (2013). 'Fair tax evasion', *Nordic Journal of Political Economy*, 38, 1–16.

Brehm, J. W. (1966). *A Theory of Psychological Reactance*. New York: Academic Press, Inc.

Davis, A. K., Guenther, D. A., Krull, L. K., and Williams, B. M. (2016). 'Do socially responsible firms pay more taxes?', *The Accounting Review*, 91(1), 47–68.

De Rosa, A. S. (1995). 'Le "réseau d'associations" comme methode d'etude dans la recherche sur les representations sociales: Structure, contenus et polarite du champ semantique', *Cahiers Internationaux de Psychologie Sociale*, 15, 145–57.

Dyreng, S. D., Hoopes, J. L., and Wilde, J. H. (2016). ,'Public pressure and corporate tax behavior', *Journal of Accounting Research*, 54(1), 147–85.

el Sehity, T., and Kirchler, E. (2006). 'Soziale Repräsentationen (Vorstellungen)', in H.-W. Bierhoff and D. Frey (eds), *Handbuch der Sozialpsychologie und Kommunikationspsychologie* (pp. 486–93). Göttingen: Hogrefe.

Eriksen, K., and Fallan, L. (1996). 'Tax knowledge and attitudes towards taxation: A report on a quasiexperiment', *Journal of Economic Psychology*, 17, 387–402.

Gangl, K., Kastlunger, B., Kirchler, E., and Voracek, M. (2012). 'Confidence in the economy in times of crisis: Social representations of experts and laypeople', *Journal of Socio-Economics*, 41, 603–14.

Groenland, E. A. G., and van Veldhoven, G. M. (1983). 'Tax evasion behavior: A psychological framework', *Journal of Economic Psychology*, 3, 129–44.

Kinsey, K. A. (1984). 'Survey data on tax compliance: A compendium and review', Working Paper 84, American Bar Foundation, Chicago.

Kirchler, E. (1998). 'Differential representations of taxes: Analysis of free associations and judgments of five employment groups', *Journal of Socio-Economics*, 27, 117–31.

Kirchler, E. (2007). *The Economic Psychology of Tax Behaviour*. Cambridge: Cambridge University Press.

Kirchler, E., and Maciejovsky, B. (2001). 'Tax compliance within the context of gain and loss situations, expected and current asset position, and profession', *Journal of Economic Psychology*, 22, 173–94.

Kirchler, M., Maciejovsky, B., and Schneider, F. (2003). 'Everyday representations of tax avoidance, tax evasion, and tax flight: Do legal differences matter?', *Journal of Economic Psychology*, 24, 535–53.

Moscovici, S. (1973). 'Foreword', in C. Herzlich (ed.), *Health and Illness: A Social Psychological Analysis* (pp. ix–xiv). London: Academic Press.

Moscovici, S. (1976). *Social Influence and Social Change*. London: Academic Press.

Moscovici, S. (1981). 'On social representations. Perspectives on Everyday Understanding' in J. Forgas (ed.), *Social Cognition* (pp. 181–209). London: Academic Press.

Moscovici, S. (1984). 'The phenomenon of social representations', in R. Farr and S. Moscovici (eds), *Social Representations: European Studies in Social Psychology* (pp. 3–70). Cambridge: Cambridge University Press.

Nelson, D. L., McEvoy, C. L., and Dennis, S. (2000). 'What is free association and what does it measure?', *Memory & Cognition*, 28, 887–99.

OECD (2015). 'OECD/G20 base erosion and profit shifting project', 2015 Final Reports, Executive Summaries.

Oishi, S., Schimmack, U., and Diener, E. (2012). 'Progressive taxation and the subjective well-being of nations', *Psychological Science*, 23(1), 86–92.

Peabody, D. (1967). 'Trait inferences: Evaluative and descriptive aspects', *Journal of Personality and Social Psychology Monographs*, 7, Whole No. 644.

Peabody, D. (1985). *National Characteristics*. Cambridge: Cambridge University Press.

Stark, J., el Sehity, T. & Kirchler, E. (2017). Soziale Repräsentationen – soziale Vorstellungen, in H.-W. Bierhoff & D. Frey (eds), *Kommunikation, Interaktion und soziale Gruppenprozesse*. (Enzyklopädie der Psychologie, Sozialpsychologie, pp 63-81). Göttingen: Hogrefe.

Vergès, P. (1992). 'L'evocation de l'argent: Une méthode pour la définition du noyau central d'une représentation', *Bulletin de Psychologie*, 45, 203–9.

Wagner, W., Duveen, G., Farr, R., Jovchelovitch, S., Lorenzi-Cioldi, F., Marková, I., and Rose, D. (1999). 'Theory and method of social representations', *Asian Journal of Social Psychology*, 2, 95–125.

Wagner, W., Valencia, J., and Elejabarrieta, F. (1996). 'Relevance, discourse and the "hot" stable core of social representations - a structural analysis of word associations', *British Journal of Social Psychology*, 35, 331–52.

Wenzel, M. (2003). 'Tax compliance and the psychology of justice: Mapping the field', in V. Braithwaite (ed.), *Taxing Democracy: Understanding Tax Avoidance and Evasion* (pp. 41–69). Aldershot: Ashgate.

20

TAXING HIGH-INCOME EARNERS

Tax avoidance and mobility

Alejandro Esteller-Moré, Amedeo Piolatto, and Matthew D. Rablen

> Moving to an open economy creates another avenue by which individuals might reduce or eliminate their income-tax burdens: they may move abroad.
>
> Wilson (2009: 285)

Introduction

Economic agents respond to a tax system by trying to maximise the trade-off between costs (i.e. paying tax) and benefits (i.e. social security, public goods, etc.). One way to reduce one's tax liability is to engage in tax avoidance. In the words of Piketty and Saez, "[we] can define tax avoidance as changes in reported income due to changes in the form of compensation but not in the total level of compensation. Tax avoidance opportunities typically arise when taxpayers can shift part of their taxable income [...] [to receive] a more favourable tax treatment" (Piketty and Saez 2013: 417).

Modern tax systems are designed to redistribute among taxpayers and to reduce inequality in society. Hence, the tax burden is much heavier for high-income earners, who therefore have an especially strong motive to try to contribute less by engaging in tax avoidance. Such taxpayers could well be mobile, and interjurisdiction mobility has proved to be an effective way to avoid taxes both in the case of labour and capital taxation. In this way, mobility becomes a means through which avoidance can be carried out. High-income earners are more likely to also have the opportunity to avoid taxes: their cost of moving is often smaller than for other agents and the need for skilled labour has pushed many countries to compete through tax discounts to attract them. This chapter focuses, for the most part, on labour mobility – mainly of high-income earners – as this issue has recently received much attention in both the theoretical and the empirical economics literature.

The rigorous approach to normative taxation finds its foundation in the seminal papers of Mirrlees (1971) and Diamond and Mirrlees (1971). There, the main concern is to account for the distortion that taxation may produce on labour supply, and therefore on efficiency and welfare. However, the empirical literature could not identify a strong response to taxes, at least for the labour supply of white males. The idea that other factors are relevant took hold, therefore. Over the last five decades, the economic literature on taxation proposed increasingly rich models. The standard model of optimal taxation was quickly augmented with the possibility that tax payers do not comply and the tax authority responds by choosing the optimal level of enforcement. Allingham and Sandmo (1972); Yitzhaki (1974); Pencavel (1979); Reinganum and Wilde (1985); Chander and Wilde (1998) are just a few notable examples of such studies.

Feldstein (1995, 1999) are considered the seminal papers introducing the idea that the behavioural response to a change in taxation is not necessarily through labour supply and, therefore, that the empirically relevant component is the elasticity of reported income with respect to true (gross) income. Saez et al. (2012) critically review the literature that analyses the behavioural response to changes in marginal taxation following Feldstein's intuition. The main idea is that agents respond to a change in the marginal tax rate through a variety of different channels other than labour supply, including the intensity of work, career choices, form of compensation (e.g. fringe benefits, stock options, pension plans), mobility and tax compliance. The aforementioned elasticity, without disentangling the different components, computes the total behavioural response to a change in the marginal tax rate.

Factor mobility is a key element that an optimal tax scheme cannot disregard. Under free mobility, any factor should tend to relocate where it is more productive. Mobility induces tax competition, for where factors locate depends on the comparison of net-of-tax returns. Hence, distortionary tax schemes combined with mobility may produce an inefficiency by affecting factor location choice. Furthermore, they may also affect tax proceeds, for outwards mobility erodes the tax base.

Labour and capital mobility differ in several aspects, which explains why the literature treats them separately. Capital – compared to labour – can be relocated more easily and at lower cost, although the cost of labour mobility may have decreased over the last decades. More importantly, the labour force (as opposed to capital) has location preferences that must be considered when computing equilibrium and the social optimum. Location preferences are orthogonal to productivity, which means that agents may face a trade-off between these. Factor productivity can only be observed ex-post. A specificity of labour productivity is that it depends on an ex-ante characteristic (skills) that is: (i) heterogeneous among individuals, (ii) unobservable by the tax authority, and (iii) possibly dependent on location. Skills may be correlated with the cost of mobility: arguments can be put forward in favour of either a positive or a negative correlation between skills and mobility costs. Empirically, it may be harder to track labour migration than to track capital migration (for instance, when agents are free to circulate among different tax jurisdictions, as for example within the Schengen area).[1]

The mobility of the labour force as a relevant factor in shaping the optimal tax schedule appears for the first time in the modern optimal (income) taxation literature with Wilson (1980). With this notable exception, the early literature mainly focused on capital mobility (e.g. Wilson 1986; Zodrow and Mieszkowski 1986). Keen and Konrad (2013), and Zucman (2013, 2014) provide an extensive review of the literature and a discussion of the issues related to firm mobility, tax competition, and tax avoidance. Labour mobility has been mainly (and extensively) considered in the literature as a consequence of wage differentials (net of local amenities and welfare benefits). Borjas (1999) provides a survey of this literature. Part of the empirical literature focuses on tax-induced mobility within a federal country: the cases of Canada (Day and Winer 2006), Switzerland (Kirchgassner and Pommerehne 1996; Liebig et al. 2007) and the United States (Feldstein and Wrobel 1998; Young and Varner 2011) have been considered. However, the question of how taxation has affected international mobility is quite new to the literature.

---

1 International tax avoidance may be reduced by means of international cooperation and information sharing (see, e.g., Keen and Ligthart 2006 for more on this point).

International labour mobility has changed substantially over the last decades, mainly because of a sharp decrease in its cost. Globalisation has reduced both the psychological cost of emigrating (because countries are increasingly similar to each other), and the cost of adapting to a new working environment (because production processes have become more homogeneous, language skills have improved significantly, and barriers to entry have fallen – especially within OECD countries). Meanwhile, several countries started to offer tax discounts to skilled immigrants: the Beckham law in Spain (the eponymous football player was one of the most famous people to benefit from it) is only one example. The list of European countries that offer (or have offered) tax reductions to skilled immigrants also includes, among others, Belgium, Denmark, Finland, Italy, the Netherlands, Romania and Sweden. Such special regimes increase tax competition and the opportunities for tax noncompliance. Their popularity among policymakers explains the growing interest in the literature on the mobility of high-skilled workers. In this analysis we provide an overview of the most well-known contributions to the study of the impact of mobility, given that it is an important potential source of tax avoidance and that it has a major impact on the optimal design of national tax laws.[2]

Labour force movements are not easily tracked, especially – but not only – when it comes to high-skilled workers with appointments in different tax jurisdictions. This implies that mobile workers can enjoy an informational rent that can be exploited to reduce the tax burden. Indeed, when location (or time spent in a jurisdiction) is private information, tax arbitrage and tax avoidance can increase whenever there are differences across countries in the tax legislation. Osmundsen (1999) models precisely this framework. In his model, skills and time abroad are not observable by the tax authority, and therefore both moral hazard and adverse selection problems arise, with the immediate consequence that workers obtain an informational rent and distortions are generated. However, with a continuum of types, the results differ from the well-known ones of the standard principal-agent model in that distortions occur both at the top and at the bottom of the skills distribution, while the decision of the agent with the average skill level is not distorted. This is due to the presence of countervailing incentives by skilled agents who have an incentive to pretend that they are both very mobile and unskilled, although mobility is assumed to be increasing in skills.

Even when mobility is not observed in equilibrium, agents may be very mobile and simply decide not to move because the local tax authority is able to retain them through an attractive tax scheme. From a global perspective, mobility is welfare enhancing when it relocates production factors towards where they are more productive (although optimal relocation should account for some possible tensions between individuals' productivity and location preferences). However, any mobility that is induced (or restrained) by taxes is likely to imply an inefficient distribution of factors and, therefore, to lower total welfare. Nevertheless, it may be welfare maximising for an individual country to attract some agents by offering a suitable tax scheme, although this puts at risk the ability of other countries to collect taxes.

Before moving to the introduction of the simplest theoretical framework that can be used to study mobility, the next section presents a feature of mobility that is yet to receive much attention in the literature but that will have a major impact on any model's policy recommendation.

---

2 Mobility may certainly be an instrument to avoid taxes. Its consequences, however, impact several domains of the economy that are not related to taxes. The literature on the so-called brain drain developed in the late 1960s (see, for instance, Adams 1968). While the early literature focused on the cost of emigration for those countries that lose their skilled workers (e.g., Miyagiwa 1991), some more recent contributions point out that the opportunity for skilled workers to emigrate may also become a relevant incentive for young people to invest in education in developing countries (Beine et al. 2001).

Objective function: whom should we care about?

When it comes to mobility, and in particular to the design of optimal tax schemes and optimal policies, the first problem to solve consists in agreeing upon the objective function that the jurisdictions maximise; that is, their Social Welfare Function (SWF).

A mobile labour force can only be conceived within a multijurisdiction framework. The issue with multijurisdiction frameworks is that the perspective (i.e. the objective function) matters. To fully understand the problem, let us first consider a federation of states, such as the United States, with mobility among the different states. In such a case, it may be natural to think that we want to maximise the total welfare of the whole population, regardless of their initial and final location. However, when facing a group of neighbour and independent countries, each of them designs its own "optimal" tax scheme, accounting for mobility, disregarding spillovers and externalities on other countries, and adjusting its own strategy so as to best respond to the others' choices. In such a framework, regardless of the type of interaction among states (sequential, simultaneous or nonstrategic decisions), a relevant issue is deciding whose utility should enter the social welfare function. Four different principles can be identified:

1 *citizens principle*: all and only citizens count in the SWF, and this regardless of their location
2 *residents principle*: all and only residents count in the SWF, and this regardless of their citizenship
3 *resident-citizens principle*: only inland (resident) citizens count in the SWF. Citizens living abroad are excluded.
4 *citizens and immigrants principle*: all citizens and all foreign residents (immigrants) count in the SWF.

The choice of principle may crucially affect outcomes. To fully understand this point, we consider some extreme cases. Suppose that the state authority has a Rawlsian welfare function and compares the optimal strategy when either the *citizens* or the *residents principle* is adopted. In the former case, poor agents negatively affect the value of the SWF, regardless of their location choice. The authority will try to transfer them as many resources as possible. If we consider that redistribution may be easier to implement when agents reside within the country, such an authority would either be indifferent or prefer poor agents to stay in the country. The opposite is true when the *residents principle* is adopted. When poor agents emigrate, they disappear from the SWF count, which means that an inexpensive way to increase Social Welfare would simply consist of letting the poorest in the population emigrate.

This example shows the relevance of the choice of welfare function for the authority. A normative analysis of mobility would probably call for the maximisation of global welfare; hence, we would expect the planner to consider all agents' well-being. However, tax authorities operate at the tax jurisdiction level, usually without cooperating with neighbouring jurisdictions. Any positive analysis needs therefore to introduce some assumptions on the objective function of the tax authority, and such assumptions may lead to opposing policy recommendations. The choice of the objective function is fully arbitrary: it should be considered as a political, ethical and cultural choice with no economic grounds but with important economic consequences.

In the two-skill model in Hamilton and Pestieau (2005), decisions are taken by majority voting, hence the tax authority is controlled by the largest skill-community within the jurisdiction. When low-skill agents represent the majority in a jurisdiction, the tax authority is therefore maximising a Rawlsian (i.e. maximin) social welfare function. In the opposite case of a majority of skilled agents, decisions reflect the preferences of the most productive agents in the economy and the authority follows a maximax social welfare function. In both cases, voters maximise their own utility, which means that they follow the residence principle. Osmundsen (1999) analyses the location decision of agents that can allocate their working time between two jurisdictions. The tax authority is unable to observe their location decision: indeed, the authority only observes domestic income. In the model, all agents are resident-citizens, although they may spend part of their time abroad. The authority's utilitarian social welfare function accounts for the utility of all citizens, considering homeland public good provision and agents' total consumption; therefore, it includes citizens' foreign income. Simula and Trannoy (2012) and Lehmann et al. (2014) also study the optimal taxation scheme under the threat of migration. The authors compare the results under different Rawlsian SWFs. In particular, they consider the *citizens*, the *residents* and the *resident-citizens* principles. Simula and Trannoy (2010) also consider a Rawlsian SWF, and focus on the *residents* principle. To avoid the government's perverse incentive to push all the unskilled out of the country discussed previously, they include a participation constraint in the government's maximisation problem, according to which the authority must ensure that none of its citizens will want to leave the country.

Theoretical framework

In the literature on tax-induced mobility, the basic structure of the model can be summarised as follows: two competing countries A and B are inhabited by economic agents who are identical in all aspects except productivity, which is defined by the parameter $\theta \epsilon \left[\underline{\theta}, \bar{\theta} \right]$. The density of agents of productivity θ resident in country A is $\varphi(\theta)$: this distribution coincides with the initial probability distribution if there is no mobility, while it differs from it if some agents migrate. In the simplest case (e.g. Hamilton and Pestieau 2005), productivity is binary, with a group $\underline{\theta}$ of unskilled agents, and another one $\bar{\theta}$ of skilled. Each country is assumed to be able to only tax residents.[3]

The agent's utility function, U, depends on their type, location, and consumption level $x = \left[1 - T(y) \right] y$, where y is gross income and $T(y)$ is the tax function. Taxes are usually considered as a redistribution device only, in which case the tax authority's budget constraint requires that the sum of all the taxes is zero (hence, that some agents receive a subsidy): $\int_{\underline{\theta}}^{\bar{\theta}} T(\theta) \varphi(\theta) d\theta = 0$.

The basic model can be extended to allow for the production of a publicly provided good or service (possibly a public good), in which case the tax authority needs to collect a fixed and positive amount. In the presence of a pure public good, nonrivalry implies that the per-capita cost is decreasing in the number of agents residing in a country. However, in the case of a rival good, a larger population would affect the budget constraint of the tax authority, or the quality of the provided good.

Before analysing the shape of the utility function, we note that an agent who has to decide where to locate will base his/her decision on the comparison between his/her total utility in either country; that is, (s)he will locate in country A if and only if $U_A \geq U_B$. This means, in practical terms, that the location decision depends on the total utility of an agent and not on the marginal one. This binary choice occurs when agents reside in only one country. A notable

---

3 Bhagwati (1976a, 1976b) proposes a model of international taxation in which countries tax their citizens on their income generated abroad. The difficulties in enforcing such a model may account for why almost no country has ever implemented it, the United States being a notable exception.

alternative is proposed in Osmundsen (1999), where agents share their time between two jurisdictions, and therefore their location decision is based on the marginal tax rate.

The standard model assumes that the production function exhibits constant returns to scale, and that agents are paid at their marginal productivity $f(\theta)$. An agent's productivity may depend on the location. For instance, it may be that an agent is less productive abroad. Furthermore, there may be some costs of moving: adaptation costs, learning the language, etc. The loss in productivity and the displacement costs may be independent of the skill level, or they may be either positively or negatively correlated with it. All the costs related to moving, including any location preference, may be summarised in the cost of moving function $C(\theta) = c_0 + c_1 V(\theta)$, where $V(\theta)$ is a generic function that describes the variation in the cost of moving depending on agent type. Then, an agent locates in country A (rather than moving to B) if $U_A(\theta) \geq U_B(\theta) - C(\theta)$. Clearly, if $c_1 = 0$ then the cost to migrate is orthogonal to skills. From the previous equation, we can define $R(\theta) = U_A(\theta) - U_B(\theta) + C(\theta)$ as the location rent; that is, the utility differential of an agent of type θ who does not migrate.

One important difference with the standard closed-economy taxation models is that an agent's average tax rate also plays a role: indeed, the location decision depends on the total level of utility and hence on the total (or average) tax burden. Suppose that the two countries are perfectly symmetric, and that agents' labour supply is constant (that, is, agents do not choose labour/leisure optimally). Then, all that matters for an agent is the average tax burden. Accordingly, in the unique equilibrium with symmetric countries the average tax paid by an agent of skill θ is the same regardless of their location. The standard optimal tax rule in a closed economy depends on the marginal tax rate. Allowing for mobility, the marginal tax rate matters as soon as agents must decide their labour supply. Again, if the two countries are symmetric, in equilibrium the optimal marginal tax rate is the same in the two countries (given agents' skill). However, this does not need to be true when asymmetries are introduced, e.g. when some agents face a cost of moving, or when they are not equally productive abroad. For instance, if an agent of skill $\tilde{\theta}$ has a productivity $\tilde{\theta}$ at home but $\alpha \tilde{\theta}$, with $\alpha < 1$ when abroad, clearly the domestic country can safely increase the tax burden of this agent, who nevertheless will not leave the country.

Hamilton and Pestieau (2005) and Bierbrauer et al. (2013) consider the case of countries competing against each other, all acting strategically. However, most of the theoretical literature (e.g. Wilson 1980; Simula and Trannoy 2010, 2012; Lehmann et al. 2014) focuses on the simplified framework of one country (without loss of generality, country A) that chooses the optimal tax function, assuming that country B adopts a fixed policy, which is often assumed to be *laissez-faire* (i.e. no redistribution).

As discussed in the previous section, the social planner's objective function plays an important role in the design of the optimal strategy. Hamilton and Pestieau (2005) consider three cases: the one of a Rawlsian planner, the one in which the utility of the top earners is maximised, and finally the utilitarian case. Wilson (1980) and Bierbrauer et al. (2013) restrain the SWF to be a weighted sum of utilities, but while Wilson (1980) uses the citizens principle, the planner in Bierbrauer et al. (2013) accounts only for the utility of residents. Simula and Trannoy (2010, 2012) and Lehmann et al. (2014) focus on the case of a Rawlsian welfare planner who cares only for residents. This should imply that the social planner's best strategy is to push all the unskilled agents to leave the country, as previously explained. In Simula and Trannoy (2010, 2012), the authors avoid this perverse equilibrium by introducing a participation constraint in the social planner's maximisation problem. The participation constraint implies that the planner must ensure that all citizens are willing, in equilibrium, to locate in the home country. Using the previous notation, the participation constraint imposes the condition $R(\theta) \geq 0$ for any and all θ. In Lehmann et al. (2014) some agents have an infinite cost of moving, and so will never migrate, regardless of the tax function chosen by the Rawlsian social planner (who therefore has no shortcut to increase social welfare).

Simula and Trannoy (2010) show that the Mirrlees (1971) results are no longer valid when agents are mobile. In particular, when the participation constraint is binding (i.e. $R(\theta)=0$) the planner must reduce the tax burden to avoid migration. Analysing the optimal tax formula in Simula and Trannoy (2010), we notice that an increase in the marginal rate of tax at a given level of productivity becomes more costly when some agents are mobile. The standard result implies that a marginal increase in the tax rate for agents with productivity $\tilde{\theta}$ generates an increase in tax proceeds due to the higher rate, which in equilibrium is compensated by a decrease in proceeds due to their elasticity of labour supply. However, in a mobile-labour framework the increase in the tax affects the average tax burden of all agents with skill $\theta \geq \tilde{\theta}$, hence it becomes more costly to retain those agents. As a consequence, the optimal tax rate at all productivity levels is affected by mobility. In the words of the authors "two qualitative features of the closed-economy optimal marginal tax rates are lost: they can be non-positive at interior points and strictly negative at the top. Consequently, individual mobility does not only render the tax schedule less progressive, but can also make the tax liability decreasing with gross earnings" (p. 164).

Lehmann et al. (2014) advance further in the understanding of the shape of the optimal tax schedule in the presence of mobility. Denoting $\eta = \dfrac{\partial \varphi(R(\theta),\theta)}{\partial R(\theta)} \dfrac{1}{\varphi(R(\theta),\theta)}$ as the semi-elasticity of migration, the authors show that the optimal tax schedule implies that $\dfrac{T'}{1-T'} = \xi \dfrac{X(\eta)}{\varphi}$, where ξ is the ratio between the elasticities of gross earning with respect to productivity (θ) and the retention rate $(1-T')$, while $X(\eta) = \int_{\theta}^{\bar{\theta}} (1-\eta T) \varphi(\theta) d\theta$ is the intensity of the tax liability effects for all skill levels above θ; that is, the overall impact — through the average tax rate — of a change in the tax level at productivity θ for all agents with productivity above this level. Lehmann et al. (2014) show that the shape of the tax schedule is hence characterised by the semi-elasticity of mobility (as opposed to its elasticity). Even under a monotonicity assumption on the elasticity (increasing in productivity), the semi-elasticity can be increasing or decreasing, and this factor determines whether the marginal tax rates are always positive or if they become negative at the top of the skill distribution.

The results in Lehmann et al. (2014) represent a challenge for the empirical analysis of top-earner mobility. Indeed, even the most recent analyses of Kleven et al. (2013, 2014), which are reviewed later in "Empirical literature", study the elasticity of mobility. A new empirical approach, based on the semi-elasticity is therefore compelled.

Productivity

A maintained assumption in the theoretical literature on optimal taxation under mobility is that the production function exhibits constant returns to scale and there are no peer effects or spillovers. This is the case in, among others, Wilson (1980); Osmundsen (1999); Hamilton and Pestieau (2005); Simula and Trannoy (2010) and Lehmann et al. (2014).

These assumptions, combined with the competitive labour market assumption that implies that wages are equal to marginal productivity, are at odds with what is observed empirically. Indeed, especially when thinking of highly skilled workers, it is natural to expect some bargaining power at the wage negotiation stage. Furthermore, skilled workers are likely to be highly productive, to produce positive externalities (by increasing others' productivity), and possibly to modify the internal labour demand (displacement effect).

These factors are particularly important in the context of tax avoidance: the empirical results in Kleven et al. (2014) suggest that both employers and employees enjoy some market power and that mobile highly skilled workers bargain for their wage. Within this framework, any difference between the tax systems of different jurisdictions alters the bargaining power of agents. Indeed, any opportunity to avoid taxes or to change the after-tax wage of an agent inevitably affects the willingness to accept a contract of a worker and his/her willingness to relocate. In the context of high-skilled workers (but without considering mobility) Kreiner et al. (2016) show, for instance, clear evidence of intertemporal bargaining that allows tax avoidance.

Either a nonlinear production function or the presence of peer effects and spillovers would affect workers' productivity and wage and thereby impact upon both the level of mobility and mobility-related tax avoidance. Meanwhile, the positive effects of the brain drain (to those where brain drains towards) make governments willing to compete harder to attract skilled workers. This is likely to result in tax policies that allow top earners to avoid taxes in their origin country.

The theoretical literature on optimal taxation with mobility and tax avoidance or evasion should explore the consequences of relaxing the assumption of competitive labour markets. Our guess is that peer-effects and increasing returns to scale amplify the negative impact of mobility for countries that are not able to reach a sufficient mass of skilled agents, and relax the constraint for those countries that are able to attract the most productive agents.

Empirical literature

Mobility – or at least its threat (Brueckner 2003) – is largely ignored in the empirical work on taxation, despite being a key issue for tax policy design. Empirical analyses are crucial to estimate the real response of taxpayers, which can then be used to calibrate optimal tax income formulae (see, e.g. Slemrod 2010, section III.A). In this section, we focus on the empirical analysis of two issues related to individual taxation and mobility.

The first issue concerns the relocation of taxpayers. High levels of mobility erode the tax base of sovereign governments. This effect is amplified by the fact that capital and high-skill workers are the most mobile factors of production. Therefore, mobility constraints the ability of the public sector to redistribute income, with the consequence that, in the long run, taxes tend to be borne by the most immobile factors; that is, workers instead of capital, and in particular, low skilled workers. It should be noticed that the movement of both capital and labour will be a function of "effective" tax rates, which may differ from statutory tax rates when accounting for differences in the level of enforcement in alternative jurisdictions.

The next section reviews the most recent literature that has estimated the elasticity of mobility for top-earner taxpayers due to statutory tax differentials. The focus is on individual mobility, as opposed to corporate mobility, and in particular on labour income. The empirical analyses estimate the degree of mobility of relatively rich taxpayers, which are usually assumed to be the most mobile within the population. Therefore, the estimated response of this group of taxpayers should reasonably constitute an upper bound, and so be indicative of the importance of mobility for tax policy design. This group of taxpayers is a relevant target for the public sector in terms of tax collection but are also a potential source of economic spillovers within a jurisdiction, for they are likely to be the most skilled agents. This explains the preferential tax regimes that some countries have enacted to attract this taxpayer group. Indeed, these preferential tax regimes constitute an interesting source of tax policy variation for identification purposes.

The second issue concerns the difficulty of enforcing the residence-of-the-taxpayer principle (henceforth RTP). Mobility makes it difficult to tax revenues: leaving aside tax havens, taxing income obtained outside the jurisdiction under the RTP principle crucially depends on the existence of information sharing among tax administrations both at an international level and within federations with independent federal tax administrations. In the later section, titled "Tax enforcement", we focus on the importance of cooperation and data sharing among tax administrations in order to guarantee the effectiveness of tax enforcement and to reduce the possibilities of tax avoidance.

Mobility elasticity

It is widely accepted in the literature that labour migration is a non-negligible phenomenon, and that its extent may vary depending on several factors, including the regional area and the skill level (Acemoglu 2002; Bhagwati and Hanson 2009). This constitutes a major obstacle to any empirical analysis, for results may lack external validity when the sample is homogeneous, while results may be diluted when the sample is broader.

The most recent literature on mobility and/or on top-income avoidance has focused on homogeneous groups of agents. For instance, Kleven et al. (2013) consider football players, Kleven et al. (2014) and Kreiner et al. (2016) look at top-income earners in Denmark, while Akcigit et al. (2016) and Moretti and Wilson (2017) focus on scientists and inventors. Some studies focus on one country (e.g. Liebig et al. 2007; Kleven et al. 2014; Moretti and Wilson (2017); Kreiner et al. 2016), while others consider several countries (e.g. Kleven et al. 2013; Akcigit et al. 2016). Despite the very different setting and the differences in samples, the results in terms of the mobility elasticity of top-income taxpayers are non-negligible and quantitatively similar across studies.

The analysis of Liebig et al. (2007) considers tax-induced mobility within Switzerland and shows that tax-related mobility varies significantly by age and education. In particular, younger, educated agents tend to be more mobile. This is not surprising, because young age and education are both likely to be correlated with lower costs of mobility, furthermore, education is likely to be positively correlated with wages. Therefore, the expected net-gains from mobility are larger for them.

"Superstars" are another category of agents for whom mobility is likely to be particularly high (Rosen 1981). This category includes football players. The so-called "Bosman" rule (1995) significantly reduced barriers to movement within the European Union for any worker, and in particular for professional football players. Furthermore, extensive cross-country differences in tax policies (from preferential tax regimes to variation in tax rates) make this labour market especially suitable to analyse the impact of taxation (personal income tax, payroll tax and VAT) on mobility. Kleven et al. (2013) show extensive empirical evidence about how taxes have affected the allocation of football players in 14 European countries since 1985.

A different category of top-income earners are innovators and scientists. This group is analysed by Akcigit et al. (2016) and Moretti and Wilson (2017). Both focus on star inventors. Scientists are ranked according to their patent productivity. While Akcigit et al. (2016) use data both for north America and Europe, Moretti and Wilson (2017) focus on interjurisdictional migration within the United States. Innovators, in Moretti and Wilson (2017), are assumed to relocate as a consequence of differences in state personal income tax rates (neither consumption taxes nor other local taxes are considered, although there might be differences between states), controlling for differences in amenities, wages and shocks that might also condition location. The labour supply of star scientists is the share of star scientists of a given origin state who move to another state, compared to all those who remain in the origin state. Firms represent the labour demand side, for their production function requires them to employ a scientist. Labour demand variations are therefore computed as the percentage of firms moving from a given origin state to a given destination state with respect to those remaining in their origin state. Labour supply is a function of wage and productive amenity differentials between states, but also of corporate income tax rate differentials. In equilibrium, demand and supply of scientists must be equal. From this equilibrium condition, the authors derive the reduced model to be estimated, which includes all variables conditioning both supply and demand. This model is then used to estimate the impact of corporate income tax and personal income tax differentials on location between pairs of states.

Kleven et al. (2013) examine the fraction of foreign football players as a fraction of the total number of players playing in the top league of a country. They show, by means of a cross-country correlation analysis, that immigration depends on top tax rates (the results are independent of whether marginal or average tax rates are employed), with an elasticity of 1.22.[4] Before the Bosman rule – which liberalised the market for footballers in such a way that it eliminated the quota of foreign players per team – this elasticity was not statistically different from zero.

Although the pre-Bosman period looks a good placebo test to identify the particular effect of taxes on mobility, these authors provide further empirical evidence for the purpose of identification. In particular, they take advantage of preferential tax regimes enacted in two countries, Spain and Denmark. From 1 January 2004 foreign workers (not only football players) moving to Spain could opt for a preferential flat personal income tax rate of 24% (for up to five years) instead of the standard tax piece-wise schedule with marginal rates (and also average rates, for top-income earners) that exceed 40%.[5] To be eligible, workers could not have been Spanish tax resident within the previous ten years. Similarly, Denmark enacted a preferential tax regime for foreign taxpayers in 1992. Individual taxpayers (re)locating in Denmark – including native taxpayers having lived for up to three years outside the country – with earnings approximately at the 99th percentile of the distribution of individual earnings and with most of their work within the Danish borders would enjoy a 30% flat tax rate for a period of up to three years. Absent this preferential tax regime, these taxpayers would face an average tax rate of around a 60%. Therefore, both tax regimes constitute a quasi-experiment, which is an ideal setting to test for the sensitivity of (top) taxpayers to tax differentials.

The empirical analysis for each one of these two countries follows a difference-in-difference approach before and after the reform, and is estimated by two-stage least squares. The endogenous variable is the same as in the cross-section analysis of Kleven et al. (2013), the treatment group is the country under analysis (Spain or Denmark), and the control group is obtained using the synthetic control approach of Abadie et al. (2010). In Spain, the estimated elasticity is around 1.5 for top football players (defined as those that at least have played once for their national football team). In Denmark, again for top football players, the elasticity is twice the elasticity obtained for Spain, 3.01, which can be explained by the observation that prior to this reform the number of foreign players in the Danish league was very small.

Finally, these authors estimate a multinomial logit regression model for the post-Bosman period exploiting simultaneously all sources of variation in top earnings tax rates in all 14 countries over time, and using micro data. The elasticity obtained is around one. For domestic

---

4 As is common in this literature, the variables are expressed in logs to estimate an elasticity; this is why, in order that the log of the tax rate be defined at zero, the authors work with the net-of-tax rate. This point also applies to the other papers we review.

5 This so-called "Beckham" law was revoked in 2010.

taxpayers, the elasticity with respect to the net-of-tax rate is much smaller, 0.15, which is consistent with the fact that most of these players play in their home country.

A similar difference-in-difference analysis using two-stage least squares is Kleven et al. (2014). The authors take advantage of the Danish quasi-experiment, but they consider all top-income earners in Denmark instead of focusing on football players. This preferential tax regime, that has been created to attract top taxpayers, provides an ideal setting to analyse mobility due to taxation for high-income earners. The treatment group is composed of those foreign taxpayers with earnings above the threshold set in law, while the control one consists of those foreign taxpayers with earnings between 80% and 99% of the threshold. The authors employ alternative definitions of the endogenous variable, as the number of foreigners, the number of arrivals, and the number of foreigners with less of three years of presence in the country. They obtain elasticity estimates of between 1.5 and 2; the long term elasticity (1992–2005) being slightly higher than the short term elasticity (1992–1996).

To get an idea of its quantitative meaning, for the lower bound of the estimated elasticity, this means that a 1% decrease of the tax rate (from 60% to 59%) implies a 3.8% increase in the number of foreign taxpayers. This is quite a high response, but compatible with what is observed in the data, for after having decreased the tax rate by up to 30%, the number of foreign taxpayers slightly more than doubled. Using the standard formula for the linear tax rate, τ, that maximises revenue from this group of taxpayers, $\tau = (1 + \varepsilon)^{-1}$, the revenue-maximising (effective) tax rate would be between 0.4 (for an elasticity, ε, equal to 1.5) and 0.33 (for $\varepsilon = 2$).[6] These tax rates are not far from the effective tax rates that once residing in the country these taxpayers should pay, which includes not only the personal income tax rate, but also consumption taxes.

From the two studies on inventors we learn that their elasticity is comparable to the one of the Danish top-income earners and, therefore, slightly below the one of football players. This could be explained by either unobserved idiosyncratic differences, or maybe by the difference in age (football players are likely to be younger than inventors), income levels (likely to be larger for football top players) and in the expected flow of income (likely to be spread over a longer period of time, in the case of inventors). In the case of Akcigit et al. (2016), the estimated elasticity of top inventors is around 1.3, while Moretti and Wilson (2017) obtain an elasticity of 1.6 for personal income taxes; that is, a 1% decline in after-tax income in the destination state relative to the origin state is associated with a 1.6% increase in the number of star scientists who leave the origin state and relocate to the destination state. Or to make it comparable with the previous calculations, if California decreased its 2010 marginal tax rate from 9.5% to 8.5%, it would obtain a 1.8% net increase in star scientists.

This estimated elasticity, as previously mentioned, is in the range of values obtained by Kleven et al. (2013). Thus, not unreasonably, the revenue-maximising personal income tax rate, which includes the federal income tax rate, is similar to the one obtained for Denmark. As the impact of tax differentials on mobility are typically higher within a country (namely, the United States) than across countries, one might expect this elasticity to be higher than the (cross-country) elasticity measured for Denmark. In spite of the similar findings, we note that the two empirical analyses may not be fully comparable: Moretti and Wilson's results are obtained using the marginal tax rate instead of the average tax rate, and in any case, the response of star scientists does

---

6 Note, though, that according to the theoretical framework developed by Lehmann et al. (2014), to obtain optimal tax formulae it is necessary to estimate the semi-elasticity of migration, defined as the percentage change in the mass of taxpayers of a given skill level when their consumption is increased by one unit, which cannot be derived from the elasticity of migration. This will therefore require further empirical analysis.

not have to be representative of the response of all top-income taxpayers.[7] It is also interesting to notice that the analysis of the inventors' behaviour allows one to observe a decrease in mobility along the inventors' fame. For corporate income taxes, they estimate an elasticity of 2.3.

In all the papers reviewed, despite following slightly different empirical approaches, the estimated response of top-income workers to differences in tax levels is substantial, being between 1 and 2. This mobility undoubtedly tames the capability of sovereign governments to expand the size of the public sector, or at least to pursue a complete redistributive policy, as the mobile factors are precisely those at the top of the income distribution. Empirical results at the international level and within a federation are similar. However, still further empirical analyses would be interesting to confirm the robustness of these results and gauge potential heterogeneity. For example it would be interesting to ascertain whether all taxes (payroll, personal income or VAT) have the same effect on mobility, whether the elasticity is higher for small countries (the result obtained for Denmark vs. Spain regarding football players might point to this) or whether these preferential tax regimes are justified on the grounds of the spillover effects top-income taxpayers might generate on the national or on the regional economy. All these pieces of information should be useful for a better design of tax systems.

Tax enforcement

The previously-mentioned papers estimate large responses of taxpayers relocating from one jurisdiction to another due to tax differentials. As previously suggested, though, mobility might not only be a threat for sovereign jurisdictions due to differential statutory parameters, but also due to differentials in the level of tax enforcement. If mobility were only caused by differences in statutory tax parameters then to maximise global welfare tax harmonisation would be called for, so as to avoid beggar-thy-neighbour policies (see, e.g. Kanbur and Keen 1993). In the absence of a common tax administration, however, observability and enforcement difficulties with respect to the setting of a harmonised level of tax enforcement might make it impossible for independent tax administrations to credibly commit to a coordinated policy in order to avoid the negative effects of beggar-thy-neighbour policies (Cremer and Gahvari 1997, 2000).

The empirical relevance of this setting has been recently tested by Durán-Cabré et al. (2015). In contrast to the previous papers, due to the lack of data on physical mobility for a sufficiently long time span, these authors test to what extent the tax enforcement policy of a region is affected by the enforcement policy carried out by its competitors identified by the neighbouring jurisdictions. The analysis is carried out for Spain, where regions administer the inheritance and gift tax (IGT). Up until 1997, regions were only responsible for administering the tax, but since then – and especially from 2002 on – they gained the power to modify legal elements of the IGT. There is anecdotal evidence about the incentives that this has provoked on mobility of tax bases across regions. To test to what extent (the threat of) mobility conditions tax policy, the authors estimate a spatial autoregressive panel model. Results point to the existence of interdependence in tax enforcement, such that a region decreases its tax auditing probability by around 0.6% if its neighbouring jurisdictions decrease their tax auditing probability by 1%. Thus, implicitly, regions are encouraging tax evasion as a way to attract tax bases. This interdependence in tax enforcement – albeit still present – became less important when regions also achieved legal tax power after 2002. That is, there was a switch in the nature of interdependence. Although

---

7 In particular, inventors may consider spillovers from other inventors when deciding their location, and furthermore the labour demand for a very specialised research profile may not be uniformly distributed over the country. It may then be that a top inventor has more location restrictions than an average top-income earner.

from a normative point of view, this switch looks welfare enhancing due to the gain in transparency, the main conclusion from this empirical analysis is that the design of tax enforcement is also conditioned by mobility, and so confirms the theoretical framework set by Cremer and Gahvari (2000). This seems a fruitful field of research in the future, given the particular lack of similar empirical analyses for major taxes.

Mobility might also impede the complete realisation of the RTP principle unless independent tax administrations collaborate to share relevant information. Durán-Cabré et al. (2016) test the existence of collaboration between independent tax administrations taking again advantage of the Spanish institutional framework. In particular, corporations and individual taxpayers may submit their tax declaration – and so pay taxes – to the wrong tax administration. This could occur by honest mistake or it could reflect an intention to take advantage of statutory tax differentials between regions. To which administration agents should properly submit their declaration depends on the whether the residence or the territorial (or source) principle applies. When a tax declaration is submitted to the wrong tax administration, the receiving administration should automatically inform the legitimate receiver, and also tax proceeds should be transferred. However, there is ample evidence that this collaboration is far from being automatic. Such a setting is used to test whether there exists some room for a mutually beneficial agreement to cooperate between administrations.

In the authors' empirical analysis, the endogenous variable is the amount of tax revenue transferred by region i to region j conditional on pair-specific variables (related to both regions) and specific control variables of region i; similar results are obtained when the endogenous variable is defined as the number of tax returns submitted from one tax administration to another. The model is estimated through a Tobit random effects model. From the results, the authors conclude that cooperation crucially depends on the existence of reciprocity; that is, *ceteris paribus*, a one-euro increase in the tax revenues received by region i from region j in year t results in an increase of 0.4 euros of tax revenues being transmitted from i to j in year $t + 1$. Hence, once tax administrations engage in cooperative behaviour, it is maintained, fostering even closer cooperation between them. This is a crucial point because it suggests that once regional tax administrations become aware of the potential benefits of cooperation, they do not deviate from this equilibrium. The positive effects of reciprocity, though, become weaker when region i is financially constrained (measured by its public finance deficit). Again, this looks a promising field for future research.

All in all, although the empirical evidence is scarce, as expected, the impact of mobility on the tax system is not constrained to its legal elements, but also to its administration. While harmonisation of statutory tax parameters is a difficult task (countries and regions fear losing fiscal sovereignty, and there will be winners and losers), harmonisation of tax enforcement or, in general, of tax administration processes seems simply impossible. Given the empirical evidence we have reviewed in this section, collaboration might naturally arise – leaving aside tax havens – once independent governments realise the long run benefits of such collaboration. But whether this will be enough as to impede beggar-thy-neighbour policies in tax enforcement is unclear.[8] This would naturally call for more ambitious processes of integration by tax authorities, such as a World Tax Administration. This, however, seems quite unlikely in the medium run.

---

8 For example, this is in the line with the partially optimistic description of the recent evolution in international cooperation of Atkinson (2015). "Although with a good deal of fine rhetoric" (p. 276), there are some small steps, such as the Global Forum on Transparency and Exchange of Information for Tax Purposes for OECD and non-OECD economies, the OECD Common Reporting Standard, the OECD Base Erosion and Profit Shifting Project, and the Joint International Tax Shelter Information Centre (JITSIC). This remains a nascent area, though.

Conclusion

The taxation of high-income earners is of importance to every country and has been the subject of a considerable amount of recent academic research. Top-income earners are crucial in tax design because (a) they represent a large share of the total wealth; (b) they are more mobile (more educated, better language skills and outside options); and (c) countries must compete for them. Capital and labour mobility are intrinsically different, so one cannot simply assume that the large literature on the former has applicability to the latter. There is ample evidence of uncertainty among policymakers over this aspect of tax policy. Spain initiated and subsequently repealed the Beckham law designed to attract foreign talent, while the UK initiated a 50% income tax on top earners, before quickly moving to lower it to 45%.

In this chapter we reviewed research into taxation of high-income earners with the aim of providing a synthesis of existing theoretical and empirical understanding of this issue. Theoretical approaches seek to understand the optimal tax scheme from the perspective of maximising societal welfare. While models are becoming increasingly sophisticated, a fundamental problem remains that results are very sensitive to the choice of social welfare function. The optimal behaviour depends crucially on whose welfare the social planner has at heart (citizens, residents, the sum of the two, the intersection of the two, or the world population). The Rawlsian social welfare function, which is popular in the literature, yields tractability, but is normatively questionable. Other choices of the social welfare function give the social planner seemingly perverse incentives, and the present approach to mitigating this issue – imposing *ad hoc* constraints on the planner – is clearly unsatisfactory.

Empirical approaches have examined the behaviour of particular groups of high-earners (footballers, scientists) exploiting heterogeneity in income tax rates either across countries or within a country over time. Strictly speaking, however, the relevant tax rate is not the statutory one, but the effective rate, accounting for the easiness of evasion. Top-income earners display a considerable elasticity of mobility, possibly with jumps, and within top earners, it is those with the very highest earnings that are the most mobile. Moreover, observed mobility may be very different from (and substantially understate) the threat of mobility. It is truly the threat of mobility that is matters to policymakers, for if the threat of mobility is credible there are constraints on the extent to which taxes can be raised before everyone (rich) will leave.

We have identified a number of directions for future research. From a theoretical perspective, there is further scope for positive insights to inform the normative assumptions made in theoretical work (particularly around the choice of the SWF). Second, the assumption of constant returns to scale in the production function should be relaxed. From an empirical perspective, there is an apparent disjunction between the sole focus on elasticities in the empirical literature and recent advances in the theoretical literature (in which the optimal tax schedule depends on the semi-elasticity of migration and not just on the elasticity). More research to clarify this issue is therefore called for. Also, as most studies consider specific groups of top earners (scientists, football players) work is needed to test the external validity of these findings in other occupations. It might also be interesting to understand whether it is earnings in an absolute sense or in a relative sense (relative to one's peers/colleagues) that drive mobility. It might be that (relatively badly paid) top university professors are as mobile as top football players, for instance.

Last, although we have focused on the mobility of individuals, there are also clear links to the mobility of firms. For, in particular, small firms, the distinction between mobility of the firm and the mobility of its directors becomes very heavily intertwined. We see scope for more theoretical and empirical work in this area.

Acknowledgements

For their comments and suggestions, we are grateful to: Javier Vázquez Grenno and Duccio Gamannossi. Piolatto gratefully acknowledges financial support from the Generalitat de Catalunya (2014SGR420). Esteller gratefully acknowledges financial support from the Spanish Ministry of Economics and Competitiveness (grant ECO2015–63591-R) and the Generalitat de Catalunya (2014SGR420).

References

Abadie, A., Diamond, A., and Hainmueller, J. (2010). 'Synthetic control methods for comparative case studies: Estimating the effect of California's tobacco control program', *Journal of the American Statistical Association*, 105, 493–505.

Acemoglu, D. (2002). 'Technical change, inequality and the labour market', *Journal of Economic Literature*, 40, 7–72.

Adams, W. (ed.) (1968). *The Brain Drain*. New York: Macmillan.

Akcigit, U., Baslandze, S., and Stantcheva, S. (2016). 'Taxation and the international mobility of inventors', *American Economic Review*, 106, 2930–81.

Allingham, M. G., and Sandmo, A. (1972). 'Income tax evasion: A theoretical analysis', *Journal of Public Economics*, 1, 323–8.

Atkinson, A. B. (2015). *Inequality: What Can Be Done?* Cambridge, MA: Harvard University Press.

Beine, M., Docquier, F., and Rapoport, H. (2001). 'Brain drain and economic growth: Theory and evidence', *Journal of Development Economics*, 64, 275–89.

Bhagwati, J., and Hanson, G. (eds) (2009). *Skilled Immigration Today: Prospects, Problems, and Policies*. Oxford: Oxford University Press.

Bhagwati, J. N. (ed.) (1976a). *Taxing the Brain Drain Vol. 1: A Proposal*. Amsterdam: North-Holland Publishing.

Bhagwati, J. N. (ed.) (1976b). *Taxing the Brain Drain Vol. 2: Theory and Empirical Analysis*. Amsterdam: North-Holland Publishing.

Bierbrauer, F., Brett, C., and Weymark, J. (2013). 'Strategic nonlinear income tax competition with perfect labor mobility', *Games and Economic Behavior*, 82, 292–311.

Borjas, G. J. (1999). 'The economic analysis of immigration', in O. Ashenfelter and D. Card (eds), *Handbook of Labor Economics*, Vol. 3A. Amsterdam: Elsevier Science, pp. 1697–760.

Brueckner, J. (2003). 'Strategic interaction among governments: An overview of empirical studies', *International Regional Science Review*, 26, 175–88.

Chander, P., and Wilde, L. L. (1998). 'A general characterization of optimal income tax enforcement', *Review of Economic Studies*, 65, 165–83.

Cremer, H., and Gahvari, F. (1997). 'In-kind transfers, self-selection and optimal tax policy', *European Economic Review*, 41, 97–114.

Cremer, H., and Gahvari, F. (2000). 'Tax evasion, fiscal competition and economic integration', *European Economic Review*, 44, 1633–57.

Day, K. M., and Winer, S. L. (2006). 'Policy-induced internal migration: An empirical investigation of the Canadian case', *International Tax and Public Finance*, 13, 535–64.

Diamond, P., and Mirrlees, J. A. (1971). 'Optimal taxation and public production I: Production efficiency', *American Economic Review*, 61, 8–27.

Durán-Cabré, J. M., Esteller-Moré, A., and Salvadori, L. (2015). 'Empirical evidence on horizontal competition in tax enforcement', *International Tax and Public Finance*, 22, 834–60.

Durán-Cabré, J. M., Esteller-Moré, A., and Salvadori, L. (2016). 'Empirical evidence on tax co-operation among sub-central administrations', *Journal of Tax Administration*, 2, 24–46.

Feldstein, M. (1995). 'The effect of marginal tax rates on taxable income: A panel study of the 1986 tax reform act', *Journal of Political Economy*, 103, 551–72.

Feldstein, M. (1999). 'Tax avoidance and the deadweight loss of the income tax', *Review of Economics and Statistics*, 81, 674–80.

Feldstein, M., and Wrobel, M. V. (1998). 'Can state taxes redistribute income?', *Journal of Public Economics*, 68, 369–96.

Hamilton, J., and Pestieau, P. (2005). 'Optimal income taxation and the ability distribution: Implications for migration equilibria', *International Tax and Public Finance*, 12, 29–45.

Kanbur, R., and Keen, M. (1993). 'Jeux sans frontieres: Tax competition and tax coordination when countries differ in size', *American Economic Review*, 83, 877–92.

Keen, M., and Konrad, K. A. (2013). 'The theory of international tax competition and coordination', in A. J. Auerbach, R. Chetty, M. Feldstein and Saez, E. (eds), *Handbook of Public Economics*, Vol. 5. Amsterdam: North-Holland, 257–328.

Keen, M., and Ligthart, J. (2006). 'Information sharing and international taxation: A primer', *International Tax and Public Finance*, 13, 81–110.

Kirchgassner, G., and Pommerehne, W. (1996). 'Tax harmonization and tax competition in the European Union: Lessons from Switzerland', *Journal of Public Economics*, 60, 351–71.

Kleven, H. J., Landais, C., and Saez, E. (2013). 'Taxation and international migration of superstars: Evidence from the European football market', *American Economic Review*, 103, 1892–924.

Kleven, H. J., Landais, C., Saez, E., and Schultz, E. (2014). 'Migration and wage effects of taxing top earners: Evidence from the foreigners tax scheme in Denmark', *Quarterly Journal of Economics*, 129, 333–78.

Kreiner, C. T., Leth-Petersen, S., and Skov, P. E. (2016). 'Tax reforms and intertemporal shifting of wage income: Evidence from Danish monthly payroll records', *American Economic Journal: Economic Policy*, 8, 233–57.

Lehmann, E., Simula, L., and Trannoy, A. (2014). 'Tax me if you can! Optimal nonlinear income tax between competing governments', *Quarterly Journal of Economics*, 129, 1995–2030.

Liebig, T., Puhani, P. A., and Sousa-Poza, A. (2007). 'Taxation and internal migration: Evidence from the Swiss census using community-level variation in income tax rates', *Journal of Regional Science*, 47, 807–36.

Mirrlees, J. A. (1971). 'An exploration in the theory of optimum income taxation', *Review of Economic Studies*, 38, 175–208.

Miyagiwa, K. (1991). 'Scale economies in education and the brain drain problem', *International Economic Review*, 32, 743–59.

Moretti, E., and Wilson, D. (2017). 'The effect of state taxes on the geographical location of top earners: Evidence from star scientists', *American Economic Review*, 107, 1858–1903.

Osmundsen, P. (1999). 'Taxing internationally mobile individuals – a case of countervailing incentives', *International Tax and Public Finance*, 6, 149–64.

Pencavel, J. (1979). 'A note on income tax evasion, labor supply, and nonlinear tax schedules', *Journal of Public Economics*, 12, 115–24.

Piketty, T., and Saez, E. (2013). 'Optimal labor income taxation', in A. J. Auerbach, R. Chetty, M. Feldstein and E. Saez (eds), *Handbook of Public Economics*, Vol. 5. Amsterdam: Elsevier, 391–474.

Reinganum, J. F., and Wilde, L. L. (1985). 'Income tax compliance in a principal-agent framework', *Journal of Public Economics*, 26 (February), 1–18.

Rosen, S. (1981). 'The economics of superstars', *American Economic Review*, 71, 845–58.

Saez, E., Slemrod, J., and Giertz, S. H. (2012). 'The elasticity of taxable income with respect to marginal tax rates: A critical review', *Journal of Economic Literature*, 50, 3–50.

Simula, L., and Trannoy, A. (2010). 'Optimal income tax under the threat of migration by top-income earners', *Journal of Public Economics*, 94, 163–73.

Simula, L., and Trannoy, A. (2012). 'Shall we keep the highly skilled at home? The optimal income tax perspective', *Social Choice and Welfare*, 39, 751–82.

Slemrod, J. (2010). 'Location, (real) location, (tax) location: An essay on mobility's place in optimal taxation', *National Tax Journal*, 63, 843–64.

Wilson, J. D. (1980). 'The effect of potential emigration on the optimal linear income tax', *Journal of Public Economics*, 14, 339–53.

Wilson, J. D. (1986). 'A theory of interregional tax competition', *Journal of Urban Economics*, 19, 296–315.

Wilson, J. D. (2009). 'Income taxation and skilled migration', in J. Bhagwati and G. Hanson (eds), *Skilled Immigration Today*. Oxford: Oxford University Press, Ch. 10, 285–314.

Yitzhaki, S. (1974). 'A note on income taxation: A theoretical analysis', *Journal of Public Economics*, 3, 201–2.

Young, C., and Varner, C. (2011). 'Millionaire migration and state taxation of top incomes: Evidence from a natural experiment', *National Tax Journal*, 64, 255–83.

Zodrow, G. R., and Mieszkowski, P. (1986). 'Pigou, Tiebout, property taxation, and the underprovision of local public goods', *Journal of Urban Economics*, 19, 257–65.

Zucman, G. (2013). 'The missing wealth of nations, are Europe and the U.S. net debtors or net creditors?', *Quarterly Journal of Economics*, 128, 1321–64.

Zucman, G. (2014). 'Taxing across borders: Tracking personal wealth and corporate profits', *Journal of Economic Perspectives*, 28, 121–48.

21

TAX PRACTITIONERS AND TAX AVOIDANCE

Gaming through authorities, cultures, and markets[1]

Elea Wurth[2] and Valerie Braithwaite

Tax practitioners play multiple roles in our tax and financial planning systems (Devos 2012; Klepper et al. 1991). They are gatekeepers to the tax system for those who want someone else to take care of their tax affairs. Tax practitioners function as enforcers, trying to dissuade clients from actions that will likely create problems with tax authorities, either through protracted conflict or penalties. Tax practitioners also adopt the role of enablers (or exploiters), identifying financial planning arrangements that minimize tax or avoid it altogether. An established tax practitioner will have had exposure to all of these roles, either as observer or participant (Marshall et al. 2010; Niemirowski and Wearing 2003; Tan 1999).

This chapter proposes that the tax practitioner-taxpayer relationship is a micro social process to deliver tax compliance (or semblance thereof) as outlined by Tan (1999, 2014) in her tax practitioner-client role model. This relationship, however, is not insulated from broader social forces. These social forces are represented in the integrated model presented later in Figure 21.3 as cyclical markets in tax avoidance, the tax cultures with which the practitioner has contact, and governance by local and global authorities.

In order to bring these elements together, three models of the tax practitioner and taxpayer experience are reviewed, and research on the role of the tax practitioner is discussed within these frameworks. The first two models have been developed and discussed elsewhere and will be reviewed only briefly for purposes of showing the cultural, legal and market influences on tax practitioners. First, the Wheel of Social Alignments summarises the drivers of compliance and conceives of tax practitioners as alternative authorities to tax officials (Braithwaite and Wenzel 2008; Braithwaite 2009a). Cyclical markets in vice place tax practitioners within global and local markets where they must compete for their share of business, attracting sufficient clients for a sustainable practice, or meeting employer performance benchmarks (Braithwaite 2005). Finally, new data are presented on how tax practitioners operate within the tax preparation market

---

1 The original data presented in this paper was collected and analysed as part of Dr Elea Wurth's PhD thesis, undertaken at the School of Regulation and Global Governance (RegNet) and supported by the Australian Taxation Office Commissioner's scholarship.

2 Elea Wurth contributed to this book in her personal capacity. The views expressed are her own and do not necessarily represent the views of the Australian Tax Office.

with full knowledge of oversight by the tax authority. The findings are based on a survey of over 1,000 practitioners preparing and lodging returns for clients with the Australian Taxation Office (Wurth 2013). Drawing on lessons learnt from these three models, an integrated model is provided to broaden the landscape against which we view and study developments in the tax avoidance industry.

The embedding of tax practice

Empirical work collected from taxpayers and practitioners supports the idea that practitioners, like other professionals, are responsive to influences from many sources – clients, tax authorities, professional associations, governments, international bodies, and the organizations and cultures in which they work (Ayres et al. 1989; Braithwaite 2005; Braithwaite and Wenzel 2008; Cruz et al. 2000; Gracia and Oats 2012; Hite and McGill 1992; Picciotto 2007; Roberts 1998; Shafer and Simmons 2011; Tan 2011; Yetmar and Eastman 2000). Tax practitioners operate with imperatives that are not necessarily compatible: to attract clients, meet taxpayer expectations, meet performance standards set by firm partners, build reputation, abide by professional obligations and any associated regulatory standards, and operate in accordance with the rules set down by the tax authority (Attwell and Sawyer 2001; Marshall et al. 1998; Niemirowski and Wearing 2003; Shafer and Simmons 2011; Tan 2011; Walpole and Salter 2014).

A mass of data has accumulated on the types of tax advice given and why it is given. Research on whether tax practitioners or taxpayers drive decisions converges on the conclusion that this is a contextual matter (Roberts 1998; Tan 1999; Devos 2012), but few doubt that tax practitioners can influence outcomes due to their superior knowledge and status in tax matters (Hite and McGill 1992; Jackson and Milliron 1989; Tan 1999; Niemirowski and Wearing 2003; Parnaby 2009). Tan (2011, 2014) explains the variation in advice given and accepted by taxpayers in terms of the tax practitioner-client role model. The services that a tax practitioner offers to a taxpayer are in the form of knowledge and options; that which is provided and accepted is negotiated through iterative exchanges within their relationship. Tax practitioner and client constitute a unique dyad and the decisions made within that dyad are constructed by both of them. This notion is consistent with the Bourdieusian view offered by Oats and Gracia (2012) in their work on negotiating the boundaries of licit and illicit tax conduct. The dyad is held together by trust, technical proficiency and capacity to provide aggressive advice (Tan et al. 2014).

Generally, the quality of the advice can be summarized in terms of two basic concepts, degree of technical proficiency and degree of aggressiveness (Sakurai and Braithwaite 2003; Tan et al. 2014). Programs to improve the technical knowledge of tax practitioners as well as taxpayers have evolved out of the body of research on tax practitioners and their clients (Hashimzade 2015; Masken 2014; Niemirowski and Wearing 2003). Curbing aggressiveness has proven more problematic. The body of research on the reasons why aggressive advice is given, and to whom, needs to extend beyond individualistic notions of risk-taking and be integrated into a theoretical model that reflects the contemporary complex social role of the tax practitioner in revenue systems. Tax practitioners have always been considered important as intermediaries of transactions between taxpayers and tax officials. In recent decades their role has become more complicated with recognition that they, not taxpayers, hold the special knowledge required to facilitate tax avoidance, or what Lipatov (2012) calls sophisticated as opposed to simple tax evasion. That knowledge, however, is not acquired or acted upon in a social vacuum. Tax practitioners marshal networks of support, for instance, to dispute Lipatov's argument for describing avoidance as evasion.

To understand how to curb the growing acceptance of tax avoidance and the threat it poses to tax systems (Ordower 2010; Prebble and Prebble, chapter 23, this volume), the tax practitioner-taxpayer relationship must be understood within a broader social and cultural context. As tax practitioners take instructions and give advice to clients, how they use their specialist knowledge is tempered by pressures from multiple sources: governing bodies and tax authorities that make and enforce tax laws and rules; taxpaying communities; other practitioners, professional bodies and workplaces; and the ever changing markets that present opportunities for avoidance (see Gracia and Oats 2012 for a similar view from a Bourdieusian perspective).

Competing cultures, competing authorities: the wheel of social alignments

The Wheel of Social Alignments is a model (see Figure 21.1) that describes the interactions that take place between taxpayers, tax authorities and influential others such as tax practitioners, business advisers, lobby groups and other significant players in the tax system, locally and globally. All

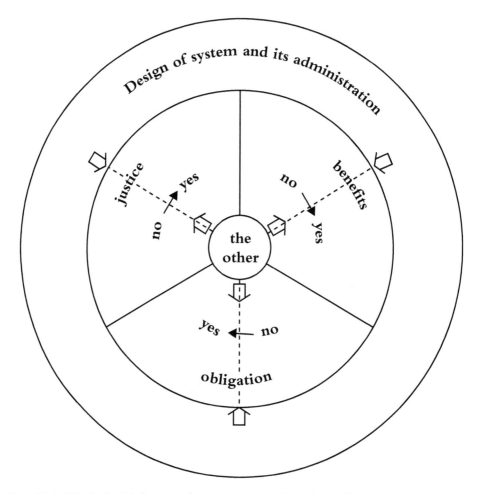

Figure 21.1 Wheel of social alignments for taxpayer cooperation and compliance.

Source: Braithwaite 2009a.

are active agents in establishing a compliant and cooperative taxpaying culture. This is not to say that everyone in the system will comply or be cooperative. Resistance in the system will always be present, and resistance often is the feedback needed for change and improved functioning (Braithwaite 2009a, 2009b). The Wheel of Social Alignments is not a model of consensus but describes the dialogic process that must take place to establish a base level of cooperation to collect tax effectively and ride out and manage cycles of aggressive tax planning and avoidance.

The middle band of the Wheel of Social Alignments represents taxpayers who must engage with the tax system as individuals, small businesses or large corporate entities. The tax system is represented in the outer band and comprises tax authorities and administrators with their laws, rules, and practices that guide how they collect tax and the demands and constraints they place on taxpayers. Deterrence measures are part of this outer band as are taxpayers' charters. Of particular relevance when thinking of tax avoidance are the policies and directives of parliament and the government of the day, also best represented as part of the outer band.

How taxpayers in the middle band engage with the tax system in the outer band – that is, whether they comply or cooperate with tax and government officials – varies across the population and across time (Braithwaite 2009a, 2009b). The vast literature on tax compliance points to multiple determinants of tax cooperation and compliance that can be summarized in terms of three conceptual levers: benefits, fairness and moral obligation (Braithwaite and Wenzel 2008; Braithwaite 2009a). These three types of levers are represented as segments of the middle band. When all are functioning optimally, tax administrators have the greatest chance of having the system operate efficiently with taxpayers willing and able to pay the tax that they should be paying. In other words, the wheel is primed to move forward.

Taxpayers cooperate more when they see benefits for themselves, or their family, or the collective. Taxpayers make such judgments of benefits, adopting any number of different identities from the highly individualized to the highly collectivized (Wenzel 2003). Government policy and performance affects perceptions of benefits. Taxpayers are also more likely to cooperate if the system is fair. Again fairness may be assessed from the perspective of the individual or the group. It may refer to fairness of process (procedural justice in Tyler's (1990) terms; see Murphy 2010) or fairness of outcome (distributive justice as in the question: "Are others paying their fair share of tax or am I and people like me paying more than my fair share?" See Wenzel 2002, 2003). Finally, the third lever for taxpayer cooperation is moral obligation. Taxpayers are social beings and as such are exposed to a legal sensibility: They have lifelong learning that laws are to be obeyed and adverse consequences are likely to follow from disobeying authority. At the heart of all well-governed societies is respect for law and an internalized sense of moral obligation. Repeatedly it has been shown that moral obligation is a stalwart buffer against tax evasion and avoidance (Braithwaite and Wenzel 2008; Braithwaite 2009a, 2009b; Braithwaite and Reinhart 2013).

These three factors of benefits, fairness and moral obligation shape how taxpayers react to the tax authority's expectations of compliance. The process of 'sense making' around benefits, fairness and moral obligation is ongoing and is influenced by other people and alternative authorities that put forward their own interpretations and seek to influence taxpayer decisions. The inner band represents these other forces. They may be local or global. They include lobby groups (pro- and anti-tax), political leaders, family and friends. Hasseldine et al. (2011) point to the 'Big Four' as having a major influence on the tax policies of individual countries. Their voice is heard not only in the corridors of power but also through the media, thereby shaping tax discussions across the community. International organizations such as the Organisation for Economic Co-operation and Development (OECD) and various other global non-state organizations with an interest in tax policy also exert their influence (Ring 2010). The actors in the inner band can exert their influence on both the middle band of taxpayers and the outer band of tax administrators and policy makers.

Included in the inner band are tax practitioners. Tax practitioners enter into a professional relationship with taxpayers. They also have professional relationships with the outer band (tax administrators and policy makers) and others in the inner band (financial planners, business consultants, lobby groups and professional associations to name a few). Tax practitioners are highly networked actors in the tax system; they are holders of knowledge and resources, and importantly of contacts through whom tax avoidance contagion is triggered. For this reason, tax practitioners are at the centre of any discussion about tax avoidance and the eliciting of taxpayer cooperation. The wheel will not be socially aligned to move forward without their support.

When taxpayers approach a tax practitioner to provide a service or they return to the same practitioner year after year, as is most often the case (Tan et al. 2016), they enter a relationship in which each brings a set of expectations and needs. Each practitioner-client relationship has its unique features. Yet research findings point to overarching trends and consistent sources of variation. Most taxpayers want their tax practitioner to keep them out of trouble with the tax authority (Hite and McGill 1992; Sakurai and Braithwaite 2003). They want to believe that they are honest taxpayers. To this extent there is alignment between taxpayer moral obligation and the expected service they receive from the tax practitioner.

Along with being honest is the desire to save tax: taxpayers do not want to pay more than is necessary (Sakurai and Braithwaite 2003; Niemirowski and Wearing 2003). Niemirowski and Wearing (2003) have proposed that taxpayers resolve the tension between being honest and saving tax by passing responsibility to tax practitioners. Tax practitioners protect the taxpayers' view of themselves as honest and respectable while playing aggressively backstage on their behalf. The evidence suggests tax practitioners try to be responsive to clients' needs (Bobek and Radtke 2007; Cloyd 1995; Schisler 1994) but are also mindful of possible sanctioning by the authority. Tax practitioners are likely to adopt the role of enforcer when tax law is unambiguous, but they are more likely to adopt the role of exploiter when tax law is ambiguous (Klepper et al. 1991). In other words, tax practitioners are more likely to stay within the law when it is clear in its intent and purpose, but they are more likely to test the boundaries when loopholes and ambiguities permit.

A not insignificant number of taxpayers also are not honest in dealings with their tax practitioner, failing to fully disclose their tax related activity (Attwell and Sawyer 2001; Niemirowski and Wearing 2003). This may be careless or deliberate. Whatever the case, tax practitioners are aware that taxpayers differ in their attitudes to taxation and their expectations of them, and that they must manage their clients and earn their trust if they are to be retained as their service provider (Tan 2011; Tan et al. 2016). For tax practitioners, convincing clients that their tax affairs are being managed in a proper and fair way is necessary for a sustainable practice, and if the practitioners can add aggressive tax-planning advice to those who want it, their market share can be consolidated (Tan et al. 2016). Tax practitioners have reason to establish their authority in their relationships with their clients.

Authority is enhanced in the public eye through the tax practitioner's affiliation with high-status professional associations. Some evidence suggests that membership in professional bodies such as being a qualified CPA (certified public accountant) is associated with more aggressive tax planning (Ayres et al. 1989; Erard 1993; Shafer and Simmons 2011). Working for the large global accountancy firms also has been linked with giving clients more aggressive tax-planning advice (Marshall et al. 2010). This may reflect the fact that high-status and well-networked practitioners are better positioned to know what options exist for tax avoidance and the risks they attract.

Tax practitioners working within large accountancy firms are subject to further pressures to 'capture' clients. Those seeking tax advice are encouraged to integrate tax advice with financial planning, while business owners are encouraged to use the firm's business consultancy services (Blackburn et al. 2010). The effects on tax practice can be significant. For example, the lack of auditing rigor by Arthur Andersen, formerly one of the 'Big Five' accounting firms, was the result of conflicting business arms of the organisation (Coffee 2006: 28). Arthur Andersen offered an auditing service, which promised an independent examination and verification of company accounting documents. Auditing, however, became a means of entry into businesses. Auditing staff were trained to market more lucrative consultancy services. It was this emphasis on cross-selling that impaired the independence of auditors' professional examinations (Coffee 2006).

As well as obligations that arise in relation to professional networks are the obligations that tax practitioners hold as a result of their personal ethics (Cruz et al. 2000). Work environments can give rise to tensions among obligations to the firm, obligations to the client, and ethical obligations (Shafer and Simmons 2011). Bobek et al. (2010) found that non-partners in accounting firms have a less positive view than partners of the ethics of the work environment. Doyle et al. (2013) have made a case for poor moral reasoning in the tax practitioner context and Blanthorne, Burton and Fisher (2014) have argued that tax practitioners are disconnected from moral reasoning when advising clients. These researchers make the case for why tax practitioners may function as an alternative authority that undermines the capacity of tax authorities to elicit taxpayer cooperation.

The Wheel of Social Alignments reminds us that the tax practitioner is part of a rich social network in the tax system and inevitably is influenced by and influences other actors. Importantly, the wheel is a reminder that tax practitioners are also taxpayers who are not immune to the influences of perceived benefits, fairness and moral obligation when it comes to deciding whether or not they will be cooperative players in the tax system and whether or not they will facilitate processes of evasion or avoidance through their professional knowledge and skill. The narratives they adopt around the legitimacy of tax evasion and avoidance, once shared and espoused by powerful interest groups, can derail tax systems (Addison and Mueller 2015).

Markets in vice and virtue: the cyclical nature of tax avoidance markets

The majority of tax practitioners are unlikely to purposefully engage in illegal conduct that puts their practice at risk. Yet, in a rapidly changing tax environment, there are many 'conversations' had by tax practitioners with clients, other advisers, and tax authorities that change their thinking, open their mind to new possibilities and shape the advice given to clients. The Wheel of Social Alignments does not adequately capture the change process in the financial and tax-planning environment. John Braithwaite's (2005) model of cyclical markets in vice and virtue helps fill this gap.

Tax practitioners cannot avoid being aware of cycles in the aggressive tax-planning and tax-avoidance market. The cycle is defined by fluctuations in supply and demand (J. Braithwaite 2005). Aggressive tax schemes emerge first in niche markets as highly sophisticated products for wealthy elite clients. They are designed to weave through tax law to suit the client's specific circumstances. The success of the schemes does not remain a trade secret. The idea is repackaged for mass marketing, often in a less nuanced way. The schemes offered to ordinary taxpayers catch on, and there is herding or contagion in the market. Variations of the schemes do not sidestep the law as neatly as the tailor-made originals. When tax schemes lose their sophistication on mass supply and slip from the grey area of avoidance to clearer territory of evasion, a tax crack-down becomes easier. Enforcement also may be aided through a change in law or legal interpretation or legal precedents, but often the contagion means that a serious enforcement-swamping problem has set in by the time the tax authority acts (J. Braithwaite 2003a, 2005). Crackdowns become highly visible and sometimes highly punitive (Hobson 2004; Murphy 2003, 2005). Avoidance is temporarily dampened in the population at large. Demand and supply of aggressive tax planning will swing up again when new avoidance measures are developed, successfully exploited and mass marketed; that is, until the tax authority effectively takes enforcement action once again. The spread of tax avoidance measures among tax practitioners and taxpayers is not static, but cyclical.

The model is based on the simple proposition that markets are normatively neutral. Therefore while it is expected that we will have markets in 'goods' (for example, producing efficiency in finding a trustworthy practitioner to organize our taxpaying accurately), we will also have markets in 'bads' (that is, efficiency in finding a practitioner who will get us out of paying the tax required of us). Evidence suggests that both markets exist in the tax preparation industry (Bankman 1999; Karlinsky and Bankman 2002; Sakurai and Braithwaite 2003).

While markets in vice and virtue co-exist, they are not equally strong at the same time. Aggressive tax schemes that spread in a contagion spawn a tax environment where moral obligation to pay one's fair share of tax is put on hold: Too much moral obligation is not adaptive during such times (Braithwaite 2009b; Braithwaite and Reinhart 2013) and in an aggressive cycle, taxpayers take their cue as to what is right by doing what others are doing, particularly when there is no fear of retribution from the tax authority (Wenzel 2004). The signals received by taxpayers from players in the tax avoidance market provide new social norms about the appropriate behaviour for the new circumstances. When tax authorities crack down on avoidance they risk criticism of being arbitrary and unfair, and too slow to respond (Hobson 2004; Murphy 2003, 2005). A crackdown needs commitment and collaboration from government, civil society, business, and tax practitioners. John Braithwaite (2003a, 2005) has argued that tax authorities must then follow through with a concerted effort to flip a market in vice to a market in virtue. Registering tax practitioners, holding scheme promoters accountable, introducing and demonstrating how anti-avoidance principles are to be used, introducing expanded tax returns, strengthening intelligence-gathering capacities in financial markets, and signalling enforcement intent early and openly together offer possibilities for flipping markets. These measures become more acceptable in the community at large when the public turns against markets in vice and clamours for the re-emergence of a market in virtue. In other words, tax avoidance is best reined in with a strengthening sensibility that tax avoidance is harmful for democracies and governments more generally, and seriously undermines the legitimacy of national tax systems (arguably this has occurred in the aftermath of the global financial crisis). For this project, political leadership is necessary, though not sufficient without follow-through with effective regulatory measures.

Many levers are needed to rein in tax avoidance because the tax environment is complex and not as amenable to direct control by national governments as they would wish. The tax environment comprises global networks of interests, often conflicting. In an article titled "Who is Making International Tax Policy", Diane Ring (2010) highlights the number of non-state actors influencing tax policy and administration internationally: the International Fiscal Association, International Bureau of Fiscal Documentation, International Tax Dialogue, International Chamber of Commerce, Business and Industry Advisory Committee, and the OECD. There are also international tax justice networks, taxpayer advocacy groups, and bodies that bring national governments together, such as the G20. The tax environment affects tax practitioners; indeed it affects all three bands in the Wheel of Social Alignments in Figure 21.1. The magnitude of the leadership challenge facing governments has grown not only with the number of influential actors and their capacity to organize globally, but also with a change in the ways tax avoidance is practiced. The boundary between aggressive tax planning and cautious minimizing of tax has increased in its blurriness with both seeking legitimacy under the responsible umbrella of financial planning (see chapter 23 in this volume by Prebble and Stewart).

The conversation required to rein in tax avoidance today is necessarily a political one and has been initiated internationally by the OECD Forum for Tax Administration and the G20. Reining in tax avoidance requires concerted efforts not only at the macro level but also at the micro level in the form of cooperation from tax practitioners and the firms to which they belong. The Big Four accounting firms are publicly proclaiming the need for a responsible approach to taxation ("responsible tax for the common good" is promoted by KPMG (2016)). Turning such declarations into action will require cooperation from the multinationals and large corporations. Given the public interest in tax avoidance by the 'big end of town', the media will undoubtedly keep the public engaged in how well actions meet the rhetoric of corporate social responsibility.

Needless to say, outside scrutiny and understanding tax cultures and the tax environment do not explain completely what is happening in private practices. Tan's (2014) tax practitioner-client role model underlines the complexity of interactions in the preparation and submission of an income tax return to the authority. Research discussed earlier in this chapter on the tax practitioner-taxpayer relationship suggests no certainty around who is the instigator, promoter and final decision maker of taking aggressive tax positions. Individual audits may get to the bottom of how decisions are made on a case-by-case basis. From a policy perspective, however, containing tax avoidance may be more effectively achieved by looking for regularities in the way in which a tax practitioner engages with his or her client base. Elea Wurth's (2013) Propensity and Opportunity Model of Tax Practitioner Behaviour provides insights into the form that engagement with a client base takes.

Tax practitioner market segmentation: the propensity and opportunity model

Wurth (2013) focused on non-compliance in the set of income tax returns prepared and submitted on behalf of clients by individual tax practitioners. The unit of analysis was the tax practitioners' self-reports on the legitimacy of the set of items that made up the income tax return (across the client base). There were 21 income tax return items. The first step was to identify types of tax practitioners based on regularities in the way tax practitioners reported on the legitimacy of their preparation for the 21 different income tax return items.

Once patterns were detected and clusters of tax practitioners were found, the next step was to identify the defining features of each cluster. The theoretical framework for doing so was based on Nagin and Paternoster's (1993) work on propensity and opportunity in criminal behaviour: Could the clusters of tax practitioners be differentiated in terms of the characteristics of the tax practitioner (propensity) and the characteristics of the environment (opportunity)? Nagin and Paternoster (1993) showed empirically that propensity (for example, lack of self control) and opportunity (easy pathways for illicit gain) worked in combination to predict criminal activity. From the literature, Wurth grouped predictors of tax practitioner non-compliance in terms of propensity, or opportunity. Propensity encompassed individual differences in risk-taking, tax ethics, wealth and status aspirations and professional identity. These are the personal characteristics, socially and psychologically acquired over the course of a person's life experience, that shape how that person makes sense of and acts upon the events happening in their world.

Opportunity captures environmental conditions, or what the person perceives the situation as offering in terms of tax minimization. Opportunity incorporates perception of audit and penalty rates (more generally deterrence measures), legal loopholes and ambiguity regarding tax treatment of particular items for a tax return. A large volume of research points to the importance of deterrence measures and ambiguity in tax law in explaining tax practitioner involvement in evasion and avoidance.

The centrally important finding of this research was that tax practitioners clustered into four different groups in terms of their confidence that the income tax return items had been prepared and submitted accurately. The distinctive compliance groups of tax practitioners emerged from a cluster analysis of 1,373 individuals[3] who were mailed a survey and asked to report on the legitimacy of the income tax returns that they prepared for their clients. As might be expected, the vast majority of tax practitioners reported that in general the income tax returns they lodged on behalf of their clients were legitimate. This suggested that tax practitioners on average were behaving honestly and professionally. Yet differences emerged and these differences proved insightful into how tax practitioners operate under conditions where they experience conflicting compliance pressures.

The 21 income tax return items varied in visibility. Dividends, salary and wages, government pensions and lump sum payments were subject to third-party reporting and were highly visible items. Less visible were items such as work-related expenses, rental deductions, business income and deductions, personal services income, capital gains and foreign income. The question was: How legitimate were the returns you submitted for your clients on item 1, then item 2 and so on to item 21. Responses were made on a rating scale from "absolutely confident they were all legitimate" to "pretty sure most are not completely legitimate".

Consistent with tax administration reports (Australian Taxation Office 2009; also consistent with Internal Revenue Service 1996), practitioners expressed greater confidence in their preparation decisions around the visible items than the less visible items. Differences emerged, however, in the degree to which confidence dropped around less visible items. These differences were captured statistically through a cluster analysis that grouped practitioners who had a similar pattern of confidence in the preparation legitimacy of the 21 items. Sharpening the differences between groups involved applying the propensity and opportunity variables. Wurth described the four clusters that emerged from this analysis as a teardrop (see Figure 21.2).

Duteous tax practitioners

At the bottom of the teardrop were duteous tax practitioners (22 per cent of the sample). They reported that the vast majority of their submitted returns were absolutely legitimate. Their confidence was slightly less on foreign income, but even so duteous tax practitioners most consistently hovered around absolutely confident about the legitimacy of the items they submitted for their clients.

---

3   The sample of practitioners who were sent the mail survey was selected from the Australian Taxation Office's database. Practitioners who responded to the survey were largely male, had a mean age of 53 years and had been practicing for a mean of 20 years. They were predominantly at the head of their organisation (sole practitioners, partners and company directors). Respondents were involved in tax preparation either directly or in an associated role. The final sample size of usable responses was 1,373 (response rate 25%).

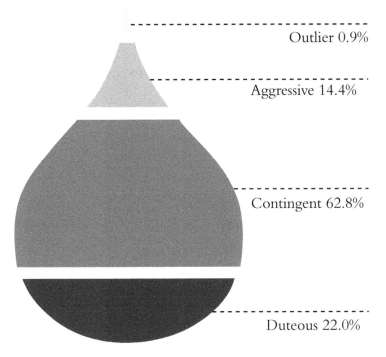

Figure 21.2 The teardrop of tax practitioner compliance with the revenue authority's expectations.
Source: Wurth 2013.

When the duteous group were interrogated as to their propensity and opportunity for avoidance and evasion, they were distinctive in their emphasis on adopting a cautious style. Their commitment to the tax system was high, as was their commitment to business best practice and tax competence. They did not see great opportunity for non-compliance. Nor did they see the preparation of individual tax returns as involving decisions that were especially ambiguous. The duteous were distinctive in their commitment to doing all parts of their job well and doing the right thing.

Contingent tax practitioners

In the middle of the teardrop were contingent tax practitioners (nearly 63%). They were similar to duteous practitioners in relation to preparation for clients on high-visibility tax return items. They professed less confidence that submitted tax items were absolutely legitimate in relation to low-visibility items and foreign income. They appeared to have greater acceptance of possible non-compliance than the duteous group.

Propensity and opportunity indicators bore this interpretation out. The contingent tax practitioners were greater risk-takers with a sense of agency or power that they could influence outcomes within the tax system. Contingent practitioners perceived a greater level of ambiguity in the tax affairs of their clients and saw opportunity to get away with non-compliant practices if they so wished. Interestingly these practitioners defined their style of preparation as being not as cautious as the duteous, but they shied away from defining their style as aggressive.

Aggressive tax practitioners

The group of tax practitioners second from the top of the teardrop were the aggressive group (approximately 14%). Their declarations of absolute legitimacy weakened from visible to less visible items, then weakened further with foreign income. Most importantly, the aggressive group were less confident than the contingent or duteous groups. They were less sure of the legitimacy of all income tax items, regardless of the item's level of visibility.

Tax practitioners in the aggressive group were distinguished by an increased propensity to compromise their preparation ethics and exploit the opportunity afforded by ambiguity within their clients' tax affairs.

Disengaged outliers

The very small top group in the teardrop, the outliers (0.9%), followed the overall pattern of the aggressive group of practitioners but were far more extreme in their responses. They were distinctive in scoring their submitted tax items as likely to be on the illegitimate side across all income items.

In terms of propensity and opportunity, the findings were intriguing. While the outliers initially were suspected of being an especially egregious group, further analyses with the propensity and opportunity factors pointed to a different interpretation. These practitioners were most clearly defined by self-reported lack of competence and a sense of powerlessness. As well as admitting to preparing client returns of extremely low compliance, they considered the likelihood of detection for such practices to be high. These characteristics suggest a state of disengagement (Braithwaite 2009b). Disengagement could possibly reflect a point-in-time crisis. More than half of this group said they would choose another career if given a chance. Possibly this group of tax practitioners had failed to adjust to an extended period of legislative and technological change in the taxation system. The outliers cluster may represent those practitioners who McKerchar (2005) found were "overwhelmed" by the demands made on them.

The teardrop model explains some of the gaps and puzzles of the tax practitioner literature. First, both propensity (willingness) and opportunity (pathways) are relevant to the bulk of preparation decisions made by a tax practitioner. But the balance of propensity and opportunity factors differs across groups. For duteous tax practitioners, a sense of what is professionally, ethically and legally correct prevails to an extent that opportunistic pathways are not on their radar. Importantly, for duteous taxpayers there is no tension between having a successful business and being an ethical professional. Duteous tax practitioners have alignment in how they manage clients and the tax environment. For aggressive tax practitioners, on the other hand, opportunity dominates any sense of moral obligation. Instead a risk-taking disposition ignites interest in tax avoidance schemes. Aggressive tax practitioners will turn to new pastures for practicing tax avoidance on behalf of their clients once a crackdown of a current scheme is mobilised by the tax authority.

This leaves the majority group of contingent tax practitioners. They have capacity to vacillate between cautious and aggressive positions. From the perspective of cyclical markets in vice, contingent taxpayers are adaptive, moving toward more aggressive positions when that appears to be what others are doing and it is safe to do so because tax authorities are tolerating such activity. This means that when a tax authority is trying to flip a market in vice into one in virtue, it is the contingent tax practitioners who are the key target group: They will be the most responsive to pressure and therefore likely to move. They will notice and heed tax authority warnings and crackdowns on what is deemed unacceptable practice.

Synthesis of the three models

The Wheel of Social Alignments sets up at a macro level the complex webs of cooperation that must be in play to steer the flow of events[4] to make a tax system sustainable and effective. Markets in vice and virtue show how these webs of relationships are washed over by market forces, with some relationships strengthening and tightening while others weaken. Contagion for tax avoidance spreads through webs of relationships that affect tax practitioners and taxpayers at a micro level. The propensity and opportunity model shows how tax practitioners carve out a market that suits them and attracts clients who want the services they offer. Some will choose to operate in a "duteous" sphere with networks that support their outlook. Some will choose an "aggressive" sphere with networks that are well informed and supportive of their operations. The majority will claim a contingent space, choosing to remain "adaptive" and tuning in to networks that will tell them which way the wind is blowing regarding avoidance, evasion and enforcement by the tax authority.

The major departure of this approach from the tax literature is that the tax practitioner is no longer seen as an individual processing incoming information and making rational decisions. The tax practitioner rather is seen as a member of a set of networks: the client practioner dyad; the workplace network; professional networks; citizen networks; family networks; friendship networks; and commercial networks. Social pressures from all these networks shape what happens when tax practitioners and their clients are making tax decisions. This suggests neither that the tax practitioner is devoid of responsibility for the advice given, nor that the taxpayer (influenced by similar sources, see Braithwaite and Wenzel 2008) is not responsible for his or her tax return to the authority. The thesis is that individuals are responsible for their decisions but that an individualistic model takes attention away from the social-relational and market forces contributing to the tax avoidance problem.

In order to understand and steer tax preparation away from avoidance and evasion, tax authorities need to understand and be able to negotiate with and manage the many sets of networks that influence outcomes. In a democracy this should be handled through reasoned argument, persuasion, effective law and competent enforcement, in accordance with the revenue authority's taxpayers' charter. Unfortunately, over-reliance on an individualistic way of analysing the problem invariably leads to domination in the tax system of politically weaker players held up as examples of moral decay. In the meantime, the system leading to such outcomes remains unexamined and the more serious promoters and carriers of avoidance measures avoid scrutiny (see examples described by Murphy 2003, 2005 and Hobson 2004, and more recently in *The Guardian*, UK (Rawlinson 2014)).

A schematic representation of the tax practitioner-client dyad as a node within sets of connected networks appears in Figure 21.3. The institutional influences discussed in this chapter are captured through the concepts of (a) authorities, (b) cultures, and (c) markets. Authorities include the government's revenue collection agency with capacity to coerce compliance through audits and deterrence responses. Deterrence can take the form of penalties, shaming, and something that is often overlooked, particularly for first-time offenders, the threat of legal action. John Braithwaite (2003a) describes the phenomenon of the taxpayer wanting "peace of mind". Persistent stress on the accused and families undergoing long, drawn-out audits and court processes, prosecutions and appeals carries weight psychologically and socially above and beyond penalties applied by the revenue authority.

---

4   The definition of regulation given by Parker and J. Braithwaite (2003) is to steer the flow of events.

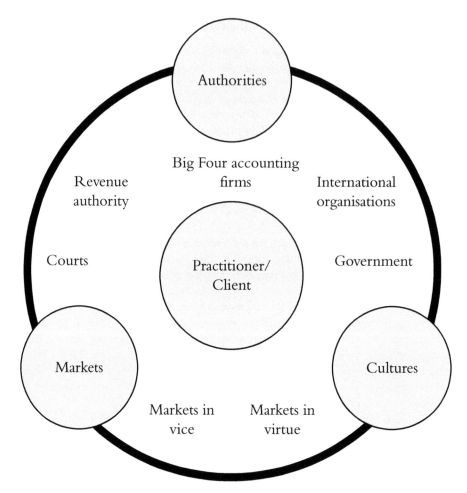

Figure 21.3 A social and economic relational model of the forces that shape the roles of tax practitioner and client and their transactions.

Authorities in Figure 21.3, therefore, include the courts and its officers, as well as barristers and others with standing in the community who can credibly support the use of particular tax avoidance measures. Defenders of avoidance schemes may extend to the Big Four accounting firms and other professional bodies. At the level of firms, the pressures that partners place on non-partners to perform certain tasks to increase income streams can also be seen as the exertion of authority on tax practitioner advice and decision-making. It would be reasonable to assume that the practices of the Big Four accounting firms set standards that are attractive to many other firms aspiring to increase their market share in the financial sector. In sum, in Figure 21.3 there are many authorities that compete for influence. Some authorities aim to contain tax avoidance, others will promote it.

Markets in Figure 21.3 represent the economic pressures on tax practitioners to enter the market of aggressive or contingent tax advice when cycles of tax avoidance gain momentum and spread through the tax community. The pressure may be felt through interactions with taxpayers, professional colleagues or employers. To the extent that a narrative of personal benefit and lawfulness develops around tax avoidance schemes, tax culture changes to promote such schemes as standard business practice. Stories of waste of taxpayers' money and bad government add to the appeal of the message of tax avoidance promoters. The executive branch of government is ideally placed to show leadership in changing the tax avoidance narrative through their capacity to direct tax policy and deliver good government, while backing up their revenue authority's efforts to uncover avoidance schemes and take action to contain them or close them down.

Flipping markets in vice to markets in virtue (also part of the story of markets in Figure 21.3) involves making an effort to re-define tax culture. Tax cultures, the third concept represented in Figure 21.3, involve a variety of norms, beliefs, attitudes and practices about taxation and the revenue authority that collects taxes. Government sets the stage for discussions of tax culture, and the business community contributes its views, as do international organizations (Ring 2010). At the heart of how culture influences compliance and cooperation with revenue authorities are the concepts of benefits, justice and moral obligation from the Wheel of Social Alignments. Stories abound of the benefits of paying tax as well as the deficits associated with wastage and economic loss through the tax system. Tax culture also can be characterised by narratives of unfairness and resistance, as told through the work of Murphy (2003, 2005) and Hobson (2004). And finally tax culture manifests itself through the all important sensibility of moral obligation, whether it is a moral imperative for the tax practitioner as is the case for those in the 'duteous' cluster, whether it depends on the clarity of the law as with the 'contingent' group, or whether it is at risk of becoming irrelevant, as is the case with those practitioners in the 'aggressive' cluster.

Implications

When tax authorities start to flip a market in tax avoidance, they need a suite of mechanisms that engage productively with tax practitioners who may be duteous, contingent, aggressive or outliers. The propensity and opportunity model explains why deterrence works in some contexts and not others and why framing around moral obligation and/or social norms can be effective, but will not necessarily be so. For duteous tax practitioners, professional ethics and commitment to their profession is paramount. Duteous tax practitioners will respond positively to being the shining light held up to contingent taxpayers: because they will have their identity affirmed as the revenue authority treats them respectfully and pursues less 'honest' practitioners. This strategy is unlikely to work with aggressive tax practitioners. Aggressive tax practitioners will respond to blocked pathways and a credible risk of penalty, albeit while searching for new ways around the law. A revenue authority that threatens a crackdown on tax avoidance will likely not dissuade aggressive tax practitioners as much as contingent tax practitioners. Contingent tax practitioners will play it safe, taking note of warnings from the revenue authority, observing what is being condoned and sanctioned, and adjusting their actions accordingly.

The difficulty for revenue authorities is in identifying their target population accurately. Taxpayers differentiate honest, no-fuss advice from cautious, minimizing advice and aggressive advice (Sakurai and Braithwaite 2003; Tan et al. 2016), and tax practitioners can be identified as duteous, contingent or aggressive (Wurth 2013). In practice, taxpayers find it difficult to clearly separate those offering cautious, minimizing advice from those offering aggressive advice (Sakurai and Braithwaite 2003). Partly this is because what is cautious and aggressive is unclear to a non-expert. The teardrop model in Figure 21.2 (above), however, provides further insight into the confusion. Most tax practitioners occupy the 'contingent' zone and can therefore cater within limits to the differential risk capacities of their clients, moving from the cautious to more aggressive ends of the spectrum depending on the tax environment, ambiguity of the law, and visibility of income tax return items. Taxpayers could well be reporting honestly when they declared their tax practitioner as giving both cautious and aggressive advice. Should a revenue authority target contingent practitioners, there is risk that honest taxpayers, cautious minimizers and aggressive taxpayers will all be caught in the web. Many of the taxpayers prosecuted in Australia's mass-marketed scheme crackdown in the late 1990s depicted themselves as honest and law-abiding and as the victims of unfair treatment by the tax authority (Braithwaite et al. 2007).

The goal is to have a net positive impact on cooperation and compliance, reining in non-compliance where necessary with enforcement action without adversely affecting non-targeted groups. Focused enforcement action needs to be made credible and legitimate through being embedded in a suite of mechanisms about which there is a central and coherent narrative. This narrative geared to discouraging particular avoidance activities needs to be shared by many authorities (government, revenue authorities, professional associations and tax practitioner boards). The narrative needs to explain why the avoidance activity is damaging (not producing benefits for the community), why it is unfair (leading some taxpayers to carry more of the burden than others with the same income, see Prebble, chapter 23, this volume) and why the responsible action for the taxpayer is to pay the tax he or she is expected to pay.

Messaging and persuasion with the community on unacceptable tax behaviour always needs to be followed up with enforcement that is signalled openly and demonstrated firmly through the willingness of a revenue authority to escalate the severity of an intervention and where appropriate its scope. One-off heavy-handed blitzes or amnesties are unlikely to change tax culture without a foreshadowed set of escalating interventions from desk audits, to partial and full audits, penalties, prosecutions and de-registration if non-compliance persists. A responsive regulatory approach of this kind incorporates educating the public, persuasion, the signalling of acceptable pathways and deterrence of unacceptable pathways (Braithwaite 2003, J. Braithwaite 2003a, 2003b, 2005). Responsive regulation is consistent with the central idea of Figure 21.3 (above) that there are multiple sources of influence on behaviour, with the result that there are multiple motives for avoiding tax. A revenue authority therefore has to have at its disposal multiple strategies and tools to elicit compliance. It makes sense to respect the commitment of the duteous through using the least intrusive sanctions should problems of avoidance or evasion arise. But it also makes sense to ratchet up levels of intrusiveness and deter the more aggressive practitioners who are not responsive to the light touch messaging from the tax authority.

Taxpayers' readiness to comply has traditionally been represented in a compliance pyramid with its base populated by honest and cooperative taxpayers who willingly defer to tax authority (Ayres and J. Braithwaite 1994; see Braithwaite 2003a for the Australian Taxation Office's Compliance Model). Other jurisdictions have followed the Australian Taxation Office's Compliance Model. Tax practitioners, however, present differently to tax authorities. Earlier work with tax practitioners who served high-wealth individuals suggested that involvement in tax avoidance distorted the pyramid shape to an egg shape (J. Braithwaite 2003b). Wurth's much larger sample of tax practitioners serving Australian taxpayers takes the next step to proposing a teardrop for the tax practitioner population more generally.

The implications for tax enforcement are significant. Bringing contingent tax practitioners on board is the highest priority, but it must be done without undermining professionalism. Indeed professionalism in the form of respect for the spirit of the law needs to be strengthened since contingent tax practitioners need to join the duteous to form the base of the pyramid to sustain cooperation. Tax authorities too often make the mistake of pursuing their target while communicating lack of trust in those who take pride in doing the right thing, generating unnecessary resistance from those who feel unfairly treated (see Braithwaite et al. 2007). The base of the pyramid weakens rather than strengthens.

A number of approaches would check movement toward more aggressiveness, while appreciating the role played by duteous tax practitioners. Registration of tax practitioners with a tax board, having penalties for scheme promoters and strengthening communication networks among professional associations and tax authorities nationally and internationally are necessary first steps to ensure that all tax practitioners are part of a conversation with tax officials around enforcement priorities. A blueprint that maps out enforcement priorities, while at the same time addressing a prioritised list of requests for clarification and certainty from tax practitioner bodies, is a sensible, mutually advantageous 'mental meeting place' to begin to rein in tax avoidance (Masken 2014 provides an account of IRS interventions of this kind). Building a shared and informed view of acceptable and unacceptable practice can only emerge from pooling intelligence and problem solving capacity (Braithwaite 2003a, 2005).

Ambiguity in tax law has long been recognised as central to the problem of tax avoidance. But equally important is a diminished sense of moral obligation to pay a fair share of tax to support national governments: Large corporations have made it very clear that the interests of shareholders rank higher than the interests of taxpayers and governments. There is little to be gained in debating ambiguity without debating moral obligation. As shown with duteous tax practitioners, ambiguity is a far greater problem for those whose moral obligation has waned than for those with a strong commitment to the tax system and the community it serves.

Along with an agenda of conversations to change culture are steps to make enforcement action more predictable and reasonable. Finding the right balance of the rules-based system with the principles-based system to counter the growth and exploitation of tax law ambiguity is ongoing (J. Braithwaite 2002; Picciotto 2007; Freedman 2010, 2012). Here the role of tax practitioners is paramount. In a hybrid system, rules must be secondary to overarching principles. Rules provide guidance on the most common transactions of business arrangements in a complex field of taxation. However, rules are used only to assist in applying the principle. In a contest between a rule and an overarching principle, it is the principle that is binding on taxpayers. In a hybrid system such as this, practitioners take on the role of enforcers for transactions of certainty while diminishing the 'penumbra' of ambiguity exposed to exploitation.

The successful implementation of a hybrid system of rules and principles-based regulation is dependent on sustaining the dominance of principles and preventing them from being converted or reduced to rules that are gamed. Reduction of principles and resurgence of rules can occur through demands for guidance on how principles will be applied in specific contexts (McBarnet and Whelan 1999) or through the build-up of legal precedent (Clayton Utz 1999). This can be neutralised through sophistication in crafting. Elegant principles must be matched to smart rulings, press releases and bright-line rules, with clarity and consistency in the relationship between principles and rulings. Badly designed principles with uncertain or confusing rules or confusion in the proffering of conflicting interpretations will exacerbate rather than resolve ambiguity. It is here that collaboration between tax practitioners, tax officials and drafters of legislation provides real benefits. The degree to which successful partnering occurs between practitioner and tax officials varies globally (see Visser 2016 on tensions in South Africa; Daly (2007 on collaboration in Ireland; Smith 2004 and Walpole and Salter 2014 on collaboration in Australia). Judith Freedman (2015) has argued for considering new institutional frameworks that can assist all players in managing the complexity that has become intrinsic to tax law. This suggests the allocation of significant resources to stay on top of the tax avoidance game. John Braithwaite (2003a: 266) hints at the need for resources in his analysis of the challenge facing revenue authorities:

> If revenue is escaping out of four open windows, closing three of them might simply see more flowing out the fourth, or a fifth window being prized open. This is not to say that it is impossible to achieve improved levels of taxpaying through a combination of measures.

Conclusion

The thesis of this chapter is that tax practitioners are central in the practice of tax avoidance and evasion. This has long been acknowledged but researchers have persisted in an individualistic model of how tax practitioners influence tax reporting. Research has focused on the 'battle' that takes place between tax practitioners and taxpayers to attribute responsibility for tax avoidance and evasion. A social and economic relational model of the kind presented here addresses this imbalance to uncover the many forces shaping tax practitioner behaviour and to point to the multiple levers that can lead to change in that behaviour. Tax avoidance becomes less attractive to the tax practitioner-taxpayer dyad when public narratives support paying tax, when ambiguities are discussed and resolved through explained application of principles over rules, when enforcement intent is signalled, explained and justified, when there is follow-through on non-compliance with readiness to sanction, and when professional practitioner networks are willing to cooperate with revenue authorities to build shared understandings of legitimate as well as suspect ways of reducing tax.

Little has been said in this chapter about international regulatory mechanisms such as the Base Erosion and Profit Shifting (BEPS) project, disclosure of profits and other transparency measures, whistle-blowing and leaks as evidenced by the Panama Papers and LuxLeaks. The contribution of the Big Four accounting firms to worldwide avoidance of tax has been widely discussed in mainstream media in recent times (see, for example, West (2016) in thenewdaily. com), as governments pursue large corporations like Google and Facebook for unpaid back taxes. The US, the UK, Indonesia, Italy, and France are just some of the countries taking this route. Whether the fight-back of these nation states and most recently of the EU serves to inspire and guide smaller nations remains to be seen. Tax has become a highly politicized issue, this time globally. Tax practitioners occupy a front seat in watching these political tussles play out and will come to their own conclusions no doubt as to whether tax avoidance is in vogue or not.

References

Addison, S., and Mueller, F. (2015). 'The dark side of professions: The big four and tax avoidance', *Accounting, Auditing & Accountability Journal*, 28(8), 1263–90.

Attwell, R. L., and Sawyer, A. J. (2001). 'The ethical attitudes of New Zealand tax practitioners – still "barely passing"', *New Zealand Journal of Taxation Law and Policy*, 7(2), 111–46.

Australian Taxation Office. (2009). *2009–10 Compliance Program*. Canberra: Australian Government. Available at www.ato.gov.au/content/downloads/COR00205435_NAT7769CP0910.pdf.

Ayres, F. L., Jackson, B. R., and Hite, P. S. (1989). 'The economic benefits of regulation: Evidence from professional tax preparers', *Accounting Review*, 64(2), 300–12.

Ayres, I., and Braithwaite, J. (1994). *Responsive Regulation: Transcending the Deregulation Debate*. Oxford: Oxford University Press.

Bankman, J. (1999). 'The new market in corporate tax shelters', *Tax Notes*, 83, 1775–95.

Blackburn, R. A., Carey, P., and Tanewski, G. (2010). 'The role of trust, relationships and professional ethics in the supply of external business advice by accountants to SMEs', Australian Centre for Financial Studies – Finsia Banking and Finance Conference 2010, 15 February. Available at http://dx.doi.org/10.2139/ssrn.1592342.

Blanthorne, C., Burton, H. A., and Fisher, D. (2014). 'The aggressiveness of tax professional reporting: Examining the influence of moral reasoning', *Advances in Accounting Behavioral Research (Advances in Accounting Behavioral Research, Volume 16)*, Emerald Group Publishing Limited, 16, 149–81.

Bobek, D. D., Hageman, A. M., and Radtke, R. R. (2010). 'The ethical environment of tax professionals: Partner and non-partner perceptions and experiences', *Journal of Business Ethics*, 92(4), 637–54.

Bobek, D. D., and Radtke, R. R. (2007). 'An experiential investigation of tax professionals' ethical environments', *Journal of the American Taxation Association*, 29(2), 63–84.

Braithwaite, J. (2002). 'Rules and principles: A theory of legal certainty', *Australian Journal of Legal Philosophy*, 27, 47–82.

Braithwaite, J. (2003a). 'Through the eyes of the advisers: A fresh look at high wealth individuals', in V. Braithwaite (ed.), *Taxing Democracy*. Aldershot: Ashgate Publishing, pp. 245–70.

Braithwaite, J. (2003b). 'Large business and the compliance model', in V. Braithwaite (ed.), *Taxing Democracy*. Aldershot: Ashgate Publishing, pp. 177–202.

Braithwaite, J. (2005). *Markets in Vice, Markets in Virtue*. Oxford: Oxford University Press.

Braithwaite, V. A. (2003). 'Dancing with tax authorities: Motivational postures and non-compliant actions', in V. Braithwaite (ed.), *Taxing Democracy*. Aldershot: Ashgate Publishing, pp. 15–39.

Braithwaite, V. A. (2009a). 'Tax evasion', in M. Tonry (ed.), *Handbook on Crime and Public Policy*. Oxford: Oxford University Press, pp. 381–405.

Braithwaite, V. A. (2009b). *Defiance in Taxation and Governance: Resisting and Dismissing Authority in a Democracy*. Cheltenham: Edward Elgar Publishing.

Braithwaite, V., Murphy, K., and Reinhart, M. (2007). 'Taxation threat, motivational postures, and responsive regulation', *Law & Policy*, 29(1), 137–58.

Braithwaite, V., and Reinhart, M. (2013). 'Deterrence, coping styles and defiance', *FinanzArchiv: Public Finance Analysis*, 69(4), 439–68.

Braithwaite, V. A., and Wenzel, M. (2008). 'Integrating explanations of tax evasion and avoidance', in A. Lewis (ed.), *The Cambridge Handbook of Psychology and Economic Behaviour*. Cambridge: Cambridge University Press, pp. 304–31.

Clayton Utz (1999). *Challenging Private Rulings*. Sydney: Clayton Utz.

Cloyd, C. B. (1995). 'The effects of financial accounting conformity on recommendations of tax preparers', *The Journal of the American Taxation Association*, 17(2), 50.

Coffee, J. C. (2006). *Gatekeepers: The Professions and Corporate Governance*. Oxford: Oxford University Press.

Cruz, C. A., Shafer, W. E., and Strawser, J. R. (2000). 'A multidimensional analysis of tax practitioners' ethical judgments', *Journal of Business Ethics*, 24(3), 223–44.

Daly, F. (2007). 'Tax advisers – undermining or enhancing the tax system?', Address given at Confédération Fiscale Européenne International Conference on Professional Affairs, Sofitel Brussels Europe, 20 November. Available at http://taxinstitute.ie/portals/0/Tax%20Policy/Institute%20Submission/2007/FD%20speech%20to%20CFE%2011%202007.pdf

Devos, K. (2012). 'The impact of tax professionals upon the compliance behaviour of Australian individual taxpayers', *Revenue Law Journal*, 22(1), 31.

Doyle, E., Hughes, J. F., and Summers, B. (2013). 'An empirical analysis of the ethical reasoning of tax practitioners', *Journal of Business Ethics*, 114(2), 325–39.

Erard, B. (1993). 'Taxation with representation: An analysis of the role of tax practitioners in tax compliance', *Journal of Public Economics*, 52(2), 163–97.

Freedman, J. (2010). 'Improving (not perfecting) tax legislation: Rules and principles revisited', *British Tax Review*, 6, 717.

Freedman, J. (2012). 'Responsive regulation, risk, and rules: Applying the theory to tax practice', *University of British Columbia Law Review*, 44(3), 627.

Freedman, J. (2015). 'Managing tax complexity: The institutional framework for tax policy-making and oversight', WP 15/08 Oxford University Centre for Business Taxation.

Gracia, L., and Oats, L. (2012). 'Boundary work and tax regulation: A Bourdieusian view', *Accounting, Organizations and Society*, 37(5), 304–21.

Hashimzade, N. (2015). 'Conference commentary: Improving tax administration through research driven efficiencies', *Journal of Tax Administration*, 1(2), 78–82.

Hasseldine, J., Holland, K., and van der Rijt, P. (2011). 'The market for corporate tax knowledge', *Critical Perspectives on Accounting*, 22(1), 39–52.

Hite, P. A., and McGill, G. A. (1992). 'An examination of taxpayer preference for aggressive tax advice', *National Tax Journal*, 45(4), 389–403.

Hobson, K. (2004). '"Say no to the ATO": The cultural politics of protest against the Australian Tax Office', *Social Movement Studies*, 3(1), 51–71.

Internal Revenue Service. (1996). *Individual Income Tax Gap Estimates for 1985, 1988, and 1992*. Washington, DC: United States Government. Available at: www.irs.gov/pub/irs-soi/p141596.pdf.

Jackson, B. R., and Milliron, V. C. (1989). 'Tax preparers: Government agents or client advocates?', *Journal of Accountancy*, May, 76–83.

Karlinsky, S., and Bankman, J. (2002). 'Developing a theory of cash businesses tax evasion behaviour and the role of their tax preparers', 5th International Conference on Tax Administration: Current Issues and Future Developments, Timebase: Sydney.

Klepper, S., Mazur, M., and Nagin, D. (1991). 'Expert intermediaries and legal compliance: The case of tax preparers', *The Journal of Law & Economics*, 34(1), 205–29.

KPMG. 'Responsible tax for the common good'. Available at https://assets.kpmg.com/content/dam/kpmg/pdf/2016/05/KPMG-2016-Tax-budget-guide.pdf

Lipatov, V. (2012). 'Corporate tax evasion: The case for specialists', *Journal of Economic Behavior & Organization*, 81(1), 185–206.

Marshall, R. L., Armstrong, R. W., and Smith, M. (1998). 'The ethical environment of tax practitioners: Western Australian evidence', *Journal of Business Ethics*, 17(12), 1265–79.

Marshall, R., Smith, M., and Armstrong, R. (2010). 'Ethical issues facing tax professionals: A comparative survey of tax agents and practitioners in Australia', *Asian Review of Accounting*, 18(3), 197–220.

Masken, K. (2014). 'IRS preparer-level treatment tests: Results from the first year of a multi-year study', unpublished report.

McBarnet, D., and Whelan, C. (1999). *Creative Accounting and the Cross-Eyed Javelin Thrower*. Chichester: John Wiley & Sons.

McKerchar, M. (2005). 'The impact of income tax complexity of practitioners in Australia', *Australian Tax Forum*, 20, 529.

Murphy, K. (2003). 'Procedural justice and tax compliance', *Australian Journal of Social Issues*, 38(3), 379–408.

Murphy, K. (2005). 'Regulating more effectively: The relationship between procedural justice, legitimacy, and tax non-compliance', *Journal of Law and Society*, 32(4), 562–89.

Murphy, K. (2010). 'Procedural justice and the regulation of tax compliance behavior', in J. Alm, J. Martinez-Vazquez and B. Torgler (eds), *Developing Alternative Frameworks for Explaining Tax Compliance*. London: Routledge, pp. 191–209.

Nagin, D. S., and Paternoster, R. (1993). 'Enduring individual differences and rational choice theories of crime', *Law and Society Review*, 27(3), 467–96.

Niemirowski, P., and Wearing, A. J. (2003). 'Taxation agents and taxpayer compliance', *Journal of Australian Taxation*, 6, 166.

Oats, L., and Gracia, L. (2012). 'Insights from Bourdieu', in L. Oats (ed.), *Taxation: A Fieldwork Research Handbook*. London: Routledge, pp. 114–19.

Ordower, H. (2010). 'The culture of tax avoidance', *Saint Louis University Law Journal*, 55(1), 47–128.

Parker, C., and Braithwaite, J. (2003). 'Regulation', in P. Cane and M. Tushnet (eds), *The Oxford Handbook of Legal Studies*. London: Oxford University Press, pp. 119–45.

Parnaby, P. F. (2009). 'Sit back and enjoy the ride: Financial planners, symbolic violence and the control of clients', *Canadian Journal of Sociology*, 34(3), 1065–86.

Picciotto, S. (2007). 'Constructing compliance: Game playing, tax law, and the regulatory state', *Law & Policy*, 29(1), 11–30.

Rawlinson, K. (2014). 'Thousands chased by HMRC debt collectors due to overpaid tax credits', *The Guardian*, 30 May [Online]. Available at http://www.theguardian.com/politics/2014/may/30/hmrc-using-a-dozen-tax-collectors-to-reclaim-overpaid-tax-credits

Ring, D. (2010). 'Who is making international tax policy? International organizations as power players in a high stakes world', *Fordham International Law Journal*, 33, 649.

Roberts, M. L. (1998). 'Tax accountants' judgment/decision-making research: A review and synthesis', *The Journal of the American Taxation Association*, 20(1), 78.

Sakurai, Y., and Braithwaite, V. (2003). 'Taxpayers' perceptions of practitioners: Finding one who is effective and does the right thing?', *Journal of Business Ethics*, 46(4), 375–87.

Schisler, D. L. (1994). 'An experimental examination of factors affecting tax preparers' aggressiveness-A prospect theory approach', *The Journal of the American Taxation Association*, 16(2), 124.

Shafer, W. E., and Simmons, R. S. (2011). 'Effects of organizational ethical culture on the ethical decisions of tax practitioners in mainland China', *Accounting, Auditing & Accountability Journal*, 24(5), 647–68.

Smith, J. P. (2004). 'Taxing popularity the story of taxation in Australia', Australian Tax Research Foundation, Research Study No. 43.

Tan, L. M. (1999). 'Taxpayers' preference for type of advice from tax practitioner: A preliminary examination', *Journal of Economic Psychology*, 20(4), 431–47.

Tan, L. M. (2011). 'Giving advice under ambiguity in a tax setting', *Australian Tax Forum*, 26, 73.

Tan, L. M. (2014). 'Understanding the tax practitioner-client relationship: Using a role theory framework', *Procedia – Social and Behavioral Sciences*, 164, 242–7. doi:10.1016/j.sbspro.2014.11.07

Tan, L. M., Braithwaite, V., and Reinhart, M. (2016). 'Why do small business taxpayers stay with their practitioners? Trust, competence and aggressive advice', *International Small Business Journal,* 34(3), 329–44.

Tyler, T. R. (1990). *Why People Obey the Law*. Princeton, NJ: Princeton University Press.

Visser, A. (2016). 'Making friends of foes to improve tax compliance', *Business Daily*, 28 June [Online]. Available at www.bdlive.co.za/national/2016/06/28/making-friends-of-foes-to-improve-tax-compliance

Walpole, M., and Salter, D. (2014). 'Regulation of tax agents in Australia', *eJournal of Tax Research*, 12(2), 335.

Wenzel, M. (2002). 'The impact of outcome orientation and justice concerns on tax compliance: The role of taxpayers' identity', *Journal of Applied Psychology*, 87(4), 629–45.

Wenzel, M. (2003). 'Tax compliance and the psychology of justice: Mapping the field', in V. Braithwaite (ed.), *Taxing Democracy*. Aldershot: Ashgate Publishing, pp. 41–70.

Wenzel, M. (2004). 'An analysis of norm processes in tax compliance', *Journal of Economic Psychology*, 25(2), 213–22.

West, M. (2016). 'Tax avoidance' masters revealed', *The New Daily*, 11 July [Online]. Available at http://thenewdaily.com.au/money/finance-news/2016/07/11/architects-global-tax-avoidance-revealed/

Wurth, E. (2013). 'A will and a way: An analysis of tax practitioner preparation compliance', unpublished PhD dissertation, ANU Canberra. Available at https://digitalcollections.anu.edu.au/handle/1885/10355

Yetmar, S. A., and Eastman, K. K. (2000). 'Tax practitioners' ethical sensitivity: A model and empirical examination', *Journal of Business Ethics*, 26(4), 271–88.

22

OPTIMAL INCOME TAX ENFORCEMENT IN THE PRESENCE OF TAX AVOIDANCE

Duccio Gamannossi degl'Innocenti and Matthew D. Rablen

We examine the optimal auditing problem of a tax authority when taxpayers can choose both to evade and avoid. For a convex penalty function the incentive-compatibility constraints may bind for the richest taxpayer and at a positive level of both evasion and avoidance. The audit function is non-increasing in reported income, and is higher for progressive tax functions than for regressive tax functions. Higher marginal tax rates increase the incentives for non-compliance, overturning the well-known Yitzhaki paradox.

Introduction

Individuals take a variety of actions to reduce their tax liabilities. In particular, one may distinguish between actions that are clearly in breach of the law (tax evasion); actions that are not explicitly ruled out under law, but which violate its spirit (tax avoidance); and actions that are legitimate (tax planning). The term "tax avoidance" is, however, sometimes used to refer to any action that changes a tax liability purely by affecting the form (but not the level) of compensation. For instance, tax avoidance opportunities arise in the context of income tax when taxpayers can shift part of their taxable income into profit or into another time period that is treated more favourably from a tax perspective – for a detailed discussion of these "form-changing" actions see, e.g. Stiglitz (1985) and Slemrod and Yitzhaki (2002). The type of tax avoidance we have in mind in this chapter is a narrower notion, in the sense that many form-changing actions are perfectly legal, and therefore fall into our notion of tax planning. Instead, we consider acts of form-changing that are so artificial in nature that the courts will deem them illegal if the tax authority mounts a legal challenge. These acts are often complex, and – unlike evasion – must be purchased from specialist providers known as "promoters". A recent example of this type of avoidance scheme is a 2012 legal case in the UK between H.M. Revenue and Customs (HMRC) and a businessman named Howard Schofield. Schofield bought an avoidance scheme to help him reduce the amount of tax due on a £10m. capital gain on a share holding. The scheme used self-cancelling option agreements that would return the seller to his original position yet create an allowable loss. Although, viewed separately, the options created exempt gains and allowable losses, when viewed together as a composite transaction they did not. HMRC (2012) described the scheme as "an artificial, circular, self-cancelling scheme designed with no purpose other than to avoid tax", and it was ultimately outlawed.

The first economic studies relating to tax compliance (e.g. Allingham and Sandmo 1972; Srinivasan 1973;Yitzhaki 1974; Christiansen 1980) utilised a general economic model of crime owing to Becker (1968). As this model lends itself much more readily to tax evasion (which is a crime) than tax avoidance (which is not outright illegal), these studies neglect the possibility of tax avoidance altogether.The economic literature that followed has largely retained this bias, even though in many countries it seems likely that loss of tax revenue due to avoidance activity is significant. For instance, according to Cobham (2005), developing countries lose $285 bn per year due to tax evasion and tax avoidance. Estimates provided by the UK tax authority put the value of tax avoidance at £2.7 bn, compared to £4.4 bn for tax evasion (HMRC 2015). Lang et al. (1997) estimate that tax avoidance costs the German exchequer an amount equal to around 34% of income taxes paid.

One of the chief lines of enquiry of economists has been to study how a tax authority can collect a given amount of income tax revenue at minimum enforcement cost, when taxpayers can illegally under-report their true income.The instruments potentially available to the tax authority to achieve this objective are (i) a tax function, which associates a tax liability to each level of income; (ii) a penalty function, which associates a level of penalty to each level of evaded tax, and (iii) an audit function, which associates a probability of audit to each level of reported income.

Like much of the literature, we focus on the audit function by exogenously assuming the form of the penalty and/or tax functions.This is justified if (i) the entity that sets the audit function (the tax authority) does not have discretion over fiscal policy and (ii) the setting of penalties is highly constrained. In practice both these conditions usually hold: the design of the tax function is typically seen as a *policy* matter to be determined by the Treasury (whereas the collection of tax is seen as an *operational* matter), while the penalty function is fixed in legislation (making it costly to change) and is bounded in its severity by the requirement that it be proportional to the perceived seriousness of the crime. Sanchez and Sobel (1993) assume that taxpayers are risk neutral, that the penalty rate on undeclared tax is constant, and that the tax function is given. They give general conditions under which tax revenue is most efficiently collected as follows: taxpayers reporting an amount of income above a threshold amount are audited with probability zero, while taxpayers reporting an amount of income below the threshold are audited with a probability that is just sufficient that they will choose to report their income truthfully.[1] Given this audit probability function, all taxpayers with true income above the threshold amount declare exactly the threshold amount, and so pay the same amount of tax. Accordingly, the "effective" tax function (after taking into account the non-payment of tax due to under-reporting) becomes flat above the threshold declaration amount.

Another strand of literature assumes that a unified entity can simultaneously set the audit, penalty, and tax functions. In this setting Chander and Wilde (1998) show that, if taxpayers are risk neutral and fines are maximal, then the effective tax function is regressive and the audit function is non-increasing. Marhuenda and Ortuño-Ortin (1994) show that these results continue to hold for a range of other (seemingly more reasonable) penalty functions. Chander (2007) generalises these results to a particular class of risk averse preferences.[2] Few other general results exist, however: for instance, Mookherjee and Png (1989) show that the introduction of risk aversion can imply that the audit function is not always non-increasing in the amount of income declared.

1 Earlier contributions that arrived at the conclusion of an audit threshold under less general assumptions include Reinganum and Wilde (1985), Scotchmer (1987) and Morton (1993).
2 See, however, Hindriks (1999) for situations in which the regressivity of the tax function is reversed.

In this chapter we investigate how accounting for the ability of individuals to avoid tax, as well as to evade tax, alters the conclusions for optimal auditing of models in which only tax evasion is possible. In our model individuals can engage in tax evasion by under-reporting their income, but can also, at a cost, participate in a tax avoidance scheme that permits them to further lower reported income. Additional to the financial cost of avoidance, both forms of non-compliance are assumed, when detected, to impose psychic harm in the form of a social stigma cost. The nature of the avoidance scheme is not unambiguously prohibited by law, but is unacceptable to the tax authority. Accordingly, if the tax authority learns of the scheme, it will move to outlaw it ex-post. If a taxpayer is audited the tax authority observes whether they are using a tax avoidance scheme and also the extent of any tax evasion. The taxpayer is fined on the evaded tax, but the tax authority has no grounds to impose a fine on the avoided tax (it can only take measures to outlaw the scheme and then recover the tax owed on the avoided income). In this context we characterise the audit function first for a linear penalty function, and later for a general penalty function. The tax authority can condition its audit function only on the amount of income declared; it does not observe the amount of non-compliance or how it is split between evasion and avoidance. We therefore look for a taxpayer such that, if this taxpayer (weakly) prefers to report truthfully rather than hide an amount of income then all other taxpayers will also wish to report truthfully.

We find that, if the penalty function is linear or strictly concave then, irrespective of the tax function, it holds that (i) if the wealthiest taxpayer is induced to report honestly, so will all other taxpayers; and (ii) at every income declaration, x, enforcement must be just sufficient that the wealthiest taxpayer does not wish to evade the amount of income $w - x$ (if evasion is more attractive than avoidance), or does not wish to avoid the amount of income $w - x$ (if avoidance is more attractive than evasion). That is, if the tax authority enforces to the point where "pure" evasion/avoidance becomes unattractive then mixtures of evasion and avoidance will also be unattractive. On the other hand, if the penalty function is convex (the marginal rate of penalty is increasing) then it is possible that the focus of enforcement is not the wealthiest taxpayer, but rather a taxpayer with intermediate wealth. The level of wealth of this critical taxpayer is an increasing function of income declared, implying that the focus of enforcement is on lower wealth individuals at lower levels of declared income, and on higher wealth individuals at higher levels of declared income. It also becomes possible that taxpayers prefer engaging simultaneously in evasion and avoidance over pure strategies. When this is so the optimal mix of avoidance and evasion moves in favour of avoidance as reported income decreases, as the competitiveness of the market for avoidance schemes increases, and as the social stigma associated with tax non-compliance falls.

In all cases we find the audit function to be a non-increasing function of declared income. When enforcement is predicated on the wealthiest taxpayer the audit function is strictly decreasing in declared income. The function is shifted upwards by an increase in wealth (of the wealthiest taxpayer), and shifted downwards by a steepening of penalties, an increase in the social stigma attached to tax non-compliance, and a lessening of competition in the market for avoidance schemes. When the focus of enforcement is not the wealthiest taxpayer, however, the audit function becomes independent of declared income and of the competitiveness of the market for avoidance. By analysing the audit function under example progressive and regressive tax functions we find that, as in Chander and Wilde (1998), lower enforcement is required to enforce a regressive tax than to enforce a progressive tax. Stronger risk aversion moves the audit function downwards, with larger downward movements for lower values of reported income.

We also find that an increase in marginal rates of tax stimulates incentives for non-compliance, such that the audit function must shift upwards to maintain truthful reporting. This is the opposite of the finding of Yitzhaki (1974), in which the incentives to be non-compliant diminish as marginal tax rates increase. The difference in predictions is of interest as Yitzhaki's finding is counter-intuitive and at variance with most empirical evidence. Whereas taxpayers can only evade in Yitzhaki's model, in our model they can also avoid. We find that the incentives to avoid unambiguously increase following an increase in marginal tax rates, so even though the incentives for evasion may worsen, nonetheless the tax system becomes more costly to enforce, and compliance falls unless enforcement is stiffened.

The chapter adds to the small, but growing, economic literature on tax avoidance (in the broad sense). Slemrod and Kopczuk (2002), Piketty et al. (2014) and Uribe-Teran (2015) analyse theoretically the elasticity of taxable income in the presence of avoidance, while Alm (1988) Alm and McCallin (1990), and Alm et al. (1990) examine the choice of an individual between evasion and avoidance. In the empirical literature, Slemrod (1995, 1996) finds pronounced tax avoidance effects in the response of high-earners to tax changes, while Feldstein (1999) finds that accounting for tax avoidance significantly increases estimates of the implied deadweight loss of income taxation. Fack and Landais (2010) show that the response of charitable deductions to tax rates is concentrated primarily along the avoidance margin (rather than the real contribution margin), while Gruber and Saez (2002) show that the elasticity of a broad measure of income is notably smaller than the equivalent elasticity for taxable income, suggesting that much of the response of taxable income comes through deductions, exemptions, and exclusions.

The plan of the chapter is as follows: the following section outlines the model; the next section performs the main analysis; then the next section considers a range of extensions. The last section concludes. All proofs are in the Appendix.

Model

A taxpayer has an income (wealth) w; w differs among individuals on the support $[0, \bar{w}]$, where $\bar{w} > 0$. Each taxpayer faces a tax on income w given by $t(w)$, satisfying $t(w) < w$ and $t' \geq 0$. Taxpayers behave as if they maximise expected utility, where utility is denoted by $U(z) = z$, with $U' > 0$ and $U'' \leq 0$. A taxpayer's true income w is not observed by the tax authority, but the taxpayer must declare an amount $x \in [0, w]$. A taxpayer can choose to illegally evade an amount of income E and to avoid paying tax on a further amount of income A, where $x = w - E - A$.

Evasion is financially costless but avoidance technology is bought in a market in which "promoters" sell avoidance schemes to "users".[3] A common feature of this market is the "no saving, no fee" arrangement under which the price received by a promoter is linked to the amount by which their scheme stands to reduce the user's tax liability. Although systematic information regarding the precise contractual terms upon which avoidance schemes are typically sold is scarce, we understand from a detailed investigation in the UK that, for the majority of mass-marketed schemes, the fee is related to the reduction in the annual theoretical tax liability of the user, not the ex-post realisation of the tax saved (Committee of Public Accounts 2013). This implies, in particular, that the monetary risks associated with the possible subsequent detection and termination of a tax avoidance scheme are borne by the user.[4] Accordingly, we assume that the promoter's fee is a proportion $\varphi \in (0, 1)$ of the tax saving accruing from the Scheme. In this way, φ may

---

3 For analyses of the market for tax advice see, e.g. Reinganum and Wilde (1991) and Damjanovic and Ulph (2010).

4 It is apparent that such arrangements give promoters incentives to mis-represent the level of risk involved in particular schemes. Consistent with this point, Committee of Public Accounts (2013, p. 11) indeed finds evidence of such mis-selling.

be interpreted as measuring the degree of competition in the market for tax avoidance schemes, with lower values of φ indicating the presence of stronger competitive forces. When a taxpayer is simultaneously evading and avoiding, the tax saving accruing to the avoidance scheme is not always unambiguous, however. To see this, note that the total tax underpayment of a taxpayer is given by $t(w) - t(x)$. This can be decomposed in two ways: one decomposition is to assign $t(w) - t(w - E)$ to be the evaded tax, and $t(x + A) - t(x)$ to be the avoided tax, but an alternative taxonomy is to assign $t(x + E) - t(x)$ to be the evaded tax and $t(w) - t(w - A)$ to be the avoided tax. These alternative approaches are equivalent if the tax function is assumed to be linear, but are distinct otherwise. As our results are not especially sensitive to which of these conventions is adopted, however, we adopt the first of these decompositions in our baseline specification. Hence, we may write the total fee paid by the taxpayer to the promoter as $\varphi[t(x + A) - t(x)]$.

We adopt a principal-agent approach in which the principal can commit to an audit and penalty function which taxpayers then take as given. Though important, as in many other contexts, we do not address the issue of how the principal can make these commitments.[5] A taxpayer reporting income x is audited with probability $p(x)$. If audited, E and A are observed. A taxpayer must then make a payment $f(t(w) - t(w - E))$ on account of the amount of evaded tax, where $f(0) = 0$ and $f' > 1$ (which, together, imply $f(k) > k$ for $k > 0$). The taxpayer cannot be fined on the avoided tax, however. The tax authority mounts a (successful) legal challenge to the avoidance scheme, giving the tax authority the right to reclaim the tax owed. Thus, instead of paying $t(x)$, the taxpayer must pay $t(x + A)$.

The experiments of Baldry (1986) provide compelling evidence that the non-compliance decision is not just a simple gamble. This can be rationalised by introducing an additional cost into the decision. This cost can be financial (Chetty 2009; Lee 2001) or psychic. We adopt a psychic cost interpretation, where the psychic cost is identified as the social stigma associated with being caught performing activities that either abuse the spirit of the law, or outright violate it. Other models to allow for costs due to social stigma include al-Nowaihi and Pyle (2000), Benjamini and Maital (1985), Dell'Anno (2009), Dhami and al-Nowaihi (2007), Gordon (1989), and Kim (2003). Social stigma is incurred when $A + E$ $(= w - x) > 0$ and the taxpayer is audited. Specifically, in the state of the world in which the taxpayer is audited we write:

$$S(w - x) = \begin{cases} 0 & \text{if } x = w; \\ s > 0 & \text{otherwise.} \end{cases}$$

One might think that the stigma cost, as well as having a fixed component, might also have a component that increases in the total amount of non-compliance $(A + E)$. We shall allow for this possibility in the section titled "Extensions" as an extension to the baseline model.[6] It might also be argued that the social stigma associated with avoidance and evasion differ. For instance, Kirchler et al. (2003) find socially positive attitudes towards tax avoidance (but socially negative attitudes towards tax evasion) among students, fiscal officers and small business owners in Austria. Recent poll evidence for the UK, however, suggests that evasion and avoidance are viewed similarly (Stone 2015). Given the mixed evidence, and that public attitudes may well vary over time, assuming that social stigma is associated equally with avoidance and evasion seems reasonable.

---

5 Reinganum and Wilde (1986) and Erard and Feinstein (1994) study the case of the principal not being able to make commitments.

6 A further line of literature (see, e.g., Hashimzade et al. 2014, 2015, 2016; Myles and Naylor 1996) relates social stigma to the prevalence of non-compliance among taxpayers. We do not explore this route here, but offer it as a possible avenue for future research.

A taxpayer's expected utility is therefore given by

$$EU = \left[1 - p(x)\right]U^n + p(x)U^a, \tag{1}$$

where U^n is a taxpayer's utility in the state in which they are not audited and U^n is a taxpayer's utility in the state in which they are audited. We then write $U^n \equiv U(w^n)$ and $U^a \equiv U(w^a) - S(w - x)$, where $\{w^a, w^n\}$ are, respectively, a taxpayer's wealth in the audit and non-audit states. Note that, owing to the equality $x = w - E - A$, we can write w^a and w^n as either functions of $\{x, A, w\}$ or of $\{E, A, w\}$. As each formulation yields separate insights we define both here. In the former case we have

$$w^n(x, A, w) = w - t(x) - \varphi\left[t(x + A) - t(x)\right];$$

$$w^a(x, A, w) = w - t(x + A) - f\left(t(w) - t(x + A)\right) - \varphi\left[t(x + A) - t(x)\right];$$

and in the latter we have

$$w^n(A, E, w) = w - t(w - A - E) - \varphi\left[t(w - E) - t(w - A - E)\right];$$

$$w^a(A, E, w) = w - t(w - E) - f\left(t(w) - t(w - E)\right) - \varphi\left[t(w - E) - t(w - A - E)\right].$$

We adopt the standard assumption of *limited liability*, whereby the tax and fine payments of a taxpayer cannot exceed their wealth w. Accordingly, to ensure that the limited liability condition always holds, we assume $w^a(x, A, w) - s > 0$, a necessary condition for which is that $w - s \geq f(t(w))$.

A *mechanism* for the tax authority consists of a set of possible income reports $M \in [0, w]$, a tax function $t(\cdot)$, an audit function $p(\cdot)$, and a penalty function $f(\cdot)$. In this chapter we focus only on *incentive compatible* mechanisms, i.e. mechanisms that induce all taxpayers to report truthfully. The standard justification for this approach is the *revelation principle*; when this principle holds, then for any feasible mechanism, one can find an equivalent mechanism that induce taxpayers to report truthfully (see, e.g., Myerson 1979, 1982, 1989). Chander and Wilde (1998) show that the revelation principle applies when the tax authority has unfettered ability to choose the tax and audit functions, while the penalty function is only constrained to be bounded above. Unfortunately, penalty functions of this type deviate significantly from those observed in practice as the penalty for under-reporting by any amount, no matter how small, is extreme. As noted by Cremer and Gahvari (1995), however, adopting more appealing but exogenously given penalties implies that one can no longer rely on the revelation principle. Whereas most of the literature has implicitly opted for tractability over realism, here we follow the lead of Marhuenda and Ortuño-Ortin (1994) in considering a setting in which the revelation principle does not hold. Implicitly, therefore, we restrict attention to the set of mechanisms that are payoff equivalent to the set of incentive compatible mechanisms we consider here. Our focus shall be primarily on the shape of the audit function for a given penalty and tax function. Accordingly, we do not allow the tax authority to choose the latter two functions.

The utility when reporting truthfully (honestly) is $U^h \equiv U(w^h)$, where $w^h = w - t(w)$. In order that the mechanism be incentive compatible, a taxpayer must never receive a utility higher than $U(w^h)$ when reporting $x < w$. This implies that

$$p(x) \geq \frac{U^n - U^h}{U^n - U^a} \text{ for all } A \in [0, w - x], \ x \in [0, w] \text{ and for all } w. \tag{2}$$

Performing an audit costs the tax authority an amount $c > 0$. Given this, a revenue maximising scheme will always minimise $p(x)$ subject to the condition in (2) holding. Define the function $p(x; A, w)$ as the smallest probability of audit that induces an (A, w)-taxpayer to report truthfully. Then

$$p(x; A, w) = \begin{cases} \dfrac{U^n - U^h}{U^n - U^a} = \dfrac{t(w) - t(x) - \varphi[t(A + x) - t(x)]}{f\big(t(w) - t(A + x)\big) + t(A + x) - t(x) + s} & \text{if } x < w; \\ 0 & \text{if } x = w. \end{cases} \quad (3)$$

The restriction $p(x; A, w) \leq 1$ holds necessarily as $U^h \geq U^a$. When $x = w$ the definition of $p(x; A, w)$ becomes arbitrary, for the condition in (2) must hold for any $p(x)$. In setting $p(w; A, w) = 0$ we follow Chander (2007: 325). In what follows we define $p(x; A, w)$ for $x < w$ unless it is explicitly stated otherwise. Note in (3) that the tax function always appears in the form $t(z_1) - t(z_2)$, with the implication that the audit function is independent of the *level* of the tax function (any vertical shift of $t(\cdot)$ must cancel). Accordingly, it is without loss of generality that we set $t(0) = 0$.

The tax authority cannot, however, utilise $p(x; A, w)$ as it observes x, but not A or w. Instead, the tax authority must choose $p(x)$ such that, for each x, reporting is truthful for all feasible A and w. Accordingly, we then define $p(x)$ as

$$p(x) = \max_{A, w} p(x; A, w).$$

The arguments of A and w that maximise $p(x; A, w)$ we write as $A^* = argmax_A\, p(x; A, w^*)$ and $w^* = argmax_w\, p(x; A^*, w)$.

Analysis

We first consider the special case in which taxpayers are risk neutral ($U'' = 0$), while the case of risk aversion ($U'' < 0$) will be considered in the "Extensions" section. We begin without restricting the form of the tax function, but restrict the penalty function to be linear: $f(k) = [1 + h]k$, $h > 0$. In this way we obtain a very simple version of the model that provides ready intuitions. For each value of x, we wish to maximise $p(x; A, w)$ in (3) with respect to A and w (allowing the suppressed variable E to vary). First, maximising with respect to A, the first order condition for a maximum is

$$\frac{\partial p(x; A, w)}{\partial A} = -\frac{\big\{\varphi s + \{\varphi - h[1 - \varphi]\}[t(w) - t(x)]\big\} t'(A + x)}{\big\{[1 + h][t(w) - t(A + x)] + t(A + x) - t(x) + s\big\}^2}. \quad (4)$$

Then (4) implies that $A^* = 0$ when

$$\varphi > \hat{\varphi} = \frac{h[t(w) - t(x)]}{s + [1 + h][t(w) - t(x)]},$$

and $A^* = w - x$ when $\varphi < \hat{\varphi}$. When $\varphi = \hat{\varphi}$ all feasible values of A weakly maximise $p(x; A, w)$. Taking the case $\varphi > \hat{\varphi}$ first, to find $p(x)$ we now maximise $p(x; 0, w)$ with respect to w. The first derivative with respect to w is

$$\frac{\partial p(x; 0, w)}{\partial w} = \frac{s t'(w)}{\big\{[1 + h][t(w) - t(x)] + s\big\}^2} > 0, \quad (5)$$

so $w^* = \bar{w}$. In the case $\varphi < \hat{\varphi}$ the relevant first derivative with respect to w is

$$\frac{\partial p\left(x; w-x, w\right)}{\partial w} = \frac{s\left[1-\varphi\right]t'\left(w\right)}{\left[t\left(w\right)-t\left(x\right)+s\right]^2} > 0,$$ (6)

so again $w^* = \bar{w}$.

Proposition 1 *If the penalty function is linear then*

$$p(x) = \begin{cases} \dfrac{\left[1-\varphi\right]\left[t\left(\bar{w}\right)-t\left(x\right)\right]}{t\left(\bar{w}\right)-t\left(x\right)+s} & \text{if } \varphi < \hat{\varphi}; \\[4mm] \dfrac{t\left(\bar{w}\right)-t\left(x\right)}{f\left(t\left(\bar{w}\right)-t\left(x\right)\right)+s} & \text{if } \varphi > \hat{\varphi}. \end{cases}$$ (7)

Summarising this analysis, when the market for avoidance schemes is sufficiently competitive ($\varphi < \hat{\varphi}$) it is sufficient to incentivise truthful reporting by all taxpayers that the wealthiest taxpayer does not wish to avoid all of their income. This holds irrespective of the shape of the tax function. If, however, $\varphi > \hat{\varphi}$ then evasion is more attractive to taxpayers than is avoidance. In this case it is sufficient to incentivise truthful reporting that the wealthiest taxpayer does not wish to evade all of their income.

The form of $p(x)$ in (7) applies more generally whenever A^* takes corner values and $w^* = \bar{w}$ (not only when the penalty function is linear). It transpires that a corner solution necessarily arises when $f'' \leq 0$, and may also arise when $f'' > 0$ under further conditions. We now analyse the comparative statics properties of $p(x)$ in (7).

Proposition 2 *In an equilibrium in which $A^* \in \{0, w-x\}$ and $w^* = \bar{w}$ then the comparative statics of $p(x)$ are given as in columns 1 and 2 of Table 22.1.*

Proposition 2 is most readily understood with respect to the expected marginal returns to evasion and avoidance. The expected return to the gamble of reporting $x < w$ (rather than w) is given, for a fixed p, by

$$R\left(A, E\right) = p\left[w^c\left(A, E, w\right) - s\right] + (1-p)w^n\left(A, E, w\right) - w^h\left(w\right)$$ (8)

In the formulation in (8) we retain A and E, by suppressing x. This allows us to consider, e.g. the effect of moving A holding E constant (with x adjusting to maintain the equality $x = w - E - A$). As taxpayers are risk neutral it must hold that $R(A^*, E^*) = 0$, for if $R(A^*, E^*) > 0$ incentive compatibility is violated, and if $R(A^*, E^*) < 0$ the tax authority could achieve truthtelling at lower cost. From (8) the expected marginal benefit to, respectively, E and A (for a fixed p) are therefore given by

$$\frac{\partial R}{\partial A} = (1-p-\varphi)t'\left(w-A-E\right);$$ (9)

$$\frac{\partial R}{\partial E} = \frac{\partial R}{\partial A} - \left\{p\left[f'-1\right]-\varphi\right\}t'\left(w-E\right).$$ (10)

The corner solution $A^* = 0$ arises when $\partial R/\partial E > \partial R/\partial A$ for all A and the corner solution $A^* = w - x$ when $\partial R/\partial A > \partial R/\partial E$ for all A. As the $p(x)$ in Proposition 2 is predicated on requiring the wealthiest taxpayer to report truthfully, it is responsive to changes in $\bar{w}$. In particular, when $A^* = 0$, if the wealthiest taxpayer chooses to evade in full an incremental increase in their income, the effect on the expected return to evasion is given by

$$\frac{\partial R}{\partial \bar{w}}\big|_{x=\text{const.}} = \left[1 - pf'\left(t(\bar{w}) - t\left(\bar{w} - E\right)\right)\right]t'(\bar{w}).$$

Note by inspection of (7) that at the corner solution $A^* = 0$ it holds that $p < [f'(t(\bar{w}) - t(x))]^{-1}$, so $1 - pf'(t(\bar{w}) - t(\bar{w} - E)) > 0$. It follows that $\partial R/\partial \bar{w}\big|_{x = \text{const.}} > 0$, so the probability of audit must necessarily rise to maintain a zero expected return to non-compliance. If instead $A^* = w - x$ then, if the wealthiest taxpayer chooses to avoid in full an incremental increase in their income, the effect on the expected return to avoidance is given by

$$\frac{\partial R}{\partial \bar{w}}\big|_{x=\text{const.}} = \left[1 - p - \varphi\right]t'(\bar{w}).$$

By inspection of (7), at the corner solution $A^* = w - x$ it holds that $p < 1 - \varphi$, so necessarily $\partial R/\partial \bar{w}\big|_{x = \text{const.}} > 0$. Again, the probability of audit must rise to preserve a zero expected return. Hence, whichever corner solution for A applies, the audit function is increasing in the wealth of the wealthiest taxpayer. As it is gainful to the wealthiest taxpayer to increase evasion (when $A^* = 0$) and avoidance (when $A^* = w - x$) it follows that to discourage the taxpayer from reporting low values of x requires more enforcement activity than does discouraging the reporting of higher values, hence the audit function is decreasing in reported income.

When the avoidance market is sufficiently competitive that avoidance is a superior instrument in reducing a taxpayer's liability than is evasion (i.e. $\partial R/\partial A > \partial R/\partial E$) a further increase in the competitiveness of the market for avoidance schemes (a fall in φ) induces the wealthiest taxpayer to wish to avoid more, and forces $p(x)$ to shift upwards to maintain truth-telling. When, however, the avoidance market is sufficiently uncompetitive that in any case avoidance is unappealing (relative to evasion) as a means of reducing one's tax liability, then the audit function becomes independent of φ. Similarly, a multiplicative shift in the penalty function (which increases the marginal rate of penalty by a fixed proportion) only affects $p(x)$ when the wealthiest taxpayer wishes to evade rather than avoid. In this case evasion becomes more costly at the margin, thereby relaxing the truth-telling constraint. We also see that an increase in social stigma results in a fall in the attractiveness of both evasion and avoidance, allowing $p(x)$ to shift downwards while maintaining honest reporting.

A proportional increase in marginal tax rates (a multiplicative shift of the tax function such that $t(\bar{w}) - t(x)$ increases for every x) increases both the expected benefits and costs of evasion and avoidance, making its effect difficult to anticipate with intuition alone. In the absence of avoidance it is well-known that the standard model of tax compliance of Yitzhaki (1974) predicts that an increase in the marginal tax rate decreases the incentive to evade, which implies (in a model without avoidance) that the tax authority would therefore be able to lower the audit function while still achieving truthful reporting. In columns 1 and 2 of Table 22.1 we observe the opposite result: as marginal tax rates increase the audit function increases. To understand this result, first consider the corner solution $A^* = 0$. Here what is crucial is how the expected return to evasion responds to a multiplicative shift of the tax function. As $t(0) = 0$ a multiplicative shift

Table 22.1 Comparative statics

	$A^* = 0$	$A^* = w^* - x$	$A^* \in \left(0, w^* - x\right)$		$w^* \in \left(x + A^*, \bar{w}\right)$	
	$p(x)$	$p(x)$	A^*	$p(x)$	w^*	$p(x)$
x	−	−	−	−	+	0
$\bar{w}$	+	+	+	+	0	0
φ	0	−	−	−	0	0
s	−	−	−	−	+	−
pivot of $f(\cdot)$	−	0	+	−	−	−
pivot of $t(\cdot)$	+	+	+	+	−	0

can equally be thought of as an anti-clockwise pivot of $t(\cdot)$ around the origin (intercept). Hence we may write $t(\cdot)$ as $\varepsilon t(\cdot)$, and then consider $\lim_{\varepsilon \to 1} \partial R / \partial \varepsilon \big|_{A\,=\,0}$:

$$\lim_{\varepsilon \to 1} \frac{\partial R}{\partial \varepsilon} \big|_{A=0} = \left[t'\left(w\right) - t'\left(w - E\right) \right]\left[1 - pf'\left(t\left(w\right) - t\left(x\right)\right) \right] > 0.$$

Hence, when $A^* = 0$, evasion is made more attractive by stiffening marginal tax rates. When $A^* = w - x$ it is instead crucial how the expected return to avoidance responds to a multiplicative shift of the tax function. We have

$$\lim_{\varepsilon \to 1} \frac{\partial R}{\partial \varepsilon} \big|_{A=w-x} = \left[1 - p - \varphi \right]\left[t\left(w\right) - t\left(w - A\right) \right] > 0, \tag{11}$$

which implies that the audit function must shift upwards to restore the expected return to zero. Noting from (9) that $1 - p - \varphi > 0$ is the condition for avoidance to be gainful in expectation, (11) implies that, when avoidance is gainful in expectation, a multiplicative shift of the tax function will increase the expected return to avoidance.

Having established that a linear penalty function always leads to a corner A^* we now examine the case in which the penalty function is kept general. In particular, we are interested in understanding the conditions under which $A^* \in (0, w - x)$. An alternative approach to differentiating $p(x; A, w)$ directly (as we did previously) is to exploit the observation that $R(A^*, E^*) = 0$. The implicit function theorem (IFT) then implies that (13) and (14) can also be rewritten more generally as

$$\frac{\partial p(x; A, w)}{\partial z} = \frac{\left[\dfrac{\partial w^a}{\partial z} - \dfrac{\partial w^n}{\partial z} \right] p(x; A, w) + \dfrac{\partial w^n}{\partial z} - \dfrac{\partial w^h}{\partial z}}{w^n - w^a + s}; \qquad z \in \left\{ A, w \right\}, \tag{12}$$

giving

$$\frac{\partial p(x; A, w)}{\partial A} = \frac{\left\{ p(x; A, w)\left[f' - 1 \right] - \varphi \right\} t'\left(x + A\right)}{w^n - w^a + s}; \tag{13}$$

$$\frac{\partial p(x; A, w)}{\partial w} = \frac{\left[1 - p(x; A, w) f' \right] t'\left(w\right)}{w^n - w^a + s}. \tag{14}$$

Using (13), at a stationary point for A we have

$$p(x; A^*, w) = \frac{\varphi}{f' - 1},$$ (15)

and, from (14), at a stationary point for w we have

$$p(x; A, w^*) = \frac{1}{f'}.$$ (16)

To verify when these define a maximum we use (13) and (14) to compute the second derivatives at a stationary point as

$$\frac{\partial^2 p(x; A, w)}{[\partial A]^2} \Big|_{\frac{\partial p(x; A, w)}{\partial A} = 0} = -\frac{p(x; A, w)\left[t'\left(x + A\right)\right]^2 f''}{w^n - w^a + s};$$ (17)

$$\frac{\partial^2 p(x; A, w)}{[\partial w]^2} \Big|_{\frac{\partial p(x; A, w)}{\partial w} = 0} = -\frac{p(x; A, w)\left[t'\left(w\right)\right]^2 f''}{w^n - w^a + s}.$$ (18)

Inspecting equations (17) and (18) we see that their sign is the sign of f', so for an interior maximum with respect to one or both of A and w it must hold that $f'' > 0$. We now investigate the case in which $A^* \in (0, w - x)$:

Lemma 1 *If $A^* \in \left(0, w - x\right)$ then $p\left(x\right) f' < 1 < \left[1 - \varphi\right] f'$ and $p\left(x\right) < 1 - \varphi$.*

In respect of the expected marginal returns to evasion and avoidance, Lemma 1 implies, first, that at an interior value of A^* the expected marginal return to evasion must equal the expected marginal return to avoidance: $\partial R(A,E)/\partial A = \partial R(A,E)/\partial E$. Second, it implies that both expected marginal returns must be positive.

Using (13) and (14), the effect of w on $p(x; A, w)$ when $\partial p(x; A, w)/\partial A = 0$ is given by

$$\frac{\partial p(x; A, w)}{\partial w} \Big|_{\frac{\partial p(x; A, w)}{\partial A} = 0} = \frac{\left[1 - \varphi - p(x; A, w)\right] t'\left(w\right)}{w^n - w^a + s} > 0;$$

where the inequality follows from Lemma 1. This implies that when A^* is interior, w^* is maximal. Substituting $w = \bar{w}$ in (15) we therefore obtain

$$p(x) = \frac{\varphi}{f'\left(t\left(\bar{w}\right) - t\left(x + A^*\right)\right) - 1}.$$ (19)

From (13) and Lemma 1 we have

$$1 - p(x) - \varphi = \frac{s + f\left(t\left(\bar{w}\right) - t\left(x + A^*\right)\right) - \left[t\left(\bar{w}\right) - t\left(x + A^*\right)\right] f'\left(t\left(\bar{w}\right) - t\left(x + A^*\right)\right)}{s + f\left(t\left(\bar{w}\right) - t\left(x + A^*\right)\right) + \left[t\left(x + A^*\right) - t\left(x\right)\right] f'\left(t\left(\bar{w}\right) - t\left(x + A^*\right)\right)} > 0.$$

Hence, it must hold that $s > \varepsilon_f (t(\bar{w}) - t(x)) - 1$, where $\varepsilon_f (z) = z f'(z)/f(z)$ is the elasticity of the penalty function with respect to evaded tax, so interior values of A^* arise for sufficiently high social stigma costs.

These findings are illustrated in Figure 22.1. We depict $p(x)$ in panel (a), the associated $\{A^*,$ $E^*, w^*\}$ in panel (b), and the expected marginal returns (denoted R_A and R_E for brevity) drawn at $p = p(x)$ and $E = E^*$ in panel (c). The figure is drawn for a linear tax function, $t(v) = 0.3v$, a quadratic penalty function of the form $f(k) = [1.1 + k/2]k$, $\varphi = 0.2$, $s = 3$, and $\bar{w} = 10$. For $x \in [0, \hat{x})$ A^* is interior – so $p(x)$ is as in (19). For $x \geq \hat{x}$ $A^* = 0$ – so $p(x)$ is as in Proposition 1.

We see in panel (a) of Figure 22.1 that $p(x)$ is decreasing and concave in x. Consistent with Lemma 1 we see that the audit function lies below $1/f'$, which is itself bounded above by $1 - \varphi$. In panel (b), A^* is initially decreasing and concave in x, and E^* is initially increasing and convex in x. In panel (c) the expected marginal return to avoidance is seen to be constant in x. This is due to the choice of a linear fine rate; more generally, it is seen from (9) that tax avoidance displays increasing/constant/diminishing marginal returns as the tax function is regressive $(t'' < 0)$/ linear $(t'' = 0)$/progressive $(t'' > 0)$. To understand the shape of the expected marginal return to evasion, observe that the variation of the expected marginal return to evasion at different levels of evasion is given at the optimum by

$$\frac{\partial^2 R}{\partial E^2} \Big|_{\frac{\partial R(A,E)}{\partial A} = \frac{\partial R(A,E)}{\partial E}} = \frac{\partial^2 R}{\partial A^2} - p(x)\left[t'\left(w - E^*\right)\right]^2 f''.$$

As $f'' > 0$ at an interior A^*, it must hold that $\partial^2 R/\partial E^2 < \partial^2 R/\partial A^2$, as seen in Figure 22.1c.

We now consider the case in which $w^* \in (x + A, \bar{w})$. Proceeding in a manner similar to Lemma 1 we obtain that $p(x) = [f']^{-1} > 1 - \varphi$. Referring to the expected marginal returns in (9) and (10), this inequality implies that $\partial R(A, E)/\partial E = 0 > \partial R(A, E)/\partial A$. At this point, the taxpayer does not wish to increase either evasion or avoidance at the margin.

Using (13) and (14), the effect of A on $p(x; A, w)$ when $\partial p(x; A, w)/\partial w = 0$ is given by

$$\frac{\partial p(x; A, w)}{\partial A} \Big|_{\frac{\partial p(x;A,w)}{\partial w}=0} = \left[1 - p(x; A, w) - \varphi\right]t'\left(x + A\right) < 0.$$

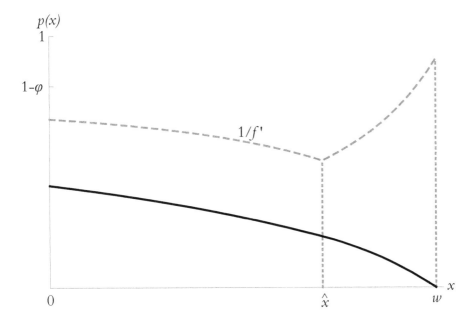

Figure 22.1(a)   Audit function for $A^* \in (0, w^* - x]$.

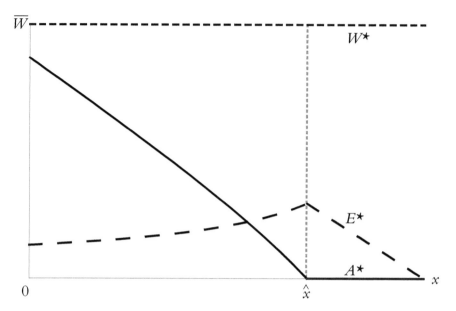

Figure 22.1(b) $\{A^{\star}, E^{\star}, w^{\star}\}$ for $A^{\star} \in (0, w^{\star} - x]$.

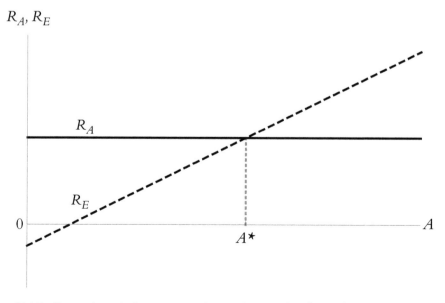

Figure 22.1(c)   Expected marginal return to avoidance and evasion for $A^{\star} \in (0, w^{\star} - x)$.

This implies that when w^* is interior, A^* takes it minimum value. Substituting $A = 0$ in (16) we therefore obtain

$$p(x) = \frac{1}{f'\left(t\left(w^*\right) - t\left(x\right)\right)}. \tag{20}$$

From (14) we have

$$1 - p(x) - \varphi = 1 - \frac{\left[t\left(w^*\right) - t\left(x\right)\right] f'\left(t\left(w^*\right) - t\left(x\right)\right)}{s + f\left(t\left(w^*\right) - t\left(x\right)\right)} < 0. \tag{21}$$

As (21) is negative, it must be that $s < \varepsilon_f(t(w^*) - t(x)) - 1$. Hence, w^* is interior when a sufficiently low level of social stigma prevails, whereas A^* is interior when a sufficiently high level of social stigma prevails.

Our findings for the case when w^* is interior are illustrated in Figure 22.2. Figure 22.2 is analogous to Figure 22.1, but to satisfy the condition in (21), we now set $s = 0.1$. For $x \in [0, \hat{x})$ A^* is interior – so $p(x)$ is as in (20). For $x \geq \hat{x}$ $A^* = 0$ – so $p(x)$ is as in Proposition 1. In Figure 22.2(a) we see that $p(x)$ is initially independent of x, but falls rapidly in a concave manner after w^* reaches the upper bound $w^* = \bar{w}$. In this example $\partial w^*/\partial x = 1$ in panel (b) but we shall show that, more generally, $\partial w^*/\partial x = t'(x)/t'(w)$. In panel (c) we see that the expected return to avoidance is negative for all w. The variation of the expected marginal return to evasion in w is given at the optimum by

$$\frac{\partial^2 R}{\partial E \partial w}\Big|_{\frac{\partial R(A,E)}{\partial E} = 0} = -p(x)t'(w)t'(w - A - E)f''.$$

As $f'' > 0$ at an interior w^*, it must hold that $\partial^2 R/\partial E \partial w < 0$, as seen in the figure.

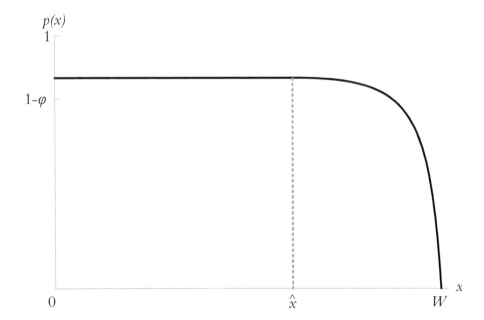

Figure 22.2(a) Audit function for $w^* \in (x + A^*, \bar{w}]$.

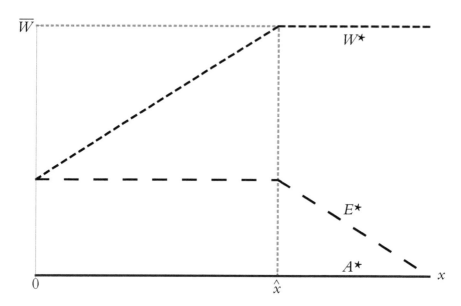

Figure 22.2(b) $\{A^*, E^*, w^*\}$ for $w^* \in (x + A^*, \bar{w}]$.

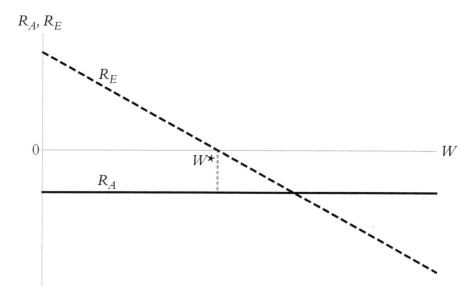

Figure 22.2(c) Expected marginal return to avoidance and evasion for $w^* \in (x + A^*, \bar{w})$.

We now formally investigate the comparative statics of the two cases analysed above:

Proposition 3 *In an equilibrium in which either A^* or w^* takes an interior value the comparative statics of $\{A^*, p(x), w^*\}$ are given as in columns 3 and 4 of Table 22.1.*

When Λ^* takes an interior value the results in Table 22.1 (column 3) for the comparative statics of $p(x)$ are consistent with those obtained in Proposition 2: the audit function is a decreasing

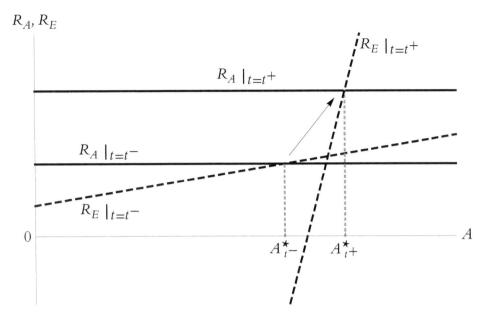

Figure 22.3 Effect of a multiplicative shift in the tax function on the expected marginal return to avoidance and evasion.

function of declared income, shifts downwards with increases in φ and s, and shifts upwards in $\bar{w}$. Moreover, $\partial A^*/\partial x$ can be written as

$$\frac{\partial A^*}{\partial x} = -1 - \frac{\{[1-\varphi]f'-1\}t'(x)}{[w^n - w^h]t'(x+A)f''} < -1,$$

with the implication that E^* is an increasing function of x (and A^*/E^* is a decreasing function of x). Whether A^*/E^* is an increasing or decreasing function of wealth depends on the shape of the tax function. If the tax function is progressive or linear then it can be shown that $\partial A^*/\partial \bar{w} > 1$, so E^* must fall, but both A^* and E^* may rise if the tax function is regressive.

When w^* takes an interior value, however, the audit function becomes independent of declared income (and this holds for any tax function). The audit function also becomes independent of $\bar{w}$ (as it is not predicated on the wealthiest taxpayer) and of φ (as avoidance is dominated by evasion as a means of reducing tax liability). In both types of interior optimum a steepening of the penalty function shifts the audit function downwards.

We now return to the question of the effects of a proportional increase in marginal tax rates (a steepening of the tax function – again by means of an anti-clockwise pivot about the intercept). Matching our finding in Proposition 2 for the case of a corner solution, the findings in Table 22.1 predict the opposite of the Yitzhaki (1974) finding: as marginal tax rates increase the tax authority must shift upwards the audit function to maintain truthful reporting. This finding is of note as Yitzhaki's result is not only paradoxical intuitively, but much empirical and experimental evidence finds a negative relationship between compliance and the tax rate (see, e.g. Bernasconi et al. 2014, and the references therein).[7] In interpreting this result it is of importance to

7 See also Piolatto and Rablen (2017) for a detailed analysis of Yitzhaki's finding, and when it is and is not overturned.

note that the Yitzhaki (1974) model can be augmented with a constant utility cost due to social stigma – as in our model – without affecting the direction of the relationship between marginal tax rates and non-compliance.[8] This difference between models is not, therefore, a part of the explanation of our differing findings. Rather, the reversal of Yitzhaki's finding relies on the idea that, even in cases where evasion becomes less attractive following an increase in marginal tax rates, tax avoidance will become more attractive for sure. Thus the overall incentives for non-compliance grow, even if the incentives for evasion weaken.

We illustrate this point graphically in Figure 22.3, which shows the effect on the expected marginal returns to evasion (R_E) and avoidance (R_A) of a multiplicative shift of a (linear) tax function. Specifically, we increase the marginal tax rate from $t^- = 0.2$ to $t^+ = 0.7$ in the model specification used in Figure 22.1. The increase in marginal tax rates is seen to increase the expected marginal return to avoidance, so that the overall expected marginal return to non-compliance at the optimum is increased (making $p(x)$ higher). In this case the expected marginal return to evasion does not uniformly increase or decrease, but rather evasion becomes subject to stronger diminishing marginal returns (recall that evasion and avoidance are inversely related for a fixed x, so the amount of evasion increases from right to left in Figure 22.3).

Extensions

In this section we consider a range of realistic extensions to the model of the previous section. As, however, these extensions reduce (often substantially) the tractability of the model, we proceed here with numerical examples, rather than general analytic solutions. As a key feature of our analysis is the incorporation of tax avoidance, we herein focus on the case in which the incentive compatibility constraints bind for an interior level of avoidance.

Optimal auditing

We now revisit the finding of Chander and Wilde (1998) that regressive tax functions are more efficient than progressive tax functions (in the sense that they cost less to enforce). In Figure 22.4 we show $p(x)$ for the linear ($t'' = 0$), regressive ($t'' < 0$), and progressive ($t'' > 0$) cases.[9] As in previous figures, A^* is interior for $x < \hat{x}$ and $A^* = 0$ for $x \geq \hat{x}$. We see that the audit function in the progressive case is everywhere above the audit function in the regressive case. Hence, the model retains Chander and Wilde's finding regarding the desirability of regressive taxation from an enforcement cost perspective. Our finding is not importantly altered if we instead employ the alternative formulation of the model whereby $t(x + E) - t(x)$ is considered the evaded tax and $t(w) - t(w - A)$ is considered to be the avoided tax.

Risk aversion

So far we have restricted the utility function to be linear. More generally, however, much evidence points towards risk aversion, which implies a utility function satisfying $U'' < 0$. Figure 22.5 illustrates $p(x)$ when taxpayers are risk neutral ($U(z) = z$) and when they are risk

---

8 If, however, social stigma is viewed as a monetary, rather than utility cost, then a negative relationship between compliance and the marginal tax rate can emerge in the Yitzhaki framework when the stigma cost is sufficiently high (see, e.g. al-Nowaihi and Pyle 2000).

9 The specific functions depicted are $t(x) = 0.3x$ (linear case); $t(x) = 0.3x - 0.01x^2$ (regressive case); and $t(x) = 0.06x^2$ (progressive case).

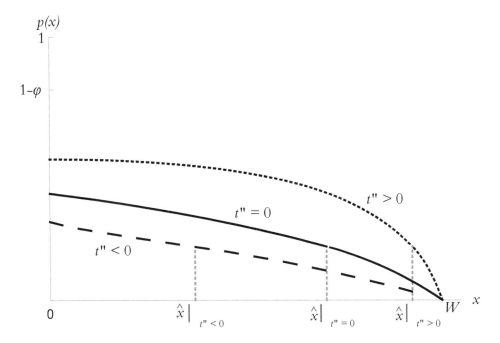

Figure 22.4   Audit function for a progressive, linear, and regressive tax function.

averse ($U(z) = z^{2/3}$). The audit function under risk aversion is seen to lie everywhere below the equivalent function when taxpayers are risk neutral. To understand this finding we apply Jensen's inequality to the condition $R(A^*, E^*) = 0$ to obtain

$$p(x)U^a + \left[1 - p(x)\right]U^n = U^h \le U\left(p(x)\left[w^a - S\right] + \left[1 - p(x)\right]w^n\right).$$

This inequality implies that $u^h \le p(x)[u^a - S] + [1 - p(x)]u^n$, which is equivalent to $p(x) \le [u^n - u^h]/[u^n - u^a + S]$. Under risk neutrality this inequality binds, so $p(x)$ must necessarily lie below the risk neutral level when risk aversion is introduced.

Furthermore, the audit function under risk neutrality is steeper than under risk aversion. Under risk neutrality an increase in declared income affects the taxpayer's payoff by the difference between the expected marginal return from truthful declaration and the expected marginal return of the lottery associated with under-declaration. However, if the taxpayer is risk averse, the expected marginal utility of an increase of x will also factor (positively) the reduction of risk. Hence, $p(x)$ in the risk aversion case is less sensitive to increases in the amount declared.

Variable social stigma

We now relax the previous assumption of a constant utility cost of social stigma by allowing for this cost to contain a variable component. We write

$$S(w - x) = \begin{cases} 0 & \text{if } x = w; \\ s + \psi[w - x] > 0 & \text{otherwise;} \end{cases}$$

where $\psi \ge 0$. When $\psi = 0$ we recover the specification of $S(\cdot)$ used in the previous section. Figure 22.6 compares the audit function in the two cases: one with a constant social stigma ($s = 3$,

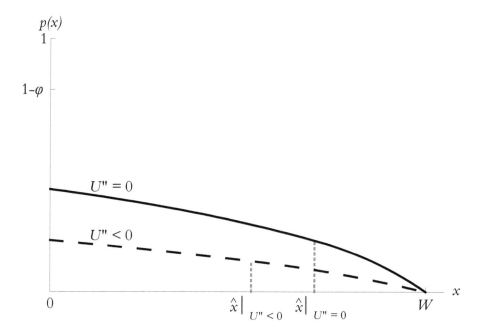

Figure 22.5 Effect of risk aversion.

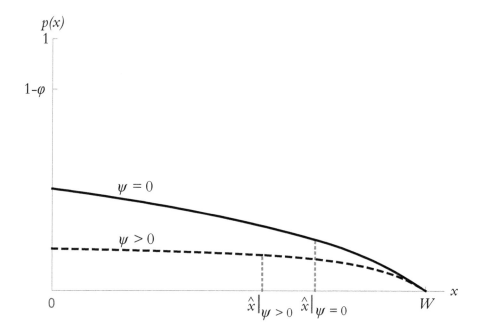

Figure 22.6 Effect of a variable component to social stigma.

$\psi = 0$) and one with variable stigma ($s = 3$, $\psi = 0.9$). As can be seen from the figure, the increase in ψ causes $p(x)$ to shift downward and become flatter. While the first effect is due to the absolute increase of the stigma cost, the second one is caused by variation in the marginal stigma cost. Indeed, for a unitary increase of declared income x, the taxpayer reduces his stigma by an amount ψ, hence, the reduction in $p(x)$ following an increase x is smaller the higher is ψ. In this way, holding the level of stigma constant, stiffer deterrence is needed when the stigma cost is dependent on evaded liabilities so as to counteract the stigma-relieving effect of an increase in the declaration.

Conclusion

In this chapter we investigated how accounting for the ability of individuals to avoid tax, as well as to evade tax, alters the conclusions for optimal auditing of models in which only tax evasion is possible. The nature of the avoidance activity we consider is not explicitly prohibited by law, but is unacceptable to the tax authority. Accordingly, if the tax authority learns of the avoidance, it moves (successfully in our model) to outlaw it ex-post.

Some key features of the literature that considers only evasion are preserved: we find that the audit function is a non-increasing function of declared income and, as in Chander and Wilde (1998), less enforcement is required to enforce a regressive tax than to enforce a progressive tax. The model does, however, also yield new insights, in particular around the relationship between tax compliance and marginal tax rates. The evasion-only literature has encountered the so-called "Yitzhaki puzzle" whereby stiffer marginal tax rates decrease incentives to be non-compliant. In our framework, however, the opposite applies: incentives to be non-compliant increase with marginal tax rates. The key to this result is that the incentives to avoid tax unambiguously increase following an increase in marginal tax rates. Thus, even though the incentives for evasion may worsen, nonetheless, the tax system becomes more costly to enforce, and overall compliance falls unless enforcement is stiffened.

We are also able to understand further questions such as "which taxpayers are the most difficult (expensive) to make compliant?"; and "should tax auditing be geared to preventing avoidance or evasion?" On the first question, we find that in plausible circumstances it is the wealthiest taxpayer who is the most difficult to make compliant. While we know of no direct empirical evidence on this matter, our result chimes with the findings of attitudinal research regarding perceptions of the compliance of the rich (e.g. Wallschutzky 1984; Citrin 1979). The answer to the second question depends critically on (i) the level and shape of the penalties for evasion; and (ii) the competitiveness of the market for avoidance schemes (for this determines the share of the possible proceeds from avoidance that must be paid as a fee). If the penalty function is linear or concave then, irrespective of the tax function, a non-compliant taxpayer will engage purely in avoidance, or purely in evasion. Thus enforcement is focused entirely on one form of non-compliance or the other. When, however, the penalty function is convex (which seems quite likely empirically, given that smaller cases of tax evasion are typically punished through fines, but larger cases are punished through prison sentences) a non-compliant taxpayer may simultaneously want to avoid and evade tax, so enforcement must reflect both of these possibilities. We have shown that a taxpayer's preferred mix of avoidance and evasion moves in favour of avoidance as reported income decreases, as the competitiveness of the market for avoidance schemes increases, and as the social stigma associated with tax non-compliance falls.

We finish with some avenues for future research. First, it would be of interest to allow for imperfect audit effectiveness, as in Rablen (2014) and Snow and Warren (2005a, 2005b), for it might be that evasion and avoidance differ in the amount of tax inspector time required to detect them. Second, it might also be of interest to model more carefully the market for avoidance. In practice there are a range of providers of tax advice, ranging from those that offer solely tax planning, to those that are willing to offer aggressive (or even criminal) methods, making it important to understand the separate supply- and demand-side effects. A last suggestion is to explore the effects of different forms of avoidance. We assume that avoidance permits some amount of income to be hidden from the tax authority, but an alternative modelling approach might be to assume that it allows some amount of income to be taxed at a lower rate.

Acknowledgements

We are grateful to Andrea Vindigni, Chris Hutcheon; and participants at the TARC Workshop on Tax Avoidance (London) and the 4th Annual TARC Workshop (Exeter) for helpful comments. This chapter was written while Gamannossi degl'Innocenti was a visitor at Brunel University London, whose hospitality he thanks. Gamannossi degl'Innocenti gratefully acknowledges financial support from the Ministero dell'Istruzione, dell'Università e della Ricerca (cycle XXVIII) and from the European Commission (Erasmus mobility grant 2015-1-IT02-KA103-013713/5).

References

Allingham, M. G., and Sandmo, A. (1972). 'Income tax evasion: A theoretical analysis', *Journal of Public Economics*, 1(3–4), 323–38.

Alm, J. (1988). 'Compliance costs and the tax avoidance tax evasion decision', *Public Finance Quarterly*, 16(1), 31–66.

Alm, J., Bahl, R., and Murray, M. N. (1990). 'Tax structure and tax compliance', *The Review of Economics and Statistics*, 72, 603–13.

Alm, J., and McCallin, N. J. (1990). 'Tax avoidance and tax evasion as a joint portfolio choice', *Public Finance/Finances Publiques*, 45(2), 193–200.

al-Nowaihi, A., and Pyle, D. (2000). 'Income tax evasion: A theoretical analysis', in A. MacDonald and D. Pyle (eds), *Illicit Activity: The Economics of Crime and Tax Fraud*. Aldershot: Ashgate, 249–66.

Baldry, J. C. (1986). 'Tax evasion is not a gamble', *Economics Letters*, 22(4), 333–5.

Becker, G. S. (1968). 'Crime and punishment: An economic approach', *Journal of Political Economy*, 76(2), 169–217.

Benjamini, Y., and Maital, S. (1985). 'Optimal tax evasion and optimal tax evasion policy: Behavioural aspects', in W. Gaertner and A. Wenig (eds), *The Economics of the Shadow Economy*. Berlin: Springer-Verlag, 245–64.

Bernasconi, M., Corazzini, L., and Seri, R. (2014). 'Reference dependent preferences, hedonic adaptation and tax evasion: Does the tax burden matter?', *Journal of Economic Psychology*, 40(1), 103–18.

Chander, P. (2007). 'Income tax evasion and the fear of ruin', *Economica*, 74(294), 315–28.

Chander, P., and Wilde, L. L. (1998). 'A general characterization of optimal income tax enforcement', *The Review of Economic Studies*, 65(1), 165–83.

Chetty, R. (2009). 'Is the taxable income elasticity sufficient to calculate deadweight loss? The implications of evasion and avoidance', *American Economic Journal: Economic Policy*, 1(2), 31–52.

Christiansen, V. (1980). 'Two comments on tax evasion', *Journal of Public Economics*, 13(3), 389–93.

Citrin, J. (1979). 'Do people want something for nothing: Public opinion on taxes and public spending', *National Tax Journal*, 32(2), 113–29.

Cobham, A. (2005). 'Tax evasion, tax avoidance and development finance', QEH Working Paper Series No. 129, University of Oxford.

Committee of Public Accounts (2013). *Tax Avoidance: Tackling Marketed Avoidance Schemes*. London: The Stationery Office.

Cremer, H., and Gahvari, F. (1995). 'Tax evasion and the general income tax', *Journal of Public Economics*, 60(2), 235–49.

Damjanovic, T., and Ulph, D. (2010). 'Tax progressivity, income distribution and tax non-compliance', *European Economic Review*, 54(4), 594–607.

Dell'Anno, R. (2009). 'Tax evasion, tax morale and policy maker's effectiveness', *Journal of Socio-Economics*, 38(6), 988–97.

Dhami, S., and al-Nowaihi, A. (2007). 'Why do people pay taxes? Prospect theory versus expected utility theory', *Journal of Economic Behavior and Organization*, 64(1), 171–92.

Erard, B., and Feinstein, J. (1994). 'Honesty and evasion in the tax compliance game', *RAND Journal of Economics*, 25(1), 1–19.

Fack, G., and Landais, C. (2010). 'Are tax incentives for charitable giving efficient? Evidence from France', *American Economic Journal: Economic Policy*, 2(2), 117–41.

Feldstein, M. (1999). 'Tax avoidance and the deadweight loss of the income tax', *Review of Economics and Statistics*, 81(4), 674–80.

Gordon, J. P. F. (1989). 'Individual morality and reputation costs as deterrents to tax evasion', *European Economic Review*, 33(4), 797–805.

Gruber, J., and Saez, E. (2002). 'The elasticity of taxable income: Evidence and implications', *Journal of Public Economics*, 84(1), 1–32.

Hashimzade, N., Myles, G. D., Page, F., and Rablen, M. D. (2014). 'Social networks and occupational choice: The endogenous formation of attitudes and beliefs about tax compliance', *Journal of Economic Psychology*, 40(1), 134–46.

Hashimzade, N., Myles, G. D., Page, F., and Rablen, M. D. (2015). 'The use of agent-based modelling to investigate tax compliance', *Economics of Governance*, 16(2), 143–64.

Hashimzade, N., Myles, G. D., and Rablen, M. D. (2016). 'Predictive analytics and the targeting of audits', *Journal of Economic Behavior and Organization*, 124(1), 130–45.

Hindriks, J. (1999). 'On the incompatibility between revenue maximisation and tax progressivity', *European Journal of Political Economy*, 15(1), 123–40.

HMRC (2012). *Court of Appeal Backs HMRC in Tax Avoidance Case*, NAT69/12. London: HM Revenue and Customs.

HMRC (2015). *Measuring Tax Gaps 2015 Edition: Tax Gap Estimates for 2013–14*. London: HM Revenue and Customs.

Kim, Y. (2003). 'Income distribution and equilibrium multiplicity in a stigma-based model of tax evasion', *Journal of Public Economics*, 87(7–8), 1591–616.

Kirchler, E., Maciejovsky, B., and Schneider, F. (2003). 'Everyday representations of tax avoidance, tax evasion, and tax flight: Do legal differences matter?', *Journal of Economic Psychology*, 24(4), 535–53.

Lang, O., Nöhrbaß, K. H., and Stahl, K. (1997). 'On income tax avoidance: The case of Germany', *Journal of Public Economics*, 66(2), 327–47.

Lee, K. (2001). 'Tax evasion and self-insurance', *Journal of Public Economics*, 81(1), 73–81.

Marhuenda, F., and Ortuño-Ortín, I. (1994). 'Honesty vs. progressiveness in income tax enforcement problems', Working paper no. 9406, University of Alicante.

Mookherjee, D., and Png, I. (1989). 'Optimal auditing, insurance, and redistribution', *Quarterly Journal of Economics*, 104(2), 399–415.

Morton, S. (1993). 'Strategic auditing for fraud', *The Accounting Review*, 68(4), 825–39.

Myerson, R. B. (1979). 'Incentive compatibility and the bargaining problem', *Econometrica*, 47(1), 61–74.

Myerson, R. B. (1982). 'Optimal coordination mechanisms in generalized principal-agent problems', *Journal of Mathematical Economics*, 10(1), 67–81.

Myerson, R. B. (1989). 'Mechanism design', in J. Eatwell, M. Milgate and P. Newman (eds), *Allocation, Information, and Markets*. New York: Macmillan Press, 191–206.

Myles, G. D., and Naylor, R. A. (1996). 'A model of tax evasion with group conformity and social customs', *European Journal of Political Economy*, 12(1), 49–66.

Piketty, T., Saez, E., and Stantcheva, S. (2014). 'Optimal taxation of top labor incomes: A tale of three elasticities', *American Economic Journal: Economic Policy*, 6(1), 230–71.

Piolatto, A., and Rablen, M. D. (2017). 'Prospect theory and tax evasion: A reconsideration of the Yitzhaki Puzzle', Theory and Decision, 82(4), 543–65.

Rablen, M. D. (2014). 'Audit probability versus effectiveness: The Beckerian approach revisited', *Journal of Public Economic Theory*, 16(2), 322–42.

Reinganum, J., and Wilde, L. (1985). 'Income tax compliance in a principal-agent framework', *Journal of Public Economics*, 26(1), 1–18.

Reinganum, J., and Wilde, L. (1986). 'Equilibrium verification and reporting policies in a model of tax compliance', *International Economic Review*, 27(3), 739–60.

Reinganum, J., and Wilde, L. (1991). 'Equilibrium enforcement and compliance in the presence of tax practitioners', *Journal of Law, Economics & Organization*, 7(1), 163–81.

Sanchez, I., and Sobel, J. (1993). 'Hierarchical design and enforcement of income tax policies', *Journal of Public Economics*, 50(3), 345–69.

Scotchmer, S. (1987). 'Audit classes and tax enforcement policy', *American Economic Review*, 77(2), 229–33.

Slemrod, J. (1995). 'Income creation or income shifting? Behavioral responses to the tax reform act of 1986', *American Economic Review*, 85(2), 175–80.

Slemrod, J. (1996). 'High-income families and the tax changes of the 1980s: The anatomy of behavioral response', in M. Feldstein and J. M. Poterba (eds), *Empirical Foundations of Household Taxation*. Chicago: University of Chicago Press, 169–92.

Slemrod, J., and Kopczuk, W. (2002). 'The optimal elasticity of taxable income', *Journal of Public Economics*, 84(1), 91–112.

Slemrod, J., and Yitzhaki, S. (2002). 'Tax avoidance, evasion and administration', in A. Auerbach and M. Feldstein (eds), *Handbook of Public Economics*, 1st ed. Amsterdam: North-Holland, 1423–70.

Snow, A., and Warren Jr., R. S. (2005a). 'Ambiguity about audit probability, tax compliance, and taxpayer welfare', *Economic Inquiry*, 43(4), 865–71.

Snow, A., and Warren Jr., R. S. (2005b). 'Tax evasion under random audits with uncertain detection', *Economics Letters*, 88(1), 97–100.

Srinivasan, T. N. (1973). 'Tax evasion: A model', *Journal of Public Economics*, 2(4), 339–46.

Stiglitz, J. E. (1985). 'The general theory of tax avoidance', *National Tax Journal*, 38(3), 325–37.

Stone, J. (2015). 'Most people think legal tax avoidance is just as wrong as illegal tax evasion, poll suggests', *The Independent*, 1 March. London: Independent Print Limited. Available at www.independent.co.uk/news/uk/politics/most-people-think-legal-tax-avoidance-is-just-as-wrong-as-illegal-tax-eva sion-10077934.html [Accessed 10 October 2016]

Uribe-Teran, C. (2015). 'Down the rabbit-hole: Tax avoidance and the elasticity of taxable income'. Unpublished manuscript. Available at https://www.researchgate.net/profile/Carlos_Uribe_Teran.

Wallschutzky, I. G. (1984). 'Possible causes of tax evasion', *Journal of Economic Psychology*, 5(4), 371–84.

Yitzhaki, S. (1974). 'A note on "Income tax evasion: A theoretical analysis"', *Journal of Public Economics*, 3(2), 201–2.

APPENDIX

Proof of Proposition 1: The proof follows immediately from (4), (5) and (6).

Proof of Proposition 2: Differentiating in (7) we obtain that, if $A^* = 0$, then

$$\frac{\partial p(x)}{\partial \bar{w}} = \frac{t'(\bar{w})\left[1 - p(x)\right]f'}{f + s} > 0;$$

$$\frac{\partial p(x)}{\partial x} = -\frac{\left[1 - p(x)f'\right]t'(\bar{w})}{f + s} < 0;$$

$$\frac{\partial p(x)}{\partial s} = -\frac{p(x)}{f + s} < 0;$$

$$\frac{\partial p(x; \varepsilon f)}{\partial \varepsilon} = -\frac{p(x)f}{f + s} < 0;$$

$$\frac{\partial p(x, \varepsilon t)}{\partial \varepsilon} = p(x)[1 - p(x)f'] > 0;$$

$$\frac{\partial p(x)}{\partial \varphi} = 0.$$

The comparative statics when $A^* = w - x$ follow similarly.

Proof of Lemma 1: We first prove $p(x)f' < 1$ From (14), (16) and (18), if there exists a $\hat{w} \leq \bar{w}$ such that $p(x; A, w)$ attains the value $p(x; A, \hat{w}) = [f'(t(\hat{w}) - t(x + A))]^{-1}$ then $p(x; A, \hat{w}) = max_w$ $p(x; A, w)$ — for if (13) defines a maximum in A, as assumed, then (13) defines a maximum in w. $p(x; A, \hat{w})$ is maximised in A when $\hat{A} = 0$ (as $f'' > 0$ for there to be an interior A^*), so $\hat{w} \neq w^*$ for, by assumption, if it were that $\hat{w} = w^*$ then $p(x; A, \hat{w})$ would be maximised for an interior value of A. Hence we have $[f'(t(\hat{w}) - t(x + A^*))]^{-1} > p(x; A^*, w^*) = p(x)$. As this will hold for every $\hat{w}$, we have $p(x)f' < 1$. If $\partial p(x; A, w)/\partial w > 0$ everywhere then there does not exist a $\hat{w} \leq \bar{w}$ such that $\partial p(x; A, w)/\partial w = 0$. We note that it cannot be that $\partial p(x; A, w)/\partial w < 0$ everywhere as $\partial p(x; A, w)/\partial w|_{A = w - x = 0} = \varphi\, t'(x)/[s + f(0)] > 0$. In this case $p(x; A, w)$ is maximised at $w = \bar{w}$ and satisfies $p(x; A, \bar{w}) < [f'(t(\bar{w}) - t(x + A))]^{-1}$. An analogous argument to that above then establishes that $p(x)f' < 1$. Then, from (15), we may set $p(x) = \varphi[f' - 1]^{-1}$ in $p(x)f' < 1$ to obtain $[1 - \varphi]f' > 1$. That $p(x) < 1 - \varphi$ follows immediately.

Proof of Proposition 3: The comparative statics of a pivot around $(k, f(k)) = (0, 0)$ are found by writing $f(\cdot)$ as $\varepsilon f(\cdot)$, differentiating with respect to ε, and then examining the resulting derivative as $\varepsilon \to 1$. The pivot of the tax function is performed analogously. The comparative statics of a shift of the tax function are found by replacing $t(\cdot)$ with $t(\cdot) + \varepsilon$, differentiating with respect to ε, and then examining the resulting derivative as $\varepsilon \to 0$. When $A^* \in (0, w - x)$ we use the implicit function theorem in (13) to obtain:

$$sgn\left(\frac{\partial A^*}{\partial s}\right) = -sgn\left(\varphi t'(A + x)\right) < 0;$$

$$sgn\left(\frac{\partial A^*}{\partial \varphi}\right) = -sgn\left(f + [t(A + x) - t(x)]f' + s\right) < 0;$$

$$sgn\left(\frac{\partial A^*}{\partial \bar{w}}\right) = sgn\left([1 - \varphi]f' - 1 + [w^n - w^h]f''\right) > 0;$$

$$sgn\left(\frac{\partial A^*}{\partial x}\right) = -sgn(\{[1 - \varphi]f' - 1\}t'(x) + [w^n - w^h]t'(A + x)f'') < 0;$$

$$sgn\left(\frac{\partial A^*(\varepsilon f)}{\partial \varepsilon}\right) = sgn(s\varphi + t(\bar{w}) - t(x)) > 0;$$

$$sgn\left(\frac{\partial A^*(\varepsilon t)}{\partial \varepsilon}\right) = sgn([t(\bar{w}) - t(A + x)][w^n - w^h]f'' + \{[1 - \varphi]f' - 1\}[t(\bar{w}) - t(x)] > 0;$$

and when $w^* \in (x, x + A)$ we use the IFT in (14) to obtain

$$sgn\left(\frac{\partial w^*}{\partial s}\right) = sgn\left(t'(w^*)\right) > 0;$$

$$sgn\left(\frac{\partial w^*(\varepsilon f)}{\partial \varepsilon}\right) = -sgn\left(\frac{st'(w^*)}{[f + s]^2}\right) < 0;$$

$$sgn\left(\frac{\partial w^*}{\partial x}\right) = sgn\left(\frac{t'(x)}{t'(w^*)}\right) > 0;$$

$$sgn\left(\frac{\partial w^*}{\partial \bar{w}}\right) = sgn\left(0\right) = 0;$$

$$sgn\left(\frac{\partial w^*(\varepsilon t)}{\partial \varepsilon}\right) = -sgn\left(\frac{f''t'(w^*)}{[f']^2}\right) < 0;$$

$$sgn\left(\frac{\partial w^*}{\partial \varphi}\right) = sgn(0) = 0.$$

Turning to $p(x)$, we use the IFT in (2) along with (13) or (14) to obtain

$$sgn\left(\frac{\partial p(x)}{\partial s}\right) = -sgn(w^n - w^h) < 0;$$

$$sgn\left(\frac{\partial p(x; \varepsilon f)}{\partial \varepsilon}\right) = -sgn([w^n - w^h]f) < 0;$$

$$sgn\left(\frac{\partial p(x)}{\partial x}\right) = \begin{cases} -sgn\left(\dfrac{1-p(x)-\varphi}{w^n - w^c + s}\right) < 0 & \text{if } A^* \in (0, w - x); \\ sgn(0) = 0 & \text{if } w^* \in (x, x + A); \end{cases}$$

$$sgn\left(\frac{\partial p(x)}{\partial \overline{w}}\right) = \begin{cases} sgn(\{[1-\varphi]f' - 1\}) > 0 & \text{if } A^* \in (0, w - x); \\ sgn(0) = 0 & \text{if } w^* \in (x, x + A); \end{cases}$$

$$sgn\left(\frac{\partial p(x; \varepsilon)}{\partial \varepsilon}\right) = \begin{cases} sgn([1-\varphi]f' - 1) > 0 & \text{if } A^* \in (0, w - x); \\ sgn(0) = 0 & \text{if } w^* \in (x, x + A); \end{cases}$$

$$sgn\left(\frac{\partial p(x)}{\partial \varphi}\right) = \begin{cases} -sgn\left([1-\varphi]f' - 1\right) < 0 & \text{if } A^* \in (0, w - x); \\ sgn(0) = 0 & \text{if } w^* \in (x, x + A). \end{cases}$$

PART V

Tax avoidance and society

23

TAX AVOIDANCE AND MORALITY

Zoë Prebble and John Prebble

Introduction

This chapter considers whether tax avoidance is moral. The authors argue that while there is a good deal of judicial authority for the proposition that the legal and moral lines between different modes of tax minimization are the same, this authority is not well reasoned; rather, it is based on unsubstantiated assumptions. After testing these assumptions, the chapter will demonstrate that not only do the assumptions fail to justify the view that tax avoidance is moral, but also that logic supports the contrary view. The discussion in the chapter follows the tri-partite analytical framework of evasion, avoidance, and mitigation, explained in Chapter 5 of this book, "General Anti-Avoidance Rules and the Rule of Law", to which readers are referred. The chapter begins by considering a common reason for the belief that avoidance is moral.

Tax evasion and tax avoidance

The distinction

Tax evasion and tax avoidance involve similar taxpayer behaviour and are each undertaken in pursuit of the same broad aim: to minimize or to eliminate tax liability. They are factually similar, but legally distinct.

Tax evasion is illegal. It consists in the wilful violation or circumvention of applicable tax laws in order to minimize tax liability.[1] Tax evasion generally involves either deliberate under-reporting or non-reporting of receipts, or false claims to deductions. This conduct is legally straightforward to identify; a taxpayer has committed tax evasion only if he or she has breached a relevant law. Indeed, evasion ordinarily involves criminal fraud.

Tax avoidance is not illegal. Rather, it is the act of taking advantage of legal opportunities to minimize one's tax liability.[2] Lord Hoffman captured the essence of avoidance in this passage:

---

1 B. A. Garner (ed.) *Black's Law Dictionary* (8th ed., St Paul, Minn: West Group 2004), 1501.
2 Ibid., 1500.

The hallmark of tax avoidance is that the taxpayer reduces his liability to tax without incurring the economic consequences that Parliament intended to be suffered by any taxpayer qualifying for such reduction in his tax liability.[3]

Since tax-avoiders engage only in legal behaviour, even when the Commissioner detects avoidance schemes, the tax-avoiders are not ordinarily subject to criminal punishment. (This is not to say that the Commissioner will allow tax avoidance schemes to stand unchallenged, and tax legislation may contain provision for penalties specific to avoidance.)

The distinction between tax evasion and tax avoidance appears to lie behind contentions that tax avoidance is not immoral. If avoidance is not illegal, how can it be immoral? There is a flaw in the assumption behind this question: it is common to find things that are not illegal but that are generally thought to be immoral. This question is considered later. Here, the authors address a prior question: if by avoidance we mean behavior that, if discovered, will be struck down by a general anti-avoidance rule, either statutory or judge-made, is it even correct to say that avoidance is legal in any robust sense?

Is tax avoidance robustly or only contingently legal?

If an avoidance scheme cannot achieve a reduction in tax liability without secrecy, it is hard to see it as legal in any robust sense. A scheme that will clearly be struck down if it should ever be challenged seems to be only weakly or contingently within the law.

Such an avoidance scheme does not seem robustly legal because usually we think of legality as involving a strong predictive aspect.[4] For example getting away with murder is of a quite different order from getting away with tax avoidance because an undetected murder is still not even weakly legal. In order properly to reflect the predictive aspect of law, it is necessary to recognize that much of tax avoidance is legal in only a weak sense.

The strict construction of tax statutes

There is a strong tradition of construing tax statutes literally.[5] That is, the Commissioner can levy tax only by bringing taxpayers within the letter of the law, and if he fails to do so, the taxpayer is free from tax even if his case appears to be captured by the spirit of the law.[6] A tax avoidance scheme can succeed if the court confines itself to the literal interpretation of the formal dimensions of the tax law. However, an avoidance scheme is likely to fail if the court looks beyond the form of transactions to whether the underlying substance is within the law's spirit, not just its letter.[7]

---

3 *C.I.R. v. Willoughby*, (1997) 70 T.C. 57, 116 (H.L.) (Eng.).

4 O. W. Holmes, The Path of Law, in J. Feinberg and J. Coleman (eds), *Philosophy of Law* (6th ed., Belmont, CA: Wadsworth Publishing 1999, first published 1897), 174.

5 *Partington v. A-G* [1869] L.R. 4 H.L. 100, 122; see also *Ormond Inv. Co. v. Betts* [1928] A.C. 143, 434 (H.L.) (Eng.); *C.I.R. v. Duke of Westminster* [1936] A.C. 1, 19 (H.L.) (Eng.); *St. Aubyn and Others v. A-G* [1952] A.C. 15, 32 (H.L.) (Eng.); *Fed. Comm'r of Taxation v. Westraders Pty. Ltd.* (1980) 144 C.L.R 55, 60 (Austl.); see generally R. Lavoie, "Subverting the Rule of Law: The Judiciary's Role in Fostering Unethical Behaviour", 75 *University of Colorado Law Review* 115, 183 (2004).

6 *Partington v. A-G* [1869] L.R. 4 H.L. 100, 122, Lord Cairns.

7 T. Rostain, "Sheltering Lawyers: The Organized Tax Bar and the Tax Shelter Industry", 23 *Yale Journal on Registration* 77 (2006).

According to the strict approach to statutory construction, courts must analyze parties' transactions by reference to the exact words of the statute. A corollary is that taxpayer motive is irrelevant when considering whether the taxpayer has remained on the safe side of the legal line.[8] The important question is whether a transaction satisfies the letter of the law; all we can learn from motive is whether a transaction coheres with the law's spirit.

Assumptions about the morality of tax avoidance

The strict approach to interpreting tax statutes appears to have contributed to the belief that while evasion may be immoral, and while tax evaders may be "bad," tax avoidance is not a moral wrong.[9] Taxpayers are assumed not only to have the legal right to avoid tax liability, but also a corresponding moral entitlement to do so.

This assumption is evident in many tax avoidance decisions. Lord Tomlin famously said in *Duke of Westminster v. Commissioner of Inland Revenue*[10] that "every man is entitled if he can to order his affairs so that the tax attaching under the appropriate Acts is less than it otherwise would be."[11] He did not expressly say whether he was referring to moral, or only to legal, entitlement, but Lord Clyde was clear on this point in *Ayrshire Pullman Motor Services and DM Ritchie v. Commissioner of Inland Revenue*.[12] He considered that an arrangement was "neither better nor worse" for the reason that it had a tax avoidance purpose, adding that "[n]o man in this country is under the smallest obligation, moral or other, so to arrange his legal relations … as to enable the Inland Revenue to put the largest shovel into his stores."[13]

Other cases have confirmed that there is "nothing illegal or immoral,"[14] and "nothing wrong" about transactions with tax avoidance purposes.[15] Tax avoidance is not in the least "fraud[ulent]" but a basic taxpayer entitlement;[16] and a tax avoider "neither comes under liability nor incurs blame."[17] In *Helvering v. Gregory*,[18] Judge Learned Hand rejected the notion that there is "even a patriotic duty to increase one's taxes."[19]

This line of authority has been very influential.[20] Many tax lawyers suggest that the idea of ethical or moral considerations impinging on the tax-planning domain is simply absurd.[21] Some in the media have promoted the view that taxpayers have "a legal and moral right to work out how to pay as little tax as possible."[22] Lawyers and taxpayers who wish to engage in tax avoidance tend wholeheartedly to agree with judges like Lords Tomlin and Clyde and Judge Learned

---

8 *Vestey's Ex'rs v. C.I.R.* [1949] 31 T.C. 1, 81(Eng.); *Craven v. White,* 3 All E.R. 495, 518 (H.L.) (Eng.).
9 *Ratzlaf v. United States,* 510 U.S. 135, 140–41 (1994).
10 [1936] A.C. 1 (H.L.) (Eng.).
11 *C.I.R. v. Duke of Westminster* [1936] A.C. 1, 19 (H.L.) (Eng.).
12 *Ayrshire Pullman Motor Servs. and DM Ritchie v. C.I.R.* [1929] 14 T.C. 754 (H.L.) (Eng.).
13 *Ayrshire,* 14 T.C. at 763–64.
14 *A-G v. Richmond* [1909] A.C. 466, 475 (H.L.) (Eng.).
15 *Jaques v. Fed. Comm'r of Taxation* [1924] 34 C.L.R 324, 362 (Austl.).
16 *C.I.R. v. G. Angus & Co.* [1889] 23 Q.B. 579, 593 (Eng.).
17 *C.I.R. v. Fisher's Ex'rs* [1926] A.C. 395, 412 (H.L.) (Eng.).
18 69 F.2d 809 (2d Cir. 1934).
19 *Helvering v. Gregory,* 69 F.2d 809, 810 (2d Cir. 1934), *aff'd Gregory v. Helvering,* 293 U.S. 465, 469 (1935).
20 See G. Lehmann, "The Income Tax Judgments of Sir Garfield Barwick: A Study in the Failure of the New Legalism", 9 *Monash University Law Review* 115 (1983).
21 R. Taylor, "Rusty Pipes Is Simply Rusty, Says Tax Practitioner", *Tax Notes Today* 135, 135 (1994).
22 See G. Monbiot, "Comment and Analysis: Publish and Be Damned: The Super-Rich Are Fleecing Us By Avoiding Taxes, and It Should Be a Matter of Public Record", *The Guardian* (28 September 2004), 21.

Hand, seeing tax avoidance "as being not only legal … which it is by definition … but [also] thoroughly respectable."[23]

There are fewer judicial pronouncements to the opposite effect, but far from none.[24] Lord Denning famously remarked that tax avoidance "may be lawful, but it is not yet a virtue."[25] Nevertheless, on the whole, arguments that tax avoidance is immoral have not caught the attention of commentators, lawyers, or taxpayers to the same degree as statements asserting the opposite.[26]

Is the moral line the same as the legal line?

It seems clear that there is a moral distinction between illegally evading tax on one hand and making a donation to charity and claiming a corresponding deduction on the other. Few would dispute that acceptable tax mitigation like charitable giving is moral and that tax evasion is immoral. Accordingly the moral line must be somewhere between these two extremes. Avoidance sits between acceptable tax mitigation and tax evasion. This means there are several possibilities as to where the moral line lies. The moral line might fall cleanly between avoidance and evasion or it might clearly separate avoidance from mitigation. The remaining possibility is that the line cuts less neatly through avoidance itself, with the result that some avoidance is morally acceptable and some is not. The issue then is where exactly the moral line is drawn.

The prevailing view previously discussed is that tax evasion is immoral while tax avoidance is moral.[27] By definition, tax evasion is illegal and tax avoidance is legal at least in the weak sense discussed earlier.[28] According to this view, then, the moral line between different types of tax minimization behaviour coincides with the legal line.

A logical error: a segue from legal to moral language

While it is true by definition that tax avoidance is legal and evasion is illegal, it is a logical confusion to draw moral inferences from legal norms. The question of whether particular conduct is moral is a matter of morality, not a matter of law. It is true that taxpayers are legally entitled, at least in a weak sense, to avoid tax, but moral entitlement does not necessarily follow from legal entitlement. It is this logical error that many judges, lawyers and commentators make when they assert that there is "nothing illegal or immoral" about tax avoidance; they have good arguments for the first claim but advance no persuasive justification for an uninterrupted segue to the second.[29]

Further analysis reminds us that, contrary to the judicial opinions collected previously in this chapter, it is a logical error to aver that an action is or is not moral as a matter of law. Legal norms

---

23 P. Clyne, *How Not to Pay Any Taxes: A Handbook for Tax Rebels* (Wellington: Professional Publications 1979), 44; see also E. Kirchler, B. Maciejovsky and F. Schneider, "Everyday Representation of Tax Avoidance, Tax Evasion and Tax Flight: Do Legal Differences Matter?" 24 *Journal of Economic Psychology 535* (2003); Discussion Paper 187, Department of Economics, Humboldt University of Berlin (2001).

24 See, e.g. *Latilla v. C.I.R.*, [1943] 1 All E.R. 265 (H.L.) (Eng.); *Ensign Tankers Ltd. v. Stokes*, [1992] 2 All E.R. 275 (H.L.) (Eng.); see also, Monbiot, n.22, at 21; Rostain, n.7, at 77; J. Thorndike, "Tax History – Civilization at a Discount: The Morality of Tax Avoidance", 95 *Tax Notes* 664 (2002); K. D. Deane, "Law, Morality and Tax Evasion", 13 *Anglo-American Law Review* 1, 7 (1984).

25 *In re Weston's Settlements*, [1968] 3 W.L.R. 786 (H.L.) (Eng.).

26 *Weston*, 3 W.L.R. at 786.

27 See previously in this chapter, at heading: "Assumptions About the Morality of Tax Avoidance."

28 See previously in this chapter, at heading: "Is tax avoidance robustly or only contingently legal?"

29 *A-G v. Richmond* [1909] A.C. 466, 475 (H.L.) (Eng.).

are in a different category from moral norms. It is no more logical for a court to judge that an action is moral as a matter of law than it would be to judge that a scientific conclusion, such as "The oceans are rising", is correct or incorrect as a matter of law. If we want a legal judgment we ask a judge. If we want a moral judgment we ask a priest, a philosopher or a pundit. Logically, the argument that tax avoidance is moral finds no support in judicial pronouncements. What line of reasoning may be employed instead? Where is the line within the field of tax minimization that separates the moral from the immoral?

The placement of the moral line: two alternatives

There are two broad alternatives regarding the placement of the line that separates moral from immoral tax minimization activity. One possibility is that the preponderance of the judicial authorities previously discussed are correct and that the legal line between evasion and avoidance maps exactly onto, or indeed defines, the moral line. According to this view, legal tax avoidance is morally permissible and we are able to conclude that tax evasion is immoral simply because it is illegal.[30]

The alternative possibility is that the moral line is different from the legal line, that is, the legality of tax avoidance is a matter separate from its morality. This view allows that it may be true both that many or all instances of tax evasion are immoral and that many instances of tax avoidance are morally permissible. But this view at the same time holds that the bald statement that "taxpayers are morally entitled to avoid tax because avoidance is not illegal" is not necessarily true.

The four assumptions behind the view that tax avoidance is moral

As has been explained, there is a good deal of judicial authority for the proposition that the legal and moral lines between different modes of tax minimization behaviour are the same. This authority is not well reasoned; rather, it is based on unsubstantiated assumptions. The rest of this chapter tests these assumptions, concluding that not only do the assumptions fail to justify the view that tax avoidance is moral, but also that logic and evidence positively support the contrary view. The four assumptions are:

1 Taxpayers are morally entitled to their pre-tax incomes and taxation is an unjustified governmental incursion onto individuals' private property rights.
2 Tax evasion and tax avoidance are not especially harmful and therefore not immoral.
3 The crime of tax evasion is *malum prohibitum* rather than *malum in se*; that is, rather than concerning conduct that is wrong by any criterion, the crime derives its only immoral quality from its legal status.
4 Morality exists wholly independently of the law.

When these assumptions are examined, we see that they should be rejected. In particular, *mala in se* and *mala prohibita* are not exhaustive categories and tax evasion is not immoral simply because it represents a breach of the general duty to obey the law. Evasion is immoral in a much deeper

---

30 A. Seldon, "Avoision: The Moral Blurring of a Legal Distinction Without an Economic Difference", in A. R. Ilersic (ed.), *Tax Avoision: The Economic, Legal and Moral Inter-Relationships Between Avoidance and Evasion* (London: Institute of Economic Affairs, 1979), 3.

sense. As will be shown, this argument leads to the conclusion that since tax avoidance is factually similar to tax evasion, and since evasion is immoral in a deep sense, then avoidance is also immoral; it is not rendered moral by a distinction from evasion that is strictly, and only, legal.

The first assumption behind the view that tax avoidance is moral: that there is a moral entitlement to pre-tax income

The traditional approach to interpretation of tax legislation is to construe it strictly and literally.[31] Tax law is often likened to penal law in this respect; just as there cannot be punishment without law, so there cannot be taxation unless "[t]he Crown … [can] make out its right to the [tax]."[32] It is said that taxpayers have the fundamental right "to arrange their affairs to minimize the taxes they must fairly pay."[33]

Implicit in this approach is the assumption that individuals have a *prima facie* moral and legal right to their pre-tax income; private property rights are viewed as the natural, free-market ordering of things.[34] From this perspective, taxation is a largely unjustified interference in the natural order and even the limited levels of taxation that are "justified" are coercive takings by the State.[35]

Nagel's and Murphy's response to the assumption

The intuition that there might be a moral entitlement to one's pre-tax income is familiar to most taxpayers who have ever looked at their pay-slips and noticed the difference between the pre-tax and post-tax income figures.[36] Liam Murphy and Thomas Nagel challenge this view,[37] arguing that the assumption that pre-tax market allocations of resources are an appropriate starting point from which to assess the morality of taxation systems needs to be substantiated, not simply asserted. Murphy and Nagel reject the philosophical underpinnings of the assumption on the ground that it is logically incoherent.

The philosophical underpinnings of the assumption

The assumption that the free-market ordering of property is morally privileged draws on the Lockean concept of natural property rights. Other philosophers of the early modern period had

31 *Partington v. A-G* [1869] L.R. 4 H.L. 100, 122; see also *Ormond Inv. Co. v. Betts* [1928] A.C. 143, 434 (H.L.) (Eng.); *C.I.R. v. Duke of Westminster* [1936] A.C. 1, 19 (H.L.) (Eng.); *St. Aubyn and Others v. A-G* [1952] A.C. 15, 32 (H.L.) (Eng.); *Fed. Comm'r of Taxation v. Westraders Pty. Ltd.* (1980) 144 C.L.R 55, 60 (Austl.); see generally Lavoie, n.5, at 183.

32 *C.I.R. v. G. Angus & Co.* [1889] 23 Q.B. 579, 593 (Eng.).

33 See generally, e.g. Revenue Provisions in President's Fiscal Year 2000 Budget: Hearing Before the Senate Finance Committee, 106th Cong. (1999) (statement of D. A. Lifson, chairman, Tax Executive Committee, American Institute of Certified Public Accountants).

34 N. Brooks, "The Responsibility of Judges in Interpreting Tax Legislation", in G. S. Cooper (ed.), *Tax Avoidance and the Rule of Law* (Amsterdam: IBFD Publications, 1997), 93, 97.

35 A. P. Simister and W. Chan, "On Tax and Justice", 23 *Oxford J. Legal Stud.* 711, 714.

36 K. A. Kordana and D. H. Tabachnic, "Tax and the Philosopher's Stone", 89 *Virginia Law Review* 647, 650 (2003); K. D. Deane, "Law, Morality and Tax Evasion", 13 *The Anglo-American Law Review* 1 (1984).

37 Kordana and Tabachnic, ibid, at 649–50; L. Murphy and T. Nagel, *The Myth of Ownership: Taxes and Justice* (New York: Oxford University Press, 2002), 35; see generally S. Holmes and C. R. Sunstein, *The Cost of Rights: Why Liberty Depends on Taxes* (New York: W.W. Norton & Co, 1999); Brooks, n.34, 97; Simister and Chan, n.35, at 714.

argued that property is not a natural kind but instead something that has been created by the state or has arisen out of society-wide convention.[38] Bentham later asserted that "property and law are born together and die together. Before the law there was no property; take away the law, all property ceases."[39]

John Locke had a different view; he believed that property could exist independently of particular politics or conventions.[40] According to Locke's account, individuals reduce resources from the natural world to their ownership through their labour.[41] Government or the state are not necessary for the creation of property. Instead, government and the state arise after property, as a necessary mechanism for protecting natural rights.[42]

The logical incoherence of the assumption

Murphy and Nagel reject the Lockean-inspired view that property rights exist independently of special legal or political conventions and that we have a moral right to our pre-tax, market-derived income. They consider such a view, which they call "everyday libertarianism," to be wholly incoherent.[43]

In a pre-legal state of nature, such as envisaged by Thomas Hobbes, there would not be a "market" to yield "free-market outcomes" in anything like the sense that the everyday libertarian uses these terms.[44] The market depends on law. A working legal system is a necessary precondition for the existence of "money, banks, corporations, stock exchanges, patents, or a modern market economy … the institutions that make possible the existence of almost all contemporary forms of income and wealth."[45] A legal system cannot exist without government; government depends on taxation.[46] Thus property rights fundamentally depend on taxation. It is therefore "meaningless" to speak of a *prima facie* property right to one's pre-tax income.[47] The distribution of resources via the free market thus has no position of moral privilege compared with other distribution models.[48]

The assumption that there is a moral right to pre-tax income arises in the context of the debate between legal positivists like Bentham, and natural law theorists like Locke, and more recently between exclusive and inclusive legal positivists, about the relationship between law and morality. It is beyond the scope of this chapter to do more than draw attention to this jurisprudential context. It is worth noting however that while Murphy's and Nagel's position is non-Lockean, it need not be construed as purely positivist.

---

38 T. Hobbes, *De Cive: The English Version 26–27*, H. Warrender (ed.) (Oxford: Clarendon Press, 1983, 1st ed., 1647); D. Hume, *A Treatise of Human Nature* 489, L. A. Selby-Bigge and P. H. Nidditch (eds.) (Oxford: Clarendon Press, 1978, 1st ed., 1739), 489.

39 J. Bentham, *The Theory of Legislation*, C. K. Ogden (ed.) (London: Kegan Paul, Trench, Trubner & Co., 1931, 1st ed., 1802), 113.

40 J. Locke, *Two Treatises of Government*, P. Laslett (ed.) (Cambridge: Cambridge University Press, 1988, 1st ed., 1689).

41 J. Waldron, *Property, Stanford Encyclopedia of Philosophy* (6 September 2004), available at http://plato.stanford.edu/entries/property/.

42 Ibid., Part 4.

43 Murphy and Nagel, n.37, at 74.

44 Hobbes, n.38, at 26–7; Kordana and Tabachnic, n.36, at 650.

45 Murphy and Nagel, n.37, at 32.

46 Ibid., 36; see also S. Holmes and C. R. Sunstein, *The Cost of Rights: Why Liberty Depends on Taxes* (New York: W. W. Norton & Co., 1999), 59; L. P. Martinez, "Taxes, Morals, and Legitimacy", 1994 *Brigham Young University Law Review* 521, 540–1 (1994).

47 Murphy and Nagel, n.37, at 36.

48 Ibid., 59.

Consequences of rejecting the assumption

If there is not even a presumptive moral entitlement to pre-tax income, then the imposition of taxes by the government is not interference in the natural or moral order; any particular scheme of taxation and government spending is simply one among many possible distribution models.[49] This alone is not to say that any particular taxation system is moral or immoral. Murphy and Nagel argue that questions of tax policy comprise just a small part of a much wider set of questions of political philosophy and conceptions of justice. We can only evaluate the justice of after-tax income by reference to the legitimacy of the wider political and social system in which it is set.[50]

Rejecting the assumption that there is a moral right to pre-tax income does not by itself allow us to conclude that tax avoidance is necessarily immoral. Nevertheless, rejecting this assumption removes part of the basis for the conclusion that tax avoidance is moral.

The second assumption behind the view that tax avoidance is moral: that tax avoidance and tax evasion are not harmful

In the context of criminal law, three key elements, or criteria, are often used to justify criminalizing particular conduct: culpability, social harmfulness and wrongfulness.[51] These three criteria for criminalizing conduct offer ways of analyzing judges' statements that tax avoidance, as compared with tax evasion, is morally permissible. These three criteria are not mutually exclusive; there is considerable scope for overlap. Nor are they exhaustive; there could be other reasons why a community might feel criminalization is justified. However, within the context of this chapter, these criteria will provide a sufficient overview of the elements from which tax evasion and tax avoidance might derive moral content.

Culpability as a moral justification for criminalizing conduct

Tax evasion and avoidance each seem to satisfy the element of culpability, in the sense of an intention to bring about the outcomes in question. They share the same sorts of causes and motivations.[52] Avoiders and evaders alike seek to reduce or to dodge their tax obligations. If anything, avoidance often requires a more involved and substantial mental element. The detailed planning of a tax avoidance scheme suggests a mind deeply engaged in the enterprise of minimizing taxes. There is some overlap here with the other two criteria for criminalizing conduct; if conduct is not harmful or wrongful, then its deliberateness need not mean that it is particularly culpable. But assuming that some harmfulness and wrongfulness can be established, tax evasion and avoidance both seem to satisfy the culpability requirement.

Harmfulness as a moral justification for criminalizing conduct

The harmfulness criterion is concerned with the quality of the act and its effects rather than with the characteristics of a particular defendant.[53] People and communities have interests, that

---

49 Murphy and Nagel, n.37, at 36.

50 Ibid., 33; see also M. Schler, "Ten More Truths About Tax Shelters: The Problem, Possible Solutions, and a Reply to Professor Weisbach", 55 *Tax Law Review* 325, 395 (2002).

51 See S. P. Green, "Why It's a Crime to Tear the Tag Off a Mattress: Overcriminalization and the Moral Content of Regulatory Offenses", 46 *Emory Law Journal* 1533, 1547 (1997).

52 A. Christopher, "The Law Is the Law Is the Law …", in Ilersic (ed.), n.30, at 80.

53 Green, n.51, at 1549–50.

is, things in which they have some stake. An act is harmful to the extent that it impinges on such interests.[54] Harmfulness is not a sufficient condition for criminalizing conduct; individuals' interests will often have some negative effect on each other but not all resulting intrusions will be harmful enough to justify criminal sanctions. Some conflicts, such as the potential conflicts of interest between competitors in a competitive marketplace, are seen as acceptable. However, harmfulness seems to be a necessary, or at least a close to necessary, condition for criminalizing conduct; many commentators doubt whether conduct that is not harmful should ever be criminalized.[55]

The assertion that tax avoidance is not morally wrong perhaps relies to a certain extent on an assumption that avoidance is not really very harmful conduct. The harm criterion can be difficult to assess in respect of so-called victimless crimes where it is difficult or impossible to identify a direct victim. However, tax evasion and avoidance cannot be described as of victimless crimes or victimless conduct; crimes tend to be considered victimless if only consenting adults are involved, for example, illicit drug use or consensual incest or consensual sexual deviancy.[56] Attempts to claim that avoidance is harmless because it is victimless cannot succeed.

Diffuse harms and harms that are difficult to identify

Tax evasion is not a victimless crime in the sense described in the foregoing paragraph but there is a superficially analogous argument that seems to be implicitly relied on to show that tax evasion is not harmful and so is morally neutral.[57] This argument is not that tax evasion is victimless in the standard sense of the term. Instead, the argument begins by posing the question, "who are these victims and what is the exact harm?" The idea seems to be that it is very difficult to pinpoint any particular victim of tax avoidance or evasion. The argument proceeds from lack of identifiable victims to the conclusion that no harm is caused by tax avoidance and evasion.

The flaw in this argument is that it assumes that a lack of individually identifiable victims is the same thing as a lack of victims altogether and that sufficiently diffuse harm is substantially similar to a total absence of harm. It is true that if taxpayer X chooses to pay less than taxpayer X's proper level of tax, we cannot point to some other individual Y who is a direct victim of this conduct. But this does not mean that no one is affected by taxpayer X's tax avoidance or evasion. Taxpayer X has caused harm, and this harm affects real people, but the harm is diffuse. These diffuse harms associated with tax avoidance and evasion are more difficult to visualize than the harms that affect the very tangible victims of street crime.[58] Nevertheless, the harm criterion is satisfied whether the harm in question is spread thinly but widely or concentrated on one identifiable victim. The harm caused by tax evasion may be significant only in the aggregate, and many of the victims of tax evasion may remain unaware of the harm that they suffer, but the harm is significant nonetheless.[59]

The problem with suggesting that diluted harms at some point cease to be real harms can be illustrated by reference to the dilemma of large numbers. The dilemma is this: for any individual

---

54 Ibid., 1550.

55 See, e.g. A. von Hirsch, "Injury and Exasperation: An Examination of Harm to Others and Offense to Others", 84 *Michigan Law Review* 700 (1986).

56 Garner (ed.) *Black's Law Dictionary*, n.1 at 400.

57 B. Bracewell-Milnes, "Is Tax Avoidance/Evasion a Burden on Other Taxpayers?" in Ilersic (ed.), n.30 at 105–7.

58 S. P. Green, "Moral Ambiguity in White Collar Criminal Law", 18 *Notre Dame Journal Law Ethics & Public Policy* 501, 510 (2004).

59 Ibid., 509.

it may appear that the harm that will result from refusing to comply with a social duty is so diluted as to be negligible; yet, if everyone followed that line and refused to comply, the negligible harms would add up to a very great harm. Eventually the system bursts; this is in no one's best interest.[60]

The harmfulness of tax avoidance in Kantian terms

Economically speaking, there is no distinction between tax avoidance and tax evasion.[61] They are motivated by the same desire to minimize tax liability and have the same economic consequences. It is very difficult to gauge the amount of revenue lost to tax avoidance schemes, but even according to conservative estimates the sum lost in the United Kingdom each year to tax avoidance runs to tens of billions of pounds every year.[62] Similarly, the United States tax avoidance boom of the 1990s was estimated to cost the federal government billions of dollars in lost tax revenue.[63]

Tax avoidance is harmful in that it results in a misallocation of resources.[64] People spend time and money devising avoidance schemes. This expenditure of effort may be profitable for the taxpayer but only because that taxpayer manages to extract an unintended tax benefit.

Tax avoidance therefore represents a deadweight loss to the economy, as the taxpayer in achieving the tax benefit undertakes no actually beneficial activity.[65] The activity is demonstrably non-beneficial according to the following thought experiment. Imagine that everyone, rather than just a subset of taxpayers, actively and aggressively pursued tax avoidance schemes wherever there was both an opportunity to do so and little chance of being found out. The effect would be that tax rates would have to be raised and no one would achieve any gain. In fact, everyone would be worse off because tax avoidance is itself a deadweight cost.[66]

This thought experiment is an application of Kant's moral principle known as the "categorical imperative", a moral requirement deduced as a rational argument. Its essential postulate is that conduct is moral only if it would be acceptable even if everyone adopted it.[67] In respect of the thought experiment, the categorical imperative would point out that tax avoidance can be beneficial only if practised by a minority. If we were all avoiders, deadweight costs from misallocation of resources, transaction costs, and compensatory increases in taxation or government borrowing would result in a net overall disbenefit. To frame the reasoning as Kant would have, avoidance would not be rational behaviour if everyone engaged in it; it therefore cannot be moral behaviour.

Whether practiced by all or by some, tax avoidance also undermines governments' revenues and governments' progressivity policies.[68] Avoidance has substantially negative distributional

60 Ibid., 14.
61 Seldon, n.30, at 3.
62 See Tax Justice Network figures quoted in Monbiot, n.22, at 21.
63 Rostain, n.7, at 77.
64 Brooks, n.34, at 96.
65 Ibid.
66 M. O'Grady, Revenue Comm'r, address at KPMG Tax Conference, "Acceptable Limits of Tax Planning: A Revenue Perspective" (7 November 2003).
67 G. Bird, "Immanuel Kant", in T. Honderich (ed.), *The Oxford Companion to Philosophy* (Oxford: Oxford University Press, 1995), 435; see also R. Johnson, "Kant's Moral Philosophy", in E. N. Zalta (ed.), *The Stanford Encyclopedia of Philosophy* (Stanford, CA: Stanford University, 2005).
68 J. Waincymer, "The Australian Tax Avoidance Experience and Responses: A Critical Review", in G. S. Cooper (ed.), *Tax Avoidance and the Rule of Law* 247, 257 (Amsterdam: IBFD Publications, 1997); D. McBarnet, "Law, Policy, and Legal Avoidance: Can Law Effectively Implement Egalitarian Policies?" 15 *Journal of Law in Society* 113, 114 (1998).

consequences.[69] Not all taxpayers are able or willing to devise or to take advantage of tax avoidance schemes.[70] Generally it is wealthy taxpayers or those with more sophisticated knowledge of tax law who are in the position to take advantage of tax avoidance opportunities.

Both avoidance and evasion risk undermining public confidence in the tax system. This can give rise to a vicious circle: as confidence falls, members of the public become less likely to comply with tax laws voluntarily.[71]

Wrongfulness as a moral justification for criminalizing conduct

In order to examine tax avoidance from an ethical perspective, this chapter has employed an analogy with the three qualities that are ordinarily required of an action before it is criminalized, namely culpability, social harmfulness, and wrongfulness. Foregoing sections of the chapter have argued that tax avoidance satisfies the culpability and harmfulness requirements at least as well as does tax evasion. It follows that the only possible point of difference between the two is in terms of their respective wrongfulness. As a quality, wrongfulness focuses on the act rather than on the actor. A wrongful act is one that violates some kind of norm or moral standard.[72] However, wrongfulness is the very question at issue here; so consideration of this criterion cannot tell us much at this stage. The chapter will revisit this factor later, in the section headed "The dependence of morality on law".

The third assumption behind the view that tax avoidance is moral: that tax evasion is *malum prohibitum*

An analytical framework that appears to have escaped earlier commentators is that tax avoidance and evasion, while legally distinct, are factually very similar. That is, the difference between evasion and avoidance is essentially a matter of law, not of relevant fact. Legal distinctions certainly provide sound bases for legal conclusions, but they cannot similarly justify moral conclusions. This observation is similar to the Humean point that one cannot derive an "ought" from an "is."[73]

To defend tax avoidance as legal and thus moral is not only to say something about tax avoidance but implicitly also to comment on evasion. People who aver that there is a moral entitlement to avoid tax often make a point of contrasting avoidance and evasion, saying that there is a moral entitlement to avoid tax but no corresponding entitlement to evade it. This argument is hard to sustain when one takes into account that, the ingredients and effect of avoidance and evasion being factually similar, they are divided from one another by a line drawn according to law, not according to the facts of the case.[74] In contrast, generally speaking we expect that if two actions are factually similar, then they will be morally similar as well. There must be some basis for morally distinguishing two factually similar actions. If the only difference between evasion and avoidance is one of legality, and if avoidance is wholly moral, then the immorality of evasion

69 Brooks, n.34, at 96.

70 Ibid.

71 O'Grady, n.66.

72 Green, n.58, 551; P. Aranella, "Convicting the Morally Blameless: Reassessing the Relationship Between Legal and Moral Accountability", 39 *UCLA Law Review* 1511, 1530 (1992).

73 R. Cohon, "Hume's Moral Philosophy", in *The Stanford Encyclopedia of Philosophy* (29 October 2004), available at http://plato.standford.educ/entries/hume-moral/.

74 S. H. Kadish, "Some Observations on the Use of Criminal Sanctions in Enforcing Economic Regulations", 30 *The University of Chicago Law Review* 424, 425 (1963).

must be entirely attributable to its illegality. Put another way, it is not the content of the conduct itself that makes judges think that tax evasion is immoral, but simply that the evader has breached an overriding moral obligation to obey society's laws. Thus, judges return to the comparison between tax avoidance and evasion. Tax avoidance lacks the one characteristic that renders evasion immoral. People conclude that since avoidance is legal it must also be moral.

Mala prohibita *and* mala in se

There is a longstanding conceptual distinction between acts that are *mala in se* and those that are *mala prohibita*. An act that is *malum in se* is an evil in itself. For instance, murder, theft, and rape are *mala in se*; such conduct is immoral because of its inherent nature, not because of its legal status.[75] Murder or rape would still be immoral even if not criminalized.[76] On the other hand, an act that is *malum prohibitum* is a crime only because the law prohibits it. For instance, jaywalking and not carrying a driver's licence while driving are *mala prohibita*.[77] Such conduct is criminal simply because it is prohibited by statute; it is not necessarily immoral in its own right. *Mala prohibita* and *mala in se* have customarily been understood as mutually exclusive terms:[78] acts are either wrong because of their inherent nature or only wrong because they have been prohibited.

Mala prohibita *and* mala in se: *mutually exclusive concepts*

Although judges who identify tax avoidance as moral have not expressly used the terms *malum in se* and *malum prohibitum*, these concepts seem to underlie at least some judicial views on the respective moral statuses of tax avoidance and tax evasion.[79] Since the terms are supposed to be mutually exclusive and exhaustive, any wrong that would not be a wrong independently of its illegality is by definition not *malum in se*, but is necessarily *malum prohibitum*.

It is at least technically or trivially true that tax evasion is not *malum in se*. Tax evasion is the wilful attempt to defeat or circumvent the tax law so as to reduce one's tax liability.[80] If there is no tax law, there is nothing wilfully to defeat; that is, no conduct that could even arguably be independently immoral. For instance, unlike many jurisdictions, New Zealand does not have a comprehensive capital gains tax. While there are circumstantial or policy reasons for the presence or absence of capital gains tax in any particular country, from the point of view of an individual taxpayer it is fairly arbitrary whether such a tax exists. Consider two identical taxpayers, each with the same business and earnings structures. One is resident in the United States and the other in New Zealand. Each makes an identical capital gain, which neither taxpayer reports. Only the American taxpayer is liable to capital gains tax. Neither taxpayer reports the gain. The American taxpayer is therefore guilty of evasion, but the New Zealander is not, simply because of the absence of any law that taxes capital gains. But more than this, we are sure that the taxpayer has done nothing that is morally wrong.

Judges who assert a moral entitlement to avoid tax seem to assume that it follows from the observations earlier in this chapter that the United States taxpayer who evades the capital gains

---

75 Garner (ed.) *Black's Law Dictionary*, n.1 at 978–9.
76 Green, n.51, at 1571; see also P. Devlin, *The Enforcement of Morals* (Oxford: Oxford University Press, 1968), 33.
77 Garner (ed.) *Black's Law Dictionary*, n.1 at 978–9.
78 Ibid., 979.
79 See R. Romano, *The Advantage of Competitive Federalism for Securities Regulation* (Washington, D. C.: AEI Press, 2002), 60.
80 Garner (ed.) *Black's Law Dictionary*, n.1 at 1501.

tax is morally culpable for breaking a valid law, but would not be morally culpable had that law not existed. Accordingly, if tax evasion is not *malum in se*, it must be *malum prohibitum*. If it is *malum prohibitum*, it is only immoral by virtue of its illegality. In contrast, it is said, tax avoidance, which is not illegal, is morally permissible.

The "Arbitrariness" of tax law

Judges who say that tax avoidance is moral do not think that tax evasion is excluded from being *malum in se* in only a trivial or technical sense. They further suggest that even where there is a tax law relating to the conduct in question, the conduct's moral content does not extend beyond that which it derives purely from its illegality. They draw on tax law's perceived arbitrariness: tax law is arbitrary and an arbitrary law surely cannot be *malum in se*. Judges' persistent reference to line drawing in tax law seems calculated to suggest this arbitrariness.[81] If tax is an area governed by no universal moral imperative, then a legal line, wherever it is drawn, has no necessary relation to the facts that it governs.[82] Legal rules like the rules of taxation are not logically deduced, but posited: "the claim of our [tax] code to especial respect is simply that it exists, that it is the one to which we have become accustomed, and not that it represents an eternal principle."[83]

Is it true that tax evasion is only malum prohibitum? *a third category of wrongfulness*

We have seen that tax evasion logically cannot be *malum in se* in the strict sense of that term; any talk of tax evasion where there is no tax law is meaningless. However, it is dangerous to proceed from that observation to the conclusion that tax evasion is necessarily *malum prohibitum* and that the conduct itself is therefore morally neutral.

The division of all wrongs into *mala in se* and *mala prohibita* has a long history. It is appealing because it seems to capture some observable truths: some wrongs do seem to be immoral independently of their legal categorization; some crimes do seem largely regulatory. However, the flaw that seems to have accompanied the terms *mala prohibita* and *mala in se* throughout their history is the notion that they are mutually exclusive and exhaustive. Most particularly, it is not self-evident that the categories are exhaustive of the possible relationships between the legality and morality of various types of acts.

Tax evasion may not be *malum in se*; however, it seems a quite different type of conduct from paradigmatic *mala prohibita*.[84] Even if tax evasion is not *mala in se*, there seems to be more wrong with it than is wrong with purely regulatory violations.[85] Tax crimes are generally classed as "regulatory" because they are governed by statutes that are administered by an administrative agency, that is, by an official state organization charged with collecting revenue.[86] But mere definitional sleight of hand is not enough to justify the alleged moral entitlement to avoid tax. The very questions at issue are first, whether there is a moral duty not to evade tax and secondly,

---

81 *Bullen v. Wisconsin*, 240 U.S. 625, 630 (1916).
82 See L. Oliver, "Judicial Approaches to Revenue Law", in M. Gammie and A. Shipwrite (eds.), *Striking the Balance: Tax Administration, Enforcement and Compliance in the 1990s* (London: Institute for Fiscal Studies, 1996), 174.
83 O.W. Holmes, "Law in Science and Science in Law", 12 *Harvard Law Review* 443, 460 (1899); see also A. Schotter, *The Economic Theory of Social Institutions* (Cambridge: Cambridge University Press 1981), 21.
84 Garner (ed.) *Black's Law Dictionary*, n.1 at 1501.
85 Devlin, n.76, at 16.16.
86 Green, n.51, at 1544.

whether there is a similar duty not to avoid it. Blindly assuming that *mala in se* and *mala prohibita* are exhaustive of the moral landscape does not take us far in answering these questions.

It is similarly circular to identify tax evasion as a "regulatory offence" and then to assume that all regulatory offences are *mala prohibita* such that their content is morally neutral.[87] Concepts like *malum prohibitum* and "regulatory offence" seem often to be called upon to do more explanatory work than they are logically capable of. The mere fact that a statute is administered by an administrative agency is no necessary indicator that the statute lacks moral content. The concepts *malum in se* and *malum prohibitum* may have the weight of tradition on their side, but any proposition that they are exhaustive is based on assumption, not on reason. Averments that tax avoidance is not immoral seem to rely on a false dichotomy: it is not correct to say that unless an action is immoral entirely independently of all law its content must be morally neutral, nor that the sole claim of an action to moral weight must be derived from a general obligation to obey the law. There is plenty of logical space between these two paradigms for other hybrid types of relationship between law and moral obligation. The final part of this chapter discusses this logical space.

The dependence of morality on law

Most commentators and judges who assert a legal and moral right to avoid taxes would not go as far as to say there is also no moral duty not to evade taxes. That is, they are not sceptics in respect of existence of at least a *prima facie* moral duty to obey the law.[88] In their legal decisions, judges do not usually engage in detailed theoretical discussions of political obligation. The authors have found no tax decisions in which a judge has discussed the relative merits of social contract theories of political obligation as compared to fairness theories or to any other model. It is a rare judge who would deny any *prima facie* obligation to obey valid law. It is beyond the scope of this chapter to analyze all the possible derivations of such a duty to obey the law.[89] For the purposes of this chapter, it will be sufficient to proceed on the same assumption as that embraced by judges, that is, that there is a general moral obligation to obey the law.

Judges who assert a moral entitlement to avoid tax derive a specific duty to obey tax law in particular from a general obligation to obey the law. They agree that since tax evasion is illegal there is a moral duty not to engage in it.[90]

The fourth assumption: that all aspects of political morality are determinate and independent of the law

The picture of tax evasion as *malum prohibitum* and thus morally neutral is flawed. As previously discussed, *mala prohibita* and *mala in se* are not necessarily exhaustive categories. Professor Tony

---

87 Aranella, n.72, 1530.
88 For some sceptical perspectives see M. B. E. Smith," Is There a Prima Facie Obligation to Obey the Law?" 82 *Yale Law Journal* 950 (1973); R. Wasserstrom, "The Obligation to Obey the Law", 10 *UCLA Law Review* 780 (1973); A. D. Woozley, *Law and Obedience: The Arguments of Plato's Crito* (Chapel Hill, NC: University of North Carolina Press, 1979); J. Raz, "The Obligation to Obey the Law" and "Respect for Law" in *The Authority of Law: Essays on Law and Morality*, Vol. I (Oxford: Oxford University Press, 1979), 233 and 250; A. J. Simmons, *Moral Principles and Political Obligations* (Princeton, NJ: Princeton University Press, 1979).
89 See generally A. J. Simmons, "Obligations, Political", in E. Craig (ed.), *Routledge Encyclopedia of Philosphy* (London; New York: Routledge, 1998), /6.
90 T. Honoré, "Must We Obey? Necessity as a Ground of Obligation", 67 *Virginia Law Review* 39, 48 (1981).

Honoré's writing helps to explain why these categories are not exhaustive. The view that tax evasion is morally neutral, except for its illegality, seems predicated on the assumption that we can always determine the moral status of an act independently of a community's laws.[91] According to this assumption, we can determine whether an act is immoral through rational moral argument without the need to draw any firm conclusions from what the formal legal system has to say on the matter.[92]

Like many unspoken assumptions, this one has *prima facie* plausibility. In a great many cases we do seem to know the moral value of an act independently of its legal status; we do not need to trawl through the statute books to know that murder, rape, or theft are wrong. It is true that some conduct, for example tax evasion and avoidance, is impossible to evaluate, or even to define, if removed from its legal context. However, it begs the question to assert that, because such conduct relies on legal definition, its content is necessarily morally neutral. It begs the question to assert that this conduct's only moral component comes from its legal status. Such an argument could only be logically sound if it first established that legally independent wrongfulness, in a *mala in se* sense, and moral content derived only from legal status, in a *mala prohibita* sense, exhausted the moral landscape.

For Honoré, a "picture of morality as a blueprint and law as a structure put up either according to or in disregard of it is … misleading."[93] We live in collective groups or political communities. A large part of morality relates to questions of how to co-exist and to cooperate with others: "[t]he core of morality is, in a broad sense, political."[94] It follows that in a complex society, a viable morality necessarily has a legal component. That is, the morality of a complex society will be incomplete without a legal system containing certain types of laws.[95]

Broadly speaking, when we consider moral questions we are concerned with the ways in which our actions may significantly impact on other people, either individually or collectively. We are interested in how these impacts do, or should, limit or restrain our behaviour.[96] For Honoré, law relates to morality in two central ways. First, law can form a part of morality. Secondly, laws are open to moral criticism.[97] The second of these assumptions is fairly uncontroversial from a legal positivist standpoint; if there is no necessary connection between morality and law, then it is possible to criticize an existing law on moral grounds. However, the first assumption requires further explanation.

Honoré: some aspects of morality depend on external definition

Moral principles are normative in the sense that they tell us how we should or should not act or behave. However, such principles are not always determinatively prescriptive. Moral principles are often quite general; while they provide a guide to the sorts of ways individuals should generally act, they do not always contain enough information to allow them to tell individuals exactly what is required of them in particular situations. For instance, there may be a general principle that individuals should be "generous" or "kind" or should "not always put their own interests first" but these principles are fairly open ended and vague. These broad duties are not

---

91 T. Honoré, "The Dependence of Morality on Law", 13:1 *Oxford Journal of Legal Studies* 1 (1993).
92 Ibid.
93 Ibid., 3.
94 Ibid., 2.
95 Ibid.
96 Ibid.
97 Ibid.

always sufficient to define individuals' particular duties to each other when their interests con-flict.[98] Particularly when a moral requirement is considered compulsory, it requires a measure of specificity in order that individuals may know just what they are morally required to do. If the core of morality is interacting with others, then our morality, as a set of general principles, is incomplete or lacks specificity. For morality to be complete and meaningful in practice it needs some additional definition from a source outside of itself.

Primitive and pre-legal societies

By Honoré's account, a "primitive" society is one without the formal legal institutions that are present in "complex societies."[99] In primitive, tribal, small-scale or pre-legal societies, individu-als' moral duties to each other tend to be well defined. Individuals in a small-scale community tend to know each other or to be closely linked.[100] Their social roles are defined by fairly rigid customary or conventional practices and are clearly understood.[101] It is rare for anyone to doubt how to act in any particular situation because there will generally be clear social norms to which individuals understand that he or she must adhere.[102] Despite the indeterminacy of general moral principles, it is unusual for individuals in a primitive society to experience moral conflict.

Modern legal societies

A complex, larger, modern society involves more independence and separation of individuals. While it is still a collective, the links between the members are less direct, more abstract.[103] The links between members of a complex society are too numerous and varied for convention to determine or to settle the content of individuals' moral obligations to one another.[104] In a com-plex society there are more "others" to consider. Moral codes need to become more specific.[105] Individuals tend not to feel that they have links to a great number of "others." Instead, they feel as though, since there are so many seemingly faceless "others," they are not linked to any of them.[106]

Making vague moral norms precise is just as necessary in a complex society as in a primi-tive one, but convention and social pressure will be sufficient neither to define nor to enforce particular moral requirements.[107] Honoré argues that law fulfils this determinative role in complex societies.[108]

It is hard to see why an individual's duties to others in a small, close-knit group would cease merely because the group reaches such a size that an individual no longer has direct links with

98 R. Sugden, *The Economics of Rights, Co-Operation and Welfare* (New York: Palgrave Macmillan, 2004), 150.
99 Honoré, n.91, at 2. Note, this distinction is similar to the distinction drawn by Popper between "closed" and "open" societies. See K. R. Popper, *The Open Society and Its Enemies: Volume 1 – The Spell of Plato 172–90* (2nd ed., London: Routledge, 1952).
100 Popper, ibid, at 176.
101 Ibid., 172.
102 Ibid.
103 Popper, n.99, at 174.
104 Honoré, n.91, at 8.
105 J. H. Petersen, "The Moral Foundation of the Welfare State Versus the Mechanism: A Contribution to the Discus-sion of Philosophical and Theoretical Issues in Social Security Today" 52J. Welfare & Soc. Security 12, 14 (1998).
106 Ibid.
107 Honoré, n.90, at 49.
108 Honoré, n.91, at 11.

every member. Certainly, that individual's duties take on a more abstract nature and may be less straightforwardly conceptualized by individuals, but they remain duties. Judicial statements that have reflected a belief in the moral dubiousness of tax avoidance often invoke such notions of duties of good citizenship and duties to other taxpayers.[109]

Tax evasion and the middle ground between mala in se *and* mala prohibita: *a legally constructed moral wrong?*

If some moral obligations need outside determinants, then the problem with viewing *mala in se* and *mala prohibita* as exhaustive categories becomes clear. Legally defined crimes like tax evasion are not necessarily morally neutral.

In cases where either convention or law is required to give an abstract moral norm sufficient definition to be socially prescriptive, the defined moral obligation cannot be said to be universal or wholly or causally distinct from the convention of law that shapes it. Within the context of a modern, complex society such us our own, convention will be insufficient for this purpose; so we will necessarily be dealing with a moral duty defined by law. The abstract moral duty that relates to tax evasion is something like "to contribute to one's cooperative society." Taxation law gives shape to this moral duty by defining the measure of the tax that a taxpayer must pay.

Such a legally defined moral duty does not clearly fit within the *malum in se* category: tax is by definition something that is legally imposed; it is logically impossible to pay a tax if there is no tax law to impose it; to fail to do something that is logically impossible cannot be immoral. However, while this thought experiment tells us that tax evasion is not *malum in se*, it does not establish that, given that we do have tax laws, there is not something wrong with evading these laws beyond the general obligation to obey the law. To class tax evasion as *malum prohibitum* and therefore morally neutral seems to fail to take proper account of the fact that, although legally defined, the duty is a moral one.

When tax evasion is understood this way, we can see that evasion is morally wrong not only because it is illegal but also because, within our legal and societal context, our broad moral obligation to contribute to the collective has taken the specific shape of a duty to pay our taxes. Tax evasion is thus a wrong in a deep sense. Considering that tax *evasion* is morally wrong in virtue of its content as well as its legal status, it is not convincing to suggest that the mere fact that tax *avoidance* is not illegal means that it is also not immoral. From this perspective, the factual similarity between avoidance and evasion and the fineness of the legal line between them suggest the opposite conclusion from the one drawn by judges. If tax avoidance is factually almost indistinguishable from tax evasion, and if despite being a legal construct tax evasion is in a deep sense immoral, then tax avoidance is similarly immoral.[110]

Conclusion

Judges and commentators have made much of the legal difference between evasion and avoidance. Many judges have considered that while evasion is immoral because it breaks the law, legal avoidance involves no such moral misstep. But to draw moral conclusions from legal observations constitutes logical confusion. The fact that conduct is not illegal does not necessarily mean

---

109 *Latilla v. C.I.R.* [1943] 1 All E.R. 265, 381 (H.L.) (U.K.).
110 W. B. Barker, "The Ideology of Tax Avoidance", 40 *Loyola University Chicago Law Journal* 229, passim (2009) comes to similar conclusions via arguments that relate to political economy and democracy.

that it is also moral. It is legal to sell cigarettes, but this observation does not tell us whether selling cigarettes is moral. It is true that conduct that is legal cannot be immoral in one special sense: that is, since it is not illegal, it cannot be immoral for the reason of illegality. But conduct can be immoral for many reasons other than that it breaches the law. Evasion is immoral for more than legal reasons alone.

The current assumptions behind the view that tax avoidance is moral are proven to be unsubstantiated. Therefore, it becomes clear that *mala in se* and *mala prohibita* are not exhaustive categories and that tax evasion is not immoral simply to the degree that it represents a breach of the general duty to obey the law; it is immoral in a much deeper sense. Since tax avoidance is very similar factually to tax evasion, and since evasion is immoral in a deep sense, then avoidance is also immoral; it is not rendered moral by a distinction from evasion that is strictly, and only, legal.

Acknowledgement

This chapter draws on Zoë Prebble and John Prebble 'The Morality of Tax Avoidance', 20 *Creighton Law Review* (Symposium Issue: Estate Planning, Moral, Religious, and Ethical Perspectives) 693–745 (2010). The authors thank Zainab Radhi and Hanneke van Oeveren for their invaluable editorial assistance.

24

THE IDEOLOGY OF
TAX AVOIDANCE

William B. Barker

Over and over again the courts have said that there is something sinister in so arranging one's affairs so as to keep taxes as low as possible. The rich do so, but they do
wrong; for everybody owes a public duty to pay what is fair and equitable. Taxes are
exactions for the general welfare; they should not be voluntary contributions for the
rich and forced exactions for the poor. To demand less in the name of the people is
to recant the values of democracy.[1]

Introduction

Tax avoidance is recognized today by practically all governments as a serious threat to the
integrity of tax systems in democratic societies. However, effective deterrence in a manner that
comports with the principles of a free society is an awesome task. This task cannot be accomplished without identifying and challenging the ideological basis that fosters tax avoidance in
order to begin the process of establishing the democratic core value of equality as an insinuating
principle of income tax law.[2]

Tax avoidance is a common term in tax law and scholarship. Though the concept is sometimes explicitly used in statutes,[3] it is more often an underlying premise for legislative, administrative, or judicial action targeting taxpayer conduct that is perceived to undermine fair and
equitable taxation.

The term tax avoidance does not have a limiting and definite meaning. Instead, the term is
a label for describing pragmatic decisionmaking, which by "pricking a line through concrete
applications"[4] identifies abusive situations. The results of experience have led to a kind of predictability under US law that supports propositions such as, "[e]xperienced tax professionals

---

1 The foregoing intentionally reverses the sentiment found in Judge Learned Hand's statement in *Comm'r v. Newman*,
   159 F.2d 848, 850–51 (2d Cir. 1947) (Hand, J., dissenting). See text preceding n.33 for the actual statement.
2 See generally W. B. Barker, "The Three Faces of Equality: Constitutional Requirements in Taxation", 57 *Cage Western Reserve Law Review* 1 (2006) (arguing that the power to tax is naturally circumscribed in constitutional norms
   between the people and government such as equality).
3 See, e.g. I.R.C. §§ 269, 482 (2000).
4 *Bazley v. Comm'r*, 331 U.S. 737, 741 (1974).

can usually readily distinguish tax shelters from real transactions" and "[g]ood tax lawyers know when they are pushing hard at the edge of the envelope."[5]

Sophisticated guesswork is not the same as the legal certainty expected of tax law under the rule of law. The result is that it is difficult to treat tax avoidance as a category, like negligence, that is a normative legal prescription demanding action. Ultimately, even in the case of anti-avoidance legislation, it is the legal profession, and the judge in particular, who determines what really constitutes impermissible avoidance. Dealing with the problems of tax avoidance involves actions traditionally considered outside the conventional role of the judge.[6] This leaves legislatures, administrators, and jurists confronting an ever shifting landscape of taxpayer responses to taxation with a principle that, while found in taxation, is really not part of the law. Consequently, the judicial response to legislative and even judicial antiavoidance regimes has been that they are dealing with something extraordinary - a remedy that should be used sparingly because of an essential arbitrariness which always borders on opening Pandora's Box.[7]

In the United States, the shift in judicial attitudes toward tax avoidance has been profound. Early in the history of income taxation in America, as the nation was confronting the overwhelming problems resulting from the Great Depression, Congress and the courts faced significant planning by taxpayers that deprived the government of revenue at a time when it could ill afford to lose income.[8] The result was a more substantive, open-ended legal method for tax legislation that was a radical departure from previous interpretation methods.[9] This development in tax jurisprudence reached its apex during the years of the Warren court. It should come as no surprise that the court responsible for the highest advancement of the human rights of those who were most traditionally disadvantaged by our system would be the same court that purposefully interpreted tax law restricting its abuse by those who are traditionally advantaged by our system.

Since then, the tide has turned. Literalism in the interpretation of tax legislation now dominates. Though the US Tax Court has recently adopted a more intentionalist approach to tax legislation, it has not met with success on appeal.[10] Tax law is now dominated by the approach of the US district courts, courts of appeal, and the Supreme Court, which have turned increasingly to a plain meaning approach.[11]

---

5 J. Braithwaite, *Markets in Vice, Markets in Virtue,* Oxford: Oxford University Press (2005), 126.

6 See W. B. Barker, "Expanding the Study of Comparative Tax Law to Promote Democratic Policy: The Example of the Move to Capital Gains Taxation in Post-Apartheid South Africa", 109 *Penn State Law Review* 703, 726–7 (2005)

7 See Y. Grbich, "Does Spotless Exorcise Barwick's Ghost?" in R. L. Deutsch (ed.), *Tax Catch-Ups: A Prospect Intelligence Report*, St Leonards, New South Wales: Original, Prospect Media (1997), 88, 105–12 for an excellent account of the judiciary's struggles with implementing Australia's General Anti-Avoidance Rule.

8 President Roosevelt's *Message to Congress on Tax Evasion and Avoidance* (17 June 1937), reprinted in US Revenue Acts 1909–1950, 20 The Laws, Legislative Histories and Administrative Documents 2 (B. D. Reams, ed., 1979).

9 See W. B. Barker, "Statutory Interpretation, Comparative Law, and Economic Theory: Discovering the Grund of Income Taxation", 40 *San Diego Law Review* 821, 830–2, 850–9 (2003) (tracing the change from formalism to intentionalism in the US Supreme Court's approach to interpretation that took place from 1930–1956).

10 See generally D. F. Shores, "Textualism and Intentionalism in Tax Litigation", 61 *Tax Law* 53 (2007). Shores' study of the appeals of ten Tax Court cases that used an intentionalist approach showed in every case a reversal by the court of appeals using a plain meaning or textualist approach to statutory interpretation. *Id.* at 62–4.

11 *Id.* at 63; see also N. B. Cunningham and J. R. Repetti, "Textualism and Tax Shelters", 24 *Virginia Tax Review* 1 (2004); D. A. Geier, "Commentary: Textualism and Tax Cases", 66 *Temple Law Review* 445 (1993); D. A. Geier, "Interpreting Tax Legislation: The Role of Purpose", 2 *Florida Tax Review* 492 (1995); M. L. Heen, "Plain Meaning, the Tax Code, and Doctrinal Incoherence", 48 *Hastings Law Journal* 771 (1997); R. Lavoie, "Subverting the Rule of Law: The Judiciary's Role in Fostering Unethical Behavior", 75 *University of Colorado Law Review* 115 (2004);

A legal method based on strict or literal interpretation is the prop that sustains tax avoidance. It, in turn, is nurtured by the ideology of liberty.[12] The consequence is that in the United States, the federal courts have readopted the ideology that underpins tax avoidance.

This paper takes a small step. As suggested by its beginning quote, this paper shall examine tax avoidance by challenging the traditional starting point. This paper will show that the ideology underpinning tax avoidance is in direct conflict with core democratic values. This ideology leads to a moral perspective that supports a right to avoid over a duty to pay a fair share of taxes. In a democratic society that values taxation in accordance with fairness, that moral perspective is wrong. It exalts individual license over democratic ideas about what income tax law requires of citizens. Freeing tax law from this ideology will promote a moral perspective of compliance, thus providing a new starting point for developing a sustainable approach to curbing avoidance.

Values in conflict

The nature of tax avoidance can best be understood in terms of the conflicting values that seek their meaning through income tax law. To discover these essences, start with the notion that tax avoidance deals with the incongruence between the intent or object of the statute in taxing a particular situation the way it does or the purpose of the statute in giving a particular benefit to the taxpayer, and the tax outcome advanced by the taxpayer.[13] In most cases, it is said that the taxoutcome determined on the basis of the taxpayer's situation is supported by a reading of the statute but not necessarily with the statute's intent or policy.[14] As President Franklin Roosevelt stated in an address to Congress:

> All [methods of avoidance] are alike in that they are definitely contrary to the spirit of the law. All are alike in that they represent a determined effort on the part of those who use them to dodge the payment of taxes which Congress based on ability to pay. All are alike in that failure to pay results in shifting the tax load to the shoulders of those less able to pay.[15]

These taxpayer outcomes achieve tax results that seem to defy the logic of taxation.[16] These results are in accordance, however, with the logic of another value system. This other value system promotes the individual value of liberty over the individual and collective value of equality. Thus, tax avoidance operates in the limbo created by the antagonism between the ideology underpinning income taxation and the ideology underpinning tax avoidance.

The ideology of income taxation

Ideologies are systems of ideas about the goals, values, and aspirations of a society or of a particular social group. Comprehensive income taxation derives its legitimacy from its democratic

---

A. L. Smith, "The Deliberative Stylings of Leading Tax Law Scholars", 61 *Tax Lawyer* 1 (2007); L. Zelenak, "Thinking About Nonliteral Interpretations of the Internal Revenue Code", 64 *North California Law Review* 623 (1986).

12 See Part ll.B.

13 See R. W. Parsons, *Income Taxation in Australia: Principles of Income, Deductibility and Tax Accounting.* Sydney: Law Book Co. (1985), 844–5.

14 *Id.*; see also Heen, n.11, at 771 (explaining that a literal interpretation ignores "the rich range of contextual and policy considerations that inform" the tax law).

15 President Roosevelt's *Message to Congress on Tax Evasion and Avoidance*, n.8, at 2.

16 President Roosevelt's *Message to Congress on Tax Evasion and Avoidance*, n.8, at 2.

ideological values. Income taxation was believed to advance the value of equality in accordance with ability to pay.[17] Taxation in accordance with ability to pay or means is a constitutional requirement in many countries and in several American states.[18] American legislative history singled out the justice of ability to pay as the most important reason for the adoption of the federal income tax system pursuant to the Sixteenth Amendment.[19]

Progressive income taxation in America was the result of a bitter class struggle to reduce the role of regressive consumption taxes and impose larger levels of tax on those with greater means and wealth.[20] History confirms that the income tax law was social legislation that had the strongest claim to democratic legitimacy because it was the result of the demands of public opinion at a time when, in the words of Thomas Jefferson, the "spirit of the people [was] up."[21]

The ideology of tax avoidance

Frustrating these social and legislative goals is the fact that many persons with significant means do not pay a fair share of taxes consistent with the values of income taxation.[22] One reason for this is a common judicial antagonism to the values of income taxation. A leading jurist expressed the opinion that tax legislation lacked moral values:

> Law is all about the rules which society imposes upon its members for the regulation of their conduct. Elementary fairness dictates that if rules are to be imposed in an area in which there is no universal moral imperative to aid understanding, they shall be clear and unequivocal, so that the subject may know with certainty what he or she may and may not do and what are the legal consequences of any projected course of action.[23]

The concept of tax without a concept of right fosters tax avoidance because tax avoidance, in the value system of the legal profession, has a strong ideological basis.

The ideological support for tax avoidance is the right of liberty, that is, the liberty of the subject to be free from an overreaching government, the freedom of property, and the freedom to contract.[24] Liberty in the context of tax is the value system of a particular social group, those with means, who follow the philosophy that "the prosperity of the middle and lower classes depend[s] upon the good fortunes and light taxes of the rich."[25] Liberty here masks the under-

---

17 H.R. REP. NO. 63–5, at XXXVII (1913). See generally Barker, n.9, at 860–1.

18 See Barker, n.2, at 8–10.

19 H.R. REP. No. 63–5, at XXXVII. See generally Barker, n.9, at 860–1.

20 H.R. REP. No. 63–5, at XXXVII; see also Barker, n.9, at 860.

21 Thomas Jefferson, "Letter to Judge Spencer Roane" (6 September, 1819), in Memorial (ed.), *The Writings of Thomas Jefferson*, Vol. 10 (1904), 140, 141.

22 See generally Dep't of the Treasury, "The Problem of Corporate Tax Shelters" (1999) (addressing the "growing level of tax avoidance behavior"); see also President Roosevelt's Message to Congress on Tax Evasion and Avoidance, n.8, at 2.

23 Lord Oliver of Aylemerton, "Judicial Approaches to Revenue Law", in M. Gammie and A. Shipwright (eds), *Striking the Balance: Tax Administration, Enforcement and Compliance in the 1990s*, Conference Report. The Institute for Fiscal Studies, London (1996), 174 (emphasis added).

24 See, e.g. R. A. Epstein, "Taxation in a Lockean World", 4 *Social Philosophy and Policy* 49 (1986). See generally G. Brennan and J. M. Buchanan, *The Power to Tax: Analytical Foundations of a Fiscal Constitution*, New York: Cambridge University Press (1980).

25 Louis Eisenstein, *The Ideologies of Taxation*, Cambridge: Harvard University Press (1961), 63 (quoting Secretary of the Treasury Andrew Mellon).

lying goal of this class to reestablish the incidence of the tax burden on others. Thus, liberty provides the security to pursue an unfettered life as a consumer. Liberty grants to every person who has the wherewithal to pay the right to treat tax savings as a commodity in civil society that can be invented, patented, and purchased just like a new car. In fact, one can obtain insurance that compensates when one does not receive the intended tax benefit.[26]

The differences between the liberal rights ideology of liberty and the ideology of equality are critical. Equality in taxation stands squarely on the shoulders of a progressive movement in taxation that asserts that the political goals of taxation are substantive equality and redistributional justice.[27] Though the modem advocates of ability to pay may have abandoned its class basis[28] and thus robbed the concept of much of its force, the class politics of the Sixteenth Amendment to the Constitution and the Revenue Act of 1913 were clear.[29] In those more truthful times, Dr. T.S. Adams, a former high treasury official, concluded that "[c]lass politics is of the essence of taxation."[30] Henry Simons set forth the political nature of the case for progressive income taxation as follows: "The case for drastic progression in taxation must be rested on the case against inequality - on the ethical or aesthetic judgment that the prevailing distribution of wealth and income reveals a degree (and/or kind) of inequality which is distinctly evil or unlovely."[31]

Equality is not simply an ideology; it is the purpose acknowledged by Congress for the adoption of the income tax law.[32] The purpose of the legislation, taxation in accordance with ability to pay, is as much a part of the law as the language of the text itself. In contrast, liberty uses the ideology of formal equality, or equality before the law, as a mask for one class's political goal of shifting the burden of any significant taxes from the few to the many. It is not the democratic political process, but rather the neutral concept of legal certainty that leads to this outcome. The ideology of liberty, however, is not part of the tax law and is derived by the legal profession in accordance with the liberal conception of the rule of law. Thus, liberty is the ideological basis of legal methodology in taxation.

Liberty has prevailed against a strong democratic mandate of substantive equality due to the adoption by the legal profession of the liberal ideology of tax avoidance. Legal methodology is outside legislation yet has the power to negate its essential purpose.

The morality of tax avoidance: turning tax avoidance upside down and inside out

> Over and over again courts have said that there is nothing sinister in so arranging one's affairs as to keep taxes as low as possible. Everybody does so, rich or poor; and all do right, for nobody owes any public duty to pay more than the law demands: taxes are enforced exactions, not voluntary contributions. To demand more in the name of morals is mere cant.[33]

---

26 See Braithwaite, n.5, at 113–14.

27 See Barker, n.9, at 864. See generally J. D. Buenker, *The Income Tax and the Progressive Era,* New York and London: Garland Publg., Inc. (1985).

28 See Eisenstein, n.25, at 12.

29 See Barker, n.9, at 860–1.

30 T. S. Adams, "Ideals and Idealism in Taxation", 18:1 *American Economic Review* (1928), 1.

31 H. C. Simons, *Personal Income Taxation,* Chicago: Univesity of Chicago Press (1938), 18–19. Henry Simons also believed that the purpose of taxation in accordance with ability to pay, that is mitigating disparities of wealth, was too settled to require further debate. *Id.*; see also H. C. Simons, *Federal Tax Reform* (1950), 144.

32 See Part H.A.

33 *Comm'r v. Newman*, 159 F.2d 848, 850–51 (2d Cir. 1947) (Hand, J., dissenting).

Judge Learned Hand's famous lines have been quoted so often that their point of view must clearly be that of the judiciary.[34] The social judgment of the tax professional is that tax avoidance is not bad behavior.[35]

The incidence of tax avoidance is explained and justified as "a market response by the tax-payer to a tax structure that is non-neutral and discriminatory."[36] Loopholes and tax planning opportunities are seen as safety valves for systems that overtax persons and enterprises. The human proclivity to evade or avoid has been described as follows:

> The attempt to avoid paying taxes is a reaction against the constraints imposed by any tax. It is universal and an inevitable consequence of the very existence of taxes. "Tax and eva-sion are as inseparable as a man and his shadow." Payment of taxes symbolizes submission. It provokes a feeling of powerlessness by creating a direct bufferless relationship between the isolated, defenceless individual and the state Moloch. It is experienced as a restriction on a person's freedom and interference with his fundamental aspirations for power and prestige. It strikes at the very core of the tax-payer's being, provoking an affective and wholly irrational reaction similar to "a child's reactions to parental domination."[37]

Consequently, failing to gain a tax advantage and having one's taxes increase due to unsuccess-ful tax avoidance is deemed to be a penalty.[38] Though these sentiments may not be publicly shared by all,[39] tax counsel consider themselves morally justified and economically compelled to develop tax savings strategies for the benefit of their clients.[40]

In general, nations recognize a right of tax planning.[41] In some countries this right to choose lesser taxed alternatives is understood as a general exception to constitutional rules that specifi-cally prohibit the strict or literal interpretation of laws.[42] Courts in Belgium state that taxpayers

34 B. I. Bittker and M. J. Mcmahon, Jr., *Federal Income Taxation of Individuals*, New York: Warren Gorham & Lamont Tax Series (1988), 1–26 (noting that Judge Hand's "central message … is widely accepted").

35 See P. F. Olson, *Now That You've Caught the Bus, What Are You Going to Do With It? Observations From the Frontlines, the Sidelines and Between the Lines, So to Speak.* 2006 E. N. Griswold Lecture Before the American College of Tax Counsel, 60 *Tax Law* 567 (2007). Ms. Olson, former Undersecretary for Tax Policy, opined that tax avoidance is not evil. *Id.* at 567.

36 M. Brooks and J. Head, "Tax Avoidance: In Economics, Law and Public Choice", in G. S. Cooper (ed.), *Tax Avoid-ance and the Rule of Law*, Amsterdam: IBFD Publications (1997), 78.

37 G. Trixier, "Definition, Scope and Importance of International Tax Evasion", 1 *Council of Europe, Colloquy on International Tax Avoidance and Evasion* 1 (1980).

38 See J. C. L. Huiskamp, "Definition, Scope, and Importance of International Tax Avoidance", *Council of Europe*, n.37, at 1, 7 (referring to a tax increase as a fiscal law penalty).

39 Former ABA Tax Section President James Holden stated:

Many of us have been concerned with the recent proliferation of tax shelter products marketed to corpora-tions. … The marketing of these products tears at the fabric of the tax law. Many individual tax lawyers with whom I have spoken express a deep sense of personal regret that this level of Code gamesmanship goes on.

J. P. Holden, Dealing With the Aggressive Corporate Tax Shelter Problem, 1999 Erwin N. Griswold Lecture Before the American College of Tax Counsel, 52 *Tax Law* 369 (1999).

40 See Braithwaite, n.5, at 117.

41 S. Plasschaert, "Ways and Means to Improve European and Wider International Cooperation Against Tax Evasion and Avoidance, With Particular Reference to Transfer Pricing Within Multinational Enterprises", in *Council of Europe*, n.37, at 1, 9; F. Vanistendael, "Judicial Interpretation and the Role of Anti-Abuse Provisions in Tax Law", *Tax Avoidance and the Rule of Law*, n.36, at 131, 132.

42 G. Cooper, Conflicts, "Challenges, and Choices – the Rule of Law and AntiAvoidance Rules", *Tax Avoidance and the Rule of Law*, n.36, at 13, 27. Belgium and France are examples. *Id.*

are free to choose "la voie la moins imposée."[43] This is also known as the "fiscally least burdened" route.[44] Even today in countries like Australia, which statutorily requires that a purposeful interpretation of tax law must be preferred to a literal interpretation,[45] the general right to plan is recognized.[46] Planning to reduce one's tax liability is fully ingrained in the legal and social culture.

Judges around the world have proclaimed that tax planning to reduce one's liability to pay tax is an entitlement.[47] No one has a moral duty to pay any more than the law requires;[48] taxpayers consequently pay less than they would otherwise owe.[49] Indeed, transactions that have no apparent purpose other than to avoid tax are justified because "there is nothing wrong in companies or shareholders entering, if they can, into transactions for the purpose of avoiding or relieving them from taxation."[50] Tax planning is accomplished through the freedom to choose the *form* of the transaction that the taxpayer enters into.[51] The most illuminating description of this process was provided by Judge Barwick of the Australian High Court when he stated, "[T]he [taxpayer] has every right to *mould* the transaction into which he is about to enter into a *form* which satisfies the requirements of the statute."[52]

Thus, tax avoidance accomplished by gaming the system is not only acceptable, but legitimate. In the words of Judge Learned Hand, tax avoiders "do right."[53] Case law at times even suggests a kind of admiration for the clever scheme.[54] This is because the traditional view is that the duty to pay tax is perceived in a most limited way because tax legislation is mere pragmatism lacking any "universal moral imperative."[55] Many perceive legislation in general, and tax legislation even more so, as being the result of political compromise without any claim to universal truth.[56] Tax avoidance, to the contrary, is rooted in a core individual right. The right can be seen in the light of two principles: "the freedom to engage in contractual arrangements and the rule that only laws, adopted by [the legislature], legitimate the levying of taxes."[57] The first principle recognizes a taxpayer's right to choose the form of the transaction. The second principle contains the implicit assumption that tax statutes must be certain of scope and that they are subject to strict or literal interpretation.[58] The underlying moral principles that support tax avoidance restrict the value of argumentation based on intent and purpose of the act. Even where legislative purpose in the interpretation of tax statutes is required, it is still viewed with skepticism.[59]

---

43 The lesser taxed way. See Plasschaert, n.41, at 9; Vanistendael, n.41, at 136. This standard led Belgium to enact a GAAR in 1993. *Id.*

44 Plasschaert, n.41, at 9.

45 Acts Interpretation Act of 1901, 1984, ss. 15AA (Austl.) (requiring courts to interpret federal legislation to prefer an interpretation that promotes the purpose or object of the Act to one that does not).

46 J. Waincymer, "The Australian Tax Avoidance Experience and Responses: A Critical Review", *Tax Avoidance and the Rule of Law*, n.36, at 247, 250.

47 *Comm'r of Taxation of Austl. v. Westraders Proprietary Ltd.* (1980) 144 C.L.R. 55 (Austl.).

48 *Helvering v. Gregory*, 69 F.2d 809, 810 (2d Cir. 1934).

49 *Inland Revenue Comm'rs v. Westminster* [1935] A.C. I (H.L.).

50 *Jacques v. Comm'r of Taxation of Austl.* (1924) 34 C.L.R. 328, 362 (Austl.).

51 Westraders, 144 C.L.R. at 60.

52 *Id.* (emphasis added).

53 *Comm'r v. Newman*, 159 F.2d 848, 850–51 (2d Cir. 1947) (Hand, J., dissenting).

54 Lord Tomlin spoke of the "ingenuity" of the taxpayer: Westminster, [1935] A.C. 1.

55 See Oliver, n.23, at 174.

56 This is what leads textualists today to favor literal interpretation of statutes. See, e.g. A. Scalia, *A Matter of Interpretation: Federal Courts and the Law*, A. Gutmann (ed.), Princeton: Princeton University Press (1997), 17.

57 Plasschaert, n.41, at 9.

58 For a general history of interpretation of tax statutes in the US and the UK, see Barker, n.9, at 826–32.

59 Grbich, n.7, at 105–12.

The twin objects of literal interpretation, certainty and continuity – that is, that the status quo should not be disturbed – support the view that a tax savings generated by a legal form is a property right. A rights theory of avoidance treats the tax statute as "a value-neutral tool to be used by lawyers, administrators, or judges for particular ends of their choosing."[60] In addition, all debate is fairly well contained in a setting dominated by the legal profession and sequestered from the public, who are largely ignorant of the particulars.

The benign attitude towards avoidance and aggressive tax planning is widespread and exerts a powerful influence on societies.[61] Phillip Jans suggested, "*[l]a fraude est contraire aux droit aux fisc, l'evasion s'oppose seulement à ses interests*."[62] Whereas evasion deprives governments of what is legally theirs, avoidance merely raises the state's concern that taxes may not be imposed properly.

The moral posturing of tax avoidance relies on a deception. Tax law in the modem democratic world is based on each citizen's duty as a citizen to pay a fair share of the burden of government without privilege or exemption from tax.[63] Democracies are founded upon the critically important principles of fairness and equality in tax. These principles were inextricably linked to representative government.[64] Indeed, the public duty to pay taxes is established in many constitutional provisions that provide that each person is bound to contribute his proportion, or that each person is bound to contribute in proportion to his means.[65]

The importance of these norms of taxation to the contribution of the sometimes painful birth of democracies, in cases like the United States and the French Republic, and the importance of the principle of ability to pay leading to the income tax system cannot be understated.[66] These core values of democratic societies are in direct contrast with the lack of moral censure of the traditional, accepted view of tax avoidance.

Most people recognize their duty to file the most accurate return possible and to pay their appropriate share to the government.[67] A sizeable minority, however, state that their primary goal is to minimize their taxes,[68] and these attempts at minimization sometimes take the form of evasion or avoidance. For those who primarily derive income from wages and who therefore bear the brunt of taxes, tax avoidance is not a victimless crime. A legal rule that views tax savings in accordance with formal compliance with the statute establishes a right for one group that raises at the same time a corresponding obligation for another group.[69] The majority of dutiful taxpayers end up assuming a larger portion of the costs of government than do the avoiders and evaders. This outcome mocks the social values of the income tax in a democratic society.

---

60 J.W. Hurst, *Dealing With Statutes,* New York: Columbia University Press (1982), 39.

61 See Braithwaite, n.5, at 13–14, 142–3.

62 English translation: "Evasion runs counter to the rights of the state, avoidance harms its interests." Plasschaert, n.41, at 9. Les transtats indirects des benefies entre soci6t6s interdependentes, 118 Bruylant, Brussels 1976 (translated in Plasschaert, n.41, at 9).

63 For example, the Bolivian Constitution declared, "[t]he Taxes shall be fairly imposed, without either exception or privilege." Const. of the Bolivian Republic of 1826, tit. XI, cl. 1H, reprinted in *Constitutions That Made History,* A. P. Blaustein and J. A. Sigler (eds), New York: Paragone House Publishers (1988), 180.

64 See J. Locke, *Two Treatises of Government,* T. I. Cook (ed.), New York: Haffner (1947), 193.

65 See generally Barker, n.2, at 8–9 (discussing the notion of equality and the Constitution).

66 See generally *Id.* at 9. See also Barker, n.9, at 860–1.

67 K. A. Kinsey, "Measurement Bias or Honest Disagreement?" Problems of Validating Measures of Tax Evasion 6, Am. B. Found., Working Paper No. 8811 (1988).

68 *Id.*

69 See W. Hohfeld, "Some Fundamental Legal Conceptions as Applied in Judicial Reasoning", 23 *Yale Law Journal* 16 (1913).

The problem with tax avoidance is the problem of a moral perspective that leads to an equality of tax opportunity for only a few. The liberal tradition of law guarantees the same possibilities to avoid for all taxpayers. This, however, is formal equality only, or equality before the law, and only the well-to-do and well-informed can realize this advantage. The law thus protects the strong. With due regard to Learned Hand, he got it wrong. Democratic society will never be able to effectively tax income according to a taxpayer's means without turning the perceived morality of tax avoidance upside down and inside out.

The distinction between tax evasion and tax avoidance

The liberal rights view of law also biases the way avoidance and evasion are perceived. It does this by misconceiving the problem of avoidance-making avoidance separate from and unrelated to evasion. Examining avoidance without the lens of liberal moral ideology will show its underlying affinity to evasion.

Tax avoidance can be approached by determining what it is not-that is, criminal tax fraud or evasion. In examining the approach different nations take to distinguish between tax avoidance and evasion, care must be taken with vocabulary because certain terms are used differently. It is safe to say that there are three different categories of conduct involved. The first is tax evasion, fraud fiscal in France and Steuerhinterziehung in Germany, which describes criminal behavior. The second is tax avoidance, called simply tax avoidance in the UK and called illegitimate, impermissible tax avoidance in the US, evasion fiscale in France and Stearumaehung in Germany.[70] Tax avoidance describes "legal" but unsuccessful tax planning.[71] Last, there is permissible or legitimate tax avoidance, tax planning, or tax minimization, which denotes fully appropriate, successful tax planning. In order to keep the discussion intelligible, I shall refer to criminal conduct as evasion, to unsuccessful tax planning as avoidance, and to successful tax planning as minimization.

National laws on tax evasion are commonplace. In the United States, the tax code criminalizes the "willful" violation of the tax law. Section 7201[72] imposes criminal sanctions on "any person who wilfully attempts … in any manner to evade or defeat any tax."[73] Criminal sanctions can be imposed for the willful failure to collect or pay tax under Section 7202[74] or for the willful failure to pay an estimated tax, file a return or supply information under Section 7203.[75] Section 7206 prohibits the willful making or aiding in the preparation of a false or fraudulent statement or return.[76]

In a criminal prosecution under Section 7201, the government must prove beyond a reasonable doubt that the taxpayer voluntarily failed to report transactions that he was engaged in truthfully and accurately, that the taxpayer's conduct was intentional and willful, and that this led to an understatement of tax or a tax deficiency.[77] In a criminal prosecution under Section 7206, the government must prove the defendants made or aided in filling a return that was false or fraudulent as to a material matter.[78]

---

70 See Vanistendael, n.41, at 131 n. 1.
71 See *Id.* at 131; Plasschaert, n.41, at 9; C. Whitehouse, *Revenue Laws: Principles and Practice* (Croydon: Tolley, 2001, 1983).
72 I.R.C. § 7201 (2006).
73 I.R.C. § 7201.
74 I.R.C. § 7202 (2006).
75 I.R.C. § 7202 (2006).
76 I.R.C. § 7206(a) (2006).
77 *Sansone v. United States*, 380 U.S. 343, 351 (1965).
78 I.R.C. § 7206(1), (2). See *United States v. Dahlstrom*, 713 F.2d 1423, 1426–27 (9th Cir. 1983).

The unifying principle of criminal liability is the wilfulness requirement.[79] Though at one time willfulness was understood in terms of "an act done with a bad or evil purpose,"[80] the modern judicial standard is phrased in terms of "a voluntary, intentional violation of a known legal duty."[81] Three elements are clearly required in order to establish willfulness: (1) a voluntary action, (2) intentional conduct, and (3) knowledge of that which is required by law.[82]

The traditional approach to distinguishing tax avoidance and tax minimization on the one hand from tax evasion on the other hand, is to recognize that tax avoidance and tax minimization are attempts to reduce one's taxes by "lawful" means. Whether or not the conduct is successful, the view is that the "behavior is perfectly legal."[83] Thus, tax avoidance, as contrasted with tax effective minimization, is a lawful activity that is simply not effective (does not accomplish the expected result) for tax purposes.

These confident assertions are simply not a complete and accurate reflection of the nature of tax avoidance, however. To say that evasion is illegal whereas illegitimate avoidance that does not work is legal is terribly misleading. Where a taxpayer is not entitled to the fruits of his plan, it can hardly be said that the taxpayer's position is "legal," that it conforms to the law, is according to the law, is not forbidden or discountenanced by the law, is good and effectual in law.[84] It is instead "illegal," that is, not authorized by law, contrary to the law, contrary to the principles of the law.[85] The difference between avoidance and evasion is not about the legal outcome but is about the characterization of the taxpayer's conduct, that is, a description of the legal consequences of having engaged in tax avoidance. Tax avoidance is properly described as noncriminal behavior, not as legal behavior.[86]

Doctrine recognizes a clear line between noncriminal avoidance and criminal evasion. The Internal Revenue Service Manual provides that the distinction between evasion and avoidance is fine, but definite.[87] The line, however, cannot be drawn in respect to the first requirement of a voluntary and intentional action that leads to an understatement of tax liability since that standard is easily satisfied by the avoider.[88] The line must be drawn in regard to the truthfulness or accuracy of the taxpayer's representations and in regard to the question of whether the conduct results in a violation of a known legal duty.

---

79 *United States v. Murdock*, 290 U.S. 389, 397–98 (1933), overruled on other grounds by *Murphy v. Waterfront Comm'n of N.Y. Harbor*, 378 U.S. 52 (1964).

80 See *United States v. Bishop*, 412 U.S. 346, 359–61 (1973).

81 *United States v. Pomponio*, 429 U.S. 10, 12 (1976). See also Bishop, 412 U.S. at 359–61. Though Pomponio dealt with a prosecution under Section 7206, the same standard for willfulness has been applied under Section 7701. See *United States v. Kinig*, 616 F.2d 1034, 1039 (8th Cir. 1980).

82 See M. I. Salzman, *IRS Practice and Procedure*, ch. 7, rev. 2d ed., New York: Warren Gorham & Lamont Tax Series (2002).

83 Vanistendael, n.41, at 132.

84 *Black's Law Dictionary*, 4th ed., St. Paul: West Publishing Co. (1968), 1038.

85 *Id*. at 882.

86 The distinction can be important. Even though tax avoidance may not be subject to criminal sanctions, it may well be subject to civil penalties. For example, a bill is before Congress to codify the economic substance test. The bill would add Section 6662B, which would add a substantial penalty where transactions lacked economic substance. Export Products Not Jobs Act, S. 96, 1 10th Cong. §§ 201–02 (2007), available at www.govtrack.us/data/us/bills.text/I 10/s/s96.pdf

87 Internal Revenue Service Manual § 9.1.3.3.2.1 (1997).

88 Tax avoidance is sometimes defined as an activity purposefully entered into to avoid taxes. See Cooper, n.42, at 28. The presence or absence of this particular motive is not relevant to the issue of whether the taxpayer engaged in voluntary and intentional acts.

A legal conclusion that the proper tax treatment is not in accord with the taxpayer's representation of the transaction is, in a sense, a finding that the taxpayer's representations were not true. Doctrine, however, tends to mix the notion of truthfulness with that of knowledge; these notions are often depicted indirectly as questions of openness and disclosure versus secrecy and concealment. "[T]he term 'tax evasion' can be reserved for conduct that entails deception, concealment, destruction of records and the like, while 'tax avoidance' refers to behavior that the taxpayer hopes will serve to reduce his tax liability but that he is prepared to disclose fully to the IRS."[89]

Others make this point as to the different nature of tax avoidance even more forcefully: In engaging in tax avoidance, the taxpayer has no reason to worry about possible detection; quite the contrary, it is often imperative that he makes a detailed statement about his transactions in order to ensure that he gets the tax reduction he desires.[90]

This assessment is only valid from a very limited perspective. Dissimulation is the handmaiden of avoidance. Whereas the "tax avoider" may have nothing to worry about in terms of criminal prosecution, he is still concerned about detection because undiscovered tax avoidance is successful tax avoidance. Taxpayers have substantial incentives to conceal. After all, the taxpayer's goal in tax planning is tax savings, and these savings are not only an important factor to ensure the profitability of the transaction but, in many cases, may have been the only reason for entering into the transaction in the first place.[91] Additionally, in many cases, in order to achieve significant tax savings, taxpayers incur substantial transactional costs that would not have been incurred but for the tax savings.[92] For example, in a recent case, a taxpayer incurred $24,783,800 in transaction costs to carry out a prearranged purchase-sale transaction that was planned to yield tax savings of $93,500,000.[93] These costs amounted to 26.5 per cent of the expected tax savings.

What is really meant when it is said that taxpayers disclose? Taxpayers do report the results of the transactions on their tax returns in accordance with their construction of the applicable tax results. Returns may not disclose, however, the details about the transactions that the administration and courts may consider critical elements for understanding the "true" nature of the activity in terms of the statutory provisions. Relevant information may also be presented in different parts of the return, thus making it difficult for administrators to comprehensively grasp the plan.

To illustrate, take the case of captive insurance companies.[94] In *Carnation Co. v. Commissioner*,[95] the company entered into casualty and property insurance contracts with American Home, a recognized independent insurance company.[96] As part of a prearranged deal, American Home reinsured ninety percent of the risks with Three Flowers, Carnation's wholly-owned Bermuda subsidiary.[97] Due to American Home's concerns about Three Flowers' ability to meet its

---

89 Bittker and Mcmahon, n.34, at 1–25.

90 A. Sandmo, "The Theory of Tax Evasion: A Retrospective Review", 58 *National Tax Journal* 643, 645 (2005).

91 See, e.g., *Compaq Computer Corp. v. Comm'r*, 277 F.3d 778 (5th Cir. 2001) (analyzing a prearranged transaction to buy shares before the declaration of a dividend and sell those shares immediately after in order to obtain the dividend and increase the taxpayer's foreign tax credits).

92 See U.S. Dep't of the Treasury, *The Problem of Corporate Tax Shelters: Discussion, Analysis and Legislative Proposals* (1999), 23, available at www.treas.gov/offices/tax-policy/library/ctswhite.pdf.

93 See *ASA Investerings P'ship v. Comm'r*, 76 T.C.M. (CCH) 325 (1998).

94 For an account of captive insurance and tax avoidance, see W. B. Barker, "Federal Income Taxation and Captive Insurance", 6 *Virginia Tax Review* 267 (1986).

95 640 F.2d 1010 (9th Cir. 1981).

96 *Id.* at 1012.

97 *Id.*

commitments, Carnation undertook to provide $3 million in additional capital to Three Flowers on demand.[98]

Carnation reported the tax results of the transactions to the Internal Revenue Service (IRS) according to its claimed construction of the transaction. Thus, Carnation's return disclosed deductible insurance premiums. Any examination of Carnation's accounts would have revealed that these payments had been made to an unrelated insurance company. Three Flowers' accounts would have disclosed insurance income and expenses, which, if ever repatriated, would have been included in Carnation's consolidated income as foreign source dividend income and increased Carnation's foreign tax credit limitation.[99] The information provided at the time would not likely have included the facts that Three Flowers "insured" its parent's risk or that Carnation had provided a guarantee of additional capitalization in order to ensure that Three Flowers could cover its parent's risks.[100]

The court found that Carnation's contract with American Home was not insurance and that the premiums received by Three Flowers were not income derived from insurance.[101] The critical facts necessary to that conclusion were the parent-subsidiary relationship and the capitalization guarantee. Though the taxpayer was willing to disclose this information upon audit, it certainly would have benefited from the government's ignorance because assessment of Carnation's situation for tax purposes without these facts was misleading and would have made the assessment of Carnation's proper liability for tax impossible. Discovery by the Internal Revenue Service without careful auditing was not possible.[102] Yet, there is no duty to disclose unless required by statute.[103]

One reason Carnation's tax plan went awry was because the accommodation party, American Home, insisted that Carnation guarantee the losses of its captive insurance company. It was that guarantee that labeled the transaction a sham. A guarantee by Carnation of its own losses establishes a lack of relation between the legal form of the transaction, insurance, and its obvious consequences. In other words, no one could honestly believe that he had "insured" himself if he were responsible for his own losses. However, there was never any hint of wrongdoing in this case.

The absence of disapproval is even more remarkable in even more questionable tax avoidance planning. An illuminating example comes from *E.L. Du Pont de Nemours & Co. v. United States*,[104] a case that involved the proper application of the transfer pricing regime of the Code. Section 482 empowers the Secretary of the Treasury to reallocate income and deductions among related entities in order to prevent evasion or to clearly reflect the income of the entities.[105] Du Pont's plan, which was subsequently executed, was to set up a wholly-owned subsidiary [DISA]

---

98 *Id.*

99 See I.R.C. § 904 (2006).

100 See n.102.

101 Carnation Co., 640 F.2d at 1013–14.

102 Section 6038 requires that taxpayers who are in control of a foreign corporation report certain information with respect to the activities of that corporation to the IRS. I.R.C. § 6038 (2006). This includes information on related party transactions. In the early days of captive insurance companies, taxpayers assumed that the use of intermediary unrelated insurance companies shielded them from this reporting requirement. [Author's experience.]

103 For example, under US law, information with respect to certain "reportable and listed" transactions is required to be reported. I.R.C. § 6407 (2006). See also I.R.C. § 6662A (2006) (accuracy-related penalty).

104 608 F.2d 445 (Ct. Cl. 1979)

105 I.R.C. § 482 (2006).

in Switzerland to purchase US manufactured goods from the parent company and to sell these goods to related European distributors.

In the process of developing the strategy, those promoting it faced substantial opposition from Du Pont's operating divisions due to their view that the scheme conflicted with the appropriate allocation of profits among the divisions of Du Pont.[106] Consensus was achieved only because all were convinced that the plan would achieve significant tax savings and because it was agreed that the profits of the various divisions would be recalculated ignoring the role of DISA, showing the economic contributions of the various divisions for performance evaluation and compensation purposes.[107]

It was openly acknowledged that the resulting price to DISA was "artificially low"[108] or "fictitious."[109] There was also concern that these prices were significantly lower than those charged to other related entities.[110] Du Pont's Treasury Department, however, argued as follows:

> It would seem to be desirable to bill the tax haven subsidiary at less than an "arm's length" price because: (1) the pricing might not be challenged by the revenue agent; (2) if the pricing is challenged, we might sustain such transfer prices; (3) if we cannot sustain the prices used, a transfer price will be negotiated which should not be more than an "arm's length" price and might well be less; thus we would be no worse off than we would have been had we billed at the higher price.[111]

At trial, the key Treasury Department officer, instead of being a little embarrassed over the terms of the scheme, nonchalantly admitted that Du Pont would have transferred ninety-nine percent of the profit to DISA if they could have gotten it by the Internal Revenue Service.[112]

The conduct in Du Pont suggests a close affinity between tax avoidance and evasion. How close to the line did Du Pont go? Apparently, not even close. The court reported that the reason it described "the special status of DISA as a subsidiary intended and operated to accumulate profits without much regard to the function it performed or their real worth" was simply to show how difficult it was to show comparable arm's length prices."[113] The court explained that "[i]t was not that there was anything 'illegal' or immoral in Du Pont's plan; it is simply that the plan made it very difficult, perhaps impossible, to satisfy the controlling Treasury regulations under Section 482."[114] In one sense, it was completely proper to ignore the taxpayer's motivation because Section 482 is concerned with the economic substance of intergroup transfers and not with the taxpayer's intent or purpose. The court's gratuitous remarks on the taxpayer's morality, however, illuminate the moral perspective of the judge. The liberal moral perspective evidenced in Du Pont goes to the very heart of the avoidance/evasion question. In order to be evasion, the taxpayer's conduct must be willful. Willfulness depends on whether the taxpayer intentionally violated a known legal duty. Though the court in Du Pont extensively quoted the somewhat brazen comments on gaming the tax system which analyzed the risks of failure and

---

106 E.I. Du Pont de Nemours & Co., 608 F.2d at 447.
107 *Id.*
108 *Id.*
109 *E.I. Du Pont de Nemours & Co. v. United States*, 42 A.F.T.R.2d 78-5081, 78-5089 (Ct. Cl. 1978).
110 El. Du Pontde Nemours & Co., 608 F.2d at 447.
111 *Id.* at 447, n.4.
112 *Id.* at 448, n.7.
113 *Id.* at 449.
114 *Id.*

the likelihood of success,[115] and those that acknowledged that one would have done more if one thought one could get away with it, or cited the fact that Du Pont kept two sets of books – one for tax purposes and one for economic purposes, these factors were irrelevant to the question of whether Du Pont violated a known legal duty. The morality of tax avoidance has made this kind of subjective intent irrelevant. Even more surprising is the irrelevance of the taxpayer's expression of the opinion that the resulting price was "artificially low" or "fictitious" where the essence of the issue under Section 482 is whether the taxpayer had transferred at an arm's length price. The reason is that these statements are only the subjective views of taxpayers. It is only the objective characterization of taxpayers' conduct that matters. This objective characterization is from the point of view of the legal characterization of a taxpayer's representation of his situation.

The Supreme Court stated in *United States v. Bishop* that the reason Congress provided a willfulness requirement for criminal tax evasion was to "construct penalties that separate the purposeful tax violator from the well-meaning, but easily confused, mass of taxpayers."[116] Sophisticated tax planners who intentionally game the system hardly fit into this category of "the well-meaning, but easily confused, mass of taxpayers." Yet sophisticated taxpayers receive the equal protection of this doctrine. That is because an actual bona fide misconception of the law is a defense if "the ignorance or mistake negatives the purpose, knowledge, belief, reckless-ness or negligence, required to establish a material element of the offense."[117]

Du Pont illustrates the breadth of protection that a misconception of law can afford. When one reviews the rationale behind the plan, one cannot help but see expressed an unbridled optimism that this plan will work. Tax avoiders bolstered by a certain moral perspective are confident that they are on the side of right. Practically any argument will establish a bona fide misconception and save them from a charge of fraud. Their confidence is not unrealistic, for they employ attorneys who have been trained to argue any side in an adversarial system. President Roosevelt's cynical remarks are close to the mark: "'[t]ax avoidance' … means that you hire a $250,000-fee lawyer, and he changes the word 'evasion' into the word 'avoidance.'"[118] Accord-ing to the court in Du Pont, there is not even the slightest moral duty to try to get the transfer price right.[119]

The captive insurance company issue demonstrates a quite different aspect of the miscon-ception of law defense. The tax law, then and now, distinguishes provisions for self-insurance reserves, not deductible by taxpayers, and insurance premium payments, which are deductible.[120] The captive insurance industry represented a high degree of tax sophistication. At the time when captive insurance companies started to become popular, those involved with setting up

---

115 Indeed, books on tax planning recommend that one must consider the odds of success just as a businessman considers them on making normal business decisions every day. *Michie's Federal Tax Handbook*, Vol. 1, J. E. Gibson (ed.), Charlottesville, VA: The Michie Company (1970), 451.

116 412 U.S. 346, 361 (1973).

117 Model Penal Code § 2.04 (1985). See *Battjes v. United States*, 172 F.2d 1, 4 (6th Cir. 1949).

118 A. M. Schlesinger, Jr., *The Politics of Upheaval,* Boston: Houghton Mifflin & Co. (1960), 333.

119 Section 482 is a mixture of several important principles and policies of income tax law including tax avoidance principles, the assignment of income doctrine, general deduction theories, and clear reflection of net income under the parties accounting method. Boris I. Bittker and James S. Eustice, "Federal Income Taxation of Corpo-rations and Shareholders I 13.20(1)(b)" (7th ed., 2006). Though the use of Section 482 is only available to the government (Treas. Reg. § 1.482–1A(b)(3) (1968)), it does not follow that the taxpayer can disregard general tax principles and policies in setting its prices. Indeed, Treas. Reg. § 1.482-1 A(a)(3) permits taxpayers to report a price different from those actually charged on a timely filed return if necessary to reflect an arm's length result.

120 See Barker, n.94, at 274–6.

these corporations were aware of captive insurance's essential nature. For example, in *Mobil Oil Corp. v. United States*,[121] the employee responsible for planning explained:

> Outside insurance, of course, refers to covering insurable risks by paying a premium to a non-affiliated insurance company in return for an agreement that the insurance company would indemnify the insured for losses suffered. Self insurance is usually handled by setting aside premiums out of current earnings into a reserve for self-insurance; losses are charged against this reserve. Self-insurance can also be worked through an insurance affiliate. Under this system, operating subsidiaries pay premiums to an affiliated insurance company.[122]

From the point of view of those in the industry, captive insurance arrangements were unequivocally self insurance, not insurance. But lawyers know that that understanding is immaterial to the question of willfulness because these statements only represent the truth of captive arrangements from the point of view of economics, finance, commercial dealings, or even just plain common sense. It is only, however, from the point of view of the legal characterization of a taxpayer's representation of his situation that willfulness for criminal purposes is determined.

Tax avoidance, as defined in this paper, is the unsuccessful attempt to reduce one's taxes.[123] Though taxpayers are proven wrong in their conclusion, it is obvious that taxpayers do not engage in tax fraud under current doctrine. This is true because, even though taxpayers engage in voluntary tax planning, even though taxpayers intentionally engage in artificial and manipulative conduct in an attempt to reduce their taxes, and even though taxpayers may report strained versions of the facts or little fact at all, taxpayers lack the knowledge of the legal requirements of the tax laws and believe, even though sometimes foolishly, that the plan they have created could work.

Though tax planners might be wrong, their defense to tax fraud is predicated on "an actual, bona fide misconception of the law."[124] Such a misconception is a defense to tax fraud if it negates "the purpose, knowledge, belief, recklessness or negligence required to establish a material element of the offense."[125] In *United States v. Critizer*, the court concluded that "[i]t is settled that when the law is vague or highly debatable, a defendant - actually or impliedly - lacks the requisite intent to violate it."[126] There, even though the defendant was told by the Internal Revenue Service that rent from Indian lands was income, the Bureau of Indian Affairs had informed her that in their opinion it was tax exempt. The result of this intra-governmental disagreement was that the taxpayer did not report the income and, thus, concealed the facts necessary for any IRS determination. According to Critizer, this was not fraud.[127] Similarly, novel questions of tax law[128] or unique legal questions have been held as a matter of law to negate fraud.

Yet tax planners by necessity often knowingly operate close to the line. Just as obviously, those who do not succeed have crossed the line, whether they are detected or not. The Supreme

---

121 8 Cl. Ct. 555 (1985).
122 See Barker, n.94, at 284.
123 See Part III.
124 See *Battjes v. United States*, 172 F.2d 1,4 (6th Cir. 1949).
125 Model Penal Code § 2.04 (1985).
126 *United States v. Critizer*, 498 F.2d 1160, 1162 (4th Cir. 1974).
127 *Id*.
128 *United States v. Critizer*, 498 F.2d 1160, 1162 (4th Cir. 1974).

Court once concluded that in criminal matters it is not unfair "to require that one who deliberately goes perilously close to an area of prescribed conduct shall take the risk that he may cross the line."[129] This doctrine has not been applied to tax avoidance, however.

Thus, whereas the tax evader solely exploits the uncertainty of detection and not the law, the tax avoider exploits both the uncertainty of the tax law and of detection. As long as a case for uncertainty of the law can be established in tax, the case is one of avoidance. The liberal tradition's ideological insistence on certainty in the application of tax laws is also the basis for distinguishing tax avoidance from evasion. For many, this result is obvious. It relies, however, on a one-sided or incomplete view of tax legislation.

Tax law's domain is not simply the domain of the finite words of the statute. The tax law is a totality of language, purposes and intent that aims to achieve certain social goals. Tax avoidance's domain is the shadow world that results from the incongruence between statutory language and the context, intent or purpose of the legislation.[130] Words separated from their context and divorced from their purposes are words without a point of view. Or, to put it another way, they are words that the interpreter can choose any point of view from which to interpret them. Conscious tax avoidance exploits this discontinuity. The tax avoider's art may be described as the discovery either before or after the fact of formal or subjectively possible interpretations creating a veritable twilight zone of ambiguity outside the real possibilities of the statute that accord with the legislature's intent and purpose. The accepted ideology of tax avoidance conditions the judge to accept these other constructions at face value, thus formally rendering the statute vague. Consequently, there can be no fraud.

Conclusion

In America, the liberal ideology of individual liberty has been rejuvenated. Strict or literal interpretation of tax statutes is now the norm. This has two consequences for tax avoidance. The first is that courts are much more likely to reach a decision based on the "plain meaning" of the statute. In such cases, taxpayers are free to exploit interpretations that contradict the context, intent and purpose of the act. The second involves the situation where there is no plain meaning. Literalism is only a preferred mode of interpretation. Where the statute is ambiguous, the context, intent and purpose of the legislation may be considered.

In these cases, courts recognize the mandate to make the norm actual in terms of the legislation's intent and purpose.[131] When the law uses concepts like arm's length pricing, the interpreters, including the taxpayer, are directed to report their transactions in accordance with legislative values. Whether these values are described in terms of legislative intent, purpose or the spirit of the law, they are generally acknowledged to be part of the law. Yet the liberal ideology of individual rights robs these values of their full normative force. A taxpayer may safely disregard these values without being accused of fraud.

Rethinking tax evasion can change the incidence of avoidance in our society because some avoiders clearly cross the line. Putting avoiders in jail is not the point of this essay, however. Instead, the purpose of this essay is to expose the ideology that underpins tax avoidance. It is also to confront a system that tolerates aggressive game playing. Exposing this ideology to the

---

129 *Boyce Motor Lines, Inc. v. United States*, 342 U.S. 337, 340 (1952).

130 *See* n.9 and accompanying text.

131 See *Johnson v. United States*, 163 F. 30, 32 (1st Cir. 1908). See also *Corn Prods. Ref. Co. v. Comm'r*, 350 U.S. 46, 52 (1955) (gains from hedging transactions held analogous to inventory sales in order to achieve Congress' purpose).

forces of democracy is the first step to dealing with tax avoidance. A focus on this ideology can make it the object of a struggle that can produce considerable advances in applying tax law in a fair and equitable manner. Because this ideology encourages taxpayers to try to avoid taxation, and discourages the government from dealing effectively with avoidance, its demise can change the power of avoidance to undermine taxation.

Democratic societies recognize that individual freedom is only possible under the rule of law, but individual freedom means more than the rights of private autonomy. Real liberty's truest expression can only be found in a democratic society; it depends on the social rights of citizens, acting together, to determine the content of the law under which all individuals are to exercise their freedom. The American people acting through Congress have mandated taxation under a principle of equality. The task of jurists is to make both aspects of freedom real through their decisions. The principle thrust of this paper's critique is that jurists have failed to advance through tax a society that is committed to maintaining and enforcing substantive equality for its entire people.

Acknowledgements

This paper was first published in the Loyola University Chicago Law Journal (Volume 20, Issue 2, Winter 2009). The substance of this paper was presented at the Loyola University Chicago Law Journal Conference, Tax Law in a Liberal Democracy: Exploring the Relationship Between Tax and Good Governance. The author wishes to express special thanks to his co-panelists Lawrence Zelenak and Leo Martinez. Research for this paper was undertaken as part of an ATAX Research Fellowship as a visiting professor at the University of New South Wales.

25

ETHICAL ISSUES IN THE USE OF TAX INTERMEDIARIES

Jane Frecknall-Hughes

Overview

The work of tax intermediaries continues to attract attention and generate significant studies, particularly because of the alleged involvement of tax practitioners in tax avoidance. A 2008 study by the Organisation for Economic Co-operation and Development (OECD) of the role of tax intermediaries in tax compliance acknowledges that while intermediaries play a vital role in all tax systems by helping taxpayers to understand and comply with their tax obligations in an increasingly complex and regulated world, nevertheless the behaviour of intermediaries also gives rise to ethical concerns, related chiefly to their involvement in facilitating tax avoidance deemed aggressive or unacceptable by revenue authorities. The cases of Starbucks, Amazon, Google and Facebook, highlighted by the media initially in 2012, emphasise the continuing relevance of examining the work of intermediaries, as senior members of large accounting and tax firms were interrogated by the UK Government's Public Accounts Committee as to the exact nature of their advice to such multinational clients and why it resulted in so little tax being paid to the UK tax authorities.[1] The activities of intermediaries proved, arguably, a significant driver behind the OECD's work on Base Erosion and Profit Shifting. Thus tax intermediaries help taxpayers comply with the law and at the same time appear to help taxpayers find ways of not complying. This chapter explores in depth these complex dimensions within the work of tax intermediaries, by reference to the extensive literature on this topic.

Introduction

It is accepted that tax intermediaries have a very important role to play in all tax systems, as they help taxpayers to comply with their tax obligations – regulations which are rendered increasingly complicated by their volume and nature and which taxpayers often have difficulty in understanding (Doyle et al. 2013; OECD 2008). However, tax intermediaries are also often responsible for orchestrating artificial schemes that achieve compliance with the letter of the law but which undermine the spirit of the law and (often unstated) government policy and

---

1 This does inherently bring into question the quality of the advice provided. See Frecknall-Hughes and Moizer (2015) for a discussion of quality issues.

intention. Such schemes are now frequently referred to as 'unacceptable' or 'aggressive' tax planning, and if unchecked, negatively impact on the amount of tax revenue authorities can collect and impair the functioning of global tax systems (OECD 2008: 4). This type of activity was described by the UK Chancellor of the Exchequer in his 2012 Budget speech as "morally repugnant" (Krouse and Baker 2012). Reduced tax revenues result in a reduction in the provision of public goods and services (such as unemployment benefits, hospitals, policing, roads, etc.). Tax intermediaries who devise and promote tax avoidance schemes thus deprive society (especially the less well-off) of those goods and services, which is unethical, particularly when a continuing global economic crisis has put governments worldwide under immense pressure to maximise tax revenues and thus mitigate the reduction in the provision of public goods and services.

There is, however, a lack of clarity about what is meant by the term 'spirit of the law'. Freedman (2012: 635–6) notes:

> If by 'spirit of the law' is meant simply the proper intention of the legislature as discovered by the application of permissible purposive construction, then of course the courts should be finding the spirit of the law and the taxpayer should be abiding by this. But others suggest that the spirit of the law may be found outside the decision of the courts, in terms of what is acceptable to the revenue authorities or current government, or perhaps even non-governmental organizations. This means that there may be a gap between the quite proper interpretation given by the courts (based on the limitations of the system, on language and on the legislative process) and the view of the current revenue authorities on the meaning and intent of the law.

Thus for a tax intermediary aiming to comply with both the letter and spirit of the law, the need to interpret what he/she should do or report may result in attempts to elevate the spirit of the law to a state somewhere beyond legal compliance, although this is a "vague and unenforceable notion" (Freedman 2012: 651). Freedman (2012: 629) also cautions that the solution is not:

> The old cat-and-mouse game of detailed legislation, which often provides opportunities for taxpayers and their advisers to find ways of subverting that very legislation – the game of 'creative compliance' [i.e. 'schemes'].

The involvement of tax intermediaries in avoidance schemes has contributed to an increasing concern about whether their behaviour is ethical or not (Shafer and Simmons 2008). The marketing of dubious tax shelters has resulted in many US firms being investigated for facilitating tax avoidance that revenue authorities have found unacceptable (see Herman 2004).[2] The KPMG tax shelter fraud case in the United States evidences the involvement of tax professionals in such approaches (see Sikka 2010; Sikka and Hampton 2005). Companies too, with the active involvement of their senior executives, have faced allegations of using 'tax havens' or tax shelters to avoid or evade their tax obligations (Sikka 2010; Wilson 2009; Dyreng et al. 2007, 2010; Godar et al. 2005). Additional evidence of ongoing concerns is provided by the 2012 cases of Starbucks, Amazon, Google and Facebook, reported in the British press (see, for example Barford and Holt 2012), with both company executives and their tax advisers being summoned to

2 UK Revenue authorities describe this kind of avoidance variously as 'unacceptable', 'illegitimate', 'illegal', 'aggressive', 'abusive', etc., as discussed in Chapter 2 of this volume.

explain to the UK government's Public Accounts Committee the reason why these companies have allegedly paid little or no corporation tax to the UK revenue authorities (Armitstead 2013; Fuller 2013). At the date of writing this chapter, there are further reports about the alleged agreement made by Google to pay £130m in back taxes relating to the previous ten years – an amount still felt by some to be too little (see, for example Rawlinson 2016).

The term 'tax intermediary' is a relatively recent addition to the list of terms used to describe persons who work in taxation, so it is worthwhile spending a little time considering the various terms and the nature of the market for tax services and looking in more depth at why taxpayers employ professional assistance. The chapter continues by considering these issues.

What is a tax intermediary?

There are many different terms used to describe someone who works in the area of taxation – tax practitioner, tax preparer, tax professional (common in academic literature), tax adviser, tax agent and most recently, tax intermediary. The terms are used interchangeably without any real distinction of meaning (including in this chapter), although, strictly speaking, not all individuals offer the same kind of services. Some terms suggest involvement in work of greater complexity and scope than others; that is, more than just completing a tax return. According to Arzoo (1987, citing the US Joint Committee on Taxation, 1976) a tax professional is any person, or any such person's employee, who prepares, for compensation, all or a substantial portion of a tax return or claim for refund. According to Devos (2012: 5), 'tax practitioner' is a term that:

> covers a diverse group of individuals, business structures and professional groups who provide a range of tax services for their clients. Self-employed and in-house account-ants, tax advisers and registered tax agents, tax agent franchises and legal practitioners in the tax area are all embraced by the term 'tax practitioner'.

Tax practitioners play different roles within the taxation system, ranging from preparing tax returns to send to the tax authorities; responding to queries on such returns from the tax authorities; advising on the arrangement of a taxpayer's affairs (often to minimise the tax payable); acting as a valuer/mediator if disputes over valuations occur (where the tax practitioner is more overtly a negotiator with the revenue authorities); in the UK, sometimes acting as a servant of the tax authorities in situations when Her Majesty's Revenue & Customs (HMRC) might seek to investigate a taxpayer and request a report; and, lastly, as employees of a revenue authority, in the public sector.

The idea of tax practitioners being 'intermediaries' is derived, perhaps, from them occupying a 'space' between taxpayers and a revenue authority, as shown in Figure 25.1. This diagram is used by Frecknall-Hughes and Kirchler (2015) in their argument that the basic relationship among taxpayers, tax practitioners and revenue authorities is one of negotiation.

As Frecknall-Hughes and Kirchler (2015: 300) comment:

> In terms of a tax scenario, the negotiators are the tax practitioner (negotiator 1) and the individual tax authority figure (negotiator 2), acting respectively on behalf of a client (constituent 1) and the taxing authority (as an arm of government, constituent 2). In Figure 25.1, there are six potential relationships, as indicated by the six sets of double arrows, which also indicate possible information flows or exchanges. Each party derives benefits or incurs costs as a result of interaction with other parties. The difference between benefits and costs yields a net outcome to any given party for each

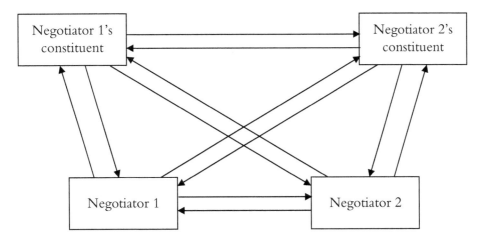

Figure 25.1 Negotiation paradigm.

Source: Developed from Wall Jr (1985: 23).

interaction (*i.e.*, a trade-off). In any interaction, the benefits and costs arise from two sources, namely, the interactions between parties as part of the on-going exchange and the agreement that results from this exchange (the process itself and the outcome of the process). This may vary according to the aims of the individuals involved.

While the authors acknowledge that other theories may explain how tax work operates, negotiation theory is, they contend, better than others, though it is not without flaws.

Tax practitioners working in the private sector will consider that their first duty is to their clients, though there may be some debate or confusion as to whom tax practitioners serve (Hammer 1996; Jackson and Milliron 1989). Devos's 2012 Australian study on the impact of tax practitioners on tax compliance indicated that tax practitioners have been considered to be representatives of both taxpayers and the government; they must act as advocates for their clients but also act as intermediaries in the tax system (see also Yetmar and Eastman 2000; Brody and Masselli 1996; Tomasic and Pentony 1991; Duncan et al. 1989). This creates a multifaceted role with complex ethical dimensions; tax professionals thus owe, in various degrees, a duty to their clients, the government, their firm, their profession, the wider public, and to themselves as individuals or as members of a firm. Some consider that in the United States practitioners act as an arm of the Internal Revenue Service (Brody and Masselli 1996; Duncan et al. 1989). This may reflect the fact that a competent practitioner will consider a taxing authority's likely stance, especially where disputed or unclear issues may be under consideration, which will be reflected in information/advice given to a client about his/her position and the concomitant risks.

Tax professionals will act on behalf of one or more parties, usually one or more clients, who may be clients of long standing where there is regular representation/interaction or may be individuals who seek assistance for a particular, one-off problem. It is common to see a tax practitioner acting on behalf of a client referred to a taxpayer's agent, but an agent, in the true sense of the word, is legally empowered to act without referring matters to his/her principal, although the agent ultimately will be answerable to the principal. In the UK a tax intermediary does not have this power; all taxpayers (including corporate taxpayers, especially under self-assessment) must sign their own tax returns and are ultimately themselves responsible for the information contained therein.

Before going on to analyse conceptually the work of tax practitioners, it is first necessary to examine the nature of the taxation services market in which they work, to establish who exactly is at work there, and also the literature on tax practitioners, to consider what they do and to determine how and why they interact with others.

The nature of the taxation services market

Tax intermediaries offer their services in a very fragmented market, although the extent of this fragmentation varies from country to country. There are many different types of individuals involved; for example, members of professional accountancy bodies whose studies have included taxation (in the UK, members of five different accountancy institutes, one of which has also a Tax Faculty); members of professional taxation bodies (e.g. the UK Chartered Institute of Taxation (CIOT), which has different grades of membership);[3] members of the legal profession, both solicitors and barristers; and former members of a taxing authority who have moved into private practice. Such individuals may work in a variety of entities; for example, as a general accounting, sole practitioner, or as part of a small- or medium-sized accounting firm or a Big Four firm (Deloitte, EY, KPMG and PricewaterhouseCoopers). Persons who have received professional legal training in tax tend to remain within the legal profession, although some are employed in accountancy practices. Practitioners are also found working within the tax/ financial function of commercial enterprises, the size and complexity of which can support such specialist functions – typically multinational groups. Revenue authorities also employ considerable numbers of taxation practitioners, who typically receive internal training within such bodies. The chief characteristics displayed by the tax services' market are a lack of professional monopoly and fragmented professional regulation.

Practitioners who are members of professional bodies are subject, though, to the professional codes of conduct issued by those bodies. For example, in the UK:

> A member is required to serve his client with professional competence and due care within the scope of his engagement letter. The recent public debate on tax avoidance has not changed the member's responsibility to his client. This has been highlighted in the debate surrounding *Mehjoo v. Harben Barker (a firm) and another company* [2013] EWHC 1500 (QB).
>
> *Chartered Institute of Taxation [CIOT] 2014: 38, Section 8.10*[4]

As the above shows, rules tend to be phrased as a series of duties that are morally obligatory for members of the profession, which has always been the case (see Barbour and McDougall 1997; Harwood 1996). However, it remains the case that anyone can set up in business as a tax

---

3 There are six other main bodies professionally involved in taxation in the UK, namely the Association of Taxation Technicians (ATT), the Association of Chartered Certified Accountants (ACCA), the Institute of Chartered Accountants in England and Wales (ICAEW, which has a separate Tax Faculty), the Institute of Chartered Accountants of Scotland (ICAS), the Institute of Indirect Taxation (IIT) and the Society of Trust and Estate Practitioners (STEP). IIT decided in 2012, however, to merge with CIOT. There is also the Worshipful Company of Tax Advisers.

4 The Chartered Institute of Taxation regularly updates its *Professional Code of Conduct*, and a revised version was issued in November 2016, to come into effect from 1 March 2017. The general sentiment of the paragraph cited here from the 2014 version is retained in the 2016 document.

practitioner in the UK, with the same being true elsewhere. The United States, for example, has certified public accountants (CPAs), accountants without the CPA designation, enrolled agents and nationwide tax-preparation chains, such as H. & R. Block (Hemans 1996; Fisher 1994). A similar lack of monopoly and fragmentation of regulation was found by Thuronyi and Vanistendael (1996: 160–3) in their examination of the organisation of the tax profession in Europe, the United States, Canada and Australia. Increasingly, however, this situation is liable to localised variation and change. For example, in the United States, Oregon has required registration of paid tax preparers since 1973, California since 1997, and Maryland since 2008 (see McKerchar et al. 2008), while Federal registration of tax intermediaries became mandatory from 1 January 2011. A range of compliance checks (related to good standing) is also mandatory and, for those intermediaries not licensed by certain professional bodies, competency tests and requirements regarding continuing education have been introduced (see Frecknall-Hughes and McKerchar 2013: 276). Other countries in general have in place more regulation requirements than the UK, of which HMRC are aware: their 2009 consultation document, *Modernising Powers, Deterrents and Safeguards. Working with Tax Agents: A Consultation Document*, does suggest in Chapter 5 that there should be some form of registration for the 12,000 estimated tax practitioners who are currently unregulated by any professional body.

Although, as previously mentioned, increasing regulation is being implemented, it would appear to meet with varying degrees of success, especially in the United States (see Hopkins 2014). Levy (2015: 438–9) comments:

> Of the 142 million individual income tax returns filed in 2011, 79 million were completed by paid preparers, and a majority of those, 42 million, were filled out by preparers who were neither licensed nor regulated. With few – if any – barriers to entry, the field of tax preparation has drawn unscrupulous players.

According to Levy (2015: 439), this kind of tax practice exploits those in reduced financial circumstances, with fraud and incompetence being common. Brock and Russell (2015) also comment that tax professionals – despite being members of professional institutes – use their skills and abilities to manipulate the letter of the law to produce abusive avoidance schemes, stepping outside existing "accepted standards of professional integrity" (p. 7) and thus contributing to institutional corruption and fraud, a point also stressed by Benshalom (2014). In this context, examining the different kinds of work that tax practitioners undertake is helpful in illuminating the types of dilemmas that may arise and the concomitant ethical implications.

Analysing the work of tax practitioners

As is inherently evident from the previous discussions, tax practitioners attract much criticism in respect of their advice to clients on tax avoidance, although this is just one aspect of their work.[5] However, differences in types of work may create different ethical implications.

---

5 Frecknall-Hughes and Kirchler (2015: 292–4) review in detail the reasons taxpayers may have for consulting a tax professional, which include ensuring that a tax return is correctly prepared, linked to avoiding penalties, investigations, *etc.*; the increasing complexity of the tax system; legal ambiguity over the type of income they receive; and, of course, a wish to pay the least tax required, though the latter does not predominate. In the United States, over half of taxpayers pay for professional assistance in completing their tax returns (see Leviner and Richison 2011).

Frecknall-Hughes and Moizer (2015) divide the work done by tax professionals into two types: tax compliance and tax planning/avoidance advice.[6]

Tax compliance work most usually will include the preparation/completion of tax computations on the taxpayer's behalf to submit to the relevant tax authority, and subsequently dealing with and resolving any uncertainties or queries. Compliance work will involve reporting economic events that have occurred, in accordance with the requirements of the relevant tax legislation. Sometimes that legislation may contain 'grey' or unclear areas, but on occasion it is the event or transaction to which the law must be is applied that is less than clear. For instance, tax law is clear that repairs must be treated differently from capital expenditure, but the distinction may not be so obvious in practical applications. For example, would the renewal, say, of a chimney on a given building be a repair or a new capital item? The specific circumstances and an opinion about the nature of the work undertaken would dictate the answer, so a tax professional may have to make a judgement about how information should be disclosed and presented. There will undoubtedly be areas too where the figures that need to be filled in on tax returns are genuinely uncertain and subject to negotiation with revenue tax authorities, as a usual and expected element of the process, such as in deciding on the worth of private company shares or other types of property.

Tax planning/avoidance (or mitigation) work would include tax practitioner attempts to reduce a taxpayer's liability. On many occasions, this would be non-contentious and would accord with the letter and spirit of the law. An instance would be devolving estates under UK inheritance tax law by making lifetime transfers, which would be non-taxable if the transfers were made seven years prior to death.

Tax practitioners can go further than this, though, and devise schemes which test or stretch tax statutes that may be subject to interpretation because they are unclear or ambiguously written, or where they are dealing with something that is not dealt with by a specific law, or indeed, case law precedent. These kinds of stretching or 'financial' engineering (with no other objective than to avoid tax) have frequently come to the courts for a decision on whether they are legitimate – witness the many well known cases such as *Ayrshire Pullman Motor Services and D.M. Ritchie v CIR, IRC v Duke of Westminster, Ramsay (W.T.) Ltd v CIR, etc.*: sometimes the taxpayer won, but sometimes HMRC did. All have contributed, however, to a change of opinion towards tax avoidance (see Wyman 1997; Frecknall-Hughes 2007), now reflected explicitly in the guidance published by HMRC on the recent UK General Anti-Abuse Rule (GAAR) (HMRC 2013, Section B2.1), which rejects the courts' decisions "in a number of old cases".

Tax schemes within the UK are now usually filtered out by the disclosure of tax avoidance scheme rules (DOTAS) which the Finance Act 2004 introduced, but the continuing cases of Starbucks, Amazon, Google and Facebook show that international schemes remain problematic. They should, perhaps, be more accurately designated as 'tax arbitrage', as their undoubted aim is to take advantage of the distinctions between the different treatments and rates offered by different tax jurisdictions.

Given the number of cases that have come before the courts, it is, perhaps, unusual that relatively little may be deduced about tax practitioner ethics from the decisions in such cases, as there is only occasional comment about such duties. This may seem rather at odds with the legal decisions themselves. The 1997 case of *Hurlingham Estates Ltd v Wilde & Partners*, for instance, inherently suggested (at p. 628) that a solicitor owed a duty to a client to structure a property

---

6 This is not the only possible analysis. Thuronyi and Vanistendael (1996: 148–51) identify six different functions performed by tax practitioners (see the discussion by Frecknall-Hughes and Kirchler (2015: 295–6)).

transaction so as to avoid a tax charge. A similar view predominated in the long-running case of *Mehjoo v Harben Barker*, until the final Court of Appeal judgement in 2014. Considerable significance was placed on Mr Mehjoo "accept[ing] in evidence that he would not have gone ahead with the [scheme] if he had been advised that there was a substantial risk of it being challenged by HMRC" (Rayney 2014) and on the fact that Harben Barker (under the terms of its engagement letter) was only obligated to provide a limited amount of tax planning advice. Comments like these create some confusion, ethically speaking, as to the nature of a practitioner's duty – a situation which is clearly open to manipulation and exploitation by less scrupulous practitioners who, if not members of any professional body, would not be duty bound to abide by a code of professional ethics.

Studies on tax practitioners and ethics

Existing studies looking at ethics and tax practice seldom explain what 'ethics' means in regard to practitioner behaviour or decision making, taking it for granted that the meaning is self-evident. Recent press coverage of alleged tax 'scandals' links ethics more specifically to avoidance (see, as referred to earlier, Armitstead 2013; Barford and Holt 2012; Fuller 2013). However, ethical issues arise across the full range of a practitioner's work, both compliance and avoidance/planning. In a survey of 2,156 managerial and professional business personnel, Longenecker et al. (1989a) found that respondents under the age of 40 were "significantly more permissive in their views regarding ethics in a variety of situations", including issues concerning overstating expenses and evading taxes, although they were under no significant pressure to act unethically. Longenecker et al. (1989b), in considering differences in ethical behaviour between large and small firms of advisers, found that although small firms were more lenient in tolerating overstatement of expenses, evasion of taxes, collusion in bidding and insider trading than large firms, they took a more severe view on things such as faulty investment advice and misleading financial reporting. Marshall et al. (1998) in a Western Australian study find that the most important ethical failure is a lack of ensuring confidentiality in respect of privileged client information, followed by inadequate technical competence, failure to make reasonable enquiries/conduct research, continuing to act for a client where there is incorrect information and conflicts in distinguishing between tax planning and tax avoidance. Stainer et al. (1997) note the empirical studies undertaken from the viewpoint of the tax adviser in respect of ethical issues in taxation, highlighting generally the controversial nature of certain tax planning/avoidance practices. Increasingly aggressive tax avoidance (that is, how willing tax practitioners are to challenge revenue authorities' own interpretation or application of tax law in their adoption of reporting positions or promotion of avoidance schemes) has emerged over time as a dominant theme (see, for example Roberts 1998; Cloyd 1995; Bandy et al. 1994; Cuccia 1994; Schisler 1994, 1995; Hite and McGill 1992; Reckers et al. 1991; Duncan et al. 1989; LaRue and Reckers 1989; Sanders and Wyndelts 1989; Jackson et al. 1988) and is now targeted by governments worldwide (see Frecknall-Hughes 2007). Such studies indicate that aggressive tax avoidance is unethical, but do not specify why it is unethical, perhaps, assuming again that it is self-explanatory that the outcome is less tax revenue collected with the consequence of the provision of fewer public benefits, with a deleterious effect on needy members of society. Brock and Russell's more recent (2015) study stands out as one of the few identifying the effects of the reduced revenue resulting from aggressive (or abusive) avoidance.

Although there is a substantial body of research which examines the reasons why taxpayers comply or do not comply with their filing/reporting obligations (see Frecknall-Hughes and Kirchler 2015), it is only relatively recently that this body of research has begun to consider the effect of employing a tax practitioner. Several studies find that practitioner-prepared returns are less compliant than those prepared by the individual taxpayer (Erard 1990, 1993; Klepper and Nagin 1989; Smith and Kinsey 1987). This reinforces the idea that tax practitioners are important in the compliance process, as they can encourage clients to be compliant or deter them (LaRue and Reckers 1989). The literature shows both effects. Klepper and Nagin (1989) and Klepper et al. (1991) suggest that it is the dual role inherent in tax law that creates this duality for practitioners: they act as 'enforcers' in unambiguous contexts and as 'exploiters' in ambiguous ones (supported by the findings of Spilker et al. 1999; Hite et al. 2003). Doyle et al. (2013), when investigating the ethical reasoning processes of tax practitioners in social contexts and in tax contexts, found no differences between tax practitioners and non-tax practitioners in ethical reasoning in social contexts, but when the context changed to tax, differences in ethical reasoning were significant: tax practitioners utilised a significantly lower level of ethical reasoning than non-practitioners. Little difference was made by the size of the firm for which practitioners worked (Doyle et al. 2014). Several studies (e.g. Erard 1993; Reinganum and Wilde 1988; Ayres et al. 1989; Jackson and Milliron 1989; McGill 1988; Westat, Inc. 1987) indicate 'aggressiveness' from tax practitioners being involved. However, Tan (1999), when considering small business owners in New Zealand, found that they preferred conservative advice from a tax practitioner rather than aggressive advice – with a strong wish for a correct return to be prepared (Tan 1999; Hite and McGill 1992; Collins et al. 1990). Several studies report on the factors affecting tax practitioners' levels of aggressiveness. These have been discovered to be client attributes (quality of records, dependability, etc.), the preparer's own concerns about penalties, possible loss of (an important) client, opinions of others in the firm, advocacy posture, client risk preferences, levels of ambiguity in a particular issue, whether tax is due by the client, tax authority experience, probability of tax investigation, type of firm, certified public accountant (CPA) status or not, education level, whether the decision was taken by one practitioner or a group and ethical concerns. Practitioners can be influenced by one or more different factors, and one or more factors may operate in conjunction.[7]

Doyle et al. (2013) establish that tax practitioners apply a less principled level of reasoning in considering tax dilemmas (as opposed to social dilemmas) with little difference made by the size of firm for which they work (Doyle et al. 2014). Further work by Frecknall-Hughes et al. (forthcoming) considers the types of ethical influences on the work of practitioners by looking at the main streams of Western ethical philosophy that relate to that work, namely deontology and consequentialism.[8] They conclude (by means of an innovative use of the Defining Issues Test, a scenario-based instrument borrowed from moral psychology and used here to assess both the levels and type of moral reasoning) that practitioners in tax scenarios give a higher weight to deontological considerations than non-tax practitioners in those same scenarios, which may reflect a greater appreciation of the fundamentally legal nature of tax, though they also concluded that much more work remains to be done here.

Conclusion

This chapter has reviewed existing literature on ethical issues in respect of the work of tax professionals – or intermediaries. While tax avoidance is the area that currently dominates

---

7 See Schmidt 2001; Cruz et al. 2000; Carnes et al. 1996a, 1996b; Burns and Kiecker 1995; Bandy et al. 1994; Schisler 1994; Johnson 1993; Newberry et al. 1993; Cloyd 1991; Reckers et al. 1991; Duncan et al. 1989; Helleloid 1989; LaRue and Reckers 1989; Kaplan et al. 1988; McGill 1988; Milliron and Toy 1988; Roark 1986.
8 Relatively few studies have examined the type of ethical thought that practitioners might use – see Burns and Kiecker (1995) and Cruz et al. (2000).

discussions on practitioner ethics (and indeed, has caused concerns in the past), there are other areas in practice where issues can arise. What becomes abundantly clear is that this is an area that is far from straightforward – and ethics overall for the individual practitioner is a multifaceted concept, not easily defined and rendered made complex by the large number of different aspects that need to be considered.

Acknowledgements

Much of this chapter draws on earlier research, particularly J. Frecknall-Hughes and E. Kirchler, "Towards a General Theory of Tax Practice", 24:2 *Social & Legal Studies* 289–312 (2015); J. Frecknall-Hughes, P. Moizer, E. Doyle and B. Summers, "An Examination of the Ethical Influences on the Work of Tax Practitioners", *Journal of Business Ethics* (forthcoming), doi:10.1007/s10551-016-3037-6; and J. Frecknall-Hughes and P. Moizer, "Assessing the Quality of Services Provided by Tax Practitioners", 13:1 *eJournal of Tax Research* 51–75 (2015).

Table of statutes

Great Britain. *Finance Act 2004. Elizabeth II. Chapter 12.* (2004) London: The Stationery Office.

Table of cases

Ayrshire Pullman Motor Services and Ritchie v CIR (1929) (14 TC 574).
Hurlingham Estates Ltd v Wilde & Partners [1997] STC 627.
IRC v Duke of Westminster [1936] AC 1.
Mehjoo v Harben Barker (a firm) & Anor [2014] EWCA Civ 358.
Ramsay (W. T.) Ltd v. CIR [1982] AC 300.

References

Armitstead, L. (2013). 'Big four accountants blast tax scheme claims', *The Telegraph*, 26 April [Online]. Available at www.telegraph.co.uk/finance/personalfinance/consumertips/tax/10018397/Big-Four-accountants-blast-tax-scheme-claim [Accessed 18 August 2013].
Arzoo, G. A. (1987). 'Preparer penalties and compliance', *Tax Adviser*, January, 36–43.
Ayres, F. L., Jackson, B. R., and Hite, P. (1989). 'The economic benefits of regulation: Evidence from professional tax preparers', *Accounting Review*, 64(2), 468–87.
Bandy, D., Betancourt, L., and Kelliher, C. (1994). 'An empirical study of the objectivity of CPAs' tax work', *Advances in Taxation*, 6, 1–23.
Barbour, C., and McDougall, A. (1997). 'Conduct unbecoming', *Taxation*, 28 August, 592–5.
Barford, V., and Holt, G. (2012). 'Google, Amazon, Starbucks: The rise of "tax shaming"' [Online]. Available at www.bbc.co.uk/news/magazine-20560359 [Accessed 29 December 2012].
Benshalom, I. (2014). 'Who should decide whether the apple is rotten? Tax disclosure and corporate political agency', *Columbia Journal of Tax Law*, 6, 86–117 [Online]. Available at SSRN: http://ssrn.com/abstract=2569509 [Accessed 1 May 2015].
Brock, G., and Russell, H. (2015). 'Abusive tax avoidance and institutional corruption: The responsibilities of tax professionals', Edmond J. Safra Working Paper No. 56 [Online]. Available at SSRN: http://ssrn.com/abstract=2566281 or http://dx.doi.org/10.2139/ssrn.2566281 [Accessed 10 May 2015].
Brody, R. G., and Masselli, J. J. (1996). 'Tax preparers: Whose team are they on?', *National Public Accountant*, 41(3), 18–46.
Burns, J. O., and Kiecker, P. (1995). 'Tax practitioner ethics: An empirical investigation of organizational consequences', *Journal of the American Taxation Association*, 17(2), 20–49.

Carnes, G. A., Harwood, G. B., and Sawyers, R. B. (1996a). 'The determinants of tax professionals' aggressiveness in ambiguous situations', *Advances in Taxation*, 8, 1–28.

Carnes, G. A., Harwood, G. B., and Sawyers, R. B. (1996b). 'A comparison of tax professionals' individual and group decisions when resolving ambiguous tax questions', *Journal of the American Taxation Association*, 18(2), 1–18.

Chartered Institute of Taxation (2014). 'Professional conduct in relation to taxation' [Online]. Available at www.tax.org.uk/Resources/CIOT/Documents/2014/02/Professional%20Conduct%20in%20Relation%20to%20Taxation%20190214%20final.pdf [Accessed 6 May 2014].

Chartered Institute of Taxation (2016). 'Professional conduct in relation to taxation' [Online]. Available atwww.tax.org.uk/professional-standards/professional-rules/professional-conduct-relation-taxation [Accessed 29 November 2016].

Cloyd, C. B. (1991). 'The effects of accounting method, ambiguity type and client risk preferences on recommendations of tax preparers', paper presented at Midyear Meeting of the American Taxation Association, Albquerque, New Mexico, February.

Cloyd, C. B. (1995). 'The effects of financial accounting conformity on recommendations of tax preparers', *Journal of the American Taxation Association*, 17(2), 50–70.

Collins, J. H., Milliron, V. C., and Toy, D. R. (1990). 'Factors associated with the household demand for tax preparers', *Journal of the American Taxation Association*, 12(1), 9–25.

Cruz, C. A., Shafer, W. E., and Strawser, J. R. (2000). 'A multidimensional analysis of tax practitioners' ethical judgments', *Journal of Business Ethics*, 24(3), 223–44.

Cuccia, A. D. (1994). 'The effects of increased sanctions on paid preparers: Integrating economic and psychological factors', *Journal of the American Taxation Association*, 16(1), 41–66.

Devos, K. N. H. (2012). 'The impact of tax professionals upon the compliance behavior of Australian individual taxpayers', *Revenue Law Journal*, 22(1), 1–26 [Online]. Available at http://epublications.bond.edu.au/cgi/viewcontent.cgi?article=1223&context=rlj [Accessed 10 April 2013].

Doyle, E., Frecknall-Hughes, J., and Summers, B. (2013). 'An empirical analysis of the ethical reasoning process of tax practitioners', *Journal of Business Ethics*, 114(2), 325–39.

Doyle, E., Frecknall-Hughes, J., and Summers, B. (2014). 'Ethics in tax practice: A study of the effect of practitioner firm size', *Journal of Business Ethics*, 122(4), 623–41.

Duncan, W. A., LaRue, D. W., and Reckers, P. M. J. (1989). 'An empirical examination of the influence of selected economic and noneconomic variables in decision making by tax professionals', *Advances in Taxation*, 2, 91–106.

Dyreng, S., Hanlon, M., and Maydew, E. L. (2007). 'Long-run corporate tax avoidance', *Accounting Review*, 83(1), 61–82.

Dyreng, S., Hanlon, M., and Maydew, E. L. (2010). 'The effects of executives on corporate tax avoidance', *Accounting Review*, 85(4), 1163–89.

Erard, B. (1990). 'The impact of tax practitioners on tax compliance: A research summary', paper presented at the 1990 Internal Revenue Service Research Conference, Washington, DC, November.

Erard, B. (1993). 'Taxation with representation: An analysis of the role of tax practitioners in tax compliance', *Journal of Public Economics*, 52(2), 163–97.

Fisher, A. (1994). 'Finding the right tax adviser', *Fortune*, 21 March, 159–60 and 161.

Frecknall-Hughes, J. (2007). 'The validity of tax avoidance and tax planning: An examination of the evolution of legal opinion', unpublished LLM dissertation, The University of Northumbria.

Frecknall-Hughes, J., and Kirchler, E. (2015). 'Towards a general theory of tax practice', *Social & Legal Studies*, 24(2), 289–312.

Frecknall-Hughes, J., and McKerchar, M. (2013). 'Historical perspectives on the emergence of the tax profession', *Australian Tax Forum*, 28(2), 276–88.

Frecknall-Hughes, J., and Moizer, P. (2015). 'Assessing the quality of services provided by tax practitioners', *eJournal of Tax Research*, 13(1), 51–75.

Frecknall-Hughes, J., Moizer, P., Doyle, E., and Summers, B. (forthcoming). 'An examination of the ethical influences on the work of tax practitioners', *Journal of Business Ethics*. doi:10.1007/s10551-016-3037-6.

Freedman, J. (2012). 'Responsive regulation, risk, and rules: Applying the theory to tax practice', *UBC Law Review*, 44(3), 627–62; Oxford Legal Studies Research Paper No. 13/2012 [Online]. Available at SSRN: http://ssrn.com/abstract=2027406 [Accessed 9 May 2015].

Fuller, C. (2013). 'Big four to appear before public accountants committee', *Accountancy Age*, 21 January [Online] Available at www.accountancyage.com/aa/news/2237667/big-four-to-appear-before-public-accounts-committee [Accessed 18 August 2013].

Godar, S. H., O'Connor, P. J., and Taylor, V. A. (2005). 'Evaluating the ethics of inversion', *Journal of Business Ethics*, 61(1), 1–6.

Hammer, S. (1996). 'AICPA statements on responsibilities in tax practice', *The CPA Journal*, (January), 43.

Harwood, R. (1996). 'Ethical training', *Accountancy*, August, 118.

Helleloid, R. T. (1989). 'Ambiguity and evaluation of client documentation by tax professionals', *Journal of the American Taxation Association*, 11(1), 22–36.

Hemans, D. (1996). 'Choosing the right tax professional', *Black Enterprise*, November, 127–9.

Herman, T. (2004). 'IRS to issue rules on tax shelters; ethical guidelines target "opinion letters" often used to justify questionable transactions', *Wall Street Journal*, 8 December [Online]. Available at http://online.wsj.com/news/articles/SB110246789556693907 [Accessed 23 December 2013].

Hite, P., Hasseldine, J., Al-Khoury, A., James, S., Toms, S., and Toumi, M. (2003). 'Tax practitioners and tax compliance', in A. Lymer and D. Salter (eds), *Contemporary Issues in Taxation Research*. Warwick: Ashgate Publishing Limited, 17–43.

Hite, P. A., and McGill, G. A. (1992). 'An examination of taxpayer preference for aggressive tax advice', *National Tax Journal*, 45(4), 389–401.

HMRC (2009). 'Modernising powers, deterrents and safeguards. Working with tax agents: A consultation document', HMRC.

HMRC (2013). *HMRC's GAAR guidance* [Online]. Available at www.hmrc.gov.uk/avoidance/gaar-part-abc.pdf [Accessed 7 May 2014].

Hopkins, J. P. (2014). '*Loving v. IRS*: The IRS's Achilles' heel for regulated tax advice?', *Virginia Tax Review*, 34, 191–228 [Online]. Available at SSRN: http://ssrn.com/abstract=2547716 [Accessed 6 May 2015].

Jackson, B. R., and Milliron, V. C. (1989). 'Tax preparers: Government agents or client advocates?', *Journal of Accountancy*, 167(5), 76–83.

Jackson, B. R., Milliron, V. C., and Toy, D. R. (1988). 'Tax practitioners and the government', *Tax Notes*, 41(3), 333–41.

Johnson, L. M. (1993). 'An empirical investigation of the effects of advocacy on preparers' evaluations of judicial evidence', *Journal of the American Taxation Association*, 15(1), 1–22.

Kaplan, S. E., Reckers, P. M. J., West, S. G., and Boyd, J. C. (1988). 'An examination of tax reporting recommendations of professional tax preparers', *Journal of Economic Psychology*, 9(4), 427–43.

Klepper, S., Mazur, M., and Nagin, N. (1991). 'Expert intermediaries and legal compliance: The case of tax preparers', *Journal of Law and Economics*, 34(1), 205–29.

Klepper, S., and Nagin, N. (1989). 'The role of tax practitioners in tax compliance', *Policy Sciences*, 22, 167–92.

Krouse, S., and Baker, S. (2012). 'Osborne clamps down on tax abuse', *Financial News* [Online]. Available at www.efinancialnews.com/story/2012-03-21/osborne-clamps-down-on-tax-abuse-in-budget [Accessed 29 December 2012].

LaRue, D., and Reckers, P. M. J. (1989). 'An empirical investigation of the influence of selected factors on professional tax preparers' decision processes', *Advances in Accounting*, 7, 37–50.

Leviner, S., and Richison, K. (2011). 'Tax preparers and the role they play in taxpayer compliance: An empirical investigation with policy implications', Buffalo Legal Studies Research Paper Series, Paper No. 2011-021 [Online]. Available at SSRN: http://:ssrn.com/abstract¼1884188 [Accessed 10 April 2013].

Levy, A. H. (2015). 'Believing in life after *Loving*: IRS regulation of tax preparers', *Florida Tax Review*, 17(5) [Online]. Available at SSRN: http://ssrn.com/abstract=2585595 [Accessed 5 May 2015].

Longenecker, J. G., McKinney, J. A., and Moore, C. A. (1989a). 'The generation gap in business ethics', *Business Horizons*, 32(5), 9–14.

Longenecker, J. G., McKinney, J. A., and Moore, C. A. (1989b). 'Do smaller firms have higher ethics?', *Business and Society Review*, 71(Fall), 19–21.

Marshall, R. L., Armstrong, R. W., and Smith, M. (1998). 'The ethical environment of tax practitioners: Western Australian evidence', *Journal of Business Ethics*, 17(12), 1265–79.

McGill, G. A. (1988). 'The CPA's role in income tax compliance: An empirical study of variability in recommending aggressive tax positions', PhD Thesis, Texas Tech University.

McKerchar, M., Bloomquist, K., and Leviner, K. (2008). 'Improving the quality of services offered by tax agents: Can regulation help?', *Australian Tax Forum*, 23(4), 399–425.

Milliron, V. C., and Toy, D. R. (1988). 'Tax compliance: Investigation of key features', *Journal of the American Taxation Association*, 9(2), 84–104.

Newberry, K. J., Reckers, P. M. J., and Wyndelts, R. W. (1993). 'An examination of tax practitioner decisions: The role of preparer sanctions and framing effects associated with client condition', *Journal of Economic Psychology*, 14(2), 439–52.

OECD (2008). 'Study into the role of tax intermediaries', Fourth OECD Forum on Tax Administration, Cape Town, South Africa.

Rawlinson, K. (2016). 'Google agrees to pay British authorities £130m in back taxes', *The Guardian*, 21 January [Online]. Available at www.theguardian.com/technology/2016/jan/22/google-agrees-to-pay-hmrc-130m-in-back-taxes [Accessed 8 February 2016].

Rayney, P. (2014). 'Case report: How the Mehjoo decision affects tax advisers' [Online]. Available at www.accountancylive.com/case-report-how-mehjooo-decision-affects-tax-advisers [Accessed 5 May 2014].

Reckers, P. M. J., Sanders, D. L., and Wyndelts, R. W. (1991). 'An empirical investigation of factors affecting tax practitioner compliance', *Journal of the American Taxation Association*, 13(2), 30–46.

Reinganum, J. F., and Wilde, L. L. (1988). 'Tax practitioners and tax compliance', Social Science Working Paper No. 666, Pasadena: California Institute of Technology.

Roark, S. (1986). 'An examination of risk attitudes in legal tax research', PhD Thesis, Arizona State University.

Roberts, M. R. (1998). 'Tax accountants' judgment/decision-making research: A review and synthesis', *Journal of the American Taxation Association*, 20(1), 78–121.

Sanders, D. L., and Wyndelts, R. W. (1989). 'An examination of tax practitioners' decisions under uncertainty', *Advances in Taxation*, 2, 41–72.

Schisler, D. L. (1994). 'An experimental examination of factors affecting tax preparers' aggressiveness – a prospect theory approach', *Journal of the American Taxation Association*, 16(2), 124–42.

Schisler, D. L. (1995). 'Equity, aggressiveness, consensus: A comparison of taxpayers and tax preparers', *Accounting Horizons*, 9(4), 76–87.

Schmidt, D. (2001). 'The prospects of taxpayer agreement with aggressive tax advice', *Journal of Economic Psychology*, 22(2), 157–72.

Shafer, W. E., and Simmons, R. S. (2008). 'Social responsibility, Machiavellianism and tax avoidance', *Accounting, Auditing and Accountability Journal*, 21(5), 695–720.

Sikka, P. (2010). 'Smoke and mirrors: Corporate social responsibility and tax avoidance', *Accounting Forum*, 34(3–4), 153–68.

Sikka, P., and Hampton, M. (2005). 'The role of accountancy firms in tax avoidance: Some evidence and issues', *Accounting Forum*, 29(3), 325–43.

Smith, K. W., and Kinsey, K. A. (1987). 'Understanding taxpayer behavior: A conceptual framework with implications for research', *Law & Society Review*, 12(4), 640–63.

Spilker, B. C., Worsham, R. G., and Prawitt, D. F. (1999). 'Tax professionals' interpretations of ambiguity in compliance and planning decision contexts', *Journal of the American Taxation Association*, 21(2), 75–89.

Stainer, A., Stainer, L., and Segal, A. (1997). 'The ethics of tax planning', *Business Ethics: A European Review*, 6(4), 213–19.

Tan, L. M. (1999). 'Taxpayers' preference for type of advice from tax practitioner: A preliminary examination', *Journal of Economic Psychology*, 20(4), 431–47.

Thuronyi, V., and Vanistendael, F. (1996). 'Regulation of tax professionals', in V. Thuronyi (ed.), *Tax Law Design and Drafting*. Washington, DC: International Monetary Fund, 135–63.

Tomasic, R., and Pentony, B. (1991). 'Taxation law compliance and the role of professional tax advisers', *Australian & New Zealand Journal of Criminology*, 24, 241–57.

Wall Jr, J. A. (1985). *Negotiation Theory and Practice*. Glenville, IL: Scott Lovesman.

Westat, Inc (1987). 'A survey of tax practitioners', prepared for the Internal Revenue Service.

Wilson, R. (2009). 'An examination of corporate tax shelter participants', *Accounting Review*, 84(3), 969–99.

Wyman, P. (1997). 'Upholding the law', *Tax Journal* (10 November), 3–4.

Yetmar, S. A., and Eastman, K. K. (2000). 'Tax practitioners' ethical sensitivity: A model and empirical examination', *Journal of Business Ethics*, 26(4), 271–88.

26

DISTINGUISHING TAX AVOIDANCE AND EVASION

Allison Christians

Introduction

Lawmakers around the world are facing political pressure to address the problem of "tax dodging" by wealthy elites and multinational firms. Media coverage, social protest, and sustained campaigns for tax justice by activist individuals and global nongovernmental organizations (NGOs), have all contributed to this pressure. Central to the story is the concept of "tax dodging": does it mean tax evasion, implying a breach of law? Or can it encompass actions that are strictly legal yet breach social mores in some fashion? At a hearing in the United Kingdom regarding successful tax-minimizing strategies employed by Amazon, Google, and Starbucks which later led to EU-level investigations, Parliamentary Accounts Committee Chair Margaret Hodge clearly embraced the latter view, stating that: "We are not accusing you of being illegal; we are accusing you of being immoral."[1]

Hodge's statement suggests morality is an extra-legal standard that tax administrators ought to interrogate as a matter of their authority to compel or forbid certain behaviours. This echoes a trend among tax justice advocates that is often reflected in the popular press, namely, a conflation of actions alternatively described as planning, minimization, avoidance or evasion within a single tax compliance framework that describes the relationship between the state and the taxpayer.

Advocating a role for morality as a direct constraint on taxpayer behaviour introduces non- and quasi-legal or "soft law" standards where law appears to fail. The desire of civil society to intervene in governance is understandable if the problems of tax avoidance and evasion are conceptually linked in a narrative that casts the beleaguered state as a relatively feeble rival to an aggressive taxpayer class that seeks only to undermine the tax system. In this narrative, avoidance and evasion are two forms of the same category of behaviour. However, the narrative is not as clear when viewed through the lens of tax competition among states.

While most governments would like to capture some tax revenue from their part of the global economy, most also want to attract foreign investment capital from the global economy. These two goals pull governments in opposing policy directions, as lawmakers fluctuate between

---

1 Public Accounts Committee – Minutes of Evidence, HC 716 (12 November 2012), available at www.publications. parliament.uk/pa/cm201213/cmselect/cmpubacc/716/121112.htm

seeking revenues and using their tax systems to lure investment away from other jurisdictions that impose higher tax burdens. Tax competition might be healthy – some argue it is an appropriate way to check the state's otherwise unrestrained tendency to expand itself. Whether that is true is debatable, but it is clear that tax competition sends a signal to taxpayers that lawmakers accept tax avoidance as legitimate behaviour. With state sanction thus made explicit for tax avoidance, the conflation of avoidance with evasion in the public imagination is problematic.

This chapter therefore makes three points: first, that tax avoidance and evasion are, like other behaviours, actions that must be assessed and managed through legal processes; second, that law has the tools necessary to address both avoidance and evasion as systemic issues; and finally, that in any policy analysis, tax avoidance and evasion must be recognized as different categories of behaviour because the former is often facilitated, motivated, and encouraged in a world of aggressive tax states.[2]

Conflating tax avoidance and evasion

To understand how we got to a place where tax avoidance and tax evasion have been characterized as questions of morality and why these concepts should instead lead us invariably toward the rule of law, a brief review of the contemporary tax policy landscape is required. Two media-based exposés of international taxation combine to produce the source material for this exploration. The first, involving the "offshore leaks" database obtained and reported on by the International Consortium of Investigative Journalists (ICIJ), taught the public about an epidemic of tax evasion spreading across the globe.[3] The second, the ongoing media coverage of single-digit effective tax rates paid on a global basis by household brand companies like GE, Google, Apple, Starbucks, and Amazon taught the public about an epidemic of tax avoidance, often characterized as "aggressive" to move it conceptually closer to the concept of evasion.[4]

---

2 As the corporate social responsibility literature attests, social sanction, such as through naming and shaming, can have enormous impact on shaping behaviour for the social good. For an analysis of why corporations should consider their tax planning strategies in light of corporate social responsibility norms, see H. Gribnau, "Corporate Social Responsibility and Tax Planning: Not By Rules Alone", 24 *Social and Legal Studies* 225 (2015).

3 See ICIJ, "Secrecy for Sale: Inside the Global Offshore Money Maze", *Int'l Consortium Investigative Journalists*, available at www.icij.org/offshore. Recent revelations of the ICIJ have raised allegations of facilitaiton of tax evasion by law firm Mossack Fonseca in Panama and intimations of tax evasion by politcans and others through the use of holding company structures in the Bahamas. See ICIJ, "Former EU Official Among Politicians Named in New Leak of Offshore Files From the Bahamas" (21 September 2016), available at www.icij.org/offshore/former-eu-official-among-politicians-named-new-leak-offshore-files-bahamas.

4 See D. Kocieniewski, "GE's Strategies Let It Avoid Taxes Altogether", *New York Times* (24 March 2011), available at www.nytimes.com/2011/03/25/business/economy/25tax.html?pagewanted=all&_r=0; C. Duhigg and D. Kocieniewski, "How Apple Sidesteps Billions in Taxes", *New York Times* (28 April 2012), available at www.nytimes.com/2012/04/29/business/apples-tax-strategy-aims-at-low-tax-states-and-nations.html; M. Warman, "Google Pays Just £6m UK Tax", *The Telegraph* (8 August 2012), available at www.telegraph.co.uk/technology/google/9460950/Google-pays-just-6m-UK-tax.html; C. Patterson, "Google, Starbucks, and Amazon ... For These Multinationals Immorality Is Now Standard Practice", *The Independent* (13 November 2012), available at www.independent.co.uk/voices/comment/gogoog-starbucks-and-amazon-for-these-multinationals-immorality-is-now-standard-practice-8313038.html; V. Barford and G. Holt, "Google, Amazon, Starbucks: The Rise of 'Tax Shaming'", *BBC News* (21 May 2013), available at www.bbc.co.uk/news/magazine-20560359; "Tax Paid By Some Global Firms in UK 'An Insult'", *BBC News* (3 December 2012), available at www.bbc.co.uk/news/business-20559791.

The evasion story

The evasion story is a simple one, involving a clear question of governance failure for which the moral case seems virtually unambiguous.[5] Reporters who analyzed the ICIJ offshore leaks database found that "alongside perfectly legal transactions, the secrecy and lax oversight offered by the offshore world allows fraud, tax dodging and political corruption to thrive."[6] Related stories abound, including the ongoing saga between the United States and Switzerland with respect to marketing efforts by UBS to secrecy-seeking American customers,[7] a similar dispute between Germany and Lichtenstein,[8] and the "Lagarde list" furnished to Giorgios Papakonstantinou – then the Greek Finance Minister – with the names of some 2,000 Greek residents, many with top government credentials, who were holding cash in secret Swiss bank accounts.[9] The information contained in this steady stream of leaks produced a flood of media coverage that has moved activists to take issue with how governments manage the financial affairs of high-net-worth individuals.

The question this story clearly raises is why governments cannot or will not prevent this patently illegal and obviously objectionable behaviour. One possibility is that governments cannot prevent this behaviour; the other is that they can do so but choose not to for political reasons. The media coverage itself, and the response of activists in using such coverage to rally for a very specific set of tax policy reforms, suggests that the clear answer to tax evasion is greater public oversight to oversee the efforts (or lack thereof) of governments to fairly enforce their own laws, and to pressure governments to remedy past practices of lax enforcement, if better enforcement is possible.[10]

One place where activists have sought avenues for such oversight is within the architecture of the Organization for Economic Cooperation and Development (OECD). Formed as part of the

---

5 Leaving aside those for whom all taxation is simplistically viewed as either theft or slavery or both.

6 A. Ohlieser, "The Secret World of Tax Havens Just Got a Whole Lot Less Secret", *Slate* (3 April 2013), available at www.slate.com/blogs/the_slatest/2013/04/04/offshore_leaks_tax_haven_report_over_2_5_million_document_leak_reveals_details.html.

7 See, e.g. N. Mathiason, "Tax Scandal Leaves Swiss Giant Reeling", *The Observer* (28 June 2008), available at www.guardian.co.uk/business/2008/jun/29/ubs.banking.

8 See "Germans Admit Tax Evasion as Scandal Widens to US", Australia, *Deutsche Welle* (26 February 2008), available at http://dw.de/p/DDmr. This scandal became so widespread that it became popularly known as the "Lichtenstein tax affair." See 2008 Liechtenstein Tax Affair, *Wikipedia*, available at http://en.wikipedia.org/wiki/2008_Liechtenstein_tax_affair.

9 The story of the Lagarde list was broken by investigative journalist Kostas Vaxevanis, who published the list after learning that the Greek government had altered it to remove key names and was otherwise disinclined to pursue prosecutions based on its contents. See Editorial, "Greece Arrests the Messenger", *New York Times* (29 October 2012), available at www.nytimes.com/2012/10/30/opinion/greece-arrests-the-messenger.html. Vaxevanis was arrested for violating the privacy rights of those named in the list and is currently facing a second trial on the same issue after being acquitted in November 2012. "Greek Bank List Editor Costas Vaxevanis Acquitted", *BBC News* (1 November 2012), available at www.bbc.co.uk/news/world-europe-20172516; H. Smith, "Greek Editor Kostas Vaxevanis Faces Retrial Over 'Lagarde List' Revelation", *The Guardian* (16 November 2012), available at www.theguardian.com/world/2012/nov/16/greek-editor-kostas-vaxevanis-retrial; H. Smith, "Greek Journalist's Retrial Over Lagarde List Postponed", *The Guardian* (8 October 2013), available at www.theguardian.com/world/2013/oct/08/greek-retrial-kostas-vaxevanis-lagarde-list-postponed.

10 See, e.g. R. S. McIntyre, M. Gardner and R. J. Wilkins, *Corporate Taxpayers & Corporate Tax Dodgers 2008–10* (2011), available at www.ctj.org/corporatetaxdodgers/CorporateTaxDodgersReport.pdf; Fact Coalition, *Tax Reform*, available at http://tjn-usa.org/storage/documents/FACT_Tax_Policy_101911.pdf; Fact Coalition, *Inconvenient Realities on Corp. Tax: Loopholes, Tax Breaks & Subsidies Tell the Real Story on the Corp. Tax Rate*, available at http://tjn-usa.org/storage/documents/FACT_Sheet_CORPTAX_DRAFT.pdf.

reconstruction effort in the post-war era, the OECD is not primarily a source of international law but rather a forum for consensus-building among its member nations, which include the United States, Canada, and EU countries, but not Brazil, China, or India. The OECD is thus a transnational network, and its tax division is a tightly knit epistemic community whose main purpose is to create spaces for government officials to collaborate with business and industry leaders to frame issues of international tax policy, formulate norms, and syndicate these norms globally through domestic lawmaking procedures.[11] This institutional structure has had tremendous consequences for the formation of global tax policy, and serves as a warning about the role of norms, non-state actors, and institutions in tax policy matters more generally.[12]

The OECD began addressing the problem of offshore tax evasion in 1996, when it developed an appreciation of how certain jurisdictions – many of which are controlled possessions and territories of OECD member countries – were seen as eroding the revenue-raising ability of many of the member countries.[13] Two years later, the OECD published a report that developed criteria to identify harmful tax competition and recommended as a counteractive solution a proposed blacklist of countries that were to be targeted with various sanctions unless they started sharing tax information with leading OECD countries pursuant to OECD standards.

After extensive lobbying against the project by the United States, Switzerland, and Luxembourg, the OECD ultimately reduced its work to an easily attainable compliance threshold. A country would be removed from tax haven blacklists by having in place at least twelve tax information exchange agreements (TIEAs) pursuant to OECD-drafted model language.[14] These TIEAs arranged actual information exchange among countries in such a way as to continue the status quo unabated; indeed, tax justice advocates claimed that evasion may have even increased in countries that had not been subjected to OECD scrutiny, such as the United States, the United Kingdom, and Switzerland.[15]

Consequently, despite aspirational declarations by world leaders that the OECD had ended the era of bank secrecy in 2009, in fact, the opposite was true.[16] Yet because the institution had set the parameters of its own success, little recourse was available. The Tax Justice Network – a civil society organization formed from a coalition of researchers and activists focused on harmful tax practices – together with other NGOs and activists, took on the issue in various ways. Recent developments suggest that their constant public criticism, combined with reports on

---

11 A. Christians, "Networks, Norms, and National Tax Policy", 9 *Washington University of Global Studies Law Review* 1, 22 (2010).

12 The OECD is capable of exercising centralized coercive authority even if it does not dispense international "law," and many commentators have gone so far as to accept OECD declarations in tax matters as largely equivalent to law in practice. See Christians, *Hard Law & Soft Law in International Taxation*, n.2 at 325–9.

13 For a more thorough review of the OECD's work on tax evasion, see A. Christians, "Sovereignty, Taxation, and Social Contract", 18 *Minnesota Journal of International Law* 99 (2009).

14 L. A. Sheppard, "News Analysis: Don't Ask, Don't Tell, Part 4: Ineffectual Information Sharing", 53 *Tax Notes International* 1139 (2009) ("The standard OECD information exchange agreement is nearly worthless."); M. McIntyre, "How to End the Charade of Information Exchange", 56 *Tax Notes International* 255 (2009) (outlining why OECD exchange agreements are ineffective and the OECD list of tax havens a "joke").

15 See, e.g. "TIEAs: A Norwegian Update", *Tax Justice Network* (20 April 2011, 5:57 AM), available at http://taxjustice.blogspot.ca/2011/04/tieas-norwegian-update.html; see also "TIEAs: 23 Is the Magic Number", Tax Justice Network (8 September 2010, 9:24 AM), available at http://taxjustice.blogspot.com/2010/09/tieas-23-is-magic-number.html.

16 London Summit 2009, *Global Plan for Recovery & Reform* (2 April 2009), available at http://web.archive.org/web/20100310215453/www.londonsummit.gov.uk/resources/en/news/15766232/communique-020409 ("We stand ready to deploy sanctions to protect our public finances and financial systems. The era of banking secrecy is over."); McIntyre, n.14, at 255 ("Well, it's not over yet.").

the growing amount of cash believed to be hidden offshore, may be having some effect.[17] For instance, the United States has adopted punishing new rules for tax evaders and the institutions that enable them.[18] Other countries enacted similar legislation,[19] and the OECD has a similarly motivated project.[20]

Activists may see these developments as reasons for optimism, yet some glaring deficiencies remain in these regimes. The apparent unwillingness of leading nations to curb their own appeal as tax havens to the rest of the world continues to present obstacles to meaningful reform.[21]

One may well wonder if the same governments that produced the circumstances for global tax evasion, and then pronounced its death after a highly contested global battle that lasted over a decade, can be believed when they say that this time things are different.[22] But perhaps the even more troubling inquiry is what this process says about the possibilities for tax justice or fairness, however it may be articulated. If the rich countries of the world, gathering their full and ample resources and with apparently clear will and determination, have so much trouble just confronting – never mind solving – the problem of tax evasion, how much less should be expected when the behaviour in question is not so unambiguously objectionable, while potentially being even more valuable to its architects? The rhetoric on tax avoidance demonstrates there are no straightforward answers to this question.

The avoidance story

The avoidance story is more difficult, and it is here that the problem of ambiguity in the use of morality as a non-legal behavioural control arises. The issue is that the world's biggest multinational conglomerates manage to earn trillions of dollars around the world, yet many seem to pay virtually no tax anywhere. This is framed as a justice issue because it shifts the burden of taxpaying to those who cannot similarly avail themselves of sophisticated tax planning strategies, and it thereby delivers undue advantage to sprawling conglomerates over all other taxpaying members of society. In response to this injustice, tax justice advocates use the concept of morality to move some kinds of tax avoidance into the unambiguously immoral category of evasion despite the failure of the law to do so.

But this is a difficult move strategically in that it confronts a long tradition of tolerance, and even celebration, of tax avoidance behaviour by taxpayers that is at once political, cultural, and

---

17 James Henry, *Tax Justice Network, The Price of Offshore Revisited: New Estimates for 'Missing' Global Private Wealth, Income, Inequality & Lost Taxes* (2012), available at www.elcorreo.eu.org/IMG/pdf/Price_of_Offshore_Revisited_72612.pdf.

18 Foreign Account Tax Compliance Act, Pub. L. No. 111–147, 124 STAT 71 (2010) (codified in scattered sections of 26 U.S.C.), available at www.gpo.gov/fdsys/pkg/PLAW-111publ147/pdf/PLAW-111publ147.pdf.

19 S. Shaheen, "UK to Impose Son of FATCA on Crown Dependencies, Despite Government's Denials", *International Tax Review* (23 November 2012), available at www.internationaltaxreview.com/Article/3121964/EXCLUSIVE-UK-to-impose-son-of-FATCA-on-Crown-Dependencies-despite-governments-denials.html.

20 About the TRACE Project, *OECD*, available at www.oecd.org/ctp/exchange-of-tax-information/about-thetracegroup.htm (accessed 24 December 2013); see generally OECD, *Trace Implementation Package* (23 January 2013), available at www.oecd.org/ctp/exchange-of-tax-information/TRACE_Implementation_Package_Website.pdf.

21 See, e.g. A. Christians, "Putting the Reign Back in Sovereign: Advice for the Second Obama Administration", 40 *Pepperdine Law Review* 1373 (2013); A. Edgerton, "Miami's International Banking Clients Move Money to Protect Financial Privacy", *Miami Herald* (29 July 2012), available at www.miamiherald.com/2012/07/29/2920363/miamis-international-banking-clients.html; "Is the UK Serious About Tackling Tax Evasion?" *Channel 4 News* (UK) Television Broadcast (2 February 2012), available at www.channel4.com/news/is-the-uk-serious-about-tackling-tax-evasion.

22 See, e.g. L. Sheppard, "News Analysis: OECD Tries to Fix Income Shifting", 69 *Tax Notes International* 627 (2013).

legal in nature. In the United States, this doctrine is famously stated by Learned Hand in *Helvering v. Gregory*, as follows:

> Anyone may so arrange his affairs that his taxes shall be as low as possible; he is not bound to choose that pattern which will best pay the Treasury. There is not even a patriotic duty to increase one's taxes.[23]

The same sentiment is found in English common law, and has accordingly been adopted in the jurisprudence of other commonwealth countries, including Canada and Australia. Thus, in *IRC v. Duke of Westminster*, Baron Thomas Tomlin wrote:

> Every man is entitled if he can to order his affairs so as that the tax attaching under the appropriate Acts is less than it otherwise would be. If he succeeds in ordering them so as to secure this result, then, however unappreciative the Commissioners of Inland Revenue or his fellow taxpayers may be of his ingenuity, he cannot be compelled to pay an increased tax.[24]

Accordingly, when GE faced a public outcry over a media exposé of its global tax planning successes,[25] a company representative replied that the company is "committed to complying with tax rules and paying all legally obliged taxes. At the same time, we have a responsibility to our shareholders to legally minimize our costs."[26] Similarly, when Apple was criticized in the media for going to great lengths to avoid paying millions in taxes,[27] the company responded that, in addition to being a job creator and a contributor to charitable causes, it "has conducted all of its business with the highest of ethical standards, complying with applicable laws and accounting rules."[28] Generating public objection to tax avoidance in the face of a tradition of supportive legal jurisprudence and cultural understandings, including about the nature and the role of the corporation in society, is thus a potentially monumental task.

Making tax avoidance a question of morality is a difficult terrain for activists. It automatically invokes actual tax compliance as a ready defence. But it also involves the interplay of various legal rules enacted by sovereign (and often democratic) governments, as well as the kind of political malfunction that allows special interest groups to influence and directly author the laws that regulate themselves and their clients – at a high cost to broader society.[29] As a result, linking

---

23 *Helvering v. Gregory*, 69 F.2d 809, 810 (2d Cir. 1934).
24 See *Duke of Westminster v. IRC* [1936] 19 D.T.C. 490, 520 (Can.); see also *Ayrshire Pullman Motor Services and Ritchie v. IRC* [1929] 14 D.T.C. 754, 763 (Can.) ("No man in this country is under the smallest obligation, moral or other, so to arrange his legal relations to his business or to his property as to enable the Inland Revenue to put the largest possible shovel into his stores.").
25 Kocieniewski, n.4.
26 Ibid.
27 Duhigg and Kocieniewski, n.4.
28 "Apple's Response on Its Tax Practices", *New York Times* (28 April 2012), available at www.nytimes.com/2012/04/29/business/apples-response-on-its-tax-practices.html?_r=0.
29 The outsized influence wielded by business lobbyists is outlined in R. Alexander, S. Scholz and S. Mazza, "Measuring Rates of Return for Lobbying Expenditures: An Empirical Case Study of Tax Breaks for Multinational Corporations", 25 *Journal of Law and Policy* 401, 441 (2009), which estimates the return on investment in political influence over tax policy matters to be as high as 22,000 percent. Concerning the ability to author laws, professional firms are not always shy about their ability to shape the law when it comes to creating promotional materials. Corporations also partner with lobbyist think-tank hybrids like the American Legislative Exchange Council (ALEC) to advance their interest through legislative proposals. See, e.g. Am. Ass'n for Justice, "ALEC:

tax avoidance to morality seems to require telling a more complicated story about why an activity that is technically legal should nevertheless be publicly excoriated and ultimately punished.

Some have tried to overcome this challenge by categorizing avoidance into "acceptable" and "aggressive" or, alternatively, "intended" and "abusive" forms. It follows that some kinds of avoidance – such as putting money in a tax-deferred retirement savings account – are morally cleared because they are intended by government; but other kinds of tax avoidance – such as assigning low value to intangibles sold to corporate subsidiaries in order to assign profits to low-tax jurisdictions – must be immoral because the behaviour was not intended by legislators.[30]

This attempt to subcategorize an area of legal but objectionable tax avoidance is precarious. It involves drawing a line that governments themselves have failed to draw adequately, and places blame squarely on the taxpayer for behaviour that is later deemed to have fallen on the wrong side of the line based on a rudimentary idea about what the politicians who wrote the law "intended." This ignores the complex problem of political malfunction (or capture); namely, the outsized influence on tax lawmaking that is wielded by taxpayers who can take advantage of global financial markets and decentralized regulatory schemes to render themselves difficult or impossible to tax.[31]

Thus, when Starbucks, GE, Apple, and countless other companies pledge their fidelity to all applicable laws, they fail to mention the many ways in which they influence the direction of tax law reform on a global basis.[32] This influence not only includes direct lobbying efforts in national lawmaking processes but also involves the much more obscure yet equally important role multinational companies play in influencing tax policy through a panoply of other mechanisms.[33]

Because of this expansive influence on the legislative process, framing tax avoidance as a question of morality based on what legislators intend is therefore not only incapable of solving the problem of controlling taxpayer behaviour, it is inviting a whole new host of interpretive barriers to designing such a solution. Determining lawmaker intent with respect to tax

---

Ghostwriting the Law for Corp. Am." (2010), available at www.justice.org/cps/rde/xbcr/justice/ALEC_Report. pdf; ALEC Exposed, available at www.alecexposed.org. For a discussion of political malfunction and its various forms, see N. Komesar, "In Search of a General Approach to Legal Analysis: A Comparative Institutional Alternative", 79 *Michigan Law Review* 1350 (1981); N. Komesar, "Imperfect Alternatives: Choosing Institutions in Law, Economics, and Public Policy", 93 *Michigan Law Review* 1559 (1994).

30 See, e.g. R. Murphy, "Amazon, and Starbucks Are Struggling to Defend Their Tax Avoidance", *The Guardian* (13 November 2012), available at www.guardian.co.uk/commentisfree/2012/nov/13/amazon-google-starbucks-tax-avoidance. Some commentators argue that the transfer pricing issue is the crux of the problems surrounding the erosion of the corporate tax base. A unitary system of taxation, which would carve up multinational corporation's profits in a more substantively accurate manner, is often cited as the ideal solution to this problem. See, e.g. S. Picciotto, "Towards Unitary Tax. of Transnat'l Corps.", *Tax Justice Network* (2012), available at www.taxjustice. net/cmc/upload/pdf/Towards_UnitarU_Taxation_1-1.pdf.

31 See A. Christians, "Drawing the Boundaries of Tax Justice", in Kim Brooks (Ed.), *The Quest for Tax Reform Continues: The Royal Commission on Taxation Fifty Years Later,* Toronto: Carswell (2013), n.4 at 72–7.

32 In 2013, for example, the UK government reprimanded the Big Four accounting firms for initially playing "gatekeeper" by lending assistance to draft anti-avoidance legislation, and then subsequently for being "poachers" by systemically abusing their position by finding ways to do the very things that said legislative provisions were supposed to stop. See J. Martin, "UK Lawmakers Lambaste Big 4 Accounting Firms", 69 *Tax Notes International* 518 (2013).

33 These range from direct and indirect political spending to presenting promotional marketing as journalism or even academic research. Influence additionally extends to participation in various international networks – most notably the OECD – where access to lawmakers can be had in informal, mostly unobservable ways. While direct lobbying and some forms of political spending are increasingly well-documented and subject to public scrutiny as well as systemic academic analysis, the other forms of political influence are just as pervasive, yet most are rarely acknowledged in scholarship on tax policymaking.

policy requires a holistic approach that is both pluralistic and globalized in nature. This adds tremendous difficulties to the already extensively documented problem of determining legislative intent in general.

The OECD's own role in articulating tax norms provides one example of the difficulty. Lee Sheppard has argued that the OECD is principally responsible for at least three of the biggest tax base-eroding regimes in existence globally: the "treaty treatment of remote commerce; tax treatment of related-party financial transactions; [and] transfer pricing, especially separation of income from relevant activity."[34] If the lawmaker's intent marks the line between what is objectionable tax avoidance and what is not, these three regimes are problematic to say the least.[35]

Articulating exactly what a lawmaking body intended in enacting any one of these regimes would be difficult. Taken together, one might readily conclude that lawmakers in many of the OECD member countries intend not to tax very much of anything that touches international markets at all. If that is true, then much of the tax avoidance sought to be moderated with a moral requirement to abide by an assumed spirit of the law could be perfectly in line with that spirit. Troublingly, this is the case even if the spirit is implied from legislative intentions that go unstated for reasons having to do with the politics of self-preservation. Like native advertising, special interest group protection through favourable legislation is best accomplished when it is not done so overtly.[36] Adjudicating taxpayer behaviour on this basis provides no answer to the possibility that much tax legislation is in fact sponsored content.

The problem of interpreting legislative intent is further thwarted by the crowding out of alternative policy influences. This happens, for example, to the extent that the OECD, self-described as the world's "market leader in tax policy,"[37] quashes policymaking attempts by rival institutions.[38] Crowding out alternative viewpoints ensures institutional rigidity and adherence to status quo interests. It also ensures ongoing isolation of the issues facing poor countries in the global tax order.[39] As Michael Durst, a former IRS official, puts it:

> I have frequently observed [lobbying at the OECD] at close hand, and I believe it has been influential. The effectiveness of lobbying efforts has been enhanced, I believe, by the absence of any financially interested constituency that might serve as an effective counterweight and therefore as a political force for changes to current laws.[40]

Some activists have begun to point out the crisis for the rule of law on both a national and international level that is presented by this kind of political malfunction. For example, the Tax

34 Sheppard, n.22.
35 See, e.g. D. Spencer, "Tax Justice Network, Transfer Pricing: Will the OECD Adjust to Reality?" (2012), available at www.taxjustice.net/cmc/upload/pdf/Spencer_120521_OECD_.pdf; M. Durst, "The Two Worlds of Transfer Pricing Policymaking", 61 *Tax Notes International* 439 (2011).
36 See, e.g. C. Warzel, "The Real Problem With the Atlantic's Sponsored Post Debacle Proves That Above All Else, Native Ads Need to Feel Native", *Adweek* (15 January 2013, 12:51 PM), available at www.adweek.com/news/technology/real-problem-atlantics-sponsored-post-146553.
37 See, e.g. OECD's Current Tax Agenda, OECD (2012), available at www.oecd.org/ctp/OECDCurrentTaxAgenda2012.pdf.
38 R. Murphy, "OECD Should Step Down and Let UN Tackle Tax Havens Say Tax Justice Network and Action Aid", Tax Research UK (1 November 2011), available at www.tax research.org.uk/Blog/2011/11/01/oecd-should-step-aside-and-let-un-tackle-tax-havens-say-tax-justice-network-and-action-aid/.
39 See, e.g. F. Horner, "Do We Need an International Tax Organization?" 24 *Tax Notes International* 179 (2001).
40 Durst, n.38, at 442.

Justice Network has questioned the outsize influence on tax policy exercised by the OECD.[41] As activists begin to tie legal tax avoidance by multinational actors to the connection between the impenetrable forum of international tax lawmaking and the inability of the public to monitor the outcomes of such lawmaking in practice,[42] they will accordingly seek public accountability for the true cost of these regimes as a remedy.

Pluralism and the soft law path

Because the message of legal tax avoidance is both complex and nuanced, and features behaviour that is not obviously objectionable when compared to tax evasion, activists typically combine tax evasion and tax avoidance into a single category when presenting the problem to the public. For example, James Henry – an American tax justice activist who was formerly Director of Economic Research (chief economist) for McKinsey – states:

> Both evasion and avoidance have the same impact on the rest of us, which is, our tax burdens are greater because the truly rich are not paying their fair share: they are able to put their money abroad, and are basically able to take advantage of a system that allows double non-taxation. And that's a real problem.[43]

Henry thus combines tax avoidance, which is the product of either intentional or inept (or both) rule-making, with tax evasion, which is the product of taxpayers flouting the rules and governments not stopping them. This allows a single message to permeate the public consciousness; namely, that whether it is avoidance or evasion, taxpayers are misbehaving and they must be stopped.

The intentionally pluralistic character of the last century of tax policy development serves as the basis for arguing that the rule of law must be central in the formulation of any solution to this problem. This pluralistic character is most clearly evidenced in the use by rich countries of non-legal methods to create and maintain the system in existence today, including facilitating the central role played by tax havens in the global financial system.[44] Because the institutional and regulatory status quo constrains the capacity of governments to respond unilaterally to problems involving international taxation, the OECD – as its chief architect – has been criticized for perpetuating a democratic deficit in tax lawmaking, for skewing tax policy to favour its members and their constituencies, and for advancing an agenda that is inconsistent with other global social goals within the safely ensconced parameters of black-box policymaking.[45]

---

41 Taxcast Edition 14, *Tax Justice Network* (February 2013), available at www.tackletaxhavens.com/taxcast/.

42 For an anecdotal account of the difficulties related to observing OECD deliberations, see A. Christians, "What an OECD 'Public Briefing' Teaches About the Rule of Law", *Tax, Society & Culture* (18 February 2013), available at http://taxpol.blogspot.com/2013/02/what-oecd-public-briefing-teaches-about.html.

43 Carroll Trust, "Gibraltar Offshore Accounts Tax Evasion Scandal", *YouTube* (14 November 2012), available at www.youtube.com/watch?v=Cv6d9b9Z9C4.

44 C. M. Boise and A. P. Morriss, "Change, Dependency, and Regime Plasticity in Offshore Financial Intermediation: The Saga of the Netherlands Antilles", 35 *Texas International Law Journal* 377, 429 (2009); T. Freyer and A.P. Morriss, "Creating Cayman as an Offshore Financial Center: Structure & Strategy since 1960", 45 *Arizona State Law Journal*, 1297 (2013) ; R. Eccleston, *The Dynamics of Global Economic Governance: The Financial Crisis, the OECD and the Politics of International Tax Cooperation* (2012), 2; Christians, n.11.

45 For a discussion, see A. Christians, "Global Trends and Constraints on Tax Policy in the Least Developed Countries", 42 *UBC Law Review* 239 (2010).

Since the OECD is not a lawmaking body but instead deals in "norms" and "standards," there exist in law no remedies for any of its perceived misdeeds, no matter how far-reaching or damaging. Anyone who disagrees with the OECD's global grip over tax policy has little choice but to mount a challenge through another institution or mechanism that will inevitably be out-matched in financial and institutional support. Some may even be overtly thwarted in such an effort by those who seek to sustain the primacy of the OECD in preserving its own brand of tax policy against any would-be competitors. The OECD's continued tax policy domination sug-gests that its member countries have to date been well served by using these non-legal methods to shape tax practices on the ground around the world.

Given the massive resource difference between tax justice advocates and the OECD member governments, it seems clear the latter will employ their well-resourced and highly motivated supporting constituencies to clear the way for OECD-based policy views to continue to prevail. This power difference must be acknowledged as real, even while it is vigorously protested as a fundamentally unjust way to decide how states can and should exercise taxation, and continu-ously countered with comprehensively justice-oriented policy alternatives. Starting from the premise that the status quo is a product of decades of soft law, a convincing case can be made that governments can and should contain the mechanisms for controlling inappropriate behaviour within the structure of law instead.

Using law to constrain taxpayer behaviour

The line between avoidance and evasion, like many line-drawing exercises in tax or otherwise, is fraught with difficulties.[46] It is a line that should be drawn not with soft law but with legal principles, continuously monitored and enforced through compliance with agreed upon rules and standards, backed up by judicial review, to put the taxpayers on notice as to the behavioural expectations applicable to all.

This is not to say that governments are or should be helpless against formalistic or sophisti-cated tax planning.[47] Governments are clearly not helpless in this regard: this is the point and purpose of anti-abuse rules. These may be bright-line rules, such as thin capitalization and ben-eficial ownership, or more flexible regimes that rely on weighing and balancing with judicial oversight as a backstop, such as general and specific anti-avoidance rules, sham and step trans-action doctrines, and economic purpose tests.[48] All of these are admittedly cumbersome ways to solve complex problems, but they are at least capable of collectively moving the tax system toward more coherence and consistency of application.

In contrast, suggesting that the difference between illegal and legal cannot be established in law posits that while societies are incapable of articulating the parameters of acceptable conduct

---

46 See, e.g. D. Weisbach, "Line Drawing, Doctrine, and Efficiency in Tax Law", Univ. of Chi. Law Sch. John M. Olin Law & Econ. Working Paper No. 62, available at www.law.uchicago.edu/files/files/62.Weisbach.Line_.complete. pdf.

47 It is also not to suggest that tax advisors are themselves amoral actors, mere technicians, or automatons of any kind. They clearly are not, and professional standards are regularly set and enforced with respect to their behaviour in statutory and administrative rule-making, as well as private membership association regimes. *See* M. Hatfield, *The Ethics of Tax Lawyering*, 2nd ed., Chicago: CALI eLangdell Press (2011); P. C. Canellos, "A Tax Practitioner's Perspective on Substance, Form and Business Purpose in Structuring Business Transactions and in Tax Shelters", 54 *S.M.U. Law Review* 47 (2001).

48 The literature is vast on this topic. See, e.g. L. Lederman, "W(h)ither Economic Substance?" 95 *Iowa Law Review* 389 (2010); C. M. Pietruszkiewicz, "Economic Substance and the Standard of Review", 60 *Alabama Law Review* 339 (2009).

within the law, legal sanction will nevertheless be imposed for noncompliance. This implies that punishment can and will be meted out randomly, because judgments about taxpayer behaviour will be made outside of the sphere of deliberative lawmaking and instead in the court of public opinion.

Bypassing the legislative sphere as the proper place for making and enforcing decisions about civic responsibility shifts the duty of oversight away from governments and toward civil society writ large, which includes not just NGOs, activists, and others who may be interested in promoting tax justice or fairness but also all of the lobbyists, consultants, paid marketers and promoters, and other political actors who have their own agendas and many resources and mechanisms to advance them.

Assigning the problem of categorizing taxpayer behaviour to the public in this manner has pernicious effects. The most troubling of these is that it releases legislators from responsibility too easily, allowing them to continue to benefit from sponsoring legislation that favours their constituencies while purporting to act in the interest of the public. But it also runs the serious risk of pushing against the path to good governance more systemically by turning too quickly to soft law without considering how to deal with the political influence problems that will inevitably persist and may even worsen in this scenario. Instead of turning to morality as a soft law backstop to an ongoing tax governance crisis, the better path seems to be the one most tax justice advocates recommend; namely, achieving expansive transparency in lawmaking processes so as to enable public monitoring of what the legal regime produces in terms of actual outcomes for taxpayers.

Transparency has become a buzzword in international governance in general, so it is perhaps no surprise to see it mobilized by tax justice advocates. Given the technical complexity of the regimes in question, and how those regimes interact across borders to create the related yet distinct issues of evasion and avoidance, seeking transparency in international tax is no small feat. It will involve first a clear statement of the ills to be remedied – an elusive task, given the tradition of opacity and the prevalence of soft law, as well as non-legal processes and institutions. It must then overcome the institutional hurdles presented by a global tax policy regime that restricts influence from outside the business community.

But this is precisely where the intractable problem of drawing a line between tax avoidance and tax evasion may be viewed as an opportunity to achieve systemic reform. At least two systemic tax governance traditions could be challenged on the grounds that each leads to the public's inability to distinguish between tax evasion and tax avoidance, and therefore each breaks down the legitimacy of tax law in the court of public opinion, thus furthering a cycle of incoherent and uneven application of tax laws within and across societies.

The first of these systemic tax governance traditions is the outsize influence of well-resourced special interest groups over tax lawmaking processes in both domestic and international settings. There is little doubt that tax policy suffers because too much policy influence is wielded by one particular sector; namely, the business community in the influential OECD member countries and their worldwide network of lawyers, accountants, and other advisers who are well paid and therefore highly motivated to serving in this effort. Far too much of this influence is being exerted in institutions and processes that are inaccessible to public view. This suggests, at minimum, that governments have accepted, contrary to social policy goals, an inappropriate amount of obscurity around the many ways in which well-resourced actors control the design and maintenance of tax systems across the globe.

Many of the problems for tax policy posed by opacity in political influence are solvable as governance problems through the mechanism of transparency. In this case, the transparency contemplated includes the complete documentation with respect to all government officials – at all levels (national and international included) – of every meeting had with any person not in government, disclosing time spent, issues discussed, and every dollar received in the form of campaign support, issue support, or otherwise.

This is more or less the working principle of various countries' lobbying registries, as well as open meetings and access to information laws, but it envisions a more thorough public surveillance of interactions between government officials and the public at all levels and in all capacities. This kind of transparency would enable public observation of the connection between political influence and fully compliant yet significantly low-taxed members of society, and therefore provide desperately needed data points for making the case of why full compliance with existing laws is not a benchmark for appropriate taxpayer behaviour but rather a starting point for critical inquiry regarding the accountability of lawmakers to the broader public.

A second systemic tax governance tradition that impedes the ability of the public to distinguish between tax evasion and tax avoidance is the confidentiality accorded to taxpayers' tax information. This confidentiality prevents the public from observing how the law on the books plays out on the ground, and therefore sows the seeds for outrage when the media exposes the tax affairs of yet another high profile member of society.

Again, transparency is the obvious solution, this time in the form of public disclosure of certain kinds of tax information. While there is a case to be made for favouring confidentiality over publicity in the case of individuals,[49] the same case has not been made for corporations. Tax disclosure reforms, with respect to both pertinent annual tax information and beneficial ownership, have long been advocated by academics and other tax policy observers, and the tax evasion/avoidance problem could serve as the reason to finally embrace sunlight with respect to this kind of information.

Further bolstering the case for transparency, the uneven reputational risk of naming and shaming based on celebrity status or name brand visibility ought to motivate members of society whose tax affairs tell a different story to bring their governments to account for failing to delineate between tax avoidance and tax evasion in a comprehensive manner. To the extent that the targets of naming and shaming object to the charges of immorality and point to full compliance with all regulatory regimes, they should have no objection to a transparent system of governance that would allow the public to monitor tax policy outcomes on the ground.

Conclusion

The failure to coherently delineate between tax evasion and tax avoidance is not the product of legal impossibility but rather of governance failure. The answer to this governance failure is not to turn away from law by articulating a non-legal standard of behaviour based in the language of morality and then using this standard as a means to inflict legal sanctions. Instead, the answer is to demand more from the law, which means expecting more accountability in governance. This is not a revelation but a reminder of governance lessons already learned.

Transparency has always created pressure on governments to solve line-drawing problems; in tax policy it is the same story. Tax transparency forces lawmakers to expand their engagement with society beyond their immediate sources of sponsorship by improving the feedback loop between lawmaking and policy monitoring. Mechanisms like public disclosure of tax-related data and broad public participation in tax law policymaking – at all levels and in all forms of governance – have the potential to dislodge rhetoric based on conjecture and deliver to the

---

49 J. Blank, "In Defense of Individual Privacy", 61 *Emory Law Journal* 265 (2011).

public the data needed for independent study of the tax system as it plays out in practice rather than as it is suggested by the words placed in statutes by legislators whose intentions are ambiguous at best.

It is precisely within the act of drawing a line between tax avoidance and evasion that the dire need for transparency most reveals itself. The idea that taxpayer behaviour must be managed by law, rather than social sanction, rests fundamentally on the premise that tax policy can move toward greater coherence over time if the public persistently demands a means of monitoring law-making. Transparency, therefore, becomes a tool for forcing governments to distinguish between legal and illegal behaviour within a regime that is capable of sustained public observation as well as participation that is itself observable – namely, the rule of law. The desperate need for an articulation of the difference between tax avoidance and tax evasion accordingly illustrates why transparency is consistently viewed as an essential requirement for the pursuit of tax justice.

Acknowledgements

This chapter is revised and adapted from A. Christians, "Avoidance, Evasion, and Taxpayer Morality", 44 *Washington University Journal of Law and Policy* (2013), 39–59.

27

UNACCEPTABLE TAX BEHAVIOUR AND CORPORATE RESPONSIBILITY

John Hasseldine and Gregory Morris

Introduction

Over many decades, but concerning certain specific matters, more noticeable since the financial crisis of 2008, the behaviour of corporations[1] has been subject to scrutiny and comment. Politicians (in both domestic contexts and international forums), the governments of various countries, the media, various NGOs and other social commentators have expressed their opinions on many aspects of corporate behaviour and on the types of activity in which corporations should and should not engage.

In this context, there continues to develop a number of powerful discourses which articulate an expectation that corporations have a wider remit than one that is simply focused upon the generation of profit for the benefit of the shareholders. This wide ranging discourse, which includes various themes relating to governance frameworks, ethics,[2] labour policy and practice, environmental engagement, sustainability, corporate social responsibility and various stakeholder concerns, seeks to provide a model of the purpose or role of corporations which requires that when decisions are taken in respect of using the corporation's assets and resources the interests of many, and not only the interests of shareholders, should be taken into account.

The subject matter of this chapter is part of this wide ranging discourse. It has as its particular concern certain types of corporate behaviour and whether such behaviour may be considered to be acceptable or not. More specifically, in this chapter we explore the nature of corporate behaviour which at least in part, is prompted by the existence, operation and effects of a country's tax system[3] and the assessments that are made of such behaviour.

We are not alone in expressing an interest in the relationship between the tax system of one or more countries, the types of corporate behaviour that can arise in response to such systems,

---

1 For the purposes of this chapter, references to corporations are references to commercially motivated corporations and not to, for example, not-for-profit corporations. Although a number of the issues that are discussed in this chapter are also relevant when considering not-for-profit corporations, we do not consider such matters further.

2 In this chapter we make no distinction between ethics and morals; the two words are used interchangeably.

3 A tax system of a country is the collection of rules and practices, including the tax code enacted in that country, that seeks to impose taxation and collect tax revenue ostensibly to be used by a government or state for the 'public good'. Each tax system is imperfect, it has a history, is subject to political, economic and pragmatic influences and is understood, applied and administered by human beings.

and assessments being made as to whether a corporation is socially responsible or not. In the past decade there have been a number of publications, from academics and non-academics from various backgrounds including, politicians, professional practice, NGOs, national and international bodies, civil activists[4] and civil society generally[5] in which the relationship between corporate behaviour and tax systems, the reporting of the relationship (or indeed, lack of reporting of the relationship) and the consequences of such behaviour (see for example, Christian Aid (2015) and ActionAid (2016) have been considered, evaluated and even criticised.

In recent years corporations have been accused of not paying their 'fair share' of tax (TJN (2016)), of engaging in offensive 'profit shifting' (see for example Christian Aid (2013) and Washington Center (2016)) and more generally, participating in 'unacceptable tax avoidance' and 'tax dodging' arrangements (Oxfam (2016) and Cobham et al. (2015). The relationship between tax systems, corporate behaviour and the credentials of a corporation as regards any claim it makes as to it being socially responsible is the subject matter and concern of this chapter. Our aim is to identify and discuss various types of tax-related behaviour[6] that have been considered as unacceptable and explore the nature of the criteria or standards by reference to which such an assessment is made. In so doing we consider whether or not any of the principles that are associated with the corporate social responsibility ('CSR' henceforth) movement(s) are relevant when assessing the acceptability of tax-related behaviour.

Various matters need to be addressed when exploring tax-related behaviour, and many of these matters are complex. For example, the nature of tax-related behaviour has to be understood in the context of a tax system which itself exists within the framework of a wider system of national and international law and practice. In addition, as we are primarily concerned with corporations which, although acknowledged as legal persons, are very different from human beings, it is also necessary to consider the nature of the corporate entity and the freedoms and constraints to which a corporation may be subject. We are aware that even though various opinions have been expressed and claims have been made relating to the tax-related behaviour of corporations and the principles associated with CSR there has been little acknowledgment or

---

4 There are many different groups of interested parties that have contributed to the discussions on tax related behaviour. For convenience we refer to the group of interested parties and commentators consisting of politicians, the media, civil activists and non-governmental organisations (NGOs) who have taken an interest in tax related behaviour as the 'commentariat'. We acknowledge that by combining these disparate groups into one category, some of the more subtle differences between them are obscured, but we do so in the interests of brevity. We are grateful to Professor Lynne Oats for bringing to our attention this convenient way of referring to this group of interested parties and commentators.

5 The academic literature and other publications on these topics is considerable. A number of publications are referred to throughout this chapter but our references are not exhaustive.

6 The term 'tax-related behaviour' is not a term in common usage but it is useful as it seeks to be a neutral term that encompasses many commonly used terms such as, 'tax mitigation', 'tax planning', 'tax avoidance' and 'tax evasion', terms which as will be returned to in Part 1 have developed something of a polyseme nature having become rather equivocal in acquiring different meanings in various of the discussions that address such behaviour. We use this term to refer to corporate behaviour that is intentional, is in some manner a response to the tax system (including the tax code) of one or more countries and is motivated by the beneficial consequences that are expected to result from such behaviour. In this context, tax related behaviour will include the agreements, transactions and arrangements to which a corporation is a party, (whether over a period of time, for example a period of account, or as a one-off matter), the choice of asset and resource location (including that of financial and intangible assets) and also the structures adopted (financial and location) by, for example, various members of a group of companies. Tax related behaviour can refer to (a) behaviour that considers or appraises the tax consequences of a specific matter that is being considered, or (b) the entering into or implementation of a selected agreement, transaction or arrangement, or (c) the behaviour that follows the crystallisation of a liability to tax (or an entitlement to a relief) which can be referred to as compliance.

recognition of the importance of many of the matters that we consider in this chapter. Instead there is a tendency to settle for an unexamined understanding of these matters as a consequence of which the relevance of many of the issues we discuss has not been taken into account in various of the assessments of tax-related behaviour that have been made.

This has partly resulted in discussions occurring about tax-related behaviour in which although the participants appear to be talking with common purpose and meaning, such discussions are, in fact, operating somewhat at a cross purpose. Without an exploration of the nature of tax-related behaviour as it undertaken by corporations within the context of a tax system of a state, any discussion about such matters might prove to be superficial and inadequate.

We suggest that without some form of framework within which understanding of these matters can be located, a framework that can in turn be considered and criticised by others, energy and effort expended on exploring the relationship between corporations and society that exists at the interface of taxation may prove to be misguided and could lead to the development of lines of argument that are eventually recognised as rather fruitless.

The rest of this chapter will be as follows. Part 1 discusses different types of tax-related behaviour and the terms that are used and have been used in the ongoing discussions. Part 2 provides a summary of the CSR and how the principles of CSR might be relevant to assessing certain types of tax-related behaviour. In Part 3 the relationship between a tax system, a tax payer and the state is considered. Part 4 identifies a number of key characteristics of the corporate form. Part 5 discusses a number of different types of tax-related behaviour that has been considered by various parties to be unacceptable. Finally, in Part 6 we conclude.

Part 1 Words and more words: avoidance, evasion and other terms

As indicated in footnote 6, in this chapter we use the term 'tax-related behaviour'. When seeking to understand the various narratives, comments, and criticisms that have arisen over the last couple of decades concerning the behaviour of corporations within the context of taxation what is apparent is the differences that exists in the meaning of terms that are considered important when discussing these matters. In this Part 1 we briefly consider a number of the terms which have been used to discuss what we refer to as tax-related behaviour. It is tempting to fixate on finding the most appropriate term(s) and to seek the 'correct' or 'true' definition of those term as if by so doing the important and relevant characteristics of the actual behaviour that is sought will be revealed. For reasons that we discuss in Part 1 we do not consider such an approach to be useful.

1.1 Different terms, different meanings[7]

Many different terms have been used when discussing tax-related behaviour and these terms do not have fixed or even generally accepted meanings. Such familiar terms as 'tax planning', 'tax mitigation', 'tax avoidance', 'tax shelters' and 'tax evasion' (and many others) are often used by different interested parties in different ways. In addition, such terms are often prefixed with such adjectives as 'acceptable', 'unacceptable', 'aggressive', 'artificial' 'immoral' and many others.

The use of such different terms reflects an attempt to categorise tax-related behaviour into two categories, tax-related behaviour that is acceptable and that which is not. How each of

---

7 The reasons for change in the meaning of the various terms associated with tax related behaviour are many [See Chapter 28 in this book].

these two categories is to be understood and given meaning will vary depending upon which group of interested parties[8] is seeking to provide the meaning.[9] The term 'tax avoidance' might be used by one group or in one state to refer to tax-related behaviour that is acceptable but may be used by another group or in a different state to refer to tax-related behaviour; this is unacceptable. These differences are neatly demonstrated by comparing the approach taken by the tax administration of the USA ('IRS') with the approach taken by the UK tax administration ('HMRC'). There is a taxpayer 'quiz' available on the IRS website intended to help USA taxpayers understand tax. The quiz actually states: 'Tax avoidance is perfectly legal and encouraged by the IRS …' (IRS 2016). The approach of the IRS is in stark contrast with the approach taken by HMRC in which tax avoidance is a category of tax-related behaviour which is simply not acceptable (HMRC 2016).

Many of these terms used in the discussions and commentaries which focus on corporate tax-related behaviour have become polysemes, the same term can have many different meanings, for example what HMRC understand by the term 'tax avoidance' is different from the understanding of that term held by many tax advisors, academics and various members of the commentariat (see for example Barker (2009), Prebble et al. (2010), Sikka (2010) and previous references). As a result such terms no longer provide any simple, useful and generally accepted meaning which can be of assistance when considering whether a particular example of tax-related behaviour is acceptable or not. We suggest that rather than focus on the 'true meaning' of a particular term what is more important is an understanding of the characteristics or qualities of the actual tax-related behaviour undertaken and an appreciation of the context within which the behaviour is to be understood.

1.2 Equating legality and acceptability

Although many of the terms used in the discussions about tax-related behaviour have little in the way of accepted meaning, a distinction that is often considered relevant when trying to distinguish between acceptable and unacceptable tax-related behaviour is that between lawful and unlawful behaviour. This distinction can even been reduced by some to the principle: 'tax avoidance is legal and tax evasion is illegal'. The phrase suggests that if tax-related behaviour is legal then it might also be acceptable.

This principle is founded on the understanding that behaviour involving fraud and deceit or engaging in activities that are themselves unlawful (for example a business involving the distribution of unlawful drugs), is unacceptable. In contrast if there is no fraud or deceit associated with the tax-related behaviour and the activities undertaken are lawful, then the relevant tax-related behaviour must be legal. It is through the application of this principle ('tax avoidance is legal and tax evasion is illegal') that a link has been made between the acceptability of various types of tax-related behaviour and the lawful nature of such behaviour, as if the criterion of legality was sufficient to capture acceptability. Many interested parties, particularly some members of the commentariat, have found this approach to be unsatisfactory and have claimed that

---

8 Examples of different groups of interested parties would include academics, tax advisors, taxpayers, tax administrators, economists and members of the commentariat (see footnote 4).

9 We are not claiming however that each identifiable group of interested parties has necessarily has a distinct and homogeneous framework of principles and rules to which the group subscribes. Indeed at times it is difficult to grasp the coherence of the principles proposed by some interested parties, as the principles take on a random or somewhat irrational character. For example tax related behaviour undertaken by an associated subsidiary within an MNE may be considered unacceptable but effectively the same behaviour undertaken by a non-associated corporation is acceptable.

even if tax-related behaviour is legal (i.e. does not involve fraud and deceit or unlawful activities) it might still be unacceptable (see for example Tax Justice Network: FAQ).

1.3 Identifying legal but unacceptable tax-related behaviour

As a result of a dissatisfaction voiced by many with the principle that seeks to equate acceptable tax-related behaviour with the legality of that behaviour attempts have been made in more recent years to identify tax-related behaviour which is legal but is to be classified as unacceptable. Many of these attempts have focused on offering different terms in order to capture and refer to different types of tax-related behaviour, as if by naming something in a particular manner significant differences are brought into existence.[10] Such terms as 'tax planning' and 'tax mitigation' have been used to refer to acceptable and legal tax-related behaviour, and this type of behaviour is contrasted with unacceptable but legal tax-related behaviour, which may even be referred to by such terms as 'tax avoidance'[11] or 'aggressive tax planning'.

The relationship between various types of tax-related behaviour has even be represented visually using a line, a continuum, at one end of which is acceptable tax-related behaviour (whether referred to as tax mitigation, tax planning or another similar term), at the other end of the line there is located what is clearly illegal and therefore unacceptable behaviour, often identified as some form of tax evasion. Unacceptable but legal tax-related behaviour appears somewhere along the line, in the 'grey area' between tax evasion and tax planning (Frecknall-Hughes 2014). Taking such an approach to categorising tax-related behaviour is not altogether helpful. At the very least it conceals, through an appeal to a visual representation which claims explanatory power, the difficulties that exist in any attempt to identify the characteristics that tax-related behaviour which is accepted as being legal but unacceptable possesses.

For the purposes of this chapter, we consider that the term(s) used by any interested party to refer to tax-related behaviour which is considered to be unacceptable even though it is legal is not overly important. What is more important is to identify and understand the reasons that support such a classification and to explore the relationship between the supporting reasons and any assessment that is made of a corporation being considered socially responsible or not.

One of the purposes of this chapter is to identify and evaluate various assessments that have been made of tax-related behaviour. The evaluation will be by reference to principles often associated with a CSR perspective of corporate behaviour by exploring whether the CSR narrative is sufficiently developed to provide standards by reference to which certain types of tax-related behaviour can be considered as unacceptable. In order to understand the relationship between possible categories of tax-related behaviour and these principles we now turn to the wide ranging umbrella discourse of CSR (Prieto-Carron et al. (2006)).

Part 2 Corporate social responsibility

2.1 CSR and corporate behaviour

In the introduction to this chapter we noted that the behaviour of corporations has been subject to considerable scrutiny over many decades. The language in which such scrutiny is

10 An example of this type of response to tax related behaviour can be seen in the UK published report that considers the introduction of a General Anti Abuse Provision into the UK tax system. The word 'egregious' was used to identify a type of unacceptable but legal tax related behaviour (Aaronson 2011).
11 See Chapter 28 of this volume.

couched has become commonplace and is used with abandon within the commentariat and various other commentators. At least in part, the scrutiny has been prompted and inspired by demands that corporations, in addition to being value seeking, should also be, in some manner, socially responsible. That is, corporations have obligations (responsibilities) not only to shareholders but also to others. These demands are applied to many and varied issues, from considering the constituent parts of supply chains, through labour practices and a corporation's relationship with the environment to the location of units of production. Indeed there appears to be little to limit the types of corporate behaviour which are considered to fall under the umbrella provided by the CSR movement.[12]

Corporations have responded to these demands and CSR reports are now commonplace. A CSR report tends to focus on the disclosure of a corporation's activity as regards the environment, the community, labour practices, sustainability etc., but little is reported about the taxation practices and policies of those same corporations. As a result, this perceived lack of reporting on tax matters has focussed the attention of some within the wide ranging CSR community on the tax-related behaviour of corporations (Avi-Yonah, R. (2008), Jenkins, R. et al. (2013), Sikka, P. (2010), McIntyre, R. S. et al. (2011)).

For some commentators, it is by reference to the more ethically focussed principles found within CSR discourse(s) that certain types of tax-related behaviour are condemned as being unacceptable (see references in previous paragraph). As part of this approach it is even suggested by some (Christensen et al. (2004), Preuss (2010) and Sikka (2010)) that engagement with what is classified as unacceptable tax-related behaviour severely taints the overall CSR status of a corporation. This is the case even if many of the other CSR focussed activities of the corporation have merit and are to be encouraged.

If some types of tax-related behaviour are considered unacceptable by reference to ethical principles that are linked to CSR it would be helpful to identify, explain and critically examine any such principles. However when CSR ethical principles that might possibly be applicable to taxation are sought in order to examine their content and status we are immediately confronted by what considered a major problem: there is not one fixed understanding, description or explanation of CSR.

2.2 *What is CSR?*

There have been some rather bizarre definitions of CSR,[13] but perhaps the major issue that arises when trying to pin down the nature of CSR is well captured by Votaw (1973): 'The term [corporate social responsibility] is a brilliant one; it means something, but not always the same thing, to everybody.' This lack of consensus creates concerns in respect of both theory and practice.

A recent review of theoretical perspectives in the field of CSR identified six major and different theoretical frameworks that have been used in articles published in leading academic

---

12 In this chapter, we do not consider the history and development of the principles to be found within the CSR movement, (the claim(s) that corporations, in some manner, have obligations or duties to society and other stakeholders (the right holders) that go beyond the legal obligations that exist in such circumstances. For further information on the development of CSR see, for example, Crane et al. (2008).

13 Here is one definition of CSR which is rather wide ranging in the duties it suggests are imposed upon corporations by the principles underlying CSR: 'We define CSR as the duty of the companies (sic) to the development of its stakeholders, and to the avoidance and correction of any negative consequences caused by business activities' (Muthuri and Gilber (2011)). This definition is bizarre because it suggests a corporation has a duty to the 'development of its stakeholders and also a duty to correct *any* consequences of corporate activity, whether deliberate or not'.

journals between 1990 and 2104 to discuss CSR (Frynas et al. (2016)). Such a proliferation of approaches suggests there that may be little in the way of consistency as regards the ethical principles that are commonly attributed to CSR behaviour by reference to which tax-related behaviour can be assessed. It is easy to claim, that corporations are subject to ethical considerations concerning their tax-related behaviour, but such a lack of consistency and coherence in the identification of any such ethical considerations can lead to doubts as to the robustness of such claims.

In addition to the different theoretical perspectives that have been identified, a further concern is that CSR as practiced by corporations might have no foundation whatsoever that can be identified as ethically based. The editors of a special issue of Organization on CSR, whilst remaining positive, acknowledged that three general areas of research (and hence understanding) exist concerning CSR. 'CSR is viewed as a) undesirable given the profit imperative of the firm (e.g. Friedman (1970)); b) a possible panacea for taming the negative externalities of the business enterprise (e.g. Porter and Kramer (2011)) or c) an ideological tool designed to cloak (or "green wash") an otherwise uncaring corporation in the garb of ethicality and environmental friendliness.' (Fleming et al. (2013)) This analysis suggests that CSR in practice is little more than an instrumental behaviour set with little normative content other than that provided by law and an economic requirement to seek value (see for example Banerjee (2008)).

2.3 CSR: ethics and philanthropy

The view of CSR presented in Part 2.2 does not sit easily with other models of CSR, for example the analysis provided by Carroll (Carroll 1991) which offers an understanding of CSR that is perhaps more attuned to 'folk' understandings, recognising as it does the importance of normative principles. Carroll distinguishes four categories: the economic, legal, ethical and philanthropic principles which prompt corporate behaviour. He suggests that although all of these four categories of principle are important when considering corporate behaviour it is the latter two which are crucial and distinctive when categorising corporate behaviour as socially responsible (see also Schwartz et al. (2003) in which Carroll revisits this analysis). It is also recognised by many commentators that in addition to whatever ethical and philanthropic principles are linked to CSR compatible behaviour, there is also appears to be a voluntary character to the behaviour, captured by the phrase, CSR 'goes beyond the law' (see for example BIS (2014) and European Commission (2011)). That is, once legal and economic obligations have been satisfied there remains a space within which corporate choice can be exercised and the motive or reason for the decisions then made are grounded in principles of ethics or philanthropy.

Notwithstanding the lack of clarity and consistency that appears to be present in the very notion of CSR, combining the principles identified by Carroll and the voluntary nature of CSR might be considered to offer a means of understanding of what it is for some types of tax-related behaviour to be considered unacceptable within the context of CSR. This chapter seeks to identify and discuss the aptness of any principle which prompts or guides the voluntary choices of corporations, (after all legal obligations imposed by the tax system of a state have been satisfied), where such a principle is an ethical or philanthropic principle as understood by the CSR movement.

It is might be expected that commentators who have addressed the unacceptability of certain types of tax-related behaviour and have an affinity for analysing corporate behaviour which leans on the discourses and practice of CSR (and similar narratives) will have tried to identify relevant CSR principles and used these to explain how unacceptable tax-related behaviour is to be identified and why this type of behaviour is unacceptable. However, as we will discuss in

Part 5 this does not appear to be the case. As a result, claims that corporations are not socially responsible because they engage in lawful but unacceptable tax-related behaviour, where such claims seek justification by reference to principles located within CSR may prove to be empty and as a focus of corporate criticism may have no content.

Before identifying and discussing the type of tax-related behaviour that is considered unacceptable we provide a brief explanation of the relationship between the operation of a tax system and corporate behaviour.

Part 3 Tax systems

It is a truism to state that without a state adopting and operating a tax system (which will include a tax code) there would be no tax-related behaviour. However this is a truism that is often forgotten when discussing the behaviour of corporations and the tax-related behaviour in which they engage. Without a tax system, corporations operating within a state would almost certainly select between options concerning future arrangements on grounds that were primarily prompted by principles based on value seeking and value creation[14] tempered where necessary in order to maintain some form of legitimacy. By definition, corporations would have no regard to the tax consequences of the selected behaviour.

However, by far the majority of states in the world have some form of tax system to which the activities of corporations may be subject. The written down legal tax code adopted by a state is a vital part of the tax system of a state. It is the tax code, the collection of various tax laws approved (either directly or indirectly) by the legislature of the state, that is the primary source for identifying who is to be taxed, what is to be taxed, how it is to be taxed and the reliefs and credits that are available. A tax code may also contain provisions that deal with the practicalities of the operation of a tax code, including the administration and timing of the satisfaction of tax liabilities and the receipt of the benefit of tax credits and reliefs. It may also contain provisions relating to the processes for the settling of disputes.[15]

3.1 The operation of a tax code: a taxpayer and the state

Although rather daunting in terms of its length, perceived complexity and technical nature, the purpose of a tax code is to identify certain things (but not all things) that exist or happen in the world, states of affairs that exist or are brought about, and attach tax significance to such happenings. Something happens and a tax liability is crystallised. Something else might happen and a different tax liability or even no tax liability will be crystallised. In an analogous manner, something happens and a tax credit or relief might arise. The things that happen that are accorded tax significance by a tax code can be many and varied. A tax code might attach significance to a thing that happens only once (the sale of an asset for example) or to a collection of things that happen over time (for example all of the trading activity of a corporation that takes place over a period of time). When a thing (or things)[16] with tax significance occurs, a tax code will usually

---

14 We assume that in any form of market economy the principles of value seeking and value creation would still be relevant and important. We also assume that value seeking and value creating behaviour operates within a framework of law with which a corporation complies.

15 Although a tax code (and related regulations) might contain provisions that address practical and administrative issues, these topics are not the focus of this chapter. Rather this chapter will focus on the parts of a tax code that relate to tax liabilities and tax reliefs or credits.

16 What usually happens is that a corporation enters into a contract or agreement, participates in an arrangement or transaction, adopts a structure or brings about an event. A corporation engages in actions of one type or another.

provide a mechanism for identifying the value[17] that is to be taxed or relieved and the amount of tax that is due or relief that arises.

Based on the previous description a significant characteristic possessed by any tax code is that a tax code seeks to identity and delineate the collection or class of states of affairs, (to set boundaries on the membership of the set or collection of states of affairs), in respect of which a liability to taxation may crystallise or an entitlement to a relief or credit might arise under each part of a tax code.

This characteristic reflects in part, the relationship between a state and any potential taxpayer who falls within the scope of that state's tax system. The state, through the adoption, interpretation and application of the tax code, usually seeks to make clear those arrangements and resultant states of affairs to which the provisions of a tax code is to apply. There exists an implicit understanding between potential tax payers and a state. Rhetorically, the tax payers asks: 'what are the circumstances in which I have to pay taxation?'.[18] The state answers: 'you are obliged to pay taxation in these, and only these, circumstances'.[19] It is important to note that at present the rhetorical answer is not 'you are obliged to pay taxations in *all* possible circumstances unless there is a specific tax relief or credit provided in the tax system'.

This implicit understanding reflects the nature of the tax system as it exists within the general system of law, (including property law and contract law), operating within a state that supports the principle of the 'rule of law'. As a result, the crystallisation of a liability to taxation (or the arising of an entitlement to a relief) cannot simply be arbitrary, imposed or arising on the whim of a politician, a member of a government, a government official or even a NGO or civil activist, even though some commentators within these various groups might prefer that such an arrangement was indeed the case.

This characteristic also means that the structure and content of a tax code, is of necessity discriminatory. A tax code identifies, collates and distinguishes between different things that can happen in the world. Due to different parts of a tax code focussing on different collections of things that could happen in the world, the tax consequences of the various different things that are identified under a tax code will often be different. One part of a tax code will only have applicability if certain types of things occur and not all things that might occur have tax consequences under that particular part of the tax code. However this does not mean that a particular arrangement when it occurs will not be subject to taxation at all, there might be another part of the tax code under which tax consequences do arise when such an arrangement occurs. The

---

A tax code accords significance to some of these actions whether considered in the singular or in combination. In the rest of this chapter, rather than refer to 'arrangement, structure, situation, event, transaction, action or agreement' we will simply refer to 'arrangements'.

17 A common understanding of a liability to taxation is that it is usually imposed on some form of value whether that be identified as some form of income, profit or gain as defined in the relevant part of the tax system. The value identified might have accrued over a period of time or arisen as a result of a one-time arrangement. The concepts of taxable income, profit or gain will differ from state to state and have to be understood within and depend upon the tax system that operates within that state. The type or the amount of value that is taxable in one state might not be taxable in another state. A liability to taxation may also be imposed on transactions where there is no obvious value being created, for example wealth taxes or property taxes imposed on the transfer of property.

18 The question: 'what are the circumstances in which an entitlement to a tax credit or relief arises?' can also be asked and an analogous answer provided by the state.

19 When considering the tax related behaviour of different corporations that are part of a group of companies it is important to be aware that answer given by one state might be different from the answer given by a second or third state. These differences can be significant when choices are to be made between different options and the different tax consequence of each option being considered.

parts of a tax code that deal with the availability of tax reliefs and credits operate in an analogous manner. A collection or set of states of affairs is identified under a part of a tax code and if any state of affairs within the specified collection or set obtains then an entitlement to the relief or credit will arise.

3.2 Appraising a tax code

For the provisions of a tax code to be applicable, something must happen in the world which is capable of being identified and described. As previously discussed, if the state of affairs that occurs is within a set or collection of state of affairs that is contained with a part of the tax code then there will be tax consequences. The tax consequences of such a state of affairs obtaining will either be the crystallisation of a liability to tax or an entitlement to some form of tax credit or relief.[20] Until a state of affairs is brought about no crystallisation of a liability to taxation or entitlement to a relief or credit will occur.[21] Accordingly there exists a point in time, which can be termed the tax determination point, before which no tax consequences arise but following which tax consequences do arise.[22]

Before a tax position crystallises, that is before a tax determination point, it is possible for a potential tax payer to consider and appraise the expected tax consequences of a particular course of action that may or may not be undertaken.[23] The wide ranging nature and complexity of a tax code provides a tax payer with an opportunity to appraise the expected tax consequences of various options when considering utilisation of the assets and resources it owns. In addition appraisal of the tax code of different states might be relevant to different courses of action that are being considered.

For example, if an investment in a new capital machine is being contemplated, then consideration can be given as to whether the acquisition of the machine should be self-funded, or funded through borrowing or acquired through a leasing arrangement. Before any tax determination point each of these different options can assessed and the expected tax consequences of each option appraised. The expected tax consequences may have an effect on the option selected.

The process of appraisal seeks to understand the purpose of the relevant part(s) of the tax code and how it is to be applied to things that happen in the world. The method of understanding how the tax code applies will take into account any uncertainty in the tax code and the existence of any anti avoidance or anti abuse provisions that form part of the tax system. Appraisal requires understanding how the tax code is to be applied within the context of the tax system and the general framework of law that exists in the state. It also requires the realistic and careful appraisal of the different options that are being considered in order to discover the

---

20 It might be possible for some types of arrangement to be undertaken and no tax consequences will arise under a tax code.

21 This understanding is applicable whether the relevant state of affairs occurs following a one off arrangement etc. being entered into or as a result of many arrangements etc. being entered into over a period of time, i.e. during a taxable accounting period.

22 In respect of tax consequences that are attributable to arrangements that are undertaken over a period of time such as a taxable accounting period, a tax code will define a relevant period of time and before this defined period ends (the tax determination point) no tax consequences will have crystallised although tax consequences will have accrued.

23 It is possible for a corporation to make a decision which has no regard for the tax consequences of such a decision. In the terms of this chapter such a decision would not be an example of tax related behaviour.

manner in which tax consequences might arise. In the words of Ribeiro P.J. (Arrowtown[24] para 35): 'the ... question is whether the relevant statutory provision construed purposively, were intended to apply to the transaction viewed realistically'. What is important is manner in which the tax code is to be understood and applied ('purposively') and the view taken ('realistically') of the arrangement being considered.[25]

3.3 Choosing between possible options

Before a tax determination point occurs, before a tax position crystallises, corporations are able to consider any options that might be of interest.[26] Potential tax payers are able to consider or appraise the expected tax consequences of each option and make a choice having taken into account such appraisal[27] and any other duties or restrictions that might exist. The expected tax consequences of one option might be assessed as offering advantages to a tax payer as compared to the tax consequences of a different option. The advantages identified will usually take the form of (i) a reduction in the amount of taxation that crystallises as a liability, (ii) a postponement of the crystallisation of a liability to taxation, and/or (iii) an entitlement to a tax relief or credit arising. In each case a comparison is made with the expected tax consequences of a different course of action (a different option). It is only when a choice has been made, any arrangements selected have been implemented and the selected state of affairs occurs[28] that a liability to taxation crystallises (or an entitlement to a relief or credit arises).

3.4 A tension within tax systems

The characteristics of a tax system as previously summarised can give rise to situations which are not ideal. A tax system is intended by a state to set out in a clear manner the circumstances in which liabilities to taxation will crystallise or an entitlement to a tax relief or credit will arise. Not only is such an approach to a tax system important for the successful implementation of the fiscal policies of a state but it is also important for each tax payer. Under the principle of the 'rule of law' a tax payer has an expectation that the state will set out the terms on which the tax payer is to be dealt with in a manner that is clear and understandable. The taxpayer is required to understand and apply a tax code in a way that recognises the purpose(s) of the tax code. Obfuscation or vagueness in a tax code and the principle of the rule of law, which requires a reasonable measure of certainty, do not sit easily together.

---

24 *Collector of Stamp Revenue v. Arrowtown Assets Ltd* [2003] HKCFA 66.
25 This approach to appraising a tax code has regard to the intention of the lawmaker and the spirit of the law, it is concerned with both purpose and realism.
26 It is assumed for this chapter that corporations only consider that are lawful.
27 We believe it is not controversial that a tax payer is entitled to make such an appraisal; that is, a tax payer has a legal, ethical and social right to consider the tax consequences of a possible arrangement etc. that might be undertaken. Indeed, before a decision is made, providing the option being considered does not require or entail illegal acts it is difficult to envisage a society in which a potential taxpayer is not entitled to consider the tax consequences of such an option. We do however acknowledge that there are academics, members of the commentariat and even tax authorities who object to this notion of entitlement. This matter is discussed further in Part 5.
28 This chapter does not consider in detail the situation in which a choice is made based in part on an ex ante appraisal of the tax consequences of the choice and yet the execution of the selected option is lacking in some manner and a state of affairs obtains which is different (and actually has different tax consequences) from the state of affairs that was expected to obtain.

A tax code relies on words to convey meaning and understanding. It is only when the meaning of a tax code is understood and how it applies has been determined that an appropriate appraisal can be made of the tax consequences of a particular arrangement. Sometimes words can be vague or uncertain[29] and this has the effect that on occasions either the tax consequence of a particular arrangement are not known or an assumption is made concerning the tax consequences of a particular arrangement and it transpires that the assumption made is incorrect.

As a result, there is an inherent and unavoidable tension that exists within any tax system. A tax system is meant to offer certainty and yet at times uncertainty may be present. For practical purposes this tension is resolved by accepting a presumption that when something happens in the world, when an arrangement occurs that has tax consequences, the tax consequences crystallise at that time (the tax determination point) even if the actual tax consequences are not known at that time but are only determined afterwards. This presumption that a tax position crystallises at the time that the arrangement occurs even though the actual tax consequences of the arrangement may only be ascertained afterwards is important when considering whether certain types of tax-related behaviour are unacceptable.

3.5 Categorising tax-related behaviour

Based on the description previously offered, the occurrence of tax-related behaviour may be considered as relating to three different periods or times.

Firstly, tax-related behaviour which involves *appraising* a tax code with the aim of ascertaining the tax consequences of a particular course of action takes place. This type of tax related behaviour takes place before any arrangement is *implemented*, before anything with tax consequences happens, it takes place ex ante the tax determination point.

Secondly, the corporation engages in tax related behaviour when it enters into agreements, adopts arrangements or creates structures in order to bring about what has been decided. The bringing about of what has been decided usually involves entering into contracts and usually also involves the disposition of property and resources. The taxpayer *implements* the option that has been selected.

Finally there is the tax related behaviour that occurs after the tax determination point. Through this category of tax related behaviour a corporation seeks to satisfy any liability to tax that has crystallised or enable the utilisation of any entitlement to a tax relief or credit. This can be termed ex post tax related behaviour and is linked to the *compliance* behaviour of a corporation.

The categorisation of tax-related behaviour into these three types, *appraisal*, *implementation* and *compliance*, will assist the reader in understanding the various types of tax-related behaviour which have been assessed as being unacceptable. Unacceptable tax-related behaviour may occur at appraisal, implementation or compliance and the principles or standards by reference to which such behaviour is considered unacceptable may be different in each case.

Part 4 Corporations, qualities and attributes

To state the obvious once more, a corporation[30] is an arrangement that can only be recognised and can only exist if there is a system of law within a state that allows and provides for its existence. The system of law that the enables the creation, operation and cessation of a corporation

---

29 See Endicott (2000) for a discussion about vagueness in law.

30 There are many types of corporation in existence around the world. For the purpose of simplicity this chapter focuses on corporations with limited liability that are created within a corporate code. It does not consider other

is referred to in this chapter as a corporate code[31] and exists and is to be understood as part of the wider legal system[32] that operates within a state. Although the corporate code of each state is different,[33] the corporate codes of most states are similar as regards the important characteristics of a corporation, particularly those related to a corporation being separate from its owners (the shareholders or stockholders) and providing limitations for its owners in respect of the liabilities that accrue to the corporation. In this Part we discuss various aspects of a corporation that are relevant when considering tax-related behaviour.

4.1 Corporation: an artificial legal person

A corporation is the owner of assets and resources which has been referred to by Kraakman et al. (2009) as a form of 'entity shielding'. Entity shielding involves

> the demarcation of a pool of assets that are distinct from other assets owned, singly or jointly, by the firm's[34] owners (the shareholders), (footnote excluded) and of which the firm itself, acting through its designated managers, is viewed in law as being the owner. The firm's right of ownership over its designated assets include the rights to use the assets, to sell them.
>
> *Kraakman et al. (2009)*

A corporation is recognised as a 'fictional' legal person to which can be attributed the rights and obligations of ownership. The agents of the corporation, primarily the directors (who then share their power with other employees), use the powers of ownership of the corporation to use the assets and resources belonging to the corporation for specific purposes.

Constraints apply to the corporation and its agents that limit what can be done with the assets and resources of a corporation. There are legal constraints derived from both the general law of the state,[35] and from the corporate code. The directors (and by extension other employees of the corporation) cannot use the assets and resources of the corporation in any manner whatsoever, they need to have regard to the legal duties and responsibilities to which they are subject. The legal duties and responsibilities identify certain types of tax-related behaviour as being unacceptable. This will be considered further in Part 5. What will also be considered in this chapter is whether there are any ethical or philanthropic duties and responsibilities to which a corporation and its agents are subject which might also limit the tax-related behaviour which a corporation may undertake.

---

types of corporations such as unlimited corporations, semi-'transparent' corporations or corporations created by a state directly.

31 A corporate code is not limited to specific legislation related to corporations. A corporate code may also include various regulations, guidelines and understandings of the courts.

32 The wider legal system will include the law relating to agreements, property, noncontractual obligations, crimes against the state (for example murder, rape, theft) etc. in addition to the administrative mechanisms required to give effect to the legal system.

33 A corporate code can be adopted by a country and operate throughout that country. In respect of countries that are composed of separate regions or states (such as the United States), each region or state might have its own corporate code.

34 This reference to a 'firm' is a reference to a limited corporation formed under a particular corporate code and is not a reference to an unincorporated organisation.

35 Examples would be the legal requirement to refrain from unlawful activities and to comply with health and safety laws, employment law and environmental protections laws etc.

4.2 Corporate aims

An important legal and economic constraint on the use to which the assets and resources can be put is related to the key aim(s) or objective(s) of most commercially focussed corporations. The key aim is usually, in some form or another, to maintain or increase the value of the corporation, ultimately for the benefit of its owners. It is this aim that informs and shapes the freedoms and constraints, the duties and responsibilities, that directors (and other employees) have in respect of what can be done and what cannot be done when acting as agents of the corporation.[36]

An expression of the principle which captures the fundamental purpose of the corporation can be found in a phrase taken from the UK corporate code which provides a guide as to the aim or purpose of a corporation. Subject to the owners of the corporation agreeing otherwise, a primary obligation of directors (and other employees) under the UK corporate code is that any such behaviour should be focussed on the promotion of 'the success of the company for the benefit of its members (owners) as a whole'.[37] From a legal perspective and also economic perspective, for most corporations, it is this principle, or one that is recognisably very similar, that provides the guidance for the type of corporate behaviour (including tax-related behaviour) that should be undertaken.

It should be noted that this principle as contained in the UK corporate code does not require the directors to maximise profit or maximise value or even minimise taxation, instead it is phrased in terms of success. It is the directors who, acting in good faith, decide the nature and measure of what is to be counted as success. Almost certainly, success will be understood in a manner that is related to the creation and maintenance of value in some form but what is identified as success by the directors is not imposed by the UK corporate code itself. The requirement in other states, under other corporate codes, might be somewhat different but it will almost certainly be similar.

4.3 Corporations: rights and privileges

As artificial legal persons, corporations are accorded many legal rights and freedoms that are available to human beings. Right of ownership, rights to enter into contracts, rights to borrow, to sue in courts of law, to fair treatment under the law. In respect of human beings, many states through either national legislation, the national constitution or even through international agreements protect important aspects of human activity through what is often is often referred to as human rights legislation.[38] Human rights legislation intends to constraint the power of the state by, in part, protecting the liberty of those that fall under the control of the state.

Human rights legislation addresses many matters but for the purpose of this chapter we focus on one aspect this protective legislation. Under the European Convention on Human Rights human beings have a right to enjoy their possessions, that is, their assets and resources.[39]

---

36 Because a corporation is a fiction that only exists within a system of law, it is important to recognise and accept that directors (and other employees) should only act within the confines provided by that system of law. It is acknowledged that directors (and other employees) do not always have regard to the legal obligations to which they are subject, but that enables condemnation to take place in such circumstances as there is a standard (the legal obligations to which the corporation and the directors are subject) by reference to which their actual behaviour can be assessed.

37 These words are taken from the UK corporate code: Companies Act 2006 section 172.

38 Human rights legislation can take the form of specific legislation such as the European Convention on Human Rights or the UK Human Rights Act. It can also take the form of being embedded in the constitution of a state.

39 See Article 1 of the Protocol to the European Convention on Human Rights, available at www.echr.coe.int/ Documents/Convention_ENG.pdf.

Provided that the assets and resources are used for lawful purposes, humans have the right to use their possessions as they wish. However this rights is not unlimited, a state does have the power to interfere in this right in certain circumstances, through a tax system for example. A state can curtail the enjoyment of a human's possession of his or her assets and resources by levying a tax liability in accordance with the terms of the tax code adopted in that state.

When considering and assessing whether certain types of tax-related behaviour may be unacceptable it is necessary to acknowledge that in a number of states corporations are granted many of the rights that are accorded to human beings under human rights legislation, corporations have human rights. In the UK a corporation, just as a human being has the right to enjoy its possessions, which means that a corporation can own assets and resources and contract freely in respect of those possessions. This provides a corporation with a legal right to consider different options as to how its assets and resources can be used, what structures can be adopted, what arrangements can be entered. This legal right will be relevant when discussing what constraints are applicable when a corporation selects between options, one or more of which may offer tax advantages. Although the relationship between law and morality is complex and subject to considerable debate, it is not unreasonably to accept that many legal rights reflect moral or ethical rights. In which case not only do corporations have a legal right to enjoy their possessions but also a moral right to enjoy such possessions.

4.4 Combinations of corporations

It is usual that under a corporate code, each validly created corporation is considered to be a separate artificial legal person. A consequence of this treatment is that a corporation can have ownership rights over one or more other corporations. A group of companies may consist of two or more corporations with the ownership, in whole or part of a particular corporation being held by another corporation.

There is no requirement that each corporation within a group must have been created under a particular corporate code. Groups of companies often consist of many corporations created under different corporate codes and even located in different countries. Each corporation, whatever corporate code it has been created under and wherever it is located is usually treated as a separate artificial legal person that has the power to own and use assets and resources. Groups of companies that are located in more than one country are often referred to a 'multinational enterprises'[40] or 'multinational corporations' and it is often the tax-related behaviour of the corporations within such groups of companies that is considered unacceptable by many of the interested parties. The tax-related behaviour of groups of companies is often coordinated through different subsidiaries so as to provide tax benefits to the group of companies considered as a whole. This is only possible because each corporation may be considered to be a separate artificial legal person that is capable of owning assets and resources and entering into contracts.

---

40 There is no single accepted understanding of the term 'multinational enterprises'. It is often used as a generic term to mean at least two identifiable organisations (whether or not taking the form of a corporation) each of which is located in a different country. The identification of an organisation and the location of such an identified organisation might be dependent upon facts, rules or regulations or even on the person or persons engaging in such identification. See P. T. Muchlinski, *Multinational Enterprises and the Law*, 2nd ed. (Oxford: Oxford University Press, 2007), for a discussion on different types of multinational enterprises.

Part 5 Unacceptable tax-related behaviour

In Part 5 we describe a number of different types of tax-related behaviour each of which has been assessed as unacceptable by one or more interested parties. We identify and discuss characteristics of these various types of behaviour with a view to identifying the principles or reasons that might be used to justify the behaviour as being unacceptability. In part 6.1 we briefly discuss tax-related behaviour that is considered unacceptable because of failures in the ex post *compliance* behaviour of the corporation (see Part 3.5.3). In Parts 5.2 and 5.3 we identify and discuss various types of tax-related behaviour that are considered to be unacceptable as a result of the characteristics of the ex ante *appraisal* and *implementation* behaviour of the corporation (see Parts 3.5.1 and 3.5.2). Finally in Part 5.3 we describe a type of tax-related behaviour that is unacceptable for reasons that might be considered pragmatic or expedient.

5.1 Ex post compliance behaviour

At the tax determination point the tax consequences of the arrangements that have been undertaken will crystallise (see Part 3.5) whether that be a liability to taxation or an entitlement to a tax relief or credit. A taxpayer will have an obligation within a tax system to satisfy any liabilities to taxation that have crystallised and only claim tax reliefs or credits in respect of which an entitlement has arisen. Taxpayers might fail to comply with this obligation and it is possible to identify different types of failure, a number of these different types are discussed in the next section. It should be noted that all of this behaviour takes place ex post the tax determination point which means that the arrangement selected has been *implemented*.

5.1.1 Intentional non compliance

If a taxpayer intentionally fails to satisfy the liability to taxation that has arisen or claims a tax relief or credit to which there is no entitlement then the tax payer is engaging in intentional non-compliance. Such behaviour, which is ex post tax-related behaviour, in almost all states is recognised as being illegal.

   This type of behaviour will involve fraud and deceit. Things have happened in the world and tax consequences have crystallised. The taxpayer intentionally fails to comply with the requirements of the tax system. The taxpayer might achieve this through an intentional failure to declare income, profit, gains or transactions that are taxable, by intentionally misdescribing what has happened, by claiming something has happened which has not actually happened or by simply not being concerned about the tax consequences of the arrangements undertaken. This type of behaviour is referred in some states as tax evasion. Tax evasion cannot occur ex ante as before the tax determination point no tax consequences have yet crystallised. Tax evasion can however be planned for ex ante, a taxpayer might have no intention of declaring to the tax authority that any income, profit or gains has arisen. The socially responsible nature of a corporation is flawed when this type of tax-related behaviour occurs. Not only is such behaviour unlawful but there is an ethical expectation that a corporation will not engage in behaviour that necessitates deceit and fraud in order to achieve its ends.

5.1.2 Negligent compliance behaviour

Another category of ex post *compliance* behaviour which might prompt some commentators to consider that corporations that engaging in such behaviour are not socially responsible is one in which the corporation's compliance behaviour is inadequate in some manner but the failure to comply is not intentional. Rather the corporation can be said to be negligent. Whether the appraisal of the tax code and/or the implantation of the chosen arrangement was flawed or the corporation simply lacks understanding of the tax consequences of what has happened, there is an inadequacy in the *compliance* process.

Recognising that taxpayers can (and do) make mistakes, tax systems often contain mechanisms and procedures that focus on such types of inadequate compliance. Provided the taxpayer is acting honestly and transparently, disclosing any information requested and seeking to satisfy any liabilities to taxation that have actually crystallised and only claim tax reliefs and credit to which an entitlement has arisen, a taxpayer is not acting illegally. A tax system may however contain provisions that impose penalties or fines on the taxpayer if it is considered that the taxpayer has not taken sufficient care with its tax affairs. Based on the CSR requirement to comply with legal obligations, it is difficult to justify classifying corporations as socially irresponsible when they engage in negligent compliance behaviour as no intentional deceit is present.[41] However commentators might consider that a corporation has some form of ethical duty to act with integrity in matters of tax compliance and might consider corporations to be socially irresponsible when they act in this manner.

5.1.3 OECD and compliance

In addition to intentional noncompliance and negligent compliance the OECD, working closely with the tax authorities if its member states, has identified a third type of unacceptable compliance behaviour. This type of compliance behaviour forms part of what the OECD identifies as 'aggressive tax planning'. The OECD suggest that sometimes a taxpayer might have formed a view on the tax consequences of the arrangement that is not altogether justified by the relevant parts of the tax code. For the OECD it is unacceptable for a taxpayer to take 'a tax position that is favourable to the taxpayer without openly disclosing that there is uncertainty whether significant matters in the tax return accord with the law.'

The OECD refers to a failure to 'openly disclose that there is uncertainty' which suggests two conditions must be satisfied before this unacceptable type of tax-related behaviour can exist. The first is that the taxpayer must be aware of the uncertainty and the second is that there must be some form of requirement to disclose any such uncertainty. Within the tax system of some states there may be a legal provision which requires such a disclosure, in which case an intentional failure to disclose would suggest that the behaviour falls within the type of behaviour discussed in Part 5.1.1, a form of 'tax evasion' and is therefore unacceptable because it is, in some manner, illegal. However, if there is no such legal provision within a tax system and the taxpayer is aware of any such 'significant matters' then any requirement or obligation for a corporate taxpayer to 'openly' disclose would have to be located within ethics,[42] possibly within ethical principles that may be expected to be included within CSR narratives. Failure to comply with any such perceived ethical principles might justify some interested parties, particularly those within the commentariat, to consider that a corporation engaging in this type behaviour is socially irresponsible.

---

41 If intentional deceit was present then the tax related behaviour would be illegal and identified as 'tax evasion', see Section 5.1.1.

42 Section 5.4 below discusses the possibility of pragmatism or expediency providing reasons for openly disclosing information in such circumstances.

It is to be acknowledged however that sometimes the tax consequences of an arrangement may be uncertain. This might be due to the nature of the tax code or to the nature of the arrangement undertaken or even a combination of both. A taxpayer might have formed an opinion concerning the expected tax consequences of the arrangement during the appraisal process. The taxpayer will engage with the compliance process with the aim of seeking that the tax outcome expected by the taxpayer is not challenged by the tax administration. In order to achieve this aim, during the compliance process the corporation will act in a manner and provide information that supports an understanding of the tax consequences of the arrange-ment which delivers the tax consequences expected by the taxpayer. On the assumption that the appraisal of the tax code has been conducted with integrity and the compliance process is undertaken with honesty it may be difficult to identify any ethical principle which requires a corporation to inform the tax administration of uncertainty as to the tax consequences of the arrangement undertaken. Undeniably the corporation does have a legal and ethical obligation not to act in a fraudulent or deceitful manner and provided there is an adherence to these ethical requirements there appears to be no ethical grounds upon which a corporation can be criticised for not 'openly disclosing' any uncertainty that exists.

5.2 *The OECD, tax authorities and ex ante tax-related behaviour*

In recent years many tax authorities have focused on tax-related behaviour in an attempt to constrain or even guide the choice of corporations. In addition to introducing relationship arrangements[43] that encourage corporations to engage in co-operative tax behaviour with tax authorities, choices can be constrained by making changes to tax codes and impose a tax charge on arrangements that were not previously taxed or withdraw or change tax reliefs and credits. An additional approach taken by a number of tax authorities is based upon identifying types of tax-related behaviour that are considered unacceptable by the tax authority. If a type of tax-related behaviour is unacceptable then a corporation should not engage in such behaviour.

In addition to the compliance behaviour referred to in 5.1.3 forming part of what the OECD refers to as 'aggressive tax planning', the OECD in conjunction with its member's tax authorities identified a category of ex ante tax-related behaviour as being unacceptable. Tax-related behaviour (*appraisal* and *implementation*) is considered to be unacceptable if it consists of: 'Planning involving a tax position that is tenable but has unintended and unexpected tax rev-enue consequences' (OECD 2008). Although it is 'tenable' for the taxpayer to undertake such an arrangement,[44] because the tax consequences that crystallise are not what the relevant tax authority expects, such tax-related behaviour is unacceptable.

The OECD report acknowledges that the concern of various tax authorities is that the tax consequences that actually crystallise 'were not foreseen by the legislators' (OECD 2008). This view of how a tax system operates does not sit easily with the discussion contained in Part 3.1. To the rhetorical question of the taxpayer: 'what are the circumstances in which I have to pay taxation?', the OECD (and the tax authorities of its member states) answers: 'you are obliged to pay taxation in accordance with the tax code but also to refrain from any tax related behav-iour which would provide a tax advantage under the tax code but such tax advantage was not

---

43 See for example Freedman et al. (2014)

44 For a position to be tenable a taxpayer must have appraised the tax code in a diligent and informed manner such that the expected tax consequences of the proposed arrangement can be justified. If a taxpayer is acting on the basis of a view that it tenable it is inappropriate that the taxpayer be accused of impropriety concerning any ex post compliance behaviour undertaken.

foreseen by the tax authority'. This is not an answer which is consistent with the importance placed on the principles upon which the rule of law rests or the protection provided to taxpayers by human rights provisions. In short, a taxpayer is required to accept that a tax authority's understanding of the application of a tax code is correct.

Unfortunately for tax authorities, the understanding that a tax authority might have in respect of a particular part of the tax code is not necessarily correct. There are many, many examples of the courts of a state disagreeing with the views of the tax authority and deciding that a taxpayer's understanding of the tax code is correct. Equally there are also many examples of courts deciding that the view of tax authorities is correct. In all such cases that are decided by the courts, it is always necessary for both the taxpayer and the tax authority to provide reasons why one understanding of the tax code is more appropriate than the other.[45] Tax consequences arise as a result of how a tax code is to be understood and applied not as a result of what a tax authority determines. A tax system that depends upon the view of a tax authority, an approach that is taken by many tax authorities, does not provide a robust foundation for its operation.

If the provisions of a tax code have tax consequences that are not in accordance with the views of a tax authority then a reasonable response is either the tax code should be amended or the views of the tax authority should change. It is unfortunate that on occasion, rather than either of this solutions being adopted the relevant tax authority will resort to the use of its power and even make reference to two 'principles' which are used to justify the position it takes. The 'principles' which are used to justify classifying such tax-related behaviour as unacceptable are that the behaviour:

'Principle' 1: it is not in accordance with the intention of the lawmaker; and/or,
'Principle' 2: it complies only with the letter of the law and not the spirit of the law.

These 'principles' or principles that are very similar have been relied upon and used, in one form or another, by academics, civil activists, the media, tax justice organisations and NGOs (see previous references). The intention of the lawmaker and the spirit of the law is being offered as standards by reference to which tax-related behaviour may be assessed. Tax-related behaviour (*appraisal* and *implementation*) has been categorised as unacceptable by accusations or claims that a corporation has engaged in tax-related behaviour which does not comply with intention of the lawmaker or has ignored the spirit of the law whether or not such accusations or claims are justified. In this context there is little need for the 'accusers' to make reference to any principles of CSR. When a tax authority and others that take this approach the behaviour of any corporation acting in this way is considered to be 'beyond the pale'.

A weakness with this approach is that the phrases used and the matters to which they refer are primarily rhetorical and are intended to provide beguiling metaphors that are to be simply accepted and not critically examined. Unfortunately when the phrases are considered carefully they are found to be wanting. In particular no content is given to the concepts upon which 'Principles' I and II rest, that is, no explanation is offered of how the intention of the lawmaker is to be discerned or how the spirit of the law is to be recognised and understood.

Undeniably there can be uncertainty present when a taxpayer is appraising part of a tax code with a view to understanding how the tax code will apply to a particular arrangement (see Part 3.5). Corporations and tax advisors do however manage to make such appraisals and when

---

45 On occasion neither the view of the taxpayer nor the view of the tax authority is correct, the courts provide the correct understanding.

appraising do try to discern the intention of the lawmaker and do take into account both the 'spirit' and the 'letter' of the law. In most tax systems the intention of the lawmaker has to be discerned from and is to be found within the tax code itself as it is understood in the context of the tax system as a whole. In the words of Lord Hoffman: 'The only way in which [a lawmaker] can express an intention to impose a tax is by a statute which means that such a tax is to be imposed. If that is what [the lawmaker] means, the courts should be trusted to give effect to its intention.' (Hoffman (2005)). Corporations and tax advisors who seek to understand how a tax code is to be applied will try to discover the intention of the lawmaker by using the same principles and mechanisms that would be used by judges in the courts. Mistakes might occur, even judges can disagree as to effects of a tax code because sometimes how a tax code is to be understood and applied may simply be difficult to discern.

Similarly there is nothing apart from the tax code itself, (which is in turn part of a tax system), that can be considered when trying to understand how the tax code applies. No distinction between the letter of the law and the spirit of the law is either required or to be found, there is only the law, the tax code that is to be understood within the context of the tax system. In the main, corporations and tax advisors do seek to appraise a tax code in the manner suggested by Ribeiro (see Part 3.2). To act otherwise would result in a very inadequate grasp of the actual tax consequences of the proposed arrangement.

Even so a number of tax authorities persist with promoting this approach as a method of identifying unacceptable tax-related behaviour. Corporations have even been 'encouraged' by this approach to refrain from certain type of tax-related behaviour[46] which would otherwise provide tax advantages to the corporation in accordance with the relevant provisions of the tax code.

Although lacking in substance, the promotion of 'Principles' I and II is indicative of a particular approach to tax-related behaviour being taken by some tax authorities. For a number of tax authorities, the ability to discern the intention of the lawmaker and appreciate how the spirit of law is to be understood and applied are matters reserved to those with a special insight into the nature of the tax code. Tax authorities claim to possess such insight. By emphasising 'Principles' I and II above, a tax authority is announcing that tax-related behaviour is unacceptable if it is based on an understanding of the tax code that is different from the tax authority's understanding of the tax code. In other words, it is the tax authority that knows what the intention of the lawmaker is and it is the tax authority that also knows what is within the spirit of the law. If a taxpayer has the temerity to act on an understanding of the tax code that is different from the understanding possessed by the tax authority then the tax-related behaviour of the taxpayer is unacceptable.

5.3 Unacceptable corporate actions and unacceptable tax codes

In Part 5.3 we identify and discuss reasons why some interested parties that are to be found primarily within the commentariat, consider that certain types of tax-related behaviour are not acceptable. The types of tax-related behaviour discussed in Parts 5.1 or 5.2 are not re-considered in Part 5.3 as the reasons why those types of tax-related behaviour are considered to be unacceptable have already been discussed.

Instead for the purposes of this Part we assume that all liabilities to taxation that arise as a result of entering into the arrangements that have been selected are satisfied in accordance with

---

46 Banking Code (2016).

the requirements of the relevant tax system. In addition we assume that no tax credits or reliefs are claimed unless an entitlement exists. We also assume in Part 5.3 that choosing to undertake a particular arrangement only takes place after the tax code has been appraised so as to discern the intention of the lawmaker and also having taken into account the 'spirit' of the law in addition to the 'letter' of the law. Accordingly in respect of the tax-related behaviour considered in Part 5.3 a tax authority would consider that the behaviour is acceptable.

5.3.1 Illustrations of tax-related behaviour

In order to explain the types of tax-related behaviour that are considered unacceptable by various members or the commentariat we provide a brief description of two corporate structures that contain types of tax-related behaviour that are commonly adopted by MNEs. The illustrations draw upon structures and arrangements that are similar to those adopted by a number of corporations that have been subject to public scrutiny in the UK and other countries over the last five years or so. We will however not make reference to specific corporations, rather the illustrations are intended to be generic. Aspects of the tax-related behaviour adopted by these corporations has been categorised by various members of the commentariat as being unacceptable. We seek to identify and discuss the reasons that underlie such assessments of unacceptability and explore whether the assessment of such behaviour can be linked to principles that are located within a CSR framework.

5.3.1.1 COFFEECO: UK OPERATION

In this example a UK trading corporation is a member of a multinational group of companies. The UK trading corporation is supplied with necessary raw materials, including coffee beans, by another corporation within the Coffeeco group of companies which is located outside the UK. The right to use the Coffeeco logo and obtain benefit from the Coffeeco brand is also granted to the UK trading corporation by another Coffeeco group corporation, again located outside the UK. The UK trading corporation pays the relevant associated group companies for the goods or services supplied. In accordance with relevant transfer pricing provisions the UK tax authority would insist on an arms length price being used when considering the tax deductibility of the expenses incurred by the UK trading corporation for the coffee beans bought and the licence fee paid. As a result of these arrangements and similar arrangements, the tax profit accruing to the UK operations of Coffeeco UK is minimal.

5.3.1.2 SEARCHCO: UK OPERATION

The Searchco group of companies offer services to businesses in many countries in the world. The success of the online search and linked advertising services it offers depends on complex software. The software, as an intangible asset is owned by a corporation within the Searchco group and licensed to users for a fee. The Searchco UK Corporation is based in London and seeks to expand the revenue base for the Searchco group by encouraging more businesses to pay for the services Searchco can provide.

A Searchco corporation in Ireland has software licensing rights in respect of Searchco's proprietary software which it allows UK businesses to use in exchange for a fee. In simple terms, Searchco UK finds potential customers based in the UK, explains the advantages that using Searchco's software can offer and if the potential customer wants to use the services available

Searchco UK introduces the potential customer to Searchco Ireland. Searchco UK has no ownership rights in respect of the software that a UK based business might wish to use. Searchco Ireland has those rights and if a UK business wants to use Searchco's services, the UK business will enter into a contract with Searchco Ireland. There are significant profits to be made out of licensing the Searchco software, and these profits initially accrue to Searchco Ireland. The employees of Searchco UK work hard to generate business for the Searchco group of companies and Searchco UK makes a profit based on the support services it provides to Searchco Ireland. However the taxable profit accruing to Searchco UK is very small relative to the taxable profit that would accrue within the UK if Searchco UK had ownership rights in the Searchco proprietary software and received the licence fee from the UK businesses that used the software. Searchco has structured operations in the UK in such a manner that very little taxable profit accrues in the UK.

5.3.2 *Tax beneficial structures*

Structuring the UK operations in the manner adopted by both Coffeeco and Searchco is considered to be unacceptable tax-related behaviour by many of the commentariat. (see previous references) The tax codes of various countries have been appraised and arrangements adopted that offer tax benefits to the Coffeeco and Searchco group of companies. Undeniably the structures and arrangements adopted reduce the amount of taxable profit accruing within the UK as compared to the taxable profit that would have accrued within the UK if different structures that did not involve non UK based companies had been adopted.

In both cases to have selected the structure that actually exists is considered to be instances of unacceptable tax-related behaviour because, (by comparison to a non-existent counterfactual, the alternative structure(s) that might have existed) a lower tax liability crystallises in the UK than would otherwise have been the case. Tax has been avoided and the avoidance of tax is unacceptable.

5.3.3 *Characteristics of unacceptability*

We suggest that those who consider such structures to be unacceptable do so for a number of reasons which are not always (if ever) clearly stated. We have identified a number of characteristics that can be gleaned from the works of a number of the commentariat. The characteristics we have identified are associated in some manner with an objection to either (i) the nature and consequences of the corporate form existing as it does within a wider legal framework or (ii) to the way in which tax systems are structured. We do not discuss at length any of the reasons we identify in the following sections, instead make a number of observations at the end of Part 5.3.

5.3.3.1 THE CORPORATE FORM

As discussed in Part 4 a corporation can own assets and resources and through its agents make use of the assets and resources to maintain and increase the value attributed to the corporation. Assets owned can be tangible or intangible and if intangible assets are owned then use of certain types of intangible asset can be licensed for use by others. Each corporation is treated as a separate artificial legal person that is capable of entering into contracts, including loan agreements, supply and distributions agreements and can also own all or part of other corporations. Two or more corporations that are members of a group of companies can enter into arrangements one with another, even if each of the corporations is located in a different country. A corporation is able to realise its aims through selecting between options. A corporation makes choices after appraising the consequences, including the expected tax consequences, of the options being considered. A corporation, just like a human being, has the right to make such choices.

It is the characteristics of a corporation as summarised in the previous paragraph that enable the Coffeeco and Searchco structures to exist and benefit from the tax consequences that follow from those structures. The structures adopted were at least in part selected because of the tax consequences that were expected to arise. It is these characteristics that the certain parties within the commentariat object to, in particular;

- each corporation within a group is treated as a separate legal person that can own assets;
- a corporation can enter into contracts with other corporations whether they be members of the same group or independent third parties;
- corporations located within different countries can enter into contracts with one another for the supply of goods or services;
- a corporation can own and exploit intangible assets[47] even if the owner of the intangible asset is in one country and the user is in another country;
- corporations can make choices between two or more options and in so doing take into account the tax consequences of each option being considered.

It is the characteristics identified in the bullet points above that enable tax efficient arrangements, such as the Coffeeco and Searchco structures to be effective.

5.3.3.2 NATIONAL AND INTERNATIONAL TAX SYSTEMS

It is not only the characteristics of the corporate that enables the Coffeeco and Searchco structures to offer tax advantages. Fundamental features of tax systems also facilitate such tax advantages. Many of these features are considered to be unacceptable by certain members of the commentariat, these include:

- the recognition by tax systems of each corporation as a separate taxable entity;
- the rules that exist for determining when a corporation is to be treated as resident for tax purposes in a particular country;
- the deductibility[48] for tax purposes of the expenses incurred by a corporation in connection with supplies of goods and services made by a corporation within the same group of companies;[49]the deductibility for tax purposes of the license fees for the use of intangible assets.

---

47 This is related to a more profound disdain for the existence of intangible assets. Certain members of the commentariat do not accept the existence or the exploitation of intangible assets hence the nonrecognition of intangible assets when calls for unitary taxation are made (Picciotto (2012)).

48 The deductibility of these expenses assumes that the arms length principle has been appropriately applied when necessary.

49 The sometimes inconsistent nature of the grounds upon which tax related behaviour is considered unacceptable by certain members of the commentariat can be illustrated by expenses incurred in respect of loans made to a corporation tax resident for example in the UK. If the lender is a fellow group company resident outside the UK then the tax related behaviour which, as a consequence of the payment of interest to the lender, results in a reduction in UK taxable profits is unacceptable. If instead the lender, still a fellow group company, is tax resident in the UK, the tax related behaviour which reduces the taxable profit accruing in the UK to the borrower is

5.3.3.3 THE COMMENTARIAT, UNACCEPTABLE TAX-RELATED BEHAVIOUR
AND THE PRINCIPLES OF CSR

Without the characteristics identified in the bullet points the tax consequences of the structures adopted by Searchco and Coffeeco would not be as they are. The existence of each characteristic is not however necessary, it can be readily acknowledged that each one, if not all, of the characteristics identified could be different. For example, a tax code could contain a provision that interest paid by a corporation within a group of companies to another corporation within the group but which is located in a different country is not a deductible expense for tax purposes. If such a tax provision existed within a tax code then the location of the lender might be relevant to the financing structure adopted.

The tax-related behaviour reflected in these illustrative tax structures and other structures adopted by many MNEs is considered to be unacceptable by many members of the commentariat (see footnote for references). The purpose of this chapter is to identify and discuss the reasons that underlie such unacceptability and discuss whether, as a result of engaging in such behaviour, a corporation can still be considered to be socially responsible by reference to principles that fall within CSR discourses. The structures of Coffeeco and Searchco are intended to be illustrative but what both structures demonstrate is that the underlying tax-related behaviour is legal. In addition these two illustrative structures are consistent with the economic principles associated with the maintenance and pursuit of value.

Claims by certain members of the commentariat that tax-related behaviour of the type illustrated by the Coffeeco and Searchco structures is unacceptable cannot be justified by reference to the illegal nature of the arrangements or by reference to the reasons discussed in Parts 5.1 or 5.2. If any reasons are offered by the commentariat, it is often by reference to morality'.[50] Other than moral principles (which overlap with legal requirements) to act honestly without fraud or deceit, it is very difficult however to locate any principles of morality within CSR discourse(s) that can be called upon to justify such assessments. Indeed it is possible to present a very robust case which demonstrates that the structures adopted by Searchco and Coffeeco are based on profound and important moral principles. The moral principles that are intended to protect and enhance human rights, the right to ownership of property and freedom to choose between options are being displayed by the Searchco and Coffeeco structures.

It is unfortunate that the views expressed by the commentariat on matters of unacceptable tax-related behaviour is accepted in an uncritical manner. The claims that are made about the unacceptability of these types of tax-related behaviour are acceded to by many within the media, NGOs, trade unionists and others to the detriment of the careful consideration of the nature of the corporate form and the role that corporations have within society that should be taking place. A discussion of the background and motives of the commentariat is to be found in Chapter 28 of this volume.

5.4 Prudence and pragmatism

This chapter now considers one further type of tax-related behaviour that is considered to be unacceptable. As explained in Part 4.2 directors have a duty or responsibility to 'promote the

---

acceptable. This apparent inconsistency suggests that it is not the arrangement itself that is objected to (the payment of interest) but a wider context within which such an arrangement can exist.

50 In connection with the tax related behaviour of one MNE, Google, the chair of the Public Accounts Committee in the UK stated: 'We are not accusing you of being illegal; we are accusing you of being immoral' (PAC 2012).

success of the company' where 'success' is likely to be understood in terms of value maintenance and creation.

Following the appraisal of a tax code it might be concluded that a particular arrangement might provide tax advantages to the corporation. However the directors consider that implementing the arrangement would not promote the success of the corporation and therefore a different option is actually undertaken. The directors do not have an obligation or responsibility to select the arrangement that maximises any possible tax advantage, a possible tax advantage can be overridden by the commercial aims of the corporation and the related duties of directors.

There can be many reasons why a particular arrangement with greater tax advantages might not promote the success of the corporation. For example, even though a diligent appraisal of the tax code has occurred and a very tenable conclusion has been reached as to the tax consequences of the arrangement, the directors might be aware that the tax authority of the state would disagree with the view of the tax consequences as understood by the corporation. The directors are not prepared to engage in a dispute with the tax authority and simply forgo the tax advantage that is thought to be available.

Alternatively, the directors might decide that if the arrangement was selected and a tax advantage obtained there is a possibility that the tax code would be changed in order to eliminate the possibility of the arrangement producing the same beneficial tax consequences in the future. Such a change to the tax code would require a restructuring exercise in the future which the directors wish to avoid. Yet another reason why a tax advantageous arrangement is not pursued is that if it became known generally that the corporation had implemented the arrangement the reputation of the corporation might be damaged even if the criticisms made of the corporation are made from a position that relies upon the views of some within the commentariat.

There are many other but similar reasons why tax-related behaviour might be assessed as unacceptable by a corporation. All are based on the principle that the directors have responsibilities that focus on the commercial success of the corporation (however measured). Any tax advantages that might be available have to be assessed not only terms of the relevant tax code but also on the more general commercial consequences of implementing such an arrangement for the corporation. The directors have to be both prudent and pragmatic when assessing tax-related behaviour and behaviour that detracts from achieving the 'success of the company' is unacceptable and to be avoided.

Part 6 Conclusion

In this chapter we have considered a specific type of corporate behaviour, behaviour that is prompted by the existence of tax codes. We have sought to locate such behaviour within a framework bounded by an understanding of the nature of tax systems and an appreciation of a number of important characteristics of the corporate form, including identifying key human rights that benefit corporations. In addition we have attempted to identify principles within CSR discourses, in particular those of law, economics and ethics,[51] and understand the manner in which such principles are relied upon when particular types of tax-related behaviour are assessed as being unacceptable.

Undeniably there are certain types of tax-related behaviour which considered unacceptable and such assessment can be justified. Corporations that engage in such behaviour are not

---

51 These principles are taken from Carroll's analysis, see Section 2.3. We consider that the Carroll's principle of philanthropy has requirements that do not sit easily with the primary purpose of a corporation.

being socially responsible (see Part 5.1 generally). However there are other types of tax-related behaviour which are assessed as being unacceptable but the grounds of such assessment are not clearly expressed and/or are very weak and lack substance. It is very easy to claim that a type of tax-related behaviour is unacceptable particularly if the claim is made by reference to a moral standard that is never clearly articulated. But if such a claim does not take into account the nature of a tax system or the rights, freedoms and duties which apply to a corporation then such a claim may be unreliable.

We consider that there are two main issues associated with the discussions that currently focus on the relationship between corporations, tax systems and society in general. The first is that there is too little critical thinking about the subject matter being discussed, there is too much reliance on the work of those that 'shout loudest' or have the most power (see Chapter 28 in this volume). A considerable part of the output of the commentariat is unclear, incoherent and misguided and yet is very influential. In a similar manner the work of the OECD and the pronouncements of various tax authorities relies upon the authority possessed by those institutions for its effect. When carefully examined, it too can be seen to be lacking in substance.

The second is that understanding the relationship between corporations, tax systems and society in general has to take into account the wide ranging framework of law, practice, rights, freedoms and obligations within which corporations, tax systems and society exist. It is importance to recognise that corporations possess certain human rights, that corporations have purposes set out (and sanctioned) by society and that tax systems have limitations. Arrangements can be devised and implemented which are tax efficient without those arrangements breaching the 'spirit' of the law or the 'intention of the lawmaker' and yet such arrangements are condemned as unacceptable.

We do not object to a call for changes in the tax system or changes in the corporate form or the nature of property that is recognised in law (for example the non-recognition of intangible assets) or even the imposition of additional constraints on the freedom to enter into contracts. All things change over time. What is of concern is when a desire to change such matters is masked by claims that certain types of tax-related behaviour is unacceptable.

We hope that this chapter has provided a clarity on understanding the very important relationship that exists between corporations, tax systems and society.

References

Aaronson (2011). 'GAAR study: A study to consider whether a general anti-avoidance rule should be introduced into the UK tax system'. Available at http://webarchive.nationalarchives.gov.uk/20130605083650; http://www.hm-treasury.gov.uk/d/gaar_final_report_111111.pdf.

Action Aid (2016). 'Leaking revenue: How a big tax break to European gas companies has cost Nigeria billions'. Available at www.actionaid.org.uk/sites/default/files/publications/leakingrevenue.pdf.

Avi-Yonah, R. S. (2008). 'Corporate social responsibility and strategic tax behavior', in W. Schoen (ed.), *Tax and Corporate Governance*. Berlin: Springer Verlag, pp. 183–98.

Banerjee, B. (2008). 'Corporate social responsibility: The good, the bad and the ugly', *Critical Sociology*, 34(1), 51–79.

Banking Code (2016). 'The code of practice on taxation for banks – consolidated guidance'. Available at www.gov.uk/government/uploads/system/uploads/attachment_data/file/566119/The_Code_of_Practice_on_Taxation_for_Banks_HMRC_consolidated_guidance.pdf.

Barker, W. (2009). 'The ideology of tax avoidance', *Loyola University of Chicago Law Journal*, 40(2), 229–51.

Business, Innovation and Skills (2014). 'Corporate responsibility: Good for business & society: Government response to call for views on corporate responsibility'. Available at www.gov.uk/government/uploads/system/uploads/attachment_data/file/300265/bis-14-651-good-for-business-and-society-government-response-to-call-for-views-on-corporate-responsibility.pdf.

Carroll, A. B (1991). 'The pyramid of corporate social responsibility: Toward the moral management of organizational stakeholders', *Business Horizons* (July–August), 39–48.

Christensen, J., and Murphy, R. (2004). 'The social irresponsibility of corporate tax avoidance: Taking CSR to the bottom line', *Development*, 47(3), 37–44.

Christian Aid (2013). 'Multinational corporations and the profit-shifting lure of tax havens by P. Jansky and A. Prats'. Available at www.christianaid.org.uk/Images/CA-OP-9-multinational-corporations-tax-havens-March-2013.pdf.

Christian Aid (2015). 'Getting to good: Towards responsible corporate tax behaviour'. Available at www.actionaid.org.uk/sites/default/files/publications/getting_to_good_towards_responsible_corporate_tax_behaviour_0.pdf.

Cobham, A., and Jansky, P. (2015). 'Measuring misalignment: The location of US multinationals' economic activity versus the location of their profits', ICTD Working Paper 42. Available at www.ictd.ac/index.php/ju-download/2-working-papers/91-measuring-misalignment-the-location-of-us-multinationals-economic-activity-versus-the-location-of-their-profits.

Crane, A., Matten, D., McWilliams, A., Moon, J., and Siegel, D. S. (eds.) (2008). *Oxford Handbook of Corporate Social Responsibility*. Oxford: Oxford University Press.

Endicott, T. A. (2000). *Vagueness in Law*. Oxford: Oxford University Press.

European Commission (2011). 'Communication from the commission to the European Parliament, the council, the European economic and social committee and the committee of the regions: A renewed EU strategy 2011–14 for corporate social responsibility'. Available at http://eur-lex.europa.eu/legal-content/EN/TXT/PDF/?uri=CELEX:52011DC0681&from=en.

Fleming, P., Roberts, J., and Garsten, C. (2013). 'In search of corporate social responsibility: Introduction to special issue', *Organization*, 20(3), 337–48.

Frecknall-Hughes, J. (2014). *The Theory, Principles and Management of Taxation*. London: Routledge, 13 October.

Freedman, J., Ng, F., and Vella, J. (2014). 'Cooperative compliance and the litigation and settlement strategy; results from a survey'. Available at www.sbs.ox.ac.uk/sites/default/files/Business_Taxation/Events/conferences/2014/tax-risk/freedmanvella-slides.pdf.

Friedman, M. (1970). 'The social responsibility of business is to increase profits', *The New York Times Magazine*, 13 September.

Frynas, J. G., and Yamahaki, C. (2016). 'Corporate social responsibility: Review and roadmap of theoretical perspectives', *Business Ethics: A European Review*, 25(3), 258–85.

HMRC (2016). 'Tax avoidance: An introduction', Her Majesty's Revenue and Customs, 27 September. Available at www.gov.uk/guidance/tax-avoidance-an-introduction. Word copy in author's files.

Hoffman, L. (2005). 'Tax avoidance', *British Tax Review*, 2, 197–206.

Internal Revenue Service. 'Activity 1: Tax avoidance and tax evasion'. Available at https://apps.irs.gov/app/understandingTaxes/whys/thm01/les03/ac1_thm01_les03.jsp. Word copy filed with author.

Jenkins, R., and Newell, P. (2013). 'CSR, tax and development', *Third World Quarterly*, 34(3), 378–96.

Kraakman, R., Armour, J., Davies, P., Enriques, L., Hansmann, H., Hertig, G., Hopt, K., Kanda, H., and Rock, E. (2009). *The Anatomy of Corporate Law: A Comparative and Functional Approach*. Oxford: Oxford University Press.

McIntyre, R. S., Gardner, M., Wilkins, R. J., and Phillips, R. (2011). 'Corporate taxpayers & corporate tax dodgers 2008–10', A Joint Project of Citizens for Tax Justice & the Institute on Taxation and Economic Policy. Available at www.ctj.org/corporatetaxdodgers/CorporateTaxDodgersReport.pdf

Muchlinski, P. T. (2007). *Multinational Enterprises and the Law*, 2nd ed. Oxford: Oxford International Law Library.

Muthuri, J. N., and Gilber, V. (2011). 'An institutional analysis of corporate social responsibility in Kenya', *Journal of Business Ethics*, 98, 467–83.

OECD (2008). *Study Into the Role of Tax Intermediaries*. Paris: OECD.

Oxfam (2016). 'Broken at the top: How America's dysfunctional tax system costs billions in corporate tax dodging'. Available at www.oxfamamerica.org/static/media/files/Broken_at_the_Top_FINAL_EMBARGOED_4.12.2016.pdf

Picciotto (2012). 'Towards unitary taxation of transnational corporations', *Tax Justice Network*. Available at www.taxjustice.net/cms/upload/pdf/Towards_Unitary_Taxation_1-1.pdf

Porter, M., and Kramer, M. (2011). 'Creating shared value', *Harvard Business Review*, 89(1/2), 62–77.

Prebble, J., and Prebble, Z. (2010). 'The morality of tax avoidance', *Creighton Law Review*, 20, 101–58.

Preuss (2010). 'Tax avoidance and corporate social responsibility: You can't do both, or can you?', *Corporate Governance: The International Journal of Business in Society*, 10(4), 365–74.

Prieto-Carron, M., Lund-Thomsen, P., Chan, A., Muro, A., and Bhusan, C. (2006). 'Critical perspectives on CSR and development: What we know, what we don't know and what we need to know', *International Affairs*, 82, 977–87.

Public Accounts Committee. (2012). 'Public accounts committee – minutes of evidence'. 12 November. Available at Parliament UK: www.publications.parliament.uk/pa/cm201213/cmselect/cmpubacc/716/121112.htm.

Schwartz, M. S., and Carroll, A. B. (2003). 'Corporate social responsibility: A three-domain approach', *Business Ethics Quarterly*, 13(4) (October), 503–30.

Sikka, P. (2010). 'Smoke and mirrors: Corporate social responsibility and tax avoidance', *Accounting Forum*, 34, 153–68.

Tax Justice Network: FAQ. 'Tax Justice Network FAQ on "tax avoidance"'. Available at www.taxjustice.net/faq/tax-avoidance/.

Tax Justice Network (2016). 'Why Google (and other multinationals) are still not paying their fair share of corporation tax', 16 February. Available at www.taxjustice.net/2016/02/16/why-google-and-other-multinationals-are-still-not-paying-their-fair-share-of-corporation-tax/.

Votaw, D. (1973). 'Genius becomes rare', in D. Votaw and S. P. Sethi (eds.), *The Corporate Dilemma*. Englewood Cliffs, NJ: Prentice-Hall.

Washington Center (2016). 'Profit shifting and U.S. corporate tax policy reform', Kimberly A. Clausing, Washington Center for Equitable Growth. Available at http://equitablegrowth.org/report/profit-shifting-and-u-s-corporate-tax-policy-reform/.

28

TAX AVOIDANCE, POWER, AND POLITICS

Lynne Oats and Gregory Morris

> This is a deeply, as far as tax is concerned, a deeply political time. It is a profoundly
> political time. A more political time in relation to tax across a broader range of coun-
> tries than I can ever remember.[1]

This chapter is concerned with opening up new avenues of thinking about tax avoidance. The
current discourse,[2] particularly in relation to corporate tax avoidance, is on one level confused,
and on another superficial. Missing from the various debates that are taking place is a more
sceptical perspective that inquires more deeply into the hidden power plays at work; how different parties are using the discourse(s) of tax avoidance for different purposes. In order to bring
questions of power into the debates, we need conceptual tools to allow for a different form of
analysis. In this chapter we explore ways of thinking about power and how they can help us
approach tax avoidance debates with a more critical eye. We identify three key actions in the
corporate tax avoidance debate, appropriation, adaptation and mobilisation, and observe the
operation of power playing out differently in each.

There are many different interpretations and understandings of 'tax avoidance' as a socio-
economic phenomenon, in terms of its substance, its consequences and the responses that it
engenders. Many conversations take place ostensibly about tax avoidance as a singular concept,
but on closer inspection it can often be found that the participants are actually talking about different things (Morris and Hasseldine this volume). Differences arise because of jurisdiction and
culture,[3] including language, as well as the disciplinary background of the speakers: economists
think very differently about tax avoidance than lawyers for example. As a consequence of the
connotations that can be associated with the term, 'tax avoidance', one particular struggle in the

---

1 W. Morris, 'Global Tax Policy Director GE and Chairman BIAC Tax and Fiscal Affairs Committee, Speaking at the
   Oxford University Centre for Business Taxation "Taxing Multinationals"' Conference (April 2013).
2 We use the term 'discourse' to mean a particular way of talking about the world.
3 For example, the approach taken by other countries to such a term as 'tax avoidance' might be very different from
   the approach taken in the UK. In New Zealand, the term 'tax avoidance' would not be used to refer to tax related
   behaviour which any potential tax payer would consider undertaking. This is because in New Zealand, 'tax avoidance' refers to a category of tax related behaviour which is unacceptable and ineffective (Hasseldine et al. (2012)).

tax field is for control over the prevailing definition, or understanding, of tax avoidance. This struggle is notably acute in the area of corporate tax avoidance, which is the focus of this chapter.

One matter that most tax scholars are agreed upon is that in recent years there has been a significant change within the tax field in the discourse(s) that exist about tax avoidance. Such change has occurred in both lay (non-expert) and specialist terms. In the UK we have moved from a settled, traditional, view of tax avoidance as being behaviour that is linked to arranging one's affairs so as to reduce (not necessarily minimise) consequent tax liabilities. Such a conception of tax avoidance relied upon a legal understanding of the relationship between a tax code and a tax payer and stood in sharp contrast to fraudulent behaviour identified as tax evasion. This traditional view was well understood by taxpayers, their advisers and tax authorities, albeit with disagreements at the margins. More recently, however this status quo has been disrupted. We now witness new visions of the types of behaviour that constitute tax avoidance resulting in what can be viewed as a fundamental shift. In this chapter, we argue that this shift is so profound that it makes many of the current debates about the nature of tax avoidance and how best to 'tackle' it fragmented if not incoherent. The discussions have become adulterated because of the confusion about and dilution of the term tax avoidance. This has not been helped by the various ways in which tax scholars use the term differently according to disciplinary background and geographical location.

There are related three fields in which the corporate tax avoidance debate has been, or is becoming, prominent. First is the UK domestic tax field. In the UK over the past decade, many new initiatives have been introduced to deal with behaviour that is labelled tax avoidance, including the Banking Code of Conduct, a General Anti Abuse Rule (GAAR), proposals to name and shame promoters of tax avoidance schemes, requirements for increased transparency including publication of a tax strategy, and even new forms of tax such as the diverted profits tax. It seems Government, in the UK at least, has been empowered by the 'public outrage' stimulated, or even arguably manufactured, by, amongst others, media coverage and by the work of political committees as part of their inquiries into tax avoidance by multinationals. HMRC, like many tax authorities, are under significant pressure to be seen to be 'tackling tax avoidance' (however defined), and 'getting tough'; which signals a specific change in approach, and in many ways runs contrary to their other contemporaneous efforts to foster cooperative compliance, and collaborative ways of working.

Second is the international field, where concerns about the detrimental effects of tax avoidance have led to the OECD Base Erosion and Profit Shifting (BEPS) project, which in turn has given impetus and support to an ongoing questioning of international tax norms and has resulted in proposals for a series of 'fixes' to modify but not fundamentally change international tax rules for multinational businesses (MNEs). This ambitious project could be more aptly named Base *Expansion* and Power *Shifting*, a point to which we return later in this chapter. The challenge of tackling 'profit shifting' has been enthusiastically taken up in Europe and we now see European versions of various initiatives designed to 'curb' corporate tax avoidance.

Thirdly, in an interesting twist and in part spurred on by 'public outrage', in the intellectual or scholarly field, promotors of corporate social responsibility, human rights, and even sustainability, have seized on the corporate tax avoidance debate as being symptomatic of a wider malaise in society, and are lining up with tax campaigners to promulgate sweeping reforms.

How can we unravel the complex interrelationships in this new, dynamic environment? It would seem that many of the more recently arrived commentators both from within and outside of the academy have approached the issue of tax avoidance from a largely uncritical perspective, not questioning or even seeking to understand the underlying currents of power or the principles which have motivated the changes to the discourse(s) that are now evident. How then can we reveal the hidden power plays that potentially obstruct sensible developments in the design and practical operation of tax systems? And importantly, how can we make sense of academic scholarship that takes tax avoidance as an object of investigation? Too little attention is given to who wins and who loses, and in what ways, in controlling the direction and scope of debates about tax avoidance. In this chapter the question of, and the importance of recognising the role of power, both overt and hidden in this ongoing discussion, is brought to the fore. As Boden (2012) states: 'only by viewing tax structures, policies and practice through the prism of the power relationships that shape them, can we understand how and why they are constituted and what their effects are likely to be.' And as Laasonen et al. (2012) note in their discussion of NGO and business relations, '[o]nly by seeing the taken-for-granted articulations as contingent can we start to problematise the potential power effects that these articulations may have'.

This chapter traces *how* the adulteration of the discourse of corporate tax avoidance has occurred, by reference to our three key actions of appropriation, adaptation and mobilisation. The chapter then asks *why* this happened, by drawing on theories of political power. In conclusion, the chapter offers some reflections on the consequences of the discursive shift and calls for greater transparency from tax scholars to highlight the assumptions and limitations in their work.

Three fields and three actions

As noted, this chapter explores developments in three interrelated fields, the domestic UK tax field, the international tax field and the field of tax scholarship. When the corporate tax avoidance debate within each of these fields is scrutinised with a more critical eye, it is possible to identify three different types of behaviour or actions. These actions overlap to some extent and are not necessarily sequential but will nonetheless assist in our analysis and understanding of recent changes in the ongoing discussion about corporate behaviour and tax avoidance. The three actions are next discussed in turn.

Action 1: appropriation

By appropriation we mean the adoption of the concept of tax avoidance for strategic purposes. We use the term 'strategic' here to denote not only actions motivated by party politics and political ideology, but also in a wider sense of actions motivated by the accumulation of status, reputation, power or capital in a wide ranging Bourdieusian sense. In this chapter, we observe that many of the contributors to the ongoing discussion about tax avoidance are motivated by interests that are not necessarily based on principles related to the 'public interest' but rather are often motivated by more narrow self-serving interests. The most obvious appropriation of the term tax avoidance in the UK was by tax campaigners and the media and came to the fore in 2010, as the ramifications of the global financial crisis became clearer and attention turned to various taxpayers and entities not paying a 'fair share' of tax.

In the early stages of the UK debates about corporate tax avoidance, for example the 2010 UK Uncut protests against selected large MNEs (Oats and Onu 2016) and the Reuters revelations about Starbucks (Bergin 2012), there can be clearly seen appropriation of the term 'tax avoidance' by actors outside of the 'tax world', that is, the community of tax specialists in both academia and practice. As momentum built in the years following 2010, an eclectic mix of commentators (but importantly not tax advisors or HMRC) began to repeat rhetoric drawn from many diverse fields, such as politics, economics and accounting, as if it was established fact. This group of commentators consisted of the media, tax activists and non-governmental organisations (NGOs) who began to take an interest in corporate tax avoidance (collectively 'the commentariat'[4]).

The increased attention focused on corporate tax avoidance was initially based largely on misunderstandings about the way in which MNEs report their tax obligations in their annual accounts and some spurious correlations, for example between taxes paid and sales or turnover. The political field, through the hearings of the UK Public Accounts Committee (PAC)[5] contributed to the spread of misinformation about the nature of tax avoidance in an MNE context. It was accepted by the commentariat without question that the PAC had sufficient understanding to pass judgment on the tax arrangements of MNEs, and very little, if anything, was said about whether the scrutiny by the PAC was within its remit and/ or existed within a robust and appropriate framework. In 'tax world' the allegations by the PAC of moral bankruptcy being exhibited by MNEs were initially met by tax specialists in practice and in government with incredulity, with a pinch of outrage but not, unfortunately, with rejoinder.

In the international field, we can see the term tax avoidance appropriated by a variety of international organisations to various ends. For example, international charities such as Christian Aid, which had not previously expressed interest in corporate tax avoidance, began to sponsor inquiries into the practices of various MNEs and publish reports (for example Christian Aid 2009).

In the scholarly field, more recently, appropriation of the term tax avoidance can be found in a range of intellectual work, for example by human rights and corporate social responsibility (CSR) scholars. As a result of the popularisation of the term tax avoidance, academics with no prior record of research or scholarship in tax matters appear to have become empowered (by themselves and others) to pass judgement on these issues, and are possibly inadvertently, perpetuating the misinformed perspectives and in some cases, urban myths promulgated by the commentariat.

In a recent paper, for example, Darcy (2016), whose research interests are international humanitarian and criminal law and business and human rights, writes of the 'mechanics of corporate tax avoidance and the human costs of such practices'. He suggests that current international tax rules 'allow companies to avoid paying taxes where economic activity takes place and where value is created', referring to the 2013 OECD document *Addressing Base Erosion and Profit Shifting*. Other sources cited in support of this statement include the UK PAC reports and an IMF staff report (IMF 2014). The arguments subsequently put forward in relation to the 'human costs of tax avoidance' are premised on the accuracy and relevance of this 'evidence', which is far from well established. He suggests that '[t]o advance the potential of a business and human rights approach to addressing corporate tax avoidance, further research and analysis is required'. Unfortunately, this appears to entail uncritical acceptance of various understandings and definitions of tax avoidance without reference to the (equivocal) scholarly work in the field. It is undoubtedly

---

4   We acknowledge that by combining these disparate groups into one category, many of the more subtle power plays are obscured, but we do so in the interests of brevity. We also note that the level of sophistication of tax specific expertise varies considerably to members of these groups, for example some journalists are well versed in tax law whereas others are not. Unpacking the 'commentariat' is a task for the future.

5   The Public Accounts Committee is responsible for examining 'reports produced by the Comptroller and Auditor General on value for money studies of economy, efficiency and effectiveness with which government departments and other bodies have used their resources', available at www.parliament.uk/business/committees/committees-a-z/commons-select/#P. See Freedman (2015) in relation to the role of the PAC.

the case that more research is needed, in which case greater circumspection may be necessary in relation to conclusions reached in advance of such further research.

Tax avoidance is portrayed as a 'sustainability problem' by Bird and Davis-Nozemack (2016). These scholars have an academic background in business ethics, corporate social responsibility, but not, it seems, tax, but do, at least undertake a careful analysis of a wide range of academic tax scholarship. Unfortunately, they do not acknowledge the various ways in which tax scholars from different disciplines use the term tax avoidance differently, nor do they question the underlying assumptions of that research. Reference is made, for example to Lanis and Richardson (2012) who apparently find that more socially responsible firms are likely to engage in less tax avoidance than their less socially responsible counterparts. However what Lanis and Richardson arguably find is a correlation between something they designate as a proxy for tax avoidance and something they designate as proxy for social responsibility. These designations or proxies are not necessarily the same as those used by other scholars using the same terminology.

This is not to denigrate such work; on the contrary, any attempt to probe an issue of such importance to most societies is welcome. Indeed, the embrace of tax avoidance by scholars outside of 'tax world' is important because, amongst other things, it creates impetus for reflection among tax scholars. Rather, we seek to point out the dangers of drawing conclusions which are based on assumptions about the robustness of what is taken to be the relevant underlying research and commentary. A particular difficulty for scholars outside of 'tax world' arises as a result of the fragmentation of tax scholarship (Oats 2012) and arguably its own myopia (Infanti 2008; Blouin 2014) and marginalisation (Bankman and Caron 2014; Livingston 1998; Turnier 2000).

The appropriation of the term tax avoidance for various political purposes successively by the commentariat, the PAC and intellectuals from outside of 'tax world' follows a clear upward trajectory. At various points along this trajectory, the term has been adapted to achieve strategic goals. It is to this process of adaptation that the next part of the chapter turns.

Action 2: adaptation

As indicated, within the domain of practical tax expertise, in practice and industry, there had for many years been a tacit understanding of what tax avoidance as a phenomena comprised. This may well have differed between jurisdictions and also over time, but on the whole tax administrators, tax advisers and taxpayers themselves generally had a shared understanding of what constituted unacceptable behaviour in terms of designing arrangements and structures in order to reduce tax liabilities.

Separately, but running alongside the appropriation of the term tax avoidance by those operating outside of the mainstream field of tax practice and scholarship, HMRC, and other tax authorities, accelerated the adaptations that they had started to impose upon the term some time earlier. From the mid-2000s, HMRC began to deal with large corporates in a different way, for example through the Tax on the Boardroom Agenda campaign, and leading on the 2008 OECD Tax Intermediaries project. At this point the beginnings of a shift in the 'official' meaning can be seen, when for example, a distinction between the 'letter of the law' and the 'spirit of the law' was made and promulgated as being of importance and significance. Of course, HMRC had no prior need to appropriate the term 'tax avoidance', it was already part of their lexicon, but it did set about to redefine its scope and crystallise the category of circumstances in which the use of the term was considered appropriate. The term 'tax avoidance' which previously had been a neutral term started to become a term of condemnation. The 2012 HMRC publication entitled *Lifting the Lid on Tax Avoidance*, according to Davidson (2014) marked a move away from traditional approaches and foreshadowed the use of 'subtler approaches' to discourage avoidance and encourage good behaviour, including persuasive communication, additional legislation and more sophisticated intelligence gathering.

The appropriation of the term tax avoidance by the commentariat and politicians, and its insertion into the 'public imagination' giving rise to claims of public outrage was linked to this adaptation and spoke to a number of closely aligned agendas. It was able to infiltrate public consciousness because in part it leant upon the change in the narrative being promoted by tax authorities. The narrative created by tax campaigners and journalists tapped into anti-capitalist and anti globalisation sentiments and also into a rather anti-liberal, anti-establishment (indeed anti-power) ideology.[6] Social media played a big role in this shift, as more and more commentators became beguiled by the charisma and apparent earnestness of tax campaigners. Arnold and Wilson (2014) note that 'the bad publicity generated by the attacks of politicians in Europe and the United States against multinationals has generated a public perception that multinational corporations are engaged in tax avoidance activities that are probably illegal, and certainly immoral; multinationals have been put on their back feet'. The authors go on to observe that the public reaction in Canada has been more muted than in Europe and the US. The contribution to the adaptation to the scope of the term tax avoidance from this group is primarily a blurring of the notions of tax avoidance and evasion and the demands that consideration should be given to notions of morality and justice without specifying in any detail what constitutes such notions. In general this is heralding a move away from the acceptance that the principle of the rule of law[7] is a standard by reference to which tax administrations and tax payers should be assessed.

The adaptation of the term tax avoidance by the commentariat to be used as an almost blanket term of condemnation, is complemented by a further adaptation of the term in the international tax field. Tax avoidance thus becomes associated with 'profit shifting'. Russo (2016) recounts the emergence of BEPS from its inception on 5 November 2012 when G20 Finance Ministers called for a report detailing the root causes of base erosion and profit shifting. The report delivered in February 2013 was endorsed and the G20 asked for an action plan; duly delivered in July 2013. The final communique of the G20 emanating from the July 2013 Russia meeting stated 'we call on member countries to … ensure that international and our own tax rules do not allow or encourage multinational enterprises to reduce overall taxes paid by artificially shifting profits to low-tax jurisdictions.' This adaptation of 'tax avoidance' becomes blurred with economic notions of value chains and places of economic activity, a further move away from the rule of law. Vanistendael (2016) argues that the traditional concept of tax avoidance is not adequate to tackle base erosion. The BEPS initiative is redefining 'tax avoidance' based on what appears to be a new principle in international tax. The principle is that all economic activity, all economic betterment should be taxed somewhere and the rate of tax imposed should be at an appropriate level, it should not be too low. What is called, double non taxation or even reduced taxation should not be allowed at an international level. BEPS is therefore seeking to draw new lines, introduce new principles for tax jurisdictions in international tax law. It is perfectly acceptable for such new principles to be adopted by the international community, but what we seek in this chapter is that the reasons why such changes are promoted should be recognised, understood and debated. We suggest however that this is not happening due to the appropriation, adaptation and as we argue next, the mobilisation that has taken place in the tax avoidance debate.

---

6 These sentiments still appear to be exerting significant influence, witness the Brexit vote in the UK and the election of Donald Trump in the United States.

7 Prebble and Prebble, this volume.

In addition, at the international level, NGOs in particular have used the term 'tax avoidance' as a synonym for behaviour labelled as 'tax dodging' and 'tax cheating' and sought to create a link between MNE structures, illicit financial flows and tax havens, which operate to the detriment of global society and in particular developing countries. The response of the NGOs appears to be based in part on a rather crude cost-benefit or utilitarian analysis which does not take into account other principles that NGOs place high value upon, such as human rights.[8]

The adaptations of previous shared understandings (although admittedly not agreement) of the scope and extent of activities that constitute 'tax avoidance' have several directions of travel. Adaptation through appeals by HMRC to the spirit of the law and parliament's intention move the concept of tax avoidance into the political sphere and carve out a space in which HMRC (and other tax administrations) are the possessors of the authority to decide what constitutes tax avoidance. Blurring the distinction between avoidance and evasion by the commentariat allows for the interjection of fairness, as in 'fair share', justice and morality into the debates, without articulating the content of such fairness. Conflation of tax avoidance and profit shifting in the context of international taxation brings economics into a more prominent position. Conflation of tax avoidance with illicit financial flows constitutes another blurring with illegal activities. And finally, adaptations by scholars outside of 'tax world' move the concept into another realm, that of debates around corporate behaviour (CSR) and human rights.

These adaptations of understandings of what the term tax avoidance denotes are part of a process of mobilisation. In each of the fields, domestic, international and intellectual, and for each of the actors, tax authorities and practitioners, politicians, the commentariat and scholars, the appropriation of the term tax avoidance and its various adaptations are for a purpose. We describe this purpose as mobilisation, as discussed in the next section.

Action 3: mobilisation

In the third action, the appropriation and adaptation of the term 'tax avoidance' are used by the various appropriators and adapters to achieve specific, strategic aims. These strategic aims include increased power, for example for charitable bodies a raised profile leading to increased financial support from donors, and for politicians, increasing the likelihood of re-election. Mobilisation therefore means mobilising the (adapted) discourse of tax avoidance to incite a change in behaviour, in this case the behaviour of large MNEs.

An early mobilisation was by HMRC, who as noted earlier, began a concerted campaign to tackle tax avoidance (as understood by HMRC) in the early to mid-2000s, and in so doing created a space for the commentariat to enter the field by appropriating the term tax avoidance and additionally extending its meaning by adaptation.

As acutely observed by Forstater (2015) mobilisation of the term tax avoidance, and its many variants, 'tax dodging', 'tax cheating', etc. by the commentariat has given rise to unrealistic expectations in the minds of the public, governments and even the commentariat itself about the extent of the potential gain that might arise from 'tackling tax avoidance'. Van den Hurk (2014) refers to a Dutch newspaper reporting the participation exemption as being disadvantageous to developing countries and points out that in the absence of a participation exemption, the tax

---

8 There exists a very tenable link between the protection and defence of human rights and the importance of recognising and accepting the freedoms associated with such rights, including the freedom to own property and benefit from that property within a framework of law. It is sometimes forgotten that the important laws that offer protection to human beings also offer protection to corporations, in a phrase, however unpalatable to some, 'corporations have human rights too'.

benefits granted by developing countries to attract foreign direct investment (FDI) would be negated and FDI could then be expected to reduce, to the disadvantage of developing countries.

In an instance of what appears to be parasitical reciprocity, the subsequent adaptations in scope of tax avoidance by commentators outside of 'tax world', including the media, politicians and NGOs, was seized upon by government; by politicians and administrators and mobilised for a variety of ends. Indeed, it arguably suits political agendas to allow the various unsubstantiated myths and misconceptions promulgated by the commentariat to be perpetuated.

This phenomenon is not confined to the UK, but also appears in the international field, for example via the OECD BEPS project. The 'public outrage' most visibly expressed in the UK and enthusiastically adopted by the government of the day came at a particularly opportune time for the OECD. Pascal Saint-Amans took over as Director for the Centre for Tax Policy and Administration on 1 February 2012, having previously been involved in the transparency agenda through its Global Forum work. The OECD BEPS project was initiated by concerns about tax avoidance, the understanding of which had already started to shift (OECD 2008) and the subsequent adaptations to broaden its scope even further are now resonating around the globe. The mobilisation of the significantly redefined notion of tax avoidance has enhanced the role of the OECD on the international tax stage but is echoed in Europe, at the level of the Commission and the Parliament arguably to further the integration (political) agenda of the latter.

The mobilisation of tax avoidance as an object of intellectual inquiry by scholars outside 'tax world' is, certainly in the UK, in part a reflection of the need for academics to demonstrate the impact of their research on wider society. By exploring issues that are apparently of great public interest, scholars are able to meet the requirements of funding bodies to show value for money. It is also, however, part of a much wider move towards interdicisplinarity, which is to be welcomed, albeit with some caution as previously noted.

Each of the tax fields, domestic UK, international and intellectual, and each of these actions, appropriation, adaptation and mobilisation, can be seen to create shifts in the meaning attached to the term tax avoidance as it is brought into use by different groups within society for different purposes. The traditional, well understood view of tax avoidance has largely disappeared from the agenda, leaving those who subscribe to such a view marginalised. But identifying the occurrence of such discursive shifts only goes part of the way towards understanding their significance. A more difficult question is why these shifts have occurred. One way of probing the 'why' question is to think about the exercise of power and how that plays out across the various adaptations and mobilisations. In order to bring power into the analysis, the following section provides a very brief overview of some of the debates within political science.

Theories of political power – rethinking tax avoidance

There are numerous theories of power. At a crude level, power is usually thought of as something that actors possess; society is divided into those with power and those with less, maybe even powerless. Thinking about power in this way reinforces ideas of hierarchy, particularly in modern democratic societies: power is possessed by the elite. For the purposes of this chapter, the focus is on political power. One of the important contributions of scholars of political power such as Stephen Lukes (2005), and more recently Mark Haugaard, is the recognition that power is not actually a singular phenomenon but is complex and multifaceted; does not possess a single essence but rather a 'cluster of concepts' (2015: 12). Lukes portrays power as an essentially contested concept, such that there will be continual disagreement over its definition. The original article on essentially contested concepts was by Gallie (1956), in which democracy, Christian doctrine and works of art are presented as three examples of concepts that can be seen to be continually contested. Haugaard (2010) on the other hand suggests that power is not essentially contested, and portrays it instead as a 'family resemblance concept', which recognises that meaning depends on the particular language game in which it is used. Wittgenstein used the term to denote concepts that cover a wide range of behaviour or activities in respect of which there are shared and overlapping characteristics that can be recognised. Although overlapping such characteristics may not be common to all behaviours, both tennis and football are games but each is very different from the other.

The development of thinking about power in political science in recent years (see Boden 2012) starts from Dhal's early (1961) behaviouralist formulation of power as something that is observable through actual outcomes of decision. Lukes (2005) describes this as the first face of power. The first face or dimension of power has been referred to as an 'agenda setting approach' in which the object of study is 'who gets what, when and how'. This type of power is instanced when one or more individuals is/are able to 'dictate' what happens to one or more others, the actions, behaviour or choices of one is constrained by another. Bachrach and Baratz's (1962) slightly more nuanced view that 'non-decisions', that is the decision to do nothing, are also important in terms of agenda setting by excluding certain items from discussion. Lukes (2005) describes this as the second face of power. This second face of power has been referred to as the mobilisation of bias, and is generally additionally concerned with 'who gets left out of debates and how'. It can operate in practice by limiting the choices and opportunities available to an actor by not providing an opportunity to consider other options.

Lukes, initially in 1974 and then revised in 2005, introduced a self-styled 'radical' third dimension of power: in addition to decision outcomes, and non-decisions, there is a hidden dimension of power by which we succumb to domination through false consciousness, to use the Marxian phrase, that is the misrecognition of the exercise of power resulting in domination. This third face of power, or foundational level of power, goes beyond actual behaviour and concrete decisions of the first two faces. The third, hidden, face of power involves the crafting of the fundamental framework within which people's preferences are shaped. It has been referred to as 'hegemonic power' (Johal et al. 2014 cited in Akram et al. (2015)), in that 'the whole policy debate occurs within a social, cultural, economic, political and institutional framework which favours some interests over others' (Akram et al.: 346). Although using the terms 'faces' or 'dimensions' of power, Lukes can be read as referring to 'layers' of power. A surface layer of explicit identifiable power covers more subtle forms of power in the form of a deeper layer of agenda setting and even more deeply, value constitution (Hearn 2012: 3). The surface layer of power maps on to more popular or everyday conceptions of power, whereas the deeper layers are not so readily recognised or understood. As Hearn further notes (2012: 21):

> Lukes presents power as also, and more importantly, a matter of how and why conflicts of interest remain latent and unarticulated, and how the very desires, and preferences and motives of the less powerful get formed in the first instance to suit the interests of the dominant.

What is important is the recognition that there is some deeper aspect to power that is not readily observable, like Bourdieu's idea of doxa in its relationship to habitus. Doxa for Bourdieu is shared knowledge that is taken for granted and not contested; it is the foundational principles which are accepted and inform action with no requirement for them to be routinely identified or acknowledged. In his description of fields as analogous to a 'game', Bourdieu states that fields follow rules, or regularities, and the field actors, as players in the game, 'concur in their belief (doxa) in the game and its stakes; they grant these a recognition that escapes questioning'

(Bourdieu and Wacquant 2002). Indeed, Bourdieu suggests that each field has its own unique doxa and 'is characterised by the pursuit of a specific goal' (Bourdieu 2000).

Habitus is our internalised way of being in the world, how we think and act within our social environment and is shaped by our past experiences and our interactions with society's structural features as well as doxa. Individual actors in social fields carry with them a habitus which is a 'set of attitudes, values and behaviours that dispose agents to behave in particular ways' (Gracia and Oats 2012). Akram et al. (2015) suggest that habitus can be understood as the mechanism through which the third face of power influences agency. Bourdieu uses the term 'symbolic power' as something that emerges from 'the recognition of authority as legitimate which confers its carrier with an additional 'value added' power above and beyond the specific form and amount of power upon which that authority is originally based' (Loveman 2005). Symbolic power is 'the capacity that systems of meaning and signification have of shielding, and thereby strengthening, relations of oppression and exploitation by hiding them under the cloak of nature, benevolence and meritocracy' (Waquant 1993: 1–2). Symbolic power is used to create a framework within which the 'rules of the game' operate in favour of one or more actors. In the case of law, which Dezalay and Madsen (2012) suggests has symbolic power, common language can be transformed into specialised legal terms which then provide 'a tool for ordering politics without necessarily doing politics'.

There are, of course, other theorists of power as a social phenomenon as well as other possible categorisations of their ideas but for the purposes of this chapter, we confine ourselves to the three faces, dimensions or layers of power. What key messages, then, can we take from this outline sketch of selected theories of power? Power can be either obvious or hidden. It is not evenly dispersed throughout society but is concentrated in certain sections of society, and this concentration shifts over time. These three observations can help us re-think tax avoidance.

The first face of power as a surface level, coercive power, is visible in the actions of government in recent years; the UK government coercing, for example, corporate taxpayers to do things they would otherwise not do such as sign up to the UK Banking Code of Conduct. By adapting the concept of tax avoidance HMRC is exercising its power (given that it can be very expensive for a taxpayer to disagree with HMRC) in order to constrain the behaviour of corporations.

The commentariat have raised public awareness to the point where politicians, and the OECD have been forced to respond; to be seen to be addressing certain types of corporate behaviour. The agenda for debate is now defined in terms of corporate tax avoidance (as adapted by the commentariat) being endemic and symptomatic of wider problems caused by MNEs. Coercive power is also reflected, for example in the European Commission's actions in relation to Apple. The Commission is seeking to exercise its authority in order to ensure that Apple engages in behaviour that is assessed as being acceptable by the Commission. Christians (2015) notes, for example, that the European Commission's state aid inquiry into Apple 'is a cautionary tale for both tax planners and tax authorities, whose confidence in past practices must give way as traditional compromises and well-worn assumptions suddenly become subjects of intense negotiation on a global stage.'

Several features of the post 2010 tax activist led debates also reflect the operation of the second dimension of power – that is, the mobilisation of bias. 'Avoidance' of corporate income taxes by companies is portrayed as similar to tax avoidance by individuals, as is the attribution of personhood to the corporate form. This thereby precludes discussions of corporate responsibility that should be understood within a wider framework of understanding that includes corporate law, commercial and economic drivers, the interests of various stakeholders (including shareholders) that are associated with ownership and value retention and, importantly, the social contract that sets the relationship between the state and a taxpayer at the interface of a tax code (Morris and Hasseldine, this volume). Corporations are different from human beings and matters that are relevant to the choices made by human beings, such as social and moral considerations, may not be relevant to choices made by entities that exist and operate with a highly artificial and society-created system of law, that is, the corporation. These differences are not discussed; the exercise of power by the commentariat has taken them off the agenda.

The elision of tax avoidance and tax evasion has made robust debate problematic, arguably de-emphasising the latter and even taking compliance with the law, as a legitimate way of meeting regulatory obligations, off the table. The focus of opprobrium on the corporates leaves politically motivated tax policy choices and inadequacies in legislation largely unquestioned. The very existence of tax on corporate profits can no longer be debated; it is taken to be an essential feature of domestic and global tax systems. Within the public debates, the often very practical concerns of tax professionals and experts are dismissed and their voice has largely been silenced. While concerns about regulatory capture are unquestionably valid, there is an argument that the pendulum has swung too far in the other direction.

The third dimension of power; that leads us to accept certain ways of thinking and being as natural and inevitable, is unsurprisingly difficult to observe and requires a more critical analysis of events. It can be glimpsed in the way a new, arguably warped, narrative has come to be accepted by such a wide range of actors. Ironically, HMRC's apparent complicity in allowing the commentariat to redefine tax avoidance has been turned against it and attempts to use an adapted view of tax avoidance to increase its own power are now being undermined by accusations of incompetence existing within HMRC (e.g. Sikka et al. 2016). In addition, tax professionals now must be seen to be paying due regard to new norms and expectations and begin to think differently about their own practices as advisers. Again, in the early 2000s there was evidence of malfeasance among tax professionals, and no doubt change was needed, but now there is a danger that the pendulum has swung too far and the constraints being placed on tax practitioners will lead to increased costs, the burden of which will be difficult to trace.

The headlong rush in the international field to 'deal' with newly defined inappropriate practices is being internalised by governments and reflected in new laws such as the diverted profits taxes in the UK and elsewhere. A new and unacknowledged framework of fundamental principles that has changed the criteria by reference to which corporate tax behaviour is to be assessed has been introduced and accepted by many actors that are engaged in the discourse, including some tax scholars.

Importantly, power in the corporate tax field is no longer linked to position: knowledge and experience gained over time and a reputation based on honesty and integrity. The commentariat and politicians have seized the power to redefine tax avoidance for their own stategic ends. Charitable NGOs have used the concept to raise awareness and thereby increase donations to their various causes, news outlets have used heightened interest to increase circulation and therefore profit, and both activists and politicians have increased their political capital.

Where next?

A failure to distinguish between different forms of behaviour that are undertaken within the framework of a tax code, coupled with an uncritical acceptance of superficial and emotive arguments has led us down a particular path and closed off opportunities for more balanced and well informed debate among experts on appropriate reforms. Even the gathering of experts in the name of BEPS has started from the position that 'profit shifting' is a knowable, measurable and therefore controllable phenomenon.[9] In this conclusion, we take stock of where the debates around corporate tax avoidance have taken us so far and where they are likely to go next.

The spotlight on specified high profile MNEs in the retail sector, carefully chosen by the commentariat so as to maximise public attention, leaves MNEs with lower public profiles unnamed and therefore potentially unchallenged. Similarly, smaller companies, which potentially pose much greater risk to the public purse through non compliance, stay largely under the radar. The criteria for determining which organisations are to be investigated and publicly denounced is being increasingly defined by interests outside of 'tax world'. But a failure to properly investigate root causes of problems will invariably lead to inadequate solutions. Arguably inadequate solutions will play into the hands of those who are accused of wrongdoing; creating new opportunities for large MNEs to find new ways of reducing their tax liabilities, ably facilitated by their advisers.

In the scholarly sphere, it is entirely conceivable that the well-meaning commentators writing from outside 'tax world' about tax avoidance in the context of CSR, ethics, human rights, are muddying the waters. By conflating and decontextualising issues, by accepting without question the politically motivated rhetoric of similarly well-meaning tax campaigners, these scholars may well be creating an environment where governments can eschew their responsibility for creating and enforcing robust tax laws and funding tax authorities sufficiently well to equip them to deal with misconduct – in the true sense of misconduct, and not just what tax campaigners label as misconduct. We risk diluting government accountability.

One possible interpretation of the current developments in relation to corporate tax avoidance is that considerable energy and resources are now being expended in tackling a problem that has been created outside of 'tax world' on some questionable and shaky foundations. Ironically we do not even agree about the purpose of corporation tax – to some it is only a mechanism for collecting tax from shareholders and equally the notion of fairness is difficult to apply to an artificial entity.

Undoubtedly the term tax avoidance has become toxic. We have witnessed an unhealthy conflation of issues, failures to properly investigate, and a failure to acknowledge the political power seeking aspects of the whole corporate tax avoidance debate in recent years. One cannot imagine for an instant a similar scenario in the hard sciences, where policy recommendations are made based largely on the opinions of journalists and politicians.

Will the world be a better place now that these issues are debated more openly and adaptations being made to the international tax rules for taxing the profits of multinational enterprises? Probably, but maybe not. MNEs and their advisers will quickly adapt to the new environment as they always have done; new risks will emerge and the costs of additional regulatory burdens will be eventually passed on to employees, shareholders and importantly consumers, rich and poor alike. Will developing countries be able to tap into newfound wealth because the tax rules for international corporation tax are changed? That is unlikely because fundamental issues such as corruption and institutional capacity are being glossed over in the rush to increase political and other forms of capital.

Modernity, or post modernity, is a dynamic and complex environment and it is important not to cling on to old ways of thinking and doing things. Considerable time and effort is expended in trying to understand how things are now, and how they came to be, but often without probing deeply enough into the political power at play along the way. There is no turning back from the current trajectory, and no doubt some good has come from recent deliberations and

9 Notwithstanding disagreements that emerged in discussions around BEPS Action 11.

proposed changes. Certainly, putting tax at centre stage through demands for greater transparency from both taxpayers and tax authorities has created an environment in which productive discussion can take place. What we need to do now is to manage the current uncertainty, and over time develop new discourses that better reflect the nuances of tax compliance behaviour.

An important, but maybe overlooked, element of re-thinking tax avoidance, however, is re-thinking tax avoidance research. Demands for transparency need to be extended to tax scholarship. There is enormous potential for interdisciplinary endeavour to enhance debates, but only if the limitations of prior research are acknowledged. Opening the black box of tax practice is healthy, but the same needs to happen to tax research, indeed the current state of tax scholarship leads to considerable misunderstanding. We need to recognise that tax scholars are no longer only talking to one another, in closed disciplinary bubbles where assumptions and proxies and limitations do not need to be made explicit because they are well understood within those bubbles. The subject matter that is of concern to tax scholars is now of great interest to a much wider audience, including non-academics. The work of academics is now available much more quickly and no longer hidden, for example behind journal subscription barriers. For the benefit of the new wider readership of scholarly work, there is much work to be done to make clearer what we mean by tax avoidance, and the implications of, and limitations to, that meaning, to each other as well as to wider society.

References

Akram, S., Emerson, G., and Marsh, D. (2015). '(Re)conceptualising the third face of power: Insights from Bourdieu and Foucault', *Journal of Political Power*, 8(3), 345–62.

Arnold, B.J. & Wilson, J.R. (2014). 'Aggressive International Tax Planning by Multinational Corporations: The Canadian Context and Possible Responses', *School of Public Policy Research Papers*, 7(29). University of Calgary.

Banking Code (2016). 'The code of practice on taxation for banks – consolidated guidance'. Available at www.gov.uk/government/uploads/system/uploads/attachment_data/file/566119/The_Code_of_Practice_on_Taxation_for_Banks_HMRC_consolidated_guidance.pdf.

Bankman, J. and Caron, P. L. (2014). 'California dreamin': Tax scholarship in a time of fiscal crisis', *University of California Davis Law Review*, 48, 405.

Barach, P., and Baratz, M. (1962). 'The two faces of power', *American Political Science Review*, 56, 947–52.

Bergin, T. (2012). 'Reuters special report: How Starbucks avoids UK taxes'. Available at http://uk.reuters.com/article/us-britain-starbucks-tax-idUKBRE89E0EX20121015.

Bird, R., and Davis-Nozemack, K. (2016). 'Tax avoidance as a sustainability problem', *Journal of Business Ethics*. DOI 10.1007/s10551-016-3162-2.

Blouin, J. (2014). 'Defining and measuring tax planning aggressiveness', *National Tax Journal*, 67(4), 875–900.

Boden, R. (2012). 'Tea Parties, Tax and Power', in Oats, L. (ed.) *Taxation: A Fieldwork Research Handbook*. London and New York: Routledge.

Bourdieu, P., and Waquant, L. (2002). *An Invitation to Reflexive Sociology*. Cambridge: Polity Press.

Christian Aid (2009). 'False profits: Robbing the poor to keep the rich tax free'. Available at www.christianaid.org.uk/Images/false-profits.pdf

Christians (2015). 'Friends with tax benefits: Apple's cautionary tale', *Tax Notes International*, 15 June, 1031.

Dahl, R. (1961). 'The concept of power', *Behavioural Science*, 2(3), 201–15.

Darcy, S. (2016). '"The elephant in the room" corporate tax avoidance & business and human rights', *Business and Human Rights Journal*, published online. Vol 2, pp. 1–30. doi: https://doi.org/10.1017/bhj.2016.23.

Davidson, C. (2014). 'HMRC's anti avoidance strategy: the next squeeze', *Tax Journal*, 1 August 2014.

Dezalay, Y., and Madsen, M. (2012). 'The force of law and lawyers: Pierre Bourdieu and the reflexive sociology of law', *Annual Review of Law and Social Science*, 8, 433–52.

Digeser, P. (1992). 'The fourth face of power', *The Journal of Politics*, 54(4), 977–1007.

Forstater (2015). 'Can stopping "Tax Dodging" by multinational enterprises close the gap in development finance?', Centre for Global Development Policy Paper 069.

Freedman (2015). 'Lord Hoffmann, tax law and principles', in P. S. Davies and J. Pila (eds.), *The Jurisprudence of Lord Hoffman*. Oxford: Hart Publishing.

Gallie, W.B. (1956). 'Essentially contested concepts', *Proceedings of the Aristotelian Society*, 56, 167–198.

Gracia, L., and Oats, L. (2012). 'Boundary work and tax regulation: A Bourdieusian view', *Accounting Organisations and Society*, 37, 304–21.

Hasseldine, J., Holland, K., and van der Rijt, P. (2012). 'Companies and taxes in the UK: Actions, consequences and responses', *eJournal of Tax Research*, 10(3), 532.

Haugaard, M. (2010). 'Power: A family resemblance concept', *European Journal of Cultural Studies*, 13(4), 1–20.

Haugaard, M. (2015). 'The concept of power', in M. T. Gibbons (ed.), *The Encyclopedia of Political Thought*. Malden, MA and Oxford: John Wiley & Sons Ltd.

Hearn, J. (2012). *Theorizing Power*. Basingstoke: Palgrave MacMillan.

IMF (2014). 'Staff report; spillovers in international corporate taxation'. Available at www.imf.org/external/np/pp/eng/2014/050914.pdf

Infanti (2008). 'Tax as urban legend', *Harvard Black Letter Law Journal*, 24, 229.

Laasonen, S., Fourère, M., and Kourula, A. (2012). 'Dominant articulations in academic business and society discourse on NGO-business relations: A critical assessment', *Journal of Business Ethics*, 109, 521–45.

Lanis, R., and Richardson, G. (2012). 'Corporate social responsibility and tax aggressiveness: A test of legitimacy theory', *Accounting, Auditing and Accountability Journal*, 26(1), 75–100.

Livingston, M. (1998). 'Reinventing tax scholarship: Lawyers, economists, and the role of the legal academy', *Cornell Law Review*, 83, 365.

Loveman, M. (2005). 'The modern state and the primitive accumulation of symbolic power', *American Journal of Sociology*, 110, 1651–83.

Lukes, S. (2005). *Power: A Radical View*, 2nd ed. Basingstoke: Palgrave Macmillan.

Morris, G., and Hasseldine, J. (this volume).

Oats, L. (2012). *Taxation: A Fieldwork Research Handbook*. Abingdon: Routledge.

Oats and Onu (2016). 'Cozy deals, social media, and tax morale', *Tax Notes International*, 84 (1), 69–75.

OECD (2008). *Study Into the Role of Tax Intermediaries*. Paris: OECD.

Ordower, H. (2010). 'The culture of tax avoidance', *St Louis University Law Journal*, 55, 47–114.

Prebble and Prebble (this volume).

Prebble, Z., and Prebble, J. (2010). 'The morality of tax avoidance', *Creighton Law Review*, 43(3), 693–746.

Russo (2016). 'Three BEPS years, a (very) personal perspective'.

Sikka, P., Christensen, M., Christensen, J., Cooper, C., Hadden, T., Hargraves, D., Haslam, C., Ireland, P., Morgan, G., Parker, M., Pearson, G., Picciotto, S., Veldman, J. & Wilmott, H. (2016) *Reforming HMRC: Making it fit for the twenty-first century*, Report commissioned by the Shadow Chancellor of the Exchequer, John McDonnell, MP. Available at www.scribd.com/document/323334007/Reforming-HMRC-Making-it-Fit-for-the-Twenty-First-Century

Turnier, W. J. (2000). 'Tax (and lots of other) scholars need not apply: The changing venue for scholarship', *Journal of Legal Education*, 50(2), 189–212.

Wacquant, L. (1993). 'On the tracks of symbolic power: Prefatory notes to Bourdieu's "State Nobility"', *Theory Culture and Society*, 10, 1–17.

Wittgenstein, L (1958). *Philosophical Investigations*. Translated by G.E.M. Anscombe. Oxford: Basil Blackwell.

Van den Hurk, H. (2014). 'Starbucks versus the People', *Bulletin for International Taxation*, 68(1), 27–34.

Vanistendael, F. (2016). 'Is Tax Avoidance the Same Thing under the OECD Base Erosion and Profit Shifting Action Plan, National Tax Law and EU Law?' *Bulletin for International Taxation*, 70(3), 163–72.

INDEX